THE POLITICAL PHILOSOPHY OF

ROUSSEAU

THE POLITICAL PHILOSOPHY OF

ROUSSEAU

BY ROGER D. MASTERS

PRINCETON, NEW JERSEY
PRINCETON UNIVERSITY PRESS
1968

PREFACE

I · The Intention of this Study

Another book on Jean Jacques Rousseau? Apart from historical research on the details of his life—on which a great deal of new work
has already been done since the Second World War—of what use is
continued debate concerning texts which have been so divergently interpreted that a consensus of opinion on their meaning seems impossible? Whatever the necessities of academic life, the response of the
satiric author quoted by Rousseau in the *Émile* is hardly a suitable
justification.[1]

This volume has a very specific end in view. A commentary on
philosophic texts, based on a number of years of careful study, is justifiable because the first reading is often insufficient to convey the author's thought fully. Toward the end of his life, Rousseau objected to
the misinterpretations of his writings on precisely this ground:

> These particular books are not, like those of today, groups of sep-
> arate thoughts on each of which the reader's mind can rest. They
> are the meditations of a solitary man; they demand a continued at-
> tention which is not too much to the taste of our nation [i.e.,
> France: it is "le Français" who is speaking]. When one insists on
> wanting to follow their thread well, it is necessary to come back to
> them with effort and more than once.[2]

Since few students of philosophy have the time to devote "continued
attention . . . more than once" to every philosopher, a secondary
work can be helpful in providing readers with some of the insights
they might gain from their own rereading of the texts.

The present book is therefore an exegesis of the major works of
political philosophy written by Rousseau. That he was a philosopher
worthy of study today will be assumed. That it is legitimate to study

---

[1] "*Monseigneur, il faut que je vive,* disait un malheureux auteur satirique
au ministre qui lui reprochait l'infamie de ce métier. — *Je n'en vois pas la
nécessité,* lui repartit froidement l'homme en place." *Émile,* Book II (Paris:
Garnier Frères, 1961), p. 223.

[2] *Rousseau Juge de Jean Jacques,* Dialogue II, in Jean Jacques Rousseau,
Oeuvres Complètes, 3 vols. published to date (Paris: Bibliothèque de la
Pléiade, 1959-64), I, 932.

his thought primarily from the political perspective will also not be examined, since Rousseau himself noted that, before writing any of the books for which he became famous:

I had seen that everything was fundamentally connected to politics, and that, however one considered it, no people would ever be anything but what the nature of its government would make it.[3]

Finally, it will be assumed that his philosophical writings form a coherent whole, since Rousseau himself said that the appearance of "inequalities" and "contradictions" in his different works, as well as his "very paradoxical maxims," become comprehensible when careful study reveals his "system."[4]

My approach will differ from many, though by no means all, of the existing commentaries on Rousseau, which tend to fall into two categories. On the one hand, there are numerous introductions to his life and thought, of which Charles W. Hendel's *Jean-Jacques Rousseau: Moralist*[5] can be taken as the model; these works tend to summarize the thought of Rousseau for those who have not previously studied it in great detail. On the other hand, there are the multitude of writings presenting a *thesis*, which is proposed as the key—or at least a key—to Rousseau's meaning; such titles as *Le Rationalisme de Rousseau*,[6] *Le Pélagianisme de Rousseau*,[7] or *La Philosophie de l'Existence de Rousseau*[8] suffice as indications of this type of analysis. The former approach often merely provides a résumé of Rousseau's works; while offering much useful information (for example, with reference to sources), this method does not totally satisfy the needs of the serious student who is simultaneously reading the texts for himself. The latter approach suffers from the opposite disadvantage and tends to be too specialized; while frequently of great utility (and re-

[3] *Confessions*, IX (Pléiade, I, 404). This realization is explicitly dated from "when, being in Venice [i.e., between September 1743, and August 1744, when Rousseau was Secretary to the French Ambassador to the Venetian Republic, M. de Montagu] I had some occasion to notice the defects of this so highly praised government." *Ibid.*

[4] *Rousseau Juge de Jean Jacques*, III (Pléiade, I, 932).

[5] (New York: Oxford University Press, 1934), reprinted by the Library of Liberal Arts Press (Philadelphia and New York: Bobbs Merrill, 1962). For a shorter introduction, see J. H. Broome, *Rousseau: A Study of His Thought* (London: Edward Arnold, 1963).

[6] Robert Derathé, *Le Rationalisme de Rousseau* (Paris: Presses Universitaires de France, 1948).

[7] Jean-François Thomas, *Le Pélagianisme de Jean-Jacques Rousseau* (Paris: Nizet, 1956).

[8] Pierre Burgelin, *La Philosophie de l'Existence de J. J. Rousseau* (Paris: Presses Universitaires de France, 1952).

lied upon in the present work), such commentaries seem directed primarily at the scholar whose life's work is the study of Rousseau.

The present book, intended for those who have read or are reading Rousseau's works, differs from these two kinds of studies in a number of respects. The most immediately striking will perhaps be the extensive quotations and the multitude of references which pepper the textual analysis. This procedure may expose me to the objection, made against many scholars, that I cannot take a step without leaving a footnote. These constant references should not be taken as evidence of a servile attitude toward the texts, but as an attempt to provide the reader with the equivalent of that second or "more reflective reading" which Rousseau said his works demand.[9]

My objective also explains the organization of the exegesis, which is divided according to the texts studied (rather than in terms of analytical problems). At the risk of being repetitive, a detailed examination of Rousseau's major works, in which some of the most relevant passages of other texts are cited, seems the most useful way of satisfying the student's needs. Hence this book can either be read through consecutively or consulted as the chapters are relevant.

II · ROUSSEAU'S LIFE AND WORK

It will be apparent that I intend to treat Rousseau as a philosopher worthy of his fame; this approach requires no excuse, although it does raise the often discussed question of the relationship between "the man" and his work. Because Rousseau himself suggested that "the natural man" discussed in his philosophy is none other than himself,[10] the claim to interpret his thought in terms of his personal character and experience demands consideration (especially since it is such a recurring theme among commentators).[11]

---

[9] *Rousseau Juge de Jean Jacques*, III (Pléiade, I, 934-35). My own analysis could therefore be judged according to the standard Rousseau himself proposed in the Preface to the *Émile* (see the passage quoted below, p. 57).

[10] *Rousseau Juge de Jean Jacques*, III (Pléiade, I, 936).

[11] E.g., Daniel Mornet, *Rousseau: l'Homme et l'Oeuvre* (Paris: Boivin, 1950); Georges May, *Rousseau par lui-même* (Paris: Seuil, 1961); Jean Guéhenno, *Jean-Jacques* 3 vols. (Paris: Grasset, 1948 [vol. 1]; Paris: Grasset, 1950 [vol. 2]; Paris: Gallimard, 1952 [vol. 3]), English trans. (New York: Columbia University Press, 1966); Jean Starobinski, *Jean-Jacques Rousseau: le Transparance et l'Obstacle* (Paris: Plon, 1957) and "Tout le Mal vient de l'inégalité," *Europe* (Nov.–Dec., 1961), pp. 135-49; F. C. Green, *Jean-Jacques Rousseau: A Study of His Life and Writings* (Cambridge: University Press, 1955); Ronald Grimsley, *Jean-Jacques Rousseau: A Study in Self-Awareness* (Cardiff: University of Wales Press, 1960).

There is no question that Rousseau's personality was unique, if not bizarre; as he himself put it at the outset of his *Confessions*:

> I am not made like any of those I have seen; I dare think I am not made like any of those who exist. If I am not worth more, at least I am different. Whether nature did well or ill to break the mold in which it formed me, is what cannot be judged until after having read me.[12]

There is also much to be said for the view that Rousseau's personal experience had much to do with his substantive thought. For example, Jean Guéhenno has argued that the condemnation of the arts and sciences in the *First Discourse* was derived from Rousseau's realization that his personal enlightenment had resulted in moral corruption; "he only spoke concerning himself and yet he decided about the absolute, as if something within him was that absolute."[13] Such a motive can hardly be excluded, and, if true, would certainly illuminate the character and biography of Jean Jacques.

Although it would be unjust to condemn those who have devoted their scholarly efforts to an analysis of Rousseau's life—what other writer has devoted as much attention to the faithful presentation of his own character as did the author of the *Confessions*, the *Dialogues,* and the *Reveries?*—one must ask whether these matters are essential for an understanding of Rousseau as a philosopher. Given the peculiarities of Rousseau's personality and thought, many commentators have been tempted to conclude that the former is the only proper explanation of the latter. For example, Groethuysen attempts to resolve one of the most fundamental problems in Rousseau's philosophy as follows:

> Let us leave to one side the theoretical formulas, which often contradict each other in Rousseau anyway, and limit ourselves to his personal experience, which alone can make us understand how the nostalgia for nature was united in his soul with the aspiration toward a happiness that man could only realize in abandoning himself to social life without reserve and without restriction.[14]

But does such a method of interpretation help us to understand the

[12] *Confessions*, I (Pléiade, I, 5).
[13] Guéhenno, *Jean-Jacques*, I, 273-82, 289. Cf. Broome, *Rousseau*, p. 10.
[14] Bernard Groethuysen, *Jean-Jacques Rousseau* (Paris: Gallimard, 1949), p. 120. Cf. p. 131 as well as the apt remarks concerning Rousseau's personal religion as distinct from his philosophy (Ch. IX, esp. p. 309).

reasons which led Rousseau to write as he did? Since Rousseau himself explicitly asserted that the contradictions in his writings were only "apparent," doesn't this approach imply that Rousseau did not know what he was doing?

However impressive the influence of Rousseau's life experience on his writing, it will necessarily remain true that he was an enormously learned man.[15] To cite but one historically important fact, Rousseau's erudition appears to have had a very great impact on the thought of Diderot during their friendship; in a sense the *Second Discourse* and parts of the first draft of the *Social Contract* (to mention only the most relevant examples) can be seen as a dialogue between Rousseau and Diderot which was to have a broad influence on French intellectual life in the eighteenth century.[16] To reduce the philosophical and political issues that divided Rousseau and Diderot—and perhaps hastened their personal break—to a conflict of personality would falsify even the biographical question of what Rousseau's private existence truly was.[17]

Rousseau himself took the problems on which he wrote very seriously; his major works were intended to "live beyond" his century and were directed to the discovery of "truths which matter for the happiness of the human race."[18] It may be true, as many have claimed, that Rousseau's philosophic insight was the product of his own psychological problems and defects, not to say insanity. But such an interpretation—even if revealing the "efficient causes" of Rous-

[15] For an attempt to reconstruct the readings of Rousseau, see Marguerite Reichenberg, *Essai sur les lectures de Rousseau* (Philadelphia: [n. p.], 1932); reprinted in part as "La Bibliothèque de Jean-Jacques Rousseau," *Annales*, XXI (1932), 181–250. See also Robert Derathé, *Jean-Jacques Rousseau et la Science Politique de son temps* (Paris: Presses Universitaires de France, 1950), esp. Ch. II.

[16] E.g., see Jacques Proust, *Diderot et l'Encyclopédie* (Paris: Armand Colin, 1962), Ch. X, esp. pp. 341-42. See also below, Ch. VI.

[17] In fact, it would not be difficult to show that Rousseau's personality was quite distinct from his philosophical thought. He himself consistently emphasized the gap, remarking that during the years he composed his philosophical works, he was "completely transformed" and in "the condition in the world most contrary to [his] natural temperament." *Confessions*, IX (Pléiade, I, 416-17). Throughout his career, Rousseau insisted on distinguishing the works of any author from the man himself—e.g., "Le Persefleur" (Pléiade, I, 1107); "Lettre à Lecat" (Pléiade, III, 100); *Lettre à M. Christophe de Beaumont* (Garnier, pp. 440–41); it is no accident that, in the Dialogues, Rousseau tells his interlocutor that the works of Jean Jacques can be judged without seeing the author in person. *Rousseau Juge de Jean Jacques*, III (Pléiade, I, 939-42).

[18] *Émile*, Pref. (Garnier, p. 3); *Second Discourse*, Exordium (Pléiade, III, 131, 133); *First Discourse*, Pref. (Pléiade, III, 3).

seau's thought—neither explains the specifically philosophical character of works like the *Social Discourse* and *Social Contract* nor permits one to judge them as intellectual products addressed to perennial human problems.

Lest we assume from the outset that we are more intelligent than Rousseau—a hazardous assumption, if only because few of us are likely to write books that will be taken seriously two centuries after their publication—it is best not to reject out of hand the possibility that the philosophical system we are studying contains elements of truth, or is at least directed to philosophic questions that are still of relevance. Whether out of an interest in Rousseau's life, as a means of understanding his philosophy, or in the course of studying the history of Western thought, if we are to read Rousseau's major works, it must be without the presumption that they are merely the result of personal eccentricity.

III · THE ORGANIZATION OF MY ANALYSIS

Since Rousseau claimed that his writings require careful study, the present work is merely intended to supplement the student's own efforts by providing insight into Rousseau's "system." In the *Dialogues,* Rousseau's imaginary interlocutor describes his efforts to do precisely this:

> I had felt from my first reading that these writings advanced in a certain order that had to be found in order to follow the chain of their contents. I had thought I saw that this order was retrograde to that of their publication, and that the author, moving from principle to principle, did not reach the first until his last writings. It was therefore necessary, in order to advance by synthesis, to begin with the latter, which is what I did in beginning with the *Émile*, by which he finished, the two other writings which he has since published being no longer part of his system and only destined to the personal defense of his country and his honor.[19]

We have here not only a classification of Rousseau's works, but Rousseau's own suggestion on the proper method of rereading them. This suggestion should be taken seriously, and has been, at least to a certain extent, the basis of this book's organization.

It is, of course, impossible to analyze in detail every work written

[19] *Rousseau Juge de Jean Jacques,* III (Pléiade, I, 933). The two subsequent works are, respectively, the *Lettres Écrites de la Montagne* and the *Lettre à M. Christophe de Beaumont.*

PREFACE

by Rousseau, or even all of the major works published in his lifetime.[20] The passage just cited from the *Dialogues* suggests a solution, for the "Frenchman" who summarizes his "second reading" speaks only of the *Émile* and of Rousseau's "first writings" dealing with man's "primitive condition" (i.e., the *Second Discourse*) and with the dangers of corruption created by "sciences, arts, theatres, acade-

[20] At the time he wrote the *Dialogues* (1772-76), Rousseau had published the following; in each case, it is the year of publication which is given:

"Chanson" (poem and music, published in *Mercure de France*)	1737
"Le Verger de Madame la Baronne de Warens" (poem)	1739
Dissertation sur la Musique Moderne	1743
"Épitre à M. Bordes" (poem, published in *Journal de Verdun*)	1743
"Allée de Silvie" and "Imitation Libre d'une Chanson Italienne de Metastase" (poems, *Mercure de France*)	1750
Discours sur les Sciences et les Arts (called the *First Discourse*)	1750
"Lettre à M. l'Abbé Raynal" (*Mercure de France*)	1751
"Observations sur la Réponse . . ." (often called "Réponse au Roi de Pologne," *Mercure de France*)	1751
"Lettre à M. Grimm sur la réfutation de son Discours par M. Gautier"	1751
"Dernière Réponse . . . " (often called "Réponse à Bordes")	1752
"Lettre sur une Nouvelle Réfutation . . ." (called the "Lettre à Lecat")	1752
Narcisse (play, first performed in 1752; published with an important Preface)	1753
Le Devin de Village (opera, first performed in 1752)	1753
Lettre sur la Musique Francaise	1753
"Lettre sur l'usage dangereux des Ustensils de cuivre" (*Mercure de France*)	1753
Discours sur l'origine et les fondements de l'inégalité (called the *Second Discourse*)	1755
"De l'économie politique" (article in *Encyclopédie*, vol. v)	1755
"Lettre à M. Voltaire" (published against Rousseau's wishes in *Mercure de France*)	1755
Lettre à M. d'Alembert sur les Spectacles	1758
"La Reine Fantasque" (conte, published without authorization)	1758
Julie, ou la Nouvelle Héloïse	1761
Extrait du Projet de Paix Perpétuelle de l'Abbé St. Pierre	1761
Du Contrat Social, ou Principes du Droit Politique	1762
L'Émile, ou de l'Éducation	1762
Lettre à M. Christophe de Beaumont	1763
Lettres Écrites de la Montagne	1764
"Vision de Pierre de la Montagne, dit le Voyant"	1765
Dictionnaire de la Musique	1767
"Discours sur la vertu la plus nécessaire au Héros" (written 1750, published without authorization in *l'Année Littéraire*)	1768
"Pygmalion" (text of lyrical scene, first performed in 1772, published in *Mercure de France*)	1771

Although this list does not claim to be exhaustive, it permits the identification of Rousseau's major works; leaving aside writings published without authorization, poems, plays, operas, and works on music (which show the breadth of Rousseau's interests and talent), this list suggests that we should

mies" (i.e., the *First Discourse*).[21] Without denying the importance of the *Social Contract*, on which Rousseau worked for at least ten years as part of the projected *Political Institutions* (which he hoped would "put the seal" on his reputation),[22] it would seem that the essential structure of Rousseau's thought can—and indeed should—be studied first in terms of the *Émile* (which contains a summary of the *Social Contract*) and the two *Discourses*.

Although such a procedure must certainly seem shocking given the importance customarily attached to the *Social Contract*, it is supported by Rousseau's own discussion of his works. In an autobiographical letter to M. de Malesherbes (12 January 1762), Rousseau described the source of his thought as "a happy chance" which ended years of indecision in his mind and character:

> I was going to see Diderot, then prisoner at Vincennes; I had in my pocket a *Mercure de France* that I leafed through on the way. I fell on the question of the Academy of Dijon, which gave rise to my first writing. If ever something was like a sudden inspiration, it is the movement which occurred in me at that reading; suddenly I felt my mind dazzled by a thousand lights. . . . Oh Monsieur, if I had ever been able to write a quarter of what I saw and felt under that tree, with what clarity would I have shown all the contradictions of the social system; with what force would I have exposed all the abuses of our institutions, with what simplicity would I have demonstrated that man is naturally good, and that it is by these institutions that men become wicked. All I could retain of these crowds of great truths which, in a quarter of an hour, illuminated

---

reread his important books in the following order: *Émile, Contrat social, Nouvelle Héloïse, Lettre à d'Alembert, Économie Politique, Second Discourse,* the various defenses of the *First Discourse*, and the *First Discourse* itself. To treat each of these works separately—not to mention the writings on the Abbé St. Pierre, the posthumous works, and those in self-defense—would preclude anything but a summary of their contents.

[21] *Rousseau Juge de Jean Jacques,* III (Pléiade, I, 934-35).

[22] Rousseau claimed to have first thought of writing the *Political Institutions* while in Venice (1743-44), and he explicitly says that he had been working on the *Social Contract* for "five or six years" when he left Paris to live at Madame d'Épinay's Hermitage in April 1756 (*Confessions,* IX [Pléiade, I, 404-05]). Since the manuscript was in final form in 1761 (see letter to Rey, 9 August 1761, C. G., VI, 186), the figure of ten years seems correct, and is used by Rousseau himself in his letter to Moultou of 18 January 1762 (C. G., VII, 64). These biographical details are worth mentioning, because they suggest that it is dangerous to speak of an "evolution" or shift in Rousseau's thought which is merely inferred from the dates of publication of his major works. Cf. the commentaries cited below, p. 248, and the argument developed in Ch. v, §§ 2E and 3.

me under that tree, has been weakly distributed in my three principal writings, namely that first discourse, the one on inequality,
and the treatise on education, which three works are inseparable,
and form a single whole.[23]

Since, by Rousseau's own statement, the essence of his philosophic
position is stated in his *Émile*, *Second Discourse*, and *First Discourse*, it appears that the order of reading suggested in the *Dialogues*
is indeed primarily directed to these "three principal writings."

It is possible that the failure of Rousseau to mention the *Social
Contract* as one of his "principal writings" in the letter to Malesherbes is due to Rousseau's extreme reluctance to mention it to anyone, "even my friends," prior to his letter to Moultou of 18 January
1762.[24] This fact is not decisive, however. According to the letter to
Malesherbes of 12 January 1762, Rousseau considered that the fundamental unity of his work lay in his assertion of man's "natural
goodness"; as Rousseau's imaginary French interlocutor in the
Dialogues says, summarizing his reconsideration of the texts:

> In this second reading, better ordered and more reflective than the
> first, following the thread of his meditations as best I could, I saw
> everywhere the development of his great principle that nature
> made men happy and good, but that society depraves him and
> makes him miserable.[25]

The effort to create standards of a legitimate regime in the *Social
Contract* is not, strictly speaking, an integral part of this "great principle," but rather a mitigation of the ineluctable depravation of man
by society.[26] Since Rousseau's search for a solution of man's political

---

[23] (Pléiade, I, 1135-36). In Book VIII of the *Confessions*, Rousseau explicitly
refers to this version of the so-called "illumination of Vincennes" as authoritative (Pléiade, I, 351).

[24] See C. G., VII, 64. Whereas Malesherbes helped see the *Émile* through
the press (C. G., VI, 199, 258-63, *et passim*), Rousseau did not mention the
Social Contract to him until his letter of 8 April 1762 (C. G., VII, 178), having spoken only of the *Émile* in his letter of 8 February 1762 (C. G., VII,
102-03).

[25] *Rousseau Juge de Jean Jacques*, III (Pléiade, I, 934).

[26] Writing to his French publisher, Rousseau said of the *Contrat social*:
"this work, having been cited several times and even summarized in the
treatise on education [*Émile*] should be considered as a kind of appendix to
it. . . ." Letter to Duchesne, 23 May 1762 (C. G., VII, 233). This does not
mean, of course, that Rousseau viewed his political teaching as a contradiction of his other works; in the letter just quoted, Rousseau went on to insist
that the *Émile* and *Contrat social* "together make a single whole" and hence
could be published together (*ibid.*).

problem antedates the "illumination of Vincennes," which provided the impetus to his philosophical career, the suggested method of reading Rousseau's works, based on his own remarks, seems perfectly justifiable.

Another reason supports the organization I have adopted. As a practical matter, it would be awkward to combine an analysis of Rousseau's philosophy (which tries to show the place of his political principles in a larger "system") with an examination of Rousseau's own application of his political principles to concrete problems.[27] It will, therefore, be more convenient and more logical (as well as consistent with Rousseau's own advice to the reader) to analyze the general structure of his thought from the perspective of political philosophy before discussing the connection between his principles of political right and their practical realization.

These considerations have led to a division of this commentary into two parts. Part I, devoted to the "three principal writings" mentioned in the letter to Malesherbes, shows their coherence in presenting Rousseau's "great principle" of man's natural goodness. This part has been entitled "The Limits of Politics" because it is primarily in these three works that Rousseau establishes his sweeping critique of society in the name of nature; in "proving" that the creation of civil society inevitably caused human misery, Rousseau establishes a claim against all political orders—even the best and most virtuous—and suggests the necessary imperfection and impermanence of all forms of government. The analysis will begin with two chapters on the *Émile*: the first deals with Rousseau's analysis of the physical and mental development of men as we see them (i.e., living in societies); the second with Rousseau's natural religion, his metaphysics, and his proposals for the best life for the private individual. Chapter I thus roughly corresponds with the first half of the *Émile* (up to the "Profession of Faith of the Savoyard Vicar"), and Chapter II with the remainder of the work. This division is all the more natural because the philosophic implications of Rousseau's famous novel, the *Nouvelle Héloïse*, could best be treated in the context of Rousseau's descrip-

[27] However attractive it might be to apply the reverse chronological order to the seven works identified above (see n. 20), it would be difficult to organize a commentary on this basis; at some point, one must consider how Rousseau applied his principles of political right to the specific conditions of Poland (in the *Considérations sur le Gouvernement de Pologne*), Corsica (in the fragmentary *Projet de Constitution pour la Corse*), and Geneva (in the *Lettres Écrites de la Montagne*). Since the first two works were only published posthumously and the last written in self-defense, they do not enter into the ordering suggested in the *Dialogues*.

tion of the life chosen by Émile as the model of a "natural man" living in society; the division of the analysis of the *Émile* thus permits us to refer to the *Nouvelle Héloïse* at precisely the point of the "retrograde" order which Rousseau himself proposed.[28]

Assuming that a detailed analysis of Rousseau's political thought can properly be deferred, I will turn to the *Second Discourse*, in which Rousseau first had "the occasion to develop [his principles] completely in a work of the greatest importance."[29] Chapter III analyzes the First Part and the celebrated concept of the state of nature developed therein; Chapter IV, the Second Part, with its "hypothetical history of governments" and introduction to Rousseau's conception of political right. The elaboration of Rousseau's "system" concludes, in Chapter V, with the consideration of the *First Discourse*, treating Rousseau's original critique of the morally corrupting effects of enlightenment together with the series of essays he wrote defending this thesis between 1751 and 1753. At the end of this chapter, the reader will find a summary of the main features of Rousseau's philosophic system.

Part II will deal with Rousseau's political philosophy proper, tracing the development of Rousseau's prescription for political legitimacy—or, as I have called this Part, his conception of "The Possibilities of Politics." Since it is not possible to study separately each of the many works in which Rousseau elaborated and applied his political teaching, I will focus on the *Social Contract*, without question the most famous and most important of them; other works will be mentioned primarily when they clarify Rousseau's thought.

Chapter VI analyzes the first draft of the *Social Contract*—the so-called *Geneva Manuscript*—in order to formulate more precisely

[28] No attempt will be made to analyze *La Nouvelle Héloïse* in detail. Although this may in part be justified by the character of Rousseau's novel—by his own account begun in "continual ecstasy" and written in a "tender delirium" of "romantic transports" (*Confessions*, IX [Pléiade, I, 426-27, 436])—it is primarily dictated by the orientation of the work to popular or vulgar opinion, especially that of "rustics," rather than to philosophers and truth as such. See *La Nouvelle Héloïse*, Second Preface (Pléiade, II, 16–27). The same reasoning accounts for my decision not to discuss the *Lettre à d'Alembert* which, according to the Preface, is concerned with a "practical truth"; "it is no longer a question of speaking to the small number, but to the public; nor to make others think, but to explain clearly my thought" (Garnier, p. 126). On *La Nouvelle Héloïse*, see the Introduction and notes by Bernard Guyon in the Pléiade edition (and the works there cited). For a perceptive analysis of the *Lettre à d'Alembert*, see Allan Bloom's introduction in *Politics and the Arts: Rousseau's Letter to d'Alembert* (Glencoe, Ill.: The Free Press, 1960).

[29] *Confessions*, VIII (Pléiade, I, 388).

Rousseau's conception of the status of political right and the knowledge necessary for successful political action. Chapter VII treats the "principles of political right" as they were developed in the definitive version of the *Social Contract*. Departing from the orientation of many commentators, I will stress the way these principles convert the traditional question underlying political philosophy—What is the best regime?—into a much narrower question: What is law?[30]

This analysis, which will show the necessary relationship between Rousseau's "principles of political right" in the abstract and their application to specific political circumstances, leads to a consideration of Rousseau's conception of the art of politics—i.e., the rules or "maxims" which should guide the legislator and statesman—in Chapter VIII. Focusing on the least-studied aspects of the *Social Contract* (for example, Rousseau's analysis of Rome in Book IV), I hope to provide the reader with the necessary background for a fuller appreciation of Rousseau's secondary political works. Of the Conclusion, in which an effort will be made to judge the relevance and persisting validity of Rousseau's philosophy, little need be said at this point.

Before concluding these prefatory remarks, some of the details of presentation should be mentioned. I am responsible for all translations of Rousseau's texts.[31] Reference in the notes will be to French editions, selected in terms of the best possible resolution of the student's needs. All works which have appeared in the first three volumes of the Pléiade edition of Rousseau's *Oeuvres Complètes* will be cited from these definitive texts, which have the additional advantage of extensive critical notes. For the remainder of Rousseau's extensive writings, the problem is more complex: for several, the Garnier edition will be used, despite its multiplicity of errors, simply because it is the only one currently available which the student can easily purchase. In addition to the one-volume edition of the *Émile*,

[30] In Book IX of the *Confessions*, Rousseau says: "this great question of the best possible government seemed to me to reduce itself to this: what is the nature of government appropriate to form a people which is the most virtuous, most enlightened, wisest, and finally best, taking this word in its largest sense. I had thought I saw that this question was very closely connected to this other question, even if it was different: What is the government which is always held the closest to the law? From that, What is the law?, and a chain of questions of this importance" (Pléiade, I, 404-05).

[31] Translations from the *First* and *Second Discourses* are (with occasional modification) taken from *Jean-Jacques Rousseau: The First and Second Discourse*, trans. by Roger D. and Judith R. Masters (New York: St Martin's Press, 1964). Permission to reprint is hereby gratefully acknowledged.

the Garnier volume entitled *Du Contrat Social, et al.* will be used for the *Lettre à d'Alembert* and the *Lettre à M. Christophe de Beaumont*.[32] Other writings are, at this time, simply unavailable except in one of the many "vulgate" editions of Rousseau's *Oeuvres Complètes*. Although the Hachette edition has been for many years the standard one, it is impossible to buy, is as erroneous as any other, and will be rendered obsolete by the Pléiade edition; I have therefore taken the liberty of citing the edition I personally own.[33]

It is a custom in academic prefaces to thank those individuals who have been of assistance and inspiration in writing one's book. Since this practice has always seemed to me, despite the equally traditional disclaimer, to be a kind of exchange in which those so-named receive a slim recognition in return for the subtle attribution of error, I would prefer to thank, anonymously, those of my teachers who tried to show me how to read, and those many commentators who have so greatly illuminated the works of Rousseau.

A more specific expression of gratitude is due to the institutions that, without being in any way responsible for what I have written, made my research possible. My first concentrated study of Rousseau's political philosophy was undertaken while on a Fulbright Fellowship to France in 1958-59; my first effort to set down an interpretation, in the form of a doctoral dissertation, was supported under an Asher Fellowship from the University of Chicago. The present volume, however, would have been simply impossible without a Fellowship in Political Theory and Legal Philosophy from the Social Science Research Council and a Junior Faculty Grant from Yale University, which permitted me to devote the academic year 1964-65 to undisturbed restudy and writing. For the expressions of confidence implied by this support, I am sincerely thankful.

ROGER D. MASTERS
Maussane, France

---

[32] Attention should be drawn to the fact that the pagination in the notes is to recent editions in the "Classiques Garnier" series, set from different plates than those published before the war; these editions should not be confused with the new "Garnier-Flammarion" paperback series (in which the *Contrat Social*, *Émile*, and *Lettre à d'Alembert* were published after this volume went to press).

[33] Jean Jacques Rousseau, *Oeuvres Complètes*, 21 volumes (Paris: Emler Frères, 1826). It would have been possible, at considerable effort or cost, to cite a more famous (albeit less complete) edition, such as the one of 1782 prepared by Rousseau's friends Du Peyrou and Moultou. This seemed hardly practical as few libraries have these editions, and fewer students are in the position to buy them (at the current price of over $1,000 for those fortunate enough to locate a copy).

CONTENTS

CONTENTS

CONTENTS

ABBREVIATIONS

Annales—*Annales de la Société Jean-Jacques Rousseau* (1905-present).

C. G.—*Correspondence Générale de J. J. Rousseau*, ed. Th. Dufour and P. P. Plan, 24 vols. (Paris: Armand Colin, 1924-34).

E.—Jean Jacques Rousseau, *Oeuvres Complètes*, 21 vols. (Paris: Emler Frères, 1826).

G.—Editions of the *Émile* (1 volume) and *Contrat Social, et al.* (1 volume) currently published by Garnier Frères, Paris.

P.—Jean Jacques Rousseau, *Oeuvres Complètes*, 3 vols.; (Paris: Bibliothèque de la Pléiade, 1959-64).

V.—C. E. Vaughan, ed., *The Political Writings of Rousseau* (Cambridge: Cambridge University Press, 1915), reprinted by Basil Blackwell (Oxford, 1962).

"AND, THEREFORE, AQUILINE PEDANTS FIND
THE PHILOSOPHER'S HAT TO BE PART OF THE MIND..."
WALLACE STEVENS

PART I

THE LIMITS OF POLITICS

—I—

THE NATURAL DEVELOPMENT
OF THE INDIVIDUAL
(EMILE, BOOKS I-IV)

1 · The Character of the Émile

If we should begin a careful analysis of Rousseau's thought, as he himself suggests, by rereading the *Émile*, we must first determine what kind of a book it is. The *Émile* bears as its subtitle: *or, of Education*, and it is unquestionably one of the most influential works on pedagogy ever written. Yet Rousseau himself denied that the book was "a true treatise on education"; on the contrary:

> It is a rather philosophic work on the principle, advanced by the author in other writings, *that man is naturally good*. To reconcile this principle with that other no less certain truth that men are wicked, it was necessary to show the origin of all the vices in the history of the human heart.[1]

Since Rousseau considered man's natural goodness to be the central thesis of his works, the *Émile* appears to be the most philosophical analysis of Rousseau's fundamental principle.[2]

The *Émile* is thus clearly written on at least two levels: while Rousseau describes the proper education for the "natural man," he also analyzes the nature of man. On both levels, Rousseau begins from the fundamental criticism that his contemporaries do not understand childhood; "they always seek man in the child, without thinking about what he is before being man."[3] Since the education man receives from nature—"the internal development of our faculties and organs"—is beyond human control, a consistent plan of human education must be based on the natural pattern of development.[4] Rousseau was therefore forced to analyze the stages of the child's natural growth, if only

[1] Letter to Philibert Cramer, 13 October 1764 (C. G., XI, 339).
[2] According to *Rousseau Juge de Jean Jacques*, I (P, I, 687), the *Émile* is Rousseau's "greatest and best work."
[3] *Émile*, Pref. (G, 2).   [4] *Ibid.*, I (7).

— 3 —

to avoid the vices of an education which sacrifices the present to an uncertain future.[5]

The organization of the *Émile* directly follows from the natural pattern of human development as seen by Rousseau: each of the five books covers the education corresponding to a distinct stage in man's life. Book I treats infancy (the first two years, during which the child neither talks, eats solid foods, nor walks); Book II the child from about the age of 2 to 12 or 13; Book III "pre-adolescence" (the stage between 12 or 13 and 15 years of age); Book IV adolescence proper (15 to 20 years); and Book V young manhood—the period of courtship, marriage, and the final education for adult responsibility (ages 20 to about 23).

The structure of the book is, however, somewhat more complex than this, for each of the last two Books contains three distinct parts. The "Profession of Faith of the Savoyard Vicar," ostensibly a report of the religious beliefs of another man, divides Book IV into three sections: the first dealing with the personal and moral attributes of adolescence prior to sexual maturity, and the education suited to this stage; the second being the exposition of religious education (the "Profession of Faith" itself); and the third concerning education at the time of sexual maturity. Similarly, Book V is divided by explicit breaks in the exposition: the first part is entitled "Sophie, ou la femme" (discussing the proper education of women); the second— which does not have a formal title—describes the courtship of Émile and Sophie and the appropriate choice of a spouse; and the last, entitled "Des Voyages," presents a summary of Rousseau's political teaching as well as his concluding remarks on marriage and the good life chosen by Émile.

For the moment, it suffices to note that the structure of the book provides a kind of "history" of "human nature," albeit in a form like that of a "novel" (especially in the last book).[6] This history is, however, to be distinguished from a "history of the human species" like that presented in the *Second Discourse*; the *Émile* traces the development of the natural man as an individual, and not the historical development by which the species reached its present condition.[7] Pre-

[5] *Ibid.*, II (62).

[6] *Ibid.*, V (528). On the transformation of the *Émile* from an objective "treatise" into something approaching a novel, see Peter D. Jimack, *La Genèse et la rédaction de l'Émile de J. J. Rousseau*; *Studies on Voltaire and the Eighteenth Century*, Vol. XIII (Geneva: Institut et Musée Voltaire, 1960), Part 2, esp. chap. VIII.

[7] Note, however, that Rousseau implies in the *Émile* that some such de-

suming the evolution and perfection of the species and the irreversible destruction of the state of nature, Rousseau thus analyzes "the human condition" of men as we see them.[8]

By studying man as a being who develops, Rousseau introduces *history* (whether of the species, of a society, or of the individual) as a crucial element in political philosophy. Although the contribution of Rousseau to later philosophy is not here at issue, it is worth mentioning that this historical dimension became the basis of much Western thought in the nineteenth century (not only in the work of Hegel and Marx, but also for such diverse thinkers as Tocqueville, Comte, Spencer, and Mill). For us, however, the developmental emphasis reveals a characteristic of Rousseau's own philosophy: the understanding of human nature depends decisively on man's beginnings, not on his end or perfection.

Rousseau insisted on this view because only man's beginnings are certain:

> The first point from which each of us departs to arrive at the common degree of understanding is thus known, or can be known; but who knows the other extreme? . . . I do not know that any philosopher has yet been bold enough to say: This is the limit that man can reach and that he cannot pass. We do not know what our nature permits us to be; none of us has measured the distance that can be found between one man and another.[9]

Our understanding of human nature must derive its principles from the origins of man, which alone are certain for all men; it is not possible to argue that man has a naturally defined end, since nature merely permits human perfection without establishing the limit to which men may develop themselves.

Whatever the philosophical merits of Rousseau's approach, it poses an immediate problem of great theoretical significance: a man, at the beginning of his development (i.e., at birth) is not truly human. Indeed, Rousseau himself defines education broadly as that which provides "everything that we do not have at our birth and which we need when grown."[10] During the "first period of his life," discussed in Book I, the infant "is nothing more than what he was in the womb of his

---

velopment—or creation—of man must necessarily be presupposed because the human species cannot have been eternal in its present form (*Émile*, V [G, 479–80 and 480n.]).

[8] *Ibid.*, I (12).
[9] *Ibid.*, I (41). Cf. *Second Discourse*, Part 1 (P, III, 160–61).
[10] *Émile*, I (G, 7).

mother; he has no sentiment, no idea; he barely has sensations; he does not even feel his own existence."[11] Hence we are faced with a fundamental question: which faculties and attributes of the human adult, although lacking in the child, are acquisitions which are naturally necessary?

One might be tempted to restate the question more simply: what is man? But Rousseau's formulation of this question is different from that of most previous philosophers; it would be more accurate to say: what does man naturally become? Although a long philosophic tradition distinguishes between nature and convention (or nature and education), Rousseau attempts to define the natural education. Since he treats human nature in terms of the development and acquisitions of the individual, it is fitting that his most systematic analysis of human nature takes the form of a treatise on education.

2 · The Definition and Objectives of a Natural Education

A · NATURE AND THE NATURAL EDUCATION

The foregoing comments are sufficient to indicate that in writing the Émile, Rousseau did not propose an educational system that was based merely on convenience or utility. He set out to establish the *natural* education, and claimed that the systematic part of his work "is nothing else here except the movement of nature."[12] Thus he insisted on the necessity, when teaching his imaginary student, of considering "man in the abstract" (*l'homme abstrait*); "the natural education should make a man suited for all human conditions."[13] It is crucial, therefore, to determine what Rousseau meant by "nature" and a "natural education."

For anyone who has already read the major philosophic works of Rousseau, it is no surprise that he begins by making a sharp distinction between the natural and that which has been added or changed in nature by man himself.[14] Rousseau distinguishes three sources of the educational process of acquiring faculties lacking at birth:

> This education comes to us from nature, men, or things. The internal development of our faculties and organs is the education of nature; the use that we are taught to make of this development

[11] *Ibid.*, I (58).   [12] *Ibid.*, Pref. (1–2).   [13] *Ibid.*, I (27). Cf. I (12).
[14] It seems hardly necessary to cite the famous apostrophe which opens the *Émile*: "Everything is good leaving the hands of the Author of things, everything degenerates in the hands of man" (I [5]). The equally famous opening sentence of the *Contrat social*, I, i, is, of course, a variation on the same theme.

is the education of men; and the acquisition of our own experience on the objects affecting us is the education of things.[15]

Since this threefold classification is as fundamental as it is exhaustive, it may serve as a key to Rousseau's conception of nature.

The necessary physical development of man is, quite obviously, the product of nature as it is most commonly understood. Insofar as the natural is that which happens necessarily, in all times and places, one can say that man's physical growth to maturity is natural—just as Aristotle remarked that, in one sense, "that which is by nature is unchangeable and has everywhere the same force (as fire burns both here and in Persia)."[16] But Rousseau does not simply equate physical development and nature. Despite his remark that the education of nature is the only one which, in its entirety, does not depend on ourselves,[17] Rousseau insists that many human characteristics generally attributed to physical nature are in fact the consequence of human action.

For example, since the timing of puberty "is not so determined by nature that it does not vary in individuals . . . and peoples," life in civilized society produces sexual maturity at an earlier age than would otherwise be the case.[18] Hence the natural sequence of development not only varies due to physical causes such as climate;[19] it is also vulnerable to considerable change as the result of social institutions— "the education of men" as Rousseau puts it. In general, civilized peoples are physically weaker and more frequently subject to illness because men have developed the art of medicine, luxury, and mutual interdependence.[20]

When Rousseau defines the three sources of education, therefore, he does not conceive of nature as merely physical, or bodily characteristics. On the contrary, he is distinguishing the developments within man's body that are beyond individual control from those due to

[15] *Émile*, I (G, 7). It will be noted that divine revelation is omitted, and that according to Rousseau's analysis of the state of nature in the *Second Discourse*, primitive man has both the first and third kinds of education.

[16] *Nicomachean Ethics* v. 1134b.

[17] *Émile*, I (G, 7).

[18] *Ibid.*, IV (251). At this point, when speaking of the effects of climate and individual physique on the timing of puberty, Rousseau remarks: "but one can be mistaken on the causes, and often attribute to the physical that which must be imputed to the moral; this is one of the most frequent abuses of the philosophy of our century."

[19] *Ibid.*, I (26–27).

[20] *Ibid.*, I (29–32); II (69); *First Discourse*, Part 2 (22–24); *Second Discourse*, Part 1 (138–39) and n. IX (203–07).

social custom and individual experience. Since the latter—"the education of things"—is also partially attributed to nature,[21] Rousseau seems to view the natural as both broader than physical necessity (i.e., nature determines part of man's learning from experience even though these experiences are not always physically necessary) and narrower than physical necessity (i.e., man's internal physical characteristics, as we see them, are partly attributable to non-natural causes).

It is no accident that, in Rousseau's list of the three sources of education, "the education of men" occupies the central position; human nature can only be defined by isolating those human attributes that are not the creations of man himself. If the *Second Discourse* is an attempt to isolate the natural element in mankind, viewing the purely human acquisitions in terms of the historical evolution of the entire species, the *Émile* treats the same problem within the somewhat narrower confines of the individual, taking such evolution as given.[22]

The conception of a natural education is thus based on a fundamental dichotomy between nature and society: that which depends solely on man's own creations, as the result of social experience and custom, must be carefully removed if one is to discover human nature. In this sense, nature appears to be a residual category, the remainder after a process of subtraction; and indeed it is in this sense that Rousseau analyzes the natural man in the *Second Discourse*. One must, therefore, read with great care the passage in which Rousseau defines nature in the opening pages of the *Émile*, just prior to the contrast between natural man and civil man (to which we will turn in a moment).

In analyzing the verse "Believe me, nature is only habit" (*La nature, crois-moi, n'est que l'habitude*),[23] Rousseau speaks of some habits as "conforming to nature," calling them "primitive dispositions":

> As soon as we have, so to speak, the consciousness of our sensations, we are disposed to seek or flee the objects that produce them,

[21] *Émile*, I (G, 7); *Second Discourse*, Part 1 (P, III, 135, 140); Part 2 (164–65).

[22] See, for example, Rousseau's criticism of Hobbes for having imputed to man in the state of nature characteristics originating only in civil society (*ibid.*, Part 1 [153–54]). Cf. *Émile*, I (G, 48); II (73).

[23] As Pierre Burgelin has indicated (*Annales*, XXXV, 367), Rousseau cites inexactly a verse from Voltaire's *Mahomet*, Act IV, scene 1: "*La nature n'est rien que l'habitude*." See also Helvetius (*De l'Esprit*, II, xxiv): "the sensible man agrees that nature . . . is nothing other than our first habits" (*Oeuvres Complètes de Helvétius* [Paris: Lepetit, 1818], I, 211).

first according to their pleasantness or unpleasantness for us, then according to the appropriateness or unappropriateness that we find between ourselves and these objects, and finally according to the judgments that we make of them based on the idea of happiness or perfection that reason gives us. These dispositions are extended and strengthened to the extent that we become more sensitive and more enlightened; but constrained by our habits, they are altered more or less by our opinions. Before this alteration, they are what I call nature in us.[24]

For the reader who recalls the conception of human nature in the *Second Discourse*, it is crucial to distinguish between the natural dispositions of primitive man (animal impulses of self-preservation and pity, lacking thought and judgment) and the primitive dispositions of natural man (who, as described here, ultimately judges objects on the basis of the "idea of happiness or perfection that reason gives us").[25] When Rousseau explicitly includes both increased physical sensibility and increased enlightenment as factors which strengthen man's basic dispositions, he does not reject the latter as unnatural; here the natural includes all such dispositions before "they are altered more or less by our opinions."

The unnatural or human acquisitions of man are thus viewed more narrowly in the *Émile* than in the *Second Discourse*. In Rousseau's earlier work, man's nature is treated as a residual category, to be discovered after the subtraction of social acquisitions. In the *Émile*, the procedure is somewhat reversed: the unnatural is here almost a residual category—the elements which remain after the natural dispositions of man have been released from artificial constraint and studied in their entirety. To put it differently, the natural man described in the *Émile* has faculties and characteristics which can be attributed to human opinions and habits, provided that such humanly created opinions and habits do not distort man's basic nature. This approach to human nature explains Rousseau's emphasis on a natural education as one which is free from the prejudices of a given time or place. Since Rousseau does not here reject *all* acquired habits as unnatural, he merely limits "the word nature to habits conforming to nature" (i.e.,

---

[24] *Émile*, I (G, 8).
[25] See *Second Discourse*, Part 1 (P, III, esp. 142–44). Note that of the three elements which underlie the development of man's dispositions, only the first (seeking or fleeing objects "according to their pleasantness or unpleasantness for us") completely belongs to men in the earliest stage of the state of nature.

habits which do not require artificial support in order to subsist).[26]
That social education depends precisely on the support of prejudices
and opinions can be easily proven by the immense variability of human institutions and practices; if such prejudices are changed—for
instance, if one moves from one society to another—man's way of
acting also changes. In seeking to establish the natural education,
Rousseau therefore tries to emancipate man, as we see him under
present conditions, from all social prejudice in order to determine the
true direction of his natural dispositions.[27] What is natural for man is
"common to all."[28] This does not mean, of course, that Rousseau's
educational proposals could be implemented without reference to circumstances of time and place, but merely that his analysis rests on an
understanding of all classes, ages, and types of men.[29]

B · NATURAL MAN AND CIVIL MAN

The foregoing comments on Rousseau's conception of nature serve

[26] The example that Rousseau gives is very revealing: "Are there not
habits which are only contracted by force? Such is, for example, the habit of
plants whose vertical direction has been hindered. The plant left in freedom
retains the inclination that it was forced to take, but the sap has not thereby
changed its primitive direction; and if the plant continues to grow, *its pro-
longation becomes vertical again*. It is the same with the inclinations of men"
(*Émile*, I [8], italics added). Rousseau has in mind the practice of training
trees in the form called an "espalier." Note that the effects of external constraint (in the example, the artificial direction given to a plant's growth) are
not destroyed when this restraint is moved; the unnatural character of the
forced direction of growth is proven by its failure to persist in *new* growth,
but nature is incapable of reversing that part of the development which
has been completed in an unnatural manner. If the parallel with man is considered, one might compare this unnatural growth with the acquisition, by
the species, of all the attributes lacking in the animal-like state of nature.
How far this interpretation reveals the connection between the *Second Discourse* and the *Émile* must be reserved for later comment.

[27] It follows, from the example in the preceding note, that the specific form
of these emancipated natural dispositions need not be in all ways identical
to the natural dispositions before they were forcibly altered. Using the
analogy of the plant, after artificial training has caused horizontal growth,
the return of the natural inclination to grow vertically occurs in a different
place (i.e., from the point where horizontal growth is no longer coerced,
rather than from the roots themselves). Note, incidentally, the frequency
of botanical analogies in the opening pages of the *Émile* (I [5, 6, 8, 12–13,
26–27]).

[28] "After having compared as many ranks and peoples as I could see in
a life passed in observing them, I have removed as artificial all that be-
longed to one people and not to another, to one condition and not to another,
and I have only considered, as incontestably belonging to man, what was
common to all, of whatever age, whatever rank, and whatever nation he
might be" (*Ibid.*, IV [306]). Cf. IV (279); V (495).

[29] Cf. *ibid.*, I (12–13, 26–27), with Pref. (3).

to clarify his distinction between natural man and civil man. Émile is to be "natural man," and in a well-known passage, Rousseau explains this notion by posing the option between bringing up a "man" or a "citizen":

> The natural man is all for himself; he is the numerical unity, the absolute whole, who only has relations with himself or his fellow. Civil man is only a fractional unity who depends on the denominator, and whose value is in his relations with the whole, which is the social body. The good social institutions are those which know best how to denature man, to remove his absolute existence in order to give him a relative one, and to transport the *me* to a common unity; so that each private person no longer believes himself to be one, but is part of the unity, and is no longer sensitive except in the whole.[30]

From the opposition between "nature" and "social institutions," Rousseau does not conclude that one must choose between the totally isolated man of the pure state of nature and social man; the natural man is explicitly described as having relations with either himself *or* "his fellows" (i.e., other natural men but not other citizens).

Rousseau frequently insists that Émile, as the natural man, is not anti-social; he is brought up in order to live with other men. "There is a great difference between the natural man living in the state of nature, and natural man living in the state of society."[31] Émile lives *in* civil society, but he is not *of* civil society:

> In wanting to form the man of nature, it is not a matter of making a savage and sending him to the depths of the woods; but enclosed in the social vortex, it is sufficient that he does not allow himself to be carried away either by the passions or the opinions of men.[32]

Because the state of nature is a stage of human evolution which has been irretrievably destroyed,[33] the conflict between nature and society, so essential to Rousseau's entire thought, now necessarily occurs within society itself.

Thus the fundamental choice in man's education is whether he will

---

[30] *Ibid.*, I (9). On the arithmetical implication of this passage, see the "continuous proportion" in *Contrat social*, III, i (analyzed below, chap. VII, § 2E).

[31] *Émile*, III (G, 239). Cf. the similar formulation in V (514): "One must not confuse what is natural to the savage state with what is natural to the civil state."

[32] *Ibid.*, IV (306). Cf. III (211).

[33] *Second Discourse*, Part 2 (P, III, 178); *Émile*, III (G, 223).

become a citizen or simply a man, and this choice concerns the relationship between the individual and social prejudices or opinions. Émile is free from such prejudice, being entirely independent of the opinions of others; the civil man, because he has completely given himself to the political community in which he lives, conforms all his judgments and actions to the opinions of his fellow citizens and loves his fatherland rather than himself.[34] It is necessary to choose between natural man and civil man as the objective of education because, to create the latter, man must be "denatured" by transforming love of oneself, the first principle of natural man, into selfless patriotism.[35]

It is therefore impossible, according to Rousseau, to combine public education and private education. The result of such a combination is a man who is torn by contradictory impulsions:

> Anyone who wants to preserve the primacy of natural sentiments on the civil order does not know what he wants. Always in contradiction with himself, always floating between his inclinations and his duties, he will never be either a man or a citizen; he will not be good either for himself or for others.[36]

As the distinction between natural "impulses" and "duties" suggests, the incompatibility between the natural man and the citizen is connected to the fundamental distinction between "goodness" and "virtue" which is central in Rousseau's thought. The clearest form of this distinction is, of course, the contrast between man in the state of nature (who is good without the possibility of being virtuous) and the citizen (who is virtuous without the legal possibility of being merely good).[37]

While it will be appropriate to postpone the analysis of Rousseau's conception of "goodness" and "virtue," the mere indication of this distinction serves to emphasize a crucial problem implicit in the natural education designed for Émile. At the outset, as has just been

[34] *Émile*, I (9–10). Cf. *Contrat social*, II, xii (P, III, 394) and the formulation of the social contract, *ibid.*, I, vi (361). Although the term "fatherland" has been debased and rendered offensive in recent times by Nazi propaganda, it is the etymologically—and philosophically—proper translation of *patrie* and will be used here. Note that "country'" is *not* a sufficient translation because Rousseau explicitly distinguishes *patrie* from *pays* (*Émile*, v [G, 605]).

[35] See the praise of Lycurgus, *ibid.*, I (10) and *Contrat social*, II, vii (P, III, 381–82). Cf. the analysis below, pp. 21–23.

[36] *Émile*, I (G, 10).

[37] *Ibid.*, III (223); v (567, 605); and *Contrat social*, I, viii (P, III, 364–65). In principle, the patriotic citizen may not have sentiments of natural pity for foreigners (*Émile*, I [G, 9]), nor for those convicted of crime (*Contrat social*, II, v [P, III, 377]).

seen, Rousseau denies the possibility of combining the public education of the citizen and the private or domestic education of the natural man, on the grounds that the duties of the true citizen are incompatible with man's natural sentiments. But although Émile is clearly
to be given a "domestic or natural education,"[38] he is not (like the
savage) merely good; on the contrary, the last part of the Émile is
devoted to making him virtuous—a task supposedly prepared by the
"Profession of Faith."[39] Émile is subjected, by his love for Sophie, to
at least one external attachment which, according to Rousseau, did
not exist in the pure state of nature.[40] The mere act of marriage imposes the duties of a citizen upon Émile;[41] and what is even more surprising, he is educated so that, if called upon, he will be a just and
upright magistrate.[42]

The question of how a natural man can be educated to live in society, given the ultimate contradiction between society and nature,
leads to a reassessment of Rousseau's conception of a natural education. As Rousseau points out to his imaginary pupil in two important
speeches in Book v, such a natural man, to insure his freedom, must
choose where he will reside; even if he establishes the most independent means of livelihood possible, a man's freedom ultimately
depends on the political order under which he lives. One cannot be a
free private individual without choosing the society in which he can
be at peace, but the free choice to live in a civil community is the essential act which constitutes the citizen.[43] Paradoxically, to be a natural man, Émile must be at least capable of being a citizen. The project of educating a man according to his nature alone, totally free
from all social prejudice and yet living in society, is internally
contradictory.

It is now easier to understand the ambiguous passage which follows Rousseau's rejection of a civil or public education as a relevant
objective in modern times:

> Finally there remains domestic education or that of nature, but
> what will a man raised uniquely for himself become for others? If
> perhaps the double objective that people propose could be reunited

[38] Émile, I (G, 11); IV (410).
[39] Ibid., III (244); IV (388–89 and n., 402–03); v (567).
[40] Ibid., v (545–49), and the passage of the Second Discourse cited there.
[41] Émile, v (G, 571).
[42] Ibid., v (607). Cf. also I (12).
[43] Ibid., v (581, 583–84; 605–06); cf. Contrat social, IV, ii (440 and n.),
and Émile, v (G, 452–53).

in a single one, in removing the contradictions of man a great obstacle to his happiness would be removed.[44]

Despite the fundamental tension between civil man and natural man, Rousseau admits that he will attempt to raise a *man* who can also be a *citizen*—that is, "if perhaps the double objective which people propose could be reunited in a single one."[45] But is this possible? Is Rousseau's project merely the result of the "dreams of a visionary,"[46] or does it truly resolve the dilemma facing man?

C · THE OBJECTIVE OF A NATURAL EDUCATION

In part, the *Émile* can be considered as a salutary public teaching which attempts to resolve "the double objective that people propose": Rousseau apparently begins from an acceptance of common opinions, and merely tries to apply them to practice in a new way which will avoid the failures of existing customs.[47] But a serious philosophic work cannot be so dismissed in its entirety, especially since the *Émile* goes so far beyond common opinions and questions of mere practice. Rousseau himself seems to indicate the objective of his work by comparing it to Plato's *Republic*, the "noblest treatise on education ever written."[48]

What Plato attempted for the city, Rousseau does for the individual; like Plato, Rousseau creates the best possible condition of man (in speech as distinguished from deed).[49] Rousseau's education is the best that could be hoped for within the limits of human nature; the feasibility of its realization under concrete circumstances is irrelevant as long as the "absolute goodness of the project" lies "in the nature of the thing."[50] Similarly, Plato's *Republic* presents a model of the best political regime, which is justified on the basis of its possibility, granted that its realization is extremely doubtful.[51] Since there can be no doubt that for Rousseau a natural education is virtually im-

---

[44] *Ibid.*, I (11).

[45] Note the references to "l'homme et le citoyen" as if there were no internal contradiction between being a man and a citizen. E.g., *ibid.*, III (225); IV (415). Cf. V (453).

[46] *Ibid.*, Pref. (2).

[47] Compare *ibid.*, II (64): "This principle is common, it will be said; I agree; but the practical application is not common, and it is uniquely of practice that it is here a question."

[48] *Ibid.*, I (10).

[49] Cf. *Republic* II. 369c with *Émile*, I (G, 24–25).

[50] *Ibid.*, Pref. (3).

[51] *Republic* VI. 499b–502c. Émile is a "model to propose" (*Émile*, I [G, 26]).

possible to achieve,[52] the parallel seems valid and his objective clarified: Émile, like the best city described in the *Republic*, is the naturally possible, but virtually unattainable aim or perfection of the human condition.

The ultimate objective of Rousseau's projected natural education is thus not merely a philosophic understanding of what man is, but a moral (as well as political) analysis of what men should be.[53] The natural man is not here primitive man, nor even merely the abstraction of what is common to all socialized men, but the man who is not in contradiction with himself and whose faculties are in "equilibrium."[54] Like Plato, Rousseau saw that human perfection was unlikely because of the internal contradictions of man in society; the educational proposals are not, as a whole, immediately practicable. But Rousseau was not simply a modern Platonist, and to appreciate the specific character of Rousseau's thought, we must take into consideration his explicit decision not to write the *Émile* in the form of a "metaphysical and moral treatise."[55] Hence, before analyzing the philosophical implications of the book, we must return to its surface intention and consider Rousseau's proposals strictly as educational reforms.

3 · The Émile *as a Treatise on Education*

A · THE INTENTION OF ROUSSEAU'S EDUCATIONAL PROPOSALS

Rousseau's philosophical analysis of the natural man is cast in the form of a book on education, and from the outset he seems to direct the work to a nonphilosophic audience, with the apparent hope that his readers will profit in a practical way by reading the *Émile*. Both the subtitle and the epigraph are indications of this intention,[56] and in

[52] *Ibid.*, I (7); II (84). Cf. IV (393).

[53] Cf. *ibid.*, V (585). Note also that the natural education is not simply natural; Rousseau adds "art" to "nature" (*ibid.*, III [199]).

[54] *Ibid.*, IV (247, 313, 388). Such an equilibrium defines human happiness and true freedom, and was present in the state of nature but has been destroyed in society (II [63–70]).

[55] *Ibid.*, IV (278–79). Cf. II (107).

[56] The epigraph is taken from Seneca's *De Ira* XI. 13: *Sanabilibus aegrotamus malis; ipsaque nos in rectum genitos natura, si emendari velimus, juvat* ("We suffer from a curable ill; and since we are born upright nature aids us if we wish to correct ourselves.") This citation, coming from what can be called a moral essay rather than a philosophic work, expresses Rousseau's thesis of man's natural goodness in the form of an exhortation to self-improvement. Rousseau later indicates that this epigraph can be considered as a summary of the book's thesis (*Émile*, V [G, 600]). On the importance of

the Preface Rousseau explicitly addresses the book to "fathers and mothers" who are responsible for education.[57] In fact, one can consider the *Émile* as a dialogue between Rousseau and all those who are capable of improving the education of children: Book I is explicitly addressed to mothers, whose role in education is described as decisive;[58] in Book II Rousseau speaks directly to fathers;[59] and frequently he addresses the teacher (whether the father or mother performing this task).[60]

That Rousseau's direct address is intended to have practical effects is equally apparent. For example, in Book I he argues that the practice of finding a wet nurse to feed the infant is contrary to nature, and promises mothers who breast-feed their own children not only the affection of their offspring, but the respect and love of their husbands.[61] Moreover, Rousseau asserts that this one reform, by itself, would have extensive moral effects:

> But let women deign to nourish their infants, morals will be reformed by themselves, natural sentiments will reawaken in all hearts; the State will be repopulated: this first point, this point alone will reunite everything.[62]

As is appropriate for the author of the *First Discourse*, the possibility of rediscovering the best in human nature is not treated as a metaphysical problem distinct from the way men actually live; Rousseau's work is intended to have a salutary moral effect on his readers by leading them to the "route of nature."

It does not follow, however, that Rousseau speaks to all of his contemporaries indiscriminately. On the contrary, at the level of educational reform, the *Émile* is quite specifically directed to the wealthy in France, and especially the nobles.[63] Apart from the many examples clearly adapted only to this audience, the characteristics of Rousseau's imaginary student, who is explicitly described as French,

---

Rousseau's epigraphs, see below, pp. 112–13, 208, 211, n. 21; and cf. *Rousseau Juge de Jean Jacques*, III (P, I, 941).

[57] *Émile*, Pref. (G, 3).

[58] *Ibid.*, I (5–6 and n.). See also I (17–20); III (226, 235).

[59] *Ibid.*, II (62). See also I (16–17, 23).

[60] *Ibid.*, II (120); III (184–85, 202–03, 212–13); IV (294); *et passim.* Note also the extent to which Rousseau directly addresses the "reader": e.g., III (193, 207, 216); IV (314, 390, 396); V (509). On the intention of Rousseau's direct address to "mothers and fathers," which he later described as a means of "either making myself better understood or expressing myself in fewer words," see *Lettres Écrites de la Montagne*, V (P, III, 783).

[61] *Émile*, I (G, 19).   [62] *Ibid.*, I (18).   [63] See *ibid.*, III (226).

wealthy, and of high birth, are sufficient evidence of this intention.[64] Given Rousseau's well-known republican and anti-aristocratic sentiments, it is all the more necessary to explain why his "model" education, supposedly suited to all men, is given to the son of a wealthy French nobleman.

One reason for Rousseau's appeal to the French upper classes could be that only the wealthy have the means to attempt the private education proposed for Émile, prescribing as it does a tutor for each child and extensive travels. Or perhaps Rousseau directed his work to the French nobility because it was, *par excellence*, the example of a class which set the tone of a whole society; since this group seemed to be the only one which truly mattered in eighteenth-century France, any reform had to begin with the young nobles. Even if these reasons occurred to Rousseau, however, such practical considerations are, by his own admission, marginal to the elaboration of the natural education for man.[65]

Rousseau himself explains why he wants Émile to be a wealthy child:

> The natural education should make a man suited to all human conditions; now, it is less reasonable to bring up a poor man to be rich than a rich one to be poor, for in proportion to the number in these two conditions, there are more ruined men than parvenus. Let us therefore choose a rich man; we will be at least sure to have made one more man, whereas a poor one can become a man by himself.[66]

An education which is suited to a child only on the assumption that he retains the high status of his birth is likely to be catastrophic if the "mobility of human things" forces him to change his way of life.[67] Social position in civil society, especially in modern times, is necessarily unstable. Rousseau therefore warns the French upper classes:

> You have faith in the present order of society without thinking that this order is subject to inevitable revolutions, and that it is impossible for you to foresee or to forestall that which can effect your children. The great becomes little, the rich becomes poor, the mon-

---

[64] *Ibid.*, I (27). Cf. II (181); V (601–02). Note also that Rousseau's example of the natural tastes he would exhibit if wealthy is directed to this audience (IV [430–43]). It need hardly be added that not all classes of French society could afford wet nurses.

[65] Cf. *ibid.*, Pref. (3).

[66] *Ibid.*, I (27). Rousseau immediately adds that the same reason explains his preference for a well-born student.

[67] *Ibid.*, I (11–12, 13); III (225–26).

arch becomes subject: are the blows of chance so rare that you can count on being exempt? We approach the state of crisis and the century of revolutions. Who can tell you what will become of you then?[68]

The rich and noble have an interest in adopting Rousseau's proposed educational scheme precisely because it is intended to suit men for all social conditions, and is thus their only protection against the possibility of social revolution.

This appeal to the self-interest of his specific audience, which sets the tone of the *Émile*, is clearly related to Rousseau's belief that private interest is the motivating factor of most human action. He never tires of insisting that however preferable virtue may be to vice, the attempt to base morality and right on pious exhortation and reasoning alone is bound to fail.[69] Having thus formulated his practical proposals so that they will be most useful and will appear to the benefit of some readers, Rousseau could claim that his criticism of prevailing educational practices was not merely negative.[70]

B · THE PROPER METHODS OF EDUCATION

Rousseau's attack on the way his contemporaries educated their children could be said to derive, at least in part, from his attack on the enlightenment in the *First Discourse*: again and again he criticizes the substitution of idle knowledge for the teaching of the duties appropriate to manhood.[71] The violence of Rousseau's attack on learning from books[72] is also related to a more specific fault of educational practice, namely the attempt to teach children without understanding their nature and pattern of development. He argues that children are placed under continual constraints which run counter to natural impulses; subject to adult caprice and authority from earliest youth, the child seeks to escape the bonds imposed on him and learns to disrespect his elders. Forced to learn before he can understand, the child uses words with no idea of their meaning. What passes for precocity is thus merely vain memorization, or an occa-

[68] *Ibid.*, III (224). Cf. I (13).

[69] E.g., *ibid.*, II (88, 116); IV (278, 356). Cf. *Contrat social*, I, Intro. (P, III, 351); III, ii (400–01).

[70] *Émile*, Pref. (G, 1–2). On the foregoing, compare Rousseau's correspondence with the Duke of Wurtemberg, esp. C. G., X, 205–17.

[71] *Émile*, Pref. (G, 1–2); I (12); II (128). Cf. *First Discourse*, esp. Part 2 (P, III, 24, 30).

[72] E.g., "I hate books; they only teach how to talk about what one does not know" (*Émile*, III [G, 210]). Cf. II (176); IV, "Profession of Faith" (373).

sional happy remark which does not deserve the praise it is unfailingly given. The child thus learns that only appearances count; precisely because such educational practices make a great show of teaching morality through reason, they result in immorality.[73]

Rousseau's educational methods are intended to avoid these failings. His fundamental principle is that the child should always be treated according to the stage of his natural development and capacities.[74] Rousseau calls his basic method "negative education": it is mainly necessary to waste time at first, being more concerned with preventing the child from learning error and vice than trying to teach him any specific information.[75] In place of constraints and formal lessons, it is essential to allow the child to grow up freely; Rousseau controls and directs his pupil solely by what he calls "well-regulated freedom" (liberté bien reglée).[76] All artificial restraints on the child's activity, from swaddling clothes to the commands of his elders, must be removed. In their place, Rousseau controls Émile by the "necessity of things," always placing him in circumstances where physical objects limit his behavior impersonally. When he is punished or rewarded, it is as a necessary consequence of his own action; the pupil is never subjected to the overt will of another person.[77]

Instead of being forced to take lessons that he would not freely choose, the child does only what interests him; natural curiosity must be stimulated by sensually perceptible objects and lessons which the student finds useful and in his own interest.[78] He learns only that which he can understand by himself, remaining in "absolute ignorance" of whatever is beyond his capacity and never accepting anything on the authority of another.[79] The child's own experiences, especially with his physical environment, thus replace formal lessons that are beyond his comprehension and represent memorization rather than true learning; hence Rousseau's well-known emphasis on "lessons of things" (leçons des choses).[80] Since reasoning is not a

---

[73] E.g., ibid., Pref. (2); I (47, 49–50); II (60, 73–79, 95–116); et passim.
[74] Ibid., II (63, 174); III (201–02, 222); IV (273–74).
[75] Ibid., II (82–83). Cf. I (54–56); II (96, 117, 151); IV (274).
[76] Ibid., II (80). Cf. I (50); II (69, 121, 179, 292). The argument that restraint is needed early in life to prepare for later experience is sharply rejected by Rousseau, who refuses to sacrifice the immediate happiness of his pupil to some presumed future good, especially because the ever-present threat of death makes it uncertain that the child will even live to become an adult (ibid., II [61–63]; V [532]).
[77] Ibid., I (14–16, 38–39, 51–52); II (70–71, 93–94). See also the examples, II (122–27) and III (193–97).
[78] Ibid., II (116, 160, 176); III (192). See the example, II (150–53).
[79] Ibid., III (186, 201–02, 242).   [80] Ibid., II (127–28); III (185–90, 203).

necessary consequence of man's physical nature, and requires a development of man's body and the senses, one cannot begin with rational lessons.[81] Rather than teaching the young the sciences, Rousseau insists that the object of education must be sound judgment.[82]

C · THE EDUCATION OF ÉMILE

In applying this method, Rousseau specifies the treatment, activities, and studies suited to each period of the child's development. During infancy he prescribes, in addition to maternal breast-feeding and clothing which allows freedom of movement, the appropriate foods and medical treatment, the response to crying, and the methods of weaning and teething; walking and talking should be learned by the child in his own due time, and not as a consequence of forced lessons (which often do more harm than good).[83] The child between 2 and 12 learns only that which is necessary or of immediately sensed utility: his "moral" education is limited to objects related to himself whose intelligibility is unquestionable (the simplest notion of property and the single precept of never harming another), without the study of languages, history, or any form of reasoning going beyond the child's "present and sensible interest."[84] At this stage the emphasis is on physical education: bodily exercise, development of the senses, and accurate judgment of sensations.[85]

During the third stage, between 12 or 13 and puberty, Émile is taught how to learn and given a love of learning by himself, without formal education in the sciences.[86] Continuing to be motivated by his own sense of utility, he studies first his physical environment,[87] and then the most rudimentary elements of society (the character and value of the various arts),[88] ultimately learning a trade so that he will be capable of working to support himself.[89]

At adolescence, the youth is first capable of natural passion and hence of sensing his relations with others; it is at this point that what Rousseau calls "moral" education truly begins.[90] While retarding the moment of sexual maturity as long as possible, the student starts to study other men, first in terms of the weakness common to all (to develop his sentiments of pity, friendship, and generosity), then in terms of the differences of human character (with the aid of histori-

[81] *Ibid.*, II (76–79, 117–18).   [82] *Ibid.*, III (222). Cf. V (584–85).
[83] *Ibid.*, I (14–21, 31–40, 42–48, 50–58).
[84] *Ibid.*, II (87–99, 103–06, 178).
[85] *Ibid.*, II (117–20, 127–74).   [86] *Ibid.*, III (191–92).
[87] *Ibid.*, III (185–209).   [88] *Ibid.*, III (212–21).
[89] *Ibid.*, III (225–36).   [90] *Ibid.*, IV (246–50).

ans like Plutarch).[91] Only at this point, having led Émile to experience the pleasure of helping others,[92] does Rousseau introduce religious education[93] and instruction in social matters and taste.[94] In the final stage of education, in which the young man prepares to take his place in adult social life, courtship is interrupted by travel and political studies, which lead Émile to a knowledge of the best life for man.[95]

D · THE EDUCATION OF WOMEN

Inserted in this educational scheme at the beginning of Book V is Rousseau's description of the proper education for women. Based on his analysis of the differences between the sexes, Rousseau proposes an education for girls which is markedly different from his proposals for bringing up Émile. Whereas the male child must be allowed the largest possible freedom, the female must be trained to accept constraint and social opinion; instead of learning to judge independently, she is taught that her virtue depends decisively on the prejudices and judgments of others.[96] Despite many superficial similarities (such as emphasis on physical exercise), the education of women is based on principles radically opposed to those in Rousseau's natural education for men.

This sharp dichotomy between the treatment of the two sexes reveals the impossibility of considering the *Émile* merely on the level of an educational treatise. To be sure, one could say that Rousseau's comments on female education are due to his own prejudices, from which modern man has since been emancipated by the doctrine of the equality of all human beings, regardless of age, class, *or* sex. But since Rousseau based his entire education of Émile on the principle that the natural man is and must be free from social prejudice, such a criticism would reduce Rousseau to the status of a bumbling radical in contradiction with himself. Before coming to such a conclusion—especially with reference to the philosopher who had so much to do with the adoption of the notion of human equality (not to mention "progressive" education)—one must consider his reasons for treating men and women so differently. Hence one is led to the surprising conclusion that the status of the *Émile* as an educational treatise can only

---

[91] *Ibid.*, IV (260–78, 280–92).   [92] *Ibid.*, IV (299–304).
[93] *Ibid.*, "Prof. of Faith" (320–87).
[94] *Ibid.*, IV (407–43).   [95] *Ibid.*, V (564–607).
[96] *Ibid.*, V (454–97). Cf. Pierre Burgelin, "L'Éducation de Sophie," *Presence de Jean-Jacques Rousseau, Annales*, XXXV, 113–37.

be fully understood by analyzing the work's least-studied part, "Sophie, ou la femme." But this means that we must return to a consideration of the *Émile* as a philosophic work.

4 · The Émile *as a Philosophic Analysis of Human Nature*

A · THE IMPLICATIONS OF THE DISTINCTION BETWEEN THE SEXES

At the beginning of his analysis of the natural woman, Rousseau presents his reasons for giving each sex a distinct education. In so doing, he criticizes Plato's *Republic* on grounds that require consideration, especially since we have already seen a certain kinship between this work and the *Émile*:

> Plato, in his *Republic*, gives women the same training as men; I can well believe it. Having removed private families from his government and no longer knowing what to do with women, he found himself forced to make them men. This noble genius had combined everything and foreseen everything; he forestalled an objection that perhaps no one would have thought of raising; but he poorly resolved the [objection] that was raised. I do not speak of that supposed community of women, of which the oft-repeated reproach proves that those who make it have never read him; I speak of that civil promiscuity which everywhere confuses the two sexes in the same activities and the same labors, and cannot fail to engender the most intolerable abuses; I speak of that subversion of the sweetest sentiments of nature, immolated to an artificial sentiment which can only exist by means of them. As if a natural hold was not necessary in order to form conventional bonds! as if the love that one has for those who are close was not the principle of that which one owes the State! as if it was not by the small fatherland, which is the family, that the heart is attached to the large! as if it was not the good son, the good husband, the good father, who makes the good citizen![97]

This passage shows, if nothing else, how acute a reader Plato found in Rousseau, who here puts his finger on an essential characteristic of the *Republic*, namely its abstraction of *eros* or love from the political

[97] *Émile*, v (G, 452–53). Cf. *Republic* iv.423d–424a; v.449c–466d. It is a paradox worthy of note that Rousseau, whose thought seems so "modern" because of his democratic political orientation, adopts an "archaic" view of feminine inferiority, whereas Plato, seemingly outmoded politically, takes the currently fashionable view of the equality between sexes. Perhaps this paradox in itself justifies the perennial relevance of political philosophy.

realm. Rousseau counters Plato's egalitarian treatment of women with the observation that love of one's own is essential to political life and patriotism: one cannot love one's own country unless one is capable of loving one's own wife, children, and family.[98] Plato's attempt to abolish the family, in the name of the unity of the city, is untenable because good citizenship is impossible if "the sweetest sentiments of nature" have been destroyed.[99]

The criticism is curious, however, when compared with the passage in Book I that we have already noticed in discussing the distinction between the natural man and the citizen:

> If you want an idea of public education, read Plato's *Republic*. . . . When one wants to refer to the country of chimeras, the institution of Plato is named: if Lycurgus had only written his, I would find it even more chimerical. Plato only purified the heart of man; Lycurgus denatured it.[100]

Just before this remark, Rousseau has given two examples of true citizenship; since both are from Sparta, they show us what Rousseau meant in saying that Lycurgus had "denatured" man. Paedaretus, the Spartan citizen who was joyous at his failure to be elected to the Council of Three Hundred, represents a love of one's fatherland which has completely absorbed man's natural love of himself and self-interest; the Spartan woman who is more concerned with her city's victory than the death of her five sons reveals the subordination of love of one's own family to patriotism.[101]

What is striking, of course, is that Lycurgus' "denaturing" of the Spartans, by substituting a conventional patriotism for their natural love of themselves and their families, is the same fault for which Rousseau criticizes Plato in the passage of Book V of the *Émile* just

[98] Cf. Aristotle's criticism of the *Republic* on similar grounds in *Politics* II.1261a–1264b, esp. 1262b: "Whereas in a state having women and children common, love will be watery; and the father will certainly not say 'my son,' or the son 'my father.' "

[99] We cannot go into the question of how far this criticism of Plato is related to Rousseau's own personal experience, and especially to the act of putting his five children in a foundling home at birth—which Rousseau originally justified as "an act of the citizen and father" in Plato's *Republic*. See *Confessions*, VIII (P, I, 357).

[100] *Émile*, I (G, 10). On Plato's claim to have "purified" the men in his best city, see *Republic* III.399e.

[101] See *Émile*, I (G, 9–10). For the sources, see Plutarch's *Sayings of Kings*, 191F; *Sayings of Spartans*, 231B; *Sayings of Spartan Women*, 241C; in *Moralia*, trans. Frank Cole Babbitt (Loeb Classical Library; Cambridge: Harvard University Press, 1956), III, 135, 385–87, 461–63.

cited. Yet in Book I, Rousseau says that Plato merely "purifies" man's heart, whereas Lycurgus went further in "denaturing" it. This contradiction requires explanation,

A partial explanation may be that, in Rousseau's mind, Plato did not fully destroy man's love of himself, but merely redirected self-interest and enlarged the guardians' familial ties so that they coincide with the city.[102] Be that as it may, the criticism of Plato's *Republic* in Book V of the *Émile* forces us to reconsider the conception of the citizen put forth in Book I: if Plato's best regime destroys the natural root without which the conventional bonds of civil society cannot stand, what is one to say about Sparta, where this "subversion of the sweetest sentiments of nature" went even further?[103] The answer is that the laws of Sparta did not abolish the family, and treated the two sexes quite differently; although Lycurgus denatured Spartan citizens by putting disinterested love of country in place of self-interest, he did not destroy love of the family and the natural sentiments flowing from it. The Spartan woman described in Plutarch and cited by Rousseau runs to the temple to give thanks for her city's victory, but this merely means that she *subordinated* love of her children to patriotism—it does not imply that, as a mother, she did not love her sons nor privately grieve at their death.

This distinction between the actuality of Sparta and the best regime of Plato is in many ways decisive for Rousseau's thought. While we cannot go into all the implications of this distinction, it explains more deeply his conception of the difference between nature and society as these concepts are used in the *Émile*. Rousseau appears to insist that there must be "a natural hold" in order to establish "conventional bonds." However much human nature was reformed by Lycurgus, Spartan institutions did not annihilate the natural human sentiments as they manifest themselves in social man, and indeed could not do so.

What Rousseau means when he speaks of the Spartans as "denatured" is clear from his remark that "every patriot is hard on strangers: they are only men, they are nothing in his eyes."[104] As Rousseau

[102] For evidence that such an interpretation is possible, consider *Republic* v.461d–466b, 468b–d, and vii.518d–521b. The reluctance of the "philosopher-king" to rule is obviously a limit on the extent to which all members of the best regime are animated by love of their city or their fellow citizens.

[103] Cf. *First Discourse*, Part 2 (P, III, 24), where Rousseau cites Montaigne's remark that the laws of Lycurgus were "in truth monstrously perfect"; and *Second Discourse*, Part 2 (P, III, 187–88).

[104] *Émile*, I (G, 9). Rousseau adds: "Outside, the Spartan was ambitious,

argues later in the *Émile*, the natural man is animated by a love of humanity, and his virtuous actions of benefaction are directed to other men as men, not as citizens.[105] The citizen, in contrast, recognizes only his fellow citizens, and exhibits a patriotic virtue which is opposed in its spirit to love of humanity. Thus Rousseau's radical distinction between nature and society cannot be interpreted to mean that the citizen, as such, lacks all natural sentiments; on the contrary, citizens are still men, and their love of country can only replace or absorb their self-love if patriotism is connected to sentiments of love of others which arise naturally in the family.

We can now see somewhat more clearly how Rousseau conceived of nature in writing the *Émile*. To return to the status of women, which seems to be critical for his concept of a natural education, Rousseau insists that there is a fundamental difference between male and female due to the nature of the sexual act:

> The one must be active and strong, the other passive and weak: it is necessary that the one wants and can, it is sufficient that the other resists little. This principle established, it follows that the woman is made specially to please the man. If the man should please her in turn, it is out of a less direct necessity: his merit is his power, he pleases by the sole fact of being strong.[106]

Rousseau immediately adds that this relationship is "the law of nature, prior to love itself"; the sexual distinction between male and female is a natural necessity even in the pure state of nature (where true love for a single mate is not yet present).[107]

Rousseau argues that feminine resistance to the advances of the male is a natural result of this difference between the sexes; such reserve is especially necessary because the human species lacks the instinctive limits on sexual activity of other animals.[108] It follows that the male, despite his superior force, effectively depends on the female, who can vary the extent of her resistance and hence the pleasure of the male; again, Rousseau calls this relationship "an invariable law of nature."[109]

---

avaricious, iniquitous: but disinterestedness, equity, and concord reigned within the walls." This remark shows how far Rousseau was from thinking that self-interest among the Spartans had been totally destroyed; the laws of Lycurgus banished self-interest within the city, but they did not "purify the heart of man."

[105] *Ibid.*, IV (258–68, 299–304).   [106] *Ibid.*, V (446).
[107] *Ibid.* Cf. *Second Discourse*, Part 1 (P, III, 157–58).
[108] *Émile*, V (G, 446–47). Cf. *Lettre à d'Alembert* (G, 189–92).
[109] *Émile*, V (G, 448–49).

Rousseau adds to these natural distinctions the radically different consequences of sexual intercourse for males and females in order to show that the different perfections and duties of the two sexes have their origin in nature. For example, Rousseau asserts that infidelity is a far more serious vice for a woman than for her husband:

This inequality is not a human institution, or at least it is not the work of prejudice, but of reason: it is appropriate for the one of the two [sexes] to which nature entrusted the deposit of children to answer for it to the other.[110]

In this remark, Rousseau makes it clear that the distinction between the duties (and therefore the education) suited to men and women arises from nature, even though it did not fully exist in the state of nature. The natural origin of sexual differences was indeed fully present in the pure state of nature in the form of the reciprocal relationship between the force of the male and the weakness of the female. But it is imprecise to say that the true inequality of the sexes is "not a human institution": the exact formulation is that this inequality is "not the work of prejudice, but of reason."[111]

Once again we see that in the *Émile*, as distinct from the *Second Discourse*, Rousseau considers as natural those characteristics of the species which do not depend on social prejudice, assuming that evolution necessarily forces man to live in society. Whatever the origins of the species, it is a "law of nature" (i.e., one of the ineluctable principles which reason discovers as the explanation of natural phenomena) which *now* forces men to live in society.[112] The same natural principles which governed the pure state of nature still operate in socialized human nature, but their consequences are somewhat different and can only be discovered by reason. The specific education which is natural for socialized woman is, like the natural education given Émile, a human institution based on the primitive dispositions of na-

[110] *Ibid.*, v (450).
[111] Cf. *Geneva MS*, I, v: "For several reasons derived from the nature of the thing, the father should command in the family" (P, III, 299). The paragraph devoted to this proposition is used, virtually without change, in *Économie Politique* (P, III, 242–43). The decisive reasons for paternal authority, rather than joint authority of both parents, are the temporary "incommodities" of women and the father's need to be certain that the children for whom he is responsible are his own.
[112] "In leaving the state of nature, we force our fellows to leave it also; no one can remain in it in spite of the others, and it would actually be leaving it to want to remain there in the impossibility of living in it, for the first law of nature (*loi de la nature*) is the care of self-preservation" (*Émile*, III [G, 223]). On the term "law of nature," see below, pp. 77-80.

ture, freed from the artificial variations due solely to the peculiar human institutions found in various societies.[113]

We are thus led to recognize that, despite the apparent contradiction in Rousseau's methods of teaching men and women, the same conception of human nature underlies a natural education for both sexes. Whether or not we are tempted to reject his subordination of the female to the male as an anachronistic prejudice, it is not inconsistent with Rousseau's own understanding of the human condition. This conclusion has a double importance. First, it permits us to return to the philosophical analysis of Émile's education with the assurance that Rousseau's remarks on the natural development of the human male are relevant to the entire species "in anything that does not depend on sex."[114] Second, the moral implications of the natural sentiments and affections, created by the sexual difference between man and woman, will have to be considered carefully when we come to study the basis of political life; if the emotions on which civil society is founded are rooted in natural sentiments arising in the family, we will be forced to reconsider the extent to which nature and society are in contradiction to each other. But before examining Rousseau's political teaching as such, we must first complete our study of his understanding of human nature—the "systematic part" of the *Émile*, in which the "movement of nature" in man's development is described.[115]

B · THE NATURAL STAGES OF HUMAN DEVELOPMENT: INFANCY

For Rousseau, human nature is not a constant, but a continuous pattern of development in which, as has been noted, he distinguishes five major stages leading to maturity. In Book I of the *Émile*, Rousseau analyzes infancy, the period of radical dependence (from birth to the age when the child walks, talks, and eats solid food) during which the infant's physical needs greatly exceed his own forces.[116] The newborn exhibits only mechanical movements, without consciousness or will; the bodily senses are imperfect and "the soul, enchained in imperfect and half-formed organs, does not even have the sentiment of its own existence."[117] The infant "has no sentiment, no idea; he barely has sensations."[118] Like any animal having anima-

---

[113] Cf. § 2 of this chapter.
[114] *Émile*, v (G, 445).
[115] *Ibid.*, Pref. (2).
[116] *Ibid.*, I (50, 58).
[117] *Ibid.*, I (40).
[118] *Ibid.*, I (58). The terms *"sentiment"* and *"sensation"* recur throughout Rousseau's analysis and are of great importance. If the use of the cognate to

tion and sensitivity the infant must learn to use its senses and does so from the moment of birth.[119] "The first sensations of infants are purely affective; they only perceive pleasure and pain"; these sensations, expressed respectively by silence and by crying, are at first diffuse, for the infant does not distinguish the sensation caused by an object from the object itself.[120]

From the moment of birth, the infant begins to learn. Bodily movement, a necessary "impulse of the internal parts of a body which tends toward growth,"[121] is connected both with the development of imperfect physical organs and with the learning of the difference between external objects and the sensations they cause in the child. Just as the infant learns of space by moving his body, so the motion of objects teaches him that these objects exist outside of himself.[122] The process by which bodily sensations are developed is described by Rousseau in terms of matter in motion, and he insists that the physically determined movements of the infant have no moral element; if a baby destroys objects, this is an accidental consequence of his bodily motions and not an indication of natural wickedness.[123]

Rousseau does not, however, restrict his analysis of the infant to bodily sensation and movements; as has been noted, he contrasts the imperfection of the infant's senses with the virtual absence of what he calls "sentiments," expressed in the "looks" of the eyes rather than facial grimaces or cries.[124] It is clear that such sentiments or consciously felt states of being are closely connected with ideas.[125] It does not follow, however, that sentiments or ideas are unnatural merely because infants do not have them; as Rousseau remarks in the *Second Discourse*, "every animal has ideas, since it has senses."[126] Thus, referring to the supposition of an infant born with "the stature and strength of a grown man," Rousseau concludes that:

---

translate the latter seems unobjectionable, the proper English equivalent for "*sentiment*" is more difficult to find, for it means not only feeling or sentiment (which are not totally synonymous), but also, on occasion, opinion. Here the cognate will be used unless the latter meaning is unambiguous.

[119] *Ibid.*, I (41–42). Note that although Rousseau speaks of the "soul" of the newborn, he treats the infant as if he were indistinguishable from any other animal. At the outset, therefore, Rousseau leaves open the question of whether man is simply an animal or whether he has an immaterial soul distinct from his body.

[120] *Ibid.*, I (42, 45).

[121] *Ibid.*, I (14, 49).   [122] *Ibid.*, I (44–45).

[123] *Ibid.*, I (48–49).   [124] *Ibid.*, I (45–46).

[125] *Ibid.*, I (40, 58); IV, "Prof. of Faith" (353–54n.).

[126] *Second Discourse*, Part 1 (P, III, 141).

this man-child would be a perfect imbecile, an automat, an immobile and almost insensible statue . . . he would only have a single idea, namely that of *me*, to which he would relate all his sensation; and this idea, or rather this sentiment, would be the only thing he would have that the ordinary infant lacks.[127]

Since this supposition, like Condillac's *homme-statue* to which it refers,[128] represents man's primitive and natural stupidity,[129] the sentiment of one's own existence is the natural root of all ideas, even if it does not truly emerge until the second stage of human development.[130]

Rousseau explicitly indicates that, despite the virtual absence of sentiments in the infant, occasional manifestations of moral sentiment are possible:

Before the age of reason, we do good and evil without knowing it; and there is no morality in our actions, even though there is sometimes [morality] in the sentiment of the actions of another that are related to us.[131]

The infant has neither reason nor conscience, but he is capable of feeling moral outrage at physically sensible injustice done to him. Rousseau gives the example of a nurse who slapped a crying infant:

He was immediately silenced: I thought he was intimidated . . . I was mistaken: the unfortunate one was suffocated with anger. . . . A moment later came sharp cries; all the signs of the resentment, furor, despair of that age were in his accents . . . when I might have doubted that the sentiment of the just and the unjust was innate in the heart of man, this example alone would have convinced me. I am sure that a burning coal which fell by chance on the hand of that infant would have been less sensible than this rather light slap, given with the manifest intention of offending him.[132]

While we cannot yet discuss the status of the conscience and the innate moral sentiments to which Rousseau here refers, it is essential to

---

[127] *Émile*, I (G, 40).

[128] See L'Abbé de Condillac, *Traité des Sensations*, esp. "Dessein de cet ouvrage," in *Oeuvres* (3rd ed.; Paris: Libraires Associés, 1777), III, 1–6.

[129] "However little one has reflected on the order and progress of our knowledge, one cannot deny that this was just about the primitive state of ignorance and stupidity natural to man before he learned anything from experience or his fellows" (*Émile*, I [G, 41]). Rousseau thus implicitly endorses the analysis of the *Second Discourse*.

[130] *Émile*, II (G, 61).

[131] *Ibid.*, I (48).   [132] *Ibid.*, I (46–47).

recognize that he saw observable evidence of such sentiments in infants.[133]

C · EARLY CHILDHOOD: THE DEVELOPMENT OF THE SENSES

The second basic stage of life, childhood proper, is marked by development toward an equilibrium between the child's needs and his forces.[134] With increased strength develops self-consciousness:

> Memory extends the sentiment of identity over all moments of existence; he becomes truly one, the same, and consequently already capable of happiness or misery.[135]

In the natural order of development, sensual perception leads first to memory, then to reasoning; all mental processes originate in the senses.[136] The child learns to attach meanings to linguistic signs and gestures on the basis of their sensual effects: his brain retains words and images, but not ideas—and "in whatever study there may be, without the idea of the things represented, the representative signs are nothing."[137]

This distinction between signs or images and the ideas they represent for the adult is important:

> Before the age of reason, the infant does not receive ideas, but images, and there is the following difference between them: images are only absolute pictures of sensible objects, and ideas are the notions of objects, determined by relationships. An image can be alone in the mind which reproduces it, but any idea presupposes others. When one imagines, one only sees; when one conceives, one compares. Our sensations are purely passive, whereas all our

---

[133] See also Rousseau's note on animal instinct, in which he implies that dogs have something like a moral instinct when threatened (*ibid.*, IV, "Prof. of Faith" [348–49n.]).

[134] *Ibid.*, II (69–71, 179).

[135] *Ibid.*, II (61). Rousseau adds that one must consider the child as "a moral being" from this time on. This use of the adjective *moral* must be distinguished from the noun *morale* (morality); here Rousseau uses *moral* to mean "conscious" or capable of thought, referring to the basic dichotomy between the adjectives *physique* and *moral*. See below, chap. III, § 3B; and cf. the passage cited at n. 88 of chap. II.

[136] *Émile*, II (117–18, 128).

[137] *Ibid.*, II (106). Cf. 59, 103. It is for this reason that Rousseau insists that a child can only really learn one language (105), and that much education is useless, being merely the learning of words whose meaning is not understood. See particularly the masterful analysis of La Fontaine's "Le Corbeau et le Renard" (*ibid.*, II [111–14]).

perceptions or ideas arise from an active principle that judges. That will be demonstrated later.[138]

Since the only "demonstration" of the difference between passive sensation and active judgment occurs in the "Profession of Faith," an examination of Rousseau's analysis of human reason must be deferred until the next chapter. For the moment, we can limit ourselves to the distinction between the child's "sensitive reason," based primarily on sensible objects and the images representing them in the brain, and "intellectual reason" (which depends on ideas properly so-called).[139] Or, to use a later formulation:

> What I called sensitive or childlike reason consists of forming simple ideas by the combination of several sensations; and what I call intellectual or human reason consists of forming complex ideas by the combination of several simple ideas.[140]

During childhood, the mind is capable of forming "images" or "simple ideas," but nothing more; hence the decisive developments until the age of 12 or 13 are the perfection of the five senses.

Rousseau thus devotes a large section of Book II to the education of the child's senses and the possibility of training his judgment of sensual objects.[141] The implications of this discussion will be somewhat clearer if we compare it to the treatment of the five senses in the *Second Discourse*. The natural savage learns primarily to use senses necessary for his self-preservation:

> He will have extremely crude touch and taste, and sight, hearing, and smell of the greatest subtlety. Such is the animal state in general; and according to the reports of travelers, such also is that of most savage peoples.[142]

In contrast, in the *Émile* Rousseau gives priority to touch and sight, which he calls "the two senses whose usage is the most continuous and the most important";[143] much of the training of the senses is not merely concerned with animal self-preservation.[144] The ordering of the

---

[138] *Ibid.*, II (103). Cf. *Second Discourse*, Part 1 (P, III, 147–51).

[139] *Émile*, II (G, 128). Cf. 156.

[140] *Ibid.*, II (174).

[141] The five senses are discussed in the following order: touch (*ibid.*, II, [138–48]), sight (148–50), hearing (161–64), taste (164–72), and smell (172–74).

[142] *Second Discourse*, Part 1 (P, III, 140–41).

[143] *Émile*, II (G, 160). Cf. 153.

[144] Note particularly the importance attributed to games at night (*ibid.*, II, 139–42), drawing and geometry (154–58), and singing (162–64).

senses of the natural man in the *Émile* is no longer that of natural man in his "animal state."

In developing Émile's bodily senses, Rousseau is primarily concerned with the two senses that produce erroneous judgments subject to correction in children. Of the three types of sensation which are of secondary importance in the *Émile*, both hearing and taste are "passive" senses for which there is less need to train one's judgment;[145] because the sense of smell depends decisively on imagination, it is not too important in the sensual judgments appropriate for children.[146] In contrast, judgments of touch and sight are necessarily made by children and need to be perfected. Although touch is the most frequently used and the surest sense (because it is the most limited one), judgments of touch are "imperfect" and "crude" because its usage is habitually mixed with that of sight.[147]

> Thus sight is the most faulty of all our senses precisely because it is the most extended and because, preceding all the others by a great deal, its operations are too quick and too vast to be able to be corrected by them.[148]

The illusions of perspective, while necessary to permit judgments of extension, introduce erroneous judgment because a small nearby object can be confused with a large, distant one.[149]

Unlike savage man, who along with other animals necessarily develops those senses which insure self-preservation (sight, hearing, and smell), Émile is taught to perfect his sensual perception so that he will judge external objects correctly; the former has accurate sensations, the latter accurate sensual judgments.[150] This difference between the analysis of physical sensation in the *Second Discourse* and the *Émile* is an additional proof that the natural man of the latter work is the perfected human being, not a primitive one. Rousseau's attempt to train the sense of touch, a "crude" sense in the state of nature, is connected to his conception of correct sensual judgment as the basis of physical science; the combination of accurate tactile and visual sensation is needed for a true perception or "knowledge" of natural phenomena because vision needs to be corrected by touch, "of all the

145 On hearing (*ibid.*, II [161]); on taste (166). Note that Rousseau trains Émile's ear (a "passive" organ) by his voice (an "active" one)—*ibid.* (161).
146 *Ibid.*, II (173).
147 *Ibid.*, II (146).   148 *Ibid.*, II (149).
149 Cf. *ibid.*, II (140–41n.) and (149–50).
150 See *ibid.*, III (221–22).

senses the one which instructs us the best on the impression that foreign bodies can make on our own [body]."[151] For example, one of the
decisive proofs of an experiment conducted during the next stage of
Émile's education is precisely the correction of a visual sensation by
the sense of touch.[152] And although Rousseau asserts that a man can
ultimately "judge correctly on the basis of the impressions of a single
sense," before this is possible he must have previously "verified" one
sense by another "for a long time."[153]

If we recall Rousseau's distinction between purely passive sensations and active judgments based on the comparison of sensations, it
is clear that even in the realm of sensual perception Émile does not
develop his senses as merely passive responses to matter in motion.
During the second stage of childhood, the natural human being does
not yet have truly intellectual ideas; he has only "a small number of
moral notions which relate to his present condition (*état*), none concerning the relative condition of men,"[154] and his only moral sentiments are a consciousness of himself and his own rights.[155] But he
does begin to form that aspect of thought which Rousseau calls "sensitive or childlike reason," consisting of the comparison of sensations.[156] Although this "first reason of man" is composed of simple
ideas, apparently akin to the ideas of animals, in man "sensitive reason . . . serves as the basis for intellectual reason (*raison intellec-
tuelle*)."[157] It would appear that the additional possibilities of human
reason are derived from the presence, even at a relatively early stage,
of a kind of active judgment or comparison of sensations which is, at
least, much more extensive in men than in animals, and which permits

[151] *Ibid.*, II (146). See also 153, and the passage cited at n. 142 of this
chapter.
[152] *Émile*, III (G, 241–42).
[153] "From which it follows that after having verified the relations of one
sense by another for a long time, it is necessary to verify the relations of
each sense by itself; then each sensation will become an idea for us, and this
idea will always conform to the truth" (*ibid.*, III [240]).
[154] *Ibid.*, II (178). As Rousseau adds, "of what use would the latter be to
him, since a child is not yet an active member of society?"
[155] *Ibid.*, II (61, 88, 90, 176).
[156] *Ibid.*, II (174). Obviously the idea of property, which a child of 12 supposedly has, is based on the comparison of different sensations (see 90–92).
[157] "Since everything that enters human understanding comes to it by the
senses, the first reason of men is a sensitive reason; this is what serves as the
basis of intellectual reason" (*ibid.*, II [128]). Cf. *Second Discourse*, Part 1
(P, III, 141). Hence even if man has an innate feeling (*sentiment*) of justice,
he cannot reason about justice except as an idea ultimately derived from
sense experience.

man the luxury of verifying the accuracy of his sensations in order to know and adapt to his physical environment.[158]

Toward the end of Book II, Rousseau indicates that the following stages of education will emphasize the training of the mind, for which the training of Émile's body and his sensual judgment has been only a preparation.[159] Having discussed the five bodily senses:

> It remains for me to speak, in the following books, of the cultivation of a kind of sixth sense, called common sense less because it is common to all men than because it results from the well-regulated use of the other senses, and which teaches us of the nature of things by the combination of all their appearances. As a consequence, this sixth sense does not have a specific organ: it only resides in the brain, and its purely internal sensations are called perceptions or ideas. The extent of our knowledge is measured by the number of these ideas; their sharpness and their clarity make up the precision of the mind, and the art of comparing between them is what is called human reason.[160]

Whatever its roots in nature, this "sixth sense" is developed only in perfected man; common sense is so-called because it requires the combination of the perceptions of all the senses, and not because it is common to all men.[161] Although human thought is described as a "kind" of sense with its own "sensations," human reason proper is based on an active comparison of ideas by the human mind, and not merely on a passive response to matter in motion.

D · LATER CHILDHOOD: THE DEVELOPMENT OF REASON

The emphasis on training the mind to make correct judgments of physical phenomena is pronounced in the third stage of education— the short period, from the age of 12 or 13 to puberty, when the child has an excess of force over need which permits him to learn a great deal about his environment.[162] Even though at this point the child becomes capable of having ideas properly so-called, Rousseau insists that it is not possible to begin abstract or intellectual reasoning at once:

---

[158] *Émile*, II (G, 117–18). The full impact of this difference between socialized or perfected man and primitive man or other animals will be analysed in the next chapter, when we turn to Rousseau's understanding of the status of judgment and reason.

[159] Cf. *Émile*, II (G, 127–28) and III (185–86).

[160] *Ibid.*, II (174).

[161] Cf. Descartes, *Discourse on Method*, Part I.

[162] *Émile*, III (G, 182–84).

himself to others (e.g., pity, love of another, or humanity); having only "primitive sentiments" connected with love of himself, his own preservation and pleasure, he is solely interested by "purely physical objects."[171] To the extent that a child of this age observes aspects of social life, he is to learn about industry, mechanical arts, and exchange, and not the moral implications of society (which cannot be easily represented by physical objects).[172] Thus, as Rousseau summarizes this stage of education:

> Émile has only natural and purely physical knowledge. He does not even know the name of history, nor what metaphysics and morals are. He knows the essential relationships of man to things, but none of the moral relationships of man to man.[173]

Even with respect to physical phenomena, although the natural child acquires ideas,[174] the development of reason is still limited:

> He little knows how to generalize ideas and make abstractions. . . . He does not seek to know things by their nature, but only by the relationships that interest him. He only judges what is foreign to him in relation to himself, but this judgment is exact and certain.[175]

Not only the acquisition of knowledge of social life and the virtues suited to it, but also true reasoning about nature itself is impossible prior to adolescence and the emergence of the passions which underlie human society.

E · ADOLESCENCE: THE DEVELOPMENT OF THE PASSIONS

The fourth stage of education is therefore decisive: adolescence culminates in a "second birth" when "man is truly born into life, and . . . nothing human is foreign to him."[176] It is in the analysis of this period, lasting from about the age of 15 to sexual maturity, that Rousseau elaborates his understanding of the status of human passions and the basis of the bonds between men. Whereas the child is characterized by the absence of sentiments arising out of his relations with others, during adolescence the youth goes beyond mere love of himself to acquire such sentiments.

Rousseau denies that human passion can be destroyed, but insists that it is essential to distinguish the natural source of the passions from those which have been added by man's modification of his own

---

[171] *Ibid.*, III (200–02, 244). Cf. II (88).
[172] *Ibid.*, III (212, 217–18).
[173] *Ibid.*, III (243).   [174] *Ibid.*, III (237).
[175] *Ibid.*, III (243).   [176] *Ibid.*, IV (246).

nature.[177] The animal's instinct to preserve itself produces, in man, the sentiment or passion of love of oneself:

> The source of all our passions, the origin and principle of all the others, the only one which is born with man and never leaves him as long as he lives, is love of oneself: a primitive passion, innate, anterior to all others, and of which all others are only, in a sense, modifications.[178]

This natural passion to love oneself is "always good," and as we have noted is already present in the child.[179] As long as the child's sensibility is limited to the relationships of physical objects to himself, this passion is "absolute"; since the natural child is only concerned with himself, and not with others, his behavior has no morality.[180]

An objection which might immediately be raised against Rousseau's analysis is derived from the experience of the infant in the family: is it not true that the child develops an attachment to his parents, and especially to his mother, which produces the kind of sentiment of love for another supposedly lacking in children? Since all passion originates in need, we must ascertain why the physical needs of the infant, which place him in a position of impotence and dependence, do not produce moral sentiments prior to adolescence. Rousseau does not deny that the child may in fact experience moral sentiments relating himself with others, but he insists that such a development is unnatural and can be avoided.[181] Although the physical dependence of the infant produces an extension of the infant's love of himself to those who assist him, this attachment is "purely mechanical":

> What favors the well-being of an individual attracts him; what hinders it repels him: this is only a blind instinct.[182]

[177] *Ibid.*, IV (246–47). Note that while it is "an enterprise as vain as it is ridiculous" to try to *destroy* the passions, it is not as certain that the passions cannot be prevented from emerging: "I would find anyone who wanted to prevent the passions from arising *almost as crazy* as one who wants to annihilate them" (*ibid.*, italics added). The reason for this difference, of course, is that man in the state of nature does not have human passions properly so called; savage man's only passions are "the simple impulsion of nature" (*Second Discourse*, Part 1 [P, III, 143]). Presumably, the passions could be prevented from emerging—but Rousseau indicates that this is not his objective both in the *Émile*, IV (G, 247) and in the *Second Discourse*, n. IX (207).

[178] *Émile*, IV (G, 247).

[179] *Ibid.*, II (88); IV (248).   [180] *Ibid.*, IV (248–49, 257).

[181] Cf. *ibid.*, I (47) and IV (248–50).

[182] *Ibid.*, IV (248).

The child's needs are bodily, and are naturally satisfied by things, not by people; an animal can perform the same function as the human mother and the child's attachment to it will have exactly the same character.[183]

True passions differ from such instinctive or mechanical attachments because they presuppose a consciousness of the intention or will of another being:

> What transforms this instinct into a sentiment, attachment into love, and aversion into hate, is the manifest intention to harm us or to be useful to us. One does not develop passion for insensitive beings who only follow the impulsions given them; but those from whom one expects good or evil by their interior disposition, by their will, those that we see acting freely for or against, inspire in us sentiments similar to those they show us.[184]

Normally, the child requires a long time to perceive the intention or will of others toward him, and even then the child's sentiment toward another is self-centered.[185] It follows that all human passions based on the comparison of the self to another are unnatural as long as there is no physical need which forces the individual to seek out another; since sex is the first such need, only with the coming of man's sexual drive is he fully capable of imagining and comparing the will and sentiments of another to his own.

While we must analyze in more detail the means by which the individual perceives the "interior disposition" of another to help or harm him, it will be useful to begin by discussing the relationship between love of oneself (*amour de soi*) and self-love (*amour-propre*) which Rousseau introduces at this point:

> Love of oneself, which only regards ourselves, is content when our true needs are satisfied; but *amour-propre*, which compares, is never content and cannot be because this sentiment, in preferring ourselves to others, also demands that the others prefer us to themselves, which is impossible.[186]

As readers of the *Second Discourse* will remember, there Rousseau insists that only "love of oneself" is natural, and that *amour-propre*

---

[183] Rousseau here cites the attachment of Romulus to the wolf who suckled him (*ibid.*) Cf. the examples of children brought up by animals in the *Second Discourse*, nn. III (P, III, 196) and X (212).

[184] *Émile*, IV (G, 248).

[185] Cf. *ibid.* with the exception described in I (46–47) cited above, p. 29.

[186] *Émile*, IV (G, 249).

or "self-love" is an artificial sentiment which does not exist in the state of nature:

> Love of oneself is a natural sentiment which inclines every animal to watch over its own preservation, and which, directed in man by reason and modified by pity, produces humanity and virtue. *Amour-propre* is only a relative sentiment, artificial and born in society, which inclines each individual to have a greater esteem for himself than for anyone else, inspires in men all the harm they do to one another, and is the true source of honor . . . in our primitive state, in the true state of nature, *amour-propre* does not exist; for . . . it is not possible that a sentiment having its source in comparisons he is not capable of making could spring up in his soul.[187]

This formulation connects the origin of *amour-propre* in civilized man with his ability to make comparisons with others, but it does not fully explain the source of such comparisons.

According to the *Émile*, the advent of the sexual drive is the true foundation of man's "relations with his species" and "all the affections of his soul."[188] Love is a moral sentiment or passion which presupposes the comparison of the self with another, and the moral aspect of sexual love (as distinct from the purely physical impulsion) requires a preference for a specific mate, based on comparisons which reveal a reciprocity of affections between the two lovers. In civilized man, sexual desire necessarily goes beyond the physical aspect of love to which the natural savage was limited; whereas "any woman is good" for man in the pure state of nature, the moral element of a specific preference presupposes the evolution of the human species and the acquisition of "enlightenment, prejudice, and habit."[189] But as soon as man is capable of making the comparative judgments which create the possibility of love, he is also capable of comparing himself to *any* other member of his species, and not merely to those for whom he may feel sexual desires. Paradoxically, just as man is able to feel the sweetest passions, he is also in a condition to feel envy, jealousy, and hatred—the "hateful and irascible passions" which originate from *amour-propre*. Both true love and *amour-propre* are unnatural senti-

---

[187] *Second Discourse*, n. xv (P, III, 219). In our translation of the *Discourses* (New York: St Martin's Press, 1964), *amour-propre* was rendered as "vanity"; this is imprecise since Rousseau speaks of *vanité* and *orgueil* ("vanity" and "pride") as two different forms of *amour-propre* (*Émile*, IV [G, 250]); *Constitution pour la Corse* (P, III, 937–38).
[188] *Émile*, IV (G, 249).
[189] *Ibid.*, IV (249–50) and *Second Discourse*, Part 1 (P, III, 157–58).

ments, and the basic difference between them is that the latter is inequitable, whereas love, being reciprocal, is not.[190]

In contrast to man in the state of nature, Émile or the socialized natural man necessarily develops both *amour-propre* and specific preferences for a sexual mate.[191] This of course creates a decisive problem for Rousseau: if the natural savage can be good without virtue (since love of oneself is naturally good and is not contradicted by *amour-propre* in the state of nature), the natural man living in society cannot avoid the vice which is inherent in *amour-propre* as soon as he reaches adolescence. While the last half of the *Émile* is devoted to the resolution of this problem, Rousseau indicates at this point how vice can be avoided, or at least minimized, at the present stage of human evolution:

> What makes man essentially good is to have few needs and to compare himself little with others; what makes him essentially wicked is to have many needs and to depend a great deal on opinion. On this principle it is easy to see how one can direct to good or evil all the passions of children and men. It is true that not always being able to live alone, they will be good only with difficulty: this difficulty will even increase necessarily with their relationships, and it is above all in this that the dangers of society make art and care more indispensible for us in order to prevent, in the human heart, the depravation which arises from its new needs.[192]

The necessity of "art" and "care" reveals once again the internal contradiction of educating natural man within society, and explains why Rousseau's project is virtually impossible to achieve in practice.

To preserve natural goodness in society, man's needs must be kept at a minimum and he must be dependent, insofar as possible, on things rather than on people (to whom he can compare himself, whose will can be moved, and whose prejudices are most often unnatural).[193] Rousseau is explicit in distinguishing between such a dependence on things and dependence on men:

> There are two kinds of dependence: that on things, which is from nature; that on men, which is from society. Dependence on things, having no morality, does not hinder liberty and does not engender

---

[190] *Émile*, v (G, 548).
[191] *Ibid.*, IV (250). Cf. 244.   [192] *Ibid.*, IV (249).
[193] *Ibid.*, II (63–66) and the references cited in n. 77 to this chapter. Note also that dependence on things (rather than on men) parallels Rousseau's emphasis on the "education of things" (rather than the "education of men").

the vices. Dependence on men, being disordered, engenders them all, and by it master and slave mutually deprave each other. If there is some way of remedying this evil in society, it is to substitute law for man, and to arm the general wills with a real force superior to the action of every private will. If the laws of nations could, like those of nature, have an inflexibility that no human force could ever overcome, dependence on men would then become that on things; in the republic all the advantages of the natural state would be united with those of the civil state; to the freedom which keeps man exempt from vices would be joined the morality which raises him to virtue.[194]

Rousseau's political teaching, based on the famous notion of the general will, is thus merely a development, in terms of a society as a whole, of the same concept of freedom which underlies Émile's private education; despite the polar opposition between the education suited to the natural man and that of the citizen, both are intended to free the individual from a dependence on other men *qua* individuals.[195]

To liberate either the natural man or the citizen from artificial dependence on the "private will" of another human being, it is necessary to "direct . . . all the passions." This is possible because, although passions originate in man's sensibility and cannot be completely destroyed, the objects desired depend on imagination; by reorienting man's imagination it is possible to direct human passion according to "the true relations of man, as much in the species as in the individual."[196] For example, even *amour-propre* need not necessarily produce the "hateful and irascible passions" which normally arise from it:

> Extend *amour-propre* to other beings, and we will transform it into virtue, and there is no human heart in which this virtue does not have its root.[197]

The crucial factor underlying the character of all human passions is therefore the role played by the imagination, which directs love of oneself and *amour-propre* to objects which the individual believes are

---

[194] *Émile*, II (G, 70–71). Note the use of the term *volontés générales* in the plural: when speaking of all mankind, Rousseau thereby makes clear the inevitable division of the human species into different societies, each of which has its own general will. Cf. below, chap. VI, §§ 2A–B.

[195] See *Émile*, II (70n.).

[196] *Émile*, IV (G, 256–57). Cf. *Lettre à d'Alembert* (G, 232).

[197] *Émile*, IV (G, 303).

desirable. "The errors of imagination transform the passions of all finite beings into vices"; if primitive man is naturally good, it is in large part because his imagination "does not speak" to him.[198]

All moral or relative sentiments are based upon an imagination or comparison of another's internal disposition with one's own, which develops only along with sexual sensibility and the resulting physical need for another member of the species:

> Since the child does not imagine what others feel, he only knows his own ills; but when the first development of the senses lights the fire of imagination, he begins to feel himself in his fellows, to be moved by their complaints, and to suffer with their pains.[199]

Because the development of sexual maturity in the adolescent is a slow process according to nature,[200] the imagination which is due to the earliest phenomena of sexual sensibility is not necessarily directed to sexual objects. On the contrary:

> The first sentiment of which a carefully educated young man is susceptible is not love; it is friendship. The first act of his emerging imagination is to teach him that he has fellows, and the species affects him before sex.[201]

Several pages later, however, Rousseau seems to contradict himself; when the adolescent reflects on the suffering of other sensitive beings:

> the sight of blood flowing will make him turn away his eyes; the convulsions of a dying animal will give him an indescribable anguish before he knows the origin of these new movements. . . . Thus pity, the first relative sentiment which touches the human heart according to the order of nature, is born.[202]

Even granting the possibility that sexual sensibility does not immediately produce sexual imagination and passion, how can Rousseau state that two different sentiments—friendship and pity—are the "first" to develop?

The answer to this apparent contradiction lies in a careful reading of the two passages just cited. Pity is called a "relative sentiment," friendship merely a "sentiment." Pity is a sentiment which presupposes comparison of the self with other beings; since it implies a pref-

[198] *Ibid.*, IV (257); *Second Discourse*, Part 1 (P, III, 158, 144).
[199] *Émile*, IV (G, 260).
[200] *Ibid.*, IV (257–58). See above, p. 7.
[201] *Ibid.*, IV (258).   [202] *Ibid.*, IV (261).

erence of one's own position to that of another, it seems to be connected to the general class of sentiments which Rousseau describes as *amour-propre*.[203] In contrast, friendship is, like sexual love, a sentiment which requires reciprocity; it is one of the "sweet and affectionate passions" stemming from love of oneself.[204] Moreover, friendship is the first sentiment of a young man who is "carefully educated," whereas pity is the first sentiment "according to the order of nature"; the latter is directed to any sensitive animal, the former to other men only. There is something more natural—or at least more inevitable—in the early occurrence of the sentiment of pity than in the priority of friendship.

Why this should be is explained by Rousseau's analysis:

> The weakness of man makes him sociable; our common miseries carry our hearts to humanity: we would not owe it anything if we were not men. Any attachment is a sign of insufficiency: if each of us had no need of the others, he would scarcely think of uniting with them.[205]

Human need is thus at the root of society and the feelings that unite men. But the effects of human needs are subtle:

> We attach ourselves to our fellows less by the sentiment of their pleasures than by that of their pains; for we see in the latter much more clearly the identity of our nature and the guarantees of their attachment for us. If our common needs unite us by interest, our common miseries unite us by affection. The sight of a happy man inspires in others less love than envy; he would be willingly accused of usurping a right that he lacks in creating an exclusive happiness for himself; and, moreover, *amour-propre* suffers by making us feel that this man does not have any need of us.[206]

Mutual needs may explain why men have a common interest in uniting, but as long as needs alone—and the self-interested calculation of how to satisfy those needs—are the sole basis of unity, no society or even friendship can last.[207] Insofar as one joins a group only for one's selfish motives, as soon as self-interest or pride dictates one can also

---

[203] To reveal this connection, it is sufficient to notice that on the same page Rousseau speaks of both *amour-propre* and pity as the source of the sentiment of humanity (*Ibid.*, IV [303]).

[204] *Ibid.*, IV (276 and n.).

[205] *Ibid.*, IV (259).   [206] *Ibid.*

[207] *Ibid.*, IV (386n.). Cf. *First Discourse*, Part 1 (P, III, 6–7).

leave it.[208] Indeed, it could be said that Rousseau's entire political teaching is directed, at least in part, against what he saw to be the weakness of the Hobbesian-Lockean derivation of civil society from self-interest alone; for Rousseau, such a theoretical position destroyed any bond of affection within the city, and thus replaced true patriotism and civic virtue with a base and selfish bourgeois calculation.[209]

For a human group to be truly lasting, it must be based on affection as well as interest. But the root of an affection for others cannot be the natural love of oneself, which is an absolute sentiment that only relates other objects to one's own utility. Friendship would seem to be the logical basis for man's sociability.[210] But since friendship, like love, is based on reciprocity, friendship may not stand the test of a conflict of personal interest; who has not heard of old friends who, having become business partners, fell out over a difference of interest? As soon as men can compare their own sentiments with the sentiments of others, friendship or love, were it to be based solely on the extension of love of oneself to the other, would be subject to the ever-present risk that one partner would imagine that the other was happier than he. Such a comparison, by producing envy, would thus destroy friendship by causing love of oneself to become *amour-propre*.[211]

In contrast, the sentiment of pity can serve as the basic root of affection for others, and indeed it is only by the prior development of pity that even friendship is possible. As has been shown, all true passion requires the use of one's imagination in conjunction with a comparison of the self with others. But the only natural way to imagine the sentiments felt by another is pity, which is even observed in some form in animals.[212] In men, pity involves an action of putting oneself in the shoes of another, so to speak:

In fact, how do we let ourselves be moved by pity, if it is not in

---

[208] Cf. *Second Discourse*, Part 2 (P, III, 166–67); *Préface à Narcisse* (P, II, 968 and n.).

[209] Cf. *Émile*, I (G, 10); II (93n.); IV (280). Note that, according to the *Contrat social*, the element of common interest on which civil society rests is *opposed to* the private interest of each member (*Contrat social*, II, iiin. [P, III, 371]).

[210] In classic political philosophy, this connection between sociability and human friendship was often explicit. See Aristotle, *Nicomachean Ethics* VIII.-1159bff.; Cicero, *Laws* I.xii.

[211] The possibility of such a development is clearly implied by Rousseau (*Émile*, IV [G, 276n. and 278–79n.]).

[212] *Second Discourse*, Part 1 (P, III, 154–56).

transporting ourselves outside of ourselves, and identifying ourselves with the suffering animal, leaving our being, so to speak, in order to take his? We only suffer insofar as we judge that he suffers; it is not in ourselves, but in him that we suffer. Thus no one becomes sensitive except when his imagination is animated and begins to transport him outside of himself.[213]

Pity can be stimulated by the sight of any "suffering animal"; friendship or love presupposes an imagination of the feelings of other human beings.

Any pure sentiment of love or friendship, being inextricably bound up with our own pleasure, partakes of love of oneself in a form that can easily degenerate into envy and *amour-propre*; in contrast, the sort of imagination and sentiment connected with pity does not run that risk, for it is *already*, like *amour-propre*, a comparison with another which reveals the preferability of one's own condition. To reformulate the point, pity is the only moral sentiment which partakes of the characteristics of both love of oneself and *amour-propre* simultaneously; the sentiment of pity is "sweet" because it reveals a contentment with one's own status (like love of oneself), but it is also a comparison with others to our own benefit (like *amour-propre*).[214] Yet pity is not *amour-propre*, and is prevented from degenerating into it because it depends on the imaginary transportation of the self to a less fortunate being, an act of the imagination in itself unpleasant (although the resulting sentiment is "sweet").

The decisive status of pity in Rousseau's thought should come as no surprise for those who recall that in the *Second Discourse* the sentiment of pity is Rousseau's substitute for the principle of sociability, which dominated the traditional understanding of natural law.[215] This substitution permits Rousseau to base his conception of human passions and virtues on animal-like responses, in contrast to the classic view (according to which the standard of a sentiment like friendship is derived from the perfection of virtue and goodness as understood by reason). The replacement of sociability by the prerational sentiment of pity presupposes that pity, unlike reason, is present in the state of nature. Without anticipating the analysis of the *Second Discourse*, we must consider the extent to which the treat-

[213] *Émile*, IV (G, 261).   [214] *Ibid.*, IV (259–69, 270).
[215] *Second Discourse*, Pref. (P, III, 125–26). On the extent to which Rousseau's conception of man's natural asociality is thus intermediate between Hobbes' assertion of natural anti-sociality and the view of natural sociability derived from Aristotle, see below, chap. III, § 3.

ment of this sentiment in the *Émile* casts doubt on this possibility. Pity requires an act of imagination, and apparently man in the state of nature (like a young child) has virtually no imagination.[216] If the child is incapable of pity—as Rousseau clearly indicates[217]—how is a primitive man or an animal, similarly lacking in moral sentiments, to be said to feel pity?

The difficulty is subtly admitted by Rousseau in describing the timing of Émile's first sensations of pity:

> If he had remained stupid and barbarous, he would not have them; if he was more educated, he would know their source: he has already compared ideas too much in order to feel nothing, and not enough to conceive of what he feels.[218]

Does it not seem that primitive man—"stupid and barbarous"—is as incapable of pity as the fully civilized man? If we turn again to the *Second Discourse*, we find indeed that fully civilized man, especially if he is trained to think, suppresses the sentiment of pity; as soon as men begin to live in society, even in the later stages of the state of nature, the emergence of *amour-propre* undermines pity.[219] More to the point, when Rousseau reduces natural pity to "a sentiment that puts us in the position of him who suffers," he adds that this is a "sentiment that is obscure and vivid (*obscure et vif*) in savage man, developed but weak (*developpé mais faible*) in civil man."[220] As the contradictory character of these adjectives suggests, there is something mixed about the sentiment of pity, so that it is not fully developed either in the primitive man of the pure state of nature nor in the civil man who has learned to think. It seems that pity appears in its strongest form in the early stages of the adolescence of Émile, the natural man living in society. We must see why this is so.

Pity is "obscure and vivid" to the natural savage for two different

[216] *Second Discourse*, Part 1 (144, 158). As we have seen, pity is somehow akin to *amour-propre*, since both are comparisons of the self with another, leading to the conclusion that the condition of the self is preferable to that of the other. Yet *amour-propre* is, according to Rousseau, unnatural and not present in the state of nature precisely because primitive man is incapable of the comparisons required (*ibid.*, Part 1 [158] and n. xv [219–20]).

[217] *Émile*, I (G, 48).

[218] *Ibid.*, IV (261).

[219] *Second Discourse*, Part 1 (P, III, 156); Part 2 (169–71).

[220] "Even should it be true that commiseration is only a sentiment that puts us in the position of him who suffers—a sentiment that is obscure and strong in savage man, developed but weak in civilized man—what would this idea matter to the truth of what I say, except to give it more force" (*ibid.*, Part 1 [155]).

reasons: it is vivid because it is a sentiment which arises immediately from a physical sensation—the simple perception of the suffering of another living being;[221] it is obscure because it requires an act of imagination, and primitive man seems to lack this faculty.[222] Moreover, for man in the state of nature, governed largely by impulse, the sentiment of pity is clearly subordinate to his desire for self-preservation; should the two basic impulses conflict, it is the latter which governs his action.[223] On the other hand, the sensation of seeing another suffer has a very different effect on civil man. Imagination and judgment are "developed," permitting a more conscious identification of the self with the other, but the sentiment arising out of the active response of the brain is "weak" because of the simultaneous development of *amour-propre* due to man's reasoning.[224]

In the case of the adolescent Émile, however, pity can be both "developed" (because he has been trained to compare sensations, so that his imagination leads him to feel the suffering of another being) and "vivid" (because he has not begun to reason about his own status relative to other men, and thus has not been depraved by the sentiment of *amour-propre*).[225] If—and it is an almost impossible condition—Émile can be trained to feel pity for his fellowmen without simultaneously stimulating the "sentiments which force us to compare ourselves with others" (like vanity, emulation, and glory), then his sentiment of pity can be used as the basis of his moral training.[226] We should not be surprised that this seems to be a weak reed upon which to base all human morality, for Rousseau himself points out that reason is forced to reestablish the rules of natural right which, primitively, could be derived from love of oneself and pity.[227] But for the natural man in society—the rare exception who is perfected in accordance with nature—pity can apparently become, at adolescence, the true basis of all social sentiments and morality.

5 · *The Implications of Pity: Human Virtues and Human Affections*

Since the foregoing analysis has been somewhat tortuous, a restate-

[221] See again *Émile*, IV (G, 261), cited above at n. 202. Cf. *ibid*. (267).
[222] See below, chap. III, § 2E.
[223] Note the "legitimate case" referred to in the Preface to the *Second Discourse* (P, III, 126), and cf. Part 2 (166).
[224] See *ibid*., Part 1 (155–56).
[225] See *Émile*, IV (G, 261), cited above at n. 218. Note that Rousseau's analysis presupposes the distinction between the comparison of sensations ("sensative or childlike reason") and "intellectual reason" properly so-called.
[226] *Ibid*., IV (266).
[227] *Second Discourse*, Pref. (P, III, 126); *Geneva MS*, II, iv (P, III, 329).

ment of the status of pity will clarify Rousseau's conception of the human passions. The emergence of moral sentiments relating one human being to another presupposes the emergence of sexual sensibility, but it is not necessary for the first such moral sentiment to be love (a conscious reciprocal affection between male and female). On the contrary, all human affection has its natural root in pity, the only emotion of primitive man which presupposes an act of imagination (i.e., the identification of oneself with the suffering of another). Since the object to which the imagination is directed determines the sentiment which results, pity can be called the origin of both man's "sociability" and "all the social virtues." But the sentiments derived from pity are not all of the same kind. On the one hand, the natural sensibility caused by pity creates relative sentiments which, like a purified form of *amour-propre*, are comparisons with others implying that one's own condition is preferable to that of another; the resulting sentiments are what we might call *human* or *humanitarian virtues*:

> In fact, what are generosity, clemency, humanity, if not pity applied to the weak, to the guilty, or to the human species in general?[228]

On the other hand, pity makes possible a reciprocal relation of equality between beings, each of which senses that others voluntarily chose to identify their well-being with his own; these sentiments are *human affections*: friendship, love, and patriotism.[229]

The distinction between human virtues and human affections is central, for they are intrinsically opposed to each other, even though Rousseau attempts to combine them in educating Émile. The virtues resulting directly from pity are not exclusive—clemency or humanity toward one fellowman implies, at least in principle, clemency or humanity toward all fellowmen in the same position. Human affections, on the contrary, are necessarily exclusive; the suspicion that this exclusive preference is not shared produces, in social man, the passion of jealousy which "irritates" love if it does not destroy it.[230] The human virtues need not—and indeed cannot—be reciprocal (since the emotion of pity presupposes a difference between one's own condition and that of the other being who is pitied); the human affections

---

[228] *Second Discourse*, Part 1 (155). Cf. *Émile*, IV (G, 262, 303).

[229] "Benevolence and even friendship are, rightly understood, the products of a constant pity fixed on a particular object" (*Second Discourse*, Part 1 [P, III, 155]).

[230] Cf. *Émile*, V (G, 546–49) and *Second Discourse*, Part 1 (P, III, 157–59).

are necessarily reciprocal (and the failure of reciprocity destroys the sentiment of affection). Patriotism is a love of one's fellow citizens which, in its exclusivity and reciprocity, is akin to friendship and sexual love; as we noticed when comparing natural man to denatured or civil man, patriotism is intrinsically opposed to humanitarianism.[231] Although pity itself is one of the "simplest operations" of the human soul, it produces contradictory sentiments in social man.

The opposition between the virtues and the affections derived from pity is reinforced by a paradox: although humanitarian virtues seem to be more natural than human affections, human affections are more solid than humanitarian virtues. The virtues derived directly from pity are more natural than affections because they presuppose only the direction of the imagination toward new objects; by extending the primitive identification with another from physically sensible suffering to "moral" misfortunes, the simplest natural sentiment of pity produces such virtues as humanity, clemency, and generosity.[232] But these human or humanitarian virtues, although directly based on a universal natural sentiment, are not felt by all men; the true sentiment of humanity presupposes the "abstract idea" of the human species, an idea which is not natural to primitive man and is acquired by few men even in society.[233] Indeed, in order to develop the virtue of humanity, Rousseau indicates that Émile must first have the experience of affectionate sentiments toward "those who have been made dear or necessary by habit."[234] If the virtues derived from pity seem to be more natural (because pity can sometimes exist in primitive man), it is the exclusive and reciprocal affection for others, arising out of a prior habit or mechanical attachment, which is the only reliable basis of moral sentiment. To be sure, love presupposes a kind of reflection that is akin to *amour-propre* and was absent in the state of nature. But once mankind has evolved to his present, socialized state, the kind of comparison with others represented by friendship and love is more reliable—indeed, more "natural"—than the indiscriminate generalization of pity to all other men.

As we shall see in a later chapter, a human morality based on the

[231] See above, pp. 11–13, 22–25. This connection between sexual love and patriotism as similar derivations from pity explains why Rousseau could speak of a "natural hold" for the "bonds of convention" created by society, and thereby clarifies the grounds of his criticism of Plato's *Republic*. See again *Émile*, v (G, 452–53).

[232] *Ibid.*, iv (267).

[233] Cf. *Second Discourse*, Part 1 (P, iii, 156) and Part 2 (178); *Émile*, iv (G, 276, 307); and *Geneva MS*, i, ii (P, iii, 286–87).

[234] *Émile*, iv (G, 276).

sentiment of pity directed to all men as men is insufficient for reasoning man. By proving that the sentiments of love and friendship, albeit unnatural to the species, are natural developments from pity in social man, Rousseau thus prepares the groundwork for a solid or more reliable morality, based in part on self-interest and in part on these derivative manifestations of pity. To show that the political teaching which Rousseau elaborates is grounded in sentiments originating in pity, we need merely indicate that the general will consists in the act of identifying oneself with one's fellow citizens—an act of imagination which, like primitive pity, "transports us" outside of ourselves.[235] If the resulting love of one's country is an exclusive, reciprocal passion which is intrinsically opposed to the humanitarian sentiments of the true philosopher, at least patriotism and the civic virtue which flows from it are accessible to all socialized men. Only the replacement of an impotent, humanitarian virtue by civic virtue, based on a contract which is a human creation, prevents the wicked from successfully seeking their own selfish interest at the expense of decent men.[236]

The foregoing analysis has gone to great length to show the comprehensive character of Rousseau's understanding of social man. We have seen that conscious, moral sentiments of affection, albeit lacking in the pure state of nature, are natural in the sense that they derive from the natural sentiment of pity and originate necessarily once men transform the mechanical attachment of animal habit into a truly human passion. The individual's moral sentiments are capable of taking a "good" or natural form even in society, but the control of human passion is an exceedingly delicate operation once man is no longer merely an animal. The only method of restraining a human passion is to oppose it by another passion;[237] reason alone is impotent to control desire, and only becomes a regulating force when its wisdom is supported by such sentiments as love.[238] For example, since the character of the passions depends on imagination, Rousseau directs Émile's sexual desire by encouraging his student to imagine the pleasures of true love and the perfections of the woman whom he will love.[239]

---

[235] Cf. *Contrat social*, II, iv (P, III, 373) and IV, i (437–38). Note also that both friendship and marital love, like civil society, are egalitarian contracts (*Émile*, IV [G, 276]; v [607]). Cf. also IV (405).

[236] See below, chap. VI. Cf. *Émile*, IV (G, 303–04).

[237] *Ibid.*, IV (406–07).   [238] *Ibid.*, IV (276, 398, 417).

[239] *Ibid.*, IV (408–10). Cf. 256, 415. This explains why Rousseau believed that corrupt morals could be reformed by a novel depicting the pleasures of

The natural passions of social man can only be preserved from corruption by art. In fact, the entire development of Émile's sentiment of pity presupposes that Rousseau has been able to "fool" his student's "emerging sensibility" by delaying the moment of sexual maturity and controlling sexual impulses while cultivating reason.[240] Art is necessary because it is impossible to control or redirect another's passions by formal commands:

> The heart only receives laws from itself; by wanting to enchain it one releases it; one only enchains it by leaving it free.[241]

Rousseau replaces the tutor's overt constraint by those sentiments which are freely accepted by the natural man, and uses the adroit manipulation of such sentiments to lead his student to moral virtue.[242] Rousseau's natural education is an attempt to show how the passions, if freed from the deformation caused by social opinion, can be morally upright; if the *Émile* is, as Rousseau says, a treatise on man's natural goodness, this goodness is based on his freedom, and especially on the freedom of the passions.[243]

---

true love and the virtues flowing from it. See *La Nouvelle Héloïse*, Second Pref. (P, II, 22–26).

[240] *Émile*, IV (G, 388). Cf. 256, 273–74, 393; and note that Rousseau even uses the device of exciting Émile's passion for hunting (a sport which obviously contradicts the natural sentiment of pity) to retain sexual desire (*ibid.*, IV [397]).

[241] *Ibid.*, IV (277). See also 278.

[242] *Ibid.*, IV (278–79, 303–04, 402–03). Although Rousseau calls a natural education "well-regulated liberty" (*la liberté bien reglée—ibid.*, II [80]), this manipulation requires deceit; indeed, as someone once put it informally, "Rousseau must have a make-believe world. The natural education is a make-believe education." While a few commentators have ascribed this to a totalitarian impulse (e.g., Lester G. Crocker, "Rousseau et la voie du totalitarisme," *Rousseau et la Philosophie Politique* [Paris: Presses Universitaires de France, 1965], p. 128), such an interpretation is unnecessary and unwarranted; cf. Judith N. Shklar, "Rousseau's Images of Authority," *American Political Science Review*, LVIII (December 1964), 925-30. Ultimately, the artificiality of the natural education can probably best be understood as a kind of "thought experiment," not totally unlike Condillac's *homme statue*; Rousseau attempts an experiment in which nature is controlled (or, to use Bacon's term, "tortured") in order to reveal itself. And since the experiment is impossible to conduct in practice, Rousseau contents himself with an experiment in words. See *Émile*, I (G, 24); *Second Discourse*, Pref. (P, III, 123–24); and cf. Plato, *Republic* II.369a–c.

[243] As Leo Strauss puts it: "In Rousseau, passion itself took the initiative and rebelled; usurping the place of reason and indignantly denying her libertine past, passion began to pass judgment, in the severe accents of Catonic virtue, on reason's turpitudes" (*Natural Right and History* [Chicago: University of Chicago Press, 1953], p. 252).

Rousseau's elaboration of the development of man's senses and faculties is essentially completed by the first section of Book IV; in the remainder of the *Émile*, Rousseau presents the religious teaching appropriate to the natural man, and the ways in which such an individual can be taught to live with his fellowmen, find a suitable wife, and understand the nature of politics. These aspects of the natural education, while important, consist in the response of developed human nature to those experiences which the adolescent has not previously encountered. Before considering the remainder of the work, therefore, it is necessary to pose a central question which has hitherto been ignored. Although much of Rousseau's analysis in the *Émile* can be reduced to the properties of matter in motion and the "laws of necessity," human freedom seems to be the essence of man's natural goodness. What then is the status and meaning of human freedom?

In the *Second Discourse* Rousseau argues that man's distinctive characteristic is freedom, but he then admits that this is a "metaphysical" idea which is open to objections; within the *Second Discourse* Rousseau apparently rests his argument on man's "perfectibility."[244] But is this retreat from freedom to perfectibility as the essence of human nature truly definitive, or is it merely a provisional statement? Rousseau's only elaborate treatment of the problems he himself calls "metaphysical," including "the philosophic meaning of the word freedom (*liberté*)," occurs in the "Profession of Faith of the Savoyard Vicar." It is to this section of the *Émile* that we must now turn.[245]

[244] *Second Discourse*, Part 1 (P, III, 141–42).

[245] The last paragraph of *Contrat social* (I, viii), contains what appears to be an implicit reference to the *Émile* in general, and to the "Profession of Faith" in particular: "To what has just been said, one could add to the acquisitions of the civil state moral freedom, which alone makes man truly the master of himself; for the impulsion of appetite alone is slavery, and obedience to the law one prescribes to oneself is freedom. But I have already said too much on this point, and the philosophic meaning of the word *freedom* is not here part of my subject" (P, III, 365). Since Rousseau has just distinguished between "natural freedom" in the state of nature (as analyzed in the *Second Discourse*), and the "civil freedom" in political society (which is discussed in the *Contrat social*), "moral freedom" is implicitly different from the topics discussed in these two works; the only place where Rousseau says "too much" about the latter is clearly the *Émile*, and this may be why it contains a "philosophic" analysis of the concept of freedom. Cf. Derathé's note (III, 1450, n. 1).

ROUSSEAU'S DETACHABLE
METAPHYSICS AND THE GOOD LIFE
(EMILE, BOOKS IV·V)

1 · *The Character of the "Profession of Faith"*

Of all the difficulties posed by the works of Rousseau, the status and meaning of the "Profession of Faith of the Savoyard Vicar" is one of the most complex and least carefully analyzed. On the one hand, a number of commentators have used it as evidence that Rousseau was fundamentally a Christian philosopher, whose religious thought is sometimes said to derive from the Protestantism of his native Geneva, sometimes from sentiments akin to Pascal's, and sometimes from the Pelagian heresy (especially as put forth in the doctrine of Molina adopted by certain Jesuits).[1] At the other extreme, the "Profession of Faith" is either simply ignored or assimilated into Rousseau's teaching of the civic religion in the *Social Contract*; since Rousseau speaks only in the name of the Savoyard Vicar, the status of the "Profession of Faith" is treated as necessarily doubtful and the core of Rousseau's thought found elsewhere in his works.[2]

While most attempts to derive Rousseau's philosophical orientation from theological presuppositions do not require comment, the latter view is subject to the difficulty that Rousseau himself explicitly acknowledged the views of the Savoyard Vicar as similar—though not identical—to his own.[3] Rousseau privately wrote that he believed

---

[1] E.g., see Pierre–Maurice Masson, *La Réligion de J. J. Rousseau*, 3 vols. (Paris: Plon, 1914); John S. Spink, *J. J. Rousseau et Genève* (Paris: Boivin, 1934); Jacques-François Thomas, *Le Pélagianisme de J. J. Rousseau* (Paris: Nizet, 1956). Some have even gone so far as to argue that Rousseau's thought is consistent with Thomism. See Henri Guillemin, "Présentation," in *Jean-Jacques Rousseau: Du Contrat Social* (Paris: Le Monde en 10/18, 1963), pp. 33–34, and the work of R. P. Ravier cited in his n. 40.

[2] In addition to the many works which simply ignore the "Profession of Faith," not to say the entire problem of Rousseau's thought concerning religion, see Leo Strauss, *Natural Right and History* (Chicago, University of Chicago Press, 1953), p. 288.

[3] In the *Rêveries d'un Promeneur Solitaire*, Rousseau describes the process

in God, the duality of substances, and the immortality of the soul
before he was persecuted for writing the "Profession of Faith."[4] Although there may well be, as Groethuysen has pointed out, a tension
between Rousseau's philosophy and his personal religion,[5] this only
indicates the importance of the teaching of a natural religion which
Rousseau placed at the center of the *Émile*.

If the faith of the Savoyard Vicar approaches Rousseau's own religious beliefs, how can this part of the *Émile* be related to the rest of
Rousseau's writings without thereby interpreting his entire philosophy in fundamentally religious terms? Since Rousseau did not write

by which he resolved his personal metaphysical and religious doubts: "the
result of my painful research was just about (*à peu près*) what I have since
registered in the *Profession of Faith of the Savoyard Vicar*" (Prom. III [P, I,
1018]). See also the Lettre à M. de Franquières, 15 January 1769 (C. G.,
XIX, 48–63); *Confessions*, IX (P, I, 407); and the profession of faith of Julie
in *La Nouvelle Héloïse*, VI, xi (P, II, 714–16). The similarity between Rousseau's personal views and those attributed to the Savoyard Vicar (or Julie)
does not mean, however, that the speeches attributed to these characters are
in every respect accepted by Rousseau: "In the *Émile* is found the profession
of faith of a Catholic Priest, and in the *Héloïse* that of a devout woman:
these two pieces are sufficiently in agreement that one can explain one by the
other, and from that agreement it can be presumed with some probability
that if the Author who published the books containing them does not adopt
both of them *in entirety*, at least he favors them a great deal" (*Lettres
Écrites de la Montagne*, I [P. III, 694], italics added). For further evidence that
the Savoyard Vicar's profession is not identical to Rousseau's opinion in every
respect, see *ibid.*, III (730 n., 749–50).

[4] Among the many examples in Rousseau's correspondence, see esp. the
Lettre à Jacob Vernes, 18 February 1758 (C. G., III, 286–88). On the status
of the "Profession of Faith" as a declaration of positions that Rousseau had
already asserted in private and felt compelled to take publicly, see Charles
W. Hendel, *Jean-Jacques Rousseau: Moralist* (Indianapolis and New York:
Bobbs–Merrill, 1962), II, 124–39. "I considered it a duty to say my opinion
(*sentiment*) in important and useful things . . ." (*Lettres Écrites de la Montagne*, III [P, III, 749]). See also Pierre-Maurice Masson, La "*Profession de
Foi du Vicaire Savoyard de Jean-Jacques Rousseau*" (Paris: Hachette, 1914),
Part I, chap. I. Masson's critical edition of the original, with Rousseau's manuscript draft on facing pages, is invaluable for analysis of the sources and history of the text.

[5] "He (Rousseau) was a philosopher and a Christian. He was not a Christian philosopher" (Bernard Groethuysen, *J. J. Rousseau* [Paris: Gallimard,
1949], p. 309). It must be added, however, that if Rousseau accepted "true
Christianity" because of the "purity of its morality (*morale*)," he did not thereby commit himself to belief in Jesus as the son of God. See *Lettres Écrites de la
Montagne*, I (P, III, 698, 706). Hence Rousseau speaks of "Jesus, enlightened
by the spirit of God . . ." and concludes that, "When he would not have
been the wisest of mortals, he would have been the most lovable" (*ibid.*, III
[742, 754]). It is therefore more accurate to describe Rousseau as an adherent of "theism or natural religion, which Christians pretend to confuse with
atheism or irreligion, which is the directly opposed doctrine" (*Émile*, "Prof.
of Faith," [G, 360]).

in his own name, but in the name of a Savoyard Vicar whom he claims to quote, it cannot be denied that the religious and metaphysical opinions set forth have a different status than propositions which Rousseau asserted as unquestionably his own. Even granted that the "Profession of Faith" corresponds to Rousseau's own belief, the literary device used underlines the "insuperable obstacles" and "insoluble objections" to any metaphysical system.[6] Indeed, the mere fact that this section is described as a "Profession of Faith" distinguishes it from those works where Rousseau claimed to have established undeniable "proofs" of his position.[7]

This distinction between the certainty of Rousseau's philosophic proofs and the doubt of Rousseau's beliefs in the "Profession of Faith" must, however, be viewed cautiously; to determine precisely the extent to which the former can be interpreted without reference to the latter, it is necessary to compare statements made in the name of the Vicar with those made by Rousseau himself. This is all the more imperative because, within the "Profession" itself, Rousseau added footnotes which are unquestionably his own comments on the Vicar's statements,[8] and in which the Vicar's position is reiterated on a number of important points (such as the denial that matter naturally and necessarily moves by itself, and the criticism of the atheistic position of the *philosophes*).[9]

The need for cautiously comparing the statements of the Savoyard Vicar to Rousseau's own philosophical analysis is reinforced by the explicit intention with which the "Profession of Faith" is presented. Rousseau describes it as an "example" of the religious teaching suitable for the natural man, who is treated in the *Émile* as the best or most perfect socialized man.[10] Thus, on one level, the "Profession of Faith" seems to serve a function directly parallel to the chapter on

[6] *Ibid.*, (324). "Philosophy, having on these matters neither basis nor limit, lacking primitive ideas and elementary principles, is only a sea of incertitude and doubt, from which the metaphysician never extricates himself" (Letter to Vernes, 18 February 1758 [C. G. III, 287]). Cf. *Second Discourse*, Part 1 (P, III, 151): "metaphysical" ideas, such as "matter, spirit, substance, mode, figure, movement, . . . have no model in nature."

[7] Cf. *ibid.*, Part 1 (162); Part 2 (193); n. IX (202); *Letter to M. Philopolis* (P, III, 232).

[8] This is doubly important because, as a general rule, Rousseau utilized footnotes as a device to provide clarification for "philosophic" readers as distinct from a more superficial or "vulgar" audience. Consider the addressee of the last note to the "Profession of Faith" (*Émile*, IV [G, 389n.]).

[9] *Ibid.*, "Prof. of Faith" (328 and n., 329n., 330, 385–87, 386–89n.). Cf. also 333 and n.; 337–38 and 338n.; 362 and 362–63n.; 382 and n.

[10] *Ibid.*, IV (314, 387). See above, chap. I, § 2C.

"Civil Religion" in the *Social Contract*: just as a society needs positive religion as a bond which preserves the morality of its citizens (even though this religion does not have the status of philosophic truth), so the natural man, now that all men live in society, needs religious training to reinforce the weakness of the natural sentiments like pity, which kept primitive man from being vicious.[11]

The Vicar himself insists on the nonauthoritative character of his teaching: the reader must on every point judge for himself the truth of the opinions presented in the "Profession of Faith."[12] But Rousseau used the same canon throughout the *Émile*:

If I sometimes take an assertive tone, it is not to impose on the reader; it is to speak as I think. Why should I propose in the form of doubts what I myself do not doubt? . . . In exposing freely my opinions, I so little expect to be authoritative that I always add my reasons, so that I can be judged.[13]

If this general principle indicates that the "Profession of Faith," explicitly proposed "in the form of doubts," is not entirely certain, it also suggests that anything which the Savoyard Vicar and Rousseau both state affirmatively is at least Rousseau's own "opinion." We must therefore try to define clearly the limits of these affirmatively held opinions and their connection to Rousseau's philosophy.

Before doing so, however, it will be useful to indicate the structure and outlines of the entire "Profession." This part of the *Émile* has the same form as Rousseau's *First* and *Second Discourses*: it begins with a Preface (in this case Rousseau's description of the scene of his encounter with the Savoyard Vicar), and is then composed of an introduction (the Vicar's summary of his own life, his quest for faith, and his method), and two major parts, divided by Rousseau's interruption of the Vicar. In the first part, the Savoyard Vicar elaborates the dogmas of natural religion; in the second he presents a critique of theological doctrine and a denial of the revealed status of any positive religion.[14] Each of the main parts, moreover, has the same internal

[11] See n. 2 of this chapter, and compare *Lettres Écrites de la Montagne*, I (P, III, 695, 697–700, 703–07).

[12] *Émile*, "Prof. of Faith" (G, 320, 335). But note the distinction between the Vicar's "intimate persuasion" of the dogmas of the first part of his faith and his doubts concerning the second part (360–61).

[13] *Ibid.*, Pref. (2). This passage is explicitly connected to the "Profession of Faith" in *Lettres Écrites de la Montagne*, III (P, III, 747–48).

[14] The pagination of these divisions is as follows: Pref. (*Émile*, "Prof. of Faith" [G, 314–20]); Intro. (320–25); Part 1 (325–59); Part 2 (360–87). The structure of the *First Discourse* is identical, as is that of the *Second Discourse* (with the exception of the Dedication which precedes the latter).

structure, being composed of an introductory statement, a body of substantive analysis, and then conclusions (first of a general character, and then applied to the lives of the Vicar and Rousseau). The "Profession of Faith" thus appears to be a speech addressed to all men, or at least all readers, by a man who claims not to be a philosopher; it is an exoteric discourse.[15]

2 · Rousseau's Natural Theology and Dualist Metaphysics

A · THE FIRST "ARTICLES OF FAITH": NATURAL THEOLOGY

We will not analyze here the second part of the "Profession of Faith," which criticizes the exclusive claims of all revealed religions; since all specific religions are "external" or "public cults" which are purely political matters, the only religious training necessary for natural man is the "theism or natural religion" provided in the first section of the Vicar's Profession.[16] The Savoyard Vicar introduces this teaching by describing his own state of moral and religious incertitude and the inability of the works of philosophers to resolve it; only the writings of the English theologian Samuel Clarke are supported by the kind of "direct proofs" that can balance the "insoluble objections" to which every metaphysical system is open.[17] Because reasoning is incapable of resolving the doubts inherent in all metaphysics,

[15] *Émile*, IV (G, 314); "Prof. of Faith" (320, 336, 360n.). Cf. *First Discourse*, Intro. (P, III, 5); Part 2 (30); and Strauss, *Natural Right and History*, pp. 260–61. Note that while the judges of the *Second Discourse* are explicitly distinguished from its "vulgar readers," this distinction is not made in the "Profession of Faith." Cf. *Second Discourse*, Intro. (P, III, 133) and Part 1 (163) with *Émile*, "Prof. of Faith" (360 and n.).

[16] *Ibid.*, "Prof. of Faith" (360–62, 378–81). Note that the conclusion of the Second Part of the "Profession" is the presupposition on which Rousseau's analysis of Christianity as a civic religion (*Contrat social*, IV, viii) is based.

[17] *Émile*, "Prof. of Faith" (321–24). As a comparison of the "Profession" and Clarke's *Treatise on the Existence of God* shows, the Savoyard Vicar's praise, at least in part, is an attempt to provide a respectable theological authority for the Vicar's bold religious views; Clarke insists that after he has proven the existence of God by a priori reasoning (direct proofs having been largely ignored), anyone who professes natural religion without accepting Christian revelation is certain to lapse into pure atheism. See the Ricotier translation of Clarke's work, published under the title *Traités sur l'Existence et les Attributs de Dieu: Des Devoirs de la Religion Naturelle, et de la Vérité de la Religion Chrétienne*, 3 vols. (2nd ed.; Amsterdam: Jean Frederic Bernard, 1728), II, 39–48. Cf. *Émile*, "Prof. of Faith" (360): the Savoyard Vicar is a good example of the kind of "deist" Clarke explicitly attacks. In Rousseau's mind, Clarke's principles are true only insofar as they contradict "philosophic atheism"; for practical purposes, Plato and Clarke are identical in this respect. Lettre à M. de Franquières, 15 January 1769 (C. G., XIX, 50).

the Savoyard Vicar's opinions on these matters are largely determined by feeling or sentiment:

> I return to the examination of the knowledge which concerns me, resolved to accept as evident everything to which I cannot refuse my assent in the sincerity of my heart, as true everything which seems to me to have a necessary connection to these first, and to leave everything else in uncertainty.[18]

The Savoyard Vicar here faithfully expresses Rousseau's repeated assertion that man can never go beyond the realm of opinion with reference to knowledge of the whole; it is important to have a *sentiment* for oneself, but this sentiment or opinion may merely be a prejudice as far as the reason of others is concerned.[19]

The exposition of the Savoyard Vicar's metaphysical and theological beliefs begins with a brief analysis of his own nature:

> But who am I? . . . I exist and I have senses by which I am affected. This is the first truth that strikes me and that I am forced to admit.[20]

Having revised Descartes' famous *cogito ergo sum* by substituting sensation for thought, the Vicar immediately poses a decisive problem:

> Have I a specific sentiment of my existence or do I only feel it by my sensations? This is my first doubt, which at present I cannot resolve. For being continually affected by sensations, either immediately or by memory, how can I know if the sentiment of myself is something outside these sensations, or if it could be independent from them?[21]

The terms of the Vicar's problem are derived from Rousseau's analysis of human sensitivity: men have sensations which are essentially passive responses to material objects, but they also have a "kind of sixth sense," the brain, whose sensations (if they can be so called) are merely internal. Some of these mental sensations (e.g., the memory) are clearly determined by physical sensations of external objects, but others are "ideas" which are based on the "active" comparison of various sensations or ideas. Whatever the status of such

[18] *Émile*, "Prof. of Faith" (G, 324).
[19] See *Rêveries*, III (P, I, 1017–18, 1020–23); and the Letter to Vernes cited in n. 6 of this chapter.
[20] *Émile*, "Prof. of Faith" (G, 325).
[21] *Ibid.*

ideas, the child does not begin by forming them in his brain; prior to thought is the sentiment of one's own existence—a feeling of self-consciousness—which is neither an ordinary physical sensation (since it is not the response to a specifically sensed object) nor an idea.[22]

Consistent with Rousseau's own emphasis on explaining man in terms of his origins, the simplest mental act which is not obviously a passive response to bodily sensation is the decisive question for the Savoyard Vicar. Indeed, it is decisive for Rousseau's entire understanding of human nature, which presupposes the existence of natural sentiments derived from man's sentiment of his own existence. If sentiments are merely composite sensations, the possibility of distinguishing between natural and unnatural sentiments would appear to require a prior distinction between the natural physical sensations and those sensations or combinations of sensations which are somehow not natural. But since physical sensations are all basically the product of the same five senses, such a distinction is only possible if the term "natural" is treated in a radically historical sense, and the natural sensations are described as those which were felt by primitive man in the pure state of nature. Within the *Émile*, Rousseau's analysis of the sensations and natural sentiments does not have this character and cannot, because to do so would imply that all socially acquired sensations and sentiments are equally artificial—hence that there is no possibility whatever of educating a natural man within society. The entire project of the *Émile* stands or falls according to the resolution of the first doubt of the Savoyard Vicar.

The Vicar, therefore, postpones consideration of this crucial problem momentarily in order to analyze the implications of sensation itself:

> My sensations occur in me, since they make me feel my existence; but their cause is foreign to me, since they effect me in spite of myself, and it is not up to me either to produce them or destroy them.[23]

Sensations are therefore caused by external objects whose existence is certain:

> All that I sense outside of myself and which acts on my senses I

[22] *Ibid.*, I (58); II (61, 174, 237, 240), and above, chap. I (pp. 28–30).
[23] *Ibid.*, "Prof. of Faith" (325). Note that the ambiguity of the phrase "they make me feel" (*elles me font sentir*) leaves the Vicar's first doubt still unresolved.

call matter, and all portions of matter that I conceive of as united in individual beings I call bodies.[24]

By simply becoming conscious of his sensations, the Savoyard Vicar claims that he is certain of the existence of the universe and can therefore dismiss the metaphysical debates of idealists and realists:

> Then I reflect on the objects of my sensations; and finding in myself the faculty of comparing them, I feel myself endowed with an active force that I did not previously know I had.[25]

At this point, the Savoyard Vicar restates the distinction between passive sensations and active judgments which, as we have seen, Rousseau repeatedly makes earlier in the *Émile*:

> To see is to feel; to compare is to judge; judging and feeling are not the same thing. By sensation, objects are presented to me separately, isolated, as they are in nature; by comparison I move them, I transport them so to speak, I put them on top of each other to decide about their difference or similarity and in general about all their relationships. . . . Let any name whatsoever be given to this force in my mind which brings together and compares my sensations; let it be called attention, meditation, reflection, or whatever one wishes;[26] it is still true that it is in me and not in the things, that I alone produce it even though I only produce it on the occasion of the impression that objects make on me. Without being master of feeling or not feeling, I can examine more or less what I do feel.[27]

On the purely epistemological level, Rousseau (both in his own name and in the discourse of the Savoyard Vicar) analyzes human knowledge in terms of man's freedom to judge as against his inability to be the "master" of his sensations. Since erroneous judgment thus can be imputed to man's active contribution to his own thought process, the capacity for knowledge concerning the true relations of phys-

---

[24] *Ibid.* Note that the term "conceive" (*conçois*) is still undefined at this point; the Vicar's analysis is not a rigorously deductive metaphysics.

[25] *Ibid.*

[26] As Hendel notes, the Vicar here refers to the terms used by Descartes, Locke, and Malebranche respectively, when referring to the "veritable act of reason" (*Jean-Jacques Rousseau: Moralist*, II, 141). Hendel's chapter on the "Profession of Faith" is extremely useful for the reader who seeks the sources of the metaphysics presented there.

[27] *Émile*, IV, "Prof. of Faith" (G, 326–27).

ical objects necessarily increases the likelihood that humans will judge sensations falsely. Or, to show more clearly the connection between the Savoyard Vicar's epistemology and the *First Discourse*, most men must pay the price of error for the ability of a few men to discover theoretical science.[28] Since human judgment and thought is not unambiguously good, the status of knowledge depends decisively on the status of that underlying freedom which produces it. Rousseau's epistemology cannot be fully established until the source of man's faculty for active judgment is identified.[29]

In order to resolve the metaphysical question of how man is capable of freely manipulating his sensations by an active thought process, the Savoyard Vicar must analyze the properties of matter, for the fundamental question is whether activity or movement is or can be a property of matter itself. According to the materialist view, matter can move spontaneously; if this were true, man's activity in thought could merely be a different manifestation of the universal properties of matter and the epistemological distinction between active judgment and passive sensation, set forth by both Rousseau and the Savoyard Vicar, would not imply that man's freedom is derived from an immaterial soul. Although the *Second Discourse* left this question open, the "Profession of Faith" presents an explicit rejection of materialism.[30]

[28] Cf. *ibid.*, III (239) and *First Discourse*, Part 2 (P, III, 18). Hence the perfection of the individual is inconsistent with the perfection of the human species; there is no natural end or *telos*. *Second Discourse*, Part 1 (P, III, 162); Part 2 (171); *Lettre à M. Philopolis* (P, III, 232).

[29] This explains the subordinate role of theoretical science in Rousseau's philosophy. The subordination of reason to sentiment which so many commentators emphasize is based on reason itself (*Émile*, "Prof. of Faith" [327]); reason shows that man's freedom, the source of thought, is not fully realized in thought (since thought at least presupposes materially determined sensation). Freedom is only fully realized by the approximation of a return to the state of nature by the *promeneur solitaire* (who surrenders thought for the sake of the free but passive sentiment of his existence) or by the total denial of the state of nature by the citizen (who surrenders independent thought for the freely active participation in the collective will). Theoretical science is opposed to patriotic citizenship because it undermines the healthy opinions of a free society, and it is opposed to solitary happiness because it undermines the tranquil sentiments of the free man. Cf. Strauss, *Natural Right and History*, pp. 257–58, 263, 278–79, 288–89, 291–94.

[30] On the similarity between Rousseau's formulation and that of his contemporaries, including the materialists, see the notes in Masson's edition of the "Profession of Faith," esp. pp. 79–91. As Masson notes, "all this paragraph is only the development and revision of Rousseau's annotations on several pages of the book *De l'Esprit* I, i" (*ibid.*, 79 n.). On the "Profession of Faith" as a tacit refutation of Helvetius' materialism in *De l'Esprit*, see *Lettres Écrites de la Montagne*, I (P, III, 693 n.).

The Savoyard Vicar begins from the sensations he feels, "lost in this vast universe and as if drowned in the immensity of beings, without knowing anything of what they are, neither among themselves nor in relation to me";[31] from the perspective of such ignorance, he must "study" or "observe" by comparing the objects known through sense:

Everything that I perceive by the senses is matter, and I deduce all the essential properties of matter from the sensate qualities that make me perceive it, and which are inseparable from it.[32]

This way of posing the problem, while apparently consistent with materialism, makes the Vicar's first deduction about the properties of matter decisive; his next words are therefore extremely important as the first or most basic active judgment that arises from a comparison of sense experiences:

I see it [matter] sometimes in movement and sometimes at rest, from which I infer that neither rest nor movement are essential to it; but movement being an action, is the effect of a cause of which rest is only the absence. Thus when nothing acts on matter, it does not move, and by the very fact that it is indifferent to rest and to movement, its natural state is to be at rest.[33]

This reasoning contains several steps which deserve close inspection.

The Vicar's primary sense experience distinguishes between objects that move and those at rest; his first inference is that neither rest nor motion are "essential" to matter. It is obvious, however, that the important point is a denial of motion as a natural or essential property of matter; to emphasize this, Rousseau added the following footnote in his own name after the words "sometimes at rest":

This rest is only, if you wish, relative; but since we observe more and less in the movement, we conceive very clearly one of two extreme terms, which is rest, and we conceive of it so well, that we are even inclined to take as absolute the rest that is only relative. Now it isn't true that movement is of the essence of matter if it can be conceived of at rest.[34]

---

[31] *Émile*, "Prof. of Faith" (G, 328). In the original manuscript, Rousseau had added: "what they are, neither *absolutely*, nor among themselves nor in relation to me" (ed. Masson, p. 92).

[32] *Émile*, "Prof. of Faith" (G, 328).

[33] *Ibid.* On the assertion that matter can be sensed both in motion and at rest, cf. *ibid.*, II (160–61).

[34] *Ibid.*, "Prof. of Faith" (328 n.). For the sources of this interpretation of the principle of inertia, see ed. Masson, p. 95, n. 1.

This argument implies that a human judgment or thought—the abstract conception of the state of rest—could not fundamentally contradict the "essence of matter"; while Rousseau could therefore be taxed for ignoring his own analysis of the sources of erroneous judgments, it is perhaps more useful to indicate that this particular passage seems to echo the classical assumption that there is a natural articulation between knowledge based on sense impressions and the physical universe.[35]

The Savoyard Vicar does not leave it at the inference that neither motion nor rest is "essential" to matter, however; he goes on to point out that since movement is "the effect of a cause" that is extrinsic to matter itself, "its natural state is to be at rest." Again, the argument is curious in a way, for one could presumably argue just as well that rest, being the result of a "cause" (viz., the absence of movement), is extrinsic to matter, whose natural state would then be movement. In other words, we seem here to be confronted with a circular argument that is intelligible primarily as a free or active judgment by the Savoyard Vicar (and Rousseau), denying the natural primacy of motion in matter. That this position represents a fundamental critique of materialism, pointing to the will as a source of movement not determined by external physical causes, is apparent throughout the "Profession of Faith."

The Vicar proceeds to analyze matter in motion in terms of an Aristotelian distinction:

> I see two kinds of movement in bodies, namely communicated movement and spontaneous or voluntary movement. In the first, the cause of motion is foreign to the moved body, and in the second it is within itself.[36]

Since spontaneous or voluntary movement is not a natural "state" or quality "essential" to matter, it is impossible to account for move-

[35] For the classical view, see Aristotle, *Physics* VIII.253a–b; *Metaphysics* II.993a–b. In other words, Rousseau seems to have abandoned Cartesian doubt in the footnote under consideration. Cf. *ibid.* I.983a ("the divine power cannot be jealous") and Descartes, *Discours de la Méthode*, IV; *Méditations*, I (*Oeuvres de Descartes*, ed. Victor Cousin [Paris: Levrault, 1824], I, 156–58, 235–44).

[36] *Émile*, "Prof. of Faith" (G, 328). Cf. Aristotle, *Physics* VIII.254b ff. Note, however, that while Aristotle's conception of things "that derive their motion from themselves" leads to the conclusion "that in all cases of things being in motion, that which primarily imparts motion is unmoved" (*ibid.*, 258b), the unmoved mover does not act by virtue of *will*.

ment without assuming the existence of an original cause which is non-material; matter itself is "dead."[37]

This assertion has both metaphysical and theological implications:

All movement which is not produced by another can only come from a spontaneous, voluntary act; inanimate bodies only act by movement [i.e., communicated movement], and there is no true action without will. That is my first principle. I therefore believe that a will moves the universe and animates nature. That is my first dogma or my first article of faith.[38]

The second article of faith flows directly from the first:

If matter in motion shows me a will, matter in motion according to certain laws shows me an intelligence: this is my second article of faith.[39]

The assumption that matter is naturally passive leads to the belief in God as the intelligent will which is the first cause of motion. Although the Vicar then deduces the Divine attributes of wisdom, power, goodness, eternity, and justice, he insists that these qualities of God—and hence His essence as well—are simply unknowable.[40]

While we cannot here consider the philosophical sources of this "natural theology," nor the specific conception of God that derives from it, the implications of the Savoyard Vicar's beliefs for Rousseau's thought require analysis. In so doing, it will be revealing to separate the theological aspect of the belief in God from the metaphysical understanding of the properties of matter. As has been noted, Rousseau elsewhere made it clear that he shared the Vicar's belief in God as the unknowable source of order and motion in the universe.[41] But this belief is merely an article of faith or a sentiment which other men are free to disbelieve. As Rousseau himself insists, men in the state of nature do not naturally conceive of God, and the first conceptions of the divinity are merely physical objects endowed with human sensibility; a true or noncorporeal idea of God presupposes a kind of intellectual abstraction of which few men (and no children) are capable even in civilized society.[42]

[37] *Émile*, "Prof. of Faith" (G, 328–32).
[38] *Ibid.* (330).   [39] *Ibid.* (332).
[40] *Ibid.* (335, 345–48).
[41] Cf. also *ibid.*, I (48), which explicitly indicates the authoritative character of the Vicar's belief in goodness as the most essential attribute of God.
[42] *Ibid.*, IV (307–12). Cf. *Second Discourse*, Part 1 (P, III, 149–50) with Pref. (127) and Part 2 (173–74, 186): religion is discovered only by social

Elsewhere in the *Émile*, Rousseau refers to God as the "author of things," the "author of our being," or the "author of our nature"; in Rousseau's own exposition, the identification of God with nature and the material universe would in no way change the meaning of his thought.[43] The Vicar himself makes this clear when he implies that without his articles of faith, the idea of God is "bodily and sensitive," and can be equated to "the world itself" (*le monde même*).[44] For non-believers, "God" and "nature" are apparently interchangeable concepts.[45]

B · DUALIST METAPHYSICS

Although the Savoyard Vicar's articles of faith, as well as Rousseau's own personal belief in God which they reflect, are merely personal sentiments, does it follow that the entire "Profession of Faith" has the same status? Since the Savoyard Vicar explicitly distinguishes his "first principle" (i.e., his first "metaphysical" or philosophical principle) from his "first article of faith,"[46] we must consider the relationship between the metaphysical argument of the Vicar and Rousseau's own understanding of nature.

The Savoyard Vicar's denial of materialism leads to the conclusion that man is a free being and that the soul is an immaterial substance distinct from the body—a position which can be described as "meta-

---

man as a means to preserve civil society and property. As with all learning, the idea of God only occurs to men when they have an interest in discovering it; as with other knowledge, this selfish motivation need not prove the falsity of the idea in question.

[43] E.g., *Émile*, I (G, 5, 13, 49); II (165). The first use of the word God implicitly equates God and nature (I, 28). Cf. also II (62); IV (246–47).

[44] Having established his articles of faith, the Vicar contemplates God and discovers that "God is *no longer* bodily (*corporel*) and sensitive; the supreme Intelligence who rules the world is *no longer* the world itself: I raise and exhaust my mind in vain in order to conceive his essence" (*ibid.*, "Prof. of Faith" [346], italics added).

[45] Note that, according to the Vicar, the rules of moral conduct are dictated "*by nature*" (*ibid.*, "Prof. of Faith" [348], cited at n. 72 of this chapter). Cf. the substitution of God for nature in the similar formulations, *ibid.*, II (93n.) and IV (247); and the source of the "ineffaceable characters" engraved on men's "hearts" according to *Rêveries*, III (P, I, 1021); *First Discourse*, Part 2 (P, III, 30); *État de Guerre* (P, III, 602).

[46] See again *Émile*, "Prof. of Faith" (G, 330), cited at n. 38 of this chapter. Note also that the third article of faith (the immateriality of the soul) is derived from a "principle" (man's freedom) which is not identical to it (*ibid.* [340]). Only the second or central article of faith—the intelligence of the will that moves the universe—is purely theological.

physical dualism."[47] The crucial element in the elaboration of this dualist position is the Savoyard Vicar's sentiment of his own will:

> I want to act and I act; I want to move my body and my body moves; but it is incomprehensible and without example that an inanimate body at rest begins to move by itself or produces movement. The will is known to me by its action, not by its nature.[48]

Although the relationship between will and motion, and the connection between the two substances in man is a "mystery," this dualism is the only comprehensible way of explaining motion and is at least based on direct personal experience (unlike the materialist assumption that motion is an inherent property of matter). On this basis, moreover, the doubtful status of the sentiments—and especially the sentiment of one's own existence—is resolved by the Savoyard Vicar: whereas the senses are moved by matter (a substance which is divisible and extended), the sentiments are indivisible properties of the soul.[49]

Earlier in the *Émile*, Rousseau argues in his own name that as soon as man conceives of the abstract idea of substance, a duality of substances in human nature logically follows: metaphysical dualism is prior to the idea of God.[50] Within the "Profession of Faith" itself, Rousseau's footnotes explicitly endorse the Vicar's critique of materialist metaphysics; whereas belief or disbelief in the incomprehensible idea of God is a purely personal matter, the philosophic doctrine that matter moves by itself depends on concepts which other men should be able to understand.[51] Even if Rousseau did not believe in a Christian God, it would seem that the Savoyard Vicar's metaphysical dualism corresponds to Rousseau's own position.[52]

[47] *Ibid.*, "Prof. of Faith" (337–40, 343–44). Cf. Strauss, *Natural Right and History*, p. 265.

[48] *Émile*, "Prof. of Faith" (G, 330).

[49] *Ibid.* (338 and n., 344).

[50] *Ibid.*, IV (308–09). Cf. the similar argument used by the Savoyard Vicar, "Prof. of Faith" (337–38). Elsewhere, Rousseau simply asserts the duality of the substances of body and soul (*ibid.*, IV [275]); the distinction between the two is made consistently throughout the book: I (40, 46); II (63); III (187); IV (250, 271–72). See also, I (29, 37, 49); II (120); III (228); IV (275, 388).

[51] *Ibid.*, "Prof. of Faith" (339n.). In the footnotes to the "Profession of Faith," Rousseau clearly adopts the Savoyard Vicar's metaphysical "first principle," whereas he does not similarly endorse the "dogma" of the existence of God. See *ibid.* (328n., 333–34n.); cf. 342n., 345n., 360n., 362–63n., 366–67n., 386–89n.

[52] Rousseau's personal metaphysics could thus be summarized as follows:

the notion of God as the creator of matter must be abandoned in favor of the pagan view that both matter and God are eternal. Matter in itself is neither good nor bad. God, the active cause of motion, form, and change in matter, is purely good but not omnipotent; God cannot destroy matter, but has "full power" to organize or order it. Cf. the Lettre à Franquières, 15 January 1769 (C. G., xix, 57, cited in n. 60 of this chapter). Man is a "mixed being," a material body endowed with will and a soul; although the human species can be described in terms of its unique degree of perfectibility, this faculty is in turn derived from man's active will or capacity for spontaneous motion. While other animals may be capable of spontaneous motion, only man has the potentiality of a degree of freedom similar to that of God. But perfection of the human species beyond the merely animal condition simultaneously produces evil, because man's spiritual or "active" attribute, when fully realized, is corrupted by his bodily nature. God is impotent to prevent this emergence of evil during man's earthly existence, but this evil cannot be attributed either to original man (who is by nature good largely because his spiritual faculty is not fully active) or to matter as such; although perfected man is in a sense responsible for evil, accidental material causation (extrinsic to the nature of the individual as an animal) was necessary for man to become perfected and thus corrupted. See especially the Letter to Voltaire, 18 August 1756, which is probably the most complete statement of Rousseau's own metaphysical position: "I do not see that one can seek the source of moral evil elsewhere than in free, perfected, and thereby corrupted man (*l'homme libre, perfectionné, partant corrompu*); and with respect to physical evils, if sensate and impassive matter is a contradiction as it seems to me, they are inevitable in any system of which man is a part; and then the question is not why man isn't perfectly happy, but why he exists. Moreover, I think I have shown [i.e., in the *Second Discourse*] that except for death, which is an evil almost only because of the preparations that are made for it, the largest part of our physical evils are also our own work. . . . Without doubt this material universe should not be dearer to its author than a single thinking and feeling being; but the system of this universe, which produces, conserves, and perpetuates all the thinking and feeling beings, should be dearer to him than a single one of these beings; he therefore can, in spite of his goodness—or rather by his goodness itself—sacrifice something of the happiness of individuals to the conservation of the whole. I hope, I think I am worth more in the eyes of God than the earth on a planet, but if the planets are inhabited, as is probable, why should I be worth more in his eyes than all the inhabitants of Saturne? . . . It is to be believed that particular events are nothing in the eyes of the master of the universe; that his providence is solely universal; that he contents himself with conserving the genera and the species and with presiding over the whole, without disquieting himself concerning the manner in which each individual passes this short life. . . . It seems that things should be considered relatively in the physical order and absolutely in the moral order: the greatest idea I can make of Providence is that each material being is disposed in the best way possible in relation to the whole, and that each intelligent and sensate being [is disposed] in the best way possible in relation to himself; so that, for anyone who feels his existence, it is better to exist than not to exist. . . . If I bring these various questions back to their common principle, it seems to me that they are all related to that of the existence of God. If God exists, he is perfect; if he is perfect, he is wise, powerful, and just; if he is wise and powerful, all is good; if he is just and powerful, my soul is immortal; if my soul is immortal, thirty years of life are nothing for me and are perhaps necessary for the maintenance of the universe. If one grants me the first proposition,

Traces of this dualist analysis of man are present in Rousseau's political teaching, which is based on the flat assumption that freedom is the "quality of being a man."[53] In the *Social Contract*, Rousseau insists that a free act presupposes a will distinct from physically determined power:

All free action has two causes which combine to produce it: one is moral, namely the will which determines the act, the other is physical, namely the power which executes it. When I walk toward an object, it is first necessary that I want to go there, secondly that my feet carry me there. If a paralytic wants to run, or if an agile man does not, both will remain where they are.[54]

Indeed, the freedom of man's will as distinct from physical matter is in a sense the root of Rousseau's political thought: the virtuous society must be free because citizens are slaves (i.e., not truly men) if they do not freely will the laws that govern them.[55] But since Rousseau implies that the conception of freedom in the *Social Contract* presumes his philosophic analysis of this concept elsewhere,[56] to what extent does the assertion of human freedom depend on metaphysical dualism?

We are thus forced to consider the difficulty raised when Rousseau argues in the *Second Discourse* that the human species is distinguished from other animals by man's faculty of freedom, and then immediately withdraws this argument in favor of perfectibility as the distinct quality of man. This replacement of freedom by perfectibility poses two crucial problems: first, does it mean that Rousseau himself had doubts about metaphysical dualism; and second, if this metaphysical doctrine is dubious—or merely a personal belief whose truth

the following ones will never be shaken; if one denies it, it is unnecessary to dispute its consequences" (C. G., II, 306, 315, 317, 318). For an indication of what seems to have been Rousseau's early thought on the metaphysical problem, especially as formulated by Pope, see the recently discovered Letter to Count Conzié of Charmettes, 17 January 1742; Jean Nicholas, "Une Lettre Inédite de Jean-Jacques Rousseau," in Société des Études Robespierristes, *Jean-Jacques Rousseau* (Gap: Imprimerie Louis-Jean, 1963), pp. 9–16.

[53] *Contrat social*, I, iv (P, III, 356). Cf. I, i (351); I, ii (352); *Geneva MS*, I, v (P, III, 304); *Second Discourse*, Part 2 (P, III, 180–84).

[54] *Contrat social*, III, i (P, III, 395). This passage is identical in the first draft: *Geneva MS*, III, i (P, III, 334). Cf. the Vicar's distinction between the "power to will" and the "force to execute" his will (*Émile*, "Prof. of Faith" [G, 339]).

[55] *Contrat social*, I, ii (P, III, 352–53); I, iii (354); I, viii (364); III, xv (429–31).

[56] *Ibid.*, I, viii (365), cited in n. 245 to chap. I.

cannot be proven—what is the status of human freedom according to Rousseau? In order to answer these questions it will be useful to have the relevant text before us.

After describing man in the pure state of nature, Rousseau says:

> I have to this point considered only physical man; let us now try to look at him from the metaphysical and moral side. In every animal I see only an ingenious machine to which nature has given senses in order to revitalize itself and guarantee itself, to a certain point, from all that tends to destroy or upset it. I perceive precisely the same things in the human machine, with the difference that nature alone does everything in the operations of a beast, whereas man contributes to his operations by being a free agent. The former chooses or rejects by instinct and the latter by an act of freedom, so that a beast cannot deviate from the rule that is prescribed to it even when it would be advantageous for it to do so, and a man deviates from it often to his detriment. . . . Every animal has ideas, since it has senses; it even combines its ideas up to a certain point, and in this regard man differs from a beast only in degree. . . . Therefore it is not so much understanding which constitutes the distinction of man among the animals as it is his being a free agent. Nature commands every animal, and the beast obeys. Man feels the same impetus, but he realizes that he is free to acquiesce or resist; and it is above all in the consciousness of this freedom that the spirituality of his soul is shown. For physics explains in some way the mechanism of the senses and the formation of ideas; but in the power of willing, or rather of choosing, and in the sentiment of this power are found only purely spiritual acts about which the laws of mechanics explain nothing.[57]

In this passage, which is completely consistent with the texts we have studied in the *Émile*, Rousseau flatly asserts not only that it is the essence of man's nature to be free, but that the will or free choice is a "spiritual act" which cannot be derived from the laws of matter in motion. The physical and the moral or spiritual realms are distinct; and the latter can in no way be reduced to the former.

Rousseau's endorsement of metaphysical dualism in the *Second Discourse* is, however, immediately qualified:

> But if the difficulties surrounding all these questions should leave some room for dispute on this difference between man and animal,

[57] *Second Discourse*, Part 1 (P, III, 141–42).

there is another very specific quality which distinguishes them and about which there can be no dispute: the faculty of self-perfection.[58]

As Strauss points out, this qualification is intended to free Rousseau's analysis of the state of nature from any metaphysical objections which might have been raised by materialists; perfectibility is an observable phenomenon which, unlike the spirituality of man's soul, is subject to empirical or scientific proof.[59] But since, according to Rousseau's epistemology, the very possibility of science apparently depends on the freedom of the human mind to judge sensations, Rousseau's substitution of perfectibility for human freedom cannot be definitive without simultaneously destroying the philosophic ground on which the substitution rests.[60]

One way to avoid this vicious circle is suggested by the text cited above. Perfectibility is substituted for freedom as the distinctive quality of man in a discussion of the "difference between man and animal"; it could be that freedom is an insufficient basis for such a distinction only because animals may also be, in a sense, free beings, and not because human freedom is in any way dubious. That this is a possible interpretation is indicated by the Savoyard Vicar's remark that animals may share the capacity of spontaneous actions which man feels in his own power of will.[61] If we look carefully at the treatment of the animal-like primitive man of the *Second Discourse*, we

[58] *Ibid.*, Part 1 (142).

[59] Strauss, *Natural Right and History*, pp. 265–66.

[60] Cf. *ibid.*, pp. 280–81, as well as Strauss's conclusion that Rousseau "suggests that the traditional definition of man be replaced by a new definition according to which not rationality but freedom is the specific distinction of man" (*ibid.*, pp. 278–79). Cf. below, p. 265, and consider the Letter to Franquières, 15 January 1769 (C. G., xix, 57): "I remember having long ago encountered this question of the origin of evil, and having touched upon it [i.e., in the *Second Discourse*] . . . the ease that I found in resolving these things came from the opinion that I have always had concerning the eternal coexistence of two principles: one active, which is God; the other passive, which is matter, that the active being combines and modifies with full power, but nonetheless without having created it and without being able to annihilate it. This opinion made me hooted at by the philosophers I told it to; they decided it was absurd and contradictory. That may be, but it did not seem so to me . . . . " Although it is sometimes said that Rousseau's analysis in the *Second Discourse* presupposes a materialist world-view, this letter suggests the contrary; Rousseau seems to have accounted for the emergence of evil as a consequence of man's status as a "mixed being" (*ibid.*, p. 55). Cf. n. 52 of this chapter.

[61] *Émile*, "Prof. of Faith" (G, 328). Cf. the example of the wild horse in the *Second Discourse*, Part 2 (P, iii, 181).

see clearly that Rousseau does not elsewhere raise doubt concerning the existence of freedom or will in the pure state of nature; on the contrary, just *after* the substitution of perfectibility for freedom as the characteristic separating men from beasts, Rousseau summarizes the condition of the natural savage as follows:

> To perceive and feel will be his first state, which he will have in common with all animals. To will and not will, to desire and fear will be the first and almost the only operations of his soul until new circumstances cause new developments in it.[62]

It may be true that animals *also* share freedom of some kind, just as they have the capacity to form ideas, but man, even in the state of nature, apparently had a will and a soul.[63] While Rousseau radically breaks down or at least lowers the difference between man and other animals, he does not deny the primacy of human freedom, which is a natural faculty because it is *felt* by all conscious men; freedom is described as the "quality of being a man" in the *Second Discourse* as well as in the *Social Contract*.[64]

This explanation of the retreat from freedom to perfectibility is not, however, totally satisfactory. Insofar as man's freedom is based solely upon a dualist metaphysics, the "insoluble objections" to any metaphysical doctrine can be raised not only against the dualism of body and soul, but also against freedom itself. Since Rousseau admitted this weakness of all metaphysical doctrines within the "Profession of Faith"[65] as well as in the *Second Discourse*, he could not allow his entire philosophical position to depend on a dualist metaphysics even if, as it appears, he personally preferred it to the materialist alternative. If forced to choose between freedom and science or knowledge of the whole, Rousseau insists on the priority of freedom. He can do this, of course, only because he ultimately replaces reason by sentiment, so that even if his metaphysical arguments in favor of man's spiritual or moral freedom are rejected, the incontrovertible sentiment of man's free will remains.[66] Although Rousseau's philosophy is, in a sense, based on metaphysical dualism, this metaphysical position is "detachable."

[62] *Ibid.*, Part 1 (143).
[63] Cf. *ibid.*, Part 1 (136–37); n. x (210–11); and *Émile*, II (118): the savage is "without any other law except his will."
[64] *Second Discourse*, Part 2 (P, III, 184); *Contrat social*, I, iv (P, III, 356).
[65] *Émile*, "Prof. of Faith" (G, 324).
[66] *Ibid.* (353–54).

C · ROUSSEAU'S DETACHABLE METAPHYSICS

The way in which Rousseau based his own thought on a metaphysical position which the reader is free to reject is clarified by his distinction between different meanings of the word freedom. In Book I, chapter VIII of the *Social Contract*, Rousseau explicitly distinguishes between natural freedom, civil freedom, and moral freedom.[67] The notion of moral freedom ultimately depends on a dualist metaphysics because it is a "philosophical" idea; the wise individual can achieve such freedom by becoming the "master of himself," but this may require the acceptance of a natural theology which some men reject. While this notion of moral freedom is the most convincing root of Rousseau's argument that man is by nature good (because then one can say that all evils have been freely willed by man himself),[68] there is apparently no way of proving the existence of moral freedom to the materialistic sceptic.

Rousseau's metaphysical—and hence dubious—conception of moral freedom need not, however, be totally equated with other meanings of freedom. Unlike moral freedom, natural freedom is an observable phenomenon: isolated animals are not naturally dependent on each other (however subservient they may be to natural instinct). Similarly, civil freedom is not merely a metaphysical concept because it too can be observed; if the criteria for civic freedom have been properly defined, as presumably Rousseau himself does in the *Social Contract*, any competent observer, regardless of his metaphysical beliefs, should be capable of discovering whether a given society has legitimate laws and is therefore free. Although Rousseau was hardly a modern positivist,[69] he comes close to what is now called a "value-free" approach within the realm of metaphysics; one can reject Rousseau's conception of moral freedom, based as it is on metaphysical dualism, without undermining his notions of natural freedom and civil freedom.[70]

[67] See P, III, 364–65.
[68] Cf. *Émile*, "Prof. of Faith" (G, 342) with I (48); II (63–69); IV (247–49).
[69] E.g., "one must know what should be to judge well what is" (*ibid.*, v [585]).
[70] Cf. Strauss, *Natural Right and History*, pp. 281–82. Hence the "blurring" of the distinction between moral freedom, natural freedom, and civic freedom, which Strauss emphasizes, is in part due to the ambiguous status of moral freedom in Rousseau's thought: it is essential to his own understanding of man, but it cannot be the foundation of a philosophic position because it ultimately has the status of a personal opinion.

To see how this articulation between metaphysics and Rousseau's understanding of human nature applies to the morality of the individual in society, we need merely look at what the Savoyard Vicar says after he has established his basic articles of faith:

> After having thus deduced, from the impression of sensible objects and from the interior sentiment that leads me to judge about causes according to my natural intelligence, the principle truths that it was important for me to know, it remains for me to discover what maxims I should derive for my conduct.[71]

Reasoning about truths begins from sense experience—and if limited to observable phenomena ultimately produces a nontheological and nonmetaphysical understanding of man (as in the *Second Discourse* or *Social Contract*). If one adds to sensual observation the interior sentiments which at least seem to be different from ordinary sensations, it is possible to "deduce the principle truths" that concern man. But unlike most traditional moralists of his time, the Savoyard Vicar does not try to derive rules of conduct directly from such metaphysical and moral truths:

> Still following my method, I do not derive these rules [of conduct] from the principles of high philosophy, but I find them written by nature in ineffaceable characters at the bottom of my heart.[72]

It would seem that the metaphysical and theological beliefs of the Savoyard Vicar can be detached from the rest of Rousseau's thought not only because other men will doubt them, but also because a "high philosophy" is not necessary for establishing personal rules of moral conduct. Since reason errs, individual morality can only be derived from man's natural sentiments; metaphysical reasoning leads to the abdication of reasoning in moral questions.[73]

3 · The Conscience and Personal Morality: Natural Religion as the Solution to the Problem of Natural Law

The Savoyard Vicar uses the distinction between man's body and his soul as the basis for his teaching that man's conscience is a natural faculty which plays the role often attributed to reason in traditional moral doctrines:

[71] *Émile*, "Prof. of Faith" (G, 348).
[72] *Ibid.* Cf. n. 45 of this chapter.
[73] *Émile*, "Prof. of Faith" (G, 353).

Too often reason fools us, we have only too well acquired the right to accuse it; but the conscience never fools us; it is the true guide of man: it is to the soul what the instinct is to the body.[74]

Human morality has a solid basis in the sentiments men have concerning their own action. The proof that there is a natural sentiment of morality is that when man's own self-interest is not involved, he always prefers good to evil; pity is the irreducible minimum which proves that these sentiments exist.[75] The conscience arises in socialized man from the combination of natural sentiments relating the self to others (like pity) with the self-centered natural sentiments (like love of oneself), and is therefore innate or natural. Whereas man's ideas are acquired, the sentiment of the conscience is not:

> To know the good is not to love it: man does not have innate knowledge of it, but as soon as his reason makes him know it, his conscience leads him to love it: it is this sentiment that is innate.[76]

Reason is an insufficient basis of virtue not merely because it errs, but because it discovers—and often merely reflects—a man's self-interest; reason alone can therefore never overcome the contradiction between what is good for the individual and the common good.[77]

Rousseau himself repeats this same view elsewhere in the *Émile*, explicitly endorsing the Savoyard Vicar's conception of the conscience as a natural sentiment distinct from acquired ideas:

> Reason alone teaches us to know good and evil. The conscience, which makes us love the one and hate the other, although independent from reason, can therefore not develop without it.[78]

If the conscience is not effectively present in the state of nature, it is because primitive man, like the infant, has no true or intellectual ideas; once socialized man, as a necessary consequence of living in contact with others, develops the ideas of good and evil, the innate sentiment of the conscience is released.[79] Although reason is the nec-

---

[74] *Ibid.* (348).
[75] *Ibid.* (349–51). Cf. the Vicar's use of the reaction to tragedy in a theatre with *Second Discourse*, Part 1 (P, III, 154–55).
[76] *Émile*, "Prof. of Faith" (G, 354).
[77] *Ibid.* (355–56).   [78] *Ibid.*, I (48). Cf. V (481–83).
[79] *Ibid.*, IV (257). "The same man who should remain stupid in the forests should become reasonable and sensible in cities" (*ibid.* [306]). Note that the natural sentiments of socialized man have the same direction as those of the primitive man, but they have been displaced by the perfection of the species; the conscience is a civilized form of pity. See above, nn. 26 and 27

essary prerequisite for the existence of the conscience, without an appeal to the conscience—or, more generally, to the sentiments—reason itself is incapable of moving men to action.

> Reason alone is not active; sometimes it restrains, rarely it excites, and it never did anything noble. To reason all the time is the mania of small minds.[80]

Since the appeal from reason to sentiment, and especially the conscience, is ubiquitous in Rousseau's works, here we seem to have found an aspect of the "Profession of Faith" which was fully shared by Rousseau and which is an inseparable part of his philosophic teaching.[81]

We will understand more fully the status of the conscience by looking at the kind of morality derived from it. The Savoyard Vicar remarks that, on the basis of his articles of faith culminating in the awareness of his own conscience, he is able to reestablish "all the duties of natural law" (*tous les devoirs de la loi naturelle*); his natural religion is effectively reduced to the "natural law" which establishes the moral duties of social men as individuals.[82] Although the *Second Discourse* criticizes the traditional natural law teaching and the *Social Contract* teaches that political right is independent of it,[83] within the *Émile* Rousseau speaks in his own name of a "natural law" (*loi naturelle*) which should bind all civilized men.[84] He also speaks of *devoirs de la nature, devoirs de l'homme, premiers devoirs,* and *droits de la nature* as obligations on civil man which derive from natural sentiments rather than from positive civil law or divine law.[85]

---

to chap. I, and pp. 45–48. The nonexistence of the conscience in the state of nature is emphasized by Rousseau in the *Geneva MS*, I, ii (P, III, 287).

[80] *Émile*, IV (G, 398). By "active" in this passage, Rousseau clearly means the sole cause of observable motion or activity of the body (as distinct from the activity within the mind that is implied in "intellectual reason"). Cf. Ch. I, §4C–D.

[81] See *First Discourse*, Part 2 (P, III, 30); *Dernière Réponse* (P, III, 93); *Second Discourse*, Ded. (P, III, 116); Part 1 (156); *Rêveries*, III (P, I, 1016–23); *Lettre à d'Alembert* (G, 139n.); *Rousseau Juge de Jean-Jacques*, III (P, I, 954, 965, 972, *et passim*); *Fragments Politiques*, II, 6 (P, III, 476); *État de Guerre* (P, III, 602); *Nouvelle Héloïse*, esp. III, xviii (P, II, 364).

[82] "All the duties of natural law, almost effaced from my heart by the injustice of men, are retraced in it in the name of the eternal justice which imposes them on me" (*Émile*, "Prof. of Faith" [G, 356–57]). See also 361, 385.

[83] Cf. *Second Discourse*, Pref. (P, III, 124–25); *Contrat social*, II, vi (P, III, 378).

[84] *Émile*, IV (G, 278, 279n., 300n.).

[85] E.g., "duties of nature" (*ibid.*, I [37]); "duties of man" (I [26]); "first

Some commentators have concluded that, despite appearances to the contrary, Rousseau accepted in part the traditional natural law doctrine of his time—a conclusion which, as we shall see, is explicitly denied in the *Second Discourse*. The difficulty arises because Rousseau's understanding of a moral natural law is complicated by a double objective: on the one hand, Rousseau attempted to reformulate the traditional teaching by substituting the conscience or sentiment as the means by which men learn of their moral duties; on the other, Rousseau radically restricts the importance of this natural law, which even in its new, sentimental form is impotent in the state of nature and irrelevant for the citizen. This double objective must be constantly borne in mind, because Rousseau uses his reformulated natural law as a possible basis for individual virtue in the case where civic virtue is impossible, just as he uses civic morality as a solution for the impotence of natural law.[86]

Before we turn to the limits or weakness of the natural law teaching Rousseau represents, we must clearly understand what he meant by the term and how he tried to reestablish the traditional natural law teaching. In the Preface to the *Second Discourse*, Rousseau criticizes the confusion which surrounds the conception of "natural law":

> Without speaking of the ancient philosophers, who seem to have tried their best to contradict each other on the most fundamental principles, the Roman jurists subject man and all the other animals indifferently to the same natural law (*loi naturelle*), because they consider under this name the law that nature imposes upon itself rather than that which it prescribes; or rather because of the particular sense in which those jurists understand the word law, which on this occasion they seem to have taken only for the expression

---

duties" or "duties" (ɪ [18], ɪɪ [88], ɪv [300], v [483, 488, 493]); "rights of nature" or "rights" (ɪɪ [70], ɪv [278], v [493, 507]).

[86] Many studies of Rousseau's thought have had a one-sided emphasis precisely because they have either argued that he denied all standards of natural law in the name of civil society or that he accepted the traditional view according to which natural law persists as a moral standard even within a just society. For examples of the first view, see C. E. Vaughan, *The Political Writings of Jean Jacques Rousseau* (Oxford: Blackwell, 1962), Intro., ɪ, esp. 16–18; Alfred Cobban, *Rousseau and the Modern State* (London: George Allen & Unwin, 1934) pp. 115, 147–49. For the second view, see Franz Haymann, "La Loi Naturelle dans la Philosophie Politique de J. J. Rousseau," *Annales*, xxx, 65–110; Robert Derathé, *J. J. Rousseau et la Science Politique de son Temps* (Paris: Presses Universitaires, 1950), pp. 152–71. On the inadequacy of the evidence presented by the latter, see below, chap. vɪɪ, § 2A.

of the general relations established by nature among all animate beings for their common preservation.[87]

An ambiguity results from the combination of the word "law" with the word "nature" because one can speak of a "law of nature" (i.e., the "law that nature imposes on herself") consisting of "general relationships" that are physically inevitable and inviolable, or of a "natural law" which is "prescribed" by nature to a "moral being" capable of disobedience.

While the Roman jurists are criticized for having considered *only* the former meaning, more recent writers, according to Rousseau, consider "natural law" in the second sense:

> The moderns, recognizing under the name law only a rule prescribed to a moral being, that is to say, intelligent, free, and considered in his relations with other beings, consequently limit the competence of natural law to the sole animal endowed with reason, namely man; but each defining this law in his own fashion, they all establish it upon such metaphysical principles that even among us there are very few people capable of comprehending these principles, far from being able to find them by themselves.[88]

Rousseau's implicit preference for this "modern" conception is therefore combined with the criticism that all those who have employed it base natural law on "metaphysical principles."

Rousseau thus attacks the overly rationalist orientation of all natural law teachings, both ancient and modern:

> So that all the definitions of these wise men, otherwise in perpetual contradiction to one another, agree only in this, that it is impossible

[87] *Second Discourse*, Pref. (P, III, 124).

[88] *Ibid.* (124–25). Although Rousseau appears to refer to all modern authors, this remark applies most clearly to modern *jurists*, like Grotius, Pufendorf, Barbeyrac, or Burlamaqui. Later in the *Second Discourse*, Rousseau explicitly distinguishes Hobbes from the other moderns precisely because Hobbes did not follow their procedure in treating "natural right." See *ibid.*, Part 1 (153). For the views of the "modern jurists," see Hugo Grotius, *Le Droit de la Guerre et de la Paix*, I, i, § 11 (trans. Jean Barbeyrac [Amsterdam: Pierre de Coup, 1724], 52–53); Jean-Jacques Burlamaqui, *Principes du Droit Naturel*, II, i, § 2 (Geneva: Barrilot & Fils, 1747), 142; and Samuel Pufendorf's critique of the notion of natural law in the works of Spinoza and Hobbes in *Le Droit de la Nature et des Gens*, II, ii, esp. § 3 and 9 (trans. Jean Barbeyrac [Amsterdam: Gerard Kuyper, 1706], 140–44, 150–52). Compare Pufendorf's definition of "natural law" (*ibid.*, II, iii), with Hobbes' distinction between "rights of nature" and "laws of nature" (*Leviathan*, I, xiii–xiv).

to understand the law of nature (*loi de nature*) and consequently to obey it, without being a great reasoner and a profound metaphysician: which means precisely that men must have used, for the establishment of society, enlightenment which only develops with great difficulty and in very few people in the midst of society itself.[89]

That is to say, for Rousseau all prior efforts to define natural law are absurd, cannot be used to explain either the foundation of society or man's moral obligations, and must be reformulated so as to be consistent with an understanding of natural man.[90]

Before undertaking his own study of natural man in the *Second Discourse*, Rousseau therefore summarizes the conditions that must be fulfilled by a "natural law":

All that we can see very clearly concerning this law is that, for it to be the law, not only must the will of him who is bound by it be able to submit to it with knowledge; but also, for it to be natural, it must speak directly by nature's voice.[91]

There are two criteria inherent in the "natural law" when properly defined: its quality as "law" (which requires the capacity for conscious, freely willed obedience) and its naturalness (which requires direct promulgation to all men by nature). Thus there should be no question concerning the precise meaning of the term natural law according to Rousseau: because it refers to a law which nature prescribes to man as a free agent capable of reasoning, the term must be

[89] *Second Discourse*, Pref. (P, III, 125). Cf. St. Thomas Aquinas, *Summa Theologica*, I–II, ques. 93, art. 2; ques. 94, art. 4.

[90] One might well object that Rousseau is unfair to the traditional teaching, according to which the Second Table of the Decalogue belongs to that which is necessarily known to man, especially by means of the conscience. For St. Thomas, all men know, or are capable of knowing, "the first precept of law, that *good is to be done and ensued, and evil is to be avoided*" (*ibid.*, ques. 94, art. 2, Dino Bigongiari, ed., *The Political Ideas of St. Thomas Aquinas* [New York: Hafner, 1957], p. 45). Rousseau admits that "all peoples who have recognized two principles have always regarded the bad as inferior to the good" (*Émile*, I, [G, 48]), but he denies that such a recognition was universally necessary for primitive man. Even if the traditional teaching were accurate, it would be incomplete because it does not explain how men became rational enough to discover the difference between good and bad. Moreover, the traditional teaching cannot really be satisfactory because it does not indicate that avoiding evil has a priority over doing good in one's relations with others. See *ibid.*, II (99), and *Second Discourse*, Part 1 (P, III, 156).

[91] *Ibid.*, Pref. (125).

distinguished from the notion of "laws of nature" that are physically necessary.[92]

Rousseau's belief that he could avoid the absurdity of the traditional dependence on reason to promulgate the natural law is clearly expressed in the *Émile*:

> If this were the proper place, I would try to show how, from the first movements of the heart arise the first voice of the conscience, and how from the sentiments of love and hate emerge the first notions of good and evil; I would show that *justice* and *goodness* are not only abstract words, pure moral beings formed by the understanding, but true affections of the soul enlightened by reason, and which are only an ordered development of our primitive affections; that, by reason alone, independently of the conscience, one cannot establish any natural law (*loi naturelle*); and that all right of nature (*droit de la nature*) is only a chimera if it is not founded on a natural need of the human heart.[93]

While we will consider in a later chapter whether the rights of nature

[92] In the *Émile*, Rousseau is relatively consistent in his use of the term *loi naturelle* to refer to the natural law as defined in the *Second Discourse* (see the usage cited in nn. 82 and 84 of this chapter). In contrast, he normally uses the term *loi de la nature* to refer to a physically necessary law of nature: *Émile*, II (G, 70, 134); III (199, 222, 223); v (446, 448, 455, 547, 548, 604). On some occasions in the *Émile*, however, Rousseau does not use the term in this unambiguous way: IV (403); v (605, 612); cf. n. 106 of this chapter. In other works, the usage is often consistent with the distinction between "natural law" and "law of nature" predominating in the *Émile*: e.g., *Second Discourse*, Ded. (P, III, 111), Pref. (124, 125, 126); *Letter to Philopolis* (P, III, 232), *État de Guerre* (P, III, 602); *Geneva MS*, I, ii (P, III, 284, 285); I, vi (306); II, ii (317); *Contrat social*, II, iv (P, III, 373); II, vii (383). The term *loi de nature* also often has the specific meaning of the necessary regularities controlling man in the state of nature: *Second Discourse*, Part 2 (P, III, 178); *Économie Politique* (P, III, 245); *Contrat social*, III, xvi (432); *Essai sur l'Origine de Langues*, chap. ix (E, XIII, 198). On a number of occasions, however, the terms are used ambiguously or in contradiction with the distinction here suggested: *Second Discourse*, Pref. (P, III, 125), Part 2 (174, 194); *Geneva MS*, I, iv (297); II, iv (326); *Contrat social*, II, vi (378); *Fragments Politiques*, II, 4 (P, III, 476); *Lettres Écrites de la Montagne*, vi (P, III, 807), viii (842); *Gouvernment de Pologne*, vi (P, III, 973); *État de Guerre* (610). For the sake of exposition we will follow the distinction implied in the Preface of the *Second Discourse* and generally followed in the *Émile*.

[93] *Émile*, IV (G, 278). For the reasons why the *Émile* is not the "proper place" for such a "course of study," see below, chap. II, § 4A. Cf. the similar formulation in the *État de Guerre*: "If natural law was only written in human reason, it would be little capable of directing most of our actions, but it is also engraved in man's heart in ineffaceable characters and it is there that it speaks more strongly than all the precepts of philosophers" (P, III, 602).

have a different status than reformulated natural law, Rousseau adds a footnote dealing with the latter:

> Even the precept to act toward others as we want them to act toward us has no other true foundation than the conscience and sentiment; for where is the precise reason for me to act as if I were another, especially when I am morally certain never to find myself in the same situation? And who will answer me that in faithfully following this maxim I will succeed in having others follow it toward me in the same way? . . . But when the force of an expansive soul identifies me with my fellow, and I feel myself in him so to speak, it is so that I will not suffer that I do not want him to suffer; I am interested in him out of the love of myself (*l'amour de moi*), and the reason for the precept is in nature itself, which inspires in me the desire for my well-being in whatever place I feel myself existing. From which I conclude that it is not true that the precepts of the natural law (*loi naturelle*) are founded on reason alone, they have a more solid and more certain basis. The love of men derived from the love of oneself is the principle of all human justice.[94]

Whereas in the traditional teaching the conscience merely promulgates a natural law that can only be precisely and truly established on the basis of reason, for Rousseau such a law cannot be based, even theoretically, on reason. Only if the conscience is a natural sentiment growing out of pity, which permits one man to transport himself into the place of another, can love of oneself be transformed into a love of all men; since men are endowed by nature with an active principle of freedom or will, which enables them to compare sensations and imagine the sufferings of others, a perfected form of pity is a sentiment that can naturally obligate man toward his fellowmen.

These passages show that Rousseau believed he could satisfy the definition of natural law proposed in the *Second Discourse* insofar as civilized men are concerned. A natural law based on the conscience is impossible for man in the state of nature because it presupposes the knowledge of good and evil, which can only be acquired after the social passions of love and hate have led men to reason; the natural law requires an "ordered progress of our primitive affections."[95] But precisely because primitive pity (which is only stimulated by the

---

[94] *Émile*, IV (G, 278–79n.). Cf. *Geneva MS*, II, vi (P, III, 329), where Rousseau also insists that the Golden Rule "needs a foundation" other than reason, but where this precept is derived from civil law.

[95] Cf. the passage just cited with *Geneva MS*, I, ii (P, III, 283–84).

physical sensation of seeing another being suffer) degenerates in society into the conscious comparison of the self with others, stimulated by man himself, love of oneself can be directed to love of humanity. Socialized man can discover his natural duties if his *amour-propre* is made to operate in the same way as pity; the transformation of *amour-propre* into love of all men is identical to the transformation of love of oneself into the love of all men.[96] The reformulated natural law is thus identical with the humanitarian virtue we have already discussed, and if reason is needed to discover this natural law, it is a very rudimentary form of reason.[97]

Regardless of the practical difficulty, not to say impossibility, of so transforming *amour-propre*, this conception of a natural law based on a reeducation of the natural sentiments is of great importance. This new natural law teaching is the heart of what could be called Rousseau's "romanticism": it permits him to criticize simultaneously both traditional moral doctrines and materialist philosophy on the ground that both overemphasize the role of reason. The traditional moral and religious teaching can be attacked because it presupposes that reasoning leads to knowledge of man's moral duties, whereas in fact the wicked man reasons quite well with reference to himself.[98] Indeed, the attempt to teach moral duties by reason (in the manner of Samuel Clarke, the theologian cited with apparent approval by the Savoyard Vicar) ultimately leads to materialism.[99]

Materialist philosophy, on the other hand, directly emphasizes egoistic calculation of one's own self-interest, and on this basis there is no ground for overcoming the unreformed *amour-propre* which prefers one's own happiness to the misery of others. For Rousseau, such doctrines are ultimately immoral because they teach that all morality gains its effectiveness from the prior existence of a social contract concluded between purely selfish men.[100] Although utility is indeed the first source of all contractual agreements which create mutual duties and rights, for Rousseau any contract has another basis in the *loi de la conscience*; hence he asserts when describing the agreements made by Émile as a child:

[96] Cf. *Émile*, IV (G, 303 and 279). Note also v (556), where Rousseau refers to the conscience as "the *amour-propre* of one's own self-respect" (*l'amour-propre du bon temoignage de soi*).

[97] *Ibid.*, v (483). See above, chap. I, §5.

[98] Cf. *ibid.*, II (99) with "Prof. of Faith" (356).

[99] *Ibid.*, IV (307). Cf. Clarke, *Traité de l'Existence de Dieu*, esp. chap. XIII, (trans. Ricotier, I, 209–10, 227–30).

[100] E.g., see Hobbes, *Leviathan*, esp. chap. XIV, XV (Oakeshott ed., pp. 89–90, 94, 103). Cf. *First Discourse*, Part 2 (P, III, 28).

when the duty to keep his agreements will not be supported in the child's mind by the weight of his utility, soon the interior sentiment, beginning to take form, will impose it on him as a law of the conscience, as an innate principle whose development only awaits the knowledge to which it applies. This first trait is not written by human hands, but engraved in our hearts by the author of all justice. Remove the primitive law of conventions and the obligations it imposes, and all is illusory and vain in human society. Whoever only keeps his promises for his own profit is hardly more bound than if he had promised nothing; or at most he will have the power to violate it like the trump of card players, who only delay using it in order to await the moment for using it with greater advantage.[101]

Mere calculation is insufficient as the basis of *any* morality, whether that based on a natural law binding men as men, or that based on the contract underlying civil society.[102]

The public teaching of a materialist philosophy like that of Hobbes, which tries to establish society and morality solely on the basis of the individual's calculation of his own interest, is disastrous and has even worse social consequences than religious fanaticism:

> Irreligion, and in general the reasoning and philosophic spirit, attaches souls to life, making them effeminate and vile, it concentrates all the passions in the baseness of private interest, in the abjectness of the human *me*, and thus silently saps the true foundations of all society; for what private interests have in common is so little that it will never balance what they have in opposition to each other.[103]

To be effective, morality must have a sanction binding the individual whose self-interest would lead him to ignore his obligations; without a necessary sanction, any rule of morality is merely a wish that the wicked can violate to the prejudice of the good. Materialist philosophy, by openly attacking all religion, destroys the salutary belief in punishment after death without providing morality with an equivalent basis:

[101] *Émile*, II (G, 93). Note that the last clause implies that some men in society—i.e., the rich and powerful—indeed keep the social contract for purely rational reasons as long as civil society is advantageous to them. Cf. *ibid.*, IV (280 and n.); *Second Discourse*, Part 2 (P, III, 177–78); *Contrat social*, I, ix, n. (P, III, 367).
[102] *Ibid.*, II, vii (383).
[103] *Émile*, IV (G, 386n.) Cf. *Contrat social*, II, iii, esp. n. (P, III, 371).

Philosopher, your moral laws are very beautiful, but show me, if you please, their sanction.[104]

In contrast, Rousseau argues that his education of Émile shows how man can be taught moral obligations which are truly binding:

If one waits, if one prepares the moment to be understood, then teach him the laws of nature (*lois de la nature*) in all their truth; show him the sanction of these same laws in the physical and moral evils which their violation brings on the guilty, . . . if, I say, one shows him with evidence how health, strength, courage, virtues, even love, and all the true goods of man depend on the taste for chastity, I maintain that then one will make this very chastity desirable and dear to him. . . .[105]

For the socialized natural man whose conscience is fully developed, violations of natural law are punished by evils which are necessary consequences of immorality; Rousseau's sentimental version of natural law can be supported by the law of nature.[106] As the Savoyard Vicar insists, remorse is the necessary punishment of the wicked, and it is a punishment which is effective on earth.[107] A natural law based on the conscience has a necessary or natural sanction because all men have a natural desire to secure their own well-being or happiness,[108] and any man whose natural sentiments are properly developed is aware that true happiness is an internal state of contentment with oneself. Crime is a moral evil which is not dependent on custom or opinion because the *bon temoignage de soi* is a *bien de cette vie* which is as natural as bodily strength or health.[109]

Unfortunately, Rousseau was aware that his reformulation of the

[104] *Émile*, IV (G, 389n.) Cf. *First Discourse*, Part 2 (P, III, 24, 27–28).
[105] *Émile*, IV (G, 402–03).
[106] This may explain Rousseau's use of the term *loi de la nature* to refer to what is here called natural law. Before the "Profession of Faith," Rousseau uses *loi naturelle* to describe a moral law, and *loi de nature* to describe physically necessary laws governing natural phenomena; after the "Profession of Faith," the term *loi de la nature* is used indiscriminately for both kinds of laws. The natural religion converts a *loi naturelle* into a *loi de la nature* by providing it with ineluctable sanctions. See the uses of these terms cited in n. 92 of this chapter.
[107] *Émile*, "Prof. of Faith" (G, 345, 349, 351). Note that although Rousseau criticizes materialist philosophy for destroying the healthy religious belief in punishment after death, the Savoyard Vicar's creed does not include such punishments.
[108] *Ibid.*, III (185).
[109] "Aside from strength, health, one's own self-respect, all goods of this life are in opinion; aside from bodily pain and the remorse of the conscience, all our evils are imaginary" (*ibid.*, II [66]). See also II (63–70); IV (270–71); V (556); and cf. "Prof. of Faith" (351).

natural law tradition was radically insufficient because, to be effective, all men must actually feel remorse for their evil deeds. The Savoyard Vicar—and Rousseau himself—may be perfectly convinced that the conscience exists and torments the wicked, but this conviction is not a powerful sanction for the natural law unless others also believe in the conscience and the afterlife of the soul. Ultimately, this means that natural law is impotent in the face of any man who denies that God exists and rejects a dualist metaphysics; any rational atheist who says he is not purely selfish (and, as a consequence, wicked) is either a liar or a fool.[110] But belief in God is not shared by all men, and some may not even be capable of it; moreover, private belief is purely a matter of man's will, which can in no way be coerced (any effort to force men to believe produces mere hypocrisy and effectively destroys religion).[111] Since the moral teaching of the Savoyard Vicar is impotent without "good faith," and good faith is ineffective without Socratic wisdom, the natural law which truly establishes the golden rule, although founded on natural sentiment, is only accepted by those who reason in the manner of Socrates or Jesus.[112]

As a result of the impotence of natural law, Rousseau was forced to base virtue on a stronger foundation, namely political society. In so doing, Rousseau never denies that there is another possible basis of justice; he simply insists that the alternative is impotent. The following formulation of the *Social Contract* therefore takes on a slightly different meaning than it is often given:

All justice comes from God, he alone is its source; but if we knew how to receive it from so high, we would not need either government or laws. Without doubt there is a universal justice derived from reason alone; but this justice, to be admitted among us, must be reciprocal. Considering things humanly, the laws of justice are vain among men because they lack a natural sanction; they only create the good of the wicked and the evil of the just when the latter observes them toward everyone while no one observes them toward him.[113]

[110] *Ibid.*, IV (390). Cf. "Prof. of Faith" (356); *Lettre à d'Alembert* (G, 201n.); Letter to Franquières, 15 January 1769 (C. G., XIX, 58).

[111] *Émile*, IV (G, 309–12, 387n.).

[112] *Second Discourse*, Part 1 (P, III, 156); *Émile*, IV (279n.); V (605). Cf. *Geneva MS*, I, ii (P, III, 281–87); and esp. II, iv (329), where such a natural law is called "rational natural right" (*droit naturel raisonné*).

[113] *Contrat social*, II, vi (P, III, 378). The successive versions of the second

Instead of flatly rejecting natural law, Rousseau reformulates it and keeps it in reserve, so to speak, for the man who does not insist on reciprocity because he has retired from society to the greatest extent possible; the natural law is the guide of a few wise men at the margins of society, but it is useless for the many.[114]

Rousseau's reformulation of natural law in the form of a natural religion based on sentiment denies the primacy of reason and yet seems to be inappropriate to all but the very few who reason properly. This solution to the meaning of the "Profession of Faith" is open to an important objection: how could Rousseau, who had attacked all books which undermine healthy opinions in the *First Discourse*, so boldly attack the officially accepted religious dogmas of his time (especially since, as we have seen, the "Profession of Faith" has the status of an exoteric discourse)? Rousseau could not have been unaware that the Savoyard Vicar's exposition of natural religion, particularly in the second part which flatly rejects revelation, was in contradiction to the apparent beliefs of most of his contemporaries. How could Rousseau present a rejection of religious beliefs, such as the fear of eternal damnation which he considers salutary, merely in order to present an education that might lead a few men to virtue? And why was such a teaching so directly addressed to all of his contemporaries?

The first answer to this apparent contradiction arises from Rousseau's understanding of the time in which he wrote. It is no longer dangerous to attack Christian dogmas which could serve as salutary prejudices, for in fact these beliefs have ceased to be held seriously; the Savoyard Vicar's teaching is appropriate for a corrupt age:

As long as there remains some good belief among men, one must

---

sentence of this passage reveal clearly how Rousseau viewed the problem of his reformulated natural law teaching. In the first draft, Rousseau had originally written: "As for those who recognize a universal justice derived from reason alone and founded on a simple right of humanity, they are in error. Remove the voice of the conscience and reason is immediately silent" (P, III, 1423). He then changed the first draft to read: "Without doubt there is a universal justice for man derived from reason alone and founded on the simple right of humanity, but to be admitted this justice must be reciprocal" (*Geneva MS*, II, iv [P, III, 326]). In the final form, this "universal justice" is connected more directly with God and reason (by the suppression of the reference to the conscience and "rights of humanity," and by the substitution of the phrase "among us" in the second half of the sentence for the earlier phrase "for man" in the first half). Even with a basis in the conscience, the "laws of justice" presuppose reason and a belief in God.

[114] See below, chap. VI, § 2B, and cf. *Émile*, V (G, 605).

— 86 —

not trouble peaceful souls nor alarm the faith of the simple by difficulties that they cannot resolve and that disquiet them without enlightening them. But once everything is shaken, one should save the trunk at the expense of the branches.[115]

An attack on the purely formal opinions of an age of disbelief is the only way to replace a corrupted public opinion with the kind of healthy prejudices needed to support morality. But if Rousseau wrote the *Émile* in a form appropriate to his own time, this intention is not sufficient to explain a religious and moral teaching which, as a printed book, was to outlast the conditions in which it was written.[116]

Ultimately, Rousseau considered the natural morality he presented as salutary not only in an age of disbelief, but even in a healthy society. On this level, the appeal from reason to conscience as the foundation of natural law is tenable because the natural religion (suited in principle to all men) is paradoxically the root of civil religion (which is appropriate to citizens as members of a particular, legitimate political order). The same dogmas which the Savoyard Vicar teaches the natural man are taught to all citizens by Rousseau himself:

> It is highly indifferent to the glory of God that we know [the truth] in everything; but it is important for human society and each of its members that every man know and fulfill the duties to his fellows and himself that the law of God imposes on him. . . . What interests me and my fellows is that everyone know that there exists an arbiter of human fate, of whom we are all the children, who orders us all to be just, to love each other, to be beneficent and full of pity, to keep our agreements with everyone, even our enemies and their people; that the apparent happiness of this life is nothing, that there is another life after it in which the supreme Being will reward the good and judge the wicked. These dogmas and similar dogmas are those which it is important to teach the young, and to persuade all the citizens.[117]

Because even a natural law based on the conscience ultimately de-

---

[115] *Ibid.*, "Prof. of Faith" (383). Rousseau explicitly applied the Vicar's description to the contemporary state of public religious beliefs: cf. *ibid.* (360) with the note Rousseau adds in his own name.

[116] *Rêveries*, III (P, I, 1018). Cf. *First Discourse*, Part 2 (P, III, 27–28).

[117] *Émile*, V (G, 480–81). As will be apparent in a moment, this civil religion as presented in the *Émile* is subtly different from the civil religion of a legitimate regime.

pends on a belief in God, in religious matters there is a "narrow circle of dogmas which are connected to morality" forming the basis of all virtue in society.[118]

Natural religion is therefore the basis of the civic religion elaborated in the *Social Contract*, although the two are not identical:

> Now it matters to the State that each citizen have a religion which makes him love his duties; but the dogmas of this religion only concern that State or its members to the degree that these dogmas are related to morality and the duties which those who profess it are held to fulfill toward others.[119]

The civic religion consists of that part of natural religion concerning moral duties to other men, and is silent concerning man's duties toward himself. As a result, compare the following dogmas of the civic religion as stated in the *Social Contract*, to those Rousseau summarizes in the *Émile*:

> The existence of the powerful, intelligent, beneficent, foreknowing, and provident Divinity, the life to come, the happiness of the just, the punishment of the wicked, the sanctity of the social contract and the laws: these are the positive dogmas. For negative dogmas, I limit them to a single one: intolerance.[120]

For the citizen of a legitimate regime, it is not necessary to believe that *all* men are children of the same God, nor that agreements with one's enemies must be kept; beneficence and pity toward other men as men (which Rousseau teaches Émile as part of his civil religion) are replaced in the complete civic religion by the sanctity of the social contract and the positive law. Although the natural religion or the sentimental natural law based on the conscience is, in a sense, the source of the civic religion presented in the *Social Contract*, the latter is narrower in scope and must be tolerant of whatever beliefs men add with respect to their own personal salvation. Rousseau presents the teaching of natural religion not only because it can serve as a source of civic religion, but because it includes duties which the individual with a conscience recognizes as important in private life, apart from the civil duties of the citizen of even the best regime.

---

[118] *Ibid.*

[119] *Contrat social*, IV, viii (P, III, 468). The last clause ("and the duties," etc.) was lacking in the first draft (*Geneva MS* [P, III, 340]).

[120] *Contrat social*, IV, viii (P, III, 468–69). Cf. Letter to Voltaire, 18 August 1756 (C. G., II, 321–22). Note that intolerance is also sacrilegious from the point of view of the natural man in society, even though it is not presented as a dogma in his version of the civil religion (*Émile*, v [G, 481]).

Rousseau wanted to revise the natural law doctrine of his time both to satisfy the needs of a corrupt age, and to show the basis, in the sentiments of the individual *qua* individual, of the healthy beliefs of the good society. This teaching was necessary despite—or rather precisely because of—the fact that it criticized the decadent beliefs of eighteenth-century Christianity, for there was another criticism of these unhealthy religious opinions which threatened to further corrupt the men of Rousseau's time and make impossible the return to a more healthy society. Materialism is as much the target of the natural religion as organized Christianity, not only because Rousseau personally believed in metaphysical dualism, but ultimately because such a philosophic doctrine is socially dangerous. If the only basis of morality is the public teaching of a philosophy that attacks all religion in the name of human reason, popular morality is certain to be destroyed because the mass of men cannot reason.[121] Since sentiment is the only possible basis of moral virtue for the many, both the lawgiver and the isolated philosopher must base human morality on the conscience; a healthy moral doctrine directed to the few must at the same time be suitable for the many.

4 · *The Good Life Chosen by Émile:* *Rousseau's Romantic Solution*

A · THE DUALITY OF ROUSSEAU'S INTENTION

We have seen that Rousseau's metaphysical dualism and natural religion have a deliberately ambiguous status in his thought: his personal beliefs are in some ways decisive for his philosophy, especially since they permit him to reject both traditionalist morality and a philosophic materialism, but these fundamental views are presented as subject to doubt and hence can be detached from his political teaching without changing or destroying it. One is led to wonder whether Rousseau's presentation of a politically impotent, sentimental morality merely reflects the "paranoia" some have seen in his personality,[122]

[121] *Ibid.*, v (518). Cf. C. G., xix, 58–60. On the extent to which Rousseau failed in his attempt to develop a natural religion that would provide a common ground between the *philosophes* and devout Christians, see Jean-Louis Leuba, "Rousseau et l'Orthodoxie Éclairée," in Université de Neuchatel, *Jean-Jacques Rousseau: Quatre aspects de l'homme et de l'oeuvre* (Neuchatel: Secrétariat de l'Université, 1962), pp. 48–69; Michel Launay, "La Société Française d'après la Correspondance de J.-J. Rousseau," in Société des Études Robespierristes, *Jean-Jacques Rousseau* (Gap: Imprimerie Louis-Jean, 1963), pp. 31–36.

[122] E.g., J. L. Talmon, *The Origins of Totalitarian Democracy* (New York:

or whether there is a serious justification for the ambivalence of Rousseau's thought. Evidence for the latter view can be found not only in the purely historical fact that most paranoid men do not continue to be studied seriously as philosophers over the centuries, but more to the point, within Rousseau's own writings.

In the *Confessions*, Rousseau insists that the persecution he underwent after the publication of the *Social Contract* and the *Émile* was unjustified:

> Everything that is bold in the *Social Contract* was previously in the *Discourse on Inequality*; everything that is bold in the *Émile* was previously in Julie [i.e., *La Nouvelle Héloïse*].[123]

This remark suggests that, in his own eyes, the boldness of Rousseau's thought had a double character. We can characterize this duality as, on the one hand, a radical criticism of the illegitimacy of most political regimes, and on the other, as an assertion of natural sentiment as the guide for the individual. It is perhaps justifiable to call the latter aspect of Rousseau's thought "romantic," since it was first proposed in a novel and found its most rigorous justification in a philosophic work which, especially in its concluding sections, also appeared to be novelesque.[124] Rousseau's "physical" or "scientific" analysis of man in the *Second Discourse* leads to a critique of political society according to which the only solution to human evils is, in most cases, extremely revolutionary (if indeed this political solution is applicable). But this was not Rousseau's only conclusion; the difficulty of creating or even preserving a legitimate political society under modern conditions also suggests the necessity of a purely private or domestic education. This education culminates in the natural religion presented by the Savoyard Vicar (or by Julie), and it is ultimately directed toward a certain kind of individual whose moral excellence is personal, not civic: Rousseau's "romanticism" points to retired life in the family, and in the highest case to the *promeneur solitaire* as the good life for man.[125] At the same time that Rousseau proposes a

Praeger, 1960), pp. 38–39. Cf. Irving Babbitt, *Rousseau and Romanticism* (Boston: Houghton Mifflin, 1919), pp. 73–74; Jean Starobinski, *Jean-Jacques Rousseau: La Transparance et l'Obstacle* (Paris: Plon, 1957), pp. 222–23n.

[123] *Confessions*, IX (P, I, 407).

[124] *Émile*, V (G, 528). Cf. *Rousseau, Juge de Jean Jacques* (P, I, 673): the *Émile* and the *Nouvelle Héloïse* can both be called "novels."

[125] It is no accident that the texts most frequently studied by students of French literature, insofar as they consider Rousseau as a "pre-romantic" or founder of nineteenth-century romanticism, are the *Nouvelle Héloïse*, the *Con-*

solution for man's political debasement, he provides some men with an eternal claim to reject—or at least stand aside from—this political solution; it was fitting that the *Social Contract* and the *Émile* were published in the same year.

Here we are concerned primarily with only one of the two objectives of Rousseau's thought, and the duality of his intention is stressed so that the good life for which Émile is educated can be placed in a proper perspective. The natural man of the *Émile* is in civil society, but not of it; he is free of all the opinions which necessarily underlie political life. Such a man is happy because he is independent; he is good because he is guided by conscience and reason instead of by vain prejudice; and he is even virtuous because he has the strength to overcome base passion, conforming his will to duties arising from the "eternal laws of nature and order." Although this life is not open to all men, it can be described as a desirable goal without public danger, since the natural man's goodness and virtue rest decisively on his belief in natural religion—a belief which is politically salutary in all times. But precisely because the natural religion rests on metaphysical and theological beliefs which are personal and cannot be convincingly defended against rational skepticism, the natural man in society can never be anything but an exception.

B · THE GOOD MAN AND THE GOOD CITIZEN

The character of this exception, which is of course ultimately Rousseau's justification for his own life, is clarified by summarizing the good life chosen by Rousseau's model pupil in the *Émile*. After religious teaching has made possible the combination of love of oneself with love of the "author of one's being," it is possible for the natural man to enter social relations without being corrupted by the *amour-propre* which necessarily arises in society. Since the only method of controlling such passions as sexual desire is to redirect them with the aid of other passions (and, secondarily, with reason), the quest for a sexual partner can be directed to the search for a virtuous woman; true or social love of another, precisely because it is an unnatural sentiment, can be used to control physical desire.[126] The fundamental motivation during the last period of natural education is therefore sexual love in its socialized or unnatural form: by encour-

---

fessions, and the *Rêveries* (i.e., Rousseau's least political and least philosophical writings).

[126] *Émile,* IV (G, 249–50, 389, 392, 406–10); V (514).

aging this passion and directing it toward the kind of woman who is worthy of love, Émile is prevented from imagining that there is true pleasure in the merely physical action of sexual intercourse. The opinions of others thus continue to be irrelevant for the natural man, whose choice of a sexual partner is based solely on the judgments that he has been trained to make for himself.[127]

The natural sentiment of love in its social form is the basis of the good life, for it leads to the preference for those activities and individuals that conform to one's own judgments of the good. Although comparison with others is unavoidable in society, it does not necessarily produce an exclusive preference of the self (*amour-propre*), because the natural man loves others insofar as they are similar to his own image of moral goodness; when Émile is praised, he is pleased because this praise shows that those who honor him are themselves good:

> He will not exactly say: I rejoice because they approve of me; but I rejoice because they approve of the good I have done; I rejoice because those who honor me do themselves honor: as long as they will judge so soundly, it will be noble to gain their esteem.[128]

This reformed pride is dependent on the judgments of others only insofar as their opinions are healthy, and provides the individual with grounds for withdrawing from social life whenever others cease to judge "soundly."

The social comparisons of the natural man are thus the obverse of the judgments necessary when the citizens of the legitimate regime vote on a law: in the latter case, each individual is asked if a given proposition conforms to the general will, shared by all his fellow citizens; in the former, each individual judges whether the opinions of others conform to his own personal standards of goodness.[129] Since the true citizen is happy when he conforms to the judgments of others, whereas the natural man is happy when others conform to his judgment, the natural man can be a good citizen only if the judgments of all his fellows are healthy. To restate the relationship in Aristotelian terms, although the good citizen and the good man may be the same in the best regime, there is in general a disproportion between the good man and the good citizen.[130]

[127] *Ibid.*, IV (410–15).
[128] *Ibid.*, IV (423). Cf. *Second Discourse*, Ded. (P, III, 116–17).
[129] *Contrat social*, IV, ii (P, III, 440–41).
[130] Cf. Aristotle, *Politics* VII.1333a: "But since we say that the virtue of

If Rousseau's understanding of the problem can be stated in classical terms, his solution is radically different from that of classic political philosophy; because Rousseau so radically emphasizes natural sentiment in place of reason, it is no longer possible to discuss the question of the good man and the good citizen in terms of the tension between the philosophic life and the political life (as did Plato, Aristotle, and Cicero).[131] For Rousseau, the life of natural man is not necessarily inconsistent with citizenship; for example, as a member of society he must have a productive trade.[132] But the ultimate justification of Émile's trade is derived not from civic duty, but from freedom—the man without a means of livelihood which is certain to support him in all times and places runs the risk of being dependent on others. Whereas the good life according to the classics culminated in the leisure of the philosopher, Rousseau's image of the good life apparently leads to the freedom of the independent gentleman farmer.[133]

Rousseau therefore tries to form the tastes of the natural man in terms of his independence of other men and their opinions; if the natural man has the good fortune to be rich, wealth should be used to assure, in leisure, those immediate sensual pleasures which are open to all men.[134] The appropriate choice of a wife is essential because the sentiment of sexual love has its origins in nature and, as we have seen, presupposes mutual respect: Émile's choice of Sophie reflects his own standards of goodness and provides his natural sentiments with an object that reinforces his own moral excellence. While it is virtually impossible to be assured that all of one's fellow citizens will judge soundly, with care it is possible to marry a woman whose judgments are constantly worthy of respect. The marriage contract is more likely

---

the citizen and ruler is the same as that of the good man, and that the same person must first be a subject and then a ruler, the legislator has to see that they become good men, and by what means this may be accomplished, and what is the end of the perfect life." See also 1324a, where Aristotle distinguishes between "the life of the philosopher and the life of the statesman," and 1334a, where he asserts that "the end of the best man and of the best constitution must also be the same."

[131] See Aristotle, *ibid.*; Plato, *Republic* vi.488a–497c; Cicero, *Republic* i.iv–vii.

[132] "To work is therefore an indispensable duty for social man. Rich or poor, strong or weak, any idle citizen is a rogue" (*Émile*, iii [G, 226]).

[133] *Ibid.*, iii (226–34); v (604). Cf. Aristotle, *Politics* vii.1325a: "For some renounce political power, and think that the life of the freeman is different from the life of the statesman and the best of all; but others think the life of the statesman best. . . . To both we say: 'you are partly right and partly wrong.'"

[134] *Émile*, iv (G, 430–43).

to be supported by reciprocally felt affection than the social contract, since the former can be based on a more nearly natural sentiment if one's mate has been freely chosen.[135] The priority of family life over civic obligation in the eyes of this natural man rests on his preference for those social relations based on "mutual attraction."[136]

The parallel and distinction between civil society and marriage reveals more fully the tension between the good man and the good citizen. Citizenship is virtuous only if it is based on freedom, which is to say free participation in the making of laws. But since the place of one's birth is purely accidental, the freely willed choice to live in a given society is normally merely inferred from continued residence; although men should be free to emigrate, there is at the least a sentimental attachment to the place of one's birth which produces a kind of obligation to love one's fatherland.[137] Ultimately the freedom of the good citizen depends on accidents of time and place which are not totally within his control; and this is particularly true for modern man, since good citizenship may have become virtually impossible due to the historical accident of Christianity.[138] In contrast, the reciprocal affection possible in marriage is not so radically subject to conditions beyond individual control. To be sure, external "convenience"—the circumstances that make a given marriage partner appropriate—should be considered: a man should never marry a woman whose status is higher than his, and although he should prefer a certain equality of status (if all other things are balanced), it is not against nature or reason that the woman be inferior as long as she thinks to about the same extent as her husband.[139] But these limits are of secondary importance, especially in comparison with the accidental determinations of one's native country; for all practical purposes, the prudent man can choose his mate freely. The family is a more natural society than the city because it can be based on a natural affection that is mutually shared and freely chosen.[140]

[135] *Ibid.*, v (507). Cf. *Second Discourse*, n. IX (P, III, 205): The free choice of one's marital partner is "the most sacred of [nature's] rights."

[136] *Émile*, IV (G, 435).

[137] *Ibid.*, v (605–06); *Contrat social*, III, xviii (P, III, 436 and n.); IV, ii (440 and n.).

[138] At the outset of the *Émile*, Rousseau asserts: "These two words, *fatherland* and *citizen*, should be removed from modern languages. I know well the reason, but I don't want to say it; it has nothing to do with my subject" (*Émile*, I [G, 10], original italics). The reason did, however, have something to do with the subject of the *Contrat social*, and it is not unlikely that it is presented in Book IV, chap. VIII (see esp. P, III, 462–67).

[139] *Émile*, v (G, 516–18).

[140] Cf. *Contrat social*, I, ii (P, III, 352); *Nouvelle Héloïse*, III, xviii (P, II, 356–60).

The happiness of the good man thus rests primarily on his freedom, just as does the virtue of the good citizen:

> Whoever does what he wishes is happy, if he is self-sufficient; this is the case of man in the state of nature. Whoever does what he wishes is not happy, if his needs exceed his forces.[141]

Although the state of nature is the standard of happiness and freedom to which both the socialized natural man and the citizen must be compared, each is a return to the freedom of the state of nature on a higher level. Even the natural man living in a corrupt society owes his excellence, in part, to the existence of that society.

> Born in the depths of a forest, he would have lived more happily and more freely; but having nothing to combat in order to follow his impulses, he would not have been virtuous, and now he knows how to be so in spite of his passions.[142]

Without the experience of social relations, the education described in the *Émile* would be impossible; even the natural morality is social in the sense that it could not come into being before civil society.[143]

C · GOODNESS AND VIRTUE

The best possible life of the individual *qua* individual can be characterized as a combination of virtue and goodness, since it stands midway between the goodness of man in the state of nature and the virtue of the citizen in a legitimate regime. Goodness as such is merely negative, and consists in not harming others.[144] As a child, Émile is merely good; his freedom consists in following natural impulses without artificial obstacles based on social custom or opinion.[145]

> But one who is only good stays that way only as long as he finds pleasure in it; goodness is broken and perishes under the shock of human passions; the man who is only good is only good for himself.[146]

Once men live in society, the impulsive goodness of a primitive man or a child is insufficient without the protection of virtue.

---

[141] *Émile*, II (G, 70).
[142] *Ibid.*, v (605).
[143] Cf. *ibid.* with the three kinds of freedom described in *Contrat social*, I, viii (P, III, 364–65).
[144] *Émile*, II (G, 99); *Second Discourse*, Part 1 (P, III, 154–57).
[145] See above, pp. 18–20, 29, 36–37, and the references there cited.
[146] *Émile*, v (G, 567).

The word *virtue* comes from *force*; force is the base of all virtue. ... What is, therefore, the virtuous man? The one who knows how to conquer his affections; for then he follows his reason, his conscience; he does his duty; he maintains himself in order, and nothing can entice him away from it.[147]

The socialized individual is not truly or morally free unless he has virtue because otherwise he is a slave of his passions, which have been necessarily modified and expanded by the mere existence of society. Thus Rousseau exhorts Émile:

Until now you were only free in appearance; you only had the precarious freedom of a slave of whom nothing has been demanded. Now be free in fact; learn to become your own master; command your heart, Émile, and you will be virtuous.[148]

Virtue must be added to the goodness of the natural man in the name of moral freedom, for only if one is the master of one's passions are they blameless.[149] True freedom consists in voluntary subjection to the "laws of necessity" and the self-imposed extension of such laws to moral life.[150]

In a sense, therefore, the good man living in society is even freer than he would have been in the state of nature, for he follows natural impulses by a true or moral act of freedom, and lives according to self-legislation. But for a civilized man to be free as an individual rather than as a citizen, he must restrict his needs to those he can satisfy independently with his own natural strength.[151]

The only one who acts as he wills is one who has no need, in doing so, of using the arms of another in addition to his own: from which it follows that the first of all goods is not authority but freedom. The truly free man only wants what he can do, and does what pleases him.[152]

Even marriage implies an attachment to another human being which restricts freedom; ultimately, Rousseau's "romantic" solution for individual happiness leads to the *promeneur solitaire*, the idle dreamer whose freedom consists in the unfettered enjoyment of the most natural sentiment of all, the sentiment of one's own existence.[153] In the

[147] *Ibid.*, orig. italics. Cf. *Discours sur la Vertu du Héros* (P, II, 1272–73); *Rêveries*, VI (P, I, 1052–54); C. G., XIX, 58.
[148] *Émile*, V (G, 567).
[149] *Ibid.*, V (568).　　　　[150] *Ibid.*, II (68–71); V (569, 603).
[151] *Ibid.*, II (68); IV (280).　　　　[152] *Ibid.*, II (69).
[153] *Rêveries*, I (P, I, 999–1001); II (1002–04); VII (1061–63); VIII (1075,

Émile, however, Rousseau does not go this far except in one foot-note, clearly written in defense of his own solitude (which had been criticized by Diderot):

> The precept of never harming another implies that of being at-tached to human society as little as possible; for, in the social con-dition, the good of one necessarily creates the bad for another. This relationship is in the essence of the thing, and nothing could change it. On this principle, let it be asked which is better, the so-cial man or the solitary one. A famous author says that only the wicked is alone; I say that only the good man is alone.[154]

As we have seen, Émile is explicitly educated to live with other men, and not to be solitary; he is trained to be beneficent to other indi-viduals, in direct contradiction to Rousseau's "principle."[155] Émile's freedom and goodness are therefore not as complete as they could be were he to live in total isolation; the natural education presented by Rousseau is a compromise which only imperfectly reflects the natural

---

1081–84); and esp. v (1040–49); *Émile*, v (G, 604–05); C. G., ii, 308. Cf. Strauss, *Natural Rights and History*, pp. 291–92. Note, however, that Rous-seau insists that his isolated retreat was only possible and legitimate because of the persecution to which he was subject: *Rêveries*, i (995–99); v (1045); vi (1055–56); vii (1066); viii (1075-79).

[154] *Émile*, ii (G, 99n.). The reference is to Diderot's *Le Fils Naturel*, Act iv, scene 3: "J'en appelle à votre coeur; interrogez-le; et il vous dira que l'homme de bien est dans la société, et qu'il n'y a que le méchant qui soit seul." J. Assézat, ed., *Oeuvres Complètes de Diderot* (Paris: Garnier, 1875), vii, 66. Rousseau's violent reaction to this line by Diderot has traditionally been taken as an example of Jean Jacques' overly sensitive, if not paranoid personality; even F. C. Green, who considers Diderot to have been partly at fault, remarks that "Rousseau's suspicions were baseless and even offensive" (*Jean-Jacques Rousseau* [Cambridge: University Press, 1955], p. 150). Cf. the note to the passage in the Assézat edition of Diderot; and Jean Guéhenno, *Jean-Jacques Rousseau* (Paris: Grasset, 1950), ii, 175. Rousseau himself, however, speaks of the line in question not as an isolated challenge, but as a "bitter and harsh sentence without mitigation" that was "among several unkind but tolerable things" (*Confessions*, ix [P, i, 455]). I believe it could be shown that Diderot's play and the *Entretiens sur le Fils Naturel* which follow it form a kind of *roman à clef* that would have been evident to anyone in the circle of philoso-phes at the time; the character Dorval (to whom the decisive sentence was ad-dressed) seems clearly to be Rousseau, and the speaker—Constance—seems to be Diderot himself. If this interpretation were to be proven correct, Rous-seau's reaction would appear rather justifiable, especially since Dorval is the *fils naturel* of the title. In *De la Poésie Dramatique*, Diderot says explicitly the *Le Fils Naturel* was never intended as a play that would really be per-formed; on the contrary, it is a "kind of novel (*une espèce de roman*) . . . in which the truth is continuously placed on a parallel with the fiction" (*Oeuvres* [ed. Assézat, vii, 337]).

[155] *Émile*, iv (G, 299–303); v (555–56, 561–63).

goodness and freedom of man in the state of nature. As a philosophical treatise on the thesis that man is by nature good, the *Émile* points to the *Second Discourse*, in which Rousseau's view of man's natural state is most fully developed.

5 · The Émile *as Rousseau's Answer to Plato's* Republic

Before turning to the analysis of the *Second Discourse*, we may well conclude our study of the *Émile* by trying to explain why Rousseau presents in it a model of the good life which is something of a compromise. If Rousseau's principles seem to lead to the solitary dreamer's life as the freest expression of human nature, why is Émile educated for a private life that falls short of this most complete freedom?

One reason for this compromise is the "democratic" character of Rousseau's conception of the good life of the private man. Despite the aristocratic addressee of the *Émile*, Rousseau proposes a solution for individual human happiness which is in principle open to all men, because it is the many who count:

> It is the people who compose the human species; what isn't people is so little that it isn't worth the trouble to count it . . . if all the kings and all the philosophers were removed, it would hardly be noticeable, and things wouldn't be any the worse.[156]

The retired family life of Émile presupposes only goodness based on the independence of a farmer, and the virtue derived from natural sentiments and a universally accessible natural religion; although the solitary dreamer may be an even more perfect form of the good private life, such a withdrawal from society is not possible for most men now that the state of nature has been irrevocably destroyed and human passions artificially stimulated.[157]

It could be argued that Rousseau did not openly advocate the return to the solitary enjoyment of one's own existence because such a

---

[156] *Ibid.*, IV (265–66). Cf. C. G., XIX, 52–53.

[157] Consider *Rêveries*, V (P, I, 1047): "The sentiment of existence, stripped of all other affection, is by itself a precious sentiment of contentment and peace which would alone suffice to make this existence dear and sweet for anyone who could keep away from himself all the sensual and earthly impressions which incessantly distract us from it and trouble its sweetness in this life. But most men, continually agitated by passions, little know this state. . . . It would not even be good in the present constitution of things if, avid for these sweet ecstasies, they became disgusted with the active life which their continually renewed needs prescribe as a duty."

teaching would be dangerous for public morals, especially since "any idle citizen is a rogue."[158] But whereas a solitary dreamer's concern for the morals of his fellow citizens would be purely negative (i.e., he would simply refrain from doing anything—like publishing a book—which could harm others), Rousseau's intention in writing the *Émile* was to improve the life of his fellowmen; whatever the element of reveries or idle dreams contained in his projected natural education, Rousseau himself does not write as an idle man.[159] The meaning of the *Émile* must be sought on the level of philosophy, and not in terms of the life of a solitary dreamer that Rousseau felt himself forced to adopt after he was persecuted.

For this reason it is justifiable and illuminating to consider the *Émile* as a modern response to the conception of the best life and best regime presented in Plato's *Republic*. While many commentators have emphasized the kinship between Plato and Rousseau,[160] the parallel between the *Émile* and the *Republic* deserves particular attention because Rousseau himself suggests it so explicitly, not only at the outset, but at several other important points.[161] Although it is conceivable that the *Émile* is organized so that the topics treated in each book correspond to those in the first five books of Plato's *Republic*,[162]

---

[158] *Émile*, III (G, 226), cited in n. 132 of this chapter; *First Discourse*, Part 2 (P, III, 18); and the passages in the *Rêveries* in which Rousseau justifies his own solitude (see n. 153 of this chapter).

[159] *Émile*, Pref. (G, 2–3) and v (528, 606). Cf. *Rêveries*, VII (P, I, 1066): "As long as men were my brothers [i.e., until Rousseau was persecuted after the publication of the *Émile*], I created projects of earthly felicity; these projects being always relative to the whole, I could only be happy with public felicity, and the idea of a private happiness never touched my heart until I saw my brothers seeking their [happiness] in my misery."

[160] E.g., Ernst Cassirer, *Rousseau, Kant, Goethe* (New York: Harper Torchbooks, 1963), pp. 26–27; Hendel, *Jean-Jacques Rousseau, Moralist*, I, 8–12, 16–19; II, 85, 93–94, 105, 110–12, *et passim*; Vaughan, *Political Writings of Rousseau*, I, 2–4; Jouvenel, "Essai sur la Politique de Rousseau," in Rousseau, *Du Contrat Social* (Geneva: Editions du Cheval Ailé, 1947), esp. p. 38.

[161] See above, pp. 14–15, 22–24; *Émile*, I (G, 10); II (102); v (452–53); as well as III (222–23). Note also that the Savoyard Vicar equates Plato's picture of the just man in the *Republic* with the historical person of Jesus; by implication, one function of the "Profession of Faith" is to substitute Jesus for Socrates as the model of human excellence (*ibid.*, "Prof. of Faith" [379–80]). This substitution is made explicit in the Letter to Franquières (C. G., XIX, 60–63).

[162] The first book of each work contains a critique of conventions and opinions without truly establishing human morality; Books II and III describe the basic pattern of education (dealing with such matters as the status of poets, who are in each case banished, and physical training). In Book IV of the *Republic* there is an analysis of the healthy tastes of the guardians as well as a discussion of the passions and virtues in the human soul, topics which

it would be mere speculation to assert that this is an intentional similarity; one is on safer ground if the comparisons are directed to the central themes of each work.

We have already noticed that Rousseau's private education of the natural man, like Plato's public education, is directed to the discovery of the best human condition. Plato's quest leads to the creation, in words, of the best city; and the best city must be ruled by a philosophic man—or, as it is commonly said, by a philosopher-king. But according to Plato, the idea of a philosopher who is a king is laughable; it is a paradox. Political life in actuality is based on love of one's own—whether it is the love of oneself (which leads to the quest for power) or love of one's own country (which leads to selfless patriotism); the philosophic life is animated by the love of truth. Thus, even in the best city, the philosopher does not want to rule, and in existent cities those who do have power reject the philosophers. Given the irreducible tension between civic life and philosophy, the best regime is for all practical purposes unattainable; the educational scheme of the *Republic* leads not to immediate political reform, but to the philosophic life for the few.[163]

Rousseau's attempt to describe the natural education is also directed to the development of the best human condition, but is more specifically concerned with the individual within society.[164] Generally for Rousseau, as for Plato, the best individual is not merely the citizen, since most societies are corrupt.[165] Rousseau's natural education is also, in a sense, suited to the development of the philosopher-king, surprising as this may seem: Rousseau suggests that Émile's education will make it possible for him to be both a philosopher, if he has

---

are treated in Book IV of the *Émile* (although in reverse order); the establishment of religion occurs at the center of Book IV in each volume. Just as Book V of the *Émile* has three parts (dealing respectively with inequality of the sexes, the formation of the family, and Rousseau's political solution), so Socrates faces "three waves" of paradox in Book V of the *Republic* (the equality of the sexes, the abolition of the family, and the philosopher-king as the best regime). Of the many detailed similarities which are striking, especially in Book V, one will have to suffice as an example: Book V of the *Republic* concludes with Socrates' discussion of the lover of wisdom (475b–480a), whereas Rousseau concludes the corresponding Book of the *Émile* by describing marital love (G, 607–14).

[163] See *Republic*, esp. VI.488a–502c, and IX.588b–592b.

[164] Note, however, that Socrates raises the question of the best regime only as a means to illuminate the nature of justice in the individual (*ibid.*, II.368d–369b).

[165] Cf. *Émile*, V (G, 605–07), and *Republic* VI.496b–497c.

the intelligence necessary,[166] and a ruler of others, if he has the desire.[167] Rousseau even alludes directly to the possibility that Émile might be a philosophic ruler, suggesting that this would not be the consequence of the natural education because Émile would not want to rule if he became a philosopher.[168]

If Rousseau sees the human problem in terms similar to those of Plato, his solution is fundamentally different from that of the *Republic*; the natural education of the *Émile* may be suited to create a philosopher-king if the student has the natural gifts to become one, but unlike Plato, Rousseau does not assume these natural gifts and constructs his work on the assumption that his student is of only average intelligence.[169] To see why Rousseau refuses to direct his teaching primarily to those capable of the quest for truth, it is necessary to restate Plato's position on the *Republic* in more detail, comparing it to the understanding of man set forth in the *Émile*.

Socrates' attempt to define justice in the *Republic* is based on an examination of the four principal human virtues—wisdom, courage, moderation, and justice—as they appear in the best city. This city is provisionally described in Books II and III as composed of "money-makers" or producers (artisans, freemen, and slaves), the "helpers" or military class, and the "guardians" or rulers. Wisdom is connected with the few who rule because they possess that part of knowledge which provides "good counsel" in practical affairs; courage with the soldiers who have been imbued with unshakeable "right and lawful belief" concerning what is to be feared or not feared; sobriety or moderation, extending throughout all classes in the city, with "the concord of the natural superior and inferior as to which ought to rule."[170] Justice is then defined as "the having and doing of one's own and what belongs to oneself," on the assumption that "each one man must perform one social service in the state for which his nature was best adapted."[171] Applying this understanding to the nature of the individual, Socrates develops his well-known tripartite division of the

---

[166] *Émile*, III (G, 192, 221). Hence Émile thinks and travels like a true philosopher: III (219, 236); IV (288, 291); V (523, 538, 579–84).

[167] *Ibid.*, IV (418), as well as II (180); V (585).

[168] *Ibid.*, V (597). Cf. the reluctance of the philosophers to rule in the *Republic* VII.519c–521b.

[169] *Émile*, I (G, 26) and esp. IV (293): "I chose him [i.e., Émile] among the vulgar minds to show what education can do for man. All the rare cases are outside of the rules." Cf. *Republic* II.367c–368b; VI.503b–504c as well as 492e.

[170] *Ibid.*, IV.428b–432a.

[171] *Ibid.*, 433a–434d. Cf. II.369b–370c with *Émile*, III (222–23).

human soul into the principles of appetite or desire, spirit or *thumos*, and reason (corresponding to the classes of "the money-makers, the helpers, and the guardians" in the best city); as in the city, the just man is one "in whom the several parts within him perform each their own task"—the rational part ruling, with the aid of spirit, over the appetites.[172] In principle, the best regime has the same virtue as the best individual.

This conception of the character of the virtues and their basis in human nature determines Plato's teaching of how men should live. For most men, the best and most virtuous life is found by fulfilling, in the best city, the rank and functions appropriate to their differing natural capacities; those capable of acquiring good opinions and motivated by honor can rise to be helpers or soldiers, whereas the many, dominated by their appetites, are suited only to be artisans or money-makers (if not slaves). Indeed, it could be said that the "vulgar" are far from the center of Plato's concerns: the mass of men—the "producers"—are soon lost from view in the ascent to the philosophic life which constitutes the structure of Books II through VII of the *Republic*.[173] Since the philosophic life, which is the "noblest pursuit" for man and the only intrinsically legitimate nonpolitical activity, is only possible and suited to a few, the choice for the good life can be reduced to the virtuous citizen or the virtuous philosopher; in corrupt times, it would seem that there is no practical solution of comparable dignity for the common men.[174]

Although Rousseau returns to the Platonic distinction between knowledge and opinions, and the related conception that philosophy can only be properly cultivated by the few,[175] his deep concern for a definition of the good life suited to the common man precluded an acceptance of the simple dichotomy between a good life suited to exceptional individuals—be it the life of philosophy or that of a solitary dreamer—and virtuous citizenship in a just regime. Having assumed that men are naturally equal in the most decisive respect, Rousseau cannot base the good life for the many on the civic virtues corresponding to each man's varying natural gifts; since freedom is the

172 *Republic* IV.436a–444a. Cf. 434c–d.

173 E.g., see *ibid.*, III.414d–417b, esp. 415e; IV.431b; and, of course, the famous allegory of the cave, VII.514a–521b. Note that Socrates explicitly asserts that the guardians of the best city will not learn a trade (III.395c), and compare Rousseau's insistence that Émile learn one (*Émile*, III [G, 225–36]). Cf. below, p. 241.

174 See esp. *Republic* VI.489b–502a. Cf., however, the choice of Odysseus in the Myth of Er (X.620c–d), as well as the definition of justice (IV.444c–e).

175 See below, chap. V.

distinct "quality of man," and is shared equally by all members of the species, a more egalitarian objective is necessary. Within civil society, as we shall see, Rousseau replaces the Platonic priority on virtue with a standard of civil freedom—the general will—which requires the equal participation of all citizens in the making of laws; although the citizens of the best regime need be virtuous, the form of virtue implied is the same for all. Moreover, patriotic citizenship in a free political community is insufficient as the sole end for the vulgar, for political corruption may be unavoidable under given conditions, especially in modern times.[176]

The project of the *Émile* must be seen in this perspective, for it opens up a third practical alternative—private life in the family—and gives it a status that the nonphilosophic retreat from political life did not have in classic, and especially Platonic, philosophy. The distinction between the best man and the best citizen becomes the three-fold choice between the philosopher or solitary dreamer, the virtuous private individual (exemplified by Émile or Julie), and the free citizen—forms of life based on the distinction between natural freedom, moral freedom, and civic freedom.[177] In the name of a return to nature, Rousseau thus gives all men—not merely philosophers—a claim against political life whenever it ceases to be legitimate.

The grounds for Rousseau's modification of the options open to man rest in his implicit rejection of the tripartite division of the soul developed in the *Republic*. In place of appetite, spirit, and reason as the constituent elements of human nature, Rousseau substitutes the natural impulses of self-preservation, pity, and the sentiment of one's own existence; Rousseau denies the natural status of the two higher principles described by Socrates. Spiritedness or *thumos* cannot be natural because it is too closely connected with the conventional opinions of the noble and base: honor or pride is the result of the degeneration of the love of oneself into *amour-propre* within society, whereas the sentiment of injustice, albeit innate, is ultimately derived from the conscience (the socialized form of pity). Rousseau therefore replaces the sense of nobility and baseness, on which Plato based courage and the manly civic virtues, by pity and the conscience—private or nonpolitical sentiments which do not naturally support the standards of rightful or decent behavior established by laws and social customs. This substitution of pity for honor represents the appeal

---

[176] *Émile*, I (G, 10); II (70–71); v (585–97); and below, Part II. See also "Mon Portrait," fragment 22 (P, I, 1125).

[177] See above, pp. 53 (n. 245); 73.

to individual emotions which so strongly marks Rousseau as a founder of the "romantic" movement, and permits him to justify an independent familial life as the model of natural goodness suitable for the common man.[178]

Rousseau equally rejects the Platonic conception that reason is a constituent part of the soul: while Plato agreed that most men truly reason late in life or not at all, Rousseau draws the conclusion that reason cannot be the naturally ruling principle in man because it is itself unnatural.[179] The desire to know or curiosity has its natural origins in love of oneself, not in a love of knowledge for its own sake.[180] Thus it is as permissible and natural to cultivate this curiosity in an aimless or passive reaction to the objects which most immediately and pleasantly affect our senses—to the beauties of physical nature, especially as represented by the wonders of plant life—as it is to seek philosophical knowledge about the whole and man's place in it.[181] For the rare individual who retires not merely from civil society, but from familial obligations as well, freedom is as much or more fully achieved in the solitary dreamer's idleness as in the active quest of wisdom by rigorous philosophical study.

It is therefore no mere accident that Rousseau is known as having originated a movement of thought characterized by a "return to nature." Whereas Plato asserts the priority of art over nature by trying to *create*, in thought, the best condition which is not inconsistent with nature, Rousseau insists on the priority of nature over art by using

[178] Cf. Socrates' discussion of *thumos* (*Republic* IV.439e–441c), with the analysis of pity above, chap. I, § 4E. Rousseau's substitution of pity, a supposedly natural impulse, for spiritedness—a tendency to judge in terms of "right opinion"—goes far to explain the different position of religion in the *Émile* and the *Republic*. Since standards of honor are for Plato admittedly conventional, they are most perfect when they reflect the law of the best city, instituted under the guidance of wisdom; Socrates leaves the establishment of religious laws to Apollo of Delphi ("the god of our fathers"), since in this context conventional religion suffices as a support for right opinion (*Republic* IV.427b–c). In contrast, Rousseau must prove that the existence of God is not merely a convention in order to provide the natural sentiments of common man with a sufficient support. The difference between the "Profession of Faith" (the crucial element in the education of Émile), and the religious laws of Plato's best regime (conventions which are merely mentioned in passing), indicates the extent to which Rousseau replaces the philosophic reasoning by natural sentiments which are impotent to guarantee the good life without a personal belief in God.

[179] *Émile*, V (G, 518); *Second Discourse*, esp. Pref. (P, III, 125); Part 1 (156–57). See below, chap. III, § 2D. Cf. *Republic* IV.428e–429a; VI.503c–d.

[180] *Émile*, III (G, 185), cited at n. 167 of chap. I.

[181] *Rêveries*, VII (P, I, 1061–70). Note also the intrinsic limit on the ability of reason to acquire true knowledge (*Émile*, IV [G, 428–29]).

the latter to restore the truly natural pattern of human life to its own, albeit perfected course. For Plato, nature (as represented, for example, by the natural city which Glaucon calls a "city of pigs")[182] is low and in itself imperfect; man must insure perfection through the use of intelligence which, if it imitates nature, goes beyond mere nature. For Rousseau, nature is self-sufficient and therefore good; the perfection of the human species by man's arts necessarily introduces corruption, and the prime function of Rousseau's philosophy is to use art to limit this corruption. For Plato, the natural evolution of five kinds of regimes is a decline from the best city created by art; in the *Émile*, the natural evolution of five stages is a development from animal-like infancy to self-sufficient adult life.[183]

Rousseau's reply to Plato is thus fundamentally based on his different conception of the natural development of the human individual and the human species. No longer can one speak of a natural end for man, for the perfection of the individual corrupts the species. The assertion of the unnatural status of reason, as well as the substitution of freedom for virtue as the defining character of human excellence, presupposes that human evolution was an artificial progress away from a truly natural condition in which man was an animal or little more than an animal. These developments can only be understood by an analysis which can be described as scientific in a modern or anti-classical sense. It is to the examination of nature in the *Second Discourse*, Rousseau's "boldest" and most scientific work of philosophy, that we must therefore turn.

[182] *Republic* II.372d.

[183] Compare the decline of the best city through the four imperfect regimes (with their corresponding kinds of men) (*Republic* IV.445c–V.449b; VIII, 543c–IX.576c), with the structure of the five books of the *Émile*. In some respects, however, it would be more accurate to compare the five types of regimes distinguished by Socrates with the five principle stages of the evolution of the human species described in the *Second Discourse*: the pure state of nature treated in Part 1; savage society united by "customs and character, not by laws" (Part 2 [P, III, 169]); and the three subsequent "revolutions" described respectively as "the establishment of law and right," "the institution of the magistracy," and the "change of legitimate power into arbitrary power" (*ibid.*, 187). For both Plato and Rousseau, the standard of judgment is the first form of human life; even though this stage is virtually unattainable under present human conditions, it establishes a criterion of judgment and a principle according to which the individual should live. The other four stages of evolution also have striking similarities which merit consideration.

THE STATE OF NATURE
(SECOND DISCOURSE, PART 1)

1 · *The Character of the* Discourse on Inequality

A · THE POPULAR AND PHILOSOPHIC LEVELS
OF ROUSSEAU'S INTENTION

Rousseau considered his *Discourse on the Origins of Inequality
Among Men* (traditionally called the *Second Discourse*) as the first
writing in which he "completely developed" his philosophical principles.[1] Occasioned by the Academy of Dijon's essay contest for
1754, Rousseau subsequently described the composition of this
"work of greatest importance" as follows:

> To meditate on this great subject I traveled to Saint-Germain for
> seven or eight days. . . . Deep in the forest, I sought and found the
> image of the first epochs, whose history I proudly traced; I re-
> vealed the little lies of men, I dared strip their nature nude, follow
> the progress of time and things, which have disfigured it, and com-
> paring man's man with natural man, show them in man's supposed
> perfection the true source of his miseries. . . . From these medita-
> tions resulted the *Discourse on Inequality*, a work . . . which only
> found few readers in all Europe who understood it, none of whom
> wanted to talk about it.[2]

Although written for the Academy of Dijon's competition, Rousseau
was "sure in advance" that his *Second Discourse* would not win the
prize; he considered his reply to have been too "bold" for a provincial academy.[3] Having gained literary fame with his *First Discourse*,
Rousseau was free to seek the truth without flattering the prejudices
of his contemporaries.

---

[1] See *Confessions*, VIII (P, I, 388), cited above, Pref., p. xv.
[2] *Ibid.* (388–89).
[3] Cf. *ibid.*, IX (407) with VIII (389).

The *Second Discourse* is therefore not addressed to the academicians of Dijon, but to a very different audience:

> As my subject concerns man in general, I shall try to use a language that suits all nations, or rather, forgetting the times and places in order to think only of the men to whom I speak, I shall imagine myself in the Lyceum of Athens, repeating the lessons of my masters, with Plato and Xenocrates for judges, and the human race for an audience.[4]

In context, these assumed conditions suggest the philosophic character of Rousseau's *Discourse* and his implicit rejection of revelation as an authority; the Judaeo-Christian heritage, with its biblical account of man's creation by God, the Garden of Eden, and the source of evil in Adam's sin, is not a "language which suits all nations."[5] Even more revealing, however, Rousseau's supposition indicates that such a purely philosophic quest for the nature of man is at home in ancient Greece. The academicians of Dijon are replaced as judges by Plato and Xenocrates—the latter a Platonist who was the head of the Academy at the same time (339-314 BC) that Aristotle led the Peripatetic School (335-332 BC). Moreover, the classics are Rousseau's "masters"; to some extent modern thought is deficient when compared to classic thought, and especially to Platonic thought.[6]

[4] *Second Discourse*, Exordium (P, III, 133). Note that Rousseau considers his work to be a spoken teaching, and compare Leo Strauss, *Persecution and the Art of Writing* (Glencoe, Ill.: Free Press, 1952), pp. 47–48.

[5] Cf. *Second Discourse*, Exordium (P, III, 132); Part 2 (186); Pref. (127). Cf. *Émile*, IV, "Prof. of Faith" (G, 361–83).

[6] Cf. *Lettre à d'Alembert* (G, 204–06). The superiority of classic thought is revealed by the fact, often noted, that in many ways the model for Rousseau's *Discourse* is the Epicurean account of the evolution of human nature in Book V of Lucretius' *De Rerum Natura*. On the parallel between the poem of Lucretius and the *Second Discourse*, see Jean Morel, "Recherches sur les sources du Discours sur l'Inégalité," *Annales*, V (1909), 163–64; and Strauss, *Natural Right and History* (Chicago: University of Chicago Press, 1953), pp. 264 and 271, n. 37. Of perhaps greater importance, given Rousseau's remark that Plato is his "judge," is the account of political evolution in Book III of Plato's *Laws*. According to the *Laws*, it is possible to "suppose" that men fell into an uncivilized, isolated condition as the result of a flood (III.677a)—for Rousseau, the only assumption which permits analysis of the state of nature as if it really existed without abandoning the teaching of the "Holy Scriptures" (*Second Discourse*, Exordium [P, III, 132]). Plato's dialogue speaks of the persistence of this uncivilized condition for "untold tens of thousands of years" (*Laws* III.677d); Plato is more likely to be a fair judge of Rousseau's *Discourse* than one who gives "the writings of Moses the credence that any Christian philosopher owes them" (*Second Discourse*, Exordium [132]). On the extent to which the *Second Discourse* is particularly connected with Rousseau's rejection of the position of Diderot, see Jacques Proust, *Diderot et l'Encyclopédie* (Paris: Armand Colin, 1962), pp. 359–81.

The supposed circumstances of Rousseau's discourse also reveal a distinction between the judges of the work and its audience. As a printed book—and unlike the *First Discourse,* it is clear that from the outset the *Second* was intended to be published[7]—the *Discourse on Inequality* has a potential audience of all who can read; this means, of course, that the dangers of a public dissemination of science, on which Rousseau had insisted previously, could apply to his own work. Rousseau attempts to avoid this risk by writing in such a way that philosophic judges of his *Second Discourse* will see in it problems not perceived by the vulgar or ordinary readers. Thus, in raising the question of the relationship between philosophy and history as sources of knowledge, Rousseau concludes:

> It is enough for me to offer these objects to the consideration of my judges; it is enough for me to have arranged it so that vulgar readers would have no need to consider them.[8]

This distinction is of importance not only because it shows that Rousseau could, with consistency, write a philosophic book after his *First Discourse,* but because it indicates the necessity of going beyond a superficial reading of the text if one seeks Rousseau's philosophic meaning.

This consideration is nowhere more important than in connection with the footnotes. Rousseau's emphatic assertion that his philosophic works cannot be understood without being read at least twice has already been quoted;[9] given this rule, Rousseau's seemingly playful "Avertissement sur les notes" to the *Second Discourse* takes on a very precise meaning:

> I have added some notes to this work, following my lazy custom of working in fits and starts. These notes sometimes stray so far from the subject that they are not good to read with the text. I have therefore relegated them to the end of the *Discourse,* in which I have tried my best to follow the straightest path. Those who have the courage to begin again will be able to amuse themselves the

[7] Rousseau had entered into negotiation for the publication of the *Second Discourse* in the spring of 1754, before writing the Dedication to Geneva (see C. G., II, 67). In contrast, he claims to have "forgotten" about his *First Discourse* after writing it (*Confessions,* VIII [P, I, 356]). In fact, he thoroughly rewrote it after submitting it to the Academy of Dijon (*First Discourse,* Pref. [P, III, 3]). The original text was only chosen for publication after it was given the prize for which it had been entered (*Confessions,* VIII [363]).

[8] *Second Discourse,* Part 1 (P, III, 163).

[9] *Rousseau Juge de Jean Jacques,* III (P, I, 932), cited above, p. v.

second time in beating the bushes, and try to go through the notes. There will be little harm if others do not read them at all.[10]

The footnotes are implicitly directed only to Rousseau's philosophic readers; there is no harm "if others do not read them at all," because those who lack the "courage" to reread Rousseau's work will be spared the dangerous consequences of a kind of rational analysis suited to few men.

There are then two distinct levels of meaning in the *Second Discourse*. Just as there is a distinction in the *Émile* between specific educational reforms and a philosophic analysis of the best man in society, so Rousseau's *Discourse on Inequality* speaks both to the common man and to the philosopher.[11] On the former or more apparent level, Rousseau indicates explicitly the intention of his history of the human species:

> O man, whatever country you may come from, whatever your opinions may be, listen: here is your history as I believed it to read, not in the books of your fellowmen, which are liars, but in nature, which never lies. . . . It is, so to speak, the life of your species that I am going to describe to you according to the qualities you received, which your education and habits have been able to corrupt but have not been able to destroy.[12]

As in the *Émile*, Rousseau intends to replace the written thought of men by nature as the true standard of human life; and this return to nature is possible because man's depravation due to education and habits acquired in society cannot totally destroy his natural "qualities."[13]

At this level, the *Second Discourse* is in a sense a quasi-theological revelation which attributes the source of human evil to man himself.[14] Rousseau puts it as follows in the *Confessions*:

> My soul, exalted by these sublime contemplations, rose to the divinity; and seeing from there that my fellows, in following the blind route of their prejudices, follow that of their errors, their unhappiness, and their crimes, I cried to them in a weak voice that they

[10] "Notice on the Notes," *Second Discourse* (P, III, 128).
[11] Cf. Strauss, *Natural Right and History*, p. 271, n. 38.
[12] *Second Discourse*, Exordium (P, III, 133).
[13] See above, pp. 6–10.
[14] Cf. Jean Starobinski's apt remark: "formulated as a revelation of what is human, this *Discourse* is, in its entirety, a religious act of a particular kind, which is substituted for the sacred history [of *Genesis*]" (Intro. to *Discours sur l'Inégalité* [P, III, lii]).

could not hear: Madmen, you who complain incessantly about nature, learn that all your ills come from yourselves.[15]

As this reflexion about the *Second Discourse* indicates, the popular level of meaning is somehow presented in a "weak voice" that most men "cannot hear." Whereas the *Émile* proposes a very specific kind of personal morality for the natural man in society, and the *First Discourse* concludes with a positive exhortation to virtue, the public teaching of the *Second Discourse* is merely negative. Concluding his direct address to man in general, Rousseau predicts:

> You will seek the age at which you would desire your species had stopped. Discontented with your present state for reasons that foretell even greater discontents for your unhappy posterity, perhaps you would want to be able to go backward in time. This sentiment must be the eulogy of your first ancestors, the criticism of your contemporaries, and the dread of those who will have the unhappiness to live after you.[16]

This passage does not yet suggest that such a desired return to an earlier condition of the species is impossible; the vulgar or common audience will only gain a critical sense of discontent from reading the *Second Discourse*.

It is only in the footnotes, directed to philosophic or careful readers, that Rousseau spells out in more detail the consequences of his criticism of social prejudice in the name of nature:

> What! must we destroy societies, annihilate thine and mine, and go back to live in forests with bears? . . . As for men like me, whose passions have forever destroyed their original simplicity, . . . they will respect the sacred bonds of the societies of which they are members; they will love their fellowmen and will serve them with all their power; they will scrupulously obey the laws, and the men who are their authors and ministers; they will honor above all the good and wise princes who will know how to prevent, cure, or palliate that multitude of abuses and evils always ready to crush us; they will animate the zeal of those worthy chiefs, by showing them without fear and flattery the greatness of their task and the rigor of their duty. But they will nonetheless scorn a constitution that can be maintained only with the help of so many respectable people—who are desired more often than obtained—and from which,

[15] *Confessions*, VIII (P, I, 388–89).
[16] *Second Discourse*, Exordium (P, III, 133).

despite all their care, always arise more real calamities than apparent advantages.[17]

On the deepest level, Rousseau's attack on the corruption of the human species arising from social life has a double objective: the philosophic reader, who accepts the perfection of human intelligence as a desirable thing, should act as the disinterested advisor of rulers while preserving "scorn" for the stage of human evolution in which political society is necessary. On the one hand, the philosopher must discover the principles underlying political life, in order to teach rulers "the rigor of their duty"; on the other, he must himself stand outside the political community, since only then can he understand the true status of politics and animate "the zeal of these worthy chiefs . . . without fear and flattery."

B · THE SCIENTIFIC ANALYSIS OF NATURE

Rousseau's explicit statements concerning the central thesis and addressees of the *Second Discourse* thus reveal its essentially philosophical character; it provides an analysis of the nature of man which does not accept divine revelation or traditional morality as authoritative. Unlike the natural religion presented by the Savoyard Vicar, this approach presumes neither belief in God nor any particular metaphysical explanation of the status of man in the material universe; the *Discourse* considers the existence of all morality—and, *a fortiori*, any natural law prescribing man's eternal duties—as an open question requiring rational proof.

This orientation is clear from the full title of the work: *Discours sur l'origine et les fondements de l'Inégalité parmi les Hommes.* Rousseau took care to reproduce the original question posed by the Academy of Dijon, which is printed between the "Avertissement sur les notes" and the Exordium of the text (i.e., *after* the Dedication and Preface).[18] Since Rousseau's own title is repeated at the head of the Exordium, the thoughtful reader is led to note—as indeed many commentators have—that Rousseau changes the original ques-

---

[17] *Ibid.*, n. IX (207–08). That this counsel is directed to philosophic readers is manifest, if from nothing else, by the difficulty of this paragraph; see especially the phrases omitted in the above citation, which imply that those who do not accept divine revelation, who have no unnatural passions, and who are willing to renounce all enlightenment and reasoning, may indeed be able to return to something like a state of nature—i.e., to the life of the solitary dreamer.

[18] *Ibid.* (129).

tion.[19] The academicians had asked: "Quelle est la source de l'inégalité parmi les hommes et si elle est autorisée par la loi naturelle";[20] Rousseau adds a reference to the "foundation" of inequality, and suppresses the problem of "whether it is authorized by natural law." Until one has answered the first part of the Academy's question, the second is meaningless.[21]

The connection between previous philosophic thought and Rousseau's position is made somewhat clearer by the epigraph, which emphasizes the primacy of "nature" in his thought:

Non in depravatis, sed in his quae bene secundam naturam se habent considerandum est quid sit naturale.[22]

This citation from Book I of Aristotle's *Politics*, like Rousseau's assumption that the *Discourse* is delivered in his Lyceum, implies that it is impossible to speculate on human inequalities until one has understood nature, and especially human nature, at least as well as the ancient philosophers did. Since modern writers have failed to understand human nature, Aristotle's distinction between "corruption" and "nature," summarized by the epigraph, will be used to criticize modern natural law teachings.[23]

Although Rousseau's criticism of the ideas of philosophers appears to be directed mainly against the "moderns," it extends to "ancient

[19] E.g., see Burgelin, *La Philosophie de l'Existence de Jean Jacques Rousseau*, p. 509 (cited, P, III, 1298).

[20] "What is the source of the Inequality among men, and whether it is authorized by natural law?" The program for this prize competition appeared in the *Mercure de France* in November 1753, and is reproduced in the Pleiade edition (III, 1300).

[21] As we have already seen in discussing the *Émile*, for Rousseau the natural law in its traditional definition cannot exist in the state of nature. See above, pp. 78–82.

[22] "Not in corrupt things, but in those which are well ordered in accordance with nature, should one consider that which is natural" (Aristotle, *Politics* I.1254a36–38). Although the first edition of the *Second Discourse* cites the source as "L. 2" (i.e., Book II) of the *Politics* (see P, III, 1862), it is in Book I, chap. v (according to the currently accepted, albeit conventional divisions of Aristotle's text). This is apparently due to one of the many typographical errors which Rousseau's printer, Marc-Michel Rey, did not change in the first edition (see, e.g., C. G., II, 155, 158). For some reason, both Vaughan (V, I, 125) and the editors of the Pléiade (III, 109) have written "Aris. Politic. I.2" on the title page, as if Rousseau attributed the passage to Book I, chap. ii; aside from the identical error in all "vulgate" editions, I have found no evidence to support such an attribution as Rousseau's intention, nor any Latin translations of Aristotle (in which the division into chapters varies) which place 1254a36–38 in chap. ii of Book I.

[23] *Second Discourse*, Pref. (P, III, 124–25). Cf. Exordium (132); Part 1 (136, 153–54); Part 2 (181–84); n. XII (214–18).

philosophers" as well.[24] For example, Rousseau's epigraph is drawn from the section of Aristotle's *Politics* which establishes the concept of natural slavery, and Rousseau explicitly and repeatedly rejects the argument that men could be slaves by nature.[25] Indeed, while Rousseau cites Aristotle in order to reinforce the distinction between nature and corruption, nothing marks the difference between Rousseau's thought and the classics so clearly as the radical shift in the meaning of "nature."

Aristotle speaks of the nature of a thing as its end or perfection.[26] Since full development is an essential part of that which is natural, the beginning of a thing—mere potentiality—is not in itself decisive in establishing natural characteristics; the name "nature" is most deservingly given to the end or perfection, for it is the good form of a thing which is not corrupted.[27] Although Aristotle uses the phrase "by nature" to indicate that which occurs because of physical or material necessity,[28] the understanding of nature which is most commonly associated with his teaching assumes that when things have a beginning and an end or perfection, it is the latter which is their essence or nature.

This conception of nature, which is often called "teleological," thus accepts "final causes" as an important (though by no means exclusive) way of explaining being. It could be said that the modern attack on Aristotle's physics is directed precisely against this notion of final causes, on the assumption that only "efficient causes" can be taken into consideration in an examination of nature.[29] As we will see, Rousseau shares this modern approach to nature in the *Second Discourse*; his intention can be described as a return to some of the conclusions of the classic understanding of man on the basis of modern physical science.

In his Preface, Rousseau states that the understanding of man and his nature is a question—indeed *the* question—for philosophy, because evidence derived from man as we now see him is not sufficient:

And how will man manage to see himself as nature formed him,

---

[24] *Ibid.*, Pref. (124).

[25] *Ibid.*, Part 1 (161–62); Part 2 (183–84, 193–94); *Contrat social* I, ii (P, III, 353–54); I, iv (355–58). Cf. Locke, *Second Treatise*, chap. IV.

[26] *Politics* I.1252b30–1253a1.

[27] "The nature is the end or 'that for the sake of which.' . . . For not every stage that is last claims to be an end, but only that which is best" (*Physics* II.194a27–33). Cf. 193b and Rousseau's epigraph.

[28] E.g., *Nicomachean Ethics*, II.1103a18–25.

[29] E.g., René Descartes, *Meditations*, VI. Cf. Lucretius, *De Rerum Natura* IV.822–57.

through all the changes that the sequence of time and things must have produced in his original constitution, and to separate what he gets from his own stock from what circumstances and his progress have added to or changed in his primitive state?[30]

Rousseau illustrates the necessity of discovering man's original or primitive condition with a telling modification of a Platonic image:

> Like the statue of Glaucus, which time, sea, and storms had so disfigured that it looked less like a god than a wild beast, the human soul, altered in the bosom of society by a thousand continually renewed causes, . . . by changes that occurred in the constitution of bodies, and by the continual impact of the passions, has, so to speak, changed its appearance to the point of being nearly unrecognizable.[31]

Whereas Plato refers to the sea-god Glaucus to show the difference between man's immortal soul and its degenerate "present appearance,"[32] Rousseau adapts the same image to suggest the difference between primitive and perfected, socialized man; the ordering of Platonic thought is silently reversed by substituting, as the standard of judgment, a primitive or animal condition for the divine purity of an immortal being.

To answer the question of how human inequalities originated, one must therefore consider mankind as a species in the animal world:

> It is easy to see that one must seek in these successive changes of the human constitution the first origin of the differences distinguishing men—who, by common avowal, are naturally as equal among themselves as were the animals of each species before various physical causes had introduced into certain species the varieties we notice.[33]

This presumed "common avowal" of the natural equality of man was not, of course, shared by classic philosophers (as reference to the context of Rousseau's epigraph shows); Rousseau simply assumes the

---

[30] *Second Discourse*, Pref. (P, III, 122). The three sources of human development referred to here (nature, circumstances, and man's own progress) correspond to the three kinds of education distinguished in the *Émile* (I [G, 7], cited above, pp. 6–7).

[31] *Second Discourse*, Pref. (P, III, 122). Rousseau explicitly describes primitive man as a being as "wild" as a "wild beast" (*ibid.*, Part 1 [136]).

[32] *Republic* x.611d. Plato does not speak of a statue of Glaucus, but of the God himself.

[33] *Second Discourse*, Pref. (P, III, 123). Cf. the passage by Buffon cited in n. 35 of this chapter.

— 114 —

superiority of modern natural science, which explains the current differentiation within animal species solely in terms of "physical causes." As the only footnote to the Preface indicates, the works of a scientist like Buffon are "respectable authorities for philosophers" because they are based on reasoning which is both "solid and sublime."[34]

This unquestioning acceptance of the perspective of modern science, at least insofar as an analysis of physical causation is concerned, is decisive in many respects for Rousseau's thought. Buffon's conception of the original homogeneity of each species seems to have been at least provisionally adopted by Rousseau; pending further development of "comparative anatomy," he assumed that the present physical conformation of man as a biped could be taken as a common attribute of the species.[35] But since Rousseau's formulation is intended to be rigorously scientific, even this natural "fact" is presented cautiously, and he appends a long footnote solely to indicate that there are solid "reasons," derived from anatomy as well as experience, for saying that man is naturally a biped.[36]

Because the scientific observation of the original or primitive condition of man has been rendered impossible by the very progress of human nature which permits modern science to raise the question, Rousseau poses the following problem as suited to the "Aristotles and Plinys of our century":

What experiments would be necessary to achieve knowledge of

[34] *Ibid.*, n. II (P, III, 195) in which Rousseau gives the first of three citations from Buffon's *Histoire Naturelle, Générale et Particulière.*

[35] *Second Discourse*, Part 1 (P, III, 134): "I shall not follow his organic structure through its successive developments. I shall not stop to investigate in the animal system what he could have been at the beginning to become at length what he is. . . . Comparative anatomy has as yet made too little progress and the observations of naturalists are as yet too uncertain for one to be able to establish the basis of solid reasoning upon such foundations." Buffon had suggested that "there was, originally, only a single species of men, which having multiplied and spread over all the surface of the earth, underwent different changes by the influence of climate, the difference of food, that of the way of living, epidemic illnesses, and also by the infinitely varied mixture of more or less similar individuals. . . . These alterations . . . later became varieties of the species because they became more general, more noticeable, and more constant by the continuous action of these same causes" ("Histoire naturelle de l'homme: Variétés de l'espèce," *Histoire Naturelle, Générale et Particulière* [in 12°; Paris: Imprimerie Royale, 1752, reprinted 1774], VI, 333–35, cited P, III, 1294–95). Rousseau adopts the same explanation of the variations within the human species in n. X of the *Second Discourse* (P, III, 208).

[36] *Ibid.*, n. III (P, III, 196–98).

natural man? And what are the means for making these experiments in the midst of society?[37]

The greatest ancient naturalists would, if they lived in modern times, direct themselves to an experimental analysis of the nature of man. To emphasize the importance of empirical or scientific evidence for his conception of man's primitive condition, Rousseau himself suggests such an experiment. In a long note, Rousseau raises the question of whether orangoutangs or other similar beasts are men in their purely animal state; unlike monkeys who can be experimentally shown to be unable to perfect themselves, it is not certain whether an orangoutang can develop into a man:

> There would, however, be a means by which, if the orangoutang or others were of the human species, the crudest observers could even assure themselves of it by demonstration. But besides the fact that a single generation would not suffice for this experiment, it must pass as impracticable, because it would be necessary that what is only a supposition were shown to be true before the test that ought to verify the fact could be tried innocently.[38]

Rousseau apparently has in mind the possibility of an experimental cohabitation of orangoutangs with men over several generations, since only such an experiment would be open to the criticism of being "impracticable" on the grounds of violating standards of decency or "innocence."[39]

Rousseau's desire to cast his thought in a way that could be proven —experimentally—to the "crudest observers" reveals an effort to establish philosophic proofs on more "solid" grounds than those of classic philosophers. This consideration is essential if we are to understand fully a celebrated phrase that has caused difficulty for many commentators:

> Others will easily be able to go farther on the same road, though it will not be easy for anyone to reach the end of it; for it is no light undertaking to separate what is original from what is artificial in the present nature of man, and to know correctly a state which no longer exists, which perhaps never existed, which probably

[37] *Ibid.*, Pref. (P, III, 123–24), originally in italics.
[38] *Ibid.*, n. x (211).
[39] See the note to this passage (P, III, 1371–72), which quotes Buffon's argument that the inability of two animals to produce fertile offspring is evidence that they belong to different species. Rousseau's reserve in suggesting such an experiment reflects his awareness of the conflict between science and social morality.

— 116 —

never will exist, and about which it is nevertheless necessary to have precise notions in order to judge our present state correctly.[40]

It has often been remarked that this passage shows that Rousseau's conception of the state of nature is merely a norm or criterion for man, regardless of whether or not it ever existed; because Rousseau speaks of his work as being composed of "conjectures" or "hypotheses,"[41] it is said that his analysis can be compared to the purely hypothetical image of the state of nature by such prior thinkers as Pufendorf.[42]

Because Rousseau's central thesis of man's natural goodness ultimately depends on his conception of human evolution, this point is decisive; if he considered his view of the state of nature to be merely an hypothesis, contrary scientific evidence would have forced him to abandon his entire philosophic position. Yet Rousseau seems to encourage the development of new scientific evidence,[43] and can claim that such research will not conflict with his analysis because he has *proven* that society only develops in the human species "with the aid of certain external circumstances" which do not derive "immediately" from "the nature of the human species."[44]

On several occasions in the *Second Discourse*, Rousseau claims that he has presented proof; for example, at the end of Part 1, he asserts that he has "proved" that inequality is "barely perceptible" and of little effect in the state of nature.[45] At this point, Rousseau clarifies what is meant when he speaks of "conjectures" and "hypotheses" in the Preface and Exordium. Introducing his description of the evolution of mankind from its primitive, asocial condition to its current, perfected, and social state, Rousseau remarks:

> I admit that as the events I have to describe could have happened in several ways, I can make a choice only by conjectures. But . . . the conclusion I want to deduce from mine will not thereby be conjectural, since, on the principles I have established, one could not

[40] *Second Discourse*, Pref. (P, III, 125).
[41] *Ibid.*, Pref. (123); Exordium (133); Part 1 (162).
[42] E.g., see Starobinski's note (P, III, 1295). Since, when Rousseau says that the state of nature "no longer exists" and that it "probably never will exist," he simply recognizes the irreversibility of human evolution, the entire question concerns the meaning of his remark that it "perhaps never existed."
[43] See the passages cited at nn. 37 and 40 of this chapter.
[44] *Lettre à M. Philopolis* (P, III, 232), cited below, p. 174.
[45] *Second Discourse*, Part 1 (P, III, 162). Cf. *ibid.* (152) and n. IX (202): Rousseau also "believes he has proved" that men only left the state of nature "after many centuries" and that "man is naturally good."

conceive of any other system that would not provide me with the same results, and from which I could not draw the same conclusion.[46]

The *Second Discourse* is an attempt to avoid any possible contradiction between natural science and philosophy; if the state of nature as Rousseau describes it is called an "hypothesis," this term refers to the scientific character of the analysis and not to any doubtfulness of the precivilized, prerational origins of the human species. Even if some aspects of Rousseau's description of the state of nature are shown, on the basis of future scientific inquiry, to have been incorrect, the fundamental perspective is unchallengable.[47]

Because the biblical account of human creation has the status of a "fact" based on revelation, the terms "conjecture" and "hypothesis" may be necessary to avoid scandal and persecution, but Rousseau's argument has the same status as the "hypothetical and conditional reasoning . . . of our physicists on the formation of the earth"; Rousseau's account is scientific.[48] Only by considering the human species as a natural phenomenon, living in the "animal system" and subject to purely scientific analysis, can a philosophic understanding of human nature be established.[49]

[46] *Ibid.*, Part 1 (162). In the next paragraph, Rousseau distinguishes between "hypotheses" which cannot be destroyed even though they do not have the "certitude of facts" (i.e., cannot be proven by means of experiment or observation), and the kind of "unknown facts" supposed by philosophy or discovered by history to link "two facts given as real." It is clear from this passage that Rousseau considers the state of nature as a "fact given as real" because it is "impossible . . . to destroy" (*ibid.* [162–63]).

[47] As we will see in discussing the status of the family, the main "hypothetical" or doubtful element is man's total isolation in the pure state of nature (i.e., the absence of a "kind of family" tie between male, female, and helpless infants). See § 2C of this chapter. In the main, however, evolutionary biology has substantiated Rousseau's critique of any nonhistorical account of human nature; see below, chap. IX.

[48] *Second Discourse*, Exordium (P, III, 133). In the Preface, Rousseau says that "I began some lines of reasoning, I ventured some conjectures" (123): the former may possibly refer to Part 1 of the *Discourse*, which as we have just seen is explicitly not as conjectural as Part 2. Similarly, when Rousseau speaks of the "hypothetical history of governments" (Pref., 127), he does not imply that his account of the state of nature is hypothetical. Cf. Strauss, *Natural Right and History*, p. 267, n. 32.

[49] *Second Discourse*, Pref. (124–26). When Rousseau says at this point, "leaving aside therefore all scientific books that teach us only to see men as they have made themselves" (125), he does not mean to leave aside "all scientific books," but only those "that teach us only to see men as they have made themselves." The footnotes to the *Second Discourse* are sufficient proof that Starobinski's interpretation of this phrase (P, III, 1298) is misleading. Cf. also *Émile*, V (G, 574).

2 · *The State of Nature*: *Man as a Physical Phenomenon*

A · THE BIOLOGICAL SELF-SUFFICIENCY OF PRIMITIVE MAN

The opposition between nature and society is overtly established as the basis of Rousseau's analysis at the outset of the *Second Discourse*:

> I conceive of two sorts of inequality in the human species: one, which I call natural or physical, because it is established by nature and consists in the difference of ages, health, bodily strengths, and qualities of mind or soul; the other, which may be called moral or political inequality, because it depends upon a sort of convention and is established, or at least authorized, by the consent of men.[50]

To discover the natural condition of man and the importance of inequality in the state of nature, it is therefore necessary to abstract rigorously all human attributes which can be traced to society and the developments occurring in it. All previous thinkers have failed because they did not successfully isolate the characteristics which antedate man's sociability:

> All . . . have carried over to the state of nature ideas they had acquired in society; they spoke about savage man and they described civil man.[51]

Rousseau avoids this fault by considering mankind as a biological species:

> Stripping this being . . . considering him, in a word, as he must have come from the hands of nature—I see an animal less strong than some, less agile than others, but all things considered, the most advantageously organized of them all.[52]

Since Rousseau elsewhere warned of the difficulty of "this analytical method,"[53] his argument must be studied with great care.

---

[50] *Second Discourse*, Exordium (P, III, 131). Note that Rousseau's definition answers the question of the Academy of Dijon: either inequality originates in physically necessary laws of nature or in social convention, but in no case is it "authorized" by a moral natural law discovered by reason.

[51] *Ibid*. (132). Cf. Part 1 (153–54); n. XII (218).

[52] *Ibid*., Part 1 (134–35).

[53] "I have already said and cannot too often repeat that the error of Hobbes and the philosophers (*philosophes*) is to confuse natural man with the men they see . . . it is not among the inhabitants of a great city that one must seek the first traits of nature in the human heart. Thus this analytical method only offers abysses and mysteries, in which the wisest understands the least" (*État de Guerre* [P, III, 611–12]).

In its original condition, the human animal had "all the vigor of which the human species is capable"; empirical evidence of the "strength and vigor of men in barbarous and savage nations," provided in reports of first-hand observers, proves that the development of civilization results in a physical degeneration of the species.[54] Lacking tools, clothing, houses, domestic animals, and all purely human inventions, the most primitive men faced the same obstacles and benefited from similar means of preservation as do other animals. In order to establish his thesis that human society is an accidental or externally caused phenomenon, Rousseau must prove that the human species could survive in a purely animal condition; hence he begins by considering how primitive man could overcome threats to his existence.

The first obstacle to a primitive man's existence, like that of any animal, is physical deformity at birth; since "nature renders strong and robust those who are well constituted and makes all the others perish," the early death of the weak serves to preserve the species as a whole.[55] The more general danger of being killed by other animals is no more serious for man than for other relatively weak species: first because the primitive man, being robust and more agile than other animals, is capable of defending himself on equal terms with most "wild beasts"; and second because there is no evidence that any species naturally eats man as food.[56] Indeed, primitive man has an advantage in the animal world in that he can use physical objects as "arms," can compare himself with other beasts, and can therefore choose between "flight or combat."[57] This implies, as we shall see, that Rousseau considers man to be a very particular kind of animal, different in certain respects from an ordinary beast even in the pure state of nature.

[54] *Second Discourse*, Part 1 (P, III, 135–40) and n. VI (199–201).
[55] *Ibid.*, Part 1 (135).
[56] *Ibid.* (136–37). See the example Rousseau added for the posthumous edition of 1782 as empirical evidence of this (*ibid.*, 137n.), and cf. n. X (209).
[57] *Ibid.*, Part 1 (136–37). Rousseau's characteristic emphasis on relationships instead of abstractly defined qualities is evident in this passage: in some cases, primitive man's advantage in skill over another animal is greater than that animal's advantage in strength; in such situations the dangers of combat are "reciprocal." In other cases, the beast's advantage in strength may be greater than man's superiority in skill, but in this situation primitive man's ability to flee, and his agility in climbing trees or running, permit him to preserve himself. On the need to consider things "relatively in the physical order," see the Letter to Voltaire of 18 August 1756 (C. G., II, 318, cited in n. 52 of chap. II).

The natural or physical vulnerability of the human body itself is of more danger to primitive man than attack by predatory animals:

> Other more formidable enemies, against which man does not have the same means of defense, are natural infirmities: infancy, old age, and illnesses of all kinds, sad signs of our weakness, of which the first two are common to all animals and the last belongs principally to man living in society.[58]

Illness as such is no more serious a danger to man in the state of nature than to any other animal; only in society is medicine rendered necessary by the vices of human creation, which actually create new illnesses.[59] Restricting oneself to those characteristics shared by all animals, therefore, the two principal risks are infancy and old age. For the aged, since needs decline along with strength, self-preservation becomes less difficult and is not complicated by illnesses that are created by human excess (like gout and rheumatism); in any event, death from old age is a natural necessity which can scarcely be said to threaten the species.[60] The weakness of the infant, on the other hand, is a natural risk which is of particular importance for the survival of the species, and Rousseau must show that the human child is no more vulnerable than the young of other animals.

Rousseau admits that infancy lasts longer among humans than among other species, but argues that this is due to a "rule" of nature since the length of immaturity is in proportion with the average life expectancy; the risk to the child should the mother die is common to all species.[61] More important, Rousseau argues that the human species has an *advantage* when compared to other animals:

> I even observe on the subject of infancy that the mother, since she carries her child with her everywhere, can nourish it with more fa-

[58] *Second Discourse*, Part 1 (P, III, 137).

[59] *Ibid.* (138–39) and n. IX (204–05). In the text, Rousseau refers to Plato's *Republic* (III.405dff.) for evidence that new illnesses have occurred to men living in society, and uses the example of the health of animals found by hunters as empirical proof that illness as such is not a serious danger in the state of nature. On the threat to health supposedly created by the use of copper utensils, indicated in n. IX (204), cf. Rousseau's Letter "Sur l'usage dangereux des utensils de cuivre," published in *Mercure de France*, June 1753 (C. G., II, 47–50).

[60] *Second Discourse*, Part 1 (P, III, 137).

[61] *Ibid.* (137) and n. VII (201), citing Buffon's description of this proportion between the period of growth and length of life in various animals. Cf. also n. X (209) concerning the vulnerability of infants.

cility than the females of several animals, which are forced to come and go incessantly with great fatigue, in one direction to seek their food and in the other to suckle or nourish their young.[62]

Even assuming that the female does not have the assistance of the male, Rousseau asserts that the human mother can more readily raise her young, an advantage which would clearly permit the human species to multiply more rapidly than others. Although the mother can carry her child because, as a biped, she need not use her arms for walking, the decisive advantage of primitive humans seems to lie in the "facility" with which they find food.

B · PRIMITIVE MAN'S NOURISHMENT

Rousseau devoted considerable attention to this point. Because the earth has "natural fertility," in primitive times there was an abundance of vegetable matter—and especially of trees, which "furnish animals with more abundant food than other forms of vegetation can."[63] Since humans are capable of subsisting on vegetable food alone, it would therefore have been relatively easier for humans to find food than for carnivores. But Rousseau went further than this; he tried to show, in the footnotes, that primitive man was naturally a herbivorous species and that he only became omnivorous by imitating other animals. The physiological conformation of man (especially his teeth and intestines), the number of young, and the evidence of several observers, both ancient and modern, are cited to support this view.[64] Since Rousseau also asserts in the *Émile* that "the taste of meat is not natural to man,"[65] we must explain Rousseau's desire to prove that man is not naturally carnivorous.

[62] *Ibid.*, Part 1 (137).

[63] *Ibid.* (135) and n. IV (198). In this note, Rousseau cites Buffon's reasoning that because "animals give back less than they take from the earth," the soil in areas of prolonged human habitation ultimately becomes a desert in which the vegetative earth has been transformed into "fixed salt" and "sand." Cf. Lucretius, *De Rerum Natura* v.783–92.

[64] *Second Discourse*, nn. V (P, III, 198–99) and VIII (201–02). Cf. n. XII (216) and Part 2 (164), cited at n. 193 of this chapter, as well as Lucretius, *De Rerum Natura* v.937–44.

[65] *Émile*, II (G, 168). Rousseau goes on (*ibid.*, 169-71) to add a lengthy citation from Plutarch's essay "On Eating Meat," I, i–v; *Morals*, William W. Goodwin, ed. (New York: Atheneum Society, 1905), v, 3–8. The most interesting point in this passage is Plutarch's assertion that, when the "earth was newly formed," three-quarters of its surface was flooded and "the other quarter covered with sterile woods and forests"; Rousseau's source thus casts doubt on the image of natural plenty presented in the *Second Discourse*. Cf. *Essai sur l'Origine des Langues*, chap. IX (E, XIII, 203)—"Generally, among

One reason for this may be that the species, like the orangoutang, which Rousseau considered as possible examples of the human race in its primitive state, are herbivorous.[66] Another reason, stated explicitly, is that without the need to kill other animals for food, and living amidst natural fertility which provided readily accessible vegetable food, primitive man would be a more pacific animal with less cause to leave the state of nature.[67] But if there is physiological and observed evidence in favor of man's herbivorous origins, why did Rousseau "neglect many favorable points" connected with this hypothesis, restricting himself in the text to the observed fact that man is now omnivorous?[68]

Although this reserve may merely reflect scientific caution, a further reason for Rousseau's treatment of primitive man's eating habits lies in the fact, as he indicates in the notes, that herbivorous animals have a disadvantage by comparison with carnivores:

> Animals that live only on grasses and plants, remaining almost the entire day at pasture and being forced to spend much time nourishing themselves, could not be adequate to the nursing of several young; whereas voracious ones, having their meal almost in an instant, can more easily and more frequently return to their young and their hunting, and compensate for the dissipation of such a large quantity of milk.[69]

This comparison indicates that primitive man, who produces few children like other herbivorous species, would have had this same "disadvantage" of requiring "several hours" to eat,[70] rendering the

---

all the peoples whose origin is known to us, the first barbarians are found to be voracious and carnivorous, rather than agricultural and grain-eating"—with *ibid.* (212)—"Neither the stomach nor the intestines of man are made for digesting raw flesh: in general his taste doesn't tolerate it."

[66] See *Second Discourse*, n. x; the *Histoire des Voyages*, cited by Rousseau, says of the pongo (a species Rousseau suggests may be proto-human): "Their foods are fruits and wild nuts. They never eat flesh" (209).

[67] *Ibid.*, n. v (199): "For as prey is almost the unique subject of fighting among carnivorous animals, and as frugiverous ones live among themselves in continual peace, if the human race were of this latter genus it would clearly have had much greater ease subsisting in the state of nature, and much less need and occasion to leave it." Cf. n. ix (203): "Savage man, when he has eaten, is at peace with all nature, and the friend of his fellowman."

[68] *Ibid.*, Part 1 (135). Cf. *ibid.* (161) and Part 2 (165), where it appears that men ate meat from the earliest times, with the passage from the *Essai sur l'Origine des Langues* cited in n. 65 of this chapter.

[69] *Second Discourse*, n. viii (P, iii, 201).

[70] When an unnamed naturalist criticized the passage just cited, Rousseau

infant who cannot walk especially vulnerable (at least in comparison with other herbivorous species whose young can walk at a very young age and need not be carried in the arms of the mother).

Yet in the text Rousseau describes as *advantages* the very characteristics which would present great risks to the mother and infant were the human species instinctively limited to eating vegetable foods:

> If they have only two feet to run with, they have two arms to provide for their defense and their needs. Perhaps their children walk late and with difficulty, but mothers carry them with ease: an advantage lacking in other species in which the mother, being pursued, finds herself forced to abandon her young or to regulate her speed by theirs.[71]

As a little reflection indicates, if mankind were instinctively herbivorous, the female would be forced to spend many hours daily at pasture; when attacked, she could only defend herself with her hands (thereby leaving her defenseless infant on the ground), or run away carrying the infant (thereby occupying her hands, which could not be used in self defense, and limiting her agility, most particularly in climbing trees—i.e., in the respect which is, according to Rousseau, the decisive security of primitive man against stronger beasts).[72]

Apparently man's herbivorous food preference presents a disadvantage to the human species because the mother and child are more vulnerable—and over a longer period—than other herbivores. The decisive advantage of the human species is that it is not bound by natural instincts which govern other species:

> Men, dispersed among the animals, observe and imitate their industry, and thereby develop in themselves the instinct of the beasts; with the advantage that whereas each species has only its own

---

noted, in reply: "The difficulty that carnivorous beasts have in finding their prey in land cleared and cultivated by men would perhaps not be the same if all the earth was virgin . . . but whatever assumption you make, it will always be necessary for a horse or a bull to spend several hours at pasture, and thus in general the disadvantage will always be for the latter" ("Réponse à un Naturaliste" [P, III, 237]). On these objections and Rousseau's reply, see n. 98 of this chapter.

[71] *Second Discourse*, Part 1 (P, III, 140). Cf. *ibid.* (137), quoted at n. 62 of this chapter.

[72] Consider again *ibid.* (136–37), and n. 57 of this chapter. Cf. the note Rousseau added for the edition of 1782 concerning animals who carry their young in a pouch (*ibid.*, 140n.).

proper instinct, man—perhaps having none that belongs to him—appropriates them all to himself, feeds himself equally well with most of the diverse foods which the other animals share, and consequently finds his subsistence more easily than any of them can.[73]

Primitive man has a peculiar advantage because he is not limited solely by instinct. Whether or not this is because the human species lacks specific instincts, it is undeniable that men imitate other animals and thereby have a certain kind of freedom which other species do not have:

> Thus a pigeon would die of hunger near a basin filled with the best meats, and a cat upon heaps of fruits or grain, although each could very well nourish itself on the food it disdains if it made up its mind to try some.[74]

Before reconsidering the extent of this attribute of freedom or perfectibility in the human species, further aspects of man's ability to survive by imitating other animals need to be mentioned.

If the human can subsist on meat as well as vegetable foods from a very early period of evolution, the vulnerability of the mother would be reduced during the dangerous period when she is nursing her young. Even if it is more natural for the nursing mother to eat vegetables and milk products, as Rousseau asserts in the *Émile*,[75] the possibility of deviating from this practice in times of need means that the female would not require the assistance of the male for defense or food-gathering during the infancy of her young. In this way, Rousseau was able to argue that the persistence of the "society" between male and female was not naturally necessary to the human species; precisely because humans are omnivorous and hence could easily find sufficient food in the pure state of nature, Rousseau can consider primitive man (and woman) as "alone."[76] This connection between isolation and omnivorousness probably explains why man's natural repugnance to eat meat is so strongly emphasized in the *Émile* (where social relations are assumed to exist) and is "neglected" in the text of the *Second Discourse*.

C · PRIMITIVE MAN'S ISOLATION AND THE FAMILY

It appears that Rousseau was forced to describe natural man as

---

[73] *Ibid.* (135). [74] *Ibid.* (141).

[75] *Émile*, I (G, 35–36). In a footnote to this passage, Rousseau expresses doubt that there exist "species which are absolutely incapable of nourishing themselves with anything except meat" (35n.).

[76] *Second Discourse*, Part 1 (P, III, 140).

omnivorous in order to prove that each member of the human species lived in isolation in the state of nature. As Rousseau put it elsewhere:

> Man, at bottom, has no necessary relationship with his fellows, he can subsist without their assistance in all his possible vigor; he needs the cares of man less than the fruits of the earth.[77]

This ability of the species to survive with its members totally independent of each other is of course one of the most striking and most frequently noted aspects of Rousseau's conception of the state of nature. It is based in part on his distinction, which we have already noted, between the "physical" and "moral" aspects of love:

> Let us begin by distinguishing between the moral and the physical in the sentiment of love. The physical is that general desire which inclines one sex to unite with the other. The moral is that which determines this desire and fixes it exclusively on a single object, or which at least gives it a greater degree of energy for this preferred object.[78]

Primitive man, being unable to compare different women, is "limited solely to that which is physical in love"; the preference for a given female is a social acquisition, the family does not exist in the state of nature, and jealousy is an artificial passion based on the kind of comparisons which only arise together with *amour-propre*.[79]

> Males and females united fortuitously, depending on encounter, occasion, and desire, without speech being a very necessary interpreter of the things they had to say to each other; they left each other with the same ease.[80]

The absence of language and thought in the state of nature is thus apparently connected to the nonexistence of the family, which is part of Rousseau's proof that there is no necessary relationship or interdependence between any members of the human species in its primitive condition.

In a long footnote, Rousseau cites Locke's argument in the *Second Treatise of Civil Government* to the effect that the human family sub-

[77] *État de Guerre* (P, III, 604).
[78] *Second Discourse*, Part 1 (P, III, 157–58). Note the qualifications introduced in the last clause and cf. above, p. 40.
[79] *Ibid.*, Part 1 (158–59).
[80] *Ibid.* (147). Cf. Lucretius, *De Rerum Natura* v.962–65.

sists "because the female is capable of conceiving, and is commonly with child again . . . long before the former is out of a dependency on his father's help."[81] Rousseau's main answer is that Locke "assumes what is in question" since the female, if capable of subsisting alone between the time of intercourse and that of giving birth, would have become unknown to the father:

> One goes off in one direction, the other in another, and there is no likelihood that at the end of the nine months they have any memory of having known each other.[82]

This answer presupposes, as indeed Rousseau argues in the text, that the human species is one in which each individual naturally lives in isolation.

It is therefore quite strange that, in this same footnote, Rousseau seems to present evidence that the family is natural. Locke had argued that the continued cooperation of the male in feeding the young is particularly necessary among carnivores, whereas "in animals which feed on grass, the conjunction between male and female lasts no longer than the very act of copulation."[83] In response to Locke's implication that the human species is naturally carnivorous, Rousseau replies with evidence derived from both quadrupeds and birds:

> It seems on the contrary that if the help of the male were necessary to the female to preserve her young, it would be above all in the species that live only on grass, because the mother needs a very long time to graze, and during that entire period she is forced to neglect her brood; whereas the prey of a female bear or wolf is devoured in an instant, and she has more time, without suffering from hunger, to nurse her young.[84]

If this consideration provides, when compared to Rousseau's previous distinction between carnivores and herbivores in note VIII, "one more strong reason to doubt that the human species is naturally carnivorous,"[85] it also implies that, as a herbivorous species, there would have been a continued "society" between the human male and female even in remotest times.[86] Why, then, does Rousseau add this argu-

[81] *Second Discourse*, n. XII (214–18), citing chap. VII, § 79–80 of the *Second Treatise*.
[82] *Second Discourse*, n. XII (P, III, 217).
[83] Locke, *Second Treatise*, § 79, cited in *Second Discourse*, n. XII (214).
[84] *Ibid.* (216).   [85] *Ibid.*
[86] In concluding Note XII, Rousseau says (after the sentence cited at n. 82 of this chapter): "this kind of memory, by which one individual gives prefer-

ment, which seems to contradict his denial that the human family is natural?

This perplexity is reinforced if we read, in this context, Rousseau's discussion of "paternal authority" in Part 2 of the *Second Discourse*:

> By the law of nature, the father is master of the child only as long as his help is necessary for him; . . . beyond this stage they become equals. . . .[87]

Although Rousseau asserts that such paternal authority derives its "principal force" from civil society, he implicitly admits the possibility that the father's assistance is necessary for the preservation of each individual child during early infancy.[88] In the *Essay on the Origin of Languages*, Rousseau is more explicit:

> In the earliest times, men spread over the face of the earth had no other society than the family, no other laws than those of nature, no other language than gestures and a few inarticulate sounds.[89]

Even more surprising, the *Social Contract* explicitly returns to the position for which Rousseau had criticized Locke in note XII of the *Second Discourse*:

> The most ancient of all societies, and the only natural one, is the family. Even then, the children only remain tied to the father as long as they need him for self-preservation.[90]

In these passages, Rousseau admits that the family is natural, at least in some sense of the word, apparently contradicting his assertion that

---

ence to another for the act of procreation, requires, as I prove in the text, more progress or corruption in human understanding than can be supposed in man in the state of animality in question here. . . . Therefore there is not, for the man, any reason to seek the same woman, nor for the woman, any reason to seek the same man" (217–18). Rousseau's *proof* seems to be limited to the absence of memory or thought as the basis of continued cohabitation; his example of herbivorous species who do so cohabit shows that "in the state of animality" the male may aid the female without having a "reason" to do so.

[87] *Ibid.*, Part 2 (182).

[88] *Ibid.* Cf. *Économie Politique* (P, III, 241): "The father being physically stronger than his children, as long as his assistance is necessary for them, paternal power passes with reason as being established by nature." The same sentence occurs in the first draft of the *Social Contract* (*Geneva MS*, I, v [P, III, 298]).

[89] *Essai sur l'Origine des Langues*, chap. IX (E, XIII, 198). Cf. *ibid.* (218).

[90] *Contrat social*, I, ii (P, III, 352). Cf. Locke, *Second Treatise*, chap. V.

man in the state of nature is isolated and need not assist the female in raising the young.

Our perplexity increases further it we read, in this context, Rousseau's analysis of jealousy in the *Émile*:

> The example derived from animals has been previously examined in the *Discourse on Inequality*; and now that I reflect on it, that examination seems solid enough to refer readers to it.[91]

Having endorsed his analysis of the *Second Discourse*, Rousseau pushes it further:

> I will only add to the distinctions I made in that work that the jealousy which comes from nature depends a great deal on the power of sex, and that, when that power is or seems unlimited, such jealousy is at its highest. . . . In these same species, the females always obey the first comer, only belong to the males by the right of conquest, and cause eternal combats among them. On the contrary, in species where one unites with one, where the conjunction produces a sort of moral link, a sort of marriage, . . . the male, having as guarantee of her fidelity this preferential affection, is also less disquieted by the sight of other males, and lives more peacefully with them.[92]

Rousseau immediately applies this distinction between two kinds of species, and what he explicitly calls the "law of nature" binding the male and female in the latter type, to human beings:

> Now to consider the human species in its primitive simplicity, it is easy to see, by the limited power of the male and by the temperance of his desires, that he is destined by nature to content himself with a single female . . . the children are for so long crawling and weak, that the mother and they could only with difficulty dispense with the attachment of the father, and the cares which result from it.[93]

---

[91] *Émile*, v (G, 547). In the passage here referred to, Rousseau argues that one cannot deduce, from the violence arising from sexual desire among some animals, that the same thing occurred among primitive humans; in some species, such violence arises because "nature has manifestly established other relations than among us," and in others because there are more males than females or because the latter have "times of heat and exclusion" (*Second Discourse*, Part 1 [P, III, 159]).

[92] *Émile*, v (G, 547).

[93] *Ibid.* Rousseau also argues that equality of the numbers of human males and females, "at least in our climates," seems to support this view. Note that according to the *Second Discourse*, human sexual desire is naturally limited (Part 1 [P, III, 158]).

On the very page of the *Émile* in which Rousseau cites his *Second Discourse* with approval, he presents an argument which denies a central aspect of the analysis to which he refers, namely the necessary solitude and self-sufficiency of primitive men (and, more important, of primitive women).[94]

Before concluding that Rousseau's position was hopelessly contradictory, it would be well to restate the problem. In the text of the *Second Discourse*, Rousseau argues that the human species lives in peaceful isolation in the state of nature, lacking language, reason, and all social bonds (including those of the family). This is possible because man is not limited by instinct to any particular eating habits; by imitating other species and becoming omnivorous, humans have little or no difficulty in subsisting in the plenty of the state of nature. In the footnotes to the *Second Discourse*, Rousseau discusses the hypothesis that man is naturally herbivorous at three separate points, as if to underline the importance of the question. This hypothesis, supported by physiological evidence, ancient authorities, and reasoning derived from "the most general system of nature,"[95] is attractive because it implies that primitive man was peaceful and could subsist in plenty, as do other herbivores (some of whom, like the orangoutang or the pongo, may be primitive men). But this hypothesis also undermines Rousseau's argument for two reasons: first, it would increase the vulnerability of the isolated female (and her infant child); and second, it would suggest, by comparison with other herbivorous quadrupeds, that some sort of family indeed existed in the pure state of nature.[96] In Part 1 of the text, Rousseau asserts that the only primitive human relationship was between the mother and her children, and ceased "as soon as they had the strength to seek their food" by themselves;[97] in the notes, Rousseau provides evidence that the father is necessary to supply the needs of the mother and her very young infants (a possibility admitted in Part 2 and accepted in other works as scientifically accurate).

---

[94] Immediately after this passage, Rousseau also cites with approval the fundamental distinction between the physical and moral elements of love (on which Rousseau's argument for the absence of the family in the state of nature was based). Cf. *Émile*, v (548) and *Second Discourse*, Part 1 (P, III, 157–58), cited at n. 78 of this chapter.

[95] *Ibid.*, n. VII (201).

[96] According to the passage of the *Histoire des Voyages* cited by Rousseau, the pongos (who are considered as possible examples of primitive men) "sometimes walk in groups" and, although adults are never captured, "the Negroes take many young ones after killing the mother" (*ibid.*, n. X [209]).

[97] *Ibid.*, Part 1 (147).

These considerations show that Rousseau must have been aware that some scientists might reject his hypothesis that natural man is a solitary being without a family.[98] But, as we have noted, Rousseau flatly states at the end of his description of the pure state of nature that "one could not conceive of any other system that would not provide me with the same results";[99] even if the family is natural to the human species, Rousseau's conclusions from his account of the state of nature will be unchanged.

Whether or not the male assists the female in caring for the young in the state of nature, it is incorrect to imagine (as Condillac does) that "the family gathered in the same habitation":

> Instead, in this primitive state, having neither houses, nor huts, nor property of any kind, everyone took up his lodging by chance, and often for only one night.[100]

Apparently there are two different meanings to the assertion that the family did not exist in the pure state of nature: according to the first —more radical but also more debatable scientifically—each member of the species, with the exception of dependent infants, lives in virtually total isolation; according to the second, the family cannot be said to exist in the precise sense until, having a fixed habitation, its members acquire "a union as intimate and permanent as among us."[101] Although this second view is less radical (and not as explicitly adopted as the first in Part 1 of the *Discourse*), it is implicitly adopted when Rousseau describes "the epoch of a first revolution, which produced the establishment and differentiation of families and which introduced a sort of property."[102] Since the family arises only when men first make "huts from branches," the cooperation of a male and female, "wandering in the forests . . . without domicile" but bringing up their young children together, would not be inconsistent with Rousseau's conception that primitive man is "without speech, . . . without war and without liaisons, with no need of his fellowmen"; it

---

[98] This is proven by his citation of Locke's argument in n. XII. In fact, an unnamed naturalist is known to have objected to this point as well as two others; Rousseau wrote out answers to the other two objections, but not to the one touching the absence of the family in the state of nature. See the transcription of the manuscript (V, I, 512–14). It is entirely possible that this manuscript contains the objections made by a M. Leroi, transmitted to Rousseau by Condillac in a letter of 7 September 1756 (C. G., II, 332).

[99] *Second Discourse*, Part 1 (P, III, 162), cited at n. 46 of this chapter.

[100] *Ibid.* (146–47).

[101] *Ibid.* (146).

[102] *Ibid.*, Part 2 (167).

is only "perhaps" true that savage man never recognized another member of his species "individually."[103]

It is useful, therefore, to suggest the following interpretation concerning the family: it is conceivable, especially if humans are naturally omnivorous and live in plenty, that the family did not exist in the state of nature; this possibility, because it is the most radically asocial condition imaginable, must be the basis of a scientific analysis of natural man. "Perhaps" this state of nature "did not exist,"[104] but even if there is "a kind of marriage" in the state of nature, there are no further "moral" ties between men, and the family bond itself has no natural necessity as soon as the young are capable of seeking food and preserving themselves on their own. If the latter situation is ultimately shown to be correct, all references to "savage man" in his original condition could be extended to the primitive nuclear family (male, female, and helpless children) without thereby changing any of the fundamental conclusions of Rousseau's analysis. In this way, scientific evidence concerning the mating and child-rearing habits of the human species in its animal state could be easily accommodated by Rousseau even if his boldest, most asocial hypothesis were incorrect. To see if this interpretation is tenable, we must review the remaining aspects of Rousseau's description of the state of nature.

D · PRIMITIVE MAN'S FACULTIES:
THE STATUS OF LANGUAGE AND REASON

According to Rousseau, primitive man is at first characterized by "purely animal functions"; his desires and fears are determined by "the simple impulsion of nature":[105]

> The only goods he knows in the universe are nourishment, a female, and repose; the only evils he fears are pain and hunger. I say pain and not death because an animal will never know what it is to die; and knowledge of death and its terrors is one of the first acquisitions that man has made in moving away from the animal condition.[106]

This passage indicates why Rousseau believed that man's fear of vio-

[103] *Ibid.*, Part 1 (159–60). Cf. Part 2 (166): primitive man perceives the "conformities" among his fellowmen, *"his female,* and himself" (italics added). Cf. *Essai sur l'Origine des Langues,* chap. IX, cited at n. 89 of this chapter: the existence of the family does not imply that of speech or moral duty.

[104] See again *Second Discourse,* Pref. (P, III, 123), cited at n. 40 of this chapter.

[105] *Ibid.,* Part 1 (143).   [106] *Ibid.*

lent death, on which Hobbes (at least in part) based the origins of political society,[107] is an unnatural passion which can only emerge within society; it also points to the decisive characteristic of primitive man according to Rousseau—namely, stupidity:

> His soul, agitated by nothing, is given over to the sole sentiment of its present existence without any idea of the future, however near it may be, and his projects, as limited as his views, barely extend to the end of the day.[108]

The distance from "pure sensations to the simplest knowledge" is enormous, and man in his animal state, with "neither foresight nor curiosity," had no means of filling this gap since he lacked all language except the "cry of nature."[109] Primitive man had no arts or science since, even if an individual discovered them, he would be incapable of transmitting them;[110] at first men have no tools, no clothing, no houses, and if they begin to wear animal skins when they first enter cold climates, these are things which, under the pressure of physical need, they "soon know" how to do as individuals.[111]

Rousseau devotes a long section of the text to his reinterpretation of Condillac's analysis of the origin of speech—a subject which he also studied in an unpublished *Essay on the Origin of Language*.[112] He first suggests the insufficiency of Condillac's reasoning because it assumes, as all prior thinkers have, that the family is natural; if men lived in complete isolation, according to the reasoning of the text of the *Second Discourse*, "one can conceive neither the necessity of this invention, nor its possibility were it not indispensable."[113]

But Rousseau is willing to admit that language might have been necessary for primitive men[114]—a supposition which conforms to our previous interpretation of Rousseau's treatment of the family. Even if there were a need for communication (as indeed would have been the case if, like some other herbivorous species, there were naturally a

---

[107] Cf. *Leviathan*, Part I, chap. XI (ed. Oakeshott, p. 64) and chap. XIII (84).
[108] *Second Discourse*, Part 1 (P, III, 144).
[109] *Ibid.* (144, 146–48).
[110] *Ibid.* (145–46, 160).
[111] *Ibid.* (139–40). Cf. Lucretius, *De Rerum Natura* v.953–57; 966–75.
[112] See *Essai sur l'Origine des Langues*, especially chap. IX.
[113] *Second Discourse*, Part 1 (P, III, 146).
[114] "Let us suppose this first difficulty conquered . . . and let us seek, assuming [languages] to be necessary, how they could begin to be established" (*ibid.* [147]). At this point, Rousseau adds a footnote citing Isaac Vossius to bolster his contention that language is not intrinsically necessary— or even advantageous—for the self-preservation of animals (*ibid.*, n. XIII [218]).

"domestic intercourse of fathers, mothers, and children"), its discovery is a "new difficulty, worse than the preceding one";[115] the assumption that the family exists would "fail to resolve the objections" because the lack of language in the state of nature does not depend ultimately, or even primarily, on man's isolation.

> For if men needed speech in order to learn how to think, they had even greater need of knowing how to think in order to discover the art of speech.[116]

Rousseau then proceeds to trace the kind of development necessary for men to progress from the cry of nature, "elicited only by a kind of instinct in pressing emergencies," to a fully elaborated language, which is only needed when "it was necessary to persuade assembled men."[117]

Rousseau emphasizes this problem by asking his judges to consider how difficult the discovery of substantive nouns, numbers, and other parts of speech must have been, and he adds a footnote citing Plato's *Republic* as evidence of this problem with respect to numbers.[118] While we cannot discuss this analysis in detail, one point is central; whereas Rousseau has already asserted that "all animals have ideas, since they have senses,"[119] he admits that only men develop "abstract ideas":

> Besides, general ideas can come into mind only with the aid of words, and the understanding grasps them only through propositions. This is one of the reasons why animals can neither formulate such ideas nor ever acquire the perfectibility which depends on them.[120]

Only man avoids the vicious circle of the mutual necessity of words for ideas and ideas for words, and this was apparently only possible

[115] *Ibid.*, Part 1 (146–47).
[116] *Ibid.* (147).   [117] *Ibid.* (148).
[118] *Ibid.* (151) and n. xiv (218–19). Given Rousseau's assumption that Plato is one of the judges of the *Discourse*, this reference is clearly intended to emphasize the weakness of classical thought, which assumed that men naturally speak since they are naturally sociable; the classics provide no scientifically adequate explanation of the origin of speech. (Cf. Aristotle, *Politics* I.1253a.) Even Lucretius, who denies man's natural sociability, argues that language is the product of nature and need, not human invention or custom (*De Rerum Natura* v.1028–90).
[119] *Second Discourse*, Part 1 (P, III, 141).
[120] *Ibid.* (149). Cf. the distinction between "simple" and "complex ideas" in the *Émile* (above, pp. 34–35), and Starobinski's note to the passage just cited (P, III, 1327).

over the course of a protracted and very difficult evolutionary process.

Without language and reason, and on the assumption that primitive man was isolated:

> It is impossible to imagine why, in that primitive state, a man would sooner have need of another man than a monkey or a wolf of its fellow creature; nor, supposing this need, what motive could induce the other to provide for it, nor even, in this last case, how they could agree between them on the conditions.[121]

This remark indicates subtly how Rousseau responded to the possibility that primitive man may have lived in families or even small groups. In the pure state of nature, the animal man has no need of others, but even assuming that he does, he lacks a motive for helping others; even more important, if he should have such a motive, for example arising out of animal pity (or mechanical attachment for his mate), he cannot "agree . . . on the conditions" of mutual assistance. The decisive point is that, lacking speech and reason, contract is impossible in the state of nature.[122]

Only this interpretation reveals why Rousseau was able to cite, in the footnotes, the reports of animals (like the pongo), "who sometimes walk in groups," and assert that these animals may really be men in their primitive condition.[123] Despite the exaggerated appearance of the text, which seems to imply that men must have lived in total isolation in the state of nature, the crucial characteristic of this primitive condition is man's animal stupidity, his lack of reason, and his inability to speak. Unlike the assumption of total isolation, which could conceivably be criticized by scientists on the basis of evidence that Rousseau went out of the way to present himself (especially in the footnotes), the inability of animals to articulate thought in speech is unassailable; classic thought itself agreed that even sociable animals were incapable of doing so.[124] Once it is assumed that man was once nothing but an animal, Rousseau's proof that language is a human invention which required "centuries" is unassailable.

The "proof"—and Rousseau explicitly uses the word at this point[125]—that "nature . . . little prepared" human sociability is thus

---

[121] *Second Discourse*, Part 1 (P, III, 151).
[122] See *ibid.*, Part 2 (166–67), where this interpretation is implicitly admitted with reference to the behavior of "crows or monkeys" as well as primitive men. Cf. Lucretius, *De Rerum Natura* v.958–62.
[123] *Second Discourse*, n. X (209).
[124] See n. 118 of this chapter.
[125] *Second Discourse*, Part 1 (P, III, 152).

based on the double grounds that primitive men have little need of each other (even if they do need females and vice versa) and that, in any event, as stupid animals lacking speech, no explicit agreements between them are possible. Whereas Hobbes had argued that no justice is possible in the state of nature because contracts can be broken without a sanction,[126] Rousseau goes one step further and denies the possibility of *making* such agreements in the primitive state.[127] Simultaneously, Rousseau presents scientific evidence against the major premise of traditional jurists, like Pufendorf, who assumed that justice exists in the state of nature because natural law can be discovered by the reasoning of an isolated man.[128] Rousseau's double objective of criticizing both traditional morality and Hobbesian or materialist philosophy, which characterizes the *Émile*, is prepared by the argument of the *Second Discourse*.[129]

E · THE SENTIMENTS OF PRIMITIVE MAN: SELF-LOVE AND PITY

It is in this context of a simultaneous criticism of the traditional natural law teaching and the philosophies which were opposed to it that Rousseau's analysis of the "first and simplest operations of the human soul" must be understood. In the Preface of the *Second Discourse*, after criticizing all prior conceptions of natural law in a passage that has already been discussed,[130] Rousseau summarizes his position:

> Meditating on the first and simplest operations of the human soul, I believe I perceive in it two principles anterior to reason, of which one interests us ardently in our well-being and our self-preservation, and the other inspires in us a natural repugnance to see any sensitive being perish or suffer, principally our fellowmen.[131]

This conception of the original state of nature avoids the assumption that man is naturally social or naturally rational, assumptions which Rousseau attacks as scientifically untenable.

[126] Hobbes, *Leviathan*, Part I, chap. XIV (ed. Oakeshott, p. 89).

[127] *Ibid.* (90): "to make covenants with brute beasts, is impossible; because not understanding our speech, they understand not, nor accept of any translation of right; nor can translate any right to another: and without mutual acceptation, there is no covenant."

[128] E.g., see Pufendorf, *Le Droit de Nature et des Gens*, II, ii, § 9 (ed. 1706, I, 152–53). Robert Derathé cites this passage, from a later edition with slight modifications; *Rousseau et la Science Politique de son temps* (Paris: Presses Universitaires de France, 1950), pp. 161–62.

[129] See above, pp. 82–84. [130] See above, pp. 77–80.

[131] *Second Discourse*, Pref. (P, III, 125–26).

Because man's natural impulse to self-preservation had been accepted by all prior thinkers, Rousseau did not go to any great length to prove that it exists. Instead, he had merely to show that, in a stupid and independent animal who is unable to speak, the desire for self-preservation does not have the effect of creating a "war of all against all" as Hobbes had argued:

> Savage man, when he has eaten, is at peace with all nature, and the friend of all his fellowmen. If it is sometimes a question of disputing his meal, he never comes to blows without first having compared the difficulty of winning with that of finding his subsistence elsewhere; and as pride is not involved in the fight, it is ended by a few blows; the victor eats, the vanquished goes off to seek his fortune, and all is pacified.[132]

Hobbes' analysis is different from that of the "modern jurists" Rousseau criticized in the Preface, because "Hobbes saw very clearly the defect of all modern definitions of natural right."[133] But Hobbes:

> improperly included in the savage man's care of self-preservation the need to satisfy a multitude of passions which are the product of society and which have made laws necessary. . . . Hobbes did not see that the same cause that prevents savages from using their reason as our jurists claim, prevents them at the same time from abusing their faculties, as he himself claims.[134]

Hobbes' own premises should have led him to conclude that the "state of nature . . . is the best suited to peace, and the most appropriate for the human race";[135] Rousseau's criticism of Hobbes on his own grounds is sufficient to prove that society—or at the least, the kind of society in which men have mutual needs interpreted by speech —is unnatural.

One is led to wonder why Rousseau could not leave it at that, without insisting that pity is a natural sentiment. The importance of this

---

[132] *Ibid.*, n. ix (203).

[133] *Ibid.*, Part 1 (153). Cf. the description of the "moderns," Pref. (124–25). The detailed study of *Rousseau et la Science Politique de son temps* by Derathé is weakened by a failure to emphasize sufficiently this explicit distinction between the "moderns" or "our jurists" and Hobbes, repeated by Rousseau at two other points: *Second Discourse*, Part 1 (136, 154). Cf. also Part 2 (181).

[134] *Ibid.*, Part 1 (153–54).

[135] *Ibid.* Note that Rousseau does not say, in his own name, that the state of nature is "the most appropriate for the human race" (see below, pp. 171–74).

question is underlined by the subordinate status of pity when compared to self-preservation in savage man:

> as long as he does not resist the inner impulse of commiseration, he will never harm another man or even another sensitive being, except in the legitimate case where, his preservation being concerned, he is obliged to give himself preference.[136]

A little reflection indicates that the superior demands of self-preservation, since they are "legitimate" and interpreted solely by the individual, make pity of little operative importance whenever needs conflict in the pure state of nature. According to Rousseau himself, in this state man is "taught by experience that love of well-being is the *sole* motive of human actions";[137] pity is unreliable as the source of external behavior. It is the stupidity and lack of desire of primitive men which produces their peacefulness, not the sentiment of pity:

> Thus one could say that savages are not evil precisely because they do not know what it is to be good; for it is neither the growth of enlightenment nor the restraint of law, but the calm of passions and the ignorance of vice which prevent them from doing evil.[138]

Rousseau does not need to assume the existence of pity in order to prove that primitive man has few passions and no knowledge, since these attributes are those of "an animal limited at first to pure sensations."[139]

On the basis of our analysis of pity in the *Émile*, it is necessary to go even further: it would appear that pity, although a "natural sentiment," does not really operate in the pure state of nature. As we have seen, this sentiment presupposes imagination, and in the state of nature "imagination . . . does not speak to savage hearts."[140] Rousseau makes this point explicit in the *Essay on the Origin of Languages*:

> Social affections only develop in us with our enlightenment. Pity, even though natural to the human heart, would remain eternally

---

[136] *Second Discourse*, Pref. (P, III, 126). Cf. Part 1 (156), where the same exception is noted.

[137] *Ibid.*, Part 2 (166), italics added. Self-preservation is man's "first care" (164).

[138] *Ibid.*, Part 1 (154). When Rousseau says that pity "takes the place of laws, morals, and virtue" in the state of nature (*ibid.*, 156), does he mean that pity has the same relatively impotent status as law in the state of nature?

[139] *Ibid.*, Part 2 (164). Cf. Part 1 (160), and consider *Émile*, I (G, 48–50, 58); II (70, 81–82): like primitive man, Émile as a young child is not wicked because his passions are limited, and not because he feels pity.

[140] *Second Discourse*, Part 1 (P, III, 158); see above, pp. 43–48.

inactive without the imagination, which puts it in action. How do we let ourselves be moved by pity? In transporting ourselves outside of ourselves; in identifying ourselves with the suffering being. We only suffer insofar as we judge that he suffers; it is not in ourselves, but in him that we suffer. . . . One who has never reflected can be neither clement, nor just, nor pitying; nor can he be a wicked and vindictive being.[141]

One cannot consider this passage to be a tentative formulation, written before the *Second Discourse* and representing a view subsequently abandoned by Rousseau (as one commentator has done),[142] for the striking reason that most of the passage just cited was used, almost verbatim, in the *Émile*.[143] Not merely the efficacity of pity, but its very existence in the state of nature, is open to question.

The doubtful status of pity is underlined by the curious way that the concept is introduced in the text of the *Second Discourse*, where Rousseau asserts:

I do not believe I have any contradiction to fear in granting man the sole natural virtue that the most excessive detractor of human virtues was forced to recognize.[144]

In this allusion to Mandeville as an authority, Rousseau boldly ignores Hobbes, whose "contradiction" he would have every reason to "fear" in the context of a criticism of the Hobbesian state of nature.[145]

Rousseau's evidence in favor of the existence of this sentiment, leaving to one side his paraphrase of an imaginary scene in Mandeville's *Fable of the Bees* (which hardly has scientific status[146]), is as follows:

Without speaking of the tenderness of mothers for their young and of the perils they brave to guard them, one observes daily the repugnance of horses to trample a living body underfoot. An animal does not pass near a dead animal of its species without uneasiness. There are even some animals that give them a kind of sepulcher;

[141] *Essai sur l'Origine des Langues*, chap. IX (E, XIII, 199–200).
[142] See Starobinski's note (P, III, 1330–31).
[143] *Émile*, IV (G, 261), cited above, pp. 45–46.
[144] *Second Discourse*, Part 1 (P, III, 154).
[145] This exaggeration is reinforced by Rousseau's use of the term *vertu naturelle* to describe pity: ultimately, pity is regarded as an element of man's "natural goodness," to be distinguished from "virtue" (*ibid.*, Part 1 [156]).
[146] *Ibid.* (154–55). Cf. Bernard Mandeville, *The Fable of the Bees*, F. B. Kaye, ed. (Oxford: Clarendon Press, 1924), pp. 287–94.

and the sad lowing of cattle entering a slaughterhouse announces the impression they receive from the horrible sight that strikes them.[147]

But Rousseau has just explained the mother's care for her children without any reference to pity,[148] and the reaction of cattle in a slaughterhouse could, to say the least, be attributed to the desire for self-preservation rather than pity; the "repugnance" of horses to trample living beings did not prevent such accidents from occurring frequently before the age of the automobile.

It seems that the principal natural phenomenon in support of pity is the "uneasiness" of animals when passing near a *dead* member of their species. In fact, the sole evidence in the footnotes is of this kind; in describing the proto-human animal called the pongo, the *Histoire des Voyages* relates that:

> When one of these animals dies, the others cover its body with a heap of branches or leaves.[149]

Apart from other remarks related solely to the experience of men in society (which cannot be decisive according to Rousseau's own method of reasoning),[150] the convincing natural evidence is restricted to the reaction to seeing *dead* animals—and, what is even more important, is based in part on a report concerning the cooperative behavior of at least one species that "walks in groups."

Although Rousseau unquestionably considers pity "natural to the human heart," it appears that this sentiment is "obscure" and cannot be felt as long as man lives in isolation in the pure state of nature; pity is somehow connected with sociability, and does not necessarily have to operate for the individual to preserve himself as an isolated being. This finding implies that the original state of nature is *not* Rousseau's criterion for a most decisive aspect of human nature; the sentiment of pity, like reason, seems to be an acquisition that presupposes social contact. How then can Rousseau argue that pity is natural, unlike sociability and reason?

Since the generally accepted interpretation of Rousseau's entire

[147] *Second Discourse*, Part 1 (P, III, 154).
[148] *Ibid.* (147).
[149] *Ibid.*, n. x (209). Rousseau repeats this trait as evidence of the possibility that pongos are men in a primitive state (*ibid.*, [211]).
[150] See the examples of Sulla and Alexander of Pherae, taken from Plutarch and added for the edition of 1782 (*ibid.*, Part 1 [155]); and the comparison of the philosopher with the "rabble" and "marketwomen" (*ibid.* [156]).

notion of the state of nature is at issue, it is necessary to reconsider the basic formulation concerning pity in the Preface of the *Second Discourse*:

> Leaving aside therefore all scientific books . . . and meditating on the first and simplest operations of the human soul, I believe *I perceive* in it two *principles* anterior to reason, of which one interests us ardently in our well-being and our self-preservation, and the other inspires in us a natural repugnance to see any sensitive being perish or suffer, principally our fellowmen. It is from the conjunction and combination that our mind is able to make of these two *principles*, without the necessity of introducing that of sociability, that all the rules of natural right appear to me to flow. . . .[151]

Both self-preservation and pity are introduced as "principles" that are "perceived" by Rousseau, not as sentiments that are actually felt by primitive man (who apparently could act on these principles without necessarily being conscious of them as natural sentiments). In restating man's condition in the earliest state of nature, Rousseau explicitly distinguishes between felt "sentiments" and the activities or "cares" of this epoch:

> Man's first *sentiment* was that of his existence, his first *care* was that of his preservation.[152]

Although men originally did not feel the sentiment of pity, neither did they have a conscious desire to preserve themselves; primitive man began as a stupid animal incapable of *any* feeling except that of his mere "existence."

Rousseau therefore radically revises the Hobbesian teaching not merely by his addition of natural pity, but above all by denying that self-preservation is, in the pure state of nature, a conscious desire. Both self-preservation and pity are originally "principles"—i.e., theoretical concepts discovered by Rousseau to account for the observable behavior of primitive men (even if the men themselves are at first unaware of the sentiments that will arise from self-preservation and pity).[153] On this ground, Rousseau's assertion that pity is natural

---

[151] *Ibid.*, Pref. (125–26), italics added.
[152] *Ibid.*, Part 2 (164), italics added.
[153] This explains the tenses in the sentence: "It [pity] *carries us* without reflection to the aid of those whom we see suffer; in the state of nature . . . it *will* dissuade every robust savage from robbing a weak child or an infirm old man of his hard-won subsistence if he himself hopes to be able to find his own elsewhere" (*ibid.*, Part 1 [156], italics added). For "us" (civilized men), pity is

does not depend on evidence that such a sentiment was felt in the state of nature, but rather on the supposedly observable phenomenon that uncontrolled violence between animals of a given species does not occur. Even if primitive man was at first restrained from doing needless harm to his fellow creatures by stupidity or the limited extent of his desires, Rousseau can describe this behavior in terms of pity because pity is "the simplest operation of the human soul" that could, when it ultimately emerges, produce the same result.

Rousseau's assertion of the natural status of both pity and self-preservation is thus an attempt to formulate the most economical explanation of the widest range of scientific evidence concerning human and animal behavior; his theoretical principles can best be understood, as he himself states, in terms of the canons of modern physical science.[154] Hobbes' philosophy is inadequate because it tries to reduce all human behavior to the single postulate of individual self-preservation; if applied to animals—or at least to man as an animal—this view leads to the conclusion that the state of nature is a war of all which threatens to annihilate the entire species. Since animals preserve themselves as species, and not merely as individuals, the principle of individual self-preservation is inadequate to account for the state of nature as man's original, animal condition.

The solution of the traditional natural law teaching was to speak of sociability and reason as natural restraints of man's admitted impulse to preserve himself. Granted that Rousseau abandoned the notion of natural rationality on the grounds that it was a human invention, why did he also deny that man is naturally a social animal (despite the possibility, which he clearly admits, that the family is natural)?[155]

---

active in the present; for the savage, it "will dissuade"—i.e., as soon as it appears.

[154] Ibid., Exordium (133).

[155] The general interpretation is that Rousseau sought merely to express a radical individualism, permitting an attack on all social life as morally corrupting; for example, Strauss concludes that Rousseau would have returned to the notion of man as a naturally social animal had it not been for a desire to emphasize individual freedom (Natural Right and History, pp. 277–78). However great the role of such factors, this explanation is insufficient for two reasons. First, since the postulation of self-preservation and pity as natural "principles" has the status of a scientific hypothesis, the substitution of pity for the older notion of sociability must also be considered in terms of its adequacy in describing animal behavior. Second, the presumed individualism of the Second Discourse, if pushed too far, creates a glaring contradiction between the notion of freedom in the state of nature and Rousseau's political teaching (which by contrast seems "collectivist"). Vaughan, caught in the trap, is forced to postulate an "evolution" in Rousseau's thought which seems highly

The answer seems to be that natural sociability is unnecessary—and thus scientifically undesirable—as an assumption; since some animal species preserve themselves without social cooperation, there is no need to postulate from the outset that sociability is indispensable to human survival.

On the contrary, some men at least seem to be able to survive as isolated individuals, and the scientific data, such as that concerning man's original eating habits, is sufficiently obscure that total asociability is a hypothetical possibility. By substituting pity for sociability, Rousseau could therefore claim that his conclusions would be compatible with "any other system" conceivable:[156] if man was naturally alone in the state of nature, pity represents the check on individual self-preservation which permits the species to survive; if man naturally lived in the family, pity represents the root of the affections or emotions that maintain the peaceful social bond.[157]

The connection between pity and the preservation of the *species* is therefore decisive:

> It is very certain, therefore, that pity is a natural sentiment which, moderating in each individual the activity of love of oneself, contributes to the mutual preservation of the entire species. . . . the human race would have perished long ago if its preservation had depended only on the reasonings of its members.[158]

Even assuming (as it appears we must) that there was an epoch when men were not yet conscious of the sentiment of pity, the principles of self-preservation and pity operated together, the former representing the actions that secure the survival of the individual, the latter indi-

---

unconvincing for reasons stated in the next chapter. Cf. V, 1, 2–3, 14 with below, chap. IV, §§ 2D–E.

[156] *Second Discourse*, Part 1 (P, III, 162).

[157] Compare Rousseau's description of the relation between mother and infant before the introduction of pity (*ibid.* [147]) and after it (*ibid.* [154]). In the former passage, Rousseau says: "The mother nursed her children at first for her own need; then, habit having endeared them to her, she nourished them afterward for their need." In the second, he speaks of "the tenderness of mothers for their young and of the perils they brave to guard them." Before introducing the principle of pity, one can only speak of an attachment based originally on need and later on habit (neither of which is necessarily sufficient to lead to self-sacrifice for the sake of another); only if one assumes the existence of something like pity can one speak of an affection joining individuals.

[158] *Ibid.* (156–57). Note again the tenses: pity "is" *now* a "natural sentiment"; men "would have perished long ago" if they depended on active reason. The passage immediately preceding the first of the quoted sentences clearly applies to civilized man, not savage man.

cating that such actions are restrained and do not result in needless harm to others of the same species. Sociability cannot serve the same theoretical function as pity, because if it is assumed that man is a social animal, one still has to explain why the resulting groups did not annihilate each other in the state of nature.[159]

The role of pity as a principle that explains the survival of the species explains the order in which Rousseau discusses the state of nature. As in the *Émile*, pity is discussed before sexual desire because pity appears to be the most elemental sentiment connecting one individual to another.[160] Pity and sex are the last two aspects to be treated in Part 1 of the *Second Discourse* because they are relevant to the physical survival of the species as a whole, whereas the earlier description in Part 1 (before the introduction of pity) treats primitive man's capacity to survive as an isolated individual.[161]

The priority of pity to sexual desire is necessary for Rousseau because the latter is, in its physical sense, an impulsion which the individual can satisfy without producing off-spring (and hence without preserving the species).[162] Moreover, pity serves as an additional check on the danger that sexual desire would lead to violence. To be sure, the restraint of pity is not needed to prevent such violence in the pure state of nature, because man's ignorance and limited desires prevent love from exceeding its peaceful, "physical" aspect; in the discussion of sexual desire in Part 1 of the *Second Discourse*, pity is not mentioned.[163] But as soon as the simplest fixed society is formed, men necessarily compare themselves to others, *amour-propre* emerges, and pity becomes necessary as a restraint in order to preserve the human species from the jealousy and vengeance which arise in "nascent

[159] See especially the *État de Guerre*, in which Rousseau argues that "all proportions considered, the weakest man has more force for his own preservation than does the strongest state for its preservation" (P, III, 606). As a result of "the law of conservation that nature itself establishes among the species and which maintains them all in spite of their inequalities," a group must be animated by a greater "vivacity of its passions" than an isolated individual, for this is the only way to compensate for the relative weakness when preservation depends on the cooperation of different individuals (*ibid.*). As a result, "the state of war is natural" between societies.

[160] See above, pp. 40, 43–48, 138–39, and the references there cited.

[161] Hence Rousseau's summary of the condition of the individual in the pure state of nature does not even mention pity; *Second Discourse*, Part 2 (P, III, 164–66). Cf. *État de Guerre* (P, III, 601-02), where Rousseau describes the individual in the state of nature without explicitly speaking of pity, only to introduce its equivalent after raising the possibility of an "accidental or private war that could arise between two or several individuals."

[162] Cf. *Second Discourse*, n. IX (P, III, 204–05) and n. 213 of this chapter.

[163] *Second Discourse*, Part 1 (P, III, 157–59).

society."[164] Even though "natural pity had already undergone some alteration"—indeed, precisely for this reason—it can serve as a decisive factor in the intermediate stage between the pure state of nature and civil society (i.e., the condition Rousseau calls "the best for man" in Part 2).[165] After further evolution has caused the development of the first conflicting claims to property and the resulting "state of war," pity is "stifled" and it becomes necessary to establish the laws of civil society in order to preserve the human species;[166] but prior to this stage there was apparently an intermediate era in which pity was the necessary precondition for the preservation of the species.[167]

Despite the fact that in the pure state of nature a conscious sentiment of pity directed toward other living members of the species cannot really exist, or at least be effective in producing external action, Rousseau insists that when primitive man's own self-preservation is not in question, natural pity leads him to aid others—or at least not to attack them.

> In fact, commiseration will be all the more energetic as the observing animal identifies himself more intimately with the suffering animal. Now it is evident that this identification must have been infinitely closer in the state of nature than in the state of reasoning.[168]

While such "identification" is not possible in the pure state of nature, it becomes possible as soon as the isolated savage has any experience of making "observations" concerning other animals and his own species, for then he develops "a premonition as sure as dialectic and more prompt" concerning his behavior toward others; pity can apparently emerge in the state of nature before the existence of fixed homesites establishes the family as we know it.[169] Only the argument that pity is a natural sentiment permits one to attribute "natural goodness" to man in his original condition:

[164] *Ibid.*, Part 2 (170). Cf. Lucretius, *De Rerum Natura* v.960–61, 1019–27.
[165] *Second Discourse*, Part 2 (P, III, 171). See below, pp. 171ff.
[166] *Ibid.*, Part 2 (174–76).
[167] Consider again *ibid.*, Part 1 (156–57): "The human race would have perished long ago if its preservation had depended only on the reasonings of its members." Pity is needed to check *reason*, not the love of oneself.
[168] *Ibid.* (155–56).
[169] *Ibid.*, Part 2 (166). Note that primitive man's awareness of the "conformities" among men (i.e., the capacity to make those comparisons necessary in order to feel pity) is described as arising *after* "the first movement of pride (*orgeuil*)." Cf. above, pp. 43–44, 45–48.

Instead of that sublime maxim of reasoned justice, *Do unto others as you would have them do unto you*, it [pity] inspires all men with this other maxim of natural goodness, much less perfect but perhaps more useful than the preceding one: *Do what is good for you with the least possible harm to others.*[170]

By considering the effects of natural impulses on "all men," rather than merely the isolated individual, Rousseau is able to derive a standard for man which is—at least in principle—valid in the state of nature (since it does not presuppose reasoning) and relevant even in society (where the errors of reasoning and *amour-propre* need to be restrained).

As we saw in analyzing the *Émile*, pity is decisive because it is the only natural basis for "empathy" between humans. Since Hobbes' thought is, in a sense, constructed on the premise that no individual is capable of fully sharing the feelings of others (it is for this reason that words are crucial for Hobbes as the sole means of communicating one's inner state to others), Rousseau's denial of natural rationality would have meant that the conventional status of language could be extended to all sentiments arising from the contact of one individual with another.[171] Such a conclusion would have limited natural sentiment to the "first" one, namely the "sentiment of one's own existence,"[172] which could only guide the isolated man or *promeneur solitaire*; the state of nature, without the principle of pity, could provide the standard for neither the natural man in society (as in the *Émile*) nor for the establishment of a legitimate political regime (as in the *Social Contract*).

[170] *Ibid.*, Part 1 (156), original italics. If, in the earliest stage of the state of nature, pity is relatively impotent to "inspire" men with this maxim, the limited character of the primitive love of oneself has the same effect; once men are capable of violating this maxim, in a barely developed era of the state of nature, they are restrained by the natural pity that is released by the simplest comparisons with others.

[171] Hobbes, *Leviathan*, Part I, chap. IV (ed. Oakeshott, p. 18): "But the most noble and profitable invention of all other, was that of SPEECH . . . whereby men register their thoughts; recall them when they are past; and also declare them one to another for mutual utility and conversation; without which, there had been amongst men, neither commonwealth, nor society, nor contract, nor peace, no more than amongst lions, bears, and wolves." Cf. also Intro. (6) and Part I, chap. v (24–25). Because Rousseau denies the natural status of both reason and language, speech cannot be the basis of society, and the explanation of its development is only possible once men have established permanent family ties; cf. *Second Discourse*, Part 1 (P, III, 151) and Part 2 (168–69). Need—including the sexual need for a female—cannot explain the origin of speech (*ibid.*, Part 1 [147]); both society and language presuppose a nonrational faculty of sharing the feelings of others.

[172] *Ibid.*, Part 2 (164).

3 · *Rousseau's Concept of Nature*

A · PERFECTIBILITY AS THE CHARACTERISTIC OF THE HUMAN SPECIES

We have to this point ignored Rousseau's conception of freedom in the state of nature, as well as the related question of his substitution of perfectibility for freedom as the distinguishing characteristic of the human species. When treating this question in the context of the *Émile*, it appeared that Rousseau believed in free will as an attribute of man's immaterial soul, but that he considered this position, which we have called "metaphysical dualism," to be a purely personal opinion of no scientific standing.[173] Despite this fact, Rousseau continues to describe man in the pure state of nature as a "free being."[174] At the same time, however, Rousseau says that primitive man had "in instinct alone, everything necessary for him to live in the state of nature."[175] To see how a "free being," endowed with free will even in the state of nature, could act solely by "animal impulse," we must reconsider Rousseau's distinction between natural freedom and moral freedom in the *Social Contract*.[176]

Man is free in the state of nature in an external sense which is not subject to any metaphysical doubts whatever—i.e., primitive man, as an animal, is exempt from "servitude and domination" since he has no naturally necessary need of other males to satisfy his basic needs.[177] In this sense, freedom means independence from other beings and the absence of any means to force others to do one's will:

> Is there a man whose strength is sufficiently superior to mine and who is, in addition, depraved enough, lazy enough, and wild enough to force me to provide for his subsistence while he remains idle? . . . he is obliged to expose himself voluntarily to much greater trouble than he wants to avoid and gives to me.[178]

For a man to command another to provide for his sustenance, an act of the will is required—but given man's nature and his easily satisfied needs, Rousseau implies that it would never actually occur that one individual would willingly enslave another.

---

[173] See the analysis of *Second Discourse*, Part 1 (141–42) above, pp. 69–72.
[174] *Second Discourse*, Part 1 (152). Cf. *ibid.* (162) and Part 2 (166, 171).
[175] *Ibid.*, Part 1 (152).
[176] See *Contrat social*, I, viii (P, III, 364–65) and above, p. 53, n. 245, pp. 73–74.
[177] *Second Discourse*, Part 1 (P, III, 161–62). Cf. Part 2 (167, 181).
[178] *Ibid.*, Part 1 (161).

The same animal instincts which make it virtually impossible for man to be enslaved in the state of nature would seem to imply that free will is equally impossible in that condition; natural freedom seems to contradict even the possibility of moral freedom (except insofar as the latter occurs in civil society, which is unnatural). Does Rousseau's scientific account of the state of nature simply contradict his personal belief in the immateriality of the soul and free will?

The solution to this problem lies in Rousseau's conception of perfectibility as the defining character of the human species. Savage man lives according to natural impulses, but these animal drives in man are of a unique character in the natural world. As was remarked in discussing the problem of subsistence, natural man "perhaps" lacks a distinctive instinct of his own, but *in any event* he "appropriates" the instincts of all other animals and learns to be omnivorous; man "develops in himself" the instincts that other animals receive from nature.[179]

> Savage man, by nature committed to instinct alone, or rather compensated for the instinct he perhaps lacks by faculties capable of substituting for it at first, and then of raising him far above nature, will therefore begin with purely animal functions.[180]

On two occasions, Rousseau questions whether men have any instincts at all, but the fundamental point is independent of this question.[181] Even if man has instinct, he also has "faculties capable of substituting for it at first"; even in the most animal state, man contributes something to his own behavior.

Perfectibility is:

> a faculty which, with the aid of circumstances, successively develops all the others, and resides among us as much in the species as in the individual. By contrast, an animal is at the end of a few months what it will be all its life; and its species is at the end of a thousand years what it was the first year of that thousand.[182]

[179] *Ibid.* (135), cited at n. 73 of this chapter.
[180] *Ibid.* (142–43).
[181] Cf. *Émile*, IV (G, 348–49, n.), where Rousseau argues that instincts exist in both man and animals, despite the doubts of such philosophers as Condillac.
[182] *Second Discourse*, Part 1 (P, III, 142). Cf. *ibid.* (160): for the human species, "the generations multiplied uselessly," without "progress," because "art perished with the inventor"; the stability of the pure state of nature was the result of the inability of isolated men, lacking language, to "communicate" the discoveries resulting from the faculty of perfectibility, not from a fixed instinctive limit (as with other species).

Since other species do not evolve, the decisive proof that man is perfectible lies in the observed phenomenon that only man "is subject to becoming imbecile":

> . . . while the beast, which has acquired nothing and which has, moreover, nothing to lose, always retains its instinct—man, losing again by old age or other accidents all that his *perfectibility* had made him acquire, thus falls back lower than the beast himself.[183]

If man has an instinct, it is the instinct to perfect himself insofar as is necessary for self-preservation; everything human is derived from perfectibility. Without perfectibility man is even "lower than the beast itself" and even the purely animal impulses (e.g., the desire to preserve oneself) cannot operate in man.[184]

We have already mentioned Rousseau's remark that the first men who live in cold climates "soon" learn how to wear the skins of the animals they kill.[185] Although primitive man has "neither foresight nor curiosity," lacks speech, and hence the capacity for even simple knowledge (not to mention abstract ideas and reasoning), he is capable of imitating presently visible actions by other beasts and of arming himself with "stones or a stick."[186] Although he cannot compare himself with other men as men,[187] nor compare the attractiveness of other females as possible mates,[188] primitive man can at least compare the risks of fighting another animal with the dangers of losing.[189] Such limited comparisons or "mechanical prudence" can be called "purely animal" because every animal "combines its ideas up to a certain point"; unlike the comparisons arising out of *amour-propre* (which presume that one's merit is judged by another man), such a mental operation is akin to the "simple ideas" discussed in the *Émile.*[190]

A "purely animal function" (the comparison of simple sensations

---

[183] *Ibid.* (142), original italics.

[184] Rousseau underlines the element of human initiative or "will" in perfectibility by mentioning a custom which creates a kind of imbecility among certain tribes: this custom is described as the "suggestion" of a man, to be judged according to its moral effects (*ibid.*). The faculties that primitive man had only "in potentiality" are clearly connected with reason, not with perfectibility and the free learning process connected with it (*ibid.* [152]).

[185] *Ibid.* (139–40).   [186] *Ibid.* (136).

[187] *Ibid.*, n. xv (219). But cf. Part 2 (166).

[188] *Ibid.*, Part 1 (158): the moral element of love depends on "comparisons he is not capable of making."

[189] *Ibid.* (136).

[190] *Ibid.* (141); n. xv (219); and *Émile*, III (G, 237), cited above, p. 35.

into complex sensations or simple ideas, such as the monkey's ability to remember, when seeing one nut, that a previous nut was pleasant to eat)[191] has a peculiar importance in the human species, for only men are capable of manipulating these simple ideas. Part, if not all, of man's perfectibility "depends on" the capacity to form "general ideas," a capacity which man has in potentiality at the beginning of his existence (and which other animals lack).[192] Summarizing the pure state of nature, Rousseau says:

> The products of the earth furnished him with all the necessary help; instinct led him to make use of them. . . . But difficulties soon arose; it was necessary to conquer them. The height of trees, which prevented him from reaching their fruits, the competition of animals that sought to nourish themselves with these fruits, the ferocity of those animals that wanted to take his very life, all obliged him to apply himself to bodily exercises. It was necessary to become agile, fleet in running, vigorous in combat. Natural arms, which are branches of trees and stones, were soon discovered at hand. He learned to surmount nature's obstacles, combat other animals when necessary, fight for his subsistence even with men, or make up for what had to be yielded to the stronger.[193]

The characteristics of agility which Rousseau cites at the outset of Part 1 of the *Second Discourse*, and which permit him to describe natural man as "the most advantageously organized of all" animals, are in good part *learned* by primitive man; "the gifts which nature offered" had to be "wrested" from her, and this overcoming of the "obstacles of nature" began to take place even *before* the human race expanded, causing competition for food supply between men.[194]

Perfectibility thus operated effectively—and not merely in potentiality—in the pure state of nature, independently of all natural accidents, though to be sure these accidents were a great stimulus to man's development; external factors are a necessary but not a sufficient cause of the evolution of the species.[195] Primitive man is dif-

---

[191] *Second Discourse*, Part 1 (P, III, 150).

[192] *Ibid.* (149), cited at n. 120 of this chapter. Starobinski's interpretation of this sentence (P, III, 1327) assumes that "the perfectibility" which "depends" on the ability to formulate "general ideas" is a restricted or advanced part of perfectibility; while this reading may be correct, it is possible that Rousseau means to say that *all* perfectibility arises from this "active" capacity of the human mind.

[193] *Ibid.*, Part 2 (164–65).

[194] Cf. *ibid.*, Part 1 (135–36) and Part 2 (165).

[195] *Ibid.*, Part 2 (165, 168–69). Cf. *Lettre à M. Philopolis* (P, III, 232).

ferent from the other animals, even when limited to purely "animal functions," because he has a kind of choice that they lack. Although it would be misleading to call such choices "free will" in the fullest moral sense because they are limited to the immediately sensed means of securing the individual's self-preservation, man in the state of nature has a "will" of his own.[196]

B · NATURE AND THE DISTINCTION BETWEEN PHYSICS AND MORALS

We are now in a better position to understand more fully what Rousseau called "his great principle that nature made man happy and good, and that society depraves him and makes him miserable."[197] This is, however, not as easy a principle to understand as it may appear. Rousseau says that in his primitive state man was inspired by a maxim of "natural goodness."[198] But goodness, at least in the "ordinary meaning," is a "moral quality," and Rousseau seems to describe man in the state of nature as an animal who lacks "any kind of moral relationship" and merely follows physically determined impulses.[199] Moreover, he says that primitive man was happy because, being "free," "healthy," and unable to reason, he could feel no "kind of misery."[200] But in the *Émile,* Rousseau says that it is necessary to treat a child as a "moral being" as soon as he has "consciousness of himself," because this sentiment (which is shared by primitive man and a child of two) is the precondition of happiness or misery.[201] If happiness and goodness are qualities of a "moral being," how can they be shared by a "stupid and limited animal" incapable of reasoning, whose actions lacked "morality" before the emergence of civil society?[202]

The problematic status of natural goodness in the pure state of nature is underlined by the following passage in the first draft of the *Social Contract*:

[196] Hence, if the pongos are really primitive men, their refusal to push logs into fires started by Negroes is an act of "will," but this choice is largely determined by the necessities of self-preservation in a warm climate (*Second Discourse,* n. x [P, III, 211]). Cf. Part 1 (143): primitive man is free "to will or not will."

[197] *Rousseau Juge de Jean Jacques,* III (P, I, 934).

[198] *Second Discourse,* Part 1 (P, III, 156).

[199] *Ibid.* (152).

[200] *Ibid.* But cf. *Geneva MS,* I, ii (P, III, 282), where Rousseau speaks of misery as "permanent" in a later stage of the state of nature.

[201] *Émile,* II (G, 61) and cf. I (40). According to the *Second Discourse,* primitive man is a child (Part 1 [P, III, 160]).

[202] *Contrat social,* I, viii (P, III, 364).

There is even more; this perfect independence and this unregulated freedom, even were it to remain joined to the ancient innocence, would always have had an essential vice harmful to the progress of our most excellent faculties—namely the lack of that liaison of the parts which constitutes the whole. . . . each would remain isolated among the others, each would only think of himself; our understanding would not be able to develop; we would live without feeling anything, we would die without having lived; all our happiness would consist in not knowing our misery; there would be *neither goodness in our hearts nor morality in our actions,* and we would never have tasted the most delicious sentiment of the soul, which is the love of virtue.[203]

It appears that although primitive man is "innocent," he lacks not merely the "idea of goodness," but also the *sentiment* of "goodness" in his "heart" (without which morality and virtue are impossible). Since man's primitive condition therefore seems to be irrelevant to his civilized and perfected life, it is necessary to determine with more precision the relationship between morality and nature.

We have noted that throughout Rousseau's work there is a radical distinction between nature and society; social convention, attributable to man's own works, must be "stripped away" in order to discover human nature. At the beginning of the Exordium, Rousseau applies this distinction when he separates "natural or physical" inequality from the "moral or political" inequality which depends on human convention.[204] At first sight, it appears that Rousseau's analysis of the state of nature, especially because it is so clearly intended to be consistent with modern natural science, has the character of the "reasoning of a physicist" and nothing more; the identity between "physics" and "nature" seems to be complete.[205] For example, when Rousseau distinguishes between the "moral and the physical" in analyzing the sentiment of love, he asserts that primitive man is "limited to the physical element" of sexual desire;[206] as one commentator has aptly put it, "natural man is premoral in every respect."[207]

This interpretation is, however, open to an important objection. Since, as Rousseau flatly states, morality is only possible when man

[203] *Geneva MS,* I, ii (P, III, 283), italics added. Cf. Derathé's note (P, III, 1412) and *Lettre à d'Alembert* (G, 192).
[204] *Second Discourse,* Exordium (P, III, 131), cited at n. 50 of this chapter.
[205] *Ibid.* (133).   [206] *Ibid.,* Part 1 (157–58).
[207] Strauss, *Natural Right and History,* p. 271. Cf. Starobinski's note (P, III, 1329, n. 2 for p. 152).

acquires moral freedom and reason by living in society,[208] natural goodness seems to have one meaning in the *Second Discourse* and another in the *Émile*: whereas in the former work it is not freely chosen (hence "premoral"), in the latter it is apparently freely self-imposed or at least learned by the natural man living in society (hence decidedly "moral"). But if this were the case, Rousseau's claim to have developed a coherent "system" of thought based on the single concept of natural goodness would be dangerously compromised, to say the least. How could he consider the state of nature, in which man is somewhat "subhuman," to be the criterion for judging man as we know him?

If we reconsider the *Second Discourse* with great care, it becomes apparent that Rousseau does not limit himself to a purely "physical" analysis of human nature. In the First Part, he explicitly insists on going beyond a consideration of "physical man"; it is only when looked at from the "moral and metaphysical side" that one becomes aware of perfectibility as the decisive characteristic of the human species.[209] In applying the distinction between natural and conventional inequality in the Exordium, Rousseau describes "the difference of ages, health, bodily strengths, and qualities of mind or soul" as natural; qualities like "wisdom or virtue," which are not merely physical, are contrasted with the unnatural inequalities of "wealth and power."[210]

It appears that Rousseau used the terms "physical" and "moral" in a way which is somewhat different from the "ordinary meaning." According to his explicit definition, the adjective "physical" refers to that which "harms" or "contributes" to the preservation of the "*individual*."[211] Elsewhere, he wrote that there are only two "physical needs" established by nature and "of an absolute necessity" for in-

208 E.g., *Émile*, I (G, 48), cited above, p. 29.
209 *Second Discourse*, Part 1 (P, III, 141–42). On the basis of Rousseau's approach to "metaphysics" in the *Émile*, it would appear that the "metaphysical" side is man's freedom (which Rousseau admits to be questionable), whereas the "moral" side, albeit connected, is the incontestable, objective phenomenon of perfectibility.
210 *Second Discourse*, Exordium (131–32). Cf. the lists of natural inequalities which serve as the basis of the conventional "privilege" of being "honored" by other men in the early stages of society, prior to the existence of governments and laws (*ibid.*, Part 2 [169, 174]): although physical strength is at the center of both lists, the natural inequalities which are "put into action" by social life include differences of "mind," "merit," and "talent" which are not entirely physically determined since learning and will are involved in them.
211 *Ibid.*, Part 1 (152), italics added.

dividual self-preservation, "namely food and sleep."[212] The satisfaction of sexual desire, the third need of man in the state of nature, "is not, strictly speaking, a physical need."[213] Although a "moral being," according to the conventional definition used by the modern jurists and cited by Rousseau, is "intelligent, free, and considered in his relations with other beings,"[214] for Rousseau himself only the last characteristic is decisive; intelligence is not an essential aspect of a "moral being."[215]

This peculiar conception of "moral" things as those which concern man "in his relations with other beings" (whether he be a stupid animal or civilized and rational) explains the order in which Rousseau describes the state of nature. He first treats the "physical" needs of individual survival, and shows that neither free will nor language (hence reason) is necessarily characteristic of man as an isolated animal. Before introducing his discussion of pity (a sentiment which obviously concerns man's "relations with other beings"), Rousseau tentatively describes primitive man as follows:

> It seems at first that men in that state, not having among themselves any kind of moral relationship or known duties, could be neither good nor evil, and had neither vices nor virtues; unless, taking these words in a physical sense, one calls vices in the individual the qualities that can harm his own preservation, and virtues those that can contribute to it; in which case it would be necessary to call the most virtuous the one who least resists the simple impulses of nature.[216]

But, Rousseau hastens to warn, "it is appropriate to suspend the judgment we could make of such a situation";[217] he immediately goes on

[212] "L'influence des Climats sur la Civilisation," *Fragments Politiques*, x (P, III, 529–30). "Eating and sleeping are the only needs he [natural man] knows" (*État de Guerre* [P, III, 605]).

[213] *Émile*, IV (G, 415). Cf. *Second Discourse*, Part 1 (P, III, 143).

[214] *Ibid.*, Pref. (125).

[215] See, e.g., *ibid.*, n. XII (215–16): "moral" things are concerned with the "advantage of the human species"; Part 1 (157–58): the "moral" element of love lies in the comparison of others as objects of sexual desire. (Cf. *Émile*, II [G, 61].) This use of the term "moral" without reference to intelligence or "morality" properly speaking is taken even further by Helvétius, who adopted the historical perspective of the *Second Discourse* but interpreted the "moral" things solely in terms of "physical sensibility" (see *De l'Esprit*, esp. III, ix [*Oeuvres Complètes*, ed. 1818; I, 292-96]).

[216] *Second Discourse*, Part 1 (P, III, 152). This remark cannot possibly be definitive, because "the one who least resists the simple impulses of nature" is not "virtuous" according to Rousseau; he is "good."

[217] *Ibid.*

to show that man is not "naturally wicked" merely because he lacks "the idea of goodness."[218] Only then does Rousseau argue that pity makes possible an unthinking kind of "natural goodness," different from virtue and not dependent on the reasoning it supposes.[219] Rousseau moves from the discussion of primitive man as a purely isolated being, concerned only with individual self-preservation, to the discussion of pity and sexual desire, both of which are necessary for the "mutual preservation of the species" (but *not* physically necessary for the preservation of the individual).[220] Although "it seems at first" that primitive man lacks "any kind of moral relationship," consideration of the relationship between the preservation of the individual and that of the species leads to the analysis of natural impulsions which concern other beings and are "moral" in the particular sense which Rousseau attaches to the word.

Rousseau's conception of a kind of moral impulse or sentiment, existing by nature even though directed to others, is clearly formulated in the discussion of sensibility in the *Dialogues*:

> Sensibility is the principle of all action. . . . There is a physical and organic sensibility which, being purely passive, seems to have no other end than the conservation of our body and that of our species by the directions of pleasure and pain. There is another sensibility which I call active or moral, which is nothing other than the faculty of attaching our affections to beings who are strangers to us. The latter, the understanding of which cannot be given by the study of pairs of nerves, . . . acts sometimes positively by attraction, sometimes negatively by repulsion, like a magnet by its poles. The positive or attracting action is solely the work of nature which seeks to extend and reinforce the sentiment of our being; the negative or repelling action, which compresses and forces back the sentiment of another, is a mixture that thinking produces.[221]

Negative active sensibility is an "artificial and bad passion" arising "from social relations, the progress of ideas, and the cultivation of the mind," which cause the love of oneself to degenerate into *amour-propre*; positive active sensibility is "the simple work of nature" because it "derives immediately from the love of oneself" and is "a pure matter of sentiment in which reflection has no part."[222] Nature is the

---

[218] *Ibid.* (153).   [219] *Ibid.* (156).   [220] *Ibid.* (156, 157).

[221] *Rousseau Juge de Jean Jacques*, II (P, I, 805). Note that Rousseau insists, in passing, that the study of "moral" things cannot be deduced from the study of "physical" ones.

[222] *Ibid.* (805–06). Rousseau's formulation in this passage, deriving "the

source of both passive, physical sensibility (which results in the desire for self-preservation and the purely physical element of sexual desire), *and* moral, active sensibility (which, like pity or the attachment of a mother for her infant, attracts the affections of one individual to another). The distinction between nature and society is not exactly the same as the distinction between physics and morals, even though these dichotomous terms seem to be equated in the Exordium of the *Second Discourse.*

In many respects, pity is the decisive example of the positive moral sensibility which Rousseau claimed was natural. If, as Rousseau insists, this sentiment can come into being before the establishment of civil society, the duality of pity and love of oneself creates a particular kind of choice when these two natural sentiments conflict. Although primitive man "never comes to blows without first having compared the difficulty of winning with that of finding his subsistence elsewhere," he "learns . . . to fight for his subsistence even with other men" from the earliest times. Since each individual is the judge of whether he "hopes to be able" to find food elsewhere, it is possible that pity "will dissuade every robust savage from robbing a weak child or an infirm old man of his hard won subsistence," but it is also possible that primitive man's mechanical comparison of the relative difficulties involved leads him to attack the weakest members of the species (who are of course the easiest to defeat).[223]

Precisely because pity is unreliable as a motive for action in the state of nature, Rousseau's assertion that this sentiment can be felt by primitive man underlines the kind of choice possible in the state of nature. As we have seen, according to Rousseau "animal functions" have a peculiar status in the human species, which is alone capable of the kind of choice or learning that permits its perfectibility. This capacity of imitation or invention is directed largely to the individual's preservation, which is not automatically insured by a fixed instinct. As a result, the quest for human survival in the state of nature requires comparisons of different actions and a kind of

---

loving and sweet passions" from love of oneself and the "hateful and cruel" ones from *amour-propre*, is almost identical to the passages in the *Émile* studied above (see pp. 38–41). See also *Émile*, IV (G, 262), where Rousseau distinguishes between "attractive and sweet passions which please men naturally" and "the repulsive and cruel passions which, so to speak, are not only nul, but negative."

[223] Cf. *Second Discourse*, Part 1 (P, III, 156); Part 2 (165); n. IX (203). In the note, Rousseau says that the fight is ended by "a few blows"; if one primitive man attacks another, he takes care not to pick on his equal in strength.

choice between them; once pity comes to be felt, it is at least possible that a savage could follow this relatively "obscure" impulse, which helps to preserve the species, instead of the more pressing drive to his own self-preservation. Choice exists in the state of nature, but it is of minor importance because the exercise of this freedom (if it can be so called) can neither destroy the human species nor lead men out of their primitive condition.[224]

Man is naturally good because he has, in pity, a natural impulse which—if he does not "resist" it—leads him to respect the "natural right," common to every sensitive being, "not to be uselessly mistreated by others."[225] In the state of nature, man follows only impulses and not reason, but these impulses are the basis of a "moral sensibility" founded solely in nature and directed to other beings. The decisive characteristic of such moral sensibility is that it is "a pure matter of sentiment in which reflection has no part." Primitive man, like a child living in society, is a "moral being" without "morality." Although morality in the full sense of the word presupposes thought and hence social life, Rousseau's proposals for restoring or preserving morality in society depend on his conception that man can be moral without reasoning. Only in this way could he claim that man is naturally good, and substitute sentiment for reason as the guide for man.

[224] Cf. Strauss, *Natural Right and History*, p. 271, n. 38: "natural man lacks freedom of will; hence he cannot misuse his freedom; natural man is characterized, not by freedom, but by perfectibility." Paradoxically enough, Strauss's conclusion is accurate precisely because his premise is overstated; even if primitive man *does* have freedom of will (e.g., a free choice between robbing a child or showing pity toward him), he "cannot misuse his freedom." Rousseau's "detachable metaphysics" has the same function in the *Second Discourse* as in the *Émile*: it illuminates more fully Rousseau's own conception of man, but its rejection is presumably possible without destroying that conception.

[225] *Second Discourse*, Pref. (P, III, 126).

THE EVOLUTION OF THE
HUMAN SPECIES
(SECOND DISCOURSE, PART 2)

1 · *Natural Right as a Standard of Judgment*

In the Preface to the *Second Discourse*, Rousseau asserts that the "science" of natural right is surrounded by "uncertainty and obscurity" because the nature of man has hitherto not been studied properly (i.e., in a manner consistent with physical science); Rousseau's account of the state of nature is the only method of discovering the "true definition of natural right."[1] According to this account, man was originally an animal differing from other species only by virtue of the faculty of perfectibility; human behavior can therefore be most fully accounted for as the product of two "principles"—love of oneself (the desire for self-preservation) and pity—which have the status of animal impulses.

> It is from the conjunction and combination that our mind is able to make of these two principles, without the necessity of introducing that of sociability, that all the rules of natural right appear to me to flow: rules which reason is later forced to reestablish upon other foundations when, by its successive developments, it has succeeded in stifling nature.[2]

The potential conflict between love of oneself and pity is important, because without it the "goodness" of man in the state of nature would be totally irrelevant to human beings who, having been perfected, can reason and choose between various actions.

Rousseau also claims that his conception of human nature resolves the "ancient disputes about the participation of animals in natural law"; since the modern jurist's definition of this concept is apparently correct, only man (i.e., perfected man living in society) has the "in-

---

[1] *Second Discourse*, Pref. (P, III, 124).
[2] *Ibid.* (126).

tellect and freedom" necessary to discover and be bound by a natural law.[3] But since animals are sensitive beings, "they too ought to participate in natural rights," and most particularly, the "right not to be uselessly mistreated" by men (or other animals).[4] Whereas a natural law properly so called is impossible in the state of nature (and, indeed, Rousseau never uses the term in Part 1 of the *Second Discourse*),[5] natural right inheres in animal sensibility and can be shared by men and beasts.

It is therefore with some surprise that one realizes that, in Part 1 of the *Discourse*, Rousseau does not discuss the "natural rights" of man in his primitive state; before Part 2, the term occurs only twice, once in the Exordium, when Rousseau criticizes erroneous notions of natural right, and once in Part 1, when Hobbes is credited with having seen "the defect of all modern definitions of natural right."[6] The closest that Rousseau comes to speaking of a substantive right of nature concerns civilized man as the enemy or destroyer of nature:

> Nature treats all the animals abandoned to its care with a partiality that seems to show how jealous it is of this right. The horse, the cat, the bull, even the ass, are mostly taller, and all have a more robust constitution, more vigor, more strength and courage in the forest than in our houses . . . it might be said that all our cares to treat and feed these animals well end only in their degeneration.[7]

If there is such a thing as natural right in the state of nature, man participates in it only as an animal (i.e., only insofar as he is "abandoned" to the care of nature).

In Part 2 of the *Discourse*, Rousseau makes more explicit the opposition between the consequences of human perfection and natural right. He cites the remark of Grotius that "the division of lands created a new right," adding "that is, the right of property, different

---

[3] *Ibid.* (126). Cf. 124–25.   [4] *Ibid.* (126).

[5] Note that in Part 1 Rousseau says that "the combination of divine and human laws hardly suffices" to prevent suicide in society; natural law is not mentioned as having any efficacy after man has left the state of nature, and in his primitive condition such a law is not only impossible, but unnecessary because of man's natural impulse to self-preservation (see *ibid.*, Part 1 [152]). Consider also Rousseau's alteration of the question posed by the Academy of Dijon (above, pp. 111–12).

[6] *Ibid.*, Exordium (132); Part 1 (153). In the footnotes to Part 1, the only use of the term was added by Rousseau for the posthumous edition of 1782; see *ibid.*, n. IX (205), where the right of each individual to choose his own mate is called "the most sacred of the rights" of nature.

[7] *Ibid.*, Part 1 (139). Cf. Aristotle, *Politics* I.1254b10: "tame animals have a better nature than wild."

from the one which results from the natural law (*loi naturelle*)."[8] Man creates new rights (not only to landed property, but also to the esteem of other men) which occur only after the invention of houses and arts, which could not exist in the pure state of nature. These new claims lead to a state of war because, prior to the creation of civil society, there is a "perpetual conflict" between the "right of the strongest and the right of the first occupant"; to avoid this situation in which possessions were vulnerable and violence frequent, the rich man conceives of the project of creating political society, a kind of institution "as favorable to him as natural right was adverse."[9] As a result of the establishment of societies throughout the world, the "law of property and inequality" becomes an "irrevocable right," and "civil right" replaces the "law of nature" as the rule of individual men, although different societies remain in the state of nature vis-à-vis each other.[10]

Rousseau's first use of the term "natural right" in Part 2 of the *Second Discourse* shows that it is not the basis on which civil society is founded; the most likely or most "natural" account of the establishment of laws shows them to be a conscious attempt to replace natural rights by created or conventional rights.[11] When Rousseau considers other hypotheses concerning the origins of political right, he in no case admits that a natural right could have served as the foundation of civil society.[12] It is necessary to "test the facts by right,"[13] but in so doing it appears that the importance of natural right is negative; certain explanations of the origin of civil society—notably the Hobbesian assumption, restated in a different form by Pufendorf, that men can contractually surrender their freedom to an individual—are untenable because a man has no "right" to alienate the freedom of his children, "a gift that they receive from nature by being men."[14]

The conception of natural right thus has a somewhat peculiar status in Rousseau's thought, at least in comparison with the use of the term by earlier thinkers who speak of natural rights which exist in the state of nature and are, to a certain extent, inalienable even in civil society.[15] In contrast, for Rousseau the standard by which civil

[8] *Second Discourse*, Part 2 (P, III, 173–74).
[9] *Ibid.* (176–77).   [10] *Ibid.* (178).
[11] *Ibid.* (177). Cf. Exordium (132): the question of the *Discourse* is "to indicate in the progress of things the moment when, right taking the place of violence, nature was subjected to law."
[12] *Ibid.*, Part 2 (179–86).   [13] *Ibid.* (182).   [14] *Ibid.* (184).
[15] For example, Hobbes' notion of the individual's natural right to self-preservation persists with civil society (set up to secure this basic natural right,

— 160 —

society must be judged is "the nature of the contract" underlying political life;[16] natural right is a criterion which permits criticism of political society, but only from the outside as it were. Hence Rousseau remarks that one could write a "considerable work" comparing "the advantages and inconveniences of all governments" relative to the "rights of the state of nature,"[17] and he concludes the *Discourse* by asserting that:

> Moral inequality, authorized by positive right alone, is contrary to natural right whenever it is not combined in the same proportion with physical inequality.[18]

Since Rousseau has previously admitted that "positive right alone" *is* capable of authorizing "moral inequalities," at least if these conventional rights conform to the rules of legitimacy tentatively sketched in the *Second Discourse* and fully elaborated in the *Social Contract*, natural right is here an external or nonpolitical standard of judging any society (be it legitimate or not).

In a sense, natural rights as such do not exist in the pure state of nature because a right is a claim, based on reasoning; a right cannot exist unless a violation of that claim is an "injury" or an "injustice." But primitive man, being unable to reason, is incapable of conceiving of his rights; as Starobinski puts it, "natural right is spontaneously lived by natural man."[19] As a stupid animal, primitive man may possess a bearskin, uneaten fruit or game, or a hut, but he has no claim to property; if another violently seizes such possessions, this act does not violate the property right, which can only arise from labor (i.e., a conscious transformation or acquisition of natural objects which is neither necessary nor even possible in the pure state of nature).[20] The "rules of natural right" are only discovered by reasoning, hence only in civil society, when "the mind" of a philosopher like Rousseau is

---

which is precarious in the state of nature); similarly, for Locke the natural right to property is not annihilated, but rather secured or truly established by the foundation of political society. See *Leviathan*, esp. Part 1, chap. xiv and Part 2, chap. xxi (Oakeshott, ed., pp. 91–92, 142); *Second Treatise*, esp. chap. ix, § 123; chap. xi, § 135, 138–39; chap. xvi, § 182–84, 190–94; chap. xviii, § 202.

[16] *Second Discourse*, Part 2 (P, iii, 185).

[17] *Ibid.* (189). In a sense, note ix is an outline of such a critique of society; fittingly enough, the only reference to natural rights in Rousseau's footnotes occurs at this point. (See n. 6 of this chapter.)

[18] *Ibid.*, Part 2 (193–94).

[19] See Starobinski's note (P, iii, 1299).

[20] *Second Discourse*, Part 1 (140, 145, 159, 161); Part 2 (164, 165, 167, 170, 172, 173–74); n. ix (203).

"capable" of studying the "conjunction and combination" of the animal impulses which operate unself-consciously in the state of nature.

The "rules of natural right" can thus be called "laws of nature"—and in the concluding sentence of the *Discourse* Rousseau makes this equation—because they are natural regularities that govern and explain phenomena in the state of nature, even though they are only discovered as rules by philosophers living in society.[21] Such rules permit a correct appreciation of the difference between civil society and man's primitive condition, but they are "rules which reason is forced to reestablish on other foundations" when the state of nature has been destroyed by the perfection of the human species. Although natural right no longer operates as such in civil society, it is a more solid critical standard than the traditional conception of natural law because only the former could—and did—operate before reason discovered the "rules which codify it."

One might say that a certain hardheadedness led Rousseau to focus his attention on natural rights which men act upon inevitably without even knowing they exist, rather than on duties which can be ignored or violated. To put it more succinctly, natural rights are prior to natural duties because in case of a conflict, rights take precedence. As is proven by his willingness to eat meat, primitive man will ignore natural pity (which creates a kind of "duty" toward other sensitive animals) in order to preserve himself; even in civilized man, the first sentiment of justice "does not come from that which we owe, but from that which is due us."[22] Speaking of grown children Rousseau argues that:

> By the law of nature . . . the [self-sufficient] son, perfectly independent of the father, then owes him only respect and not obedience; for gratitude is certainly a duty which must be rendered, but not a right which one can require.[23]

Rights must be enforceable, and to be enforceable, natural rights must depend on the ineluctable workings of natural impulses.

In the pure state of nature, right is inchoate; at this stage, one can say that man's animal impulses are his natural rights. Self-preserva-

[21] *Ibid.*, Pref. (126) and Part 2 (193–94). On this use of the term "law of nature," see above, n. 92 to chap. II.

[22] *Émile*, II (G, 88).

[23] *Second Discourse*, Part 2 (P, III, 182). Cf. the distinction between "simple duty" and "strict right" in the *Geneva MS*, I, vi (P, III, 306).

tion gives every man "the right he reasonably claims to things he needs" even when he is too stupid to make this claim rationally.[24] Thanks to pity, it is also untrue that primitive man "always refuses his fellowmen services" merely because "he does not believe he owes them."[25] Although pity is subordinate to the desire for self-preservation, the natural right enforced by pity (i.e., the right of all animals not to be "*uselessly* mistreated" by others) is so formulated that it fully takes into account the ordering of natural sentiments.

Since even the violent theft of food from a helpless child is authorized by natural right, one can say that what happens by nature is right or good. As a free animal, man in the state of nature has an implicit right to mate with whatever female he encounters; incest is impossible since primitive man cannot distinguish his children from other members of the species.[26] This is true even if, as Rousseau admitted in the *Essay on the Origin of Languages*, the family existed in the state of nature, for in that case:

> Each family was self-sufficient and perpetuated itself by its own blood: the children, born from the same parents, interbred . . . one became husband and wife without having ceased to be brother and sister.[27]

Since theft, adultery, incest, and even murder cannot occur in the pure state of nature unless justified by the necessities of self-preservation, the natural right of each individual is only limited by his strength.

In this sense, "the right of the strongest" effectively exists and is a perfectly legitimate natural right. To be sure, Rousseau comments that "the law of the strongest" is rendered "vain" in the state of nature by the total independence of each individual, but this remark merely indicates that "each man" is "free" because "the bonds of servitude" cannot be imposed by those with superior force as long as men lack "reciprocal needs."[28] As Rousseau put it elsewhere, describing the state of nature persisting between civil societies: "The most inviolable law of nature is the law of the strongest."[29] It is this

---

[24] *Second Discourse*, Part 1 (P, III, 153). Cf. *Émile*, II (G, 73); *Contrat social*, I, ix (P, III, 365).

[25] *Second Discourse*, Part 1 (P, III, 153).

[26] *Ibid.*, n. IX (205); Part 1 (160). Note that the equality of the sexes, community of women, and absence of the family, which Plato proposes in the *Republic*, are all characteristic of the pure state of nature according to Rousseau. Cf. above, n. 183 to chap. II.

[27] *Essai sur l'Origine des Langues*, chap. IX (E, XIII, 218).

[28] *Second Discourse*, Part 1 (P, III, 162). Cf. 161.

[29] *Gouvernement de Pologne*, xii (P, III, 1013).

law of nature which establishes the right of the father to control his children, since paternal authority ceases to be a "right" in the state of nature as soon as a child has the force to secure his own means of preservation.[30] Indeed, the right of the strongest might be called *the* natural right *par excellence*, for when civil society is corrupted and reduced to "the sole law of the strongest," Rousseau concludes that the society has turned into a state of nature.[31]

Rousseau's emphasis on force as the basis of right also characterizes the new claims or rights which arise as the consequence of the perfection of man in the later stages of the state of nature. The first fixed and vulnerable possessions acquired by men are the huts which are built at the time when the family is established:

> As the stronger were probably the first to make themselves lodgings they felt capable of defending, it is to be presumed that the weak found it quicker and safer to imitate them than to try to dislodge them.[32]

Once having acquired possession of a dwelling, the primitive family respected the similar possessions of others because they were useless and could only be secured by violence. The right of the strongest sufficed to protect possessions at this stage because it was automatically reinforced by the limited needs and passions of savage man.

The next new right which followed—the right to consideration or esteem from one's fellows—is also self-enforcing, "everyone punishing contempt shown him by another in a manner proportionate to the importance he accorded himself."[33] When men begin to cultivate the soil, the "right" to the product arises from "labor alone"; the claim to possess the soil thus tilled is a self-enforced right because the laborer is actively interested in maintaining his claim and insures it by his continued work.[34] But this claim is only a "sort of right" because, as soon as scarcity arises and social relations are developed, the dispossessed can deny the right of the first occupant through labor in the

[30] *Second Discourse*, Part 2 (P, III, 182) and *Économie Politique* (P, III, 241), both cited above, p. 128.
[31] *Second Discourse*, Part 2 (P, III, 191). Cf. the chiasmus in the sentence of Exordium (132) quoted in n. 11 of this chapter: "nature" is characterized by "violence"; *Essai sur l'Origine des Langues*, chap. IX (E, XIII, 199): primitive men, "having no other arbiter than force, considered each other enemies"; *Contrat social*, I, iii (354). Cf. Benedict de Spinoza, *Tractatus Theologico-Politicus*, chap. XVI; *Tractatus Politicus*, chap. II.
[32] *Second Discourse*, Part 2 (P, III, 167).
[33] *Ibid.* (170).   [34] *Ibid.* (173).

name of their own needs and the right of the strongest. Since the former claim can be called a "precarious and abusive right" having the status of an acquisition "by force,"[35] attempts to claim property as a right produce a war of all against all; civil society and laws are necessary to establish the "law of property" and to create an "irrevocable right" to one's possessions.[36]

The essential natural right of each individual to everything he needs for self-preservation becomes self-defeating in the last stage of the state of nature because conflicting claims to property are equally defensible in terms of natural right; faced with the violence that arises from attempts to enforce contradictory claims, men abandon their natural rights in order to preserve themselves.[37] In a sense, one can say that citizens still have a natural right to life and freedom, since these attributes are natural gifts. But the essence of the social contract is precisely an abandonment of these unconditional rights of the state of nature in order to acquire the right to property and a greater security than is possible once the war of all has broken out.[38] Strictly speaking, civilized man has natural rights only in a residual sense: if the bonds of society are destroyed, man returns to his "natural freedom," and no longer being bound by civil right, he can reclaim his natural rights. But given the risk of this claim, with its implicit reestablishment of the naked right of the strongest, natural right can never again be a feasible basis for a persisting legitimate human condition; at best, natural right helps to explain the origins of society and provides a basis for judging the difference between civil life and man's natural condition. Paradoxically, natural right is either followed without being consciously recognized (in the state of nature) or is discovered when it can no longer be claimed (in political society).

2 · The Stages of Political Evolution

A · THE EMERGENCE OF THE FAMILY AND SAVAGE SOCIETY

The "hypothetical history" presented in Part 2 of the *Discourse*

---

[35] *Ibid.* (176). Cf. *Contrat social*, I, ix (P, III, 365).

[36] *Second Discourse*, Part 2 (P, III, 178). Before the formation of civil society there is only "a kind of property," namely the possession of huts (167). Although the claim to the "right of property or of the first occupant" preceded the establishment of civil society (179), this claim must be *believed* by others (164); since this belief is tenuous and without enforceable support prior to the institution of laws, the right to property as we know it does not truly exist in the state of nature and is conventional (176, 178, 187). This is made absolutely explicit in *Contrat social*, I, viii–ix (P, III, 364–66); see also *Émile*, II (G, 89–92).

[37] *Ibid.*, III (G, 223).   [38] *Contrat social*, I, vi (P, III, 360–61).

has, according to Rousseau, a more "conjectural" character than the discussion of the pure state of nature in Part 1; by the same token it is less dependent on physical or natural science and more directed to the concerns of political philosophy or jurisprudence.[39] If we consider the stages which Rousseau explicitly describes as distinct "revolutions," this history is divided into five periods: 1) the pure state of nature is destroyed by a "first revolution which produced the establishment and distinction of families and introduced a sort of property, leading to the emergence of savage society;[40] 2) a second "great revolution," the invention of the arts of metallurgy and agriculture, which "civilized men and ruined the human race" by creating labor, claims to property, and ultimately a war of all;[41] 3) the "origin of society and laws, . . . which destroyed natural freedom for all time and established forever the law of property and inequality";[42] 4) the "institution of the magistracy," by which the people gave "private persons the dangerous trust of public authority";[43] and 5) the "changing of legitimate power into arbitrary power," which is the "corruption and extreme limit" of political evolution.[44]

Unlike the pure state of nature, in which man is "a being acting always by fixed and invariable principles,"[45] the five subsequent stages of developments are intrinsically dynamic. Since time thus becomes decisive in analyzing the successive changes in the human condition, we must constantly bear in mind Rousseau's rule for assessing this factor:

> I cover multitudes of centuries like a flash, forced by the time that elapses, the abundance of things I have to say, and the almost imperceptible progress of the beginnings; for *the more slowly events followed upon one another, the more quickly they can be described.*[46]

[39] See *Second Discourse*, Part 1 (P, III, 162–63). Rousseau appends one footnote each to the Dedication and Preface, 13 to the First Part, and only 4 to the Second Part.

[40] *Ibid.*, Part 2 (166).   [41] *Ibid.* (171).
[42] *Ibid.* (178, 187).   [43] *Ibid.* (180, 187).
[44] *Ibid.* (184, 187).

[45] *Ibid.* Pref. (122). Note that when Rousseau says that "there is always the same order" in the state of nature, he adds that "there are always the same revolutions" (Part 1 [144]). The unchanging nature of primitive man's physique is explicitly described as an assumption rendered necessary by the insufficiency of comparative anatomy; it is entirely possible that man's physical conformation was the product of an evolutionary process (Part 1 [135]). Cf. the *Essai sur l'Origine des Langues*, chap. IX, in which Rousseau insists on the natural catastrophes and "revolutions" which necessarily occurred in the pure state of nature (E, XIII, 211, 214–16).

[46] *Ibid.*, Part 2 (167), italics added.

The judges of the *Second Discourse*, knowing "the surprising power of very trivial causes when they act without interruption,"[47] will therefore perceive that it is in the various epochs prior to the establishment of civil society that the greatest changes in the human constitution take place; the stages of Rousseau's hypothetical history after the social contract are the only ones which do not require "multitudes of centuries" (even though it is in this period that the most despicable forms of human depravity occur).[48] We will see that this conception of time permits Rousseau to propose political reforms despite his criticism of the corruption inevitably caused by society.

In many respects, the epoch between the formation of the first families with a fixed residence and the invention of the civilizing arts is the decisive period in Rousseau's analysis of human evolution. It is in this period that the human animal becomes recognizably a man, since "morality" is "introduced into human actions" along with speech and the social relations which characterize human nature as we know it. Only at this period can man be said to have "natural rights" of which he is aware; "each man, prior to laws, being the sole judge and avenger of the offenses he received," the existence of consciously perceived standards of excellence can be combined with the independence enjoyed by the animal of the pure state of nature.[49]

[47] *Ibid.*, Part 1 (162).

[48] Cf. *Émile*, I (G, 41). Note that the "infinite time" and "thousands of centuries" required for the perfection of language (*Second Discourse*, Part 1 [P, III, 146]) take place largely after the establishment of the family (cf. Part 1 [146–51] with Part 2 [167–69]). In Part 2, the description of the "condition of emergent man" requires one paragraph (164); the developments resulting from the needs of self-preservation in the pure state of nature, eight paragraphs (164–67); the formation of the family, three paragraphs (167–68); the perfection of spoken or human language, but one paragraph (168); the formation of fixed group settlements and the "emergent society" found among savages, five paragraphs (169–71); the invention of the arts which cause civilization and the destruction of natural equality and independence, six paragraphs (171–74); and the resulting condition of men in the last stage of the state of nature during which a war of all breaks out, seven paragraphs (174–78). In contrast, Rousseau devotes twelve paragraphs to the explanation of the origins of society (178–84), six to the analysis of government (184–87), and seven to the necessary progress of inequality which inevitably produces tyranny (187–91). Applying Rousseau's rule concerning the inverse proportion between historical time and the length of his description of it, the most rapid events in the history of the human species would seem to be the first developments of human agility in the pure state of nature, and the conclusion of the social contract; the slowest seem to be the emergence of the human species from the rest of physical nature, the formation of fixed family settlements, and the perfection of language. Savage society, the perfection of the civilizing arts, the epoch of legitimate government, and the degeneration into tyranny seem to be relatively equal eras.

[49] *Ibid.*, Part 2 (170).

Although the condition of savage society, which is the highest development of this epoch, produced a great increase in the mutual violence among men:[50]

> The more one thinks about it, the more one finds that this state was the least subject to revolutions, the best for man, and that he must have come out of it only by some fatal accident, which for the common good ought never to have happened.[51]

Since "the human race was made to remain" in this condition of savage society "forever," and only left it "by some fatal accident," it becomes necessary to consider how the stupid and isolated human animal described in Part 1 of the *Second Discourse* could develop this social but nonpolitical condition without causing the moral corruption Rousseau attributes to civilized society.

We have already seen that Rousseau's description of primitive man as a totally isolated individual is to some extent more hypothetical than the proof of man's original inability to speak or reason.[52] The existence of human groups in the state of nature is admitted by Rousseau in such a way as to make it clear that such groups are not necessarily unnatural once the species as a whole is considered. Even when primitive man "scarcely had more intercourse" with fellow members of his species than "with other animals":

> he found himself able to distinguish the rare occasions when common interest should make him count on the assistance of his fellowmen and *those even rarer occasions* when competition should make him distrust them.[53]

Since Rousseau explicitly admits the possibility of rivalry for food in the pure state of nature,[54] his assertion that cooperation is *more* frequent than competition, even prior to the existence of distinct homesites, implies that cooperative animal behavior occurs in the earliest periods of human existence.

Rousseau apparently foresaw this objection, because after describing the way in which primitive men occasionally "united in a herd" he hastens to add:

> It is easy to understand that such intercourse did not require a language much more refined than that of crows or monkeys, which

---

[50] *Ibid.* (167, 169, 170–71).   [51] *Ibid.* (171).
[52] See above, chap. III, § 2C.
[53] *Second Discourse*, Part 2 (P, III, 166), italics added.
[54] *Ibid.*, Part 1 (156, 157); Part 2 (165); n. IX (203); n. XV (219–20).

group together in approximately the same way. For a long time inarticulate cries, many gestures, and some imitative noises must have composed the universal language.[55]

Even if men are capable of forming herds in order to secure their preservation, like monkeys or pongos, such animal sociability could not undermine Rousseau's analysis of the state of nature because animals lack both speech and reason, and are therefore incapable of having mutual obligations (which can arise only out of verbal communication).[56]

The animal-like groups of men that were possible in the pure state of nature could never have been more than "some kind of free association that obligated no one and lasted only as long as the passing need that had formed it." Since such herds were based solely on "present and perceptible interest," each individual was free to leave "his post" in a deer-hunting party in order to catch a rabbit, even if this was a violation of a kind of "mutual obligation" and resulted in the failure of the others to secure food.[57] Physical need can explain animal herds, but not societies in which men are consciously bound by duties.[58]

The existence of social groups in the state of nature is more evident when, as the consequence of the construction of permanent home-sites, the family in the precise sense was instituted. The family is not "established" until it is "differentiated" from other families as a consequence of an act which can be called a "revolution" because it depends on human inventions—the discovery of tools and the construction of huts—that are not physically necessary for the survival of man as an individual.[59] It is clear, especially if we recall Rousseau's admission that a "kind of marriage" can exist among animals, that the true family (as distinct from animal cohabitation) depends decisively on this man-made characteristic of fixed residence, since it is only the

[55] *Ibid.*, Part 2 (167).
[56] See above, pp. 134–35, and note that the first rights and duties mentioned by Rousseau in the *Second Discourse* (Part 2 [170]) presuppose the existence of speech and ideas based on it.
[57] *Ibid.* (166–67).
[58] "Whoever desires few things depends on few people; but always confusing our vain desires with our physical needs, those who have made the latter the foundations of human societies have always taken the effects for the causes, and have only been misled by all their reasoning" (*Émile*, IV [G, 280]). Cf. *Essai sur l'Origine des Langues*, chap. I-II (E, XIII, 170–73) and chap. IX (198–201).
[59] Cf. *Second Discourse*, Part 1 (140) with Part 2 (167).

sedentary life which permits the father to recognize his own children when they are grown.[60]

The distinction between the way of life of the sexes, described in the *Émile* as a result of a law of nature, is thus the consequence of an act which would have been impossible had men been restricted to merely animal instinct.[61] The human family has a peculiar status because it is not physically necessary for the individual's survival (hence man-made or unnatural in the narrowest sense of the term), yet conducive to the survival of the species and based on the "sweetest sentiments known to man" ("conjugal and paternal love") which Rousseau elsewhere calls natural.[62]

> Each family became a little society all the better united because reciprocal affection and freedom were its only bonds.[63]

The earliest group which Rousseau calls a "society" in the *Second Discourse*, and the only one he ever called "natural," is united solely by freedom and sentiment, and can arise in the state of nature without destroying the natural right of each individual to follow his natural impulses in complete freedom.

The establishment of "a fixed settlement" leads to the first perfection of language, the formation of "bands," and ultimately what Rousseau calls "nations."

> Men who until this time wandered in the woods, having adopted a more fixed settlement, slowly come together, unite into different bands, and finally form in each country a particular nation, unified by customs and character, not by regulations and laws but by the same kind of life and foods and the common influence of climate.[64]

Once men have constructed houses, natural necessity or accident pro-

[60] *Ibid.* (168): the family is "a new situation, which united husbands and wives, parents and children in a common habitation." See above, pp. 126–32; and Lucretius, *De Rerum Natura* v.1011–18.

[61] See *Émile*, v (G, 446–50) and above, pp. 25–26.

[62] *Second Discourse*, Part 2 (P, iii, 168). "If each one separately became less suited to combat savage beasts, on the contrary it was easier to assemble in order to resist them jointly" (*ibid.*). Cf. *Émile*, v (G, 452–53), cited above, p. 25. On the difference between "nature" in the narrow sense of the physical nature of the isolated individual, and "nature" in a broader meaning, which includes the "sweet" or active sentiments, see above, pp. 151–57 (and the references there cited).

[63] *Second Discourse*, Part 2 (P, iii, 168). Note the priority of an association based on affection to the emergence of virtues, and cf. above, pp. 48–51.

[64] *Second Discourse*, Part 2 (P, iii, 169).

duces "savage" or "nascent society." Although such societies are still in the state of nature (because, lacking laws and governments, each individual remains "the sole judge and avenger of the offenses he received"), at this point the first ideas of beauty, love, and jealousy developed; leisure activities, such as courtship, singing, and dancing, result in the kind of comparison between individuals which produces *amour-propre* and violence. Nonetheless, Rousseau praises savage society and says that "the human species was made to remain in it forever."[65]

Rousseau's praise of savage society is in many ways curious. Admitting that at this stage men become "bloodthirsty and cruel," he adds at once:

> This is precisely the point reached by most of the savage peoples known to us, and it is for want of having sufficiently distinguished between ideas and noticed how far these peoples already were from the first state of nature that many have hastened to conclude that man is naturally cruel, and that he needs civilization in order to make him gentler. On the contrary, nothing is so gentle as man in his primitive state when, placed by nature at equal distances from the stupidity of brutes and the fatal enlightenment of civil man, and limited equally by instinct and reason to protecting himself from the harm that threatens him, he is restrained by natural pity from harming anyone himself, and nothing leads him to do so even after he has received harm.[66]

This long sentence is one of the most confusing in the *Second Discourse* because it seems to oppose, to the conventional judgment of the cruelty of savages, a description of man's earlier or "primitive state" which conflicts with Rousseau's analysis of the "first state of nature."[67] Primitive man, when "limited *equally* by instinct and *reason*" and "restrained by natural pity," hardly seems to be the stupid animal of the First Part of the *Discourse*, who can not reason and whose natural pity is unreliable if not nonexistent. One is tempted to think that the condition "at equal distances from the stupidity of brutes and the fatal enlightenment of civil man" is identical with savage society, which Rousseau calls on the very next page "a golden mean between the indolence of the primitive state and the petulant

[65] *Ibid.* (169–71).   [66] *Ibid.* (170).

[67] Among others, Voltaire seems to have misunderstood this sentence completely; see his marginal comment (reproduced in P, III, 1345). Cf. J.-L. Lecercle, ed., Rousseau: *Discours sur l'Inégalité* (Paris: Éditions Sociales, 1954), p. 116, n. 2.

activity of our *amour-propre*."[68] But the context of the long sentence just cited and its use of the term "primitive state" contradict such a meaning; it appears that Rousseau intentionally blurs the difference between the pure state of nature (in which man is isolated and peaceful) and savage society (in which men become cruel) by calling them both a kind of "golden mean" in successive paragraphs.[69]

The only condition which could possibly fit the description of man in his "primitive state" as "placed *by nature* at equal distances from the stupidity of brutes and the fatal enlightenment of civil man" is the epoch immediately after the establishment of the family. It is only at this time that human reason begins to develop along with imagination, and as we have seen in discussing Rousseau's analysis of the passions in the *Émile*, without imagination pity is essentially inactive; the sentiment of pity as an effective restraint on human actions toward living members of the species presupposes the existence of stable family relationships.[70] Indeed, comparison with the *Émile* reveals that the condition of the isolated family with a fixed homestead is exactly parallel to that of the adolescent who learns to pity others during the short period in which sexual desire has not yet produced *amour-propre* and jealousy.[71] In the pure state of nature, man is an innocent "child" (similar to Émile before adolescence); in savage society man is in his "youth" (similar to the epoch in which Émile develops pity and his first sentiments of attachments to other beings).[72]

It is only when, after family units "slowly come together," forming savage societies or nations, that true love and jealousy arise; only then is "the goodness suitable for the pure state of nature no longer that which suited nascent society." The cruelty of the savages that are now encountered is not decisive because such savage societies are

[68] *Second Discourse*, Part 2 (P, III, 171).

[69] One reason for this blurring may be Rousseau's attempt to strengthen his argument that savage society is the "best for man." But this argument itself has to be explained, since it contradicts the assertion in Part 1 of the *Discourse* that man in the state of nature is "the most advantageously organized of all" animals (135).

[70] See *ibid.*, Part 1 (154, 158); Part 2 (167 ["the mind was enlightened"], 168 ["the first developments of the heart were the effect of a new situation"]). In Part 1 Rousseau claims that "commiseration will be all the more energetic as the observing animal identifies himself more intimately with the suffering animal . . . this identification must have been infinitely closer in the state of nature than in the state of reasoning" (155); but in the *pure* state of nature, pity is still "obscure"—it only becomes effective in an intermediate stage of the state of nature. Cf. *Lettre à d'Alembert* (G, 192).

[71] Cf. above, pp. 38–48 with *Second Discourse*, Part 2 (P, III, 167–69).

[72] *Ibid.*, Part 1 (160); Part 2 (171).

really mere collections of autonomous family units, which at an earlier stage were widely dispersed and peaceful.[73]

Even after the isolated families have formed larger units, despite the cruelty and vengeance which result from social intercourse, the decisive characteristic of the earlier, familial epoch of the state of nature remains:

> as long as they applied themselves only to tasks that a single person could do and to arts that did not require the cooperation of several hands, they lived free, healthy, good, and happy insofar as they could be according to their nature, and they continued to enjoy among themselves the sweetness of independent intercourse.[74]

In savage society, man is as "free, healthy, good, and happy" as he can be by nature. Indeed, since pity operates effectively only after the institution of the independent family unit, one might even say that the goodness of savage man is even greater (at least during the earliest epochs of this period) than it was in the pure state of nature.[75]

Rousseau's praise of the epoch of savage societies is not an anomaly, but a necessary consequence of his system, for only in this condition do the "two simplest operations of the human soul" come into full activity. Although such society is partly the result of the human invention of fixed dwellings, it is a perfection of the individual which is consistent with the "common utility" of the species (most particularly because the primitive family is better able to survive as a group even though its members are, as individuals, weaker than in the pure state of nature).[76] This distinction between the individual and the species is decisive because, after the stage of savage society:

> all subsequent progress has been in appearance so many steps toward the perfection of the individual, and in fact toward the decrepitude of the species.[77]

The perfection of the faculties of individuals in harmony with the perfection of the species reaches its culmination in savage society; once

[73] *Ibid.*, Part 2 (168–70). Cf. *Essai sur l'Origine des Langues*, chap. IX (E, XIII, 218): "there were families, but there were no nations. . . . there were marriages, but there was no love. Each family was self-sufficient."
[74] *Second Discourse*, Part 2 (P, III, 171).
[75] This explains why Rousseau can describe the Caribs—who live in savage society and not in the purely animal condition described as the pure state of nature—as the example of the self-sufficiency, goodness, and stupidity of primitive man. Cf. *ibid.*, Part 1 (144) and Part 2 (192–93).
[76] *Ibid.*, Part 2 (168, 171). Cf. Lucretius, *De Rerum Natura* v.1015–27.
[77] *Second Discourse*, Part 2 (P, III, 171).

men enter civilized or political life, individual perfectibility necessarily conflicts with the health of the species.

Rousseau relied on this distinction between the perfection of the human individual and that of the species in defending the *Second Discourse* against the criticism of Charles Bonnet (who wrote under the pseudonym of M. Philopolis):

> Since you pretend to attack me by my own system, I beg of you not to forget that, according to me, society is natural to the human species like decrepitude to the individual; and that people need arts, laws, governments just as old men need crutches. All the difference is that the state of old age derives from the nature of man alone, and that of society derives from the nature of the human species, not immediately, as you say, but only, as I have proved, with the aid of certain exterior circumstances which could be or not, or at least could arrive earlier or later, and by consequence accelerate or slow down the progress.[78]

The nature of man which Rousseau discusses in the First Part of the *Discourse* is primarily the nature of the *individual*. The nature of the species may well include not only the possibility of society, but the actuality of familial or savage society; even so, *civil* society does not result "immediately" from the nature of the species (or of its members analyzed as individuals). The human race was probably best suited to savage society even though that condition, being social, already implied some deviation from the "physical" nature of the individual as an individual.[79]

Rousseau's description of the evolution of the human species blurs the distinction between the epoch of isolated families and the slow coalescence of these groups into "troups and nations." The effect of this presentation, underlined by the curious way in which Rousseau praises the savage societies in which men become cruel, is to heighten the contrast between civil society and the independence and freedom of *all* stages preceding the discovery of the arts which "civilized men." As long as men do not depend on each other for their survival, the state of nature can be a stable condition because the self-enforce-

---

[78] *Lettre à M. Philopolis* (P, III, 232).

[79] The discovery of savage societies was added proof for Rousseau that civilized society is not natural. Political society may develop in one place and not another because of physical necessities like the presence of iron and wheat (*Second Discourse*, Part 2 [P, III, 172]), and for that very reason is not part of the nature of the human individual. Quite the reverse: since physical conditions are completely external or accidental, they are an additional argument for natural asociality.

ment of natural (or created) rights does not threaten to destroy the human race; even in those savage societies in which "it was up to the terror of vengeances to take the place of the restraint of laws," natural pity operates as an additional restraint and the subjects of dispute do not extend to day-to-day concerns of self-preservation.[80]

B · THE CREATION OF CIVILIZATION AND CLAIMS TO PROPERTY

Whereas the formation of uncivilized "nations" is treated as a slow, natural process, the discovery of "metallurgy and agriculture" is called an "invention"; it is the only step in human evolution which Rousseau calls a "great revolution."

> For the poet it is gold and silver, but for the philosopher it is iron and wheat which have civilized men and ruined the human race.[81]

The invention of the arts marks a decisive stage not merely because, like the invention of fixed homesites, it requires human ingenuity, but also—and more important—because mutual dependence on art and industry produces claims to property and destroys natural equality. Since the invention of agriculture and metallurgy make inevitable the remaining developments which "ruined the human race," Rousseau must show that this invention was caused by some "natural accident" external to man's physical nature; civilization would have been impossible had not natural phenomena intervened.[82]

The art of agriculture did not have to be discovered, properly speaking, since "its principle was known long before its practice was

[80] *Ibid.* (170–71). Note that conflicts in savage society arise from conflicting claims to "consideration" or from "jealousy," neither of which is a right necessary for physical survival.

[81] *Ibid.* (171). This remark is Rousseau's clearest hint of the parallel between his *Discourse* and Lucretius' poetic account of the history of man. Lucretius argues that the use of gold and silver is prior to the use of copper and iron, and that the discovery of gold, together with the invention of property, led to the violence which forced men to form conventions and establish civil society (*De Rerum Natura* v.1113–1296). Note, however, that according to Lucretius "Kings began to found cities" before this time (v.1108–12); Rousseau replaces this account of a primitive monarchy with a picture of an egalitarian and free savage society. Cf. n. 6 of chap. III.

[82] While the construction of houses is a "revolution" depending on human initiative, Rousseau does not describe it as a response to a natural catastrophe (*Second Discourse*, Part 2 [P, III, 167]). In contrast, the extension of speech to entire societies and the invention of the art of making iron (i.e., the sources of civilization) both seem to presuppose natural upheavals (*ibid.* [168–69, 172]). Cf. *Essai sur l'Origine des Langues*, chap. IX (E, XIII, 211): "the associations of men are in great part the work of accidents of nature . . . the revolutions of seasons are another more general and more permanent cause."

established"; the cultivation of plants for personal consumption is merely an imitation of "the ways used by nature to grow plants" and is consistent with life during the epoch of isolated family dwellings.[83] The growing of wheat for exchange, which alone can be called the "practice" of an "art," presupposes that some men devote their time to other trades instead of securing their own food; "the invention of other arts was therefore necessary to force the human race to apply itself to that of agriculture."[84] The crucial invention is the discovery of how to make iron, because peoples have become civilized only if they have discovered *both* the art of making metals and that of growing wheat.

Since neither purely human initiative nor the results of an "accidental fire" could have led savages to make iron, its discovery required the "extraordinary circumstance" of a volcanic eruption; such an unusual natural cataclysm is necessary, because one could almost say "that nature had taken precautions to hide this deadly secret from us."[85] The interdependence of men is unnatural even if men were not naturally isolated in the state of nature. Thus Rousseau can admit, as he does in the *Émile*, that the specialization of tasks and mutual cooperation in civil society is in a sense mutually advantageous while still criticizing the institution of mutual dependence and the perfection of the arts as a corruption of human nature.[86]

[83] *Second Discourse*, Part 2 (P, III, 172–73). Cf. Part 1 (145) and consider *Émile*, III (G, 216): "The first and most respectable of the arts is agriculture"; by implication "it is the freest and the nearest to independence." Cf. Lucretius, *De Rerum Natura* v.1361–78.

[84] *Second Discourse*, Part 2 (P, III, 173). Cf. Part 1 (144–45).

[85] *Ibid.*, Part 2 (172). Accidental fires, perhaps started by men themselves, could not have led to the fusion of ore because, according to Rousseau, such ore is only found "in arid spots, stripped of trees and plants"; Rousseau's account here is clearly intended as an answer to Lucretius, who had described either lightening or such fires as the cause of the discovery of how to make metals (see Lucretius, *De Rerum Natura* v.1241–96). But cf. Rousseau's quotation from Buffon concerning the origin of deserts, *Second Discourse*, n. IV (198), cited above, p. 122, n. 63.

[86] Cf. *Émile*, III (G, 222–23): "Let us assume there are ten men, each of whom has ten kinds of needs. Each must, for his own necessities, apply himself to ten kinds of work; . . . all, being appropriate for different things, will do the same ones, and will be badly served. Form a society of these ten men, and let each apply himself, for himself and the nine others, to the kind of occupation which suits him the best: each will profit from the talents of the others as if he had them all himself, each will perfect his own talent by continual training, and it will come about that all ten, perfectly well provided for, will still have enough of a surplus for others. This is the apparent principle of all our institutions. It is not my subject here to examine their consequences: I have done so in another work." The other work is, of course,

Civilization has catastrophic consequences for the human species because the perfection of metallurgy and agriculture, being unnecessary to secure individual physical survival, can never occur in natural harmony. On the contrary, at this point natural inequality, having hitherto been relatively unimportant, suddenly acts as the efficient cause of moral or political inequality:

> Things in this state could have remained equal if talents had been equal, and if, for example, the use of iron and the consumption of foodstuffs had always been exactly balanced. But this proportion, which nothing maintained, was soon broken; the stronger did more work, the cleverer turned his to better advantage; the more ingenious found ways to shorten his labor; the farmer had greater need of iron or the blacksmith greater need of wheat; and working equally, the one earned a great deal while the other barely had enough to live.[87]

Since a society's need for wheat or iron has no natural limit, the creation of such needs permits "natural inequality," like that of strength, cleverness, and ingenuity, to "imperceptibly manifest itself along with contrived inequality"; the first source of the unnatural inequalities of wealth is the operation of natural "differences of ages, health, bodily strengths, and qualities of mind or soul."[88]

To be sure, the "first step toward inequality and at the same time toward vice" occurred earlier, when natural inequalities were "put into action" by social intercourse in familial or savage society.[89] But only when wealth is a possible consequence of the operation of natural inequality do the truly corrupting effects of moral inequality appear; unlike uncivilized social groups, in which claims to prestige were enforced by the individual and hence strictly limited by the natural inequalities of strength, the kind of society based on mutual dependence "inspires in all men a base inclination to harm each other." Human vice can be attributed to civilization or civilized society, and not to social groups as such, because only after the perfection of the arts that depend on exchange does man cease to be "free and independent."[90]

---

the *Second Discourse*. Rousseau's assumption of the mutual advantage of specialization is clearly modeled on Plato's *Republic* II.369ff.

[87] *Second Discourse*, Part 2 (P, III, 174).

[88] Cf. *ibid.*, Exordium (131) and Part 2 (174).

[89] "The one who sang or danced the best, the handsomest, the strongest, the most adroit, or the most eloquent became the most highly considered" (*ibid.*, Part 2 [169]).

[90] *Ibid.* (174–75). Cf. 171.

We can now see more clearly not only why Rousseau could praise savage society as the "best" human condition and admit the possibility of natural family groups in the pure state of nature, but also why his attack on social corruption is so directly aimed at property. The claim to possess goods immediately needed for self-preservation in the state of nature or in savage society need not cause corruption because it is enforced by the natural strength of each individual (which poses a clear limit on the ability of one man to attack others) and is restricted by the direct use to which such possessions are put. Once men begin to cultivate land in order to produce a surplus of food for exchange, this condition is no longer met. Although the farmer has a claim to the produce of his fields arising "naturally" from his labor, this claim is insecure because it need not be recognized by others; claims to own the land on which food is grown, similarly arising from labor, are also not certain to be enforced by the individual's natural strength. Although the practice of agriculture precedes the establishment of civil society (which alone creates a true property right), it is impossible to imagine agricultural cultivation until land is "divided" among men, which is tantamount to an "annihilation" of the state of nature.[91]

The primary role of private property in the emergence of civil society and the corruption of the species is emphasized by the ringing critique which opens Part 2 of the *Discourse*:

> The first person who, having fenced off a plot of ground, took it into his head to say *this is mine* and found people simple enough to believe him, was the true founder of civil society.[92]

Not simple possession, but the claim to a *right* to property, is the source of human misery:

> What crimes, wars, murders, what miseries and horrors would the human race have been spared by someone who, uprooting the stakes or filling in the ditch, had shouted to his fellowmen: Beware of listening to the imposter; you are lost if you forget that the fruits belong to all and the earth to no one![93]

Although the claim to property is the foundation of civil society, there is no natural right to property in land; in the state of nature men have "neither houses nor huts, nor property of any kind."[94] Land cannot

---

[91] *Ibid.*, Part 1 (145); Part 2 (172–73).
[92] *Ibid.* (164), original italics. [93] *Ibid.*
[94] *Ibid.*, Part 1 (147). Cf. 157.

therefore be divided up without threatening some individuals with the inability of finding food, to which they have natural right as long as the claim to property has no support in conventional law.

The unnatural effect of the creation of a claim to property is underlined by Rousseau's assertion that at this stage one can no longer speak of the difference between strong and weak men:

> These words *strong* and *weak* are equivocal . . . for in the interval between the establishment of the right of property or of the first occupant and that of political governments, the meaning of these terms is better expressed by the terms *poor* and *rich*, since before the laws a man did not, in fact, have any other means of subjecting his equals than by attacking their goods or by giving them some of his.[95]

Whereas differences in strength were the essential natural inequality before the cultivation and division of land,[96] the revolutionary character of mutual interdependence is most fully revealed in its conversion of the strong man, whose rights are automatically enforced by his strength, into the rich man, whose rights are vulnerable precisely because they depend in part on the so-called "right of the first occupant" (which can be attacked by other men—and especially by other groups of men, who are collectively stronger than the wealthy individual).[97]

Even before scarcity leads the poor to attack the rich, therefore, property corrupts men by creating differences in wealth that force every man to depend on others for his survival:

> rich, he needs their services; poor, he needs their help; and mediocrity cannot enable him to do without them.[98]

As Rousseau asserts in the *Émile*, "the dependence on men, being disordered, engenders all the vices"; property forces each individual to "interest" others in "his fate," an attempt which is contrary to the natural concern of every man to provide for his own well-being:[99]

---

[95] *Ibid.*, Part 2 (179), original italics.

[96] Note that in three different lists of natural inequalities, Rousseau places "strength" in the center. Cf. *ibid.*, Exordium (131): "difference of age, health, *bodily strength*, and qualities of mind or soul"; Part 2 (169): "the one who sang or danced the best, the handsomest, the *strongest*, the most adroit, or the most eloquent"; Part 2 (174): "upon the mind, beauty, *strength* or skill, upon merit or talents."

[97] *Ibid.* (176–77): "easily crushing an individual, but himself crushed by groups of bandits."

[98] *Ibid.* (175).

[99] *Émile*, II (G, 70), cited above, pp. 41–42; *Second Discourse*, Part 2 (P, III, 164, 166, 175).

for one's own advantage, it was necessary to appear to be other than what one in fact was. To be and to seem to be (*être et paraître*) became two altogether different things; and from this distinction came conspicuous ostentation, deceptive cunning, and all the vices that follow from them.[100]

As many commentators have emphasized, this derivation of vice from the unnatural inequality arising from property was to have an enormous effect on the thought of Marx; the current conception of man's "alienation" from his fellows and from nature is largely derived from the criticism of property announced by Rousseau and emphasized in Marx's early writings.[101]

It is, however, dangerous to read back into Rousseau's work the understanding of "alienation" that was developed only after his time. Although the earliest perfection of reason and the social contacts arising in familial society destroy the perfect unity of man as an animal who is "always entirely with himself" and is limited to the "sentiment of his own existence," these developments away from the pure state of nature are not blamed as vicious; instead Rousseau attributes corruption of man to "the first effect of property and the inseparable consequence of nascent inequality."[102] Human depravity can be traced to an event which (unlike the formation of the first family) is known to be an unnatural, historical act that destroyed familial or savage society; the freedom of the pure state of nature is the criterion for man because it is the condition which most radically shows the conventional status of property and social inequality (and *not* because the first social contacts destroy man's natural goodness).[103]

Once men have become deceptive, interdependent, and vicious, the evolution of the species is merely directed to those forms of life which can permit the preservation of the species:

[100] *Ibid.* (174).

[101] See Jean Starobinski, "Introduction—*Discours sur l'origine de l'inégalité*" (P, III, lx–lxii); and his *Jean-Jacques Rousseau: le transparence et l'obstacle* (Paris: Plon, 1957), *passim*. For Marx's views, see esp. *The Economic and Philosophic Manuscripts of 1844* (Moscow: Foreign Languages Publishing House, 1961), pp. 67–83. Cf. Bronislaw Baczko, "Rousseau et l'Aliénation Sociale," *Présence de J. J. Rousseau* (Paris: Colin, 1963), pp. 223–33.

[102] *Second Discourse*, Part 1 (136); Part 2 (164, 175). The Carib, living in savage society, is the antithesis of civil man (*ibid.* [192–93]). The danger of applying the current conception of alienation to Rousseau is particularly great because he gives the term a quite different meaning in the *Contrat social*, I, iv (P, III, 355); I, vi (360).

[103] Cf. *Second Discourse*, Part 1 (P, III, 152)—where Rousseau asserts that a savage cannot be miserable because he is "free" and "healthy"—with Part 2 (171)—where he describes men in familial or savage society as "free, healthy, good, and happy."

Behold all our faculties developed, memory and imagination in play, vanity aroused, reason rendered active, and the mind having almost reached the limit of the perfection of which it is capable. Behold all the natural qualities put into action, the rank and fate of each man established, not only upon the quantity of goods and the power to serve or to harm, but also upon the mind, beauty, strength or skill, upon merit or talents. And these qualities being the only ones which could attract consideration, it was soon necessary to have them or affect them.[104]

All of man's potential faculties are released at this point of the evolutionary process, because reasoning, *amour-propre*, and even vice become necessary for survival.

It was by a very wise providence that his [savage man's] potential faculties were to develop only with the opportunities to exercise them, so that they were neither superfluous and burdensome to him beforehand, nor tardy and useless when needed.[105]

"Cultivated reason" becomes necessary because without it, men would have been incapable of responding to the disastrous war of all which arises in the last stage of the state of nature.

C · THE ESTABLISHMENT OF CIVIL SOCIETY AND LAW

Rousseau's "hypothetical history" of the human species tries to explain the efficient causes of all human attributes without introducing assumptions of what would have been convenient or useful to the human species.[106] He finds that human reflection developed out of a "mechanical prudence" directed to individual preservation, and became a devious calculation of self-interest under conditions of "competition and rivalry" in which "the opposition of interest" becomes consciously apparent to all men.[107] In the Preface, Rousseau had attacked the traditional view that man naturally reasons and can discover the natural law, asserting that such an understanding implies that:

men must have used, for the establishment of society, enlightenment which only develops with great difficulty and in very few people in the midst of society itself.[108]

---

[104] *Ibid.* (174).   [105] *Ibid.*, Part 1 (152).
[106] See *ibid.*, Pref. (125); n. XII (215–16).
[107] *Ibid.*, Part 2 (165, 175).
[108] *Ibid.*, Pref. (125), cited above, p. 79.

But it now appears that men—or rather some men—can indeed reason prior to the formation of civil society; Rousseau describes the social contract as "the most deliberate project that ever entered the human mind."[109] The political impotence of the traditional natural law follows not from the absence of reason at the moment of the creation of civil society, but from the inability of men to reason independently of their own interest; the project of establishing laws is discovered only when the rich man is "pressed by necessity" (i.e., the necessities of his own self-preservation). Since mental inequality is natural, most men are still "crude" and "easily seduced" when, under a necessary stimulus which could not be claimed for a "metaphysical" natural law teaching, the idea of inventing civil society and laws occurs to the men who will benefit most from them.

Just as Rousseau portrays the establishment of property as a fraudulent act in the opening lines of Part 2, he "invents personages and has them act out a symbolic scene" to represent the "specious reasons" underlying civil society.[110] In this vignette, "the rich man" says:

> Let us institute regulations of justice and peace to which all are obliged to conform, which make an exception of no one, and which compensate in some way for the caprices of fortune by equally subjecting the powerful and the weak to mutual duties.[111]

Curiously enough, what Rousseau here calls the "specious reasons" of the rich are those he himself gives as the foundation of legitimate political regimes in the *Social Contract*:

> I will finish this chapter and book by a remark that should serve as the basis of the entire social system: it is that instead of destroying natural equality, on the contrary the fundamental compact substitutes a moral and legitimate equality for whatever physical inequality nature could have created among men, and that, capable of being unequal in strength or genius, they all become equal by convention and right.[112]

Why then is the institution of general laws, binding all citizens equally, a tainted act?

The key lies in the effects of property and conventional inequality. Whereas the rich assert that the laws will impose mutual duties on

[109] *Ibid.*, Part 2 (177).
[110] Starobinski, "Introduction" (P, III, lxiv).
[111] *Second Discourse*, Part 2 (P, III, 177).
[112] *Contrat social*, I, ix (P, III, 367).

both the "powerful and weak," Rousseau denies that the natural in-equalities of strength accurately describe men once the introduction of property and mutual interdependence have occurred; at the moment of proposing a social contract, the crucial inequality is that of rich and poor. Even if the formal equality of civil society secures the equality of purely physical strength or weakness, it does not have the same effect in preventing abuses arising from unnatural inequalities of wealth.

> In fact, the laws are always useful to those who possess and harm-ful to those who have nothing: from which it follows that the social condition is only advantageous to men insofar as they all have something and none of them has too much.[113]

The condition of a legitimate civil society is precisely the reverse of the most likely circumstances surrounding the historical origins of civil society; one sees clearly why, in the *Social Contract*, Rousseau says he will try to show how to "make legitimate" the change which put free men into "chains."[114]

The fraudulent character of the foundation of laws does not mean, therefore, that civil society cannot be made legitimate by a thorough-going attempt to realize, in practice, the equality of mutual obligation established only in appearance by the institution of laws. Since vice arises when "to be and to seem to be became two altogether different things," civic virtue requires a return to the identity between appear-ance and reality; this return is, of course, no longer on the level of the stupid animal of the state of nature, for the social evolution of the human species must be accepted as irreversible (at least for most men).

Despite this possibility of reform, a political solution to the human problem is necessarily limited by the unnatural origins of civil society:

> There is in the state of nature a real and indestructible equality of

[113] *Ibid.* "The universal spirit of the laws of every country is to favor al-ways the strong against the weak, and the one who has against the one who has nothing: this inconvenience is inevitable and it is without exception" (*Émile*, IV [G, 280n.]). On the reappearance of the distinction between the "powerful" and the "weak" as a conventional inequality not based on physical strength, resulting from the institution of magistracies, see *Second Discourse*, Part 2 (P, III, 187).

[114] *Contrat social*, I, i (P, III, 351). If the reasons of the founders of civil society are "specious" only because the *conditions* for their realization do not exist, it would appear that the problem of legitimacy is largely dependent on these conditions (and not merely on the logic of the social contract). See below, chaps. VI–VIII.

fact, because it is impossible in that state for the sole difference from one man to another to be great enough to make one dependent on another. There is in the civil state a chimerical and vain equality of right, because the means destined to maintain it themselves serve to destroy it, and the public force added to the strongest to oppress the weak breaks the kind of equilibrium that nature placed between them.[115]

While this obstacle to a salutary political order is the most evident teaching of the *Second Discourse*, the subordinate theme of the exceptional circumstance in which conventional institutions are truly legitimate also finds its place.

After he has portrayed the origins of civil society as a fraud, Rousseau turns to other hypotheses concerning its origin; he interrupts the historical narrative to "test the facts by right."[116] Since, as Rousseau indicates in the passage from the *Émile* just cited, civil society is based on an "equality of right," the civil condition can no longer be interpreted solely in terms of "*facts*" (as can the state of nature). On the basis of apparent "facts":

> When human society is considered with calm and disinterested attention, it seems to show at first only the violence of powerful men and the oppression of the weak. . . . And as nothing is less stable among men than those external relationships which chance produces more often than wisdom, and which are called weakness or power, wealth or poverty, human establishments appear at first glance to be founded on piles of quicksand.[117]

But if one leaves it at such a "first glance," the status of social injustice would be no different than the violence of "fact" in the state of nature; viewed as mere phenomena of force without a basis in right, political life is merely tyranny.[118]

In the *Social Contract*, Grotius is criticized precisely because he did not see that civil society cannot be understood on the basis of mere historical fact:

[115] *Émile*, IV (G, 280). Cf. *Second Discourse*, Part 1 (P, III, 161–62); Part 2 (193–94).

[116] *Ibid.* (182).

[117] *Ibid.*, Pref. (127). Note again the distinction between natural inequalities of physical strength and the unnatural or conventional inequalities of power and wealth: only the latter are "external relationships."

[118] Cf. the description of conflict in the pure state of nature (*ibid.*, Part 1 [157]; n. IX [203]; n. XV [219–20]) with the description of tyranny (Part 2 [191]).

Grotius denies that all human power was established in favor of those who are governed: he cites slavery as an example. His most constant way of reasoning is always to establish right by fact. One could use a more consistent method, but not one more favorable to tyrants.[119]

Despite the historical fraud which was the most likely source of political society and laws, this act claims to establish rights; having done so, one can no longer understand "what is" without reference to "what ought to be."[120] This concern for the right underlying civil society is absolutely necessary because the historical facts which led to the foundation of civil society are actually unknown; unlike the pure state of nature, which can be shown to have existed in one form or another by natural science, the events connecting man's animal condition with his present state are hypothetical.[121]

Rousseau's account of the historical circumstances in which laws were first established is therefore inconclusive; in the *Social Contract*, he explicitly admits that:

It can also happen that men begin to unite before possessing anything, and that, after taking land sufficient for all, they enjoy it in common, or divide it between themselves, equally or according to proportions established by the sovereign.[122]

Since Rousseau was aware of a possible origin of civil society in which his "most natural" explanation would have been by definition impossible, he had to show, in the *Second Discourse*, that the choice between *all* other explanations of the historical facts "is indifferent to what I want to establish."[123] That is to say, Rousseau had to show that, however fraudulent the *motives* for establishing civil society, the political right which is thereby created establishes *reasons* for obedience which "even the wise" respect.[124]

Conquest by the most powerful could not create political right because violence merely reflects "the law of the strongest" (i.e., a relationship characterizing the state of nature) and not rights which per-

---

[119] *Contrat social*, I, ii (P, III, 353).

[120] *Émile*, v (G, 585).

[121] *Second Discourse*, Part 1 (162–63); Part 2 (179); *Geneva MS*, I, iii (P, III, 289).

[122] *Contrat social*, I, ix (P, III, 367). This passage occurs without change in *Geneva MS*, I, iii (P, III, 294). For an example of such a founding, see Locke, *Second Treatise*, chap. VIII, § 103.

[123] *Second Discourse*, Part 2 (P, III, 179).

[124] *Ibid.* (178).

mit man to transcend the state of nature.[125] A union of the weak, which at this stage would have to be called a union of the poor, is an unlikely source of law because they would have had nothing to gain from surrendering their natural freedom merely to preserve property that they did not possess:

> it is reasonable to believe that a thing was invented by those to whom it is useful rather than by those whom it wrongs.[126]

Far more important is Rousseau's rejection of the thesis that "at first peoples threw themselves into the arms of an absolute master without conditions and for all time." The Hobbesian conception of a social contract which binds the people to obey a ruler is untenable:

> For to say that the chiefs were chosen before the confederation was created and that the ministers of laws existed before the laws themselves is a supposition that does not permit of serious debate.[127]

While we will reconsider this "supposition" in discussing Rousseau's analysis of the foundation of governments, it must be noted that he uses an argument which seems akin to that of Locke in order to combat Hobbes, Grotius, and other apologists of unlimited political power; men gave themselves superiors only "to defend themselves against oppression and to protect their goods, their freedoms, and their lives, which are, so to speak, the constituent elements of their being."[128]

Although Rousseau presents as evidence the virtue of the Spartans, the preference for freedom of wild horses and barbarous men, and the historical examples of savage societies, his argument is not essentially based on such facts:

> It is therefore incontestable, and it is the fundamental maxim of all political right, that peoples have given themselves chiefs to defend their freedom and not to enslave themselves.[129]

[125] *Ibid.* (179).

[126] *Ibid.* (180). Note Rousseau's consistent tendency to connect all learning and invention with the interest of the individuals concerned.

[127] *Ibid.* In fact, Hobbes admits that there must be a tacit convention to submit to the vote of the majority before the subjects contract among themselves to obey the designated sovereign (*Leviathan*, I, xviii [ed. Oakeshott, p. 115]).

[128] *Second Discourse*, Part 2 (P, III, 180–81). Rousseau subtly indicates that his remark is directed against both Hobbes and Grotius by drawing the parallel between "our political writers" (i.e., jurists) and "our philosophers" (e.g., Hobbes). Cf. Pref. (124–25); Part 1 (153); *Émile*, v (G, 584).

[129] *Second Discourse*, Part 2 (P, III, 181). Cf. *Économie Politique* (P, III, 247): "The first and most important maxim of popular or legitimate govern-

This maxim, and Rousseau's analysis of the status of the family, is sufficient to show that parental authority cannot be the origin of "absolute government and all society"; grown children can only remain attached to their father in the state of nature by the hope of inheriting his possessions, a bond which could not possibly exist or even be imagined between the despot and his subjects.[130]

Similarly, it is in terms of right that Rousseau rejects the hypothesis of the "voluntary establishment of tyranny"; a right to divest oneself of property (which is conventional) could not extend to the alienation of one's liberty (which is an "essential gift of nature")—and even if it could, such alienation cannot extend to one's children.[131] "Arbitrary power" at the origin of civil society can be supported by neither political right nor natural right, as they can be understood by any reader (even without the support of respectable "authorities").[132]

---

ment, that is of the government which has for its object the good of the people, is . . . to follow the general will in everything."

[130] *Second Discourse*, Part 2 (P, III, 181). Note that Rousseau does not in this context treat the family as a possible origin of society, but only as the source of despotic government; since familial society was apparently the first social bond among men, parental authority must be discussed in terms of "right," and not "facts."

[131] *Ibid.* (182–84). Cf. Locke, *Second Treatise*, chap. VIII, § 116. At this point, Rousseau cites an edict "published in the name and by the orders of Louis XIV" in support of his view. This document—the *Traité des Droits de la Reine très Chrétienne sur Divers états de la monarchie d'Espagne* (1667)— was a defense of claims that the French king had explicitly renounced in his marriage contract, but which served as Louis XIV's justification for attacking the Low Countries in the War of Devolution (1667–68); Rousseau's source is not a philosophically respectable "authority." On the contrary, the same passage had been used by Sidney to criticize absolute monarchy (see *Discourses on Government*, chap. II, § 30 [London: Booksellers of London and Westminster, 1698], p. 235) and by Barbeyrac in his notes to his translation of Pufendorf (see *Le Droit de la Nature et des Gens*, VII, vi, § 10, n. 1 [ed. 1706, II, 273]). It need hardly be added that this example reveals the importance of testing "facts by right" in Rousseau's eyes. Cf. the use of another passage in the same *Traité* in the Errata to Diderot's article on "Autorité Politique," *Encyclopédie*, III, xvi, cited by Proust, *Diderot et l'Encyclopédie*, pp. 345, 356, 376.

[132] The distinction between political or conventional right and natural right as possible sources of tyranny seems to be the only explanation of the parallel arguments presented first against the assumption that "peoples threw themselves into the arms of an absolute master" (*Second Discourse*, Part 2 [P, III, 180–82]), and then against the supposedly "voluntary establishment of tyranny" (*ibid.* [182–84]). In fact, the first three suppositions considered by Rousseau are conquest, the union of the weak, and total contractual subordination to a ruler—all conventions which are analyzed in terms of political or purely conventional right; the last two hypotheses are parental power and the right to surrender one's freedom, both of which are treated in terms of natural right. Note that, in this sequence, political right is *prior* to natural right in the tem-

Rousseau's argument that, on the basis of right, political society could not originally have been ruled by individuals with arbitrary power has a double function. While this alternative must be considered because of the hypothetical character of Rousseau's historical exposition, it also serves to confirm the particular description of human evolution presented in Part 2 of the *Discourse*. If there is no ground for assuming that thinking men created the first civil society by establishing arbitrary power, it logically follows that the formation of civil society and the establishment of a formal government were separate acts.

At first society consisted only of some general conventions which all individuals pledged to observe, and regarding which the community became the guarantor for each individual.[133]

This conception of fundamental laws as conventions that are equally binding on all members of the body politic is, of course, exactly the view that Rousseau presents, in a more carefully worked out form, in the *Social Contract*.[134]

The purely "democratic" condition which characterized the first civil societies can be explained, at least by historical induction, from the fact that "the lack of philosophy and experience" prevented men from discovering, at the outset, the most effective means of organizing political power; "nascent government did not have a constant and regular form."[135] This explanation is however insufficient, if only

poral sense. Note also that in treating the Hobbesian conception of a contractual basis of arbitrary power, Rousseau cites three classical texts without apology: Pliny, a story about a Spartan (modified from the version in Herodotus and Plutarch), and Tacitus. (See *ibid.* [181], and the Pléiade edition's notes on the sources.) In contrast, when discussing the origins of civil society from the perspective of natural right, Rousseau says he will not have "recourse to the contrary proofs of Locke and Sidney" with reference to parental authority, and cites Pufendorf only to show the error of the jurists insofar as a voluntary origin of tyranny is concerned; in the posthumous edition, Rousseau adds that "I shall neglect, if one wishes, the authority of Barbeyrac, who clearly declares, following Locke . . . (*ibid.* [182–84]). Whereas classical *practice*, as reported by historians, is a reliable guide to the true nature of conventional right, modern writings on natural right are totally unnecessary for Rousseau's argument even when (as with Locke and Sidney) they do not contradict it. Cf. the pattern of Rousseau's quotations in the *Contrat social* (see below, pp. 308–09).

[133] *Second Discourse*, Part 2 (P, III, 180).

[134] *Contrat social*, II, vi (P, III, 378–80). See also I, vi–vii (360–64); II, iv (372–75); *Économie Politique* (P, III, 244–45, 248–50).

[135] *Second Discourse*, Part 2 (P, III, 180).

because Rousseau attributes to the founders of civil society the theoretically correct logic of the social contract; in any event, the factual origins of political life are of less importance than the rightful status of laws and governments.[136] It appears that the hypothetical history of governments, at least insofar as it is contrived to show the formation of a social contract and laws (or "general conventions") as distinct from the institution of government, is intended to suggest the true basis of political right.

When Rousseau turns to the establishment of a government and magistracies, he explicitly remarks that his presentation is provisional:

> Without entering at present into the researches yet to be undertaken concerning the nature of the fundamental compact of all government, I limit myself, in following common opinion, to consider here the establishment of the body politic as a true contract between the people and the chiefs it chooses for itself: a contract by which the two parties obligate themselves to observe laws that are stipulated in it and that form the bonds of their union.[137]

Although this remark has led most commentators to conclude that Rousseau's political thought was incomplete at the time he wrote the *Second Discourse*,[138] careful analysis forces one to reconsider the accepted interpretation. The passage in question is extraordinary because this "common opinion" is precisely the same as the "supposition that does not permit of serious debate," which Rousseau has just rejected.[139] It should therefore not be a complete surprise that the "common opinion" of a contract between the people and its chiefs is found untenable in the *Second Discourse*, prefiguring its explicit rejection in the *Social Contract*.[140]

Rousseau states that in such an agreement, "the two parties obligate themselves to observe the laws that are stipulated in it and that form the bonds of their union"; if so, the commonly defined contract between chiefs and subjects cannot "establish the body politic" because it merely confirms a preexisting law. Rousseau makes his criticism of

---

[136] See, however, *Contrat social*, III, x, n. (P, III, 421): the Roman republic "did not have at first a constant form."

[137] *Second Discourse*, Part 2 (P, III, 184). Note that, according to Rousseau, the "common opinion" implies a rejection of Hobbes' technical formulation of the social contract.

[138] E.g., Strauss, *Natural Right and History*, p. 285, n. 55.

[139] *Ibid.* (180), quoted at n. 127 of this chapter.

[140] *Contrat social*, III, xvi (P, III, 432–33). On the "common opinion" as representing the views of Diderot, see Proust, *Diderot et l'Encyclopédie*, pp. 376, 395.

the "common opinion" even more apparent when he argues that the contracting parties (i.e., the rulers and the people) would be free to break the contract at will "if there were no superior power." Either one must assume that "the sovereign authority" is given an "inviolable and sacred authority" by "divine will," precluding the exercise of secular political right by the citizen body, or a single contract, serving as the basis of both the body politic and the government, has the same character as the law of nature (for in the latter case "the parties would remain sole judges of their own case").[141] Because "divine will" (i.e., revealed religion) is not an acceptable authority in philosophy,[142] the "nature of the fundamental compact" accepted by "common opinion" cannot serve as a source of binding civil rights which replace natural rights and the state of nature.

Having indirectly rejected the view that a "contract" between the people and its rulers creates political obligation, Rousseau implies that the only philosophically correct foundation for civil society and government lies in his own definition of the "nature of the fundamental compact of all government." Although this "fundamental compact" is not examined in detail in the *Second Discourse*, Rousseau does describe its character clearly:

> The people having, on the subject of social relations, united all their wills into a single one, all the articles on which this will is explicit become so many fundamental laws obligating all members of the State without exception, and one of these laws regulates the choice and power of magistrates charged with watching over the execution of the others. This power extends to everything that can maintain the constitution, without going so far as to change it.[143]

Although Rousseau does not call "the single will" of the people the "general will," as he does in the *Political Economy* and the *Social Contract*, this conception of "fundamental laws" binding "all the members of the State without exception" and restricting the magistrates to the role of "ministers of the laws" is the essence of Rousseau's mature political teaching.[144] It appears that despite the ex-

[141] *Second Discourse*, Part 2 (P, III, 185).

[142] *Ibid.*, Ded. (119); Exordium (133). Divine law is politically *useful*, since popular religious belief discourages civil violence, but it has the status of a political institution and not of a transcendant rule which is certain to bind all men as men. *Ibid.*, Pref. (127); Part 1 (152); Part 2 (185); and *Économie Politique* (P, III, 264): "The voice of the people is in fact the voice of God." See also above, pp. 58, 85–89, and references there cited.

[143] *Second Discourse*, Part 2 (P, III, 184–85).

[144] Cf. *Contrat social*, IV, i (P, III, 437), where the general will is also called a "single will."

plicitly provisional character of the discussion in the *Second Discourse*, Rousseau had already thought through, at least in a rough way, his understanding of the principles of political right.[145]

A government limited by popularly enacted fundamental laws (or to use the current term, a "constitutional government") seems at first the soundest possible political regime. On the one hand, it is by definition directed to the common good and satisfies the interests of the subjects:

> The magistrate, for his part, obligates himself to use the power confided in him only according to the intention of the constituents, to maintain each one in the peaceable enjoyment of what belongs to him, and to prefer on all occasions the public utility to his own interest.[146]

On the other hand, in principle these magistrates should be "themselves the most interested" in maintaining the constitution:

> For the magistracy and its rights being established only upon the fundamental laws, should they be destroyed the magistrates would immediately cease to be legitimate, the people would no longer be bound to obey them; and as it would not have been the magistrate but the law which had constituted the essence of the State, everyone would return by right to his natural freedom.[147]

When the requirements of a legitimate political order, defined by the "nature of the fundamental compact," are not met, the body politic is *ipso facto* "destroyed" or "dissolved," and citizens regain their natural right to preserve themselves as they individually see fit.[148] Political rights, being supported by self-interest, are in principle as self-enforcing as natural rights in the state of nature.

The weakness of this constitutional solution is that it is subject to "inevitable abuse," because "experience" and "knowledge of the human heart" both reveal that the delegation of power to magistrates and rulers will ultimately be used for private rather than public

---

[145] In addition to the Dedication of the *Second Discourse*, which will be analyzed in a moment, the publication of the *Économie Politique* in the same year as the *Second Discourse* would seem to indicate this. Cf. the description of civil society before the establishment of government in the *Second Discourse* and the definition of the sovereign in the *Économie Politique* and *Contrat social* (references cited in nn. 133 and 134 of this chapter).

[146] *Second Discourse*, Part 2 (P, III, 185).

[147] *Ibid.*

[148] *Ibid.* (185–86); *Contrat social*, II, i (P, III, 369); III, x (422–23); *Économie Politique* (P, III, 245).

ends.[149] But this abuse of power is a violation of the enlightened self-interest of the magistrate himself, since a ruler who disobeys the law thereby destroys his own legitimacy; the people have an absolute right of revolution.[150] Merely by publishing the *Second Discourse*, Rousseau indicates to the citizens and magistrates of a legitimate regime —insofar as such regimes exist—that they have a mutual *interest* in preserving the sanctity of their laws against the "natural tendency" of all governments to degenerate into tyranny.

That it is possible for a "legitimate" regime to exist under modern conditions is made clear in Rousseau's Dedication, according to which "all" of the "best maxims that good sense could dictate concerning the constitution of a government" are to be found "in practice" in Geneva.[151] In order to make clear what these maxims are, Rousseau describes the characteristics of the Genevan regime as those he would have sought if he "had to choose" the place of his birth; although the Roman Republic is the "model of all free peoples," republican Geneva is the best regime to be wished for under modern conditions.[152] The best possible regime would be a small society, in which the people were sovereign and each citizen free, being subordinated to laws which no one within the city can violate and no one outside can impose. It would be an "ancient" republic, neither desiring to conquer others nor fearing conquest, in which "the right of legislation was common to all citizens," but in which "only the magistrates" had the "right" to propose new laws.[153]

Because a society in which the people themselves administer the laws is "necessarily ill-governed," Rousseau adds that he would *not* have preferred a direct democracy:

> Rather I would have chosen that Republic where the individuals, being content to give sanction to the laws and to decide in a body

[149] *Second Discourse*, Part 2 (P, III, 185, 187–88, 190); *Contrat social*, II, x (P, III, 421); *Économie Politique* (P, III, 247).
[150] *Second Discourse*, Part 2 (P, III, 185–86); *Contrat social*, III, xviii (434–36). Cf. especially *Économie Politique* (P, III, 249): "The most pressing interest of the ruler, and equally his most indispensable duty, is therefore to watch over the observation of the laws of which he is the minister, and on which all his authority is based."
[151] *Second Discourse*, Ded. (P, III, 111).
[152] *Ibid.* (113, 115). Unlike Plato and Aristotle, whose best regime exists in speech, it is characteristic of Rousseau that his best regime is closely approximated in specific cities. Note, however, the superiority of pagan Rome to Calvinist Geneva; Christianity creates an almost insuperable obstacle to the establishment of the best regime. See *Contrat social*, IV, viii (P, III, 460–69).
[153] *Second Discourse*, Ded. (P, III, 111–14).

and upon the report of their chiefs the most important public affairs, would establish respected tribunals, distinguish with care their various departments, elect from year to year the most capable and most upright of their fellow citizens to administer justice and govern the State.[154]

Unlike the "rude constitution of the first governments emerging immediately out of the state of nature," in which no distinction is made between the sovereign people and the government, Rousseau prefers a regime in which the magistrates are elected annually—as indeed he later claims was the case before governmental institutions were corrupted by inevitable abuse.[155]

The desirable regime described in the Dedication, which apparently coincides with the institutions of Geneva, is clearly consistent with the principles described in Rousseau's summary of political right. In particular, the establishment of laws by the sovereign people, binding all citizens without exception, is underlined as a decisive feature of a legitimate regime; when Rousseau mentions this aspect of his preferred homeland, he adds a footnote referring to the unusual example of a man named Otanes, who (according to Herodotus) was given the privilege of being "free and independent" within the Persian monarchy:

> If Herodotus did not inform us of the restriction that was placed on this privilege, it would be necessary to suppose it; otherwise Otanes, not recognizing any sort of law and being accountable to no one, would have been all-powerful in the State and more powerful than the king himself.[156]

The unnamed restriction was an oath to obey the Persian law; such an obligation must be assumed to have existed, even without historical evidence, because it is in the nature of laws that they must bind all citizens equally. The supremacy of law is the standard of any legitimate political order.[157]

---

[154] *Ibid.* (114).

[155] Cf. *ibid.* (114); Part 2 (180, 186). On the distinction between the government and the sovereign as a logically necessary corollary of Rousseau's principle of the general will, see below, chap. VII, esp. § 2D.

[156] *Ibid.*, n. I (195). This implicit distinction between obeying the law and obeying the government is equivalent to a rejection of the Hobbesian conception of the social contract, according to which the sovereign is precisely in the position of Otanes if his privilege were unrestricted—a position which Rousseau describes as "more powerful" than that of the king.

[157] *Second Discourse*, Part 2 (180, 185); *Contrat social*, II, iv (P, III, 374–

The relationship between the supremacy of popularly enacted laws and the powers of the government in a legitimate regime goes far to explain Rousseau's intentions in his Dedication. After summarizing the best possible regime, Rousseau addresses his fellow citizens directly, calling them "Magnificent, Most Honored and Sovereign Lords." The citizens of Geneva should preserve "a Republic so wisely and so happily constituted" by their "perpetual unity," their "obedience to the laws," and their "respect" for the magistrates whom they have chosen; the sovereign citizenry should destroy any "bitterness or distrust" toward the magistracy.[158] Rousseau then addresses the magistrates of Geneva, reminding them of the "consideration" expected by the ordinary citizens, like his own father, who are their "equals by education as well as by the rights of nature and of birth."[159] Praise of the Protestant pastors and of the women of Geneva concludes this laudatory Dedication, which on the surface seems to be evidence that at least one legitimate regime still exists in Europe.[160]

Part 2 of the *Second Discourse*, with its pessimistic analysis of the "inevitable abuse" arising in any civil society, contrasts so sharply with Rousseau's praise of Geneva that one is forced to go behind the surface of the Dedication. Although it is generally assumed that Rousseau was simply carried away by his emotions, he was in fact well aware that the description of his native city was an exaggeration that "might not please" the magistrates of Geneva; for this reason, he dated the Dedication from Chambery.[161] Since the inaccuracy of

---

75); II, vi (378–79); esp. *Économie Politique* (P, III, 249); "no exemption from the law will ever be granted, for whatever reason there might be, in a well ordered government." Cf. also *Gouvernement de Pologne*, i (P, III, 955). For the source of the story of Otanes, see Herodotus, *Histories*, III, 83.

[158] *Second Discourse*, Ded. (P, III, 115–17).

[159] *Ibid.* (117–18). Note that the magistrates are "Magnificent and Most Honored Lords"; they are not sovereign.

[160] *Ibid.* (119–20). Note that the pastors are not given an honorific title (as are the citizens and magistrates); they are praiseworthy precisely because they can be placed "in the rank of our best citizens."

[161] See *Confessions*, VIII (P, III, 392, 395). While in Geneva in the summer of 1754, Rousseau read his *Discourse* to a highly placed citizen, but took care not to read him the Dedication (*ibid.* [394]); this visit convinced him of the impossibility of gaining approval for his Dedication in advance of publication. See the Letter to M. Perdriau, 28 November 1754 (C. G., II, 132–34). After the *Second Discourse* was published, one of the first copies was sent to the magistrates of Geneva, who formally accepted the Dedication in a meeting of the Council of Two Hundred of 18 June 1755 (see C. G., II, 192–93, 196).

Rousseau's enthusiasm did not escape contemporary readers,[162] it is hard to believe that Rousseau wrote the Dedication merely as a piece of laudatory rhetoric, to be taken at face value by those who knew Genevan politics well.

In a highly personal letter to an acquaintance in Geneva, Rousseau explicitly stated his objective in writing the Dedication:

> Yes, Monsieur, struck by the parallel I see between the governmental constitution which follows from my principles and that which really exists in our Republic, . . . I took this occasion as a fortunate way of honoring my country and its rulers with just praises, of bringing to the bottom of hearts, *if possible*, the olive branch I now see only on medals, and of exciting at the same time other men to make themselves happy by the example of a people which is, *or could be, happy without changing anything in its institutions.*[163]

The Dedication of the *Second Discourse* has two functions: it presents the example of the laws of Geneva to other, more corrupted peoples, but at the same time it exhorts the Genevans themselves to live up to their laws. The constitution of Geneva is close to Rousseau's "principles," which are apparently already developed, but the actual behavior of the Genevans needs to be brought into conformity with the excellence of her laws; even legitimate laws are insufficient if the magistrates violate them and the citizens are not virtuous.[164]

E · THE DEGENERATION OF LEGITIMATE GOVERNMENT
INTO TYRANNY

The subtle implications of Rousseau's Dedication illuminate Part 2 of the *Second Discourse*, which traces "the progress of inequality"

[162] M. Dupan, who was First Syndic at the time of Rousseau's visit to Geneva in 1754, later wrote Rousseau: "You have followed the movements of your heart in the Dedicatory Epistle, and I fear it will be found to flatter us too much; you represent us as we ought to be, not as we are" (Letter of 20 June 1755 [C. G., II, 193]). Cf. also the other contemporary reactions cited by Starobinski (P, III, 1288).

[163] Letter to M. Perdriau, 28 November 1754 (C. G., II, 130), italics added.

[164] *Lettres Écrites de la Montagne*, vii (P, III, 813): "Nothing is freer than your legitimate condition; nothing is more servile than your actual condition." Letters VII, VIII, and IX are a detailed analysis of the laws of Geneva and the historical evidence of the abuses of the magistrates. Rousseau was well aware of the imperfection of Geneva long before his works were condemned there (see "Le Verger de Madame de Warens" [P, II, 1129]). Cf. also *Économie Politique* (P, III, 251, 259, 267); *Lettre à d'Alembert* (G, 176, 231).

through three distinct stages: "the establishment of law and of the right to property," "the institution of magistracy," and "the changing of legitimate power into arbitrary power."[165] This pattern is not due to the "motives for the establishment of the body politic," which as we have seen may even correspond to the true definition of political right, but are rather caused by the "form" and "inconveniences" of civil society.

> For the vices that make social institutions necessary are the same ones that make their abuse inevitable . . . it would be easy to prove that any government that, without being corrupted or altered, always worked exactly according to the ends of its institution, would have been instituted unnecessarily.[166]

The corruption of governments thus has its origins in the vices introduced together with property, and can be traced in private morals as well as political right.

Governmental institutions were at first elective, and the first magistrates were usually the wealthiest or the oldest; the difference between monarchy, aristocracy, and democracy was not a conscious choice of a form of government, but merely a result of the number of eminent men at the time of the election of the earliest governments.[167] Because the tendency to elect elders, of which historical evidence can be found, had the disadvantage of requiring frequent replacements and led to intrigue, faction, and violent conflict for power, the people ultimately assented to the principle of hereditary rule in order to preserve themselves.[168] In any event, "political distinctions necessarily bring about civil distinctions" between private individuals, resulting in the ultimate subversion of natural inequality (based on "personal merit" and "qualities") by conventional inequalities of "power," "nobility or rank," and especially "wealth" (which "is easily used to buy all the rest").[169]

The "extreme inequality of conditions," in combination with the vice inevitably produced by civil society, ultimately leads to despotism—the "fruit of an excess of corruption" in which "the law of the strongest" alone rules, as indeed had been the case (albeit with dif-

[165] *Second Discourse*, Part 2 (P, III, 187).
[166] *Ibid.* (187–88).
[167] *Ibid.* (186). This explains, incidentally, why the first governments "did not have a constant and regular form," since the original number of magistrates merely reflected the degree of inequality in various places; the "political state . . . was almost the work of chance" (*ibid.* [180]).
[168] *Ibid.* (186–87).
[169] *Ibid.* (188–89).

ferent effects) in the state of nature.[170] The conversion of "legitimate power into arbitrary power," destroying "morals and virtue," produces:

the status . . . of master and slave, which is the last degree of inequality and the limit to which all the others finally lead, until new revolutions dissolve the government altogether or bring it closer to its legitimate institution.[171]

All stages of human perfection lead ultimately to the final condition of slavery and tyranny, but this sombre picture is qualified in one respect: the stage of despotism is not necessarily permanent. New revolutions may conceivably destroy such governments or bring them back into harmony with the principles of a "legitimate institution."

The consideration of this possibility of restoring political legitimacy, or of preserving it from corruption insofar as is possible, must be deferred until we consider Rousseau's political teaching proper in Part II. For the moment, it is sufficient to note that the *Second Discourse* reveals a generally pessimistic view of the historical evolution of civil society; Rousseau shares neither the quietism of a moral critic for whom political action can never have salutary effects, nor the doctrinaire optimism that human progress is necessarily beneficial and can readily be secured by enlightenment or revolution.[172] Rousseau's thought is thus a quite original synthesis of the modern view (expressed most influentially by Hobbes, Locke, and the *philosophes*), according to which the discovery of the proper methods of organizing human society can lead to a conquest of nature permitting the virtually unlimited improvement of man's estate, and the traditional view (expressed most fully by classic philosophy) according to which the perfection of human life is a work of art, based on an imitation of nature, which can never produce perpetual progress and well-being for all men. Needless to say, such a position forced Rousseau to criticize all previous philosophic positions as inadequate, and it is only in this perspective that the *Second Discourse* takes on its fullest significance.

3 · THE ORIGINALITY OF ROUSSEAU'S POLITICAL PHILOSOPHY

It has been shown that Rousseau adopted a "non-teleological" conception of nature (i.e., that he considered nature to be primarily de-

[170] *Ibid.* (190–91). [171] *Ibid.* (187).
[172] For a consideration of the limits on perfectibility as understood by Rousseau, see esp. chap. VI, § 3 below.

fined in mechanistic or physical terms). This implies that a study of natural man must be concerned more with his beginnings than with his perfection. As a consequence, man can be conceived of as an isolated animal who was originally incapable of language, reason, and hence social obligations. Rousseau's conception of nature therefore makes it possible to speak of the "state of nature" as a condition which actually existed prior to the formation of civil society, for one can no longer speak of society as natural and its very existence requires explanation. Since it cannot be assumed that society has a natural order or perfection, Rousseau must also call into question the existence of universal standards of morality and justice; the moral guide for man can no longer be found solely in a natural law rationally discovered by all men or by philosophy, since the postulation of an animal state of nature denies the natural status of reason. The unique characteristic of man comes to be his perfectibility or his freedom, not his reason. Man's original nature becomes something which can be and is conquered by man himself.

This frame of reference leads to the search for those efficient causes which could have created civil society, joining together the naturally independent men of the state of nature. Rousseau thereby accepts some of the assumptions of what has been called the "modern natural right" teaching developed by Hobbes, Spinoza, and Locke. But in adopting this modern view, Rousseau criticizes certain fundamental assumptions of the previous "modern natural right" philosophers; in particular, he explicitly asserts that Hobbes had failed to describe a truly *natural* man, since those in a Hobbesian state of nature have faculties (reason, foresight, and calculation) and passions (*amour-propre* and fear of death) which are the consequence of social life.

Rousseau's criticism of Hobbes can be summarized as an attempt to ground the conception of the state of nature on natural science. For Hobbes, this state is not considered as the original historical condition from which the human species evolved: "I believe it was never generally so, over all the world."[173] In contrast, Rousseau tries to show that the pre-political condition of man is a historical "fact"; the evolution of the human species is a phenomenon subject to scientific analysis, based on observation, which "proves" the animal origins of man.[174] Although both Hobbes and Rousseau use the state of nature

[173] Hobbes, *Leviathan*, I, xiii (ed. Oakeshott, p. 83).
[174] "The error of Hobbes is therefore not to have established the state of war among independent men having become sociable, but to have assumed this state to be natural to the species and to have given it as the cause of the vices of which it is the effect" (*Geneva MS*, I, ii [P, III, 288]).

persisting between civil societies as evidence that it is valid to speak of such a state, the former derives his conception primarily from the experience of a civil war destroying a preexisting political society, whereas the latter seeks the condition preceding political life as such.[175]

Behind the explicit criticism of Hobbes is a less evident attack of the same order on the position of Locke, only made explicit in the footnote concerning Locke's conception of the family.[176] To be sure, when writing in self-defense later in life, Rousseau claimed that "Locke treated [these same materials] exactly in the same principles as I did," but this remark explicitly concerns the *Social Contract* and in any event refers to the method of approach and not the details of the Lockean teaching.[177] For Locke, although the right to property is imperfect until the formation of civil society fully secures it, the natural right to property is at least equal in status to the right to self-preservation;[178] ultimately Locke reduces the famous trilogy of rights to life, liberty, and property to the "right to property."[179] In sharp

---

[175] Cf. *Leviathan*, I, xiii (ed. Oakeshott, pp. 82–83) with *Second Discourse*, Part 1 (P, III, 162); Part 2 (178, 191). Rousseau's criticism of Hobbes' conception of the state of nature is thus not so much juridical or psychological (see Derathé, *Rousseau et la Science Politique*, pp. 131–41) as historical and scientific. In this respect, Locke is closer to Rousseau than Hobbes, for Locke had explicitly described the state of nature as having existed and speaks of it as "the beginning of things" (*Second Treatise*, chap. II, § 14; chap. v, § 37; chap. VIII, § 101–03, 107). See also Strauss, *Natural Right and History*, p. 230, esp. n. 96.

[176] *Second Discourse*, n. XII (P, III, 214–18). This criticism is also implicit at other points as well. For example, see the citation of "the axiom of the wise Locke, *where there is no property there is no injury*" (Part 2 [170]): in this quotation from the *Essay Concerning Human Understanding*, IV, iii § 18, Rousseau substitutes "injury" (*injure*) for the word "injustice" (*injustice*) in the original. See the French translation by Pierre Coste, *Essai Philosophique Concernant l'Entendement Humain* (Revised ed.; Amsterdam: Henri Schelte, 1723), p. 698, and the citation of this axiom by Barbeyrac in his Translator's Preface to Pufendorf's *Le Droit de la Nature et des Gens*, § 2 (ed. 1706, I, v), both of which follow the original. This substitution reflects Rousseau's irony in citing Locke when discussing the first willful "injuries" among men, since at this stage of evolution, according to Rousseau, there is merely possession or a "kind of property," and not property in the strict sense. Note also Rousseau's indication that he need not refer to Locke, and his citation of Locke through the mouth of Barbeyrac, implying that both are equally weak authorities (*Second Discourse*, Part 2 [182 and 183n.]).

[177] *Lettres Écrites de la Montagne*, vi (P, III, 812), and cf. Candaux's note (P, III, 1667).

[178] Locke, *Second Treatise*, chap. II, esp. § 4 and 6; chap. III, § 19–20; chap. IX, § 123–27.

[179] "By property I must be understood here, as in other places, to mean that property which men have in their persons as well as their goods" (*ibid.*,

contrast, Rousseau asserts that in the pure state of nature, there was no "property of any kind"; even the right to property arising from labor, although "natural" and more "real" than the right of the strongest, is essentially "usurpation" in the state of nature if any individual lacks the means of self-preservation. For Rousseau, property is an unnatural or tainted right which produced human corruption and misery, and which gained its sole respectability from civil society.[180]

In Rousseau's eyes, neither Hobbes nor Locke "arrived at" the state of nature because they did not see that natural man is an animal incapable of reason and language.[181] Rousseau's adaptation of the "modern natural right" teaching was at odds with the position of Hobbes and even of Locke because it presupposes a natural standard of "goodness," prior to civil society, which does not depend on human reason. Moreover, Rousseau's specification of the instinctive or impulsive sources of human action is not limited to self-preservation and those self-centered desires derived from it, for he insists that pity must be considered as a theoretical "principle" of almost equal status.

Pity is crucial for Rousseau because it is the basic natural sentiment capable of producing a bond between individual members of the species; in addition, pity can—at least in familial or savage societies that are still in the state of nature—restrain the desire for self-preservation. Perfected man retains some "ineffaceable" remnants of his pre-social, natural goodness, even though the animal goodness of the state of nature is opposed to—and hence not the foundation of

chap. xv, § 173). Cf. also chap. ix, § 123, 124; chap. xi, § 134; chap. xvi, § 182, 190, 196; chap. xxx, § 226. Indeed, for Locke the protection of the right to property in civil society has an even higher status than the protection of the life of every citizen: "The great end of man's entering into civil society being the enjoyment of their properties in peace and safety, . . . the first and fundamental natural law which is to govern even the legislative itself is the preservation of the society, and, *as far as will consist with the public good*, of every person in it" (*ibid.*, chap. xi, § 134, italics added). Cf. *Économie Politique* (P, iii, 256–57); *Contrat social*, ii, v (P, iii, 376–77), comparing the difference between Locke's use of the term "natural law" and Rousseau's reference to the "fundamental laws of society" or the "social treaty" (i.e., what Rousseau elsewhere calls the "nature of law").

[180] *Second Discourse*, Part 1 (P, iii, 147); Part 2 (164, 173–77); *Contrat social*, i, ix (P, iii, 365–67); and esp. *Émile*, v (G, 589): "the general will . . . can abolish [private property]."

[181] *Second Discourse*, Exordium (P, iii, 132), indirectly criticizing traditional jurists (e.g., Grotius), Locke, and Hobbes (in that order). Cf. Starobinski's notes (P, iii, 1301).

—the political order and civil justice. Hence the natural beginnings are relevant to the judgment of social man even though most human beings cannot return to the state of nature.

In this way, Rousseau tries to avoid the danger, implicit in a rigorously scientific interpretation of the "modern natural right" position, of denying any intrinsic relationship between *nature* (the physical origins of man) and virtue or justice (the moral and political perfection of man). Rousseau's attempted reformulation of the "modern natural right" teaching left him open to attack not only from the position of Hobbes or Locke, but also from the viewpoint of the traditional understanding of man as a social being subject to natural law. According to this tradition, derived from the classic and scholastic philosophy, man is a social and rational animal by nature, and standards of personal ethics and political justice are natural to him. Rousseau cannot accept such a view because he insists upon the truth of modern physics within a specified realm; natural law could not govern man while he was an independent, asocial animal, for such a man either did not know the law (being an ignorant brute) or refused to obey the law (being a calculating, selfish individual).[182]

This critique of classic and scholastic philosophy is evident from the most cursory reference to the leading representatives of the tradition. For example, according to Aristotle man is by nature able to receive virtue (since the perfection of a thing is, in a most important sense, in accordance with its nature).[183] But because the efficient cause of virtue in any particular individual is not natural necessity, but rather habit (in the moral virtues) or teaching (in the intellectual ones), Aristotle concludes: "Neither by nature, then, nor contrary to nature do the virtues arise in us. . . ."[184] In contrast, Rousseau's distinction between "virtue" and "goodness" means that human excellence is either "by nature" (i.e., natural goodness), or "contrary to nature" (i.e., virtue, which only arises in society and requires a repression of natural impulses).

The connection between Rousseau's conception of nature and his rejection of natural law as the foundation of political society is apparent if one contrasts his writings with the Thomistic teaching. For example, the traditional conception of *natural inclination* is well rep-

---

[182] See especially Diderot's restatement of the traditional view in his article *Droit naturel* in the *Encyclopédie*, and Rousseau's rejection of it in the *Geneva MS*, I, ii (both of which are analyzed in detail in chap. VI below).

[183] Aristotle, *Nicomachean Ethics* II.1103a ff. and esp. II.1109b30 ff.

[184] *Ibid.*, 1103a24.

resented by Aquinas' statement that "there is in every man a natural inclination to act according to reason; and this is to act according to virtue."[185] Rousseau's reply is evident in his oft-quoted remark that "I almost dare affirm that the state of reflection is a state contrary to nature,"[186] and in his total silence on the relevance of the "eternal law" as the source of natural law.[187]

The foundation of social morality and justice is therefore neither the "law of nature" described by Hobbes, Spinoza, or Locke, nor the "natural law" of the Thomistic or juristic tradition; it is rather the "nature of law" (i.e., the logic of obedience which is necessarily implied in any freely obeyed law, regardless of the lawless efficient causes producing political society). From the ineluctable principles on which all political relationships *must* be based, Rousseau deduces the standards of both social legitimacy ("political right") and individual morality (which he elsewhere calls "rational natural right" or "natural law"). This view permits Rousseau to treat the entire traditional natural law teaching as an existent *fact*, to be explained and grounded on the political order which must, historically, precede the philosophic formulation of universal rules of human behavior. The traditional natural law can thus be retained, in the form of the natural religion presented in the *Émile*, as an unenforceable moral guide, posterior to and derived in part from political right.[188]

This revolutionary treatment of natural law has two implications which bear emphasis. First, by taking the assumptions of the "modern natural right" doctrine to their logical conclusions, Rousseau saw that it is impossible to account for the existence of civil society apart from the evolution and history of the human species. In this sense, the

185 *Summa Theologica*, I-II, ques. 94, art. 3 (*The Political Ideas of St. Thomas Aquinas* [Bigogniari, ed.], p. 47).

186 *Second Discourse*, Part 1 (P, III, 138). Cf. the third "natural inclination" postulated by St. Thomas, *Summa Theologica*, I-II, ques. 94, art. 2.

187 Cf. *ibid.*, I-II, ques. 92, art. 2: "Wherefore since all things subject to divine providence are ruled and measured by the eternal law, . . . it is evident that all things partake somewhat of the eternal law, in so far as, namely, from its being imprinted on them, they derive their respective inclinations to their proper acts and ends. Now among all others the rational creature is subject to divine providence in the most excellent way, in so far as it partakes of a share of providence, by being provident both for itself and for others. Wherefore it has a share of the eternal reason, whereby it has a natural inclination to its proper act and end: and this participation of the eternal law in the rational creature is called the natural law" (*The Political Ideas of St. Thomas Aquinas*, p. 13). Cf. Rousseau's denial that natural man is provident, *Second Discourse*, Part 1 (P, III, 144).

188 This attitude to natural law is made more explicit in the *Geneva MS*, especially I, ii, analyzed in chap. VI below.

development of what has come to be called a "philosophy of history" by Kant, Hegel, and Marx merely elaborates what is suggested by Rousseau's criticism of previous philosophy. Secondly, Rousseau's own conception of the historical causes of social life led him to emphasize (some have said "discover")[189] the creative role of human reason; man's capacity to form ideas is a capacity to change the universe in which he lives. Social man has a "second nature," for the creation of property, law, and the mechanical arts results in the creation of a new nature (or rather, the creation of ideas and things which have their own nature).[190]

To be sure, the human institution of society does not, *ipso facto*, imply the discovery of the inner reality of conventional or human things. Many centuries are required, even within society, before the rare man can formulate clearly and correctly the true understanding of his own nature and of the nature of man-made things. Even then, the vast majority of men cannot—and need not—know the true character of human existence. Nonetheless the nature of laws can ultimately be discovered and transmitted from one philosopher to another, and this activity of philosophizing is in some sense the highest activity of which man is capable.[191]

Rousseau thus found himself in the "middle" so to speak, being opposed by two different schools of thought which were reflected among his contemporaries. To one side were those who denied any universal principles of human excellence; to the other, those who denied that physical necessity provides a satisfactory explanation for the origin of man's social life and moral life. Rousseau tried to resolve or at least rise above these opposed positions, and because of the boldness of his attempt, was forced to appear as a "man of paradoxes." Among other things, he sought to reestablish the classical conception of the *polis* on the basis of modern physics; from the modern conceptions of man as a naturally apolitical (if not antisocial)

---

[189] Cf. Eric Weil, "J. J. Rousseau et sa Politique," *Critique*, LVI (January 1952), pp. 5, 10.

[190] The originality of Rousseau's position is clearer if one compares it to that of Diderot. As Proust puts it: "for Diderot, there is not a qualitative difference between the man of the state of nature and social man; from one to the other there is neither mutation nor metamorphosis, there is only continual evolution" (*Diderot et l'Encyclopédie*, p. 361). As a result, Diderot was able to combine a thorough materialism with the traditional conception of a natural law discovered by reason. See his *Droit Naturel*, analyzed below, chap. VI.

[191] See Leo Strauss, "On the Intention of Rousseau," *Social Research*, XIV (December 1947), 455–87, esp. 473.

animal, Rousseau tried to derive a regime which approximated, in certain ways, the political order discussed by those philosophers who assumed that man was a political animal. This ambivalence of Rousseau's thought is, in a subtle way, expressed nowhere more clearly than in his *First Discourse*.

— V —

THE CONTRADICTION
BETWEEN THE SCIENCES AND MORALS
(FIRST DISCOURSE)

1 · *The Character of the* First Discourse

The title page of Rousseau's first writing of philosophic importance reveals the occasion which brought him fame and directed his energies toward a comprehensive understanding of man and society.

DISCOURS
qui a remporté le prix
à l'Académie de Dijon
En l'année 1750

Sur cette Question proposée par la même Académie:
Si le rétablissement des Sciences et des Arts a
contribué à épurer les moeurs

Par un Citoyen de Genève[1]

Rousseau did not—as was the case for the *Second Discourse*—select his own title, and indeed he published the work in its existent form solely because it received a prize.[2] Although Rousseau was evidently

[1] "Discourse/Which Won the Prize/ of the Academy of Dijon/ in the year 1750/ On the Question proposed by that Academy:/ Has the restoration of the sciences and arts tended to purify morals?/ By a Citizen of Geneva" (P, III, 1). The translation of the word *moeurs* poses a problem, because it means the way of life of a man or a people, including both moral standards and customs. In his translation of the *Lettre à d'Alembert*, Allan Bloom has used "manners [morals]" to convey the combination of an ethical assessment and a description of habits implicit in the term (*Politics and the Arts* [Glencoe, Ill.: Free Press, 1960], pp. 149–50). For the sake of simplicity, in this chapter the word "morals" will always be used in the sense of *moeurs* (both in the analysis and in translating Rousseau's texts); this use of "morals" should therefore not be confused with the meaning attached to the French word "moral" (*morale*) in chap. IV.

[2] "Little expecting the honor I received, I had, since submitting it, reworked and expanded this Discourse, to the point of making in a sense

— 205 —

far from satisfied with his essay,[3] he considered it one of his "principal writings" and it is not difficult to show that it established the orientation of his entire thought.[4]

Much scholarly research has been devoted to the circumstances surrounding the composition of the *First Discourse*, which Rousseau himself described as the result of a sudden inspiration—the so-called "illumination of Vincennes"—which he felt on reading the Academy of Dijon's question in the *Mercure de France*.[5] This has taken on particular interest because of the claim, attributed to Diderot by his friends, that Rousseau intended to answer the question in the affirmative; according to this account Diderot dissuaded Rousseau from taking this conventional view and convinced him to take the negative. The charge is important, for it implies that Rousseau's entire philosophy is derived from a paradox, adopted in order to gain fame and maintained hypocritically to retain it. Most scholars have rejected this explanation of Rousseau's fundamental criticism of the sciences and arts, which rests solely on hearsay evidence from those who had quarrelled with Rousseau and feared the publication of his *Confessions*; Diderot himself never claimed that the central thesis of the *First Discourse* was his idea and not Rousseau's.[6] It seems, therefore, that there is no reason why the *First Discourse* cannot be analyzed as representing Rousseau's views, albeit in an incomplete form.[7]

---

another work of it; today I consider myself obliged to restore it to the state in which it was honored" (*First Discourse*, Pref. [P, III, 3]). Cf. *Confessions*, VIII (P, I, 356) and above, p. 108.

[3] See the Notice which Rousseau added for the *First Discourse* when a collected edition of his works was being prepared by Duchesne in 1763: "What is celebrity? Here is the unfortunate work to which I owe mine. Certainly this piece, which won me a prize and made me famous, is at best mediocre, and I dare add that it is one of the slightest of this whole collection" (P, III, 1237). Rousseau expresses this same judgment that the work is poorly written in *Lettre à Lecat* (P, III, 98) and *Confessions*, VIII (P, I, 352).

[4] *Lettre à Malesherbes*, 12 January 1762 (C. G., VII, 51).

[5] For Rousseau's account, see *ibid.*, cited above, pp. xii–xiii; *Confessions*, VIII (P, I, 351); *Rousseau Juge de Jean Jacques*, ii (P, I, 828–29); and cf. Jean Guéhenno, *Jean–Jacques* (Paris: Grasset, 1948), I, chap. xii. For the announcement of the Academy of Dijon's contest, see P, III, 1237–38.

[6] This problem is summarized by François Buchardy, "Introduction: *Discours sur les Sciences et les Arts*" (P, III, xxvii–xxxiii). For more details, see George R. Havens, "Introduction," *Rousseau: Discours sur les Sciences et les Arts* (New York: Modern Language Association of America, 1946), pp. 6–9, 21–23; Guéhenno, *Jean Jacques*, I, 282–86; Daniel Mornet, *Rousseau, l'homme et l'oeuvre* (Paris: Hatier-Bovin, 1950), pp. 26–27; Arthur M. Wilson, *Diderot: the Testing Years* (New York: Oxford University Press, 1957), pp. 114–15. Rousseau explicitly rejected the interpretation that his thesis in the *First Discourse* was insincere; see esp. *Préface à Narcisse* (P, II, 961–63); *Lettre à Grimm* (P, III, 67).

[7] In Book VIII of the *Confessions*, Rousseau says that "I began to reveal my

Rousseau insisted, in defending the *First Discourse*, that his views in the work were carefully thought out.[8] He felt that "some precautions were necessary" in order to "make himself understood," because he wanted to be sure that the "truth" would be made "useful" in his works:

> It is only successively and for few readers that I have developed my ideas. . . . Often I gave myself a great deal of pain to try to enclose in a sentence, in a line, in a word dropped as if by chance, the result of a long series of reflections. Often most of my readers must have found my discourses poorly organized and almost entirely unconnected, failing to see the trunk of which I only showed them the branches. But it was enough for those who know how to understand, and I have never wanted to speak to the others.[9]

In order to understand fully the *First Discourse*, therefore, it will be necessary to analyze the text with more care than usual, particularly with respect to the implications of specific words and historical examples.

On the title page of the first edition, Rousseau only identifies himself as a "Citizen of Geneva," remaining anonymous (as was often done in eighteenth-century France).[10] He nonetheless continued to

principles more openly a little more than I had done up to then" in the *Préface à Narcisse* (1753), and only "completely developed them" in the *Second Discourse* (P, I, 388). That this is not a retrospective reinterpretation by Rousseau is proven by the *Préface d'une Seconde Lettre à Bordes*, written in 1753 or early 1754 (i.e., before the completion of the *Second Discourse*) but never published: "If the Discourse of Dijon itself has so excited murmurs and raised scandal, what would have happened if I had developed from the first instant the entire extent of a true but afflicting system, of which the question treated in this Discourse is only a corollary? . . . Some precautions were therefore necessary, and it is in order to be able to make everything understood that I did not want to say everything" (P, III, 106).

[8] "Before expressing myself, I meditated my subject long and profoundly, and I tried to see it from every side. I doubt that any of my adversaries can say as much. . . . I dare say that they have never made a reasonable objection that I had not foreseen and to which I had not replied in advance" (*Dernière Réponse* [P, III, 71–72n.]). Cf. *Préf. d'une Seconde Lettre* (P, III, 103).

[9] *Ibid.* (106). On the method Rousseau followed in composing the *First Discourse*, see *Confessions*, viii (P, I, 352).

[10] Although this edition gives the publisher as "Barrillot & fils" in Geneva, it was actually printed in Paris by Pissot; this device was widely used at the time to avoid some of the restrictions on publication in France. Rousseau's name first appears on the title page ("Par M. Rousseau, Genevois") in the edition which was actually published by Barrillot in Geneva later in 1750 (P, III, 1854–56). The substitution of the adjective "Genevan" for the title "Citizen of Geneva" was technically in order, since Rousseau did not formally

speak of himself as a "Genevan" or "Citizen of Geneva" even when he dropped the anonymity, in part as a means of distinguishing himself from the well-known French poet Jean-Baptiste Rousseau, but also as an indication of his status as a foreigner in the French world of letters.[11]

The latter implication is made clear by his epigraph from Ovid:

Barbarus hic ego sum
quia non intelligor illis.[12]

Rousseau writes as an outsider who tacitly identifies himself with Ovid, the Roman poet in exile among the Scythians. Although Rousseau thereby suggests that he is not an unqualified enemy of the arts, the primary implication of the epigraph is that he does not expect to be understood by most of his readers, an expectation that is reaffirmed in the Preface:

Running counter to everything that men admire today, I can expect only universal blame; and the fact of having been honored by the approval of a few wise men does not allow me to count on the approval of the public.[13]

In publishing the *First Discourse*, Rousseau thus begins by suggesting that the audience of any published work, including his own, can be divided into the "public" at large and a "few wise men."

Rousseau's attitude toward this distinction is made clear by his scorn for the volatility of popular opinions:

---

regain his status as a citizen until 1754. Jean Jacques was particularly encouraged to speak of his Genevan origin by the need to distinguish himself from the then famous French poet, Jean–Baptiste Rousseau. See *Confessions*, IV (P, I, 157); "Mon Portrait," fragment 38 (P, I, 1129); P, III, 1239, n. 2.

[11] See his *Lettre à Voltaire*, 30 January 1750, which is signed "J. J. Rousseau, Citoyen de Genève" (C. G., I, 301–02), as well as *Lettre à Lecat* (P, III, 102) and the fragment transcribed by Bouchardy (P, III, 1258). Although the title of citizen of a republic also has political overtones, they should perhaps not be overemphasized in this particular case; in the polemics raised by the *First Discourse*, Rousseau most often identified himself simply as "J. J. Rousseau de Geneve," in conformity with his legal status. See *Observations sur la Réponse*—often called "Réponse au Roi Stanislaus"—(P, III, 35); *Lettre à Grimm* (P, III, 59); *Dernière Réponse* (P, III, 71); *Lettre à Lecat* (P, III, 97); *Lettre à l'Auteur du Mercure*, 27 July 1750 (C. G., I, 305). After 1754, Rousseau used the title "Citizen of Geneva" in those "writings that I think could do honor" to his native city. See the remark concerning his failure to do so in the *Nouvelle Héloïse*, Second Pref. (P, II, 27).

[12] "Here I am the barbarian because no one understands me" (Ovid, *Tristia*, Elegy x.37 [P, III, 1]).

[13] *First Discourse*, Pref. (P, III, 3).

At all times there will be men destined to be subjugated by the opinions of their century, their country, their society. A man who plays the freethinker and philosopher today would, for the same reason, have been only a fanatic at the time of the League. One must not write for such readers when one wants to live beyond one's century.[14]

Rousseau explicitly writes in order to "live beyond his century." He apparently does not address himself to those who call themselves "philosophers" merely to be fashionable, for "such readers" must be contrasted to the "few wise men" who do not merely follow the "opinion" of the moment; in the Preface, Rousseau seems to identify himself with these "few," not with the general public.

Yet in the body of the *First Discourse*, Rousseau does not write in the guise of a philosopher or a wise man:

Which side should I take in this question? The one, gentlemen, that suits an honorable man who knows nothing and yet does not think any the less of himself.[15]

As Rousseau makes clear in the closing paragraph, he identifies himself with the nonphilosophic reader:

As for us, common men not endowed by heaven with such great talents and not destined for so much glory, let us remain in our obscurity.[16]

But by publishing the work for which he had received a prize, Rousseau can hardly remain in obscurity; quite on the contrary, in the Preface he explicitly indicates that he is writing to "live beyond his century" (i.e., for the glory of being remembered by posterity).

This paradoxical position was obviously evident to Rousseau:

How can one dare blame the sciences before one of Europe's most learned societies, praise ignorance in a famous Academy, and reconcile contempt for study with respect for the truly learned? I have seen these contradictions, and they have not rebuffed me.[17]

Rousseau's justification is based on the distinction between virtue and science:

[14] *Ibid.*
[15] *Ibid.*, Exordium (5).
[16] *Ibid.*, Part 2 (30).
[17] *Ibid.*, Exordium (5). Cf. Part 1 (16): the "contradictions" in the First Discourse are only "apparent."

I am not abusing science, I told myself; I am defending virtue before virtuous men. Integrity is even dearer to good men than erudition to the scholarly.[18]

By implication, Rousseau distinguishes between the wisdom of his academic judges and their decency as honorable men; the philosopher or scientist is also a man to whom one can appeal on the basis of virtue (as distinct from knowledge).

This method of posing before the Academy of Dijon permits Rousseau to shift the criteria of judgment to the realm of morality; in effect, the academicians are asked to judge their own scholarly pursuits in terms of the standards of virtue that Rousseau will defend. For Rousseau, this is a favorable situation in which to present his views:

> Equitable sovereigns have never hesitated to condemn themselves in doubtful disputes; and the position most advantageous for one with a just cause is to have to defend himself against an upright and enlightened opponent who is judge of his own case.[19]

The irony of this passage, evident if one reflects on the dangers of having one's opponent as judge in a legal case, is reinforced by Rousseau's own comments on the self-interest and *amour-propre* of civilized, reasoning men.[20]

Rousseau's attempt—which in fact was successful—to create a situation in which representatives of the scholarly or scientific community would condemn themselves reveals more fully his intention. In submitting his *Discourse* to the Academy of Dijon, Rousseau speaks to his judges (representing the sciences and arts) in the name of "us, common men" who "know nothing" and "yet do not think any the less" of themselves for their ignorance. In publishing the *Discourse*, so that it can be read by the general public (which holds the eighteenth-century prejudice that arts and sciences are good without qualification), Rousseau identifies himself with the poet Ovid, and makes it clear that he is really concerned with those few "wise men"

[18] *Ibid.*, Exordium (5). On the irony of this assertion, cf. *Lettre à Grimm* (P, III, 68); *Lettre à Lecat* (P, III, 102).

[19] *First Discourse*, Exordium (5).

[20] See esp. *Second Discourse*, Part 2 (P, III, 181): "Now, in the relations between one man and another . . . the worst that can happen to one is to see himself at the discretion of the other." Cf. *First Discourse*, Part 2 (P, III, 18–19), cited in nn. 78 and 79 of this chapter; *Lettre à Grimm* (P, III, 61); *Lettre à Lecat* (P, III, 97): "I was far from expecting that impartiality in an Academy."

in his audience whose philosophic concern is not merely the result of common opinions.[21]

This double perspective of the *Discourse*, although it has often not been fully recognized by commentators, requires particular emphasis: Rousseau speaks as a "common man" when addressing those who claim to be philosophers, as a philosopher when addressing true philosophers, and as a learned defender of the virtue of common men when addressing the public at large.[22] This complex intention presupposes a distinction between the kind of science respected by academicians and the general public, and the kind of science which Rousseau himself will use.

> Here is one of the greatest and noblest questions ever debated. This discourse is not concerned with those metaphysical subtleties that have prevailed in all parts of learning and from which the announcements of Academic competitions are not always exempt; rather, it is a matter of one of those truths that concern the happiness of mankind.[23]

Learning composed of "metaphysical subtleties" should be distinguished from the quest for "truths that concern the happiness of mankind" because "metaphysical" ideas have "no model in nature," are subject to error even for the few men who can understand them, and are "useless" as the sole basis of virtue.[24] The "sublime science of

[21] The distinction between Rousseau's intention in speaking to the academicians of Dijon and his intention in publishing the *First Discourse* is also made clear by the difference between the epigraph and the motto Rousseau used in submitting his work for the prize. According to the terms of the competition, "each author will be required to put, at the end of his memoire, a sentence or motto and to attach a sealed piece of paper, on the outside of which will be the same motto, and inside the seal his name, status, and address" (P, III, 1238). Rousseau's motto, which in the published *Discourse* occurs at the head of the Exordium, is "*Decipimur specie recti* (We are deceived by the appearance of right)" (Horace, *On the Art of Poetry* 25). Whereas the motto warns the academicians of the danger of error in the sciences and arts, the epigraph assumes that the general public will not understand the truth of Rousseau's position. Since Rousseau could easily have used his motto as an epigraph, his failure to do so surely indicates that his attitude in printing the *First Discourse* differs from his attitude in submitting it to the Academy of Dijon.

[22] Cf. *Lettre à Raynal* (P, III, 33); *Observations* (P, III, 37); *Dernière Réponse* (P, III, 80n.); *Lettre à Lecat* (P, III, 101n.); *Préf. d'une Seconde Lettre* (P, III, 106). Despite a slightly different formulation, the above interpretation has been greatly influenced by Strauss, "On the Intention of Rousseau," *Social Research*, XIV (December 1947), esp. pp. 463–68; *Natural Right and History* (Chicago: University of Chicago Press, 1953), esp. pp. 260–61.

[23] *First Discourse*, Pref. (P, III, 3).

[24] *Ibid.*, Part 2 (P, III, 18–19, 27); *Second Discourse*, Pref. (P, III, 125);

simple souls" or the "true philosophy," which consists in knowing how to "act well," is all that is needed for common men to live virtuously, and as a philosopher Rousseau will defend this kind of knowledge by presenting a scientific or philosophic truth consistent with virtue.[25]

Speaking for the common men, Rousseau criticizes the kinds of science for which there is no "criterion" in the name of the "sublime science" which can be known with certainty by "simple souls."

> Are not your principles engraved in all hearts, and is it not enough in order to learn your laws to commune with oneself and listen to the voice of one's conscience in the silence of the passions?[26]

This first of Rousseau's many appeals to the conscience does not reveal (as do the *Second Discourse, Émile,* and *Social Contract*) that the "laws" of true virtue are in themselves impotent since they presuppose either civil law or natural religion; at this point Rousseau merely establishes the grounds for his subsequent appeal to sentiment as the judge of reason. Rousseau thus confronts the academicians with a rhetorically astute challenge: although the "enlightenment of the Assembly that listens" to him may condemn "the construction of the discourse," it cannot openly condemn the "sentiment of the orator."

> Having upheld, according to my natural intellect, the cause of truth, whatever the outcome there is a prize which I cannot fail to receive: I will find it at the bottom of my heart.[27]

By defending virtue at the expense of claims to philosophic knowledge, Rousseau cleverly forces his academic judges to accept a senti-

---

Part 1 (151). Cf. the discussion of Rousseau's "detachable metaphysics," above, chap. II, § 2C.

[25] *First Discourse,* Part 1 (P, III, 7); Part 2 (30); *Lettre à Raynal* (P, III, 33); *Dernière Réponse* (P, III, 81); *Préface d'une Seconde Lettre* (P, III, 106). See also the distinction between two kinds of science, Strauss, *Natural Right and History,* pp. 262–63; the distinction between two kinds of ignorance, Strauss, "On the Intention of Rousseau," p. 472; and the citations in n. 32 of this chapter.

[26] *First Discourse,* Part 2 (P, III, 30). Cf. Part 2 (18); *Observations* (P, III, 42): "we have an interior guide, much more infallible than all books, which never abandons us in need"; *Dernière Réponse* (P, III, 81): "the philosophy of the soul leads to true glory, but that kind is not learned in books"; *ibid.* (86): "the testimony of a good conscience"; *ibid.* (93): "the best guides that decent men can have are reason and the conscience."

[27] *First Discourse,* Exordium (P, III, 5).

ment or feeling of the heart as criterion of truth; if they fail to award him the prize, they condemn themselves on moral grounds.

The contradiction between science and virtue in the *First Discourse* is therefore deceptive:

> What! could probity be the daughter of ignorance? Could knowledge and virtue be incompatible? What conclusions might not be drawn from these opinions? But to reconcile these apparent contradictions it is only necessary to examine closely the vanity and emptiness of those proud titles that dazzle us, and that we so freely give to human learning.[28]

It is a "prejudice" (i.e., a false opinion from the perspective of philosophy) to equate without qualification ignorance and morality; the true question concerns the distinction between the kind of knowledge which deserves to be called "science" and the "vanity and emptiness" of the learning which is given this name by common opinion.

2 · *The Contradiction between Enlightenment and Society*

A · THE CRITICISM OF MORALS IN EIGHTEENTH-CENTURY FRANCE

Rousseau's distinction between two kinds of knowledge explains why he can use scientific or philosophic reasoning and erudition in order to persuade the academicians of Dijon—and all other thoughtful men—that the arts and sciences contribute to moral corruption. The body of Rousseau's analysis, following tradition, is divided into two parts, each of which has a distinct purpose:

> After having used the first part of my Discourse to prove that these things [the dissolution of morals and the sciences] have always progressed together, I destined the second to show that in fact the former depended on the latter.[29]

Although this division is not strictly maintained, since Rousseau returns to "historical inductions" in Part 2 and includes some of his "reasoning" about the "sciences and arts in themselves" in Part 1, it will be convenient to follow this order in our analysis.[30]

---

[28] *First Discourse*, Part 1 (16). Cf. *Observations* (P, III, 38, 39).

[29] *Lettre à Grimm* (P, III, 63). At the end of Part 1 of the *First Discourse* (P, III, 16), Rousseau indicates that the First Part is devoted to "historical induction" and the Second to "reasonings" about "the sciences and arts in themselves"; cf. also *Préface à Narcisse* (P, II, 965).

[30] Cf. *First Discourse*, Part 1 (6–7 and n.); Part 2 (20, 22–23). The failure to adhere to a logical structure of argument may explain in part Rousseau's

Part 1 begins with a description of the status of the sciences, arts, and morals in eighteenth-century Europe. Rousseau praises the "marvels" of man's rediscovery of "learning" in "that part of the world which is today enlightened":

It is a grand and beautiful sight to see man emerge from obscurity somehow by his own efforts; dissipate, by the light of his reason, the darkness in which nature had enveloped him; rise above himself; soar intellectually into celestial regions; traverse with giant steps, like the sun, the vastness of the universe; and—what is even grander and more difficult—come back to himself to study man and know his nature, his duties, and his end.[31]

Newtonian physics is the model of the enlightenment, and represents a philosophic understanding of the nature of the universe which is the "glory of the human mind"; Rousseau admits from the outset that theoretical science has a valid claim to respect.[32] Moreover, the renaissance of learning rescued Europe from a kind of "barbarism of the first ages" which was "worse than ignorance"; the absence of science is not in itself sufficient for virtue.[33]

The rediscovery of literature produced not only the art of thinking, which for Rousseau results from the prior development of the art of writing, but also "the desire to please" other men, "softness of character," and "urbanity of morals."[34]

comment that "this work, full of warmth and force, absolutely lacked logic and order; of all those that came from my pen, it is the weakest in reasoning and the poorest in number and harmony. But whatever talent one may be born with, the art of writing is not learned all at once" (*Confessions*, viii [P, I, 352]).

[31] *First Discourse*, Part 1 (P, III, 6). I am indebted to Michael Lerner for the suggestion that this passage seems to reflect Plato's allegory of the Cave, *Republic* VII.514a–520d.

[32] *Ibid.*, Part 2 (18–19, 29). Rousseau insists that this praise is a sincere reflection of his intention. See *Observations* (P, III, 35-36): "Science is very good in itself, that is evident"; *Dernière Réponse* (P, III, 72): "The sciences are the *chef-d'oeuvre* of genius and reason"; *Préface à Narcisse* (P, II, 965): "Science taken in an abstract way merits all our admiration. The mad science of men is only worth laughter and scorn."

[33] *First Discourse*, Part 1 (P, III, 6); *Observations* (P, III, 54); *Letttre à Grimm* (P, III, 62); *Dernière Réponse* (P, III, 74–75 and n.). Cf. *Lettre à Lecat* (P, III, 101–02). Note the clear implication that the "first ages" were not virtuous, and cf. below, pp. 224, 244.

[34] *First Discourse*, Part 1 (P, III, 6–7). Rousseau calls the priority of the art of writing ("letters") to the art of thinking ("sciences") "an order which seems strange but which is perhaps only too natural"; the French phrase *sciences et arts* (unlike its English equivalent "arts and sciences") gives

By this sort of civility, the more pleasant because it is unpretentious . . . our century and our nation will no doubt surpass all times and all peoples. A philosophic tone without pedantry; natural yet engaging manners, equally remote from Teutonic simplicity and Italian pantomime: these are the fruits of the taste acquired by good education and perfected in social intercourse.[35]

The result of civilization and the popular cultivation of the sciences is only a false appearance, "the semblance of all the virtues without the possession of any," because art has "moulded our manners and taught our passion to speak an affected language."

Today, when subtler researches and a more refined taste have reduced the art of pleasing to set rules, a base and deceptive uniformity prevails in our customs, and all minds seem to have been cast in the same mould. Incessantly politeness requires, propriety demands; incessantly usage is followed, never one's own inclination. One no longer dares to appear as he is.[36]

The result of "artificial simplicity" and politeness is a kind of "uniformity" of customs and morals which suppresses the true genius of individuals and permits "a procession of vices" (since one is never certain of another's inner disposition).

Rousseau's criticism of the morals of his time is exceedingly condensed and sweeping. Although his attack is not directed simply or primarily against the lack of individual originality, he condemns the constraint of genius—and therewith of scientific or artistic genius in particular—by unsound public opinions; if those who judge the products of artists and scientists lack the knowledge necessary for correct judgments, the arts and sciences cannot flourish:

Every artist wants to be applauded. . . . What will he do to obtain praise, therefore, if he has the misfortune to be born among a people and at a time when the learned, having themselves become fashionable, have enabled frivolous youth to set the tone. . . . He will lower his genius to the level of his time, and will prefer to com-

the priority to theoretical science. On the reasoning behind Rousseau's remark, see Second Discourse, Part 1 (P, III, 144–51).

[35] First Discourse, Part 1 (P, III, 7). Note that in the body of the Discourse, addressing the Academy of Dijon, Rousseau speaks as one of "us"—i.e., a Frenchman or at least a European—whereas in publishing his Discourse he speaks as a Genevan—i.e., a foreigner.

[36] Ibid. (8). On the connection between vice and the distinction between "to be and to seem to be," see Second Discourse, Part 2 (P, III, 174–75).

pose ordinary works which are admired during his lifetime instead of marvels which would not be admired until long after his death. . . . And if, by chance, among the men distinguished by their talents, there is one who has firmness in his soul and refuses to yield to the spirit of his times and disgrace himself by childish works, woe to him. He will die in poverty and oblivion.[37]

Far from condemning all arts and sciences, Rousseau attempts to liberate the artist or scientist from conformity, orienting those with genius away from an attempt to please their contemporaries; his own *Discourse* is intended as a model of the "firmness" of soul needed if "one wants to live beyond his century."[38]

The most evident target of Rousseau's criticism, however, is the moral corruption represented by "politeness" and the "art of pleasing" other men:

How pleasant it would be to live among us if exterior appearances were always a reflection of the heart's disposition; if decency were virtue; if our maxims served as our rules; if true philosophy were inseparable from the title of philosopher![39]

The "politeness of our manners, the affability of our speech, our perpetual demonstration of goodwill" are morally corrupt because they hide the true intentions of men; a foreigner who judged "European morals" on the basis of appearances "would guess our morals to be exactly the opposite of what they are." A way of life in which "men of all ages and conditions . . . seem anxious to oblige one another from dawn to dark" produces vice because, in order to be polite, one must respect the opinions of others above all else. Since all men are naturally concerned primarily with their own self-interest, the exhibition of contrary sentiments merely covers "the hidden desire to profit at the expense of others" and "a secret jealousy all the more danger-

[37] *First Discourse*, Part 2 (P, III, 21). Rousseau's example of the "sacrifice" made by a genius to his own times is Voltaire, who is not referred to by his pen name but as "Arouet," his real name; Rousseau implies that to be famous in the eighteenth-century world of French letters, one must put on a false front. That Rousseau's criticism may have merit is perhaps reflected in the reviews of a recent production of Voltaire's *L'Orphelin de Chine* by the Comédie Française. See, e.g., *Nouvel Observateur*, No. 16 (4 March 1965), p. 27. Rousseau's assertion that "every artist wants to be applauded" is thus, I believe, misinterpreted by Georges May, *Rousseau par lui-même* (Paris: Seuil, 1961), pp. 54–55. Cf. Plato, *Laws* 700a–701d.

[38] *First Discourse*, Pref. (P, III, 3); Part 2 (21–22, 29–30).

[39] *Ibid.*, Part 1 (7).

ous because, in order to strike its blow in greater safety, it often assumes the mask of benevolence."[40]

Without the cover of "artificial" manners:

> men found their security in the ease of seeing through each other, and that advantage, which we no longer appreciate, spared them many vices.[41]

When it is no longer possible to sense the motives of others, one is freed to follow the basest passions with impunity as long as the prevailing standards of "decency" are maintained; whereas virtue requires the control of impulses and passion in the name of the good of others (be it the common good of a society or the good of other men as individuals), the "uniformity" of behavior produced by "politeness" is really a "refinement of intemperance" since it renders self-restraint unnecessary and legitimates self-seeking desires.[42]

By making public opinion, which is to say volatile prejudices devoid of truth, the standard of all behavior, true science and art is submitted to the judgment of incompetents and true virtue deprived of its only possible foundation in social life.

> No more sincere friendships; no more real esteem; no more well-based confidence. Suspicions, offenses, fears, coldness, reserve, hate, betrayal will hide constantly under that uniform and false veil of politeness, under that much vaunted urbanity which we owe to the enlightenment of our century.[43]

The key to Rousseau's critique may well be provided by the central term in each of these two sentences; urbanity destroys "real esteem" and produces "coldness"—i.e., it makes impossible the affections or sentiments which attach one man to another, and in so doing removes

---

[40] Ibid. (9); Lettre à Grimm (P, III, 60); Préface à Narcisse (P, II, 967–69 and 962, n.), where Rousseau puts himself in the position of the "foreigner"; Second Discourse, Part 2 (P, III, 175). Cf. Dernière Réponse (P, III, 74): "Someone who makes himself useful works for others; someone who only thinks of making himself agreeable only works for himself."

[41] First Discourse, Part 1 (P, III, 8).

[42] Ibid. (7–10); Observations (P, III, 51–52); and esp. Lettre à Lecat (P, III, 98): "I saw that men of letters spoke incessantly of equity, moderation, and virtue, and that it was under the sacred safeguard of these noble words that they surrendered themselves impudently to their passions and vices." Note that Rousseau does not explicitly distinguish between civic virtue and private virtue (the duties of a man and of a citizen) within the First Discourse; see Part 2 (24 and n., 26).

[43] Ibid., Part 1 (8–9).

the only effective check on the "more powerful motives." The corruption of morals due to politeness does not consist in mere conformity, but in the destruction of social bonds which could restrain men from following nothing but their own self-interest. Society becomes merely a "herd," devoid of both "friendship" among individuals and "love of the fatherland."[44]

B · HISTORICAL EVIDENCE OF THE COINCIDENCE OF
ENLIGHTENMENT AND CORRUPTION

Having described as moral corruption the very things that his contemporaries praised as signs of civilization, Rousseau connects the way of life of his time with the enlightenment:

> Such is the purity our morals have acquired. . . . It is for literature, the sciences, and the arts to claim their share of such a wholesome piece of work.[45]

Activities that Rousseau himself had praised at the outset of the *Discourse* now appear in a different light:

> When there is no effect, there is no cause to seek. But here the effect is certain, the depravity real, and our souls have been corrupted in proportion to the advancement of our sciences and arts toward perfection.[46]

But such moral corruption is not "a misfortune particular to our age"; since "the evils caused by our vain curiosity are as old as the world," Rousseau must seek an explanation in history, thereby intentionally enlarging the question posed by the Academy of Dijon.[47]

[44] *Ibid.* Cf. the *Préface à Narcisse* (P, II, 967), where Rousseau attributes the destruction of true affection to philosophy in particular: "The taste for philosophy relaxes all the bonds of esteem and benevolence which attach men to society . . . as a result of reflecting on humanity, as a result of observing men, the philosopher learns to appreciate them according to their value, and it is difficult to have great affection for what one scorns. . . . Family, fatherland, become for him words void of sense; he is neither relative, nor citizen, nor man; he is philosopher." Cf. *Second Discourse*, Part 1 (P, III, 156). On the decisive role of affections as the basis of virtue, see above, chap. I, § 5, and the references there cited.
[45] *First Discourse*, Part 1 (P, III, 9).
[46] *Ibid.*
[47] *Préface à Narcisse* (P, II, 964–65): "The question [of the Academy] . . . contained another more general and more important one concerning the influence of the culture of the sciences on the morals of peoples. It is the latter, of which the first is only a consequence, that I set myself to examine with care." Cf. *First Discourse*, Exordium (P, III, 5), where Rousseau adds to the question of the prize competition in restating it.

Rousseau then announces what could be called a general "law of history," of which eighteenth-century Europe is but one example:

The daily ebb and flow of the ocean's waters have not been more steadily subject to the course of the star which gives us light during the night than has the fate of morals and integrity been subject to the advancement of the sciences and arts. Virtue has fled as their light dawned on our horizon, and the same phenomenon has been observed in all times and in all places.[48]

As evidence of this rule, Rousseau describes the cultivation of the sciences and arts, and the consequent degeneration of morals, virtue, and taste, in Egypt, Greece (by implication, especially Athens), Rome, the Ottoman Empire, and China; in contrast, solid morals coincided with "disdain" for enlightenment among the early Persians, the Scythians, the Germans, the early Romans, and the modern Swiss.[49]

The historical evidence is so arranged, however, that one is led to go beyond the correlation between science and moral decay; the five corrupt peoples (assuming that "Greece" stands for fifth-century Athens) all had empires whereas the five virtuous peoples were independent and free nations. The conquest of other peoples seems to be connected to the rise of science, the corruption of morals, and the loss of freedom. Rousseau's argument is subtler than appears at first glance, for under the moralistic criticism of enlightenment is a related but quite different *political* criticism of conquest and empire.[50]

[48] *Ibid.*, Part 1 (10). Note that Rousseau compares his generalization concerning history with a physical law of nature; as a philosopher, he accepts the validity of scientific truth based on the observation of "phenomena."

[49] *Ibid.* (10–11). The central example of corruption is Imperial Rome, whereas the central example of virtue is the German people, "whose simplicity, innocence, and virtue a writer [i.e., Tacitus]—tired of tracing the crimes and foul deeds of an educated, opulent, and voluptuous people [i.e., the Romans under the Empire, who conquered the Germans]—took comfort in describing." Note the implication that a wise man living in corrupt society can understand the true virtue of an uncorrupted peoples (precisely because he is no longer bound by "love of the fatherland"); Rousseau appeals to the prior examples of Tacitus—and, as is clear in the sequel, Socrates—to justify his conception of true knowledge (i.e., knowledge consistent with virtue).

[50] Egypt had a ruler who tried to "conquer the world"; Greece was "formerly populated by heroes who twice conquered Asia"; Rome was a "world capital" which imposed a "yoke" on "so many other peoples"; Constantinople was the "capital of the Eastern Empire which seemed destined to be capital of the world"; China is an "immense country" and "vast empire." All five corrupt peoples lost their freedom after the development of the sciences and arts: "Egypt . . . was conquered"; Greece fell under the "yoke of the Macedonian,"

A similar device occurs in Part 2, where Rousseau ostensibly lists seven poor peoples who were militarily superior to civilized and wealthy ones. The Persians were conquered by Alexander the Great (referred to in the text only as "a prince who was poorer than the least significant Persian satrap"); the Scythians successfully resisted the invasions of the Persians (identified only as "the world's most powerful kings"); Republican Rome, when it "had nothing," defeated the "rich Republic" of Carthage; Imperial Rome, "after devouring all the wealth of the universe, was the prey of people [i.e., the Huns and Vandals] who did not even know what wealth was"; although poor, the "Franks conquered the Gauls, and the Saxons England"; the Swiss (identified as "a group of poor mountaineers") defeated the Austrian Hapsburgs in 1315 and 1386 and the Duke of Burgundy in 1476; and the Dutch (called "a handful of herring-fishers") successfully revolted against Philip II of Spain (1566–79). As reflection on these examples shows, however, the victors were not always poor, ignorant peoples, and the conquered not always rich, enlightened, and corrupt.[51]

If one looks carefully at this list, and compares it with the examples cited in the First Part, Rousseau's lesson is perhaps clearer. The peoples listed as having been conquered by poor or less civilized rivals

and afterwards, "always enslaved, never experienced anything in her revolutions but a change of masters"; Rome fell "under the yoke she had imposed" on others and became the "plaything of barbarians"; the history of Constantinople, full of the "most heinous in betrayals, assassinations, and crimes," is the very model of the last stage of the state of nature in which there exists only the relation of "master and slave" (cf. *Second Discourse*, Part 2 [P, III, 187, 191]); China fell under "the yoke of the ignorant and coarse Tartar" and is not "free." Five peoples are listed as having conquered Egypt: the Persians, Greeks, Romans, Arabs, and Turks; Persia, the only one of these that is also listed among the five uncorrupted peoples, is also the only one praised at that point for having "conquered" others with ease and the only one whose conquest in turn, by the Greeks, is specifically referred to (*First Discourse*, Part 1 [P, III, 10–11]). The connection between external conquest and domestic slavery is made explicit in the *Second Discourse*, Part 2 (186, 188); in the *Dernière Réponse*, Rousseau hints that there may be an "inverse proportion" between the "extent of states" and the "morals of citizens" (P, III, 87, 79).

[51] *First Discourse*, Part 2 (P, III, 20). Rousseau presents the evidence in such a way as to obscure the fact that Alexander the Great had already conquered Greece before defeating Persia, that Republican Rome no longer really "had nothing" at the time of the Punic Wars, and that the Dutch were a prosperous commercial people when they defeated the Spanish; although the Franks and Saxons were uncivilized peoples, the Gauls and the English that they conquered were not highly civilized and corrupted empires.

were, with the exception of the rich Republic of Carthage and the fifth-century Gauls and English, monarchies or empires: Persia, Imperial Rome, Austria, Spain; the victors were, with the exception of the Macedonians under Alexander the Great, either barbarian peoples (Scythians, the Huns and Vandals who conquered Rome, Franks, and Saxons) or republican states (the Roman Republic, the Swiss, and the Dutch). There is a tendency, albeit not an invariable rule, that civilized monarchies are defeated either by barbarian peoples (who are in a sense "free" even if they have kings) or republics; the only civilized form of government which is not conquered is an uncorrupted republic. Of the five peoples used as examples of healthy morals in Part 1, at least three—the Roman Republic, the Scyths, and the Swiss—are also examples of the superior military power of poor peoples in Part 2. Persia, the only one in the list of five virtuous peoples in Part 1 which is described as having sought conquest, is treated in Part 2 as a powerful kingdom which could not defeat the Scythians and was itself conquered by Alexander the Great; it is an example of a society which becomes corrupted by its political institutions (and not by the sciences and arts as such).[52]

Even granted that the tacit equation of corruption with empire or monarchy is incomplete, these comparisons reveal the extent to which Rousseau arranged examples to reinforce his central thesis, including some historical events (e.g., the victories of Alexander the Great over Persia, Rome over Carthage, and the Dutch over Spain) which are not as conclusive as they seem. The need for extreme care when comparing different societies is reinforced by the treatment of Athens and Sparta in Part 1. Having classed Greece as a whole among corrupted peoples, Rousseau suddenly admits that this is inaccurate:

> Could I forget that in the very heart of Greece rose that city as renowned for its happy ignorance as for the wisdom of its laws, that republic of demi-gods rather than men, so superior did their virtues seem to human nature? O Sparta! you eternally put to shame a vain doctrine! While the vices which accompany the fine arts entered Athens together with them, while a tyrant there so carefully col-

[52] This is all the more striking because the education of the Persian kings is used by Rousseau as the central example of the teaching of virtue as contrasted with science (*ibid.*, Part 2 [24–25n.]; see nn. 53 and 72 of this chapter). Persia is explicitly treated as a society lacking enlightenment in *Dernière Réponse* (P, III, 81). That Rousseau's principles are radically anti-monarchical but impossible to present openly, at least at this point in his career, is clearly indicated in *Observations* (P, III, 43).

lected the works of the prince of poets, you chased the arts and
artists, the sciences and scientists away from your walls.[53]

Sparta is the example of a republic of virtuous, unenlightened men;[54]
Athens, usually taken as the model of a democracy even by Rousseau
himself, is described as a tyranny whose form of government is connected to its enlightenment by the fact that Pisistratus (tyrant from
554 to 527 BC) was reputed to be the first to transcribe and organize
the poetry of Homer.[55]

The difficulty to which this contrast is exposed can be revealed by
referring to Rousseau's earlier remark concerning the corruption of
Greece:

> Consider Greece, formerly populated by heroes who twice con-
> quered Asia, once at Troy and once in their homeland. Nascent
> learning had not yet brought corruption into the hearts of its in-
> habitants, but the progress of the arts, the dissolution of morals,
> and the yoke of the Macedonian followed each other closely.[56]

If Greece was still uncorrupted at the time of the Persian wars (490
to 480 BC), when it defeated "Asia" for the second time, then clearly
the tyranny of Pisistratus in the sixth century BC is not representative
of the Athens which "became the home of politeness and good taste"
two centuries later.[57]

[53] First Discourse, Part 1 (P, III, 12). Cf. the citation of Montaigne's praise
for the education of Sparta (ibid., Part 2 [24–25n.]): whereas the Persians
educated only their kings to be virtuous and are an example of a wealthy
kingdom that was conquered, the Spartans educated their entire citizen body
to be virtuous; ignorance does not produce virtue unless it is combined with
"wise" laws.

[54] Rousseau's remark, earlier in Part 1, that before the enlightenment "human
nature, basically, was no better" (8) must be read in the light of his praise
of the Spartans as seeming "demi-gods" by comparison with modern men;
cf. Préface à Narcisse (P, II, 964n.). The argument of some commentators
that Rousseau had not developed his conception of man's natural goodness
at the time of writing the First Discourse (see P, III, 1242) cannot be confirmed by this text, and is rendered questionable by the defenses which immediately followed its publication. See esp. Dernière Réponse (P, III, 80 and
n.): Préface d'une Seconde Lettre (P, III, 106); and below, pp. 243–45.

[55] Cf. the treatment of Athens as the model of a direct democracy, Second
Discourse, Ded. (P, III, 114).

[56] First Discourse, Part 1 (P, III, 10). Note that in Part 2, Rousseau seems
to give Sparta credit for making "Asia tremble" (20), apparently ignoring
the role of Athens in the Persian wars.

[57] It cannot be said that these references are anachronistic because they
are, when carefully read, consistent; the action of Pisistratus represents a
potential vulnerability to "emerging letters" which was lacking in Sparta.
Rousseau was well aware of the details of chronology, and did not hesitate

Rousseau admitted later that the comparison between Athens and Sparta was not in itself conclusive, however revealing it may be as a symbol of the difference between enlightened and virtuous peoples.

> But since comparisons between one people and another are diffi-
> cult, because it is necessary to include a very large number of ob-
> jects and they always lack exactitude in some respect, one is much
> surer of what one does in following the history of a given people,
> and comparing the progress of its knowledge with the revolutions
> of its morals.[58]

Although Sparta provides the classic example of civic virtue which Rousseau was to use throughout his works, the argument of the *First Discourse* does not rest on the comparison of corrupt societies to the model of unenlightened patriotism, but rather on the history of each society in itself.

Rousseau's emphasis on historical development was of course to bear fruit in the radically evolutionary understanding of human nature in the *Second Discourse*, but even the apparently superficial comparisons in the *First Discourse* take on clearer meaning when looked at in this light. We have already noted the way Rousseau appears to use Persia at different epochs as an example of a virtuous people in Part 1 and a corrupted, weak monarchy in Part 2. The treatment of Rome in this regard is even more evident: in both Parts 1 and 2, Rousseau asserts that the Roman Republic was unenlightened and virtuous, the Roman Empire enlightened and corrupt.[59] Likewise, Athens itself is treated as one of "the ancient republics of Greece" which shared the virtues of the classical city until, having become enlightened, it was corrupted.[60]

The historical examination of individual societies, as distinct from comparisons between different societies, is the true basis of Rousseau's argument.

> Now the result of this examination is that the noble time, the time
> of virtue of each people, was that of its ignorance; and that in the
> measure that it became learned, artistic, and philosophic, it lost its
> morals and its probity; it fell back in that respect among the ranks

---

to pick up such errors in the works of his critics (e.g., *Observations* [P, III, 55]; *Dernière Réponse* [P, III, 81]).

[58] *Ibid.* (76). On the difficulty of comparing different societies, see also *Observations* (P, III, 43).

[59] *First Discourse*, Part 1 (P, III, 7, 10–11, 14–15); Part 2 (20, 23).

[60] *Ibid.*, Part 1 (7, 10, 12–14); Part 2 (22, 23).

of the ignorant and vicious nations which are the shame of humanity.[61]

The historical pattern of each society is more complex than appears from a superficial comparison of virtuous, unenlightened peoples to enlightened and corrupt ones; in effect, there seem to be *three* stages of history in each society: the "barbarism of the first ages" (in which a people is "ignorant and vicious"), the "time of virtue" (during which, for some peoples at least, ignorance is combined with healthy morals), and the corruption resulting from the development of the sciences, arts, and letters.

The difference between the first and last of these stages is revealing: even if both can be called vicious, at least the ignorant barbarians are capable of being reformed:

> All barbarian peoples, even those who are without virtue, nevertheless always honor virtue, whereas as a result of progress, learned and philosophic peoples finally come to hold it in ridicule and scorn it. Once a nation is at this point, one can say that corruption is at its height and it is impossible to hope for remedies.[62]

Prefiguring the conception of historical evolution on which the *Second Discourse* and *Social Contract* are based, Rousseau allows for the possibility of bringing a barbarian people to virtue by means of appropriate laws; the legislator can hope to succeed among uncivilized and superstitious barbarians, but not among corrupted, civilized nations.[63]

As Rousseau repeatedly asserted in his defense of the *First Discourse*, if "science necessarily engenders vice," it does not follow that "ignorance necessarily engenders virtue"; such "ways of arguing" may be good for "rhetoricians" or "children," but not for "philosophers."[64] Within the *First Discourse*, Rousseau is solely concerned

[61] *Dernière Réponse* (P, III, 76).

[62] *Ibid.* Note that Rousseau does not here go back to the stage prior to cruel barbarian society; the "savage society" which was the "best for man" need not be identical to the barbarian society which can be called "vicious." Cf. *Préface à Narcisse* (P, II, 964n. and 969–70n.); *Second Discourse*, Part 2 (P, III, 170–71).

[63] *Contrat social*, II, viii (P, III, 385); *Observations* (P, III, 56): "a people once corrupted has never been seen to return to virtue"; *Préface à Narcisse* (P, II, 971): "the morals of a people are like the honor of a man; it is a treasure that must be conserved, but that one no longer recovers when it has been lost."

[64] *Dernière Réponse* (P, III, 75–76 and n.); *Observations* (P, III, 54); *Lettre à Grimm* (P, III, 62).

with the conditions which render virtue impossible, not those which can create a healthy society and which were ultimately to be spelled out in the *Social Contract*. Hence his historical analysis in Part 1 concludes:

> Behold how luxury, licentiousness, and slavery have in all periods been punishment for the arrogant attempts we have made to emerge from the happy ignorance in which eternal wisdom had placed us.[65]

Enlightenment limits the possibility of salutary political action because it produces *slavery* as well as moral dissolution. Since Rousseau's audience comes from an enlightened society ruled by a monarch, he does not emphasize the political teaching implicit in his argument; Rousseau believed—but was hesitant to assert—that the only remedy was a republican regime which, to be realized in France, would require a "great revolution."[66]

C · THE SCIENCES AS CAUSES OF CORRUPTION

Historical evidence of the simultaneity of moral corruption and popular enlightenment is not sufficient for Rousseau; his intention, primarily developed in Part 2 of the *First Discourse*, is to prove that the coincidence of these phenomena is the result of a "necessary link" which can be discovered by "reasoning" about the "sciences and arts in themselves."[67] Rousseau begins by referring to the "ancient tradition" that the sciences were invented by "a god who was hostile to the tranquility of mankind," adding a footnote referring to the fable of Prometheus as it was retold by Plutarch:

> "The satyr," an ancient fable relates, "wanted to kiss and embrace fire the first time he saw it; but Prometheus cried out to him: Satyr, you will mourn the beard on your chin, for fire burns when one touches it." This is the subject of the frontispiece.[68]

When one of his critics failed to understand this scene as it was pictured in the frontispiece, Rousseau explained its relevance:

> I would have thought I insulted my readers and treated them as

[65] *First Discourse*, Part 1 (P, III, 15).
[66] *Observations* (P, III, 56).
[67] *First Discourse*, Part 1 (P, III, 16); *Préface à Narcisse* (P, II, 965).
[68] *First Discourse*, Part 2 (P, III, 17n.). Rousseau also refers to the Egyptian tradition which attributes the art of writing to the God Thoth; cf. the story as told by Socrates in Plato's *Phaedrus* 274c–275b.

— 225 —

children if I interpreted for them such a clear allegory; if I told them that the torch of Prometheus is that of the sciences, made to animate the great geniuses; that the Satyr, who seeing the fire for the first time, runs to it and wants to embrace it, represents the vulgar men who, seduced by the brilliance of letters, indiscreetly give themselves over to study; that the Prometheus who cries and warns them of the danger is the Citizen of Geneva.[69]

Reinforcing Rousseau's explicit praise of the sciences as suited to the "great geniuses," this interpretation implies that Rousseau himself is the carrier of a science which will be useful to some men—and indeed, to mankind as a whole—provided that the vulgar do not study it.

This implication is especially clear if one refers to the passage of Plutarch, of which Rousseau quotes only the first half; according to the source, Prometheus warns the Satyr:

It burns when one touches it, but it gives light and warmth, and is an implement serving all crafts providing one knows how to use it well.[70]

There is no question that the sciences and arts can be useful to man; Rousseau is primarily concerned with their effects on "vulgar men" who study without having the "genius" necessary to succeed.[71] The people at large should not be given "a foolish education which adorns our mind and corrupts our judgment"; instead of being taught foreign languages, poetry, and rhetoric, children should "learn what they ought to do as men" (i.e., "their duties").[72]

[69] *Lettre à Lecat* (P, III, 102).

[70] Plutarch, "How to Profit by One's Enemies," trans. Frank Cole Babbitt, *Moralia* (Loeb Classical Library; London: Heinemann, 1928), II, 7–8. Cf. Plato, *Protagoras* 320d–322a: "Prometheus, therefore, being at a loss to provide any means of salvation for man, stole from Hephaestus and Athena the gift of skill in the arts, together with fire—for without fire it was impossible for anyone to possess or use this skill—and bestowed it on man. In this way man acquired sufficient resources to keep himself alive, but had no political wisdom" (trans. W. K. C. Guthrie; in Edith Hamilton and Huntington Cairns, eds., *Plato: Collected Dialogues* [New York: Bollingen, 1961], p. 319). Note that Socrates later says he "follows the lead" of Prometheus (*ibid.*, 361d). Cf. also Plato, *Statesman* 274c.

[71] *Observations* (P, III, 39): "These truly learned men are few in number, I admit; for to use science well, it is necessary to unite great talents and great virtues; now this is what one can barely expect of a few privileged souls, but what one should not expect from a whole people." Cf. *Dernière Réponse* (P, III, 78); *Préface à Narcisse* (P, II, 970–71).

[72] *First Discourse*, Part 2 (P, III, 24 and 24–25n.). In the note, Rousseau

— 226 —

V · FIRST DISCOURSE

Rousseau's attempt to discourage the vulgar from scientific pursuits is subtly underlined by the order of his presentation in Part 2 of the *Discourse*, which begins with a discussion of the sciences (despite his indication in Part 1 that the letters and arts "naturally" precede true science).[73] His remarks concerning the causes of the sciences and arts are hardly concise and explicit:

> Thus the sciences and arts owe their birth to our vices. . . . What would we do with arts without the luxury that nourishes them? . . . our sciences are . . . born in idleness. . . . Luxury rarely develops without the sciences and arts, and they never develop without it. . . . Granted that luxury is a sure sign of wealth. . . . What brings about all these abuses if not the disastrous inequality introduced among men by the distinction of talents and the debasement of virtues?[74]

In one of his earliest defenses of his thesis, Rousseau reveals more fully his conception of the "genealogy" which produced the sciences:

> The first source of evil is inequality; from inequality came wealth, for the words poor and rich are relative and wherever men are equal there will be neither rich nor poor. From wealth was born luxury and idleness; from luxury came the fine arts, and from idleness the sciences.[75]

It appears that Rousseau follows an order in the *First Discourse* which exactly reverses the historical "genealogy" which he later suggested in defending it (and spelled out in the *Second Discourse*).

Since Rousseau blurs the necessary preconditions for the development of the sciences and arts, it is hard to interpret Part 2 of the *First Discourse* as a detached, scholarly examination of the causes of moral corruption; by giving priority to the corruption produced by popular enlightenment, Rousseau increases the rhetorical effect of his criticism of the study of science by the vulgar. He begins by suggesting that the objects of sciences as well as its cultivation presuppose vices:

---

quotes three paragraphs from Montaigne's "Of Pedantry" (*Essays*, I, xxv). He changes the order of these paragraphs, however, so that the account of the education of Persian kings, derived from Plato's *Alcibiades* (1.121D–122A), becomes the central paragraph in the note. On the criticism of "our education," cf. *Préface à Narcisse* (P, II, 966) and above, chap. I, § 2–3.

[73] Cf. *First Discourse*, Part 1 (P, III, 6), cited in n. 34 of this chapter, with Part 2 (16).

[74] *Ibid.*, Part 2 (17–19, 25).   [75] *Observations* (P, III, 49–50).

In a word, who would want to spend his life in sterile speculations if each of us, consulting only the duties of man and the needs of nature, had time for nothing except his fatherland, the unfortunate, and his friends?[76]

Supposing that one "seeks the truth really sincerely," which is not the case for those who actually want to "gain distinction,"[77] it is exceedingly difficult to distinguish between the "infinite combinations" of error and the "one form" of truth; even so, "it is hardest of all" to "know how to make good use of truth," whereas errors are "a thousand times more dangerous than the truth is useful." "We" (i.e., the common men) gain "so little that is useful" from the discoveries of "illustrious philosophers" that Rousseau appeals to them as judges of the dangers of enlightenment.[78]

In so doing, however, Rousseau immediately changes the target of his criticism, for he does not ask the "illustrious philosophers" to condemn their own works:

Reconsider, then, the importance of your products; and . . . tell us what we must think of that crowd of obscure writers and idle men of letters who uselessly consume the substance of the State.[79]

Rousseau attacks "futile declaimers," who attempt to distinguish themselves by being "enemies" of "public opinion,"[80] the "best known philosophers," who are like "charlatans" claiming theirs is the sole truth,[81] and above all "that crowd of elementary authors who have

[76] *First Discourse*, Part 2 (P, III, 17–18). Although Rousseau here mentions the "duties of man" and the "needs of nature" separately, he does not yet indicate that they are opposed principles of guidance for civilized man.
[77] *Ibid.* (18, 27).
[78] *Ibid.* (18–19). At this point Rousseau alludes to a series of discoveries of theoretical science in order to identify the "illustrious philosophers" to whom he appeals. While there is some question concerning the specific thinkers concerned—cf. P, III, 1249; Havens, ed., *Discours sur les Sciences et les Arts*, pp. 214–16—it is likely that Rousseau refers at least to Newton, Descartes, and Bacon, the three "preceptors of the human race" named later in Part 2 (P, III, 29). On this passage, see n. 83 of this chapter.
[79] *First Discourse*, Part 2 (P, III, 19).
[80] *Ibid.* Cf. Pref. (3): speaking as a common man to the Academy of Dijon, Rousseau shows a deference to common opinion which he explicitly denies in publishing his work; since philosophy requires "paradoxes" which, if spread, will "undermine the foundations of faith," it is necessary to present the truth in a form which will not "annihilate virtue" and only such works are consistent with the "true philosophy." Cf. Strauss, "On the Intention of Rousseau," pp. 471–73.
[81] *Ibid.*, Part 2 (27). Rousseau's attack on the "best known philosophers" is more direct and less qualified than his attack on theoretical scientists like

removed the difficulties that blocked access to the temple of the muses and . . . those compilers of works who have indiscreetly broken down the door of the sciences and let into their sanctuary a populace unworthy of approaching it."[82]

Despite the dangers of all theoretical inquiry, the "illustrious philosophers" to whom Rousseau refers indirectly are "the most enlightened of our learned men and our best citizens"; since their works contain "sublime knowledge" and there *is* a degree to which "the truth is useful," the principle that "every useless citizen is a pernicious man" does not apply as such to the "great geniuses." Rousseau does not explicitly adopt the twentieth-century distinction between "science" (i.e., natural science) and "philosophy," but his remark that the knowledge of man's "nature, his duties, and his end" is "greater and more difficult" than the understanding of "the vastness of the universe" (for example, by Newton) indicates that the consequences of studying different objects may be different. Research concerning natural phenomena has a slightly different status than the study of man's place in the whole because the latter is less likely to produce useful truths, and because the dangers of error are more radical.[83] It is "re-

Newton; after indirectly referring to four thinkers—Berkeley, Spinoza (or perhaps Holbach or La Mettrie), Mandeville (or perhaps St. Aubin) and Hobbes—Rousseau attacks by name "the dangerous dreams of Hobbes and Spinoza" (*ibid.* [28]).

[82] *Ibid.* This criticism cannot but apply, among others, to Voltaire, who had published a vulgarization of Newtonian physics.

[83] *Ibid.*, Part 1 (6); Part 2 (18–19, 29). Rousseau identifies seven discoveries of the "illustrious philosophers" to whom he appeals; the first two refer to astronomy as explained by Newtonian physics, the third to mathematics, the fourth to theological metaphysics ("how man sees everything in God"); the fifth to the metaphysical analysis of man ("how the soul and body could be in harmony"), the sixth to astronomy, and the last to biology. Rousseau then lists five possible criteria of utility for these discoveries: "had you taught us none of these things, would we be consequently fewer in number, less well governed, less formidable, less flourishing, or more perverse" (18–19). The central discovery of the philosophers, representing the little utility derived for most men, concerns theology; metaphysics is unnecessary as a basis of religious belief (cf. above, pp. 73–89). The central criterion of utility is the "formidability" of modern peoples (i.e., military power); in defending the *First Discourse* Rousseau explicitly asserts the connection between modern science or technology and the military power which permitted the conquest of America by European powers (*Dernière Réponse* [P, III, 91]). That Newtonian astronomy could be militarily useful is evident if one considers the conditions under which Athens was finally defeated in the Peloponnesian War, and especially the effect of Nicias' erroneous interpretation of a lunar eclipse, which contributed to the Athenian defeat in the Sicilian campaign. Cf. *ibid.* (83–84); *Lettre à Grimm* (P, III, 67–68); and Thucydides, *Histories*, VII, 51. It should be added that the last of Rousseau's criteria of utility appears to

flecting on humanity" and "observing men" which produces the most pernicious effects on the character of philosophers themselves, and those who "desire to distinguish themselves" in such pursuits produce "absurd systems" which are "dangerous" because they lead to "scorn for the duties of man and the citizen."[84]

The paradox that the most important subjects of knowledge are the most dangerous is particularly acute in modern times: the "dangerous dreams of Hobbes and Spinoza" (i.e., attempts to "study man and know his nature") and the "even more dangerous works that reek of the corruption of morals in our century" will be perpetuated "from age to age" by the discovery of the art of printing and by the "immortality" that a corrupted public opinion bestows on such authors. The two most dangerous forms of science are moral philosophy, because it attempts to teach the principles on which virtue is based rather than providing an example of virtuous actions, and the vulgarization of theoretical natural science.[85]

Rousseau's attack on the vulgarization of science is particularly

---

be paradoxical: Rousseau asks the illustrious philosophers if the common men would be "*more* perverse" without their scientific discoveries. Rousseau elsewhere answers this question by affirming: "Men are perverse; they would be even worse if they had the misfortune to be born learned" (*First Discourse*, Part 1 [P, III, 15]); he clearly expects the negative answer from the philosophers—a negative which would not have been possible had he asked whether men would be "*less* perverse" without science (since vice has other causes). Consider *Préface à Narcisse* (P, II, 964n.).

[84] *Ibid.* (965–67). Cf. *Observations* (P, III, 46): "was there a single one of all the [philosophical] sects that did not fall into some dangerous error; and what will we say of the distinction between two doctrines so avidly received by all philosophers and by which they secretly taught sentiments contrary to those they taught publicly. . . . The history of this deadly doctrine, written by a learned and sincere man, would be a terrible blow to ancient and modern philosophy." As a spokesman for the common man (*nous*), Rousseau criticizes the "esoteric doctrine" which is "born with philosophy"; as a philosopher, Rousseau uses this doctrine himself to a certain extent. The "pernicious maxims and impious dogmas" of philosophic sects exemplify the dangers of science, but as long as such doctrines are taught "secretly" they cannot directly corrupt the mass of men. Indeed, in a sense this note is a warning to the French *philosophes* (who were often secretly atheists): their principles were based on the assumption that popular enlightenment is salutary, yet they failed to see that their personal beliefs required an esoteric doctrine lest they be exposed to persecution.

[85] *First Discourse*, Part 1 (P, III, 6); Part 2 (18–19, 28). Rousseau connects the study of "morality" (moral philosophy) with the vice of human pride more directly than natural sciences like astronomy and physics (17); the "deadly paradoxes" of learned writers are those that "undermine the foundations of faith" and "annihilate virtue" by making ridiculous "the old fashioned words of fatherland and religion," and such thinkers "devote their talents and their philosophy to destroying and debasing all that is sacred among men" (19). The revival of enlightenment has produced "physicists, geometers,

---

strong because he implies that both "illustrious philosophers" and "us" (common men) should condemn it.[86] Rousseau thereby tacitly raises a question concerning his praise of the academies of his time, which he describes as a "remedy" for the "harmful plants" of enlightenment:

> Following this example [of nature], that Great Monarch, whose glory will only acquire new luster from age to age, drew out of the very bosom of the sciences and arts, sources of a thousand disorders, those famed societies simultaneously responsible for the dangerous trust of human knowledge and the sacred trust of morals —which these societies protect by the attention they give both to maintaining within themselves the total purity of their trusts, and to requiring such purity of the members they admit.[87]

Rousseau speaks of the Academies as a "check on men of letters"; they share the "insufficiency" of "ordinary remedies" because such institutions do not discourage popular study of the sciences and arts, and are concerned with the morals of their members rather than the moral effects of their members' writings on society as a whole.[88]

---

chemists, astronomers"; Rousseau does not speak of modern moral or political philosophers except to criticize them (26–28). It is the study of virtue—the public teaching of how men should be virtuous—which destroys the practice of virtue; popular morality depends on examples of good action and the "instruction of peoples in their duties" by those with political power, not on the "lessons" of scientific or philosophic "doctrine" (Part 1 [14]; Part 2 [27, 30]). Cf. *Préface à Narcisse* (P, II, 967–70). Although Strauss equates "metaphysics" and "purely theoretical science" as the "kind of science which is incompatible with virtue," Rousseau seems to distinguish between "metaphysics" as a kind of philosophy which has "no model in nature" (and is useless or at least unnecessary in order to produce virtue), and theoretical science, based on a philosophic understanding of natural phenomena (and a necessary "basis" of the Socratic wisdom defended by Rousseau). Granted this qualification, Strauss's conclusion is exact: "Theoretical science, which is not intrinsically in the service of virtue . . . must be put into the service of virtue in order to become good" (*Natural Right and History*, pp. 262–63).

[86] Cf. the different addressees of the rhetorical questions concerning the "crowd of obscure writers" and "that crowd of elementary authors" (*First Discourse*, Part 2 [18–19, 28–29]).

[87] *Ibid.*, Part 2 (26). This appparent praise of Louis XIV (so often called the *grand monarque*) is misleading; although he founded many Academies, including the Académie Royale des Beaux Arts (1648), Académie des Inscriptions et Belles-Lettres (1663), Académie d'Architecture (1671), Académie des Beaux-Arts at Rome (1677), and Académie des Jeux Floreaux (1694), the first and most important of these "famous societies"—the Académie Française—was founded in 1635 by Louis XIII. Cf. the indirect criticism of Louis XIV in the *Second Discourse*, Part 2 (P, III, 183), referred to above, p. 187, n. 131.

[88] *First Discourse*, Part 2 (P, III, 25–27). The result of enlightenment is

Even the exceptions to the rule seem to prove it. On two occasions, Rousseau praises the Academy of Dijon indirectly:

> There are a thousand prizes for noble discourses, none for noble actions. But let someone tell me whether the glory attached to the best of the discourses which will be crowned by this Academy is comparable to the merit of having founded the prize?[89]

And later, after describing Academies as "remedies," he adds:

> Those academies which will choose, for the prize competitions honoring literary merit, subjects suited to revive love of virtue in the hearts of citizens, will show that such love reigns among them, and will give the peoples that very rare and sweet pleasure of seeing learned societies devote themselves to disseminating throughout the human race not merely pleasant enlightenment, but also salutary teachings.[90]

---

that "one no longer asks if a man is upright, but rather if he is talented; nor of a book if it is useful, but if it is well written" (25); Academies are therefore poor guardians of the "sacred trust of morals." They are equally incompetent in their responsibility for "the dangerous trust of human knowledge" since most of their work is useless and prevents the discussion of the true problems facing philosophy. Note Rousseau's alteration of the questions posed by the Academy of Dijon (see above, pp. 111–12, and p. 218, esp. n. 47), and cf. the criticism of the Académie Française in *Lettre à Lecat* (P, III, 98–99) and *Second Discourse*, Part 1 (P, III, 148). Rousseau himself had, of course, experienced the frustration of presenting his new theory of musical notation to the Academy of Sciences, which delegated the judgment of his project to three members "assuredly of merit, but of whom not one knew music, or at least enough to be capable of judging my project . . . as soon as they wanted to speak of the foundations of the system, they did nothing but reason falsely. . . . The only solid exception that could be made against my system was made by Rameau [who was not in the Academy] . . . it is not astonishing that it was not made by an academician, but it is astonishing that all these greatly learned men, who know so many things, know so little that each should only judge concerning his own specialty" (*Confessions*, vii [P, I, 282–86]). Cf. also *Dernière Réponse* (P, III, 82); *Observations* (P, III, 56–57).

[89] *First Discourse*, Part 2 (P, III, 25).

[90] *Ibid.* (26–27). These two passages may well be the "two easily recognized additions of which the Academy might not have approved" that Rousseau mentions in the Preface (3). In both cases, the text would read smoothly without the sentences in question, which would have been base flattery in a competitive Discourse (and would have flatly contradicted Rousseau's attack on such means of gaining favor). Commentators have suggested other possible passages as the two additions to the text—see Havens' critical edition (pp. 175–76) and Bouchardy's note (P, III, 1240)—but they usually refer to passages whose omisssion would interrupt the flow of the exposition. Given the general tenor of the *First Discourse*, it is unlikely that Rousseau added his

It is a "very rare and sweet pleasure" for the people—represented by Rousseau insofar as he speaks for the common man—to see an Academy that is concerned with "salutary teachings" like those presented in the *First Discourse*. This is hardly a surprising criticism when one considers the fact that most Academies, and most especially a provincial Academy like that of Dijon, were composed of members of "the crowd of elementary authors" which Rousseau so directly attacks.[91]

Since popular enlightenment is the source of corruption, the proper remedy—at least with respect to the sciences—does not really lie in the proliferation of academies. If science is restricted to the "preceptors of the human race" who themselves need no teachers, and "Princes call the true wise men to their courts," then the "union of science and virtue" (only possible for a few) could be realized.[92]

> Only then will one see what can be done by virtue, science, and authority, animated by noble emulation and working together for the felicity of the human race. But so long as power is alone on the one side, intellect and wisdom alone on the other, learned men will rarely think of great things, Princes will more rarely do noble ones, and the people will continue to be vile, corrupt, and unhappy.[93]

Kings must "renounce the old prejudices . . . that the art of leading people is more difficult than that of enlightening them"; the true philosophers, who know how to "engage men to do good willingly," are "the men most capable of advising" rulers, and only under their guidance is it possible to create a society that is not based on "constraint."[94]

---

praise of the Swiss, his reference to "the sense of that original liberty for which [men] seem to have been born," or his reference to "disastrous inequality"; the Academy of Dijon would have had no particular reason for singling out these particular passages as having bolder implications than the remainder of the *First Discourse*.

[91] See *Lettre à Lecat* (P, III, 97–98); and esp. *Préface à Narcisse* (P, II, 967n.): "The Republic of Genoa, seeking to subjugate the Corsicans more easily, did not find a surer method than to establish an Academy among them." Cf. Bouchardy's notes (P, III, 1240–41 and 1254).

[92] *First Discourse*, Part 2 (P, III, 29–30); *Observations* (P, III, 39).

[93] *First Discourse*, Part 2 (P, III, 30).

[94] By proposing that "constraint" be replaced by "willing" or free obedience, Rousseau implicitly equates freedom and virtue; the conclusion contains perhaps the clearest condemnation of hereditary monarchy in the *First Discourse*. Cf. *Économie Politique* (P, III, 259), where virtue is treated as a means to establish freedom, not vice versa. Need it be added that Rousseau's remedy

To be sure, the restriction of theoretical science to the few with "genius" is not, according to Rousseau, as pressing or necessary in a corrupt society as it would otherwise be; once a people has become morally depraved, popular enlightenment can do little harm.

> Earthly powers, love talents and protect those who cultivate them. Civilized peoples, cultivate talents: happy slaves, you owe to them that delicate and refined taste on which you pride yourselves. . . .[95]

Since the "sciences and arts have strengthened" "thrones" (i.e., monarchies), the establishment of scientific academies and the encouragement of enlightenment by kings are consistent with the political order suited to corrupt societies in which men are no longer free.[96]

The possible utility of the public cultivation of the sciences and arts is based on two considerations: the fragility of popular enlightenment and the irreversibility of moral corruption:

> There is only one step from knowledge to ignorance; and the alternation from one to the other is frequent among peoples; but a people, once corrupted, has never been seen to return to virtue.[97]

Even if an attempt is made to reform morals by trying to prevent "vanity," "idleness," "luxury," and by reinstituting the "first equality" among men, "their hearts once spoiled will always remain so"; since reform is not likely to succeed, it is to be preferred that corrupted nations love their slavery and accept it. Moreover, since enlightenment is easily destroyed, it does not preclude the only possible method of restoring virtue in modern times.

> There is no longer a remedy, except for some great revolution almost as greatly to be feared as the evil that it could cure, and that it is blameworthy to desire and impossible to foresee.[98]

---

appears to be a return to the Platonic notion that the best possible regime requires a "philosophic ruler"? As Harry J. Benda has pointed out, however, the alliance between philosophers and kings parallels "the second best solution propounded in Plato's *Laws*" rather than the regime of the *Republic*. See "Rousseau's Early Discourses (1)," *Political Science* (Wellington, New Zealand), v (September 1953), 20, n. 30.

[95] *First Discourse*, Part 1 (P, III, 7). While Rousseau's apparently ironical recommendation to the "Earthly powers" corresponds with his own remedy, the recommendation to the "civilized peoples" fits only "slaves."

[96] *Ibid.*, Part 1 (7n.); Part 2 (26); *Observations* (P, III, 56–57).

[97] *Ibid.* (56).

[98] *Ibid.* The "almost" deserves emphasis. Cf. *Jugement sur le Projet de Paix Perpétuelle* (P, III, 599–600); *Jugement sur la Polysynodie* (P, III, 637–40).

The only solution to the political and moral depravity of enlightened Europe lies in a complete revolution which cannot legitimately be demanded openly, which might well fail to have the desired effects, and which in any event cannot hope to succeed without the guidance of the kind of theoretical knowledge contained in Rousseau's *Discourse*.

D · THE MORAL CORRUPTION CAUSED BY THE ARTS: LUXURY

Just as Rousseau's condemnation of science rests on a distinction between two kinds of science, one of which can be "good," his attack on the corrupting effect of the arts rests on a distinction between useful and pernicious kinds of art. Rousseau argues that common men ("we") would have no use for the arts without "the luxury that nourishes them"; since "luxury rarely develops without sciences and arts, and they never develop without it," Rousseau shifts his concern from the arts "in themselves" to the arts connected with luxury. He attacks the modern philosophic doctrine that "luxury produces the splendor of states" because it denies "that good morals are essential to the stability of empires, and that luxury is diametrically opposed to good morals."[99]

> What will become of virtue when one must get rich at any price? Ancient politicians incessantly talked about morals and virtue, those of our time talk only of business and money.[100]

The orientation of modern political thought toward increasing the wealth of men and nations presupposes a rejection of virtue as the end of civic life; if the value of men is measured in purely economic terms—as was, for example, suggested in Sir William Petty's *Essay in Political Arithmetick*—calculations are ultimately reduced to questions of "money," which can buy "everything except morals and citizens."[101]

[99] *First Discourse*, Part 2 (P, III, 17, 19).
[100] *Ibid.* (19). Cf. *Dernière Réponse* (P, III, 79): "I see that people always talk to me of fortune and grandeur. I myself talked about morals and virtue." It need hardly be added that the juxtaposition of these two remarks shows the extent of Rousseau's identification with the "ancient politicians."
[101] *First Discourse*, Part 2 (P, III, 19–20). Rousseau ridicules both Petty and Montesquieu without naming them: "One [of our political writers] will tell you that in a given country a man is worth the price he would fetch in Algiers; another, following this calculation, will discover some countries where a man is worth nothing and others where he is worth less than nothing." Cf. Montesquieu, *Esprit des Lois* XXIII, xvii: "Sir [William] Petty supposed, in his calculations, that a man in England is worth what he could be sold for in

Prevailing ideas, based on the assumption that economic wealth contributes to the strength of a civil society, justify luxury as a necessary means to this end; Rousseau counters with the assertion that luxury undermines not merely virtue, but the stability and power of a political society.

> Precisely what, then, is at issue in this question of luxury? To know whether it is more important for Empires to be brilliant and transitory or virtuous and durable.[102]

Rousseau does not deny that luxury produces "magnificence," "brilliance," and "surprising works" of art (as long as standards of taste permit),[103] but he argues that neither moral virtue nor political power is consistent with the cultivation of the fine arts.

> While living conveniences multiply, arts are perfected, and luxury spreads, true courage is enervated, military virtues disappear, and this too is the work of the sciences and of all those arts which are exercised in the shade of the study.[104]

Although a kind of courage is possible under modern conditions, military power ultimately depends on "force and vigor" and requires "military training" for the citizenry; the mercenary armies of Rousseau's time may be capable of establishing domestic tyranny or even of defeating an enemy at battle, but because they are vulnerable to "the rigor of the seasons and the bad weather," they cannot be used to "conquer the world and make virtue reign in it" as did the Roman legions. Even a desire to establish a "durable empire" by conquest presupposes "military regulations" which forbid "citizens the prac-

---

Algiers. That could only be true for England: there are countries where a man is worth nothing; there are some where he is worth less than nothing." (Paris: Garnièr Freres, 1949), II, 114–15. On the use of wealth to buy the "appearances of all the virtues and talents," cf. *Second Discourse*, Part 2 (P, III, 189).

[102] *First Discourse*, Part 2 (P, III, 20).

[103] *Ibid.*, Part 1 (7, 12, 14–15); Part 2 (21–22). Cf. the "brilliance" praised in the "ancient republics of Greece" (*ibid.* [23]).

[104] *Ibid.*, Part 2 (22). Note that the criticism of the "study of the sciences" in this context is subordinated to the attack on the arts and luxury, and directed against "idle and sedentary occupations" on the part of "the princes and nobility of Italy" or the citizen body as a whole. According to the *Lettre à Grimm*, true knowledge of men or of physics is impossible if one "does not leave his study" (P, III, 62). Cf. *Observations* (P, III, 55): "there are great men among us . . . which does not prevent the people from being very corrupt."

tice of those tranquil and sedentary occupations which, by weighing down and corrupting the body, soon enervate the vigor of the soul."[105]

Concentrating on the accumulation of wealth and encouraging those arts which presuppose luxury precludes true greatness:

> No, it is not possible that minds degraded by a multitude of futile concerns could ever rise to anything great, and even if they should have the strength, the courage would be lacking.[106]

The emphasis on satisfying the desires created by luxury leads to a subordination of all duties to such artificial needs:

> Someone who has once become accustomed to prefer his life to his duty will hardly delay to prefer also things which make life easy and agreeable.[107]

The possibility of subordinating individual pleasure and comfort to any noble end is therefore undermined by the development of arts oriented toward luxury; political orders based on commerce and industry necessarily become corrupt.

The justification of luxury on the ground that it "gives bread to the poor" may well be true, but "if there wasn't any luxury, there

---

[105] *First Discourse*, Part 1 (P, III, 15); Part 2 (23). Reconsider the seven examples of weak and rich nations conquered by "poor" ones (20), analyzed above, pp. 220–21: of the victors (the Macedonians, Scythians, early Romans, Huns and Vandals, Franks and Saxons, Swiss, or Dutch), only the two modern examples are known as peoples who cultivated the arts, and both were more oriented to practical or useful arts than to the "fine arts"; the Swiss and Dutch did not conquer others but established their own independence. Rousseau adds two examples taken from Montaigne's "Of Pedantry" (*Essais*, I, xxv)—the ravages of the Goths in Greece and the French victories in Italy under Charles VIII; two examples of victories of which corrupt modern armies are still capable—Hannibal's victories over Rome at Cannae and Trasimene (successful battles which did not prevent the ultimate defeat of wealthy Carthage), and Caesar's use of his army to destroy the Roman republic; and two examples of the military feats of which the moderns are incapable— Hannibal's crossing of the Alps and Caesar's conquest of Gaul (*First Discourse*, Part 2 [22–23]). Lasting conquest, as distinct from ephemeral victory or internal repression, is impossible for a society which has succumbed to luxury and wealth. Cf. *Dernière Réponse* (P, III, 82): "War is sometimes a duty and is not made to be a trade. Every man should be a soldier for the defense of his freedom; none should be one to take away that of another: and to die for one's country is too noble to be left to mercenaries."
[106] *First Discourse*, Part 2 (P, III, 20). Cf. *Dernière Réponse* (P, III, 79): modern men are even incapable of "vices which presuppose courage and firmness."
[107] *Lettre à Grimm* (P, III, 64).

wouldn't be any poor."[108] The vices which Rousseau attributes to "politeness" and "urbanity" at the outset of the *First Discourse* can equally well be attributed to luxury and "the disastrous inequality introduced among men by the distinction of talents and the debasement of virtues." The arts play a decisive role in this respect, for they are the activities par excellence which lead talented men to try to satisfy the unnecessary desires of the wealthy by conforming to "public opinions."

> Luxury cannot possibly reign in one order of citizens without soon insinuating itself in all the others . . . luxury corrupts everything— both the rich who enjoy it and the miserable who envy it.[109]

Even the virtue of the "wise man" "languishes and dies out" when he sees "glory . . . so poorly distributed."

> In the long run, this is what must everywhere be the result of the preference given to pleasing talents rather than useful ones, and what experience since the revival of the sciences and arts has only too well confirmed.[110]

There is a fundamental distinction between the "useful" and the merely "pleasant" arts, and it is the cultivation of the latter which is a principal source of vice in civil society.

Rousseau's criticism is thus directed primarily against the "fine arts" and "letters," rather than the "arts" as such; popular enlightenment is dangerous precisely because it leads men to respect those arts which have the least value in the eyes of the true philosopher.[111]

---

[108] *Dernière Réponse* (P, III, 79). Cf. *Préface à Narcisse* (P, II, 969): "Strange and fatal constitution, in which accumulated wealth always facilitates the accumulation of more, and in which it is impossible for someone who has nothing to acquire anything; in which the good man has no way of avoiding misery; in which the greatest rascals are the most honored; and in which one must necessarily renounce virtue to become a decent man."

[109] *Observations* (P, III, 51).

[110] *First Discourse*, Part 2 (P, III, 26).

[111] *Ibid.*, Part 1 (7n.): "arts of amusement and superfluities"; (8): "the art of pleasing"; (9): "letters," "spectacles"; (10): "letters," "fine arts," "obscene authors"; (11): "letters"; (12): "fine arts," "artists"; (13): "artists," "poets"; (14): "artists," "architects, painters, sculptors, and comedians"; Part 2 (19): "obscure writers and idle men of letters"; (21): "every artist," "dramatic poetry," "marvels of harmony"; (23): "paintings, engravings, jeweled vessels," "cultivate the fine arts," "letters"; (24): "compose verses," "the art of making [error and truth] unrecognizable to others by specious arguments"; (25): "statues," "paintings," "noble discourses"; (26): "poets, musicians, painters"; (27–28): "printing . . . the art of perpetuating

It would be preferable for all who could not go far in the learned profession to be rebuffed from the outset and directed into arts useful to society. He who will be a bad versifier or a subaltern geometer all his life would perhaps have become a great cloth maker.[112]

Rousseau's attack on the fine arts is thus combined with a praise of "useful arts" (even though such crafts as the making of cloth are radically unnatural and can be criticized because they create new needs and increase the mutual dependence of men).[113]

The shift of Rousseau's attention from the arts in general (i.e., all human inventions which make life more comfortable) to the fine arts or the arts based on pleasure and opinion is made clear by his long quotation from Plato's *Apology*, which presents Socrates, "the wisest of men," as an authority who endorses ignorance and criticizes the sciences and arts:

"I examined the poets," he says, "and I consider them to be men whose talent deceives themselves and others, who claim to be wise men, who are taken to be such, and who are nothing of the kind.

"From poets," continues Socrates, "I turned to artists. No one knew less of the arts than I; no one was more convinced that artists possessed some very beautiful secrets. However, I perceived that their condition is no better than that of the poets, and that they are all under the same illusion. Because the most skillful among them excel in their specialty, they consider themselves the wisest of men. This presumption altogether tarnished their knowledge in my eyes. So it was that, putting myself in the place of the oracle, and asking myself which I would rather be, what I am or what they are, to know what they have learned or to know that I know nothing, I answered myself and the god: I want to remain what I am.

"We do not know, neither the sophists, nor the poets, nor the orators, nor the artists, nor I, what is the true, the good, and the beautiful. But between us there is this difference: although those men know nothing, they all think they know something; whereas

---

the extravagances of the human mind." When Rousseau restates his thesis in the *Préface à Narcisse*, he twice speaks of "the taste for letters, philosophy, and the fine arts" as the source of moral corruption (P, II, 966).

[112] *First Discourse*, Part 2 (P, III, 29).

[113] *Dernière Réponse* (P, III, 95): "Everything beyond physical necessities is the source of evil. Nature gives us only too many needs, and it is at the least a very great imprudence to multiply them unnecessarily and thus to place one's soul in greater dependence." Cf. the context with *Second Discourse*, Part 1 (P, III, 135–36, 139–40); n. XVI (220–21).

if I know nothing, at least I am not in doubt of it. Hence all that superior wisdom attributed to me by the oracle reduces itself solely to my firm conviction that I am ignorant of what I do not know.[114]

This passage is a reorganized paraphrase of the *Apology*, in which Socrates explains to the Athenian jury that his bad reputation was the result of his effort to refute the Delphic oracle's statement that he was "the wisest man in the world."

To understand more fully Rousseau's point, it is necessary to consider the original text he claims to quote:

"I went to interview a man with a high reputation for wisdom, because I felt that here if anywhere I should succeed in disproving the oracle . . . it was one of our politicians that I was studying when I had this experience—and in conversation with him I formed the impression that although in many people's opinion, and especially in his own, he appeared to be wise, in fact he was not. . . . I reflected as I walked away: Well, I am certainly wiser than this man. It is only too likely that neither of us has any knowledge to boast of, but he thinks that he knows something which he does not know, whereas I am quite conscious of my ignorance. At any rate it seems that I am wiser than he is to this small extent, that I do not think that I know what I do not know.

After this I went on to interview a man with an even greater reputation for wisdom, and I formed the same impression. . . . After I had finished with the politicians, I turned to the poets, dramatic, lyric, and all the rest. . . . I decided that it was not wisdom that enabled them to write their poetry, but a kind of instinct or inspiration . . . the very fact that they were poets made them think that they had a perfect understanding of all other subjects, of which they were totally ignorant. . . .

Last of all I turned to the skilled craftsmen. I knew quite well that I had practically no technical qualifications myself, and I was sure that I should find them full of impressive knowledge. In this I was not disappointed. They understood things which I did not, and to that extent they were wiser than I was. But, gentlemen, these professional experts seemed to share the same failing which I had noticed in the poets. I mean that on the strength of their technical proficiency they claimed a more perfect understanding of every other subject, however important, and I felt that this error

[114] *First Discourse*, Part 1 (P, III, 13).

— 240 —

more than outweighed their positive wisdom. So I made myself spokesman for the oracle, and asked myself whether I would rather be as I was—neither wise with their wisdom nor stupid with their stupidity—or possess both qualifications as they did. I replied through myself to the oracle that it was best for me to be as I was.[115]

Although Rousseau calls this Socrates' "eulogy of ignorance," in its context it is a demonstration of his superior wisdom; more important, Rousseau's rearrangement of the passage results in a considerable shift in emphasis: Socrates' interrogation of the democratic politicians of Athens, who have "a high reputation of wisdom," is completely deleted, and the "skilled craftsmen" or "artisans" are replaced by "artists."[116]

Since these changes in Socrates' speech imply that Rousseau refuses to criticize either democratic statesmen or artisans, it is necessary to explain why Rousseau silently shifts from criticizing the arts simply (as he could well have done given his conception of the state of nature) to a criticism of the fine arts and artists.[117] The useful arts —and the craftsmen who perform them—are not subject to the same

[115] *Apology* 21b–22e, trans. Hugh Tredennick; in Hamilton and Cairns, eds., *Plato: Collected Dialogues*, pp. 7–9.

[116] Strauss has noted the implications of these changes (see *Natural Right and History*, p. 256, n. 10). Neither the substitution of "artists" for "artisans" nor the silence with respect to politicians can be taken as an accident, for Rousseau elsewhere makes the identical changes in referring to a different passage of the *Apology*. Cf. *Dernière Réponse* (P, III, 73n.): "In the trial brought against [Socrates], one of his accusers pled for the artists, another for the orators, the third for the poets, all for the pretended cause of the Gods." The *Apology* 23e–24a reads: "There you have the causes which led to the attack on me by Meletus and Anytus and Lycon, Meletus being aggrieved on behalf of the poets, Anytus on behalf of the artisans and politicians, and Lycon on behalf of the orators" (*Plato: Collected Dialogues*, p. 10). Note also that in the *First Discourse*, Rousseau has Socrates conclude that "We do not know, neither the sophists, nor the poets, nor the orators, nor the artists, nor I, what is the true, the good, and the beautiful"; this sentence is Rousseau's own invention. In the original, Socrates does not openly attack the sophists; quite the contrary, earlier in his speech, Socrates says that "I mean no disrespect for such knowledge [as is claimed by philosophers or sophists], if anyone really has it," and he proceeds to mention Gorgias, Prodicus, and Hippias (all known as sophists) as being "qualified to teach" for a fee (*Apology* 19c–e).

[117] Note also that when Rousseau quotes only half of Prometheus' speech to the Satyr as it is recorded by Plutarch, he thereby equates fire with "the sciences made to animate great geniuses," despite the fact that the fable, both in Plutarch and in Plato's *Protagoras*, explicitly connects the gift of fire with the useful crafts and *not* with the theoretical sciences. (See the passages cited above, pp. 225–26.)

criticism as the sciences and fine arts because they can be performed without engendering the risk of popular enlightenment or moral corruption. Hence Rousseau later formulated the "true rules of appreciation of art and industry" as follows:

> I say that in everything, the art whose usage is the most general and the most indispensable is the one that merits the most esteem, and that the one for which the fewest other arts are necessary merits it in addition above all the more subordinate ones, because it is freer and closer to independence.[118]

According to this criterion, agriculture is the "first and most respectable of all the arts," and indeed, Rousseau praises farming in the *First Discourse* (despite the fact that in the *Second Discourse* he treats agriculture as an art which "civilized man and ruined the human race").[119] Given the existence of civil society, only useful arts like agriculture are worthy of respect because they presuppose less interdependence of men and are therefore more compatible with equality and freedom.

Rousseau's preference for agriculture and other useful arts is thus a silent indication of his political preference for an egalitarian regime which maintains the greatest freedom of the citizens; in this context, his refusal to repeat Socrates' condemnation of the democratic politicians of Athens takes on fuller meaning. Behind Rousseau's praise for the ancient's conception of virtue is an attack on the "slavery" of modern political societies, and most particularly of monarchic government:

> While government and laws provide for the safety and well-being of assembled men, the sciences, letters, and arts, less despotic and perhaps more powerful, spread garlands of flowers over the iron chains with which men are burdened, stifle in them the sense of that original liberty for which they seemed to have been born, make them love their slavery, and turn them into what is called civilized peoples.[120]

[118] *Émile*, III (G, 216). Cf. the subordinate place of artisans in Plato's *Republic*, esp. II.274b–d; III.415a–c; and above, pp. 101–02.

[119] *Émile*, III (G, 216); *First Discourse*, Part 1 (P, III, 8, 10, 14); *Observations* (P, III, 63–64); *Dernière Réponse* (P, III, 79): "when agriculture was in honor, there was neither misery nor idleness, and there were many fewer vices"; *ibid.* (92): "the citizen whose needs attach him to the plow" is "more usefully occupied than a geometer or anatomist." Cf. *Second Discourse*, Part 2 (P, III, 171).

[120] *First Discourse*, Part 1 (P, III, 6–7).

What seems at first a rhetorical flourish condemning all civil society as "iron chains" is most particularly an attack on the destruction of freedom in highly civilized societies, which Rousseau subtly identifies with the kind of monarchy or empire based on social inequality, luxury, and enlightenment. For Rousseau, the defense of virtue is identical with the defense of political freedom under laws.[121]

E · THE *First Discourse* AS A SUMMARY OF
ROUSSEAU'S TEACHING

It appears that Rousseau's condemnation of the enlightenment is not merely a rhetorical paradox, since it is based on the "reasons" which form the "trunk" of his entire system of thought. The extent to which the *First Discourse* prefigures Rousseau's later philosophic works can be seen if his "proof" that the sciences and arts cause moral corruption is restated in terms of the historical evolution of mankind. Rousseau's point of departure is the assertion that the state of "happy ignorance" is natural to men, apart from their virtue or viciousness:

> Peoples, know once and for all that nature wanted to keep you from being harmed by knowledge just as a mother wrests a dangerous weapon from her child's hands; that all the secrets she hides from you are so many evils from which she protects you, and that the difficulty you find in educating yourselves is not the least of her benefits. Men are perverse; they would be even worse if they had the misfortune to be born learned.[122]

Nature is benevolent, caring for man as a "mother" cares for "her child." The extent to which this passage points to Rousseau's ultimate principle that nature is "good" can be recognized if one considers the three different ways in which ignorance can be compatible with uncorrupted morals. Even within the *First Discourse* Rousseau hints at the distinction between the goodness of the pure state of nature, the

---

[121] *Ibid.*, Part 1 (7n.): "Princes always view with pleasure the spread, among their subjects, of the taste for arts of amusement and superfluities. . . . For, besides fostering that spiritual pettiness so appropriate to servitude, they very well know that all needs the populace creates for itself are so many chains binding it." Consider the historical examples analyzed above, pp. 219–25; and *Dernière Réponse* (P, III, 81): Greece simultaneously "renounced virtue and sold its freedom"; "laws and morals" go together.

[122] *First Discourse*, Part 1 (P, III, 15). Cf. *Dernière Réponse* (P, III, 75): "Ignorance is neither an obstacle to good nor to evil; it is only the natural state of man."

civic virtue of the patriotic citizen, and the moral virtue of the true philosopher living in a corrupted society.

The simple goodness and freedom of ignorant men living close to nature (if not in the pure state of nature) is implicit in the contrast between those who are subjugated by kings and "the American savages who go naked and live on the yield of their hunting." Although Rousseau states that the "needs of the body are the foundations of society," the bodily needs that produce the "chains" on men are not physically necessary, and without them a people cannot be "subjugated" because no "yoke" can be "imposed on men who need nothing."[123]

> One cannot reflect on morals without delighting in the recollection of the simplicity of the earliest times. It is a lovely shore, adorned by the hands of nature alone, toward which one incessantly turns one's eyes and from which one regretfully feels oneself moving away.[124]

As the writings in defense of the *First Discourse* make clear, this praise of the "first times" refers to man's "primitive goodness" in his original status of natural ignorance, during which men were neither virtuous nor vicious in the precise sense.[125]

Prior to the era in which men are "farmers" or "courtiers" there is a more natural model of healthy morals:

[123] *First Discourse*, Part 1 (P, III, 6–7 and 7n.).
[124] *Ibid.*, Part 2 (P, III, 22).
[125] *Dernière Réponse* (P, III, 74): "The first men were very ignorant. How could one dare say that they were corrupt in times when the sources of corruption were not yet opened"; *ibid.* (78): "It is not necessary to make us so afraid of purely animal life, nor to consider it as the worse state into which we could fall; for it would be much better to resemble a lamb than a bad angel"; *ibid.* (80): "Before these frightful words *yours* and *mine* were invented, before there was that kind of cruel and brutal men called masters and that other kind of rascally and lying men called slaves; before there were men abominable enough to dare have a surplus when other men were dying of hunger; before mutual dependence forced them all to become cheats, jealous, and traitors; I would really like someone to tell me in what could consist these vices, these crimes, for which they are so emphatically reproached" (original italics); *ibid.* (92): "a heifer does not need to study botany to learn how to find her fodder, and the wolf devours his prey without thinking of indigestion. To reply to that, will one take the side of instinct against reason? That is exactly what I ask." Cf. *ibid.* (81–82); *Préface d'une Seconde Lettre* (P, III, 105); and esp. *Observations* (P, III, 42): "I am reproached for affecting to take my examples of virtue from the ancients. There is plenty of appearance that I could have found even more [examples] if I could have gone back even further."

The good man is an athlete who likes to compete in the nude. He disdains all those vile ornaments which would hamper the use of his strength, most of which were invented only to hide some deformity.[126]

Although this remark evokes the classical Greek custom of gymnastic exercises in the nude, it more directly criticizes clothing as an "invention" and points to the epoch in which men, like animals, did not need to disguise their physique in order to "use their forces" in the "combats" necessary for survival.[127]

If the "image of the simplicity of the earliest times" (i.e., the state of nature) is only indirectly suggested in the text of the *First Discourse*, the combination of ignorance and virtue in an uncorrupted society is more openly asserted.

When innocent and virtuous men enjoyed having gods as witnesses of their actions, they lived together in the same huts.[128]

Evoking the ancient custom of household gods (which was characteristic of early Greek and Roman society as well as many other primitive peoples),[129] Rousseau suggests the possibility of a "rustic" or rural society as the model of unenlightened virtue.[130] The comparison between an agricultural life and urban, commercial, and philosophic activity is of course not merely meant by Rousseau in a historical

[126] *First Discourse*, Part 1 (P, III, 8).

[127] *Dernière Réponse* (P, III, 95): "One could bet 100 to 1 that the first man who wore shoes was a punishable man, unless he had sore feet. As for us, we are too obliged to wear shoes to be dispensed from having virtue"; *Observations* (P, III, 41): "In many respects knowledge is useful, but savages are men and do not feel that necessity." Cf. the criticism of "the ancient athletes in the public games," *Préface à Narcisse* (P, II, 966); the references cited in n. 113 of this chapter; and *Lettre à d'Alembert* (G, 231).

[128] *First Discourse*, Part 2 (P, III, 22).

[129] See esp. Fustel de Coulanges, *The Ancient City* (New York: Doubleday Anchor, 1956), chap. IV, *et passim*.

[130] *First Discourse*, Part 1 (P, III, 8): "the rustic clothes of a farmer"; Part 2 (26): the remaining "citizens" in modern times are "dispersed in our abandoned countryside"; (28): "the ignorance and rusticity of our fathers"; *Lettre à Raynal* (P, III, 31): "It is true that the Author prefers rusticity to the proud and false politeness of our century, and he gave the reason for it"; *Dernière Réponse* (P, III, 74–75): "Through the obscurity of the ancient times and the rusticity of ancient peoples, one sees among a number of them very great virtues, above all a severity of morals which is an infallible mark of their purity, good faith, hospitality, justice, and what is very important, a great horror for debauchery, the fertile mother of all the other vices." Cf. *First Discourse*, Part 1 (10, 11, 14); Part 2 (27); *Lettre à Grimm* (P, III, 60, 63–64); *Dernière Réponse* (P, III, 79, 82, 92).

sense, but it does suggest that the rural character of virtuous societies was connected to their lack of enlightenment.

Rousseau does not restrict the possibility of virtuous life to "farmers, hunters, and shepherds" (like the Scythians or early Germans); Sparta and early Rome were *cities*, and civic virtue as well as military strength are attributed to republican peoples who develop arts or commerce (as did some of the early Greek cities, the Dutch, and the Swiss). The decisive point is that arts be limited to those which are useful; virtuous republics—far from "scorning agriculture"—are led and "made famous" by rustic men.[131]

The clearest statement of the civic virtue which Rousseau attaches to the republican city is, of course, the speech he puts in the mouth of Fabricius, "restored to life" to see the "pompous appearance" of the Roman Empire:

> "Gods!" you would have said, "what has become of those thatched roofs and those rustic hearths where moderation and virtue used to dwell? What disastrous splendor has succeeded Roman simplicity? . . . Let other hands win fame by vain talents; the only talent worthy of Rome is that of conquering the world and making virtue reign in it. When Cineas took our Senate for an assembly of Kings, he was dazzled neither by vain pomp nor by affected elegance. . . . O citizens, he saw a sight that could never be produced by your wealth or all your arts, the most noble sight that has ever appeared beneath the heavens, the assembly of two hundred virtuous men, worthy of commanding Rome and governing the earth."[132]

Civic virtue is to be found at its highest in an unenlightened or rustic republic like Sparta or early Rome, and the example of such cities

---

[131] *First Discourse*, Part 1 (P, III, 10): Rome was "founded by a shepherd and made famous by farmers"; (11): the Swiss are "that rustic nation"; (14): in corrupt Rome "agriculture was scorned." Cf. Part 2 (26): the contemporary French also "scorn . . . those who give us bread and who give milk to our children." Cf. *Contrat social*, IV, iv (P, III, 445–46).

[132] *Ibid.*, Part 1 (14–15). Cf. Plutarch's "Life of Pyrrhus," *Lives of the Noble Grecians and Romans* (New York: Modern Library, n.d.), p. 481f. That Fabricius' speech is an attack on monarchy in the name of republicanism is underlined when he asks: "Are the spoils of Carthage the booty of a flute player [i.e., Nero]?" Rousseau makes this even clearer when he adds: "what did I make that great man [Fabricius] say that I might not have put into the mouth of Louis XII or Henry IV?" A French king would hardly have said that the Roman Senate was "the most noble sight that has ever appeared beneath the heavens." Note that for Rousseau the Romans "subjugated other peoples as much by the veneration due to their morals as by the effort of their arms"; conquest based purely on force is not respectable. *Dernière Réponse* (P, III, 75n.).

is the most decisive historical proof that "virtue is not incompatible with ignorance."[133]

Just as the conceptions of the natural freedom and goodness of the state of nature, and the civic freedom and virtue of a legitimate republic are both implicit in the *First Discourse*, it can also be said that his model of the moral freedom of the virtuous individual in a corrupt society, ultimately developed in the *Émile*, is present in the appeal to Socrates as the "wisest of men in the judgment of God." Once civic virtue has been destroyed, those who possess the kind of science or wisdom consistent with virtue are necessarily isolated and politically impotent; it is possible that Cato "did nothing for his country," but like Socrates "he did a great deal for the human species in giving it the purest model of virtue that ever existed."[134] Unlike Cato, however, Socrates is the classic example of the private or nonpolitical virtue which is the only resource for an individual living in a corrupt time; whereas Cato exemplifies the "greatness" of a man who "leads others" and finds "his happiness in that of all," Socrates lived when "Athens was already lost" and "instructed some private persons" to find "happiness" in their own virtue.[135] Rousseau's own position is in a sense closer to Socrates than to Cato, despite his praise for the latter, because he speaks to the "human race," and particularly to the wise who live in morally corrupt societies, rather than to his own countrymen. Insofar as Rousseau does not "propose to overthrow existing society" in the *First Discourse*, his critique of the sciences and arts prefigures the attempt to lead a few men to a good life which is essentially private, based on the kind of wisdom or natural religion taught in the *Émile* and the *Nouvelle Héloïse*.[136]

---

[133] *Ibid.* (75, 83–84, 86–89); *Lettre à Grimm* (P, III, 69).

[134] *Dernière Réponse* (P, III, 87). On Socrates and Cato as models of those who leave behind "no other moral precept than the example and memory of their virtue," see *First Discourse*, Part 1 (P, III, 14); *Observations* (P, III, 55); *Lettre à Grimm* (P, III, 65); *Dernière Réponse* (P, III, 94); *Second Discourse*, Part 2 (P, III, 192).

[135] "Let us dare oppose even Socrates to Cato: the former was more a philosopher, the latter more a citizen. . . . The former instructed some private persons, fought the sophists, and died for the truth: the other defended the state, freedom, and the laws against the conquerors of the world, and quit the earth when he no longer saw a country to serve" (*Économie Politique* [P, III, 255]).

[136] *Dernière Réponse* (P, III, 95); *Observations* (P, III, 55–57); and esp. *Préface à Narcisse* (P, II, 972–73): "Insofar as my writings have edified the small number of good people, I have done them all the good I could, and it is perhaps also serving them usefully to offer the others objects of distraction preventing them from thinking about [the good people]."

Since a careful reading of the *First Discourse* shows it to contain the key elements of Rousseau's mature thought, his claims concerning the unity of his "system," his decision to reveal his principles incompletely at first, and the proper order of reading his major writings seem to be justified; there is no reason to assume that Rousseau's fundamental philosophic position changed radically between the publication of the *First Discourse* in 1750 and the appearance of the *Émile* and *Social Contract* in 1762.[137] It is therefore appropriate at this stage to summarize the essential structure of Rousseau's philosophy, using the *First Discourse* as the point of departure. In so doing, it will become evident why what Rousseau called his three "major writings" are largely devoted to the examination of the limits of political action.

Within the *First Discourse*, Rousseau suggests an alliance between political power and theoretical science as the "remedy" for the "vile, corrupt, and unhappy" condition of the people. This echo of Platonic thought, in the face of the modern belief that popular enlightenment is beneficial and unlimited progress possible, presupposes the classic distinction between "knowledge" and "opinion." Rousseau denies the possibility of true wisdom except on the part of a very few "privileged souls"; the many orient their lives in terms of public opinions or prejudices which are mere conventions devoid of philosophic truth.[138]

Rousseau's defense of popular ignorance rests fundamentally on considerations of morality, for the many are only capable of virtuous action when inspired by social prejudices and sentiments which are not, strictly speaking, rational; unlike some of the *philosophes*, Rousseau defends philosophically absurd popular prejudices pro-

[137] See again the *Préface d'une Seconde Lettre* (P, iii, 105–06), partially quoted in n. 7 of this chapter. For the contrary argument, see, among others: Vaughan, "Introduction," *Du Contrat social* (Manchester: University Press, 1918), pp. xxxiv-xxxvii; Bertrand de Jouvenel, "Essai sur la Politique de Rousseau," in J. J. Rousseau, *Du Contrat Social* (Geneva: Éditions du Cheval Ailé, 1947), p. 39; Benda, "Rousseau's Early Discourses (ii)," *Political Science*, VI (March 1954), 18, 25.

[138] See *Republic*, esp. the allegory of the ship, vi.488aff; the "divided line," vi.509dff; and the allegory of the cave, vii.514aff. Cf. *Dernière Réponse* (P, iii, 71n.): "There are very certain truths which at first glance seem absurdities, and which will always be so considered by most men. Go say to a man of the people that the sun is closer to us in winter than in summer, or that it has set before we cease to see it, and he will make fun of you." Rousseau's comparison of the "sentiment I defend" with such findings of modern natural science is indicative of the manner in which he adopts the Platonic view of knowledge.

vided that they are morally sound.[139] But in philosophy, "subjuga-
tion" to such prejudices can only produce error, whereas in civil society there is need of a guiding principle provided by the legislator—
or, more generally speaking, by good laws. Thus Rousseau's attempt
to free contemporary philosophic thought from its conventional prejudice in favor of enlightenment is simultaneously an attempt to lead
common men back to the kind of virtue which requires the subordination of personal desire to healthy conventional prejudices.[140]

Given the inability of the many to comprehend philosophic truth
and the variability of common opinion in different societies, the philosopher's view of the best human life must take into consideration
the necessary variation from one society to another and from one
man to another. In this respect, the contrast between civilized and uncivilized society is essential to an understanding of man's "nature, his
duties, and his end," for "the savage is a man and a European is a
man." Since "the government, laws, customs, and interests" characterizing European society "put private individuals in the necessity of
mutually and incessantly fooling each other, everything makes vice a
duty" for modern man. The philosopher (as distinct from the "semi-
philosopher") must therefore consider the historical fact that some
men—savages—"have no discussion of interest which divides them,"
so that "nothing leads them to fool one another." Even though "private interest speaks as loudly as among us, . . . love of society and care
of their common defense are the sole bonds that unite them"; "the
good man is the one who has no need to fool anyone, and the savage is such a man."[141]

Since the savages were good by nature, the law of history connecting moral corruption with the development of sciences and arts must

[139] For a striking example, see *Émile*, IV (G, 388–89n.).
[140] This dual perspective explains why commentators have seen Rousseau as
the defender of a bewildering array of traditional conceptions of "virtue."
For example, according to Schinz, Rousseau defends "calvinist virtue" in the
First Discourse (*État Present des Travaux sur J. J. Rousseau* [Paris: Société
d'Éditions les Belles Lettres, 1941], p. 178, and the references cited by Bouchardy [P, III, 1241]); for Georges May, it is "the virtue of silence, humility,
and obscurity" (*Rousseau par lui-même*, p. 53); for Bouchardy, following
the view that Rousseau is referring to the "famous men of Plutarch," it is a
"combatitive, active virtue" (P, III, 1241); for Henri Guillemin, Rousseau
has in mind the men "who still exist in the poor streets of Geneva, the
worker who thinks of God, who takes the Evangile seriously, and who leads
a courageous life" ("Presentation," *Contrat social, et al.* [Paris: Union Général
d'Éditions, 1963], p. 16); for Benda, the "virtuous man is, quite briefly, the
real citizen of antiquity, the *zoon politikon* of Aristotle" ("Rousseau's Early
Discourses [I]," p. 14).
[141] *Préface à Narcisse* (P, II, 969–70n.).

be seen in the broader context of human evolution. Rousseau is therefore forced to ascertain the status of savage society and to determine whether *any* bond between individual men is physically necessary, on the assumption that civil society need not be the "end" or natural perfection of the human species. He therefore transforms the "state of nature" from a philosophic abstraction into a historical epoch that must be studied from the perspective of modern natural science; when Rousseau does so, the first men appear to have been free and equal individuals who, while perfectible, lacked reason and language. The source of corruption and evil can not be attributed to man's nature, but to "ill-governed man"; the standard for judging goodness is the natural freedom of an animal who follows his own natural impulses.

Even if this conception of man's primitive state can be defended from the perspective of natural science, it is not sufficient; since humans are no longer mere animals, Rousseau must develop theoretical approximations of primitive freedom and goodness, suitable for men who have become perfected, developed reason, and can "fool each other." But given the natural science which Rousseau accepted and sought to conciliate with classical philosophy, it is impossible for him to formulate a single prescription for civilized man. Plato and Aristotle could admit a tension between the best individual life and the best society without abandoning a conception of that which is "naturally right" for thinking human beings; Rousseau could no longer leave the resolution of this tension to prudence once he had asserted that man was by nature a stupid animal. Rousseau was forced to present distinct theoretical analyses of the virtuous political regime and the virtuous civilized individual, for both are unnatural creations of man himself.

The healthy civilized society is a paradox from Rousseau's perspective because civilization tends to destroy a healthy society. Indeed, all society is subject to the risk of moral corruption and vice, which can arise among savages (who then become "barbarians") as well as civilized peoples (who then become "dissolute"). The creation of just laws and civic virtue is therefore only possible for a people which does not have "corrupted morals"; with very few exceptions, there is but one time in the history of any society when it is possible to establish a legitimate or free political regime.[142] Hence Rousseau's discovery of the pattern of human history primarily reveals the *limits* within which the legislator or statesman acts.

[142] *Contrat social,* ii, viii (P, iii, 384–86); ii, x (390–91); *Préface à Narcisse* (P, ii, 971 n.).

In the exceptional case of a people that can be given new laws, it is "necessary to begin by clearing the area and setting aside the old materials, as Lycurgus did in Sparta"—which is to say, with a "violent epoch" or "revolution"; "what makes the work of legislation difficult is less what must be established than what must be destroyed."[143] Since great wisdom and care is needed in such an enterprise, a theoretical science—what Rousseau was to call the "science of the legislator"—can contribute to the success of the founding, and it is one of the intentions of Rousseau's political writings proper to provide at least the outlines of such a science.[144] But since it is "rare" to find "the simplicity of nature joined to the needs of society," Rousseau's purely constructive political teaching cannot be solely devoted to this end, and in particular, it cannot be inconsistent with the needs of public opinion in societies which already have good laws or are already corrupt.

The rarity of the conditions necessary for establishing new laws determines the two principle objectives of Rousseau's political teaching: preservation of the morals of a healthy society and criticism of morally corrupt peoples. Indeed, the latter objective is a means to the former; because all civil society inevitably tends to foster inequality, wealth, luxury, enlightenment, urbanity, the desire for expansion, and corruption, it is necessary to preserve the small, simple and virtuous society from the specious prejudices of neighboring peoples who have become vicious.

Rousseau's task is therefore to prevent "injustice and violence from impudently taking the name of right and equity."[145] In a dissolute age, the violent and open rejection of the principles adopted by common opinion is necessary in order to show the few who are wise that public life no longer has a legitimate claim to respectability, while providing reasons that defend the morals and opinions of uncontaminated societies. This explains why Rousseau's thought could be so revolutionary in its consequences, despite his own statements that he feared revolution and merely attempted to preserve existing regimes.[146]

---

[143] *Second Discourse*, Part 2 (P, III, 180); *Contrat social*, II, viii (P, III, 385), where the founding of Sparta is given as an example of the "rebirth" of a state from "civil wars"; *ibid.*, II, x (391). Cf. *Observations* (P, III, 56), and Plato's *Republic* VI.501a.

[144] See below, esp. chaps. VI and VIII.

[145] *L'État de Guerre* (P, III, 610).

[146] Cf. *Observations* (P, III, 56); *Lettres Écrites de la Montagne*, vi (P, III, 809–12). Cf. Iring Fetscher, "Rousseau, auteur d'intention conservatrice et d'action révolutionnaire," *Rousseau et la Philosophie Politique* (Paris: Presses Universitaires de France, 1965), pp. 51–75.

Where good morals and laws still exist, their defense requires the insulation of common opinions from foreign ideas and examples that could lead to changes in existing customs:

> If I were chief of one of the peoples of dark Africa, I declare that at the frontier of the country I would raise a gallows, where I would hang without reprieve the first European who dared to penetrate the country and the first citizen who tried to leave it.[147]

This "reactionary" attitude, to use Jouvenel's phrase, rests on Rousseau's assertion that progress and change are not in themselves good:

> For customs are the morality of the people, and as soon as it ceases to respect them, it has no other rule except its passions, no other check except its laws, which can sometimes contain the wicked, but never make them good.[148]

Laws, however excellent, cannot in themselves produce a good society without a support in stable and respected customs and morals, for only the latter are truly rooted in individual habits and can lead men to virtue.

This limit on the possible efficacy of political institutions and laws is more closely related to Rousseau's concern for freedom than has usually been noted. Rousseau's notion of freedom often seems to be empty and not closely connected to virtue, even though he sometimes indicates that true civic freedom requires virtue.[149] For Rousseau, civic virtue cannot be defined in general terms (since it depends on the customs of each people, which in turn are determined to a large degree by "the nature of things"). In contrast, the prerequisites of civil freedom can be universally defined in terms of the general will. Since certain external conditions in modern times—most notably the

---

[147] *Dernière Réponse* (P, III, 90–91). Rousseau was aware of the brutality of this suggestion, and took pains to add in a note that such a policy could only be taken "by the law" (*ibid.*, 91n.); according to the *Contrat social*, in principle every citizen has the right to emigrate, but since the sovereign is bound by no higher law, the body of citizens could establish a law surrendering this right (IV, i [P, III, 440 and n.]; III, xviii [436 and n.]; II, iv [373]). If Rousseau seems to advocate what is often called today a "closed society," it should at least be pointed out that he has in mind savage societies in Africa and that to be legitimate, such isolation must be the freely willed choice of the citizen body (and not the decree of an all-powerful man or political party). Need it be added that the consequences of colonization in Africa suggest that Rousseau's advice merits consideration? Cf. *Lettre à d'Alembert* (G, 230–31).

[148] *Préface à Narcisse* (P, II, 971).

[149] Cf. esp. *Économie Politique* (P, III, 259).

popular belief in Christianity—render the most complete civic virtue impossible, Rousseau apparently believed that the defense of "virtue and truth" required a political teaching which establishes the logical priority of freedom, for a modicum of political freedom is still possible given modern opinions.

While most men act on the basis of habit, passions, or common prejudice, in the ancient cities Rousseau saw that these impulses could produce civic virtue based primarily on morally respectable customs and opinions. Such standards of action, especially once hallowed by tradition, are the only sure means "to engage men to do good willingly." Although civil freedom, which is based upon and replaces natural freedom, is the only universally valid criterion for judging different political societies, free choice is insufficient unless it is exercised in the framework of those affections, prejudices, and sentiments which are the "immoveable keystone" and "true constitution of the State."[150]

Rousseau's emphasis on the decisive role of affective sentiment as the basis of civic life explains not only why he attacked the political thought of his contemporaries, who "talk only of business and money," but why he saw no alternative for the member of a corrupt society besides the retreat to a private life based on a kind of virtue distinct from that of the citizen. In the healthy political community, each individual does not suffer from the surrender of his natural freedom because he gains civil freedom, which is to say that he enacts the laws that bind him. When one's fellows are guided by depraved prejudices, such political self-legislation becomes impossible and freedom is only possible on an individual basis; a man can still legislate for himself and be morally free if he rejects corrupted common opinions in the name of that which is natural for perfected man as a man.

For the individual who can no longer be the good citizen, the conscience and natural sentiment can provide a standard of morality, but the discovery of these guides presupposes reason or at least a kind of education that is natural (i.e., not deformed by social prejudices). The natural law or natural religion elaborated in the *Émile* is therefore based on beliefs which one cannot expect others to share, and is indeed likely to be fully accepted by only a few individuals. The virtuous private man—or, as Rousseau calls him, "the wise man"—must therefore be withdrawn from society. If he is not a "true genius" and

[150] *First Discourse*, Part 2 (P, III, 30); *Second Discourse*, Part 2 (P, III, 179–84, 187–88); *Économie Politique* (P, III, 252–60); *Contrat social*, II, iii–iv (P, III, 371–75); II, xii (394).

has only a "vulgar" or "common" degree of intelligence, he may find happiness and virtue in the kind of rural family life depicted in the *Nouvelle Héloïse* and the *Émile*.[151] If he is one of the "privileged souls" for whom science is compatible with virtue, his happiness can be combined with the "glory" due to "illustrious philosophers"; the disinterested pursuit of the truth—the life of the true philosopher— is the "honor of humanity" and, with the exception of the legislator or statesman who can render an entire society virtuous, the noblest life for man.[152] Finally, if he has a "sensitive soul," the private man can retire to the life of the *"promeneur solitaire,"* being good without virtue by surrendering himself totally to natural impulsion and the "sentiment of his own existence."[153]

Rousseau's thought thus rests on the distinction between philosophic knowledge and common opinion, and the philosophic discovery that men are naturally good and become evil only as the consequence of the perfection of the human species. The scientific study of this historical evolution reveals that freedom is the criterion linking the various conditions in which men may exist: natural freedom in the state of nature, civil freedom in the legitimate civil society, moral freedom for the civilized individual. Under modern conditions, most humans can no longer live like animals: the choice is between being a man or a citizen. Except for very rare exceptions, neither achieves virtue through philosophic reflection and reasoning; healthy sentiment is the only guide which can be usefully proposed in works directed to the general public. But the philosopher who shows others the way to goodness or virtue, who identifies the natural sentiments or healthy social prejudices they should follow, is a "preceptor of the human race"; he can legitimately hope to "live beyond his century."[154] Whatever one's judgment of Rousseau's philosophy, it must be admitted that he shared that hope, and was not mistaken in so doing.

[151] *Émile*, esp. I (G, 28); IV (430–43); V (606); *Nouvelle Héloïse*, esp. *Second Preface* (P, II, 18–23); and V, vii (602–11).

[152] *First Discourse*, Part 2 (P, III, 29); *Observations* (P, III, 39); *Dernière Réponse* (P, III, 72); *Préface à Narcisse* (P, II, 970–71); *Économie Politique* (P, III, 255); *Contrat social*, II, vii (P, III, 381).

[153] *Rêveries*, i (P, I, 995–97, 999); ii (1002–04); v (1040–49); *et passim*; *Rousseau Juge de Jean Jacques*, i (P, I, 668–73); ii (812–28).

[154] *First Discourse*, Pref. (P, III, 3); Part 2 (27, 29).

PART II

THE POSSIBILITIES
OF POLITICS

THE NATURE OF POLITICAL RIGHT
(GENEVA MS)

1 · *The Character of Rousseau's Political Writings*

In Part I of this volume, what Rousseau called his "three principal writings" have been examined in order to show the coherence and complexity of his "system." Although it may be unconventional to treat the *Social Contract* as a development of a part of that system, rather than as Rousseau's central work, we have seen that the problem of establishing a just regime is not, in fact, Rousseau's primary concern. On the contrary, he called political right "that great and useless science"[1] because the possibility of establishing political justice is severely limited by historical conditions and accident, and because in any event the political realm cannot exhaust the legitimate possibilities for a "good" human life. Nature is the standard by which any civil society can be adjudged faulty, since all political orders are imperfect human creations doomed to ultimate failure; man's nature and the demands of civil society are intrinsically opposed to each other.

Had Rousseau left it at that, he could be classed as a "moralist," albeit a politically dangerous one since his criticism of civil society might have been applied to legitimate regimes as well as despotic ones. But such a purely negative position would have represented a flat contradiction of Rousseau's primary insight that philosophy and science, insofar as they are publicly disseminated in printed books, morally corrupt the mass of men; Rousseau's moral doctrine forced him to go beyond the purely "destructive" kind of philosophic speculation for which he criticized his contemporaries.[2] Thus Rousseau

[1] *Émile*, v (G, 584). On the place of the *Contrat social* in Rousseau's system according to most commentators, see Derathé, *Le Rationalisme de Rousseau* (Paris: Presses Universitaires de France, 1948), p. 185n.

[2] See *Émile*, Pref. (G, 1): "The literature and knowledge of our century tend much more to destroy than to build."

presents an outline of his political principles both in the *Émile* (which is a treatise on the best possible life for the individual in society) and in the *Second Discourse* (which attempts to prove that all political societies are artificial). Even in criticizing social prejudice and corruption, Rousseau admitted that justice was possible—albeit not likely—in civil society.

Rousseau devoted at least ten years to the consideration of the principles on which such a legitimate political order could be built; after the publication of the *Social Contract*, he drafted proposals for constitutional legislation appropriate to Corsica and Poland, thereby proving that his political thought was in no sense merely negative. Rousseau's insistence on the possibility of salutary political action is implicit in his understanding of political right: whereas the disproportion between "fact" and "right" reveals the illegitimacy of most regimes, knowledge of what is "right" in political life can and should guide the actions of the virtuous statesman. As we will see, this connection between abstract or logical "principles of political right" and their application to political life, although until recently ignored or underestimated by critics, is the central theme of Rousseau's political teaching.

Rousseau devoted many works to politics—including the article on *Political Economy* (in which he developed explicitly for the first time his conception of the "general will" and his distinction between the "sovereign" and the "government" or "prince"), the *Letter to d'Alembert* and the *Letters Written from the Mountain* (both of which apply Rousseau's political thought to his native Geneva, the former emphasizing the corrupting effects of the arts in a still legitimate if imperfect society, the latter criticizing the injustices of Genevan politics), the writings on the works of the Abbé Saint-Pierre (including Rousseau's most extensive analysis of the possibilities of international confederation), the *Project of a Constitution for Corsica*, and the *Considerations on the Government of Poland*. Although it might be useful to discuss each of these writings in detail, such a task is beyond the scope of the present volume; our analysis must focus on Rousseau's most famous book about politics, referring to the works just mentioned only when needed to clarify the *Social Contract*.

To assess this work properly, its place in Rousseau's "system" of thought must be established with greater precision. For this purpose, it is fortunate that much of the first draft of the *Social Contract*—the so-called *Geneva Manuscript*—has survived. This early version is invaluable because it shows, with more clarity than any other single work of Rousseau's, the precise status of political right and its relationship to other standards of morality (such as those derived from Rousseau's own natural theology or from the natural law tradition of his time).[3]

In the Preface of the *Second Discourse*, Rousseau indicates that "natural right," which explains the relations between men in the state of nature, is replaced by a different standard of human action, discoverable only by reason, once men enter civil society. This rational replacement or "reestablishment" of the "rules of natural right" has a double character. On the one hand, some men can discover a "sublime maxim of reasoned justice" in the Golden Rule. But this "law of reason" (or "natural law" as Rousseau describes it in the *Émile*) is ultimately based on a natural theology or a metaphysical position which is not shared by all men; lacking a reciprocal sanction, such a natural law can have no political relevance.[4] On the other hand, Rousseau also speaks, in the *Second Discourse*, of the "nature of the fundamental compact of all government"; he hints that the principles on which every society is based, when correctly formulated, provide a valid criterion for evaluating political life. There is, moreover, a lack of clarity in the *Second Discourse* and in the *Émile* concerning the status of both the moral standard (i.e., the "natural law") and the political standard (i.e., what Rousseau later called "political right"). Fortunately, the *Geneva Manuscript* clarifies Rousseau's thinking on this crucial point and thereby provides a useful introduction to his political teaching.

The manuscript in question carries as its title: *Du Contrat Social, ou Essai sur la Forme de la République.*[5] It has been noted that in the *Second Discourse* Rousseau speaks of "researches yet to be under-

---

[3] No attempt will be made to analyze the *Geneva MS* as a running text since much of it is taken over into the final version; the relatively unchanged portions of the manuscript will be discussed in that context. Here we will emphasize those parts of the *Geneva MS* that were incorporated into the *Économie Politique* or deleted by Rousseau in the process of preparing the *Contrat social* for the press. Although it is impossible to date the *Geneva MS*, it seems incontestable that it contains material first drafted between the composition of the *Second Discourse* and the publication of the *Économie Politique* (i.e., 1754–55). This would account for the fact that, in Book I, chap. II, Rousseau answers Diderot's criticisms of the *Second Discourse* (published in *Droit Naturel* in Vol. v of the *Encyclopédie*); it might also explain why certain passages, having been used in the *Économie Politique*, were not employed in the definitive version of the *Contrat social*. But cf. Derathé, "Introduction: Première Version du Contrat social" (P, III, lxxxii–lxxxv).

[4] See above, chap. II, § 3, and consider *Lettres Écrites de la Montagne*, I (P, III, 703–07).

[5] *Of the Social Contract, or Essay on the Form of the Republic* (P, III, 279).

taken concerning the nature of the fundamental compact of all government,"[6] and it would be difficult to deny that this is the very subject referred to in the title. Moreover, the wording reveals Rousseau's conception of the nature of politics: one must define the "contract" which constitutes the social bond because any political order is conventional (i.e., it does not belong to the nature of man as defined in the First Part of the *Second Discourse*). Thus the concept of the "social contract," as used by Rousseau, refers to a question of "right" and not to an historical act which supposedly took place at the founding of every society; "I seek right and reason and do not dispute about the facts."[7] And to make this implication clear, the tentative subtitle identifies the subject as "The Form of the Republic," a phrase which suggests that the "constitution" of any society reflects the logic or "idea" of civil society in general; the conventional bonds underlying political life have a "nature" of their own which can be discovered by reason.[8]

The first chapter of the manuscript, entitled "Subject of this Work," deserves to be cited in full:

> So many celebrated authors have discussed the maxims of government and the rules of civil right that there is nothing useful left to say on the subject which has not already been said. But perhaps there would be greater agreement, and perhaps the best relationships of the social body would have been more clearly established, if one had begun by better understanding its nature. That is what I have tried to do in this work. Therefore it is not here a question of the administration of this body, but of its constitution. I make it live, and not act. I describe its springs and its parts, I arrange them in their place. I put the machine in condition to run; others who are wiser will control the movements.[9]

[6] *Second Discourse*, Part 2 (P, III, 184).

[7] *Geneva MS*, I, v (P, III, 297). Cf. *Second Discourse*, Exordium (P, III, 132); Part 2 (182). Rousseau at one point thought of using *De la Société Civile* as his title, but returned to *Du Contrat social* (which reveals the conventional origin of the body politic more directly than does the Lockean term). See P, III, 1410, where Rousseau's various tentative subtitles are also indicated.

[8] In addition to the phrase "Form of the Republic" in the subtitle, Rousseau speaks of "the idea of the civil state" (*Geneva MS*, I, iv [P, III, 297]). Note the connection between "the most exact ideas that one could have of the fundamental compact which is the basis of every true body politic" and "the nature of law" (II, v [326]) is discovered by reason and is not evident to most men.

[9] *Ibid.*, I, i (P, III, 281). Cf. the critique of Montesquieu, *Émile*, v (G, 584–85).

Apart from the analogy between society and a machine, to which we will return, the most striking thing about this chapter is its sharp distinction between the "constitution" or "nature" of political society and the "actions" or "movements" of government.[10] The latter depend on the "maxims of government" and the "rules of civil right," as applied by prudent men; there is apparently nothing useful left to say with respect to these prudential considerations.[11] The former, however, has given rise to dispute and uncertainty because no one has ever clearly formulated the "nature" or logically necessary characteristics of every political society.

2 · Justice as a Human Invention

A · DIDEROT'S *Natural Right*: A CONTEMPORARY CRITICIZES ROUSSEAU

Rousseau begins Chapter II of Book I with a question that illustrates his search for the ineluctable properties of civil society: "Let us begin by inquiring where the *necessity* for political institutions arises."[12] In order to understand this inquiry, a digression will be required, for—as Vaughan and other commentators have noted—the chapter in question is a critique of an article in the *Encyclopedia* written by Denis Diderot, at that time Rousseau's close friend. Even the title of Rousseau's chapter ("Concerning the General Society of the Human Species") cannot be fully understood without first considering Diderot's article on *Natural Right*.[13]

---

[10] In a canceled phrase in the manuscript, Rousseau said: "I say what it is, and not what it does" (P, III, 1410).

[11] "Apparently" nothing useful is left to say—but only "apparently." Cf. *ibid.*, II, iii (318), cited below, p. 292. Note also that the *Économie Politique* is primarily devoted to the "administration" of the body politic, not to its nature (P, III, 244, 250, 252, 262), and that the "rules of civil right" are not identical with "rules of political right," since the former concern the relationship of individual citizens with each other or with the state, whereas the latter deal with the body of citizens as subjects and sovereign. Cf. *Contrat social*, II, xii (P, III, 393–94); Montesquieu, *Esprit des Lois*, XXVI, xv (ed. Garnier, II, 184–85).

[12] *Ibid.*, I, ii (P, III, 281), italics added.

[13] V, I, 423–28; 445, n. 1; 450, n. 8; Robert Derathé, *J. J. Rousseau et la Science Politique de Son Temps* (Paris: Presses Universitaires de France, 1950), pp. 55, n. 4; 58, n. 3; Jacques Proust, *Diderot et l'Encyclopédie* (Paris: Colin, 1962), p. 393. In an early fragment, Rousseau entitled this chapter "Of Natural Right and the General Society" (cf. P, III, 1410–11). All references to Diderot's article (which appeared in Volume V of the *Encyclopédie*, pp. 115–16) will be to Vaughan's reproduction of the text (V, I, 429–33). It will be impossible to raise the question of the article's relationship to

After stating the importance of a correct definition of the term,[14] Diderot asserts that any unjust man must admit that, at the bottom of his soul, he wants to do to others things that he does not want done to himself.[15] The remainder of the article is then devoted to Diderot's reply to a "violent reasoner" who "intrepidly" states:

> "I know that I bring terror and trouble into the midst of the human species, but it is necessary either that I be unhappy or that I make others unhappy; and no one is dearer to me than I am to myself. ... Oh men, it is to you that I appeal. Which of you, on the point of dying, would not buy his own life at the expense of the largest part of the human race, if he was sure to do so with impunity and in secret? But," he will continue, "I am equitable and sincere. If my happiness requires that I do away with all those existences which intrude on me, it is also necessary that an individual, whoever he is, can do away with my [existence] if it intrudes on his. Reason demands it and I accept. I am not so unjust that I require of another a sacrifice that I do not want to make for him."[16]

Clearly this "violent reasoner" is in the position of a man in the last stages of the state of nature, whose reasoning leads him to the Hobbesian assertion that each man has an absolute right to judge the means of his own self-preservation (even though this leads to a war of all against all). Although today's reader might accordingly expect this statement to be attributed to Hobbes, Diderot implies that Rousseau was the "violent reasoner"; Rousseau's reply accepts this implication.[17]

Diderot insists that the answer to such a "violent reasoner" must be rational: "once the truth is discovered, whosoever refuses to conform to it is insane or wicked in a moral sense" (*méchant d'une*

Diderot's thought as a whole; cf. Proust, *Diderot et l'Encyclopédie*, chap. IX; Arthur M. Wilson, *Diderot: The Testing Years, 1713–1759* (New York: Oxford University Press, 1957), pp. 233–34. For an examination of the extent to which Diderot accepted Hobbes' premises concerning human nature, see Leland Thielemann, "Diderot and Hobbes," in Otis E. Fellows and Norman L. Torrey, eds., *Diderot Studies* (Syracuse: Syracuse University Press, 1952), II, 221–78, esp. 226, 234, 247–52 and nn. 91 and 156.

[14] *Droit naturel*, § i (V, I, 429).

[15] *Ibid.*, § II (430).   [16] *Ibid.*, § III (430).

[17] Evidence that Diderot's article was directed against the *Second Discourse* will be shown abundantly in the remainder of the analysis. Rousseau's acceptance of the role of the "violent reasoner" is proven by his citations from Diderot's formulation; for example, Rousseau quotes, in his own name, the first sentence of the passage just cited in *Geneva MS*, I, ii (P, III, 284–85).

méchanceté morale).[18] This is apparently intended to dispute the relevance of Rousseau's arguments in the First Part of the *Second Discourse*; since for Diderot "man is not just an animal, but an animal who reasons," animal sentiments are not capable of producing "goodness or badness" which is "rational" (i.e., truly moral in the conventional meaning).[19] Diderot therefore rejects the principle on which Rousseau's *Second Discourse* is based:

> What we will reply, therefore, to our violent reasoner before stifling him? That all his discourse is reduced to knowing if he acquires a right over the existence of others in abandoning his own to them. . . . We will therefore make him notice that, even if what he abandons should belong to him so completely that he could dispose of it at will and that the condition he proposes to others should also be advantageous to them, he has no legitimate authority for making them accept it.[20]

The individual is *not* the competent judge of the means to his own self-preservation when there is a conflict in the state of nature; because the rational grounds for settling such disputes are complicated, Locke, Hobbes, and Rousseau were all incorrect in granting individuals "the right to decide concerning the nature of the just and the unjust."[21] Hence the reader accustomed to the terminology of Hobbes or Locke should not be misled by the title of Diderot's article, which presents a view closer to that of the jurists or of Malebranche and Cumberland.

Now that the individual in the state of nature is considered an incompetent judge, Diderot must immediately determine the tribunal before which "we will bring this great question" of natural justice. He replies:

---

[18] *Droit naturel*, § IV (V, I, 431).

[19] *Ibid.*, § IV (430–31). Cf. § I (429–30): "if man is not free or if his instantaneous determinations, or even his oscillations, arise out of something material that is external to his soul, . . . there will not be either reasoned goodness or wickedness, even though he might have animal goodness or wickedness." This last passage is a direct attack on Rousseau's conception that a kind of goodness arising out of "something material" (namely animal impulses) is relevant to reasoning men; Diderot's interpretation of Part 1 of the *Second Discourse* confirms that given above, chap. II, esp. § 2D–3B.

[20] *Droit naturel*, § V (V, I, 431).

[21] *Ibid.*, § VI (431). Cf. § V (431): "the question of *natural right* is much more complicated than it appears to him [our violent reasoner] . . . he constitutes himself judge and adversary, and . . . his tribunal could well not have competence in this matter" (original italics).

Where? Before the human species; it is to it alone that the decision belongs, because the good of all is the only passion that it has. Individual wills are suspect, they could be good or wicked; but the general will (*volonté générale*) is always good; it has never been mistaken, and it never will be.[22]

Only the human race, as distinguished from the entire animal kingdom, participates in natural right since only men reason; Diderot rejects Rousseau's argument that natural rights, inhering in sensibility, are shared by all animals.[23] Thus the natural right of Diderot, like the "natural law" defined in the Preface of the *Second Discourse*, establishes duties on the assumption that man is a rational animal, and it is only on this basis that Diderot admits to his "violent reasoner" that he has "the most sacred *natural right* to all that is not contested against you by the entire species."[24]

According to Diderot, the "general will of the human species" is discoverable by all:

Where is this general will deposited? . . . In the principles of right written in all civilized nations, in the social action of savage and barbarian peoples, in the tacit conventions of the enemies of the human species between themselves, and even in indignation and resentment, the two passions that nature seems to have even put in animals to replace the lack of social laws and public vengeance. . . . the general will is a pure act of the understanding in each individual, who reasons in the silence of the passions concerning that which man can require of his fellowman and concerning that which his fellowman can rightfully require of him.[25]

Having asserted the universal competence of the "general will of the human species," Diderot concludes his article:

[22] *Ibid.*, § VI (431). Vaughan suggests that Rousseau may well have borrowed the term *volonté générale* from this passage, especially since Rousseau's use of the concept in the *Économie Politique* is accompanied by a reference to Diderot's article (V, I, 425). Cf. *Économie Politique* (P, III, 245) and the contrary argument in Derathé's note (P, III, 1394–95). On the term *volonté générale*, see also the references cited in n. 86 of chap. VII.

[23] Cf. *Droit naturel*, § VI (V, I, 431–32) with *Second Discourse*, Pref. (P, III, 126).

[24] *Droit naturel*, § VII (V, I, 432), original italics.

[25] *Ibid.*, § VIII–IX (432). Note the absence of natural pity, and compare Rousseau's statement that in order to discover the "laws" of "virtue" it is "sufficient" to "commune with oneself and listen to the voice of one's *conscience* in the silence of the passions" (*First Discourse*, Part 2 [P, III, 30], italics added).

Finally, that all these consequences are evident for him who reasons, and that anyone who does not want to reason, renouncing his quality as a man (*qualité d'homme*) should be treated as a denatured being.[26]

Whereas Rousseau describes freedom as the *qualité d'homme* in the *Second Discourse*, Diderot substitutes reasoning as the defining characteristic of man.[27]

B · ROUSSEAU'S REPLY: NATURAL LAW IS UNNATURAL

It has been useful to cite Diderot's article in some detail, because today's reader may tend to overlook the kind of arguments which were opposed to Rousseau's teaching in the eighteenth century. Diderot rejects the relevance of the pure state of nature analyzed by Rousseau; Diderot does not require any certainty that "natural rights" be obeyed, since these rights may not even be known by "denatured" or "beastly" men (like the "violent reasoner," who has to be "stifled" by Diderot).[28] As a result, the "natural right" described by Diderot is open to every objection which Rousseau had raised, in the Preface of his *Discourse*, against the "modern" definitions of "natural law." Under these circumstances, one might well imagine that Rousseau could have ignored Diderot's objections. Although this may explain why Rousseau's reply in Book I, chapter II of the *Geneva MS* was deleted from the *Social Contract*, the reply sheds valuable light on the status of the traditionalist conception of natural law in Rousseau's mind.

Rousseau begins the second chapter of the *Geneva MS* with a brief evocation of the independence of the individual in the pure state of nature and an affirmation that social interdependence requires the development of "unnatural" passions and intelligence. Once these developments have occurred, the last stage of the state of nature is characterized by violence and constant revolution; social contacts at this stage are not conducive to the establishment of standards of the good and the bad.[29] Rousseau tries to prove the insufficiency of Diderot's

---

[26] *Droit naturel*, § IX (V, I, 433).

[27] See *Second Discourse*, Part 1 (P, III, 141); Part 2 (184); and cf. Proust, *Diderot et l'Encyclopedie*, p. 365. Diderot's rejection of man's freedom, based on materialist determinism, helps to explain Rousseau's retreat from "freedom" to "perfectibility" in the *Second Discourse*; see above, chap. II, § 2B; chap. III, § 3A.

[28] Cf. *Droit naturel*, § V (V, I, 431) with Vaughan's remarks (V, I, 427–28).

[29] Speaking of man in this period, Rousseau says: "When his sentiments and his ideas could rise to the love of order and to the sublime notions of

supposition that before the existence of civil society the human species was a "society" or community with its own "general will"; in the state of nature, either men were too stupid to be virtuous or virtue was rendered impossible by the absence of a government and laws, which are necessary restraints on thinking men.[30]

Rousseau did not leave it at that, however. In a paragraph which he ultimately cancelled, Rousseau granted Diderot's assumption that one can conceive of the entire human species in the state of nature as forming a "general society":

> Let us conceive of the human species as a moral person having, with a sentiment of common existence which gives it individuality and constitutes it as one, a universal motivating force which makes each part act for an end which is general and relative to the whole. Let us conceive that this common sentiment is humanitarianism (*humanité*), and that the natural law is the activating principle of the entire machine. Let us then observe what results from man's constitution in his relations with others and, completely to the contrary of what we have supposed, we will find that the progress of society stifles humanitarianism in their hearts by awakening personal interest, and that the notions of natural law, which would better be called the law of reason, only begin to develop when the prior development of the passions makes all its precepts powerless. By which one sees that this pretended social bond, dictated by nature, is a true chimera since the conditions for it are always either unknown or impractical, and they must either be unknown or broken.[31]

Rousseau confirms this proof by arguing that without a "universal language that nature would teach all men" or a "kind of common sensibility that would serve as the communication of all its parts," the

---

virtue, it would be impossible for him ever to make a reliable (*sure*) application of his principles in a state of things which would never let him discern the good or the bad, nor the decent man or the wicked one" (*Geneva MS*, I, ii [P, III, 282]).

[30] He suggests in passing that Diderot's notion of natural right would, if it operated, define a golden age. But, Rousseau adds, "not felt by the stupid men of the earliest times, escaping the enlightened men of later times, the happy golden age was always a state foreign to the human race, either for not having known when they could enjoy it, or for having lost it when they could have known it" (*ibid.* [283]). Rousseau's insistence on an *historical* interpretation of the state of nature is nowhere more evident than in this rejection of Diderot's more traditional conception of that condition as a standard for perfected man.

[31] *Ibid.* (283–84).

human species could not conceivably form a single society or "moral being" (as distinct from a mere aggregation of individuals).[32]

Having shown that there is no general society of all men in the state of nature, Rousseau then directly attacks the central point of Diderot's article on *Natural Right* by arguing that every individual in the state of nature *must be* the only judge of his own self-preservation (regardless of the conflict and violence that would result once men learn to reason). Adopting the role of the "independent man" whom Diderot had called a "violent reasoner," Rousseau insists:

> "It is in vain," he could add, "that I would try to reconcile my interest with that of another; all that you tell me about the advantages of the social law could be good if, while I was scrupulously observing it toward others, I was sure that they would all observe it towards me. But what assurance can you give me? . . . It does you no good to tell me that, in renouncing the duties that the natural law imposes on me, I deprive myself of its rights at the same time, and that my violences will authorize all those which anyone would like to use against me. I consent to that all the more willingly because I do not see how my moderation could guarantee me from them."[33]

Self-interest and the general good "exclude one another in the natural order of things," and the risks of force and violence are better insurance for one's safety than dependence upon unenforced and unenforceable rules of natural law.[34]

> The proof that the enlightened and independent man would have reasoned thus is that any sovereign society which only renders account of its actions to itself reasons in this way.[35]

This proof is, of course, exactly the same one used by Hobbes, whose critique of the common understanding of natural right and natural law is accepted by Rousseau (provided that it refers only to the last stage of the state of nature).[36]

[32] *Ibid.* (284).
[33] *Ibid.* (285). Note the use of "social law" as a synonym for "natural law" in this passage, and consider the sense in which Rousseau described his natural religion (or the religion of the Evangiles) as "social" (*Lettres Écrites de la Montagne*, I [P, III, 697–706]), commenting on *Contrat social*, IV, viii [P, III, 464–67]). Diderot's general society of the human species could only be based upon natural religion, for "the perfect Christianity is the universal social institution."
[34] *Geneva MS*, I, ii, (P, III, 284).   [35] *Ibid.* (285).
[36] See Hobbes, *Leviathan*, Part I, chap. XIII (ed. Oakeshott, p. 83), and above, pp. 137–38, 197–99.

Rousseau suggests that religion is one possible reply to the "enlightened and independent man" of the last stages of the state of nature, but adds that the "multitude" is incapable of the "wise man's sublime notions of God"; popular religion would lead to the extinction of mankind if "philosophy and law did not restrain the furors of fanaticism."[37] Limiting the discussion to the solutions offered by philosophers, Rousseau then analyzes Diderot's conception of a "general will" of the human species:[38]

> "I admit that I clearly see there the rule that I can consult, but I do not yet see," our independent man will say, "the reason which is to subject me to that rule. It is not a question of teaching me what justice is, it is a question of showing me the interest I have in being just."[39]

Rousseau accepts Diderot's definition of the general will of mankind as an existent moral standard, but denies that it is binding—although one "can consult" it—because no one has a natural self-interest in obeying it.[40]

To drive home his point conclusively, Rousseau examines the kind of reasoning required for knowing Diderot's "general will of the human species":

> Moreover, as the art of thus generalizing ideas is one of the most difficult and the slowest developing exercises of human understanding, would the common man ever be capable of deriving the rules of his conduct in that manner of reasoning? And when the general will would have to be consulted on a specific act, how many times would not a well-intentioned man happen to fool himself concerning the rule or the application, and to follow only his impulses in thinking he obeyed the law? What will he do, therefore, to preserve himself from error? Will he listen to the interior voice? But it is said that this voice is only formed by habits of judging and feeling

[37] *Geneva MS*, I, ii, (P, III, 285). Cf. *Second Discourse*, Pref. (P, III, 127); Part 2 (186); *Émile*, v (605); and above, pp. 84–89: religion is only healthy when it is a civil institution, subordinate to the law, or when it is the natural religion accessible to the "wise."

[38] Rousseau quotes two sentences from *Droit naturel*, implicitly equating Diderot with the "philosopher": cf. *Droit naturel*, § VI, second sentence and § VII, first sentence (V, I, 431–32), with *Geneva MS*, I, ii (P, III, 286).

[39] *Ibid.*

[40] ". . . if the care for one's own preservation is the first precept of nature, can one force man to consider the species in general in this way, in order to impose on him duties whose link with his private constitution he does not see?" (*Ibid.*)

within society, and according to its laws; it cannot therefore serve to establish them. And then it would be necessary that there had never arisen in his heart any of those passions which speak more loudly than the conscience, cover its timid voice, and make philosophers assert that this voice does not exist. . . . It is only from the social order established among us that we derive the ideas of the one we are imagining. We conceive of the general society after our particular societies; the establishment of little republics makes us think of the large one, and we only begin to become men properly speaking after having been citizens.[41]

Natural law cannot be logically and historically prior to civil society for the simple reason that civil society is historically and logically prior to the natural law. "Virtue and happiness" result from the creation of political societies ruled by positive laws which were a means of escaping the violence of the last stages of the state of nature; "it is to law alone that men owe justice and freedom."[42]

C · THE NATURE OF LAW AS THE STANDARD OF JUSTICE

Although Vaughan concludes that Rousseau rejected natural law "root and branch," all that Rousseau himself says is that the "natural law, which would better be called the law of reason, only begins to develop when the prior development of the passions makes all its precepts powerless."[43] The political irrelevance of the natural law stems from the unnatural character of reason, but since the perfection of human faculties produces reasoning, a kind of natural law ultimately comes into being for some men; if the general society of all men exists only in the "systems of philosophers," the "systems of philosophers" really exist. The precepts of natural law formulated by the Socratic thinker, and made accessible to most men in the form of the Savoyard Vicar's natural religion, arise only in civil society; Rousseau can therefore adopt such standards as a guide to the personal morality of civilized man without abandoning the analysis of human nature in

[41] *Ibid.*, 286–87. One wonders if Kant's ethics would have been different if Rousseau had not deleted this passage when revising the *Geneva MS.*

[42] *Ibid.* (288–89) and I, vii (310)—a passage in part used in the *Économie Politique* (P, III, 248). It need not follow, of course, that the positive laws established in civil societies are themselves just merely because positive law, in general, is the foundation of justice.

[43] Cf. V, I, 16–18 and above, p. 266. For a discussion of the implications of the identification of the law of nature with a "law of reason" in the thought of Spinoza, Hobbes, and Locke, see Strauss, *Natural Right and History*, pp. 229–30 and the references there cited.

the *Second Discourse*. Rousseau rejects the "root" of the traditional natural law, but not the "branch."

Because the natural law is unnatural, the experience of political life is the only philosophically valid explanation of the origin of human justice. But since the formation of civil society is a consequence of a state of war, true morality appears to be a consequence of lawlessness; the cause of justice is not itself just.

> What reasoning demonstrates to us in this respect is perfectly confirmed by the facts, and if one goes back even a little into high antiquity one sees easily that the healthy ideas of natural right and of the fraternity common to all men were disseminated rather late, and made such slow progress in the world that it was only Christianity which generalized them sufficiently. . . . The first heroes, like Hercules and Theseus, who made war on bandits, did not fail to practice banditry themselves.[44]

But if societies are formed by "bandits" whose only rule is the "law of the strongest," how can such acts produce justice? And even more important, if the source of all virtue lies in the institution of political communities by violent, unjust means, how can there be a standard of justice superior to the positive laws of each particular civil society?

Rousseau formulates the problem in terms of the claims of the "violent reasoner," representing man at the stage of human evolution immediately prior to the formation of civil society. Once independent natural man has acquired calculating reason, there does not seem to be any means by which each individual could reasonably lay down his claim to be the sole judge of what he needs for his own preservation.

> These difficulties, which should have seemed insurmountable, were overcome by the most sublime of all human institutions. . . . How is it possible that all obey and none commands, that they serve and have no master; [that they are] in fact all the more free, under an apparent subjection, because none loses any part of his freedom

---

[44] *Geneva MS*, I, ii (P, III, 287–88). It should be emphasized that the phrase "healthy ideas of natural right," like the term "rules of natural right" used in the Preface of the *Second Discourse* (P, III, 126) or the phrase "rational natural right" used later in the *Geneva MS*, II, iv (P, III, 329), is to be explicitly distinguished from "natural right properly speaking" (*ibid.*), since the latter operates even when men have no "idea" of its existence. Cf. above, chap. IV, § 1.

except that which harms that of another? These wonders are the work of the law.[45]

It is not the specific laws, established in fact by the institution of civil society, but the logic of law in the abstract, discovered by Rousseau's analysis of *right*, which explains the origin of justice.

Thus, when Rousseau insists that his work concerns "right" and not "fact," he states:

> There are a thousand ways of assembling men, only one of uniting them. That is why I only give one method for the formation of political societies in this book, even though in the multitude of aggregations which exist under this name, there are probably not two that were formed in the same way, and not one which was formed according to the one I establish.[46]

Going beyond the historical "conjectures" presented in the Second Part of the *Second Discourse*—which serve a partly critical function of showing the conventional character of political society—the constructive elaboration of political right depends on the discovery of the "only" way of truly "uniting" a people, even if this method never occurred in fact. When men were forced to establish positive laws in order to preserve themselves, they automatically (and it is to be presumed unknowingly) established the basis of justice since the creation of any law implies the emergence of the "nature of law" as a standard of judging political institutions. Rousseau's discovery of the proper definition of this standard is thus a mental construction, only possible within society, of the principles which make civilized social life comprehensible and lead the "violent reasoner" to "become good, virtuous, sensible and . . . from the wild brigand that he wanted to be, the strongest support of a well-ordered society."[47]

No effort will be made at this point to analyze the substance of Rousseau's doctrine of the "general will," the rational principle that inheres in all political communities, defines legitimacy, and explains rightful and free obedience to positive law. Before analyzing this conception as it was ultimately presented in the *Social Contract*, it is preferable to show more clearly the functions of Rousseau's conception of political right as they are indicated in the first draft. The chapter heading of Book II, chapter IV—"Concerning the Nature of Laws and the Principle of Civil Justice" (*De la Nature des Lois et du Prin-*

[45] *Geneva MS*, I, vii (P, III, 310).
[46] *Ibid.*, I, v (297).   [47] *Ibid.*, I, ii (289).

cipe de la Justice Civile)—indicates succinctly how Rousseau himself viewed the relationship of law and justice; whereas much prior thought had tried to discover a law of nature at the root of justice, Rousseau finds the "principle of civil justice" in what he calls "the nature of laws."[48]

Having elaborated the conception of a true law according to which "the object of the law should be general as well as the will which dictates it,"[49] Rousseau adds a discussion which he did not use in the final version of the *Social Contract*.

> The greatest advantage which results from this notion is to show us clearly the true foundations of justice and natural right. In fact, the first law, the only truly fundamental law immediately derived from the social compact is, that everyone prefer, in all things, the greatest good of all.[50]

From this principle (or definition of law in the abstract) flows all political right in the strict sense:

> The specification of actions which contribute to this greatest good, by so many particular laws, is what constitutes strict, positive right.[51]

All political right can therefore be considered as the result of the single principle, implicit in any law, that "everyone prefer, in all things, the greatest good of all."

Moreover, this same principle establishes standards of civil justice which are not merely *legal*:

> Everything that is seen to contribute to this greatest good, but which the laws have not specified, constitutes the acts of civility and beneficence, and the habit which disposes us to practice these acts, even to our own prejudice, is what is called force or virtue.[52]

Virtue can best be understood as an extension of the fundamental principle of civil laws to those actions not required by "strict, posi-

[48] In addition to this chapter heading (P, III, 326), consider the phrases cited in n. 8 of this chapter.

[49] *Geneva MS*, II, iv (P, III, 327). The first part of this chapter (326–28) reappears, with some modification, in *Contrat social*, II, vi (P, III, 378–79).

[50] *Ibid.*, II, iv (328). As the sequel makes clear, the term "natural right" in this passage refers to what Rousseau calls "rational natural right" on the next page (329).

[51] *Ibid.* (328).

[52] *Ibid.* (328–29). On the identity of "force" and "virtue," see *Émile*, v (G, 567) and above, chap. II § 4C.

tive right"; both law and morality are rooted in the single principle of the individual's preference for the "greatest good of all." The morality which Rousseau has in mind at this point is clearly a *civic* one, since the collectivity in question is a political society that enacts positive law, but the same reasoning can be extended to purely humanitarian virtue:

> Extend this maxim to the general society of which the State gives us the idea; protected by the society of which we are members or by that in which we live, the natural repugnance to harm others no longer being balanced in us by the fear of receiving harm, we are brought simultaneously by nature, habit, and reason to treat other men just about like fellow citizens, and from this disposition reduced into actions arise the rules of rational natural right (*droit naturel raisonné*), different from natural right properly so-called, which is only founded on a true but very vague sentiment, often stifled by love of ourselves.[53]

Diderot's "general will" of the human species is merely an extension, in the mind of a philosopher, of the general will of a particular civil society; not only the morality and virtue of the citizen toward other citizens, but the standards of "rational natural right" (to adopt Diderot's terminology) or "natural law" (according to the definition of the *Second Discourse*) are derived from the logic underlying positive law.

It is not difficult to conjecture why Rousseau may have deleted the passages just cited when he revised the *Social Contract*, for they seem to establish a logical harmony between the virtue of the citizen and "fraternity common to all men" as men. As we have seen in analyzing the *Émile,* Rousseau insisted on the inevitable tension between civic virtue and "humanitarian virtue" (*humanité*); even if the latter is to be explained historically as an extension of the former, made possible when philosophic reason replaces natural pity, there is a difference between a man and a citizen which this passage does not fully emphasize.[54] Be that as it may, in one passage from this chapter that reappears—with some changes—in the *Social Contract*, Rousseau admits that there is a conception of "universal justice, emanating from reason alone and founded on the simple right of humanity," asserting

[53] *Geneva MS*, II, iv (329). On the words "just about like fellow citizens," which qualify the thought, cf. above, chap. I, § 2B. Note also that pity is here called a "true but very vague sentiment."
[54] See above, pp. 10–14, 24–25, 49–51, 92–94.

merely that, "lacking a natural sanction," it cannot exist for a philosopher prior to the existence of "conventions and laws."[55]

Comparison of the treatment of the "noble and sublime precept to do to others as we would have them do to us" in the *Geneva MS* and in the works analyzed in Part I reveals most clearly the difference between the optic of Rousseau's philosophic system as a whole and his political writings proper. In the *Second Discourse*, Rousseau merely describes the golden rule as a "sublime maxim of reasoned justice" accessible only to "Socrates and minds of his stamp"; natural pity is more reliable as a restraint on human action than a morality founded on reason.[56] In the *Émile*, Rousseau goes further and shows that the golden rule, while the "summary of all morality," cannot be founded solely on reason because it "has no other true foundation than the conscience and sentiment"—i.e., natural moral sentiments which only develop in society.[57] From the perspective of Rousseau's analysis of human nature, the fundamental maxim of personal morality presupposes a combination of reason and natural sentiment which renders it inaccessible to most men; only those who personally adopt something like the Savoyard Vicar's natural religion will observe the golden rule. For such "wise" men, "the eternal laws of nature and order *exist*" and "take the place . . . of positive law," which is not truly "respected" in most if not all actual political regimes; Rousseau can therefore criticize all civil society in the name of a natural or individual morality "written at the bottom of his heart by conscience and reason."[58]

In contrast, from the perspective of Rousseau's political thought, the moral precepts summarized by the golden rule are explained historically; since the conscience and morality, not to mention natural religion, are impossible in the state of nature, all human justice can be understood only as the consequence of the institution of civil society and law.

> It is therefore in the fundamental and universal law of the greatest good of all, and not in the private relations between one man and another, that one must seek the true principles of the just and unjust.[59]

Strictly speaking, even the golden rule—insofar as it is interpreted in

[55] *Geneva MS*, II, iv (P, III, 326) and *Contrat social*, II, vi (P, III, 378), cited above, p. 85.
[56] *Second Discourse*, Part 1 (P, III, 156).
[57] *Émile*, IV (G, 278–79), cited in part above, p. 80.
[58] *Ibid.*, v (605).   [59] *Geneva MS*, II, iv (P, III, 329).

terms of the relations of individuals—"is subject to a thousand exceptions for which only sophistic explanations have ever been given."[60]

> In a word, there are a thousand cases in which it is an act of justice to harm one's fellow, whereas every just action necessarily has as its rule the greatest good of all.[61]

According to the *Émile*, the golden rule "has no other true *foundation* than the conscience and sentiment" (i.e., truly moral action requires natural sentiment), whereas according to the *Geneva MS* the law of "the greatest good of all" is the "true principle" (i.e., the *reason*) explaining the extent to which the golden rule is just.

The tension between Rousseau's political teaching and his conception of natural sentiment illuminates the paradoxical character of his thought. Although standards of individual goodness and morality, formulated by the philosopher who has lived in civil society, can be used to condemn political life as a "corruption" of human nature, from the perspective of political philosophy Rousseau rejects any notion of natural law as the basis of society (on the grounds that civil society precedes all individual morality).

> It is thus that the first distinct notions of justice and injustice are formed in us; for the law is anterior to justice, and not justice to the law, and if the law cannot be unjust, it is not that justice is its basis, which need not always be true, but because it is against nature that anyone wants to harm himself, which is without exception.[62]

Since the factual origin of positive law is often unjust, the only *reason* that can be given for the existence of justice lies in the logic, which is "without exception," that "it is against nature that anyone wants to harm himself." "The love of men derived from the love of oneself is the principle of all human justice."[63] When such love of others is directed to one's political community, the calculation of enlightened self-interest produces political justice, based on the principle of all positive law that each citizen follows the "general will" and prefers "the greatest good of all" (i.e., of the citizen body); if love of oneself is "extended to the human species," natural sentiments like pity come

---

[60] *Ibid.* Rousseau adds an example which emphasizes the tension between political justice and the golden rule: "Would not a judge who condemns a criminal want to be absolved if he was himself a criminal?" Note that the principle of the "general will" cannot fully resolve this tension, for it deals only with the *laws*, not with punishment for crime (see below, chap. VII).

[61] *Ibid.* (330).   [62] *Ibid.* (329).

[63] *Émile*, IV (G, 279n.).

into harmony with justice, "the virtue . . . which contributes to the greatest good of men."[64]

A single conception, man's natural love of himself, produces radically different standards of justice depending on the relative emphasis given to reason and sentiment. The primacy of the latter (with the aid of reason) leads to the discovery of one's duties to man, whereas the primacy of the former (with the aid of the sentiments or affections which naturally attach man to those with whom he lives) is the basis of one's duties toward civil society. This explains why Rousseau's political teaching proper is so highly "rationalist" or logical in character, in sharp contrast to what has been called his "romantic" solution for individual happiness. Only because the injustices of actual political life can be "made legitimate" by Rousseau's discovery of the "nature of law" can his radical criticism of the unnatural status of social life serve as the foundation for a constructive theory of political right.

D · THE REJECTION OF ALTERNATIVE CONCEPTIONS OF POLITICAL RIGHT

In order to claim that there is but one true principle which arises necessarily out of the enactment of any positive law, Rousseau had to show that all other explanations of political obedience are untenable. In the *Geneva MS*, Rousseau—having briefly outlined his conception of the social compact—reveals the importance of this consideration by devoting Book I, chapter V to the rejection of "False Notions of the Social Bond." Because some of the material in this chapter was used in the *Political Economy* (published in 1755) and part of the remainder reworked into chapters II, III, IV, V, and IX of Book I in the final version of the *Social Contract*, it is perhaps best to consider Rousseau's critique of alternate theories of political right at this point. By so doing, it will become somewhat easier to see how Rousseau's logic of right is a universally valid principle that explains both civil obedience and personal morality.

The first of the four notions which Rousseau attacks is the family as a source of political authority. Rousseau admits, in sharp contrast to the text of the *Second Discourse*, that the family exists as a unit by nature:

> That a father's natural authority over his children extends even beyond their weakness and need, and that in continuing to obey him

---

[64] *Geneva MS*, I, ii (P, III, 288–89); I, iv (295); I, vi (306); II, iv (327–28); and *Émile*, IV (G, 303).

they finally do by habit and gratitude what they first did by necessity, can be conceived without difficulty, and the bonds that unite the family are easy to see. But that, on the father's death, one of the children usurps the power of the father over his brothers of comparable age and even over strangers, is something which no longer has either reason or foundation. For the natural rights of age, of force, of paternal tenderness, the duties of filial gratitude, all are simultaneously lacking in this new order, and the brothers are imbeciles or denatured to submit their children to the yoke of a man who, according to the natural law, must give all preference to his own children. One no longer sees here the intrinsic ties which bind the chief and the members. Force acts alone, and nature no longer says anything.[65]

The family *may* be natural, but this cannot justify the authority of an uncle over his nephews; only the father has any natural claim to obedience, and any other attempt to exercise authority is an "usurpation" which amounts to mere "force."

It is crucial at this point to note the limited extent to which physical strength can be the basis of "natural authority." Of the three "natural rights" of the father mentioned by Rousseau in the passage just cited, the central one is "force." And Rousseau proceeds to argue explicitly that the natural authority of the father rests on his physical superiority:

The father being physically stronger than his children, as long as his aid is needed by them, paternal power passes with reason as being established by nature.[66]

As with other natural rights, paternal power is self-enforcing, but force alone is not sufficient to establish a natural right: an uncle will doubtless be stronger than his infant nephews, but because he prefers his own children by nature, this superiority of force can never produce a natural right.

Rousseau goes beyond this summary of the natural rights which

---

[65] *Geneva MS*, I, v (P, III, 297–98). Note that the preference of the father for his own children is a *loi naturelle*; it is not a "law of nature" which could have operated in the pure state of nature (where grown children cannot be recognized by their parents), but it is a "law" based on the natural sentiments released by the experience of social life. Cf. above, chap. II, n. 92, and the version of this paragraph in *Contrat social*, I, ii (P, III, 352), cited in part above, p. 128.

[66] *Geneva MS*, I, v (P, III, 298). This passage reappears in *Économie Politique* (P, III, 241).

legitimize the authority of the father (and which, according to the *Second Discourse*, only come to be enforced within civil society).[67] He compares civil society to the family in a long passage used in the *Political Economy*, showing that the size, the origin of the duties imposed on those with authority, the role of property, and the "destiny" of the two kinds of society are radically different.[68]

> Although the functions of the father of a family and of the prince should tend to the same objective, it is by ways so different; their duties and their rights are so distinct, that one cannot confuse them without forming the most false ideas about the principles of society.[69]

Natural sentiments that are appropriate in the family are pernicious in civil society:

> In fact, if the voice of nature is the best counsel that a father should listen to in order to fulfill well his duties, it is for the magistrate only a false guide that works ceaselessly to lead him away from his duties. . . . To do well, the former has only to consult his heart; the latter becomes a traitor the minute he listens to his.[70]

The priority of sentiment in the realm of personal morality is sharply opposed to the priority of rational principle in political society, for the magistrate should follow no rule other than "public reason, which is the law."[71] The conventional status of the political community is thus proved by the same tension between natural sentiment and rational principle which distinguishes Rousseau's political thought from his teaching concerning individual happiness.

In the *Geneva MS* Rousseau adds, as an aside to his proof that the father has a kind of natural authority in the family, a remark concerning slavery:

[67] Cf. *Second Discourse*, Part 2 (P, III, 182).

[68] See *Geneva MS*, I, v (P, III, 298-300) and the published form of the same text, *Économie Politique* (P, III, 241-44). Note that Rousseau devotes a long paragraph to the argument that "by several reasons derived from the nature of the thing, the father should command in the family" (*loc. cit.*, pp. 299; 242-43); cf. the analysis of the inferiority of women in the *Émile*, v (G, 445-53), discussed above, pp. 25-26.

[69] *Geneva MS*, I, v (P, III, 300). In *Économie Politique* (P, III, 243) Rousseau substitutes "the first magistrate" for "the prince" and "fundamental laws of society" for "principles of society"; he deletes the words "the most."

[70] *Geneva MS*, I, v (P, III, 300); *Économie Politique* (P, III, 243).

[71] *Ibid.* See the example of Brutus "condemning his children to death" (*Dernière Réponse* [P, III, 88-89]).

I do not speak of slavery because it is contrary to nature and because nothing can authorize it.[72]

In the *Social Contract*, Rousseau enlarges on this remark by attacking
Grotius for having denied "that all human power is established in
favor of those who are governed"; shifting silently from the family
(where power is presumably so directed) to slavery, Rousseau criticizes Grotius, Hobbes, and Aristotle for not basing political right on
the natural equality of all men.[73] Slavery can only be called natural
if one mistakes fact for right, and the effects of forcible enslavement
for its cause:

> Any man born in slavery is born for slavery; nothing is more cer-
> tain. . . . If there are slaves by nature, therefore, it is because there
> were slaves against nature.[74]

Historical fact cannot be taken as the basis of right, because in a society—which Rousseau calls "the great family, all of whose members
are naturally equal"—one can describe political authority as "purely
arbitrary with respect to its institution";[75] civil society and political
right presuppose a "convention" which can only be explained by reason because the "social bond of the city could not and should not
have been formed by the extension of that of the family."[76]

The second false notion considered by Rousseau in the *Geneva
MS* is:

> That a rich and powerful man, having acquired immense posses-
> sions in land, imposed laws on those who wanted to settle there;
> that he only permitted them to do so on condition that they rec-
> ognize his supreme authority and obey all his wishes, I can even
> conceive of that.[77]

Unlike the dialogue of the rich and poor described as the most likely

---

[72] *Geneva MS*, I, v (P, III, 299). In *Économie Politique*, Rousseau substitutes "no right" for "nothing" (P, III, 243). Cf. *Contrat social*, I, iv (P, III,
358): "the right to slaves is nul, not only because it is illegitimate, but because it is absurd and means nothing."

[73] *Ibid.*, I, ii (P, III, 352–53). Originally, the criticism of Grotius was part
of Rousseau's rejection of the fourth in his list of "false notions of the social
bond," namely the "tacit consent" to usurpation (*Geneva MS*, I, v [P, III, 305]);
the extension of familial authority to political society is equivalent to "slavery,"
"usurpation," and "tyranny."

[74] *Contrat social*, I, ii (P, III, 353).

[75] *Geneva MS*, I, v (P, III, 298); *Économie Politique* (P, III, 241).

[76] *Geneva MS*, I, v (P, III, 300).   [77] *Ibid.* (300–01).

circumstance for the conclusion of the social contract in the *Second Discourse*,[78] this assumption cannot be "the first foundation of right" since it "supposes anterior rights"—namely the uncontested right of one man to "immense possessions in land," which is a "punishable usurpation" in the state of nature.[79] This hypothesis could not occur following the account of the *Second Discourse* because other men in the state of nature, having a natural right to preserve themselves, would never respect the claim of the rich man; such a conception amounts to a "double usurpation, namely over the property of the land and over the freedom of the inhabitants."[80]

Rousseau does not refer to this "false notion of the social bond" in the *Social Contract* itself, merely carrying over the discussion of the property right of the first occupant to the chapter "Of Real Property" (*Du Domaine Reel*).[81] It may be that Rousseau considered as sufficient the discussion of the *Second Discourse*, which is summarized in the *Social Contract* by the remark that:

> The right of the first occupant, although more real than that of the strongest, does not become a true right until after the establishment of the right to property.[82]

The formulation in the *Geneva MS* is, however, of interest because it is a critique of the claims to political authority by European powers who were in the process of colonizing the Western hemisphere; in addition to the reference to Balboa's claim of the entire South American continent and Pacific Ocean (which recurs in the *Social Contract*),[83] the first draft included a note of some interest:

> I read in I don't know what work, entitled I think *l'Observateur Hollandois*, a rather pleasant principle; it is that all land only in-

[78] *Second Discourse*, Part 2 (P, III, 176–77).
[79] *Geneva MS*, I, v (P, III, 301). Cf. Locke, *Second Treatise*, chap. XVI, esp. § 184.
[80] *Geneva MS*, I, v (P, III, 301).
[81] Cf. *ibid.* (301–02) and *Contrat social*, I, ix (P, III, 366). Note the distinction between a "real right" (i.e., a right to property) and a "personal right" (i.e., a right over persons).
[82] *Ibid.* (365). It seems likely that the "right of the first occupant" is more "real" than the right of the strongest not primarily in the sense of being more valid in the state of nature—a claim Rousseau explicitly denies in Part 2 of the *Second Discourse* (P, III, 164, 173, 176–77) and in the first draft of this passage, *Geneva MS*, I, iii, (P, III, 293)—but because the right of the first occupant through labor is a right to possess *land* (a "real" possession), rather than a "personal" right based solely on the physical strength of the claimant. (See the preceding footnote.)
[83] Cf. *ibid.*, I, v (301); *Contrat social*, I, ix (P, III, 366).

habited by savages should be considered vacant, and that one can legitimately take it and chase out the inhabitants without doing them any wrong according to natural right.[84]

Colonial governments can be explained with respect to the power of the King or government to grant land to subjects or immigrants, but the claim that such power is based on "natural right" is baseless. Such an attack on European colonization would doubtless have been ill-viewed by the French government at the time of the publication of the *Social Contract*,[85] but its presence in the first draft reflects Rousseau's insistence on applying his principles of political right to actual circumstances.

The third false notion studied by Rousseau in the *Geneva MS* flows logically from the preceding one: if claims to more land than is necessary for personal self-preservation are illegitimate in the state of nature, the claim to colonial territories ultimately rests on the "right of war":

> That by the right of war the conqueror, instead of killing his captives, reduces them to eternal servitude, without doubt he does well for his profit, but since he only treats them thus by the right of war, the state of war does not end between the conquered and him, for it can only end by a free and voluntary convention, as it began.[86]

The obvious thrust of this passage, which echoes Locke's treatment, is carried over into the chapter "On Slavery" in the *Social Contract*:

> I say that a slave made in war, or a conquered people, is held to nothing at all toward its master except to obey him as long as forced to do so . . . the state of war subsists between them as be-

[84] *Geneva MS*, I, v (P, III, 301). Rousseau's reference is to *L'Observateur Hollandois, ou Lettres de M. Van * * à M. H * * de la Haye, sur l'état présent des affairs de l'Europe*, 8 vols. (La Haye: no publisher, 1755–59), Eighth Letter, 2 January 1756, II, 41–48. These letters, generally attributed to Jacob N. Moreau, were an attempt to stir up anti-British sentiment among the French on the occasion of the colonial conflict that erupted into the Seven Years War (1756–63). See esp. pp. 44–45: "we can, in the present dispute, consider as vacant lands all those that are only inhabited by savages." Rousseau's footnote reference thus establishes January 1756, as the earliest possible date for Rousseau's composition of the *Geneva MS* in the form now known to us.

[85] Suffice it to mention that in 1762 England and France were still engaged in war over their rival claims to Canada and other colonial possessions; hostilities were only concluded by the Treaty of Paris in 1763.

[86] *Geneva MS*, I, v (P, III, 302).

fore, even their relationship is the consequence of it, and the usage of the right of war does not suppose any treaty of peace.[87]

The use of force can never produce a "civil state, but only a modified right of war."[88]

Rousseau's treatment of the legitimate claims arising from war goes further, as is revealed by the remark—at first curious—that the state of war "can only end by a free and voluntary convention, as it began." In his fragmentary manuscript on *The State of War*, Rousseau says:

> If I wanted to elaborate the notion of the state of war, I would easily demonstrate that it can only result from the free consent of the belligerent parties, and that if one wants to attack and the other does not want to defend itself, there is no state of war, but only violence and aggression.[89]

For Rousseau, the state of war has a conventional status in terms of right—and as such cannot exist in the pure state of nature even if a war of all against all arises immediately prior to the formation of civil society.

> By the very fact that men living in their primitive independence do not have between them sufficiently consistent relationships to constitute either the state of war or the state of peace, they are not naturally enemies. It is the relationship of things and not of men which constitutes war, and since the state of war can not arise from simple personal relations, but only from real relations [*relations réelles*], private war or war between man and man cannot exist either in the state of nature, or in the social state, where everything is under the authority of laws.[90]

War can never exist, by right, between individuals because even in the state of nature, where violence occurs, there is nothing but flux; property, which alone creates "real" things, is the necessary precondition of a state of war. Hence the rights of war in the strict or juridical sense presuppose "previously existing societies whose origin is not explained."[91]

[87] *Contrat social*, I, iv (P, III, 358). Cf. Locke, *Second Treatise*, chap. IV, § 23–24; chap. XVI, esp. § 196.
[88] *Geneva MS*, I, v (P, III, 303). Cf. *État de Guerre* (P, III, 608).
[89] *Ibid*. (615).
[90] *Contrat social*, I, iv (P, III, 356–57). Note that the phrase *relations réelles* here means proprietary relationships; cf. nn. 81 and 82 of this chapter. On this juridical critique of Hobbes' conception of the state of war, see Derathé, *Rousseau et la Science Politique*, pp. 134–37.
[91] *Geneva MS*, I, v (P, III, 303).

Although this conception of the rightful or legitimate state of war seems to be a merely technical or legal argument, it reveals the character of Rousseau's conception of civil society.

> War is therefore not a relation between man and man, but a relation between state and state, in which private persons are only accidentally enemies, not as men, nor even as citizens, but as soldiers.[92]

War is necessarily and only a condition relating different civil societies to each other because it is a concept discovered or defined by reason, unlike the mere violence occurring in the animal world. The "right of the strongest" which is automatically respected in the pure state of nature is not a true right because it has no rational meaning.

> Force is physical power; I do not see what morality can result from its effect. . . . If one must obey by force, one does not need to obey by duty, and if one is no longer forced to obey one is no longer obliged. It will therefore be seen that this word right adds nothing to force, here it doesn't mean anything at all.[93]

The right of the strongest (which alone can describe violence between individuals in the state of nature) and the right of war (which, properly defined, describes legitimate violence between political communities) could not be the foundation of civil society, for the former is not truly a right establishing correlative moral duties, and the latter does not concern individuals as such. The logic of political obedience can only be founded on a right which individual men could rationally and freely create by mutual consent.

The last of the false notions of civil society treated in the *Geneva MS* underlines the combination of will and reason which characterizes Rousseau's conception of the nature of law.

> That a violent usurpation finally becomes legitimate power by the lapse of time; that prescription alone could change a usurper into supreme magistrate and a herd of slaves into the body of a nation, is something which many learned men have dared assert, and which lacks no other authority except that of reason.[94]

Factual authority can indeed be found for the transformation of violence into civil obedience, but reason does not support such origins as

---

[92] *Contrat social*, I, iv (P, III, 357).
[93] *Ibid.*, I, iii (354). On reason as the criterion for the legitimacy of a right, cf. *ibid.*, I, iv (358), cited in n. 72 of this chapter.
[94] *Geneva MS*, I, v (P, III, 303).

the basis of respectable political right. Although Rousseau admits the possibility of a voluntary submission to arbitrary power by one generation of men, his crucial objection is his denial that "this power could possibly be transmitted to other generations."[95] In a passage similar to one in the *Second Discourse*, Rousseau distinguishes between the rights of an individual to his own life and property, and the rights of unborn children:

> It is sufficient to distinguish the rights that the son holds uniquely from his father, like the property of his goods, from the rights he only holds from nature and his quality as a man, like freedom. It is not doubtful that by the law of reason the father may alienate the former, of which he is the sole owner, and deprive his infants of them. But it is not the same for the others, which are immediate gifts of nature and which as a result no man can take away from them.[96]

The "law of reason" indicates the limits to which any man can go in freely willing to divest himself of *any* rights (be they natural or political), but there is no way of inferring a reason which could prohibit men from exercising their natural freedom (i.e., their ability to will) merely because their ancestors reached an agreement preventing them from so doing. Hence silence under a tyrant cannot be taken for consent because "it is necessary that the people speak in order to authorize him, and that they speak in full freedom."[97]

The study of political right does not concern "what is, but what is appropriate and just."[98] Whatever the role of the "law of the strongest" or brute violence as the efficient cause of man's entry into civil societies, the nature of the resulting social bond must be explained by human reason, which can discover the necessary logic of political obedience. This logic is political right properly understood; the social bond necessarily implies a voluntary union whose end is "the common interest."[99] And "if the common interest is the object of the association, it is clear that the general will must be the rule of the actions of the social body."[100] Since the concept of the general will is analyzed in detail in the next chapter, this examination of the first

[95] *Ibid.*
[96] *Geneva MS*, I, v (P, III, 304). Cf. *Second Discourse*, Part 2 (P, III, 184) and above, p. 187.
[97] *Geneva MS*, I, v (P, III, 304).   [98] *Ibid.* (305).
[99] *Ibid.* (304).   [100] *Ibid.*, I, vi (305).

draft of the *Social Contract* will have served its primary function if the character of Rousseau's principles of political right is clarified.

E · THE "IDEA OF CIVIL SOCIETY" AND THE
"SCIENCE OF THE LEGISLATOR"

Political obedience can only be legitimate if it can be explained in terms of a construct of reason, and such mental constructs—the principles of political right—must take as given the natural phenomenon that each individual has his own will and cannot be morally bound to do anything he has not freely willed to do. Human passions and needs cannot be the proper basis of principles of political right because they are historical creations or accidents that are not truly natural; if the decisive natural impulse is the desire to preserve oneself as an isolated being, in terms of right each individual's free choice of the means to survival (i.e., his freedom) is the only unquestionable assumption for political philosophy.

Developing one of the aspects implicit in Hobbes' rational construction of a "law of nature" that explains civil society, Rousseau insists that the only characteristic of man relative to the logic of civil society is his *will*.[101] This emphasis is not primarily a result of Rousseau's metaphysical belief in an immaterial soul; quite the contrary, it is intended to elaborate and correct previous modern or "scientific" political teachings.

Rousseau's principle of the general will, which defines the nature of law, might well be compared to the frictionless surface as a principle of mechanics. The frictionless surface is an "idea" which describes a relationship underlying all mechanical movement, even though no existent machine avoids friction completely; once the physical relationships have been analyzed on the assumption that friction is absent, it is relatively simple to calculate the friction which *is* present under any given circumstances. To say that the frictionless surface is an "ideal" might be misleading, for although it serves as a guide to the most efficient construction of any machine, the total absence of friction is not a feasible goal in practice.

Rousseau's principles of political justice are, like the principle of the frictionless surface, mental constructs which explain reality. These principles are "derived" from the "nature" of civil society:

These are, it seems to me, the most exact ideas that one can have of

---

[101] Cf. Strauss, *Natural Right and History*, p. 190, esp. n. 30.

the fundamental compact which is at the base of any true body politic. . . . it will be seen in the sequel how easily the entire political system is deduced from the [principles] that I have just established, and how their consequences are natural and clear.[102]

Because the correct principles are inherent in the "nature of things," they operate necessarily; because these principles are "ideas" which can never be completely realized, there is an inevitable imperfection of reality when compared to them.

Rousseau himself explicitly used this very analogy. The comparison between a political regime and a machine, with which Rousseau opens the *Geneva MS*, should be recalled in reading the following passage:

But even should the liaison of which I speak [i.e., the identity of particular wills and the general will in a well-constituted society] be as well established as it could possibly be, all the difficulties would not be removed. The works of men, always less perfect than those of nature, never go directly to their end. In politics, just as in mechanics, one cannot avoid acting more weakly or slower, and losing force or time. The general will is rarely the will of all, and the public force is always less than the sum of the particular forces; so that there are, in the parts of the State, an equivalent to the friction of machines, which one must know how to reduce to the least possible quantity, and which one must at least calculate and deduct in advance from the total force, in order to calculate exactly the proportion of the means employed to the effect desired.[103]

This analogy was apparently in Rousseau's mind at the time he was elaborating his political thought, for he also refers to it in the *État de Guerre*:

One should consider how much less, in the aggregation of the body politic, the public force is than the sum of the private forces, and how much friction there is, so to speak, in the play of the whole machine.[104]

[102] *Geneva MS*, I, vii (P, III, 309).
[103] *Ibid.*, I, iv (296–97). Cf. *Émile*, IV (G, 299): "To live in the world, one must know how to deal with men, one must know the instruments that influence them; one must calculate the action and reaction of private interest in civil society and foresee events so exactly that one is rarely fooled in one's enterprises, or that at least one always has taken the best means to succeed."
[104] *État de Guerre* (P, III, 606).

This mechanistic conception of political life, pervasive in both the first draft and published form of the *Social Contract*, provides insight to Rousseau's claim to have laid the foundations of a universally valid political teaching.[105]

The attempt to construct a theory of political life on the model of mechanics is rather different from the mode of reasoning implicit in the philosophy of Hobbes, despite the fact that both Hobbes and Rousseau have a similar objective. Hobbes had distinguished between "purely constructive or demonstrative sciences," based on mental constructs and characterized as the "consequences from quantity and motion," and the physical sciences, which apply such constructs to the experiences of bodies taken as given since they "have no dependence on man's *will*"; he apparently believed that it was possible to construct a political science, on the basis of a physical science of man, which could nonetheless have or approach the status of a "deductive" science.[106] Whereas Hobbes attempted to construct rational laws—summarized by the phrase the "nature of public law"—ultimately modeled on mathematical demonstration (and hence on the exact definition of terms and the logical deduction of consequences from these terms), Rousseau's model is an applied science or technology. In so doing, Rousseau could hope to avoid one of the major failings he found in the Hobbesian system—namely its assertion that certain phenomena are *natural* when in fact they are the consequence of social life and hence ultimately conventional.[107]

[105] See the references to political society as a "machine": *Geneva MS*, I, i (P, III, 281); I, ii (284); I, iii (292)—utilized in *Contrat social*, I, vii (P, III, 364); I, iv (296–97); II, ii (313)—utilized in *Contrat social*, II, vii (381); *Contrat social*, III, vi (408); *Lettres Écrites de la Montagne*, ix (P, III, 896). Consider also the references to political life in terms of the "resistance" and relationships of "force" (used in the mechanical sense): *Geneva MS*, I, iii (289–90)—utilized in the *Contrat social*, I, vi (360); I, iii (293)—utilized in *Contrat social*, I, ix (365); I, iv (296); II, ii (313)—utilized in *Contrat social*, II, vii (381-82); II, iii (324)—utilized in *Contrat social*, II, x (390); the analogy of centrifugal force: *Geneva MS*, II, iii (321)—utilized in *Contrat social*, II, ix (388); the analogy of levers: *Geneva MS*, II, iii (320)—utilized in *Contrat social*, II, ix (387); *Contrat social*, III, vi (409–10); III, viii (418–19 and n.); as well as *ibid.*, III, i (396–98); III, ii (400–02); III, vii (414); III, x (422); IV, i (437); IV, iv (446); IV, vii (459); *Lettre à d'Alembert* (G, 175). On the presumed universality of Rousseau's principles, see *Lettres Écrites de la Montagne*, vi (811).

[106] *Leviathan*, Part I, chap. IX (ed. Oakeshott, pp. 53–55), and Strauss, *Natural Right and History*, pp. 173–74, n. 9.

[107] See *Leviathan*, Part III, chap. XXXII: "I have derived the rights of sovereign power, and the duty of subjects, hitherto from the principles of nature only . . . that is to say, from the nature of man, known to us by experience,

Although Hobbes had compared political societies to "*automata* (engines that move themselves by springs and wheels as doth a watch)," he emphasized the characteristics of motion in the abstract rather than the empirical science based predominantly on observations of human behavior; only in this way could he claim to approximate a deductive "science of the just and the unjust," patterned on geometry and yet consistent with the given or nonconstructed character of human phenomena.[108]

For Rousseau, who admits that science must be based on human constructs, a rigorously deductive science of empirical phenomena of any sort is impossible; mathematics and geometrical proof are no longer the model for political or ethical thought because 'geometrical precision does not occur in moral quantities.'"[109] The purely rational deduction of conclusions from precise definitions must be confirmed by observation; as Rousseau himself summarized this method of proof, "I will only trust . . . reasoning insofar as it is justified by experience."[110] By approximating the approach of an experimental science, Rousseau avoided the tension between a constructed or geometric science of movement in the abstract and a science of movement based on experience. Or, to put it more precisely, this tension is displaced from the realm of philosophy itself to the relationship between theoretical constructs and their application to specific historical or political circumstances.

Rousseau's conception of science is perhaps most explicitly re-

---

and from definitions of such words as are essential to all political reasoning, universally agreed on" (ed. Oakeshott, p. 242). On the conventional character of the "experience" of civilized man according to Rousseau, see *Second Discourse*, esp. Pref. (P, III, 122); on Rousseau's denial that words can be used with "geometrical" precision, see *Émile*, II, (G, 104 n.).

[108] See *Leviathan*, Introd. and Part I, esp. chap. I–II, VI. Note that, according to the Introduction, the essential experience necessary for a deductive science of human passions is the study of oneself (ed. Oakeshott, p. 6). Compare the kind of evidence presented by Hobbes and by Rousseau to prove that "nature should thus dissociate" men: *ibid.*, Part I, chap. XIII (82–83) and *Second Discourse*, Part 1 (P, III, 151). Cf. also *Leviathan*, Part II, chap. XX (134)— "what I find by speculation and deduction"—with *Contrat social*, I, iv (P, III, 357).

[109] *Ibid.*, III, i (398).

[110] *Geneva MS*, I, iv (P, III, 296). Cf. *ibid.*, I, ii (287), cited above, p. 270; *Second Discourse*, Part 2 (P, III, 192): "what reflexion teaches us on this subject, observation confirms perfectly"; *First Discourse*, Part 1 (P, III, 16): "let us no longer hesitate to agree on all points where our reasoning will be found to coincide with historical induction"; *Contrat social*, III, x (P, III, 425–26); *Lettre à d'Alembert* (G, 192).

vealed in his criticism of Voltaire's assertion that "nature is not subjected either to any precise quantity or to any precise form":[111]

> I would have thought, entirely to the contrary, that nature alone rigourously follows this precision. . . . These apparent irregularities doubtless come from some laws that we do not know, and that nature follows just as faithfully as those known to us.[112]

The regularities discovered by science exist in the natural phenomena themselves, and are merely approximated by the construction of laws of nature by human reason; geometric figures, because they are the purest example of abstract mental constructs, can not be the model on which natural science is based.

> For mathematical figures, being only abstractions, are only related to themselves, whereas all those of natural bodies are relative to other bodies and to movements which modify them.[113]

"Demonstration" of the laws governing physical phenomena is, in the strict sense of the word, impossible even if the phenomena "have exactly the movement calculated" according to these laws; "new experiments" may at any time reveal "a more exact system" that replaces currently held theories.[114]

If modern science—despite its ability to predict natural events—is based on reasoning which approximates opinion rather than true knowledge, a science of human things cannot be based solely on the physical sciences (even though it must take them into account in analyzing the place of man in the physical world). Whereas Hobbes distinguishes between different sciences in terms of their objects and the mode of reasoning appropriate to study them, Rousseau distinguishes between the subjective certainty of knowledge concerning oneself and the lack of such certainty with respect to external phenomena. The one aspect of human nature which is certain to every man is that, as a sensitive being, he has the sentiment of his own existence; the "will" (apart from any metaphysical questions concerning its freedom) is a solid foundation for political philosophy because it is the felt manifestation of that sentiment directed toward action.[115]

This conception of science, left relatively unformulated by Rous-

[111] Voltaire made this remark in a note to his "Poem on the Disaster of Lisbon," cited by Rousseau in his "Letter to Voltaire," 18 August 1756 (C. G., II, 310 and n.).
[112] *Ibid.* (311).   [113] *Ibid.* (312).
[114] *Ibid.* (314).
[115] See *Contrat social*, III, i (P, III, 395); *Émile*, "Prof. of Faith" (G, 330).

seau and later developed by Kant, explains why Rousseau's principles of political right are so narrowly restricted to the relationship between "private wills" and the "general will." Since civil society is a
human creation—or as Rousseau puts it so often, a "moral being"
to be distinguished from the "physical beings" or men who compose
it—it is necessary to elaborate the mental construct which explains
the subordination of the latter to the former.

> At bottom, the body politic, being only a moral person, is only a
> being of reason. Remove the public convention, at that instant the
> state is destroyed without the slightest alteration in everything that
> composes it, and all human conventions could never change any-
> thing in the physical character of things.[116]

Although it is possible to discover the logical "nature of law," such a
theoretical formulation or construct is not, by itself, a "natural public
law" (i.e., a sufficient guide to practical political life) because it deals
only with the moral phenomenon of human will and not with the
physical phenomena that condition social life in time and space. Since
"it is impossible" to create a society in which each citizen "does not
have an individual and separate existence, by which he can satisfy his
own preservation by himself,"[117] the artificial logic explaining civil
obedience must be complemented by a science which treats the members of the body politic (and the circumstances in which they act) as
physical phenomena; only by means of such a combination can philosophy guide the statesman.

Immediately after elaborating the analogy between his principles of
political right and a frictionless surface in the *Geneva MS*, Rousseau
adds (with reference to the necessary "friction" which the political
man must "calculate and deduct in advance") :

> But without entering into these difficult researches which make up
> the science of the legislator, let us complete the specification of the
> idea of the civil state.[118]

[116] *État de Guerre* (P, III, 608). Cf. *Geneva MS*, I, vii (P, III, 309)—"the
state has only an ideal and conventional existence"—and *Contrat social*, II,
iv (P, III, 372–73)—"the state or the city is only a moral person . . . but
besides the public person we have to consider the private persons who compose it and whose life and freedom are naturally independent of it." But cf.
Geneva MS, I, iii (291): if the citizen "considers the moral person which
constitutes the state as a being of reason," he becomes a bad citizen; the discovery of the legal fiction underlying civil society is morally corrupting for
the many. See Strauss, *Natural Right and History*, pp. 287–88.
[117] *État de Guerre* (P, III, 606).
[118] *Geneva MS*, I, iv (P, III, 297).

This science is necessary for Rousseau if a statesman is to calculate the effects of laws:

> For the force of the laws has its measure, and that of the vices that they repress also has its measure. It is only after having compared these two quantities and found that the former surpasses the latter, that one can be assured of the execution of the laws. The knowledge of these relationships makes up the true science of the legislator.[119]

Even given a knowledge of the "nature of the social body" or the "idea of the civil state," which it is Rousseau's primary concern to discover, political action requires knowledge of the science composed of "maxims of government" that should guide the "administration" or "movement" of civil society.[120]

The articulation between the "nature of law" (Rousseau's construct establishing principles of right) and the "science of the legislator" (a guide for successful political action) is much clearer in the first draft than in the published version of the *Social Contract*. Having analyzed the social compact and shown the necessity for a legislator in Book I, the Second Book of the *Geneva MS* begins as follows:

> By the social compact we have given the body politic existence and life; now it is a question of giving it movement and will by legislation. . . . It is to this great objective that the science of legislation aims, but what is this science, where can a genius who possesses it be found, and what virtues are needed by one who dares to exercise it; this research is great and difficult; it is even discouraging for anyone who flatters himself to see emerge a well-constituted state.[121]

Without a science of legislation, the principles of political right are themselves "useless" for any purpose except the criticism of injustice, and although Rousseau himself did not claim that he had fully established such a science, he clearly intended to pose its foundations.[122]

---

[119] *Lettre à d'Alembert* (G, 175).

[120] *Geneva MS*, I, i (P, III, 281), cited above, p. 260. Cf. the distinction between "lawfulness" and the "true rules of politics" (which can resolve "inconvenience" arising from the application of "lawful" principles) in Hobbes, *Leviathan*, Part 2, chap. XIX (ed. Oakeshott, p. 129).

[121] *Geneva MS*, II, i (P, III, 312).

[122] Cf. *Émile*, v (G, 584, 597); *Fragments Politiques*, I, 2 (P, III, 474). That the elaboration of the science of legislation was not Rousseau's prime concern is indicated by the following remark in the *État de Guerre* (P, III, 611–12): "I will limit myself, as I have always done, to examining human

This intention is manifested, if by nothing else, in the order of presentation in the *Geneva MS*: the short introductory chapter to Book II is followed by a chapter "On the Legislator" (emphasizing the "superior intelligence" and "wisdom" as well as "virtue" needed by the lawgiver)[123] and another "On the People to be Instituted" (in which Rousseau distinguishes "vices" in the "substance" and "dimensions" of peoples which make a healthy institution impossible).[124] Originally, the latter of these chapters began with an indication that Rousseau was shifting from a consideration of principles of political right to the specification of the practical considerations which should guide the legislator:

> Although I am considering here right and not conveniences, I can not help glancing in passing at those conveniences which are indispensable in any good institution.[125]

In this chapter, for example, Rousseau refers to what he calls the "maxim" that "in general a small state is always proportionately stronger than a large one"; incontestably, this generalization is what Rousseau had called one of the "maxims of government" which must be distinguished from the principles of political right defining the "nature of the body politic."[126]

In its final form as well as in the first draft, the *Social Contract* contains many such "maxims." In the published version, the clearest statement of the distinction between them and principles of political right occurs in the last chapter of Book III, in which Rousseau repeats his insistence that the form of government can be changed at any time by the sovereign people:

> It is true that these changes are always dangerous, and that one should never touch the established government except when it be-

---

institutions by their principles; to correcting, if possible, the false ideas that interested authors give us about them; and to see to it at least that injustice and violence do not impudently take the name of right and equity."

[123] *Geneva MS*, II, ii (P, III, 313–18, esp. 313–14, 316–18). The bulk of this chapter appears in *Contrat social*, II, vii (P, III, 381–84). By revising the point of division between the first two books and suppressing Book II, chap. I of the *Geneva MS*, "On the Law" and "On the Legislator" became successive chapters in the middle of Book II of the *Contrat social* (thereby blurring a distinction in subject matter that had been clear in the first draft). For an explanation of this change, see below, pp. 293, 312–13.

[124] *Geneva MS*, II, iii (P, III, 318–26, esp. 319–20). This long chapter is, in the definitive version, divided into three chapters, all entitled "Of the People," *Contrat social*, II, viii–x (P, III, 384–91). For a possible explanation, see below, pp. 347–48.

[125] *Geneva MS*, II, iii (P, III, 318).   [126] *Ibid.* (320). Cf. I, i (281).

comes incompatible with the public good; but this circumspection is a *maxim of politics and not a rule of right,* and the State is no more bound to leave civil authority to its rulers than military authority to its generals.[127]

Since the maxims of politics which should guide the statesman will be discussed below in chapter VIII, the primary question here is the status of these prudential rules.

In the process of preparing the *Social Contract* for publication, Rousseau apparently decided not to call the ensemble of maxims of politics the "science of the legislator";[128] he ultimately deleted all passages in Books I and II emphasizing the difference between such a science and the principles of political right. Because this distinction is explicitly maintained in the final version of the *Social Contract*, the changes in its presentation would seem to reflect Rousseau's attitude toward the public teaching of a science of political action rather than his belief that such a science was possible and necessary. It may be that Rousseau preferred to speak of the "art of the legislator" because he was aware that he had not completed the "great and difficult" research necessary to found it.[129] Even more important, Rousseau may have become aware that his science of politics could be misused as a means of furthering personal ambition if adopted by a statesman who was not animated by virtue. Because of his fundamental attack on the principles of the enlightenment (and the relatively subordinate role of the elaboration of a political science given his conception of the limits of politics), it is not unlikely that Rousseau's revision of the draft of the *Social Contract* primarily reflects his reserve in diffusing such a potentially dangerous science.[130]

3 · *The Tension between Nature and Civil Society*

We are now in a somewhat better position to understand the con-

---

[127] *Contrat social*, III, xviii (P, III, 435), italics added. Cf. the distinction between "political considerations" and "right," *ibid.*, IV, viii (467).

[128] *Ibid.*, III, ii (402). Cf. *ibid.*, II, xi (393) with *Geneva MS*, II, vi (P, III, 333) and consider *Fragments Politiques*, II, 15 (P, III, 480).

[129] The main evidence for this interpretation is, of course, the "Notice" published at the head of the *Contrat social*, in which Rousseau says that "this little treatise is extracted from a much more extensive work, once undertaken without having consulted my strength, and abandoned a long time ago" (*Contrat social*, Avertissement [P, III, 349]). Cf. *Fragments Politiques* (P, III, 472–560).

[130] For Rousseau's emphasis on the combination of wisdom and virtue needed by any statesman who would use a "science of legislation," see *Geneva MS*, II, i (P, III, 312); II, ii (312–13, 317). On the political dangers of political science, see above, esp. chap. V, § 2C, and n. 116 of this chapter.

nection between Rousseau's philosophic teaching in general (which is characterized by the appeal from social convention to nature) and his political teaching proper (which attempts to show men how social conventions can become truly legitimate). In so doing, it will be perhaps clearer why Rousseau, who denounced tyranny so consistently, could be considered as a source of modern totalitarianism by some commentators.[131] The fundamental question to which we must turn is the relationship between Rousseau's understanding of political life and his fundamental distinction between nature and society. More precisely, how can the logic of civil society presuppose conventions which denature man, substituting "a partial and moral existence for the physical and independent existence that we have all received from nature," if it is true that "all human conventions could never change anything in the physical character of things."[132]

This apparent contradiction in Rousseau's political thought was more evident in the first draft than in the final version of the *Social Contract*. For example, in the context of the *Geneva MS*, where Rousseau asserts that "the public force is always less than the sum of the particular forces,"[133] the following passage in the chapter "On the Legislator" takes on a slightly different character than it is usually given:

> So that if each citizen can do nothing except by all the others and the force acquired by the whole is equal or superior to the sum of the natural forces of all the individuals, one can say that the legislation is at the highest degree of perfection it can attain.[134]

The "highest degree of perfection" of legislation is impossible to achieve in practice because it requires the total destruction of each man's natural independence. Laws can not completely annihilate man's nature, and indeed good laws should not even attempt to destroy or overcome nature in all things; quite the contrary:

> What makes the constitution of a state truly solid and durable, is

[131] E.g., J. L. Talmon, *The Origins of Totalitarian Democracy* (New York: Praeger, 1960), pp. 38–49; Lester G. Crocker, "Rousseau et la voi du totalitarisme," *Rousseau et la Philosophie Politique* (Paris: Presses Universitaires de France, 1965), pp. 99–136; Frederick Watkins, "Introduction," *Rousseau: Political Writings* (London: Thomas Nelson, 1953), pp. xxvii-xxxv.

[132] Cf. *Geneva MS*, II, ii (P, III, 313), repeated in *Contrat social*, II, vii (P, III, 381), with *État de Guerre* (P, III, 608), cited at n. 116 of this chapter.

[133] *Geneva MS*, I, iv (P, III, 297).

[134] *Ibid.*, II, ii (313). As published, the passage is unchanged except that it begins: "So that if each citizen is nothing, can do nothing . . ." (*Contrat social*, II, vii [P, III, 382]).

when conveniences are so well observed that the natural relationships and the laws always fall in harmony on the same points, and that, so to speak, the latter only assure, accompany, and rectify the former. But if the legislator, making a mistake in his objective, takes a principle different from the one which emerges from the nature of things, . . . one will see the laws weaken insensibly, the constitution become altered, and the State will not cease to be agitated until it is destroyed or changed and invincible nature has recaptured her empire.[135]

Although the logic of civil societies requires that the laws change the nature of *man*, practical legislation must "assure, accompany, and rectify" the "nature of *things*." But since man also has a physical nature, this distinction between the elements of "invincible nature" which ultimately recaptures "her empire" and the aspect of man which can and must be denatured requires further analysis.

According to the *Second Discourse*, the human species is distinguished from all others most noticeably by its faculty of perfectibility; men can change their own nature or give themselves a "second nature."[136] If this unique capacity permits the creation of a legitimate civil society, it also makes possible the most radical corruption of human nature. For example:

So that just as to establish slavery, violence had to be done to nature, nature had to be changed to perpetuate this right.[137]

Since Rousseau knew that, in fact, slavery had been "established" and "perpetuated," he tacitly admits that nature can be so changed that, in terms of right, "a man would not be born a man" (i.e., he would be born lacking freedom, a gift received from nature "by being a man"); what Aristotle called "natural slavery" is evidence that men can be forced or trained to act against nature almost without limit.[138]

Man's perfectibility makes possible obedience which is not based on true legitimacy or right, and a government which is obeyed, for whatever reason, can make of men virtually anything:

[135] *Geneva MS*, II, vi (P, III, 333). This paragraph appears without change in *Contrat social*, II, xi (P, III, 393). Cf. also *Geneva MS*, II, iii (325); *Contrat social*, III, viii (416), and *Lettre à d'Alembert* (G, 186): "for good laws never change the nature of things, they only follow it, and only such laws are observed."

[136] *Second Discourse*, Pref. (P, III, 122); Part 1 (142); n. x (211); *Émile*, I (G, 9–10); II (165).

[137] *Second Discourse*, Part 2 (P, III, 184).

[138] *Ibid.*; *Contrat social*, I, ii (P, III, 353); I, iv (356); III, xv (431). Cf. Aristotle, *Politics* I.1253b–55b.

It is certain that peoples are in the long run what the government makes them: warriors, citizens, men when it so wants; populace and rabble when it so pleases.[139]

This openness or freedom of man to change and create his own being has been summarized by one commentator as follows:

There are no natural obstacles to man's almost unlimited progress or to his power of liberating himself from evil. For the same reason, there are no natural obstacles to man's almost unlimited degradation. Man is by nature almost infinitely malleable.[140]

The precise question which this formulation forces us to consider is the meaning of the word "almost"; if "invincible nature" recaptures "her empire" when the legislator adopts "a principle different from the one which emerges from the nature of things," there seem to be some natural obstacles both to "man's power of liberating himself from evil" and to his "unlimited degradation." We must therefore try to see just what persisting natural characteristics Rousseau thought could limit man's almost unlimited perfectibility.

On the lowest level, man is subject to certain needs which cannot be avoided; food and sleep are, for Rousseau, the only such purely physical needs, and although sexual desire also has a moral or conventional element, it too has a physical aspect which seems impossible to destroy except in rare individual cases.[141] Of more importance is Rousseau's assertion that the perfection of man releases or activates natural impulses that were dormant in the pure state of nature; again and again he speaks of the conscience as an inborn, natural sentiment which cannot be destroyed once men have learned to reason:

These innate sentiments that nature has engraved in all hearts . . . can well be stifled in individuals by means of art, intrigues, and sophisms, but prompt to be reborn in following generations, they will always bring man back to his primitive dispositions, as the seed of a grafted tree always gives back the original stock. . . . Nature will imperceptibly reconquer her empire.[142]

[139] Économie Politique (P, III, 251).
[140] Strauss, Natural Right and History, p. 271.
[141] See above, pp. 6–8, 153–54.
[142] Rousseau Juge de Jean Jacques, III, (P, I, 972). Cf. Émile, I (G, 8), noting the botanical analogy discussed above, p. 10, nn. 26 and 27, and the references cited in analyzing the conscience, above, pp. 74–76.

The return to man's primitive and good natural dispositions is always possible for the isolated individual even in corrupt society;[143] man's natural sentiments are part of the "nature" that "will imperceptibly reconquer her empire" if the legislator fails to recognize that they are part of the nature of things.

Although for Rousseau the conscience provides at least one natural obstacle "to man's almost unlimited degradation," this obstacle is politically impotent (since it cannot serve, unaided, for anything but personal goodness or virtue). The inevitable social corruption which accompanies enlightenment and progress may render the establishment of a just political regime impossible for a given society. A people "can make itself free when it is only barbarous, but it can no longer do so when its civil energy is used up."[144] This inescapable characteristic of human evolution, which serves as a strict limit on the effectiveness of the conscience as a barrier to depravity, simultaneously serves as a kind of natural (or at least historical) obstacle to man's "power of liberating himself from evil." As a result, the possibility of creating a truly decent and virtuous human society seems to be subject to the dual limitation of the impotence of the individual's natural goodness and the irreversibility of an enlightened society's corruption.

The actualization of political justice therefore presupposes a certain harmony between natural necessity and social convention. When Rousseau speaks of the virtuous citizen as a "denatured" man, he does not mean that human perfectibility or malleability permits a total disregard for nature; on the contrary, the moulding of men (whether for good or ill) can never be truly effective unless it is consistent with nature.[145] For example, although Rousseau describes the laws of Sparta as denaturing men, in several decisive respects (such as the abandonment of weak or misformed infants and the role of women), Spartan conventions conformed to the physical "law of nature."[146]

To determine precisely the aspect of man's nature which is de-

[143] Note, for example, that the conscience is only possible for "individuals," not "collective bodies" (e.g., *Rousseau Juge de Jean Jacques*, III [P, III, 965 n.]).
[144] *Contrat social*, II, viii (P, III, 385). The term here translated by "energy" —*ressort*—also means a "spring" in a machine. See also the first draft of this passage, *Geneva MS*, II, iii (P, III, 319–20, 324): in both the *Geneva MS* and the *Contrat social*, the irreversibility of social corruption is called a "maxim"— i.e., it is part of the "science of the legislator."
[145] Cf. *Émile*, v (G, 514) with *Économie Politique* (P, III, 252).
[146] See *Second Discourse*, Part 1 (P, III, 135); *Émile*, I (G, 9); v (448, 497).

stroyed in the perfect society, one must refer to Rousseau's conception of the sentiments which are natural to man: a man is "denatured" when "the simplest operations of the human soul" have been uprooted. In this view, the ideal citizen lacks both love of himself and pity; the two naturally good impulses which characterize man and preserve the human species are intrinsically opposed to the perfection of society. Pity is, as we are told explicitly, "stifled" as man enters civil society and is "weak" within it; pity apparently contradicts the principles of a just regime, since once a criminal is legally convicted, it is doubtful whether anyone has the right to pardon him.[147] Love of oneself, the other naturally good sentiment, is even more sharply opposed to the requirements of a perfect social order: the good citizen is defined as the man who has substituted the "common self" (*moi commun*) of patriotism for the "human self" (*moi humain*).[148]

It would seem, therefore, that man is almost infinitely malleable in two senses: first, his physical nature, while it can never be destroyed, can be surprisingly changed; secondly, society can obliterate man's primitive natural sentiments. Moreover, it would seem that these two kinds of human nature have a curiously inverted relationship—in order to replace the natural sentiments by civic virtue, one must follow insofar as is possible the dictates of physical necessity; destruction or alteration of man's natural physique coincides with vice and personal pride, the unhealthy or corrupt social substitutes for love of oneself and pity. It would be radically inaccurate to apply the terms "denatured man" to those who undergo the latter combination of changes, for the true "denaturing" of the human heart is natural—or, to be less ambiguous, denatured man conforms to both the nature of the physical world and the nature of the just society.

Paradoxical as it may seem, the healthy denaturing of man does not require the destruction of *amour-propre*, the sentiment to which Rousseau attributes human corruption. Quite the contrary, as we have already seen in analyzing the *Émile*, the patriotism of the just society rests on a modified form of *amour-propre*, redirected to one's fellow citizens.[149] Because the best political order relies upon *amour-propre*, which can never be destroyed among civilized and thinking

[147] *Contrat social*, II, v (P, III, 377). Cf. *Second Discourse*, Part 1 (P, III, 154, 156); Part 2 (176); *Émile*, IV (G, 303–04).
[148] *Contrat social*, I, vi (P, III, 361)—utilizing *Geneva MS*, I, iii (P, III, 290). Cf. *Économie Politique* (P, III, 243–44)—utilizing *Geneva MS*, I, v (P, III, 300).
[149] See above, chap. I, §§ 4E and 5.

men,[150] even the perfect civil society "inevitably" tends toward decline.[151] Life is fundamentally a cycle of birth, maturity, and decay, not only for the individual and the species, but for each political society as well.[152]

The potentiality of successful political action, derived from man's perfectibility, can only operate within the natural limits posed by this pattern.

> Peoples, just like men, are only malleable in their youth; they become incorrigible in growing old.[153]

Rousseau's political teaching, far from being based on the simple enlightenment belief that "the human race is what we wish to make it," is an attempt to discover the natural factors which limit or permit the praiseworthy creation of legitimate human conventions. Rousseau's refusal to separate principles of political right from a science or art that specifies the "invincible" natural conditions surrounding successful legislation is evidence of his awareness that a doctrinaire belief in

---

[150] An indication of this impossibility may be found in the Spartan represented as the ideal citizen in the *Émile*. Rousseau says of the joy of Paedaretus upon not being elected to the council of 100: "I suppose this demonstration to be sincere; and there is reason to believe that it was. . . ." (*Émile*, I [G, 10]). Yet in one of the two versions of the story given by Plutarch, the Ephors themselves questioned the motive behind the laughter of Paedaretus: "Sayings of Spartans," 231B, *Moralia* (Loeb ed., III, 385–87). In the version followed by Rousseau, no mention is made either of this action or of laughter by Paedaretus: "Sayings of Kings and Commanders," 191F, *Moralia* (Loeb ed., III, 135). In addition, Plutarch tells another, most revealing story concerning this same Spartan general: "Chian exiles came to Sparta, and accused Paedaretus of many misdeeds; whereupon his mother Teleutia sent for them and, after listening to their complaints, feeling that her son was in the wrong, sent him this letter: 'Mither to Paedaretus. Aither dae better, or stay whare ye are and gie up hope o' gaen back safe to Sparta'" ("Sayings of Spartan Women," 241D–E, *Moralia* [ed. Loeb, III, 463]). Given Rousseau's familiarity with Plutarch, his choice of an exemplary citizen whose motives could in fact be questioned seems hardly accidental.

[151] *Contrat social*, III, ii (P, III, 401); III, x (421–22); III, xi (424); and II, xi (392)—utilizing *Geneva MS*, II, vi (P, III, 332); *Second Discourse*, Part 2 (P, III, 185, 187–88); *Lettres Écrites de la Montagne*, vi (P, III, 808).

[152] *Contrat social*, II, viii (P, III, 386); III, x (421); *Second Discourse*, Exordium (P, III, 133); Part 1 (160); Part 2 (171); n. VII (201); *Lettre à Philopolis* (P, III, 232).

[153] *Geneva MS*, II, iii (P, III, 319). Cf. *ibid.* (325): "There is almost no man nor people who does not have some best interval and some moment of his life to be given reason." Indeed, both the *Contrat social* and the *Émile* can be understood as Rousseau's prescriptions concerning how to take advantage of this possibility: cf. *Contrat social*, II, viii (P, III, 386) and Rousseau's revision of this sentence for the edition of 1782 (P, III, 1466), as well as *Émile*, IV (G, 402–03).

progress can be the foundation of the most extensive political and moral corruption. This explains why his political thought is as much directed toward preserving healthy societies where they exist as it is to prescribing the means of creating just regimes in previously "barbarian" societies.[154] Or, to put it differently, Rousseau's emphasis on realizing civil justice may explain why his works could have such revolutionary consequences despite the fact that, as one eminent critic has remarked, Rousseau was in a sense "a reactionary."[155]

[154] *Lettre à d'Alembert* (G, 216, 223, 234); *Lettres Écrites de la Montagne*, vi (P, III, 809).

[155] Bertrand de Jouvenel, "Essai sur la Politique de Rousseau," in J. J. Rousseau, *Du Contrat Social* (Geneva: Éditions du Cheval Ailé, 1947), p. 36. See also Iring Fetscher, "Rousseau, auteur d'intention conservatrice et d'action révolutionnaire," *Rousseau et la Philosophie Politique* (Paris: Presses Universitaires de France, 1965), pp. 51–76.

THE PRINCIPLES OF POLITICAL RIGHT
(SOCIAL CONTRACT)

1 · *The Character of the* Social Contract

A · THE PRACTICAL ORIENTATION OF ROUSSEAU'S PRINCIPLES OF POLITICAL RIGHT

The previous chapter should make it possible to interpret Rousseau's most famous political work without being forced to assume—as many have done—that it is riddled with "contradictions" and "confusion."[1] The title *Of the Social Contract* was, as has been suggested, chosen by Rousseau because it reflects the conventional character of all civil society.[2]

> The social order is a sacred right which serves as the basis of all others. However, this right does not come from nature; it is therefore founded on conventions. It is a question of knowing what these conventions are.[3]

Rousseau insists, from the very outset, that society can only be understood from a philosophic perspective like that of Hobbes, according to which justice is not natural. But in speaking of a social contract, Rousseau does not seek a historical convention like the Mayflower Compact; his concern with a rule of right is evident from the subtitle "Principles of Political Right"—a formula which reminds the reader

---

[1] For a typical example of such an interpretation, see George H. Sabine, *A History of Political Philosophy* (Rev. ed.; New York: Henry Holt, 1956), chap. XXVIII. For an indication of "the multifarious and mutually contradictory verdicts that have been given on the political thought of Rousseau," see Alfred Cobban, *Rousseau and the Modern State* (London: George Allen & Unwin, 1934), chap. II, and compare the varying interpretations given in the works listed in my bibliography under numbers 1 (vol. 3), 2, 8, 9, 10, 11, 12, 16, 24, 31, 34, 35, 36, 37, 38, 40, 43, 47, 48, 49, 54, 56, 57, 58, 59, 60.

[2] See above, pp. 259–60.

[3] *Contrat social*, I, i (P, III, 352). Cf. the first draft of this sentence (*Geneva MS*, I, iii [P, III, 289]), and note that in both versions Rousseau derives *"all* other" rights from the conventions of civil society.

of the jurists who derived human justice from a natural law.[4] In the title of the work, one finds the dual orientation of Rousseau's thought on which we have already insisted.[5]

Since enforceable laws of justice do not exist in the pre-political state, the founding of human society was itself an act of lawlessness. One need not rely solely on the *Geneva MS* for evidence of this view; Rousseau's epigraph, taken from Virgil's *Aeneid*, indicates this to anyone who considers the context from which it was taken:

> *Foederis aequas*
> *Dicamus leges*[6]

Although in isolation this phrase appears to refer to a historical social contract, it actually comes from a speech by the aged king of Latium, whose subjects have just been defeated in battle by the Trojans under Aeneas. The King suggests that peace be restored by a federation of the warring peoples, but his speech is of absolutely no effect; popular sentiment demands that Turnus (the great warrior of the Latins) fight a man-to-man battle with Aeneas, and the deliberations are interrupted by a new Trojan attack. Eventually Aeneas defeats Turnus and the resulting rout of the Latins permits Aeneas to establish his Trojan exiles on the site of Latium. Rome was originally founded on the "right of the strongest" and not on a social contract. And for those who might object that the epigraph comes from a poetic account, Rousseau provides another indication that force was prior to law in the founding of Rome.[7]

Although it is possible, if not probable, that political right was historically or factually founded on force, "force does not make right" philosophically speaking. The problem for Rousseau is not to de-

---

[4] E.g. Jean-Jacques Burlamaqui, *Principes du Droit Naturel* (Geneva: Barrillot, 1748); and *Principes du Droit Politique* (Geneva: Barrillot, 1751). Cf. Robert Derathé, *Rousseau et la Science Politique de Son Temps* (Paris: Presses Universitaires de France, 1950), esp. pp. 393–95.

[5] See above, pp. 77–79, 86–89, and chap. IV, § 3.

[6] "In an equitable federation / We will make laws" (*Aeneid* XI.321 [P, III, 347]).

[7] "The name *Rome*, which some pretend comes from *Romulus*, is Greek and means *force*; the name *Numa* is also Greek and means *law*. Is it a coincidence that the first two kings of that city had in advance names so well suited to what they did?" (*Contrat social*, IV, iv, n. [P, III, 444]). See *Gouvernement de Pologne*, ii (P, III, 957–58), where Romulus is described as a "brigand" and Numa as the lawgiver. If political origins are only known by fables, these fables reflect what actually happened. Cf. *Contrat social*, I, iii (354): "the right of the strongest" is "really established in principle" (or does *en principe* here mean "at the beginning"?).

scribe the establishment of political society, but to find the reasons that could make obedience *legitimate*; Rousseau must discover—or rather, create—political right.[8] Given the factual injustices of politics, the first words of the *Social Contract* show that it is necessary to satisfy two conditions in order to establish valid reasons for obedience:

> I want to seek if, in the civil order, there can be some legitimate and solid rule of administration, taking men as they are and the laws as they can be. In this research, I will always try to ally what right permits with what interest prescribes, so that justice and utility are not divided.[9]

Rousseau seeks a "rule" which is simultaneously "legitimate and solid," because without a legitimate reason for obedience human society only reveals "the violence of powerful men and the oppression of the weak";[10] and without a solid reason for obedience "the laws of justice are vain among men."[11] To be reliable, the rules of political justice must begin with the certitude that men, "as they are," are concerned only with their own interest; laws should conform to the nature of man (i.e., to a being who is not naturally just) because right merely "permits" and "interest prescribes." Political right can only replace the impotent traditional natural law teaching if utility can be combined with justice.

Since man's self-interest will never lead to the establishment of the perfect political order, Rousseau no longer seeks an ideal form of justice. Instead of describing, in words, the "best city" or the "best regime" (as in classical political philosophy, exemplified by Plato's *Republic*), Rousseau is concerned with a "rule of administration" which would be "legitimate" in the varying conditions of every actual society:[12]

---

[8] *Ibid.*, I, ii (353); I, iii (354–55). The famous opening words of Book I, chap. i of the *Contrat social* show that Rousseau "thinks" he "can resolve" the question of how to make obedience "legitimate": he does not stop to discuss the historical source of the "chains" of civil society (P, III, 351).

[9] *Ibid.*, Exordium (351).

[10] *Second Discourse*, Pref. (P, III, 127).

[11] *Contrat social*, II, vi (P, III, 378).

[12] Hence Rousseau examines the *Contrat social* (i.e., the bond that ties society together) rather than the *Republic* or *Politics* generally. No longer does political philosophy begin with the question: "What is the end of a political life?" Now the fundamental question is "Why do men obey a government?" or "What is a law?" The link between this lower question and the adoption of a materialist physics, implying that man is by nature asocial, should be evident. Cf. *Confessions* IX (P, I, 404–05), cited above, n. 29 of the Preface.

Therefore, when it is asked absolutely what is the best government, one poses a question which is insoluble because it is indeterminate; or, if one wishes, it has as many good solutions as there are possible combinations in the absolute and relative positions of peoples.[13]

Since justice must be useful, it is necessary to consider, from the outset, the human and natural necessities which serve as limits to the possible; to the objection that his principles are not realistic, Rousseau responds in advance by pointing out examples of their realization.[14]

In redirecting political speculation to that which is respectable or worthy of obedience, rather than to that which is per se desirable, Rousseau implicitly recognizes that his principles of political right must be adapted and applied to the specific conditions encountered in various societies. This concern for what happens here and now is evident in the second paragraph of the *Social Contract*:

> I enter into the matter without proving the importance of my subject. I may be asked whether I am a prince or legislator to write on politics. I reply no, and that is why I write on politics. If I were a prince or a legislator, I would not waste my time saying what ought to be done; I would do it or I would keep quiet.[15]

Although some critics have argued that Rousseau was essentially uninterested in actual political life and the practical application of his thought,[16] Rousseau himself indicates at the outset that there is a sense in which philosophical speculation is inferior to political activity.[17]

That "political right" does not exhaust the philosopher's concern

---

[13] *Contrat social*, III, ix (P, III, 419). Cf. II, xii (393).

[14] "From the existent to the possible, the logical consequence seems to me good" (*ibid.*, III, xii [426]). Cf. Exordium (351) and *Lettres Écrites de la Montagne*, VI (P, III, 809–10): "there was an existing government on my model [i.e., Geneva] . . . if I had only created a system . . . they would have been content to relegate the *Social Contract* to the land of chimeras along with Plato's *Republic*, the *Utopia*, and *Severambes*." On the relation between the *Contrat social* and the institutions of Geneva, see P, III, 1664–65 and the references there cited.

[15] *Contrat social*, Exordium (P, III, 351). This remark has ironic implications which will be considered below, pp. 306–07.

[16] E.g., Eric Weil, "J. J. Rousseau et sa Politique," *Critique*, LVI (January 1952), 17: "His theory is and wants to be unrealizable."

[17] Cf. Rousseau's preference of Cato to Socrates from the political point of view, *Économie Politique* (P, III, 255).

for politics was indicated in the *Geneva MS* by Rousseau's explicit distinction between the "science of the legislator" and the "idea of the civil state." Although many of the passages which emphasized this distinction were deleted in the final version of the *Social Contract*, we have already noted that Rousseau continues to distinguish between "principles of political right," to which the work is directed at the outset, and the "maxims of politics" which should guide the prudential application of these principles.[18] Even a superficial glance at the table of contents of the *Social Contract* shows that Rousseau does not confine himself to an exposition of the "nature of law" and abstract "principles of political right": Books III and IV are explicitly devoted to the "form of the Government" (i.e., the particular regime suitable to any given community) and the "means to strengthen the Constitution of the State" (i.e., the considerations necessary for maintaining a stable order).[19] Indeed, Rousseau turns to problems which, in the first draft, had been explicitly identified as matters of "convenience" and not of "right" as early as chapter viii of Book II, when he discusses "the People."[20]

Although most commentators have not emphasized the importance of Rousseau's distinction between the logical principles which explain the nature of law and the prudential maxims necessary for their application, there is good reason to base an examination of the *Social Contract* on this distinction. Primarily, of course, this approach is justified by our analysis of the *Geneva MS*; in addition, only this orientation explains Rousseau's extensive discussion of the Roman constitution in Book IV—a part of the *Social Contract* which has been little studied and has seemed an anomaly to some readers.[21] While many

[18] See above, chap. IV, § 2E.

[19] Book III is entitled: "In which is treated political laws, which is to say the form of government"; Book IV: "In which, continuing to treat political laws, the means of strengthening the Constitution of the State are revealed" (V, II, 22). These titles in the original table of contents are not reproduced in the Pléiade edition.

[20] Cf. *Geneva MS*, II, iii with *Contrat social*, II, viii–x. As a matter of fact, of the twelve chapters in Book II, which according to the table of contents discusses "Legislation," exactly one-half (chaps. vii to xii) deal with the general problem of implementing legislation; of the 48 chapters in the work as published, only the first 15 are devoted solely to the definition of the nature of law, which is virtually completed by Book II, chap. vi.

[21] Thus Vaughan writes: "It must be confessed that these four chapters [Book IV, chaps. iv–vii] are barely relevant to the subject and quite unworthy of the setting in which they stand. The beggarly elements of the Servian Constitution are a fitter theme for Sigonius than for Rousseau" (V, II, 109, n. 1). This view is cited with approval by Derathé (P, III, 1495), who adds: "in reality, it was for Rousseau a matter of filling out this Fourth Book, even

commentators have admitted that Rousseau was not doctrinaire in applying his political principles to "concrete" circumstances, few have realized that this prudential attitude is based on Rousseau's understanding of these principles themselves.[22] Hence, in analyzing the conceptions of the general will, the sovereign as distinct from the government, and law, it is essential to bear in mind that they are complemented by "maxims of politics" which determine the extent to which pure "right" can be approximated in "fact."

B · THE ADDRESSEE OF ROUSSEAU'S POLITICAL TEACHING

Rousseau's intention to develop principles of political right complemented by a "science of legislation" clarifies the addressee of the *Social Contract*. In a letter to his publisher, Rousseau spoke of this work as containing "difficult material, fit for few readers."[23] As noted, Rousseau begins by remarking that "if I were a prince or a lawgiver, I wouldn't waste my time saying what ought to be done; I would do it or I would keep quiet."[24] In addition to indicating that political action is in a sense superior to speculation, this remark would have seemed (at least to Rousseau's contemporaries) as a criticism of Frederick the Great, a well-known eighteenth-century ruler who had written on politics. Later in life, Rousseau frankly admitted to him

---

at the price of a digression [which has only a distant relationship with the 'principles of political right'] so that he could insert the chapter on Civil Religion." It need hardly be added that these remarks do not constitute an analysis of the chapters in question.

[22] See, e.g., Cobban, *Rousseau and the Modern State*, pp. 80–90; Ernst Cassirer, *The Question of Jean–Jacques Rousseau* (New York: Columbia University Press, 1954), pp. 65, 123; Jean Fabre, "Introduction sur le Gouvernement de Pologne" (P, III, ccxxxix–ccxlii) and "Réalité et Utopie dans la Pensée Politique de Rousseau," *Presence de Jean Jacques Rousseau* (Annales, XXXV, 181–216). To my knowledge, Bertrand de Jouvenel was the first to present a systematic discussion of Rousseau's maxims of politics in "Théorie des Formes de Gouvernement chez Rousseau," *Contrat social*, VI (novembre–décembre 1962), 343–51. Cf. Roger D. Masters, *Political Right and the Art of Politics in Rousseau's Thought* (unpublished Ph.D. Dissertation, University of Chicago, 1961). Rousseau's prudence in applying the educational proposals in the *Émile* (e.g., his correspondence with the Duke of Wurtemberg, esp. C. G., x, 205–17) is of a different order than his conception of political prudence because the latter can be based on general propositions or maxims of a scientific character, whereas the former depends more directly on individual judgments. (See *Émile*, Pref. [G, 3].)

[23] Letter to Rey, 4 April 1762 (C. G., VII, 173). For other indications that the *Contrat social* is directed to a highly select audience, and not the general public, see the footnote to "attentive readers," *Contrat social*, II, iv (P, III, 373), and the beginning of III, i (395).

[24] *Ibid.*, Exordium (351), cited at n. 15 of this chapter.

that "I have said a great deal of bad about you"; since he did not do so explicitly, it is necessary to presume that his criticisms of the Prussian king were indirect (albeit clear to the intelligent reader).[25]

The importance of Rousseau's silent criticism of a ruling monarch may be inferred from the following curious fact. Although the *Social Contract* begins with an assertion that "princes or legislators" should act and not write, Rousseau quotes a work written by a former magistrate in the French government—the Marquis d'Argenson—in no less than four footnotes.[26] Rousseau explains these quotations as follows:

[25] Letter to the King of Prussia, July 1762 (C. G., VIII, 7). Cf. his subsequent correspondence (C. G., VIII, 175, 225). One of these indirect criticisms which Rousseau later admitted was the tacit comparison of Frederick the Great to Adraste, a wicked king described in Fenelon's *Telemachus*. See *Émile*, v (G, 597) and the reference to this passage in *Confessions*, XII (P, I, 593). Frederick had written a book entitled the *Anti-Machiavel* and (as we shall see) Rousseau openly praises Machiavelli. See the passages cited below, pp. 364–65, as well as several fragments which appear to have been directed against Frederick's *Anti-Machiavel, Fragments Politiques*, VI, 9–10 (P, III, 514–15), XVI, 14 (558) and Vaughan's note to these three paragraphs (v, I, 338, n.). It is also possible that Frederick the Great was in Rousseau's mind when he referred to the bad government which results when "the State is too little for its ruler, which is very rare" (*Contrat social*, III, vi [P, III, 410]).

[26] *Ibid.*, I, ii, n. (353); II, iii, n. (371); II, xi, n. (392); and VI, viii, n. (467–68). In the first edition (1762), the author of the passages was identified solely as "M.L.M.D.A.," but Rousseau did not hesitate to supply the information that he referred to René-Louis de Voyer de Paulmy, Marquis d'Argenson (see C. G., X, 40). The Marquis was Minister of Foreign Affairs from 1744 to 1747 and died in 1757; he should not be confused with his brother, Marc-Pierre de Voyer, Count d'Argenson, who is mentioned in the *Confessions*, VIII (P, I, 384, 385–86). Cf. the notes (P, I, 1447, 1449), where the two men are confused. The manuscript from which Rousseau quotes in the *Contrat social* had circulated in numerous copies, but was not published until 1764, when Rey—Rousseau's publisher—came out with an edition under the title *Considérations sur le Gouvernement Ancien et Présent de la France* (Amsterdam: Marc–Michel Rey, 1764). Rousseau does not, however, use this title (which was apparently invented by Rey since it does not occur on any of the known manuscripts); instead, Rousseau refers to the work as the *Traité manuscrit des intérêts de la Fr. avec ses voisins* (P, III, 353, n.). In the edition of 1782, modified according to Rousseau's own notes, the reference reads: "*Traité des intérêts de la Fr. avec ses voisins, par M. le Marquis d'Argenson* (imprimé chez Rey à Amsterdam)" (see P, III, 1435). That the manuscript used by Rey had this title, though it does not appear on any of the surviving manuscripts, is perhaps indicated by the fact that, at the top of pp. 2–214 of the Rey edition, one reads "*Intérêts de la France avec ses voisins.*" Since subsequent editions of the *Contrat social* name d'Argenson explicitly—and since Rey apparently published d'Argenson's book on the basis of Rousseau's praise for it—Rousseau's reluctance to name him as the author in 1762 doubtless stemmed from the fact that he quoted from a then unpublished manuscript. In the footnotes to the *Contrat social*, d'Argenson is the first and last

I could not refuse myself the pleasure of occasionally citing this manuscript, albeit unknown to the public, to honor the memory of an illustrious and respectable man, who, even in the ministry, had conserved the heart of a true citizen and correct and healthy views of the government of his country.[27]

Rousseau's decision to "honor the memory" of an "illustrious and respectable" magistrate may well be related to his desire to convince those in political power of the way in which one gains true fame.[28] A notoriously unscrupulous king like Frederick the Great is not worthy of mention by name, whereas a man who was French Foreign Minister for only four years without becoming dishonest or corrupt is respectable and should be famous.[29]

Rousseau also cites with approval another former magistrate who is best known for having written on politics; on three occasions in the notes, and once in the text, Machiavelli is quoted with approbation.[30] Since Machiavelli only turned to writing when he was deprived of office in the Medici restoration, it would appear that magistrates may legitimately write on politics only when they are incapable of playing

---

author to be cited and his manuscript is quoted more frequently than any other single work.

[27] *Contrat social*, IV, viii, n. (P, III, 467–68, n.). Although d'Argenson proposed a liberalization of the French regime by reducing the power of the king and adding democratic elements—reforms that Rousseau would doubtless have welcomed—d'Argenson's principles come closer to those of laissez-faire than Rousseau himself adopted. On d'Argenson, see Nannerl O. Henry, *Studies in French Liberal Thought from d'Argenson to Constant* (unpublished Ph.D. dissertation, Yale University, forthcoming), chap. II. I am indebted to Mrs. Henry for pointing out to me the details concerning the title of d'Argenson's manuscript indicated in the preceding footnote.

[28] Although we do not know the wording of the manuscript consulted by Rousseau, the published versions of d'Argenson's treatise do not always agree with Rousseau's quotations (P, III, 1436, 1456, 1504). If Rousseau intentionally modified the texts, one could perhaps conclude that these references were meant as indications of d'Argenson's respectability, and not merely as proofs of his wisdom.

[29] Cf. also the passage in *Contrat social*, III, vi (P, III, 410), which Rousseau added in order to praise the Duc de Choiseul, the then Minister of Louis XV (see Derathé's note [P, III, 1482] and *Confessions*, XI [P, I, 577]).

[30] *Contrat social*, II, iii, n. (P, III, 372); II, vii, n. (384); III, ix, n. (420) and in the text of III, vi (409). See also the note to the latter passage added for the edition of 1782 (P, III, 1480) and the favorable reference in III, x, n. (422). Cf. *Économie Politique* (P, III, 247), where Machiavelli is praised, and *Émile*, IV (G, 284), where he is criticized as a poor historian; Rousseau cites Machiavelli as a "profound political writer," not as an historian (P, III, 1480).

a continued role in politics.[31] In any event, of Rousseau's direct quotations in the footnotes to the *Social Contract*, the overwhelming majority come from the works of men who had experience as magistrates (despite the explicit criticism of rulers who write about politics); the remainder are quotations from historians, not philosophers.[32] The same pattern is by and large followed in the direct quotations in the text.[33] Although this apparent preference for statesmen and historians as authorities reflects Rousseau's dissatisfaction with previous political philosophy, it may also suggest his intention to direct the *Social Contract* to statesmen or potential statesmen.

Unlike the *Émile* and the *Second Discourse*, whose addressees are explicitly indicated, Rousseau is more circumspect in the *Social Contract*. For example, he uses direct address very rarely, although in at least two instances he speaks directly to the legislator.[34] It could be objected, of course, that the *Social Contract* is intended to teach peoples of their sovereign rights, and indeed there is also one instance of

[31] This principle could be applied to the Marquis d'Argenson, whose *Traité* was written after his term as Foreign Minister; d'Argenson was also an unsuccessful competitor, along with Rousseau, in the Academy of Dijon's 1754 prize competition (P, III, 1436).

[32] In the footnotes to the first edition, Rousseau includes eleven direct quotations: four from d'Argenson, three from Machiavelli, one from the Old Testament, in which a French translation is criticized (*Contrat social*, IV, viii, n. [P, III, 461]); two from Tacitus, both in a single note in which the author is not named (III, ix, n. [420]); one from Cornelius Nepos (III, x, n. [423]). Cf. also the notes added, for the edition of 1782, to I, iv (P, III, 1441) and IV, viii (1500) as well as the addition to the note in III, v (1478). Whereas statesmen and historians are quoted, philosophers like Aristotle, Hobbes, or d'Alembert and jurists like Grotius or Bodin are merely named and discussed: e.g., *ibid.*, I, vi, n. (361); I, ii, n. (353); III, x, n. (423); IV, viii, n. (463). Cf. IV, viii, n. (468).

[33] Verbatim quotations are drawn from Montesquieu, who had experience as a magistrate (*ibid.*, II, vii [381]; IV, iii [442]); the Palatin of Posnania, speaking in the Polish Diet (III, iv [405]); Dionysius the younger, whose remark is recorded by Plutarch (III, VI [411]); Tacitus' *Histories* (III, VI [411–12]); Chardin's *Voyage en Perse* (III, viii [417]); Varro and Pliny (IV, iv [446]); a royal edict (IV, vii [459]); Jeptha in the Old Testament (IV, viii [461]); and a statement imputed to the Roman Decimvirs (II, vii [382–83]). See also the paraphrases of Philo's report of a speech by Caligula (I, ii [353]); of Montesquieu (I, ix [393]; III, iv [405]; III, viii [414]); of Grotius (I, iv [353]; I, v [359]; III, xviii [436]); and of Tacitus (IV, ii [439]). Cf. the references to Grotius, Aristotle, and Hobbes (I, ii [353]); Grotius and Barbeyrac (II, ii [370]); Plato (II, vii [381]; III, vi [412]); Warburton (II, vii [384]); Aristotle (III, v [408]); Samuel in the Old Testament and Machiavelli (III, vi [409]); the Abbé St. Pierre (IV, iii [443]); Cicero (IV, iv [452]); Hobbes (IV, viii [463]); Bayle and Warburton (IV, viii [464]). In general, Rousseau *mentions* philosophers and jurists; he *quotes* statesmen and historians.

[34] *Ibid.*, II, xi, n. (392); III, xiii (427). Cf. III, xv (431).

direct address to "you modern peoples."[35] But since Rousseau describes Machiavelli's *Prince* as the "handbook of Republicans" because "in pretending to give lessons to kings he gave great lessons to peoples," the obverse of this interpretation might well be applied to the *Social Contract*.[36]

There are other indications that Rousseau directed his political teaching to the ambitious politician. One hint of this kind is the seemingly unorthodox use of the word "prince," which Rousseau defines as "the entire body" of magistrates or governors (explicitly including more than one individual).[37] The example given to justify this usage is that of the Republic of Venice; but since Rousseau elsewhere described Venice as a most corrupt society, this example is hardly a solid basis for his unusual terminology.[38] A better explanation might be that the body of magistrates inevitably has a common interest which is different from and opposed to the general interest.[39] Since this is most clearly evident in a monarchy, where the government consists of one man (the "prince" in the conventional sense),[40] Rousseau's equation of the "prince" and the "government" may perhaps indicate that the rules guiding a government of many men are ultimately the same or similar to the rules which a single ruler should fol-

[35] *Ibid.*, III, xv (431).
[36] *Ibid.*, III, vi (409), cited below, p. 364.
[37] "The members of this body [i.e., the government] are called magistrates or *kings*, that is *governors*; and the entire body has the name *prince*" (*ibid.*, III, i [396]). Note also the chiasmus in the sequel: "I call . . . *prince* or *magistrate*, the man or the body entrusted with this administration."
[38] Cf. *ibid.*, with III, v (407); IV, iv (453); IV, v (454–55); *Émile*, IV (G, 339n.). Although many commentators have remarked that Rousseau was unique in this use of the term "prince"—e.g., J. L. Lecercle, ed., *Du Contrat social* (Paris: Éditions sociales, 1963), p. 115, n. 6; Maurice Halbwachs, ed., *Du Contrat social* (Paris: Aubier, 1943), p. 239, n. 151—in fact Machiavelli had already used the word without reference to the difference between republics and monarchies. Consider the description of the government of a republic as a "prince" in *Discourses on Titus Livy*, I, xi (ed. Max Lerner; New York: Modern Library, 1940), p. 148; the tacit identification of "princes" and "heads of republics" in *Discourses*, I, xii (150); the phrase "prince of a republic," *Discourses*, I, xviii (171); the use of the word "prince" in *Discourses*, II, i (279–80); and the application of the title "prince" to Hannibal, the general of Republican Carthage, in the *Prince*, chap. XVII (ed. Lerner, p. 62). As is clear from a close reading of these works, for Machiavelli the term "prince" ultimately refers to the leader who founds or "reorganizes" any regime, whether republican or monarchical; the usage is justifiable because only one man can establish new laws. See *Discourses*, I, x (esp. 143–44); III, i (esp. pp. 399–401); and note the blurring of the distinction between republics and monarchies in the *Prince*, esp. chaps. XIII–XIV. A man is "worthy" to be called a "prince" if he "would know how to govern states" (*Discourses*, Ded. [102]).
[39] *Contrat social*, III, ii (P, III, 400–01).
[40] *Ibid.* (401); III, vi (408).

low. The center of political life is the individual who is the highest political leader—or, in rare cases, the legislator.[41]

The assertion that the *Social Contract* is a handbook for rulers becomes more plausible if one compares this general use of the term "prince" with a passage in the chapter on monarchy:

> Much trouble is taken, so it is said, to teach young princes the art of ruling: it doesn't seem that this education is profitable for them. One would do better to begin by teaching them the art of obeying. The greatest kings who have been celebrated by history have not been brought up to rule; it is a science that one never possesses less than after having learned it too well, and that is better acquired by obeying than commanding.[42]

Since the main teaching of the *Social Contract* is that the "prince" is —or rather should be—under the law, it would seem that the book is directed to a man who, like "the greatest kings celebrated by history," is willing to begin his study of the "art of ruling" by learning to obey. If the prince fully understands Rousseau's work, he will be able to exercise the greatest power possible under the circumstances within which he rules.

Rousseau did not, however, naïvely assume that the selfish ambition of a politician armed with the *Social Contract* would automatically produce a healthy political order. On the contrary, since men have been corrupted in society and mistake their apparent interests for their true self-interest, rulers are usually blinded by their own passions. Rousseau merely tries to show that it is in the enlightened self-interest of the politician to know and practice the principles of political right; kings would be more powerful if they took a long-range view and subordinated their personal interest to the "public felicity."[43]

Similarly, in both the *Political Economy* and the *Lettres Écrites de la Montagne*, Rousseau argues that the ruler's true interest and his duty are in harmony:[44]

Ambition itself is better served by duty than by usurpation. Con-

---

[41] Cf. the "indivisible middle term" in the center of the proportion discussed in *ibid.*, III, i (398). This implication also clarifies the sentence in III, vi (408) which Derathé has difficulty interpreting (P, III, 1480).

[42] *Ibid.*, III, vi (411). Note the sole reference to the art of ruling as a "science" which remains in the published version of the *Contrat social*.

[43] *Ibid.*, III, vi (409). Note that a king would gain primarily external power, which makes him "feared by his neighbors."

[44] *Économie Politique* (P, III, 249); *Lettres Écrites de la Montagne*, vi (P, III, 811). Cf. *Second Discourse*, Part 2 (P, III, 185).

vinced that its rulers (*chefs*) only work for its happiness, the people dispenses them by its deference from working to strengthen their power; and history shows us in a thousand places that the authority it gives to those it loves and by whom it is loved is a hundred times more absolute than all the tyranny of usurpers.[45]

Since obedience to law is the only ground for respectable (i.e., legitimate) authority, usurpation of sovereignty by the government threatens that voluntary popular consent which is necessary for lasting success and justice. True legitimacy is the best means to political power—and especially to power over one's neighboring states.[46]

Rousseau's objective of influencing the statesman can also be shown by a fragment which was to serve as a preface (perhaps for the projected *Political Institutions*, of which only the *Social Contract* was published):

> I like to flatter myself that one day some statesman will be a citizen, that he will not change things solely to do otherwise than his predecessor, but to act so that they are better, that he will not have the public welfare constantly in his mouth, but that he will have it a little in his heart; that he will not make peoples unhappy to strengthen his authority, but that he will use his authority to establish the happiness of peoples; that by a happy chance he will see this book; that my unformulated ideas will lead him to think of more useful ones; that he will work to make men better or happier; and that I will have contributed something to this effect.[47]

If this passage is at all worthy of mention, it indicates that Rousseau's hopes for political reform were linked to the ambition of a rare statesman, and not merely to a general revolution originating in the citizen body.[48]

If the addressee of the *Social Contract* is the ambitious politician, Rousseau's decision to obscure the distinction between the maxims of

---

[45] *Économie Politique* (P, III, 254). Cf. the sentence that follows with Machiavelli, *Prince*, chap. XVII.

[46] "It is thus that Rome was virtuous and became the master of the world. Ambitious rulers . . . respect your fellow citizens, therefore, and you will make yourselves respectable; respect freedom, and your power will increase every day; never exceed your rights, and soon they will be without limits" (*Économie Politique* [P, III, 258]).

[47] *Fragments Politiques*, I, 2 (P, III, 474). Cf. P, III, 1515.

[48] Cf. Rousseau's practical proposal at the end of the *First Discourse* (P, III, 29–30) and above, pp. 233–34. See also *Confessions*, XII (P, I, 600); *Jugement sur le Projet de Paix Perpétuelle* (P, III, 596–600); *Gouvernement de Pologne*, VI (P, III, 974); XV (1039–41).

politics and the principles of right can perhaps be explained by the dangers of giving advice to a self-seeking man. On the one hand, the suggestions must be palatable: Rousseau could not shock the politician by denouncing the very lawless motives on which the creation of justice depends.[49] But on the other hand, one cannot praise mere selfishness without directing it to a more noble end: Rousseau had to present the moral or virtuous as part of the self-interest of the selfish politician. To satisfy these two conditions, it could be suggested that Rousseau may have blurred the distinction between principles of right (which define what is just) and maxims of art (which establish what is convenient).

Rousseau was aware that few (if any) rulers would actually follow the precept that self-interest demands justice; he describes his project as a "chimera."[50] History shows that the rulers of civil society almost always follow private interests which are opposed to the general will, but this results in tyranny which—in terms of reason—is merely the rule of the strongest:

> when one has force in hand, there is no art to make everyone tremble. . . . An imbecile who is obeyed can, like any other, punish crimes; the true statesman knows how to prevent them; it is over the wills even more than actions that he extends his respectable empire.[51]

To be worthy of respect, a politician must lead men to will voluntarily that which is in the common interest. And to be truly famous in succeeding centuries, a prince must be worthy of the respect of philosophers who understand the rational and sound basis of legitimacy.[52]

2 · The Principles of Political Right

A · THE SOCIAL CONTRACT OR THE NATURE OF LAW

It is worthy of remark that the *Social Contract* does not begin with an exposition of Rousseau's "principles of political right." Rousseau devotes the first five chapters of Book I to the proof of his assertion that "the social order is a sacred right . . . founded on conventions."[53] Recasting material in the *Geneva MS*, the unpublished *État de*

---

[49] See above, chap. VI, § 2B.

[50] Thus the fragmentary preface, cited above at n. 47, ends: "This chimera has placed my pen in hand" (*Fragments Politiques*, I, 2 [P, III, 474]).

[51] *Économie Politique* (P, III, 250). Cf. *Second Discourse*, Part 2 (P, III, 194).

[52] Cf. *Contrat social*, II, vii (P, III, 381).

[53] *Ibid.*, I, i (352), cited at n. 3 of this chapter.

Guerre, and the *Political Economy*, Rousseau denies that civil society could be derived from natural authority, be it the natural rights of parents (chapter ii) or the natural "right of the strongest" (chapter iii). He then argues that a conventional surrender of freedom cannot be the basis of political society because such an agreement, not being fully voluntary, is the same thing as slavery; neither the rights of the strongest in conquest nor the right to enslave those over whom one has the power of life and death can account for a political community (chapters iv–v). All alternative conceptions of civil obligation can thus be rejected, since they either erroneously assume that its source is natural or fail to define properly the particular conventions required for legitimacy.[54]

It is only in chapter vi of Book I that Rousseau begins to discuss the problem on the basis of his own premises. Given the impossibility of preserving human life in the last stages of the state of nature, men are forced to form civil societies. At that time, reasoning and independent men are faced with a "difficulty" which Rousseau summarizes as follows:

"Find a form of association which defends and protects the person and the goods of each associate with the common force, and by which each one, being united with all, only obeys himself and remains as free as before." This is the fundamental problem that the social contract solves.[55]

This way of posing the question indicates what can be called the "formal" character of Rousseau's principles. Although the political association is to protect its members and their goods, this end has an empty or negative quality. The uniting of men so that each wills what all will is required in order for man to obey "only himself" and remain "as free as before." But what is to be willed? The security of person and property of each citizen is the result of almost any social order in which brute force is not uncontrolled; any replacement of the law of the strongest by political institutions that protect life and property would seem to fulfill this end. But as is known by any student of politics, political institutions must be more complex than this, if only because some citizens may not respect the rights of others.[56]

Rousseau's exposition of the character of the social contract avoids

---

[54] On this rejection of all prior political theories, see above, chap. vi, § 2D as well as chap. iv, § 2C–D.

[55] *Contrat social*, I, vi (P, III, 360). Cf. the formulation of the *Second Discourse*, Part 2 (P, III, 177).

[56] Cf. *ibid.* (180).

these problems completely. Because he has stated the "difficulty" in terms of man's need to protect himself without losing his freedom, the central problem of political right is man's free consent or will. "To remove all freedom from man's will is to remove all morality from his actions";[57] politicized man must "obey only himself," for otherwise society would be equivalent to slavery.

Given the basic assumption that man cannot renounce his freedom without destroying his nature as a man, Rousseau's conception of the social contract may seem very startling:

> The clauses of this contract, . . . when well understood, are reduced to a single one: namely the total alienation of each associate with all his rights to all the community.[58]

A strictly equal surrender is made by each potential citizen, and no individual, *qua* individual, retains any right whatsoever:

> For if individuals retained some rights, as there would not be any common superior who could pronounce between them and the public, each one, being in some point his own judge, would soon pretend to be so in all; the state of nature would subsist, and the association would necessarily become either tyrannical or vain.[59]

Civil society must necessarily destroy the essential characteristic of natural freedom, namely the right to be the sole judge of the means to one's own self-preservation. If man's freedom is his "quality of manhood," however, how can such a total dependence of the individual upon society be compatible with man's nature and freedom?[60]

Since the totality of the "alienation" required by the social contract has been the basis of assertions that Rousseau was a forerunner of totalitarianism, it would be well to begin by recalling the character of the natural rights which are given up on entering civil society. In the state of nature, man possesses the natural rights of a sensitive being, enforced by the operation of the natural sentiments of love of oneself and pity; the interaction of men in the state of nature can be sum-

---

[57] *Contrat social*, I, iv (P, III, 356). On the totally secular or human basis of political life thus implied, cf. Jacques Maritain, *The Rights of Man and Natural Law* (New York: Scribners, 1943), pp. 66–67.

[58] *Contrat social*, I, vi (P, III, 360).

[59] *Ibid.* (361). Cf. *Second Discourse*, Part 2 (P, III, 180–86) and n. 1 (195); the Hobbesian conception of the social contract is untenable.

[60] Note that in *Contrat social*, I, iv (P, III, 355), Rousseau defines the verb "to alienate" as "to give or to sell," and explicitly rejects a sale or exchange of natural rights as the foundation of civil society; the alienation required in the "essential clause" of the social contract is a free gift, without reserve.

marized by the "natural right of the strongest."[61] Since these rights do not have the same moral content as the traditional natural law, the total surrender of rights to civil society should not be exaggerated; the "total alienation of each associate with all his rights to the entire community" does not involve the surrender of a pre-existing standard of justice by which civil society could be judged. Quite the contrary, all true rights—including natural rights (e.g., the rights of the father over his children and property rights)—are based on the "sacred rights" of conventional civil society.[62]

Nonetheless it would be absurd to underestimate the total character of the alienation described by Rousseau. Civil society is apparently unlimited by any higher rights prior to political law. There is no obligation which can conceivably bind the political community in advance; the total surrender of individual right creates a moral collectivity or "body politic" which has no superior:

> it is against the nature of the body politic that the sovereign impose on itself a law that it cannot break. Only being able to consider itself in a single, identical relationship, it is then in the situation of an individual contracting with himself; by which it can be seen that there is not, nor can there be, any kind of fundamental law obligatory for the body of the people, not even the social contract.[63]

Political right has both a completely secular character (i.e., no superior religious obligations are established by divine law) and an apparently unlimited sovereignty (i.e., the body politic is not limited by natural law, which is historically derived from positive law and not vice versa).

Some commentators have objected that since Rousseau speaks of natural law in his other works, he maintains the traditional distinction between positive civil laws and the natural law, superior to and binding civil society. For example, Haymann and Derathé emphasize two passages in which Rousseau, defending his own work against criticism, seems to assert that natural law limits the rightful scope of positive law. When some lawyers objected that, in the *Letter to d'Alembert*, Rousseau admits an authority superior to the Sovereign, he replied:

---

[61] Thus Rousseau's proof that social right is not natural is composed of an analysis of the natural rights of the father followed by the natural rights of the strongest (*ibid.*, I, ii–iii).

[62] See again *ibid.*, I, i (352); *Second Discourse*, Part 2 (P, III, 182).

[63] *Contrat social*, I, vii (P, III, 362).

I admit three only. First the authority of God, then that of the natural law derived from man's constitution (*la loi naturelle qui dérive de la constitution de l'homme*), and then that of honor, more powerful over an honest heart than all the kings on earth. . . . If ever sovereign authority could be in conflict with one of the three foregoing, it would be necessary that the former give way in that respect.[64]

But although these superior authorities would force the sovereign to give way "if ever sovereign authority could be in conflict with them," Rousseau does not admit that such a conflict is really possible as long as the sovereign enacts legitimate laws consistent with his principles of political right.[65]

The second major text cited to prove that the natural law limits civil law occurs in the *Letters Written From the Mountain*:

For what more certain foundation can obligation among men have than the free engagement of the one who obligates himself? . . . But by this condition of freedom, which includes others, all kinds of engagements are not valid, even before human tribunals. Thus to determine this [principle], one should explain its nature, one should find its use and its end, one should prove that it is appropriate

[64] "Réponse à une Lettre anonyme adressée à J. J. Rousseau par des Gens de Loi," 15 October 1758 (C. G., IV, 88).

[65] In effect, the laws can never violate the authority of God, because on earth *"vox populi vox dei"* (*Économie Politique* [P, III, 246]); "it is to be believed that particular events are nothing in the eyes of the master of the universe, . . . that he contents himself with conserving the genera and the species and presiding over the whole, without bothering himself about the way each individual spends this short life" (Letter to Voltaire, 18 August 1756 [C. G., II, 317]. Cf. *Lettres Écrites de la Montagne*, VI [P, III, 807n.]). Nor can the laws violate "the natural law derived from man's constitution," for this "natural law" is not the traditional law of "right reason," but rather Rousseau's construction of a new moral standard—a construction which is posterior to the emergence of civil society and only binds individuals who accept a natural religion like that of the Savoyard Vicar (see above, chap. II, § 3 and chap. VI, § 2B). If honor is "more powerful than all the kings on earth," these kings are not sovereign in Rousseau's sense. Indeed, it is surprising that Derathé and Haymann base their commentary on this letter because at this point Rousseau added a note concerning the term "sovereign authority," remarking: "We could well not understand each other on the meaning we give to this word, and as it is not a good thing that we should understand each other better, we would do well not to dispute about it" ("Réponse à une lettre anonyme" [C. G., IV, 88, n.]). This particular text is a polemic defense, not a sincere presentation of Rousseau's own views. Cf. Franz Haymann, "La Loi Naturelle dans la philosophie politique de Rousseau," *Annales*, XXX, 90–91; Derathé, *Rousseau et la Science Politique*, p. 157; Cobban, *Rousseau and the Modern State*, p. 147 n.

(*convenable*) to men, and that it has nothing contrary to natural laws (*lois naturelles*): for it is no more permissible to violate natural laws by the social contract than it is permissible to violate positive laws by the contracts of private parties, and it is only by these very laws that the freedom which gives force to the engagement exists.[66]

Rousseau plays on the ambiguity of the term "natural law" by seeming to refer to the traditional notion, but it is clear from the context that the law in question establishes the conditions under which men can freely obligate themselves.[67] This text, which was written in self-defense at a time when Rousseau was being persecuted, should therefore be read in the light of the *Social Contract*, and not vice versa.

B · THE LIMITS OF SOVEREIGNTY

In a crucial chapter of the *Social Contract*, Rousseau explicitly discusses "the Limits of the Sovereign Power."[68] He begins by asserting again that the political community has an absolute power over its members:

> As nature gives each man an absolute power over all his members, the social compact gives the body politic an absolute power over all of its [members]; and it is this very power which, directed by the general will, has the name sovereignty, as I have said.[69]

[66] *Lettres Écrites de la Montagne*, vi (P, III, 807). The Pléiade text has "*Contrat social*," in italics, as if to refer to Rousseau's work, contrary to logic and Vaughan's reading (V, II, 200). Note that this passage concerns the criteria which Rousseau's principles of political right must satisfy in order to be valid, not the criteria for judging civil society; cf. Derathé, *Rousseau et la Science Politique*, p. 158, Haymann, "La Loi Naturelle . . . ," p. 70.

[67] On the ambiguity of the terms "natural law" and "law of nature," see above, p. 80, n. 92. Despite interpretations that distinguish different "layers" of Rousseau's conception of natural law (e.g., P, III, 1662), it would seem that the "natural law" in question here is identical to the consideration of right discussed by Rousseau in rejecting alternative theories of the social bond in the *Second Discourse*, Part 2 (P, III, 179–84); *Geneva MS*, I, v (P, III, 297–304); *Contrat social*, I, ii–v (P, III, 352–59). This usage is explicit in *Gouvernement de Pologne*, vi (P, III, 973).

[68] *Contrat social*, II, iv. This chapter is taken over with relatively minor changes from *Geneva MS*, I, vi, which was entitled "Of the Respective Rights of the Sovereign and Citizen." Comparison of the two titles suggests that the "limits of the sovereign power" derive from the "respective rights of the sovereign and citizen" (i.e., from political right, not natural right or natural law).

[69] *Contrat social*, II, iv (P, III, 372). The play on the word "members" suggests the so-called "organic analogy" between a man's body and a civil society, made famous in Hobbes' *Leviathan*, Intro. (ed. Oakeshott, p. 5) to

There is an element of exaggeration in this analogy, since no man has a truly *absolute* power over his body; elsewhere Rousseau insists that man's freedom, while it may appear to be unlimited, "extends only as far as [his] natural forces," which are defined by the "hard law of necessity" and violated only at man's peril.[70] This suggests that the "absolute" power of the sovereign may have the same limit as the absoluteness of man's free will—namely the punishment for imprudence which is incurred when men violate the "nature of things."[71]

Having reasserted the absoluteness of the sovereign's will, Rousseau continues his examination of the "limits" of this power in a manner which may puzzle the reader:

> But besides the public person, we have to consider the private persons who form it, and whose life and freedom are naturally independent of it. It is therefore a matter of distinguishing well between the respective rights of the citizens and the sovereign, and the duties which the first must fulfill in their quality as subjects from the natural right which they must enjoy in their quality as men.[72]

The surrender of natural right by citizens does not annihilate that right;[73] what citizens have given up in forming the body politic is only their ability to *claim* their rights as they could in the state of nature, where each man is his own judge. This is not a sufficient explanation, however, for a right that cannot be claimed would not seem to be a true right.

In the first draft of the passage just cited, Rousseau had said:

> Everything consists in distinguishing well between the rights that

---

cite but one source. Rousseau described this analogy as "a common comparison, and inexact in many respects" when using it in *Économie Politique* (P, III, 244). Cf. Derathé, *Rousseau et la Science Politique*, pp. 410–13.

[70] *Émile*, II (G, 68).

[71] It should be added that this sanction may be virtually unnoticed by men. Hence Rousseau's argument that civil society produces more misery than happiness was consciously radical; he knew that most men would deny the truth of his assertion (see *Second Discourse*, n. IX [P, III, 202–08]). Just as few men will be "wise" enough to follow the natural religion or natural law presented in the *Émile*, few societies will follow the principles of political right developed in the *Contrat social*, but in both cases the many suffer from their errors. Cf. *Émile*, II (G, 63–71); *Gouvernement de Pologne*, VI (P, III, 973).

[72] *Contrat social*, II, iv (P, III, 373). This is a difficult sentence, as Rousseau was aware; see the note he added.

[73] For evidence that "natural right" is a criterion which can be used to judge societies, see Rousseau's surprising use of the phrase "principles of natural right" (*droit naturel*) as the basis for criticizing "feudal government" as an "absurd system" (*ibid.*, I, iv [357]). See above, chap. IV, § 1.

the sovereign has over the citizens from those it should respect in them; and the duties that they must fulfill in their quality as subjects from the natural right which they ought to enjoy in their quality as men.[74]

Of the two distinctions in this sentence, the order of the first pair of rights is reversed in the final version; in the first draft the rights of citizens against the sovereign had followed the rights of the sovereign over the citizens. It can be suggested that this change was intended to produce a chiasmus, a frequently used stylistic device in Rousseau's works. If this interpretation is correct, the key to the passage in the final version would be that a relationship of the form A:B=B:A exists, so the "rights of citizens": "rights of sovereign" = "duties of subjects": "natural rights." According to this reading, the rights of citizens have some similarity with the natural rights of men as individuals, just as the duties of the citizens have some similarity with civil or political rights.[75]

In the first draft, the passage in question is followed by the sentence:

It is certain that everything that each one alienates of his natural faculties, his goods, and his freedom by the social contract, is only the part of all these [things] whose possession is important for the society.[76]

Rousseau revised this sentence to read:

It will be agreed that everything that each one alienates of his *power*, his goods, and his freedom by the social compact, is only the part of all those whose *use* is important for the community, *but it is necessary to agree also that the sovereign alone is judge of this importance.*[77]

Although these revisions weaken the certainty of the proposition, and reduce somewhat the individual's subordination to civil society (because "power" is alienated by each citizen rather than all his "natural faculties" and because the community only claims "usage" rather

[74] *Geneva MS*, I, vi (P, III, 306).
[75] It is hardly accidental that the duties of the citizen (i.e., the demands made on the members of the political community by the sovereign) are at the center of the chiasmus (i.e., are to be emphasized in the context); see the sequel.
[76] *Ibid.*
[77] *Contrat social*, II, iv (P, III, 373), italics, indicating Rousseau's changes, are added.

than "possession"), the main thrust of Rousseau's changes is to indicate more clearly the extent to which, in fact and in right, civil society has the last word. The rights of the sovereign coexist with certain natural rights of men, but the body politic alone can determine the precise limits of both civil and natural rights.

In the *Geneva MS*, Rousseau concludes his distinction between the rights of the sovereign and those of the citizens by saying:

> Thus all the services that a citizen can render to the state, he owes to it, and the sovereign for its part cannot impose on the subjects any bonds that are useless to the community; for under the law of reason nothing happens without cause any more than under the law of nature.[78]

This passage was used in the published version of the *Social Contract* (unlike the references to the natural law in Book I, chapter ii of the *Geneva MS*); Rousseau merely adds two important qualifications:

> All the services that a citizen can render to the State, he owes to it *as soon as the sovereign demands them*; but the sovereign, for its part, cannot impose on the subjects any bonds that are useless to the community; *it cannot even will it*; for under the law of reason nothing happens without cause any more than under the law of nature.[79]

The sovereign, as such, *cannot* (i.e., is in principle unable to) go beyond the limits of public utility because it operates under the "law of reason," and according to Rousseau's discovery of that law, the only rational "cause" of law is the preference of every citizen for the common good. A positive law that violates Rousseau's principles of political right is not truly a law.

Since Rousseau substitutes his definition of the nature of law for the traditional natural law, one cannot say that there is no limit to po-

---

[78] *Geneva MS*, I, vi (P, III, 306).

[79] *Contrat social*, II, iv (P, III, 373), italics, indicating Rousseau's additions, are added. In the *Geneva MS*, this paragraph ends with a sentence that Rousseau deleted: "One ought not to confuse that which is convenient with that which is necessary, simple duty with strict right, and that which one can require of us from that which we ought to do voluntarily" (I, vi [P, III, 306]). In the first draft, Rousseau used the entire passage to contrast civic morality with strict political right; he tried to indicate both the distinction between politics and morality *and* the distinction between the rights of citizens and of the sovereign. In the final version, Rousseau simplifies the paragraph by limiting it to political right in the strict sense. That Rousseau had more than one distinction in mind in the first draft is also indicated by a canceled variant (P, III, 1420).

litical society precisely because there is no human authority above the laws.

> The clauses of this [social] contract are so determined by the nature of the act that the slightest modification makes them null and void; so that, even if they have never been formally enunciated, they are everywhere the same, everywhere tacitly accepted and recognized; until, the social compact having been violated, each one then returns to his first rights, and claims again his natural freedom, losing the conventional freedom for which he renounced it.[80]

When rulers violate the principles of political right, they are punished for so doing by the immediate and automatic destruction of the *legitimacy* of their authority in the eyes of rational men, and this sanction is more effective than any merely moral condemnation—at least once Rousseau's works have been published—because the disappearance of the duty to obey reduces such illegitimate authority to the status of pure force, without support in divine or natural right.

As in the *Second Discourse*, the rule by which political authority is judged is the nature of legitimate law; when the required logic of obedience is no longer fulfilled, men need no longer obey and the state of nature (in which each man has a complete right to preserve himself as he sees fit) can legitimately replace the civil order.

> It will be seen, therefore, that the sovereign power, completely absolute, completely sacred, completely inviolable as it is, does not exceed, nor can it exceed the limits of general conventions, and that each man can dispose fully of whatever has been left him of his goods and his freedom by these conventions.[81]

Even though social man should consider that he owes his life to the city, the claims of the city ought to be limited (since in other important respects human life is a product of nature and not of convention).[82] And since violation of Rousseau's standards of political right will return men to a state of natural freedom by dissolving the social bond, there exists a theoretical sanction should the political community attempt to exceed its proper sphere of authority. Stated more bluntly, the principle of legitimacy is enforced by an unlimited right of revolution.

[80] *Contrat social*, i, vi (P, iii, 360).
[81] *Ibid.*, ii, iv (375).
[82] Note carefully: "his life is no longer *solely* a benefit of nature, but a conditional gift of the State" (*ibid.*, ii, v [376], italics added). Cf. *ibid.*, ii, iv (375); i, iv (356).

According to Rousseau, freedom subsists within civil society—or rather, a new and more secure "conventional freedom" is created—by means of the enactment of positive laws. Because obedience must rest on freely willed subordination to the body politic, the laws can only remain binding on individuals if they are legitimate. But isn't the action forming the civil society an irrevocable surrender which in fact restricts the independence of all citizens? How can Rousseau assert that within a legitimate political community man "remains as free as before," when before (i.e., in the state of nature) each individual had what amounted to total freedom to act as he pleased? The answer to these questions is provided by Rousseau's notion of the general will.

C · THE GENERAL WILL

If read in the light of Rousseau's conception of principles of political right which define the logic of civil obedience, the difficulties that have surrounded the notion of the general will are to a large degree removed. Only after Rousseau has rejected all alternative theories of the social bond and postulated the nature of the social contract, does he speak of the body politic thereby created as having "its unity, its common *me*, its life, and its will"; in the definitive version of the *Social Contract* the term "general will" does not occur until Rousseau formulates the precise terms of the social contract in Book I, chapter vi.[83] The meaning of the concept is clarified almost at once by Rousseau's analysis of the sovereign in the next chapter:

> In fact, each individual can have, as a man, a private will that is contrary or different from the general will he has as a citizen.[84]

As is shown by the context, Rousseau introduces the concept of the general will to elucidate the necessary and inevitable tension between the sovereign, which "by the very fact that it is, is always what it should be," and the individual subject, whose "private interest could speak to him completely differently than the common interest."[85]

The notion of the general will is thus a highly voluntarist formulation of the traditional conception of the common good or the common interest (as was even clearer in the suppressed chapter of Book

---

[83] *Ibid.*, I, vi (361). This is in sharp contrast to the *Geneva MS*, in which the first discussion of the "general will" occurs in I, ii—i.e., in the context of Rousseau's reply to Diderot and *before* the rejection of other "false notions of the social bond" in I, v. See above, chap. vi, § 2B.

[84] *Contrat social*, I, vii (P, III, 363).

[85] *Ibid.*

I in the *Geneva MS*). Indeed, such a formulation was not, in itself, highly original, since Pufendorf and Montesquieu—to name but two authors whose works Rousseau knew well—had already referred to the common good or the sovereign as the reunion of the "private wills" of the subjects.[86] The radical character of Rousseau's conception can only be appreciated with reference to his understanding of science and his attempt to develop a mental construct of universal validity which would explain civil society.

Rousseau had seen that natural science could prove certain conceptions of natural right to be untenable (since man in the state of nature lacked language and reason); if so, political obligation cannot be explained without discovering a man-made logic which does not depend on the "factual" or historical "accidents" which led to social life. Since all external phenomena are only knowable by means of conceptions which, however modeled upon nature, are in themselves unnatural and subject to error, natural science cannot be the source of this explanatory theory. The only datum which is a certain and solid basis for principles of political right is the will, because it is the conscious and perceptible manifestation of man's sentiment of his own existence, the only sentiment which necessarily existed in the state of nature and is still shared by all human beings.[87]

By attempting to free the Hobbesian procedure of constructing the logic of political life from Hobbes' unscientific assumptions about human nature, Rousseau was thus forced to define the body politic and its common good solely in terms of the artificial will created when men join together to form a political community. In Rousseau's terms, this logic of *will* is rendered necessary because in order to leave the state of nature, "men cannot create new forces, but only unite and direct those that exist . . . making them act in concert."[88] Such a conversion of the physical strength of naturally independent men can only be the product of will, at least insofar as a philosophic explanation is concerned, because the resulting political community is not merely a natural phenomenon and cannot be totally explained by the

---

[86] See Pufendorf, *Le Droit de la Nature et des Gens*, VII, ii, esp. §§ 5, 13 (ed. 1706; II, 203, 213); Montesquieu, *Esprit des Lois*, I, iii (ed. Garnier, I, 10); XI, vi (166). On the prehistory of the conception of the general will, see Bertrand de Jouvenel, "Essai sur la Politique de Rousseau," in J. J. Rousseau, *Du Contrat Social* (Geneva: Éditions du Cheval Ailé, 1947), pp. 105–12. That the concept of the general will could in itself easily be consistent with the traditional natural law teaching is shown by Diderot's use of it in his article *Droit Naturel*; see above, chap. VI, § 2A.

[87] See above, chap. VI, § 2E.

[88] *Contrat social*, I, vi (P, III, 360).

discovery of the physical, historical, or natural causes which contributed to its emergence.

The social bond depends, in this view, on conventions created by an act of will on the part of each individual. The essential characteristic of such conventions is that:

> Each individual, so to speak contracting with himself, finds himself obligated in a double relationship: namely as member of the sovereign toward the private individuals, and as member of the State toward the sovereign.[89]

On the one hand, each citizen, as an individual, is a voluntary subject of the political community, and on the other, the body politic, composed of all citizens, wills its own common good. This double relationship explains why:

> one cannot apply here the maxim of civil right that no one is bound to observe engagements made with himself, for there is a great difference between an obligation toward oneself or toward a whole of which one is a part.[90]

From this relationship between the wills of individuals and the will of a body of individuals, Rousseau proceeds to deduce his conception of the "legitimate," "equitable," "useful," and "solid" conventions that create an "indestructible" general will animating the "indivisible" and "inalienable" sovereign of every civil society.[91]

Rousseau's conception that the general will is "always right and always tends to the public utility"[92] has often seemed to be a quixotic if not muddled conception. Since the majority will of the citizen body need not be equitable or just, critics have asked how one can know that a given act of sovereignty is in accordance with the general will.[93]

[89] *Ibid.*, I, vii (362).

[90] *Ibid.* Note the implication that civil right and political right are essentially different, and cf. *ibid.*, II, xii (393–94).

[91] *Ibid.*, II, iv (375) and the chapter headings of II, i (368); II, ii (369); IV, i (437).

[92] *Ibid.*, II, iii (371), cited below.

[93] E.g., F. Watkins, "Introduction," *Rousseau: Political Writings* (London: Thomas Nelson, 1953), pp. xxiv–xxv. Cf. Jouvenel, "Essai sur la Politique de Rousseau," pp. 109–10. It need hardly be added that the attribution of equity and justice to *any* act of the general will has given rise to the interpretation of Rousseau as a forerunner of totalitarianism. See esp. J. L. Talmon, *The Origins of Totalitarian Democracy* (New York: Praeger, 1960), pp. 40–48. Among the restatements of Rousseau's conception of the general will, one of the clearest is Émile Durkheim's analysis in *Montesquieu et Rousseau* (Paris: Marcel Rivière, 1953), pp. 162ff.

The context of the phrase just cited shows that Rousseau was well aware of this problem:

> It follows from what has been said that the general will is always right and always tends to the public utility; but it does not follow that the deliberations of the people always have this rectitude. One always wants one's own good, but one does not always see it. . . . There is often a great difference between the will of all and the general will: the latter only has regard for the common interest; the former regards private interest, and is only the sum of particular wills. But remove from these same wills the more and the less which destroy each other, and the general will remains as the sum of the differences.[94]

Since the will is, by definition, always oriented to that which is good for the being who wills, evil action is the result of an erroneous "judgment" of that which is good.[95] An abstract logic of obedience can be based on the properties of will—and only on these properties—for the actual interests of men are conditioned by accident and subject to error and corruption.

Rousseau asserts that the enlightened, common interest is a really existent component of the will of each man: "remove from these same [private] wills the more and the less which destroy each other, and the general will remains as the sum of the differences." If citizen A wants objects *a, b, c, d* whereas citizen B wants *d, e, f, g,* one can say that *a, b, c* form the private self-interest of A, and *e, f, g* the private self-interest of B. Although these private interests may be (and usually are) opposed to one another and cannot serve as the foundation of any common interest, Rousseau asserts that there is a part of the private interest of both A and B which is truly common (i.e., object *d*). Whereas the "will of all" is a simple "addition" of private interests, the general will is the "sum of the differences" of these interests.[96]

Far from assuming that the general will is automatically realized by the action of a majority, Rousseau insists that there is an inevitable conflict between private will or interest and the general will within every citizen:

[94] *Contrat social*, II, iii (P, III, 371). Note the chiasmus in the next to last sentence and compare Rousseau's footnote to the passage.

[95] See also *ibid.*, I, vii (363); II, vi (380).

[96] Cf. *Preface à Narcisse* (P, III, 967–68 and n.). See also the commentaries in Halbwachs, ed. *Du Contrat Social*, pp. 248–51, and Jouvenel, "Essai sur la Politique de Rousseau," esp. pp. 110–19.

"*Each interest*," says the Marquis d'Argenson, "*has different principles. The agreement between two particular interests is formed in opposition to that of a third.*" He could have added that the agreement of all interests is formed in opposition to that [private interest] of each individual. If there were no different interests, one would scarcely sense the common interest, which would never face an obstacle; all would run by itself, and politics would cease to be an art.[97]

Because the tension between private interest and the general will is inherent in political life, art is needed to direct the citizens toward the common good.

At this point it is necessary to reemphasize Rousseau's analogy between the principles of political right and the idea of a frictionless surface; as was revealed in the analysis of the *Geneva MS*, the opposition of private interest to the general will is an element of "friction" which necessarily exists in every political order.[98] This friction is intentionally ignored in the formulation of the principles underlying political obedience; hence Rousseau asserts:

For if the opposition of private interests made the establishment of societies necessary, it is the accord of these same interests that made it possible. It is what there is in common in the different interests that forms the social bond, and if there was no point on which all interests agreed, no society could possibly exist.[99]

In reading such a statement, one must never forget Rousseau's general pessimism concerning civil society: "for what private interests have in common is so little that it will never balance what they have in opposition."[100] By concentrating on the "point on which all interests" are in agreement, and treating these interests solely in terms of man's *will*, Rousseau converts the traditional concept of the common good into the revolutionary doctrine of the general will.

Although the just and legitimate end of civil society is defined in

---

[97] *Contrat social*, II, iii, n. (P, III, 371). According to the published edition of d'Argenson's *Traité*, an agreement between "two particular interests is formed by *a reason opposed* (*une raison opposée*) to that [interest] of a third" (P, III, 1456). If this is not due to a difference in the manuscripts consulted by Rousseau and used by Rey in publishing d'Argenson (which is possible—see n. 28 of this chapter), one could conclude that Rousseau substitutes the word "opposition" for "opposed reason" in order to remove the element of rationality suggested by d'Argenson.

[98] See above, chap. VI, § 2E.

[99] *Contrat social*, II, i (P, III, 368). Cf. *Émile*, IV (G, 259, 280).

[100] *Ibid.*, IV (386, n.).

terms of the general will, the general will itself is not that just end properly speaking; rather it is a formal requirement which must be fulfilled by the laws which constitute any legitimate regime. Since each citizen's varying and conflicting private interests must include an identical component (the common interest), Rousseau's logic presupposes rigorous equality in terms of right:

> By whatever side one ascends to the principle, one always finds the same conclusion: namely that the social compact establishes between the citizens such an equality that they are all obliged under the same conditions and should enjoy the same rights.[101]

Just as the individual will always seeks the good for the individual, the general will has the same object with respect to the body politic; for this to occur, it necessarily follows that "any true act of the general will obligates or favors equally all the citizens."[102]

The general will, which is to say an "act of sovereignty" or any "law," must fulfill two formal or definitional requirements: it must be willed by all members of the society, and it must apply to all members of the society.

> Why is it that the general will is always right and why do all constantly will the happiness of each one of them, if it isn't that there is not anyone who does not appropriate to himself the word *each*, and who does not think of himself in voting for all? This proves that the equality of right and the notion of justice it produces derives from the preference each gives himself, and consequently from the nature of man; that the general will, to be really such, must be [general] in its object as well as in its essence; that it must come from all to apply to all; and that it loses its natural rectitude when it tends to some individual and fixed object, because then—judging of what is foreign to us—we have no true principle of equity that guides us.[103]

The social contract itself is an act which satisfies this definition, constituting the majority of the political community as the sovereign capable of willing and enacting laws which organize the community in a continuing fashion.[104] Hence the social contract is the law which

---

[101] *Contrat social*, II, iv (P, III, 374). It needs to be emphasized that this equality of right does not necessarily require factual equality; see in particular Rousseau's praise of the highly unequal voting procedures in the Centuriate assembly in Rome (*ibid.*, IV, iv [450–52]). See below, pp. 390–91, esp. n. 134.

[102] *Ibid.*, II, iv (374).   [103] *Ibid.* (373).

[104] *Ibid.*, I, v (359); II, vi (378).

serves as the foundation and logical explanation of all other laws; it is, in itself, the "nature of law."

In the chapter "Of the Law" with which Rousseau concludes his first presentation of his principles of political right, this double generality of the "matter" and the "will," the "essence" and the "object," is explicitly repeated as the definition of all law:

> But when all the people ordain concerning all the people, it only considers itself, and if it forms a relationship, it is of the whole object from one point of view to the whole object from another point of view, without any division at all. Then the matter on which one ordains is general, like the will that ordains. It is this act that I call a law.[105]

Such laws, which are "properly speaking only the conditions of the civil association," must apply to all citizens equally or as a body; Rousseau calls them "political" or "fundamental" laws to distinguish them from other acts which also have the name "laws."[106]

Because the acts of the general will (i.e., the laws) recognize no difference between individuals, no citizen can object, on the basis of his private interest, that he is at a disadvantage. In this way, every citizen can be considered to be as free as he was in the state of nature because, in obeying the law, he is merely obeying his own will. Some critics have asserted that such conventional freedom is essentially illusory, citing as evidence Rousseau's famous remark that men can be "forced to be free."[107] To analyze this paradoxical idea, one must look at the context of this well-known phrase:

> In order that the social compact not be a vain formula, it tacitly includes this engagement, which alone can give force to the others, that whosoever shall refuse to obey the general will shall be constrained to do so by the entire body: which does not mean anything else than that one will force him to be free. For this is the condition which, giving each citizen to the fatherland, guarantees him from all personal dependence: a condition which creates the artifice and the play of the political machine.[108]

---

[105] *Ibid.*, II, vi (379). Rousseau's silence on the relation of his definition to divine law or natural law is worthy of emphasis. Cf. Aquinas, *Summa Theologica*, I-II, ques. 90–97.

[106] *Contrat social*, II, xii (P, III, 393). On the difference between Rousseau's strict definition of law and the current conception of legislation, see below, p. 339.

[107] E.g., Sabine, *A History of Political Theory*, pp. 590–91.

[108] *Ibid.*, I, vii (P, III, 364). On the identification of freedom with freedom

From Rousseau's point of view, it is evident that this requirement is necessary. If the political community lacked the right to punish violations of the law, the law-abiding citizens would be at the mercy of criminals (or "violent reasoners") who break the law in their own narrow self-interest. Since the creation of civil society replaces all pre-civil or natural rights with civil rights, the political order must have an unambiguous force capable of insuring that the sovereign is indeed the only judge of any conflict between the rights and duties of individuals.

An obvious example of such a conflict occurs in the case of warfare. If civil society is created as a means of preserving the lives of every citizen, how can the individual be obligated—by his own free will—to go into battle and perhaps be killed, thereby apparently contradicting the fundamental natural desire for self-preservation which is clearly part of the private interest of each individual (and hence in the common interest)? Rousseau responds to this objection as follows:

> The social compact has for its end the preservation of the contracting parties. He who wills the end, also wills the means, and these means are inseparable from some risks, and even some losses. He who wills to preserve his own life at the expense of others should also give it for them when it is necessary. Now the citizen is no longer the judge of the danger to which the law wills that he be exposed, and when the prince says to him that it is expedient for the State that you die, he should die.[109]

Since every individual wills his own self-preservation as part of a political community that protects all against foreign attack, the general will or the law establishes the duty of citizens—or at least those who are called to arms—to risk their lives in the common defense. An individual who claims a personal exemption from this general law "sees that which he owes to the common cause as a free contribution," and seeks to "enjoy the rights of a citizen without willing to fulfill the duties of a subject"; such an attitude is an "injustice" which can cause

---

from "personal dependence" (i.e., dependence on the will of another individual), see *Émile*, II (G, 70–71). On the psychological implications of this passage, see John Plamenatz, " 'Ce qui ne signifie pas autre chose, sinon qu'on le forcera d'être libre,' " *Rousseau et la Philosophie Politique* (Paris: Presses Universitaires de France, 1965), pp. 137–52.

[109] *Contrat social*, I, v (P, III, 376). Note that it is the "prince" (i.e., the government, not the sovereign people) which decides the practical question of war and peace. Cf. *Lettres Écrites de la Montagne*, vii (P, III, 826–27).

"the ruin of a body politic" because it denies the formal equality of the rights and duties of *every* citizen.[110]

The logic which compels free obedience even in the face of a contradiction between one's self-interest and one's duties as a subject is even clearer in the case of a crime. The death penalty inflicted on criminals has the same status as the legitimate requirement that some citizens sacrifice their lives for a common defense:

> It is in order not to be the victim of an assassin that a man consents to die if he becomes one. In this treaty, far from disposing of his own life, he only thinks of guaranteeing it, and it is not to be assumed that any of the contracting parties plans at the time to have himself hung.[111]

Every individual, in order to secure his own self-preservation, willingly consents to punish assassins and other criminals, since to fail to do so would establish the freedom of any man to kill or rob him. Even the potential murderer must will the death penalty for murder as soon as he generalizes his will and considers the effects of establishing a law permitting the murder of any citizen (hence of himself).

The use of force against a criminal or law-breaker is thus consistent with conventional or civil freedom in two related senses. First, the logic of the enlightened general will shows that it would be impossible for the guilty party to claim his own pardon as a matter of right, for to do so would destroy the generality of the law, and thereby remove his own security by effectively permitting a return to the state of nature. Second, it follows that the law-breaker is "a rebel and a traitor to the fatherland" who can be punished as an "enemy" of civil society. Man can and must be "forced to be free" precisely because conventional freedom is an artificial and fragile right which, without constraint, would relapse into a Hobbesian war of all against all.[112]

Rousseau's principle of the general will is therefore intended to introduce a certain element of rationality into the wills of all citizens. Whatever one's purely private interests, insofar as the individual states his self-interest in the form of a general law that applies equally

---

[110] *Contrat social*, I, vii (P, III, 363).

[111] *Ibid.* (376).

[112] Lest this seem to be a purely arbitrary logical construction on Rousseau's part, it is perhaps well to mention that, in fact, when the civil laws suddenly do lack force, chaos occurs even in the most civilized countries; one has only to think of the effects of the famous Boston police strike of 1919 to see that the Hobbesian argument shared by Rousseau is not necessarily totalitarian in character. Cf. Thucydides, *History of the Peloponnesian War* III.82-84 (Crawley trans.; New York: Modern Library, 1951), pp. 189–91.

to all members of the society, he cannot justly will certain things (e.g., that others run the risk of death in his defense without reciprocity, or that he may murder others without fear of punishment or retaliation). In this way Rousseau teaches the "violent reasoner" described in Diderot's *Natural Right* and the *Geneva MS* "to prefer his interest properly understood to his apparent interest"; since a calculation of self-interest at the expense of others leads man to be wicked after he has left the pure state of nature, Rousseau's principles show how "reason, which led him astray, will bring him back to humanity."[113] In this sense, the principle of the general will can be called "the law of reason," because it is the only logical basis on which reasoning men can adopt mutually binding duties.[114]

No one was less disabused than Rousseau concerning the difficulty of making man's "rational" self-interest coincide with his apparent or passionate self-interest, most particularly in political life.

> How can a blind multitude, which often does not know what it wants, because it rarely knows what is good for it, execute by itself an enterprise as noble and as difficult as a system of legislation? . . . The private individuals see the good that they reject; the public wants the good that it does not see. All equally need guides. It is necessary to obligate the former to conform their wills to their reason; it is necessary to teach the latter to know what it wants.[115]

The principle of the general will does not ensure that the laws of civil society will in fact be rational, because the substance of law must deal with complex matters which may not be understood by most men; if the people is assembled, "it is not sure that its decision would be the expression of the general will."[116]

To be sure, Rousseau seems to argue that "upright and simple men" can readily discover the general will in proposing new laws:

> The first who proposes them [i.e., new laws] only says what all have already felt, and it is not a question of either factions or eloquence to pass as a law what everyone has already resolved to do

---

[113] *Geneva MS*, I, ii (P, III, 288).

[114] *Ibid.* (284); I, vi (306); *Contrat social*, II, iv (P, III, 373).

[115] *Ibid.*, II, vi (P, III, 380). Cf. the first draft of this passage (*Geneva MS*, I, vii [P, III, 311]), and note that while the public as a body must be taught to "know what it wants," the private individuals who compose the political community must be obligated "to conform their wills to their reason"; the kind of enlightenment necessary in a healthy society is based on obedience to the laws and patriotism, not the destruction of prejudices in any simple sense.

[116] *Économie Politique* (P, III, 250–51).

— 332 —

as soon as he will be sure that the others will do it along with himself.[117]

This praise of the "herds of peasants among the happiest people in the world" (i.e., the Swiss) should be read in its context, however; Rousseau is here speaking of a civil society which is already ruled by laws, whereas it is the original legislation which largely fixes the character of each political society. The wisdom of experience teaches that direct democracy is an insufficient solution to the political problem except in rare cases; because the sovereign populace at large cannot effectively manage all the affairs of a civil society, some of the laws must be directed to the establishment of a regular government. Moreover, the circumstances which determine the most appropriate form of government for a society are so complex that only a man of "superior intelligence"—the legislator—can discover laws that satisfy the true common interest.[118]

With respect to the specific method of organizing a political community, the principle of the general will—being purely formal or definitional—is of little assistance except insofar as it indicates those institutions which are illegitimate.[119] The most important practical consequence of Rousseau's principle derives from his assertion that the assent of the general will must be "present" or "actual," "since it is absurd that the will obligate itself for the future."[120]

> It is against the nature of the will, which has no empire over itself, to engage itself for the future; one can properly be obligated to do, but not to will; and there is a great difference between executing what one has promised, because it has been promised, and willing it again, even when one had not promised.[121]

It follows that the general will cannot be presumed to speak unless it is actively consulted; "when the law speaks in the name of the peo-

---

[117] *Contrat social*, IV, i (P, III, 437).

[118] *Ibid.*, II, vii (381, 383); II, viii (384–86); II, xi (393); III, iv (404–06); III, ix (419); *Second Discourse*, Ded. (P, III, 114); Part 2 (180); *First Discourse*, Part 2 (P, III, 29–30).

[119] Cf. Watkins, "Introduction," *Rousseau: Political Writings*, p. xxv. This factor has often been stressed as an element of weakness or confusion in Rousseau's principles, especially by those commentators who failed to see Rousseau's distinction between principles of political right and the science of the legislator (e.g., Sabine, *A History of Political Theory*, pp. 586–87, 590).

[120] *Contrat social*, II, i (P, III, 368–69).

[121] *Geneva MS*, II, ii (P, III, 315–16). Rousseau continues: "Now the law of today should not be an act of yesterday's general will, but of that of today, and we are engaged to do not that which all willed but that which all will. . . ."

ple, it is in the name of the people at present and not that of previous times."[122] Because the sovereign people has the right to change the form of government at any moment, the only means of preserving a legitimate regime is the establishment of regular popular assemblies.[123]

This requirement does not, however, determine the character of the regime or the way in which it should be governed. In the legislative assemblies, Rousseau insists that the consent of the citizenry must be an individual choice, and in this spirit he presents his well-known attack on "partial associations" which claim to act in the name of groups or categories of citizens.[124] More important, the requirement that laws have a general source precludes the "formal exclusion" of the vote of any citizen—universal suffrage in the popular assemblies is necessary even though unanimity is not.[125] Within these limits, virtually any political order which rests on "authentic" acts of the general will is legitimate; a monarchy is as just as any other political institution provided it rests on a valid "act of sovereignty."[126] Moreover, the strict definition of such acts of sovereignty can, and indeed must be modified in practice; Rousseau himself admits that there are circumstances, such as those in eighteenth-century Poland, in which universal suffrage is impossible (although it should remain the ideal).[127]

[122] *Ibid.* (316).
[123] *Contrat social*, III, xiii (P, III, 426–27); III, xviii (435); *Gouvernement de Pologne*, vii (P, III, 978); *Lettres Écrites de la Montagne*, vii (P, III, 814–16, 828–30). See below, pp. 405–06, esp. n. 201.
[124] *Contrat social*, II, iii (P, III, 371–72). It is not possible here to speculate on the relationship between this requirement and the development of political parties in modern Western democracies or totalitarian regimes. Nonetheless it should be noted that Rousseau's criticism seems to apply more directly to the latter kind of party than the former; he recognized that what is today called "pluralism" is a necessary fact of political life. See especially *Économie Politique* (P, III, 245–46). Even in this chapter of the *Contrat social*, Rousseau suggests that Sparta was "unique" in being the only state in which no "partial societies" existed; in most cases it suffices to prevent gross inequality between a relatively large number of "partial associations," as was done in Rome (*Contrat social*, II, iii [P, III, 372, and esp. the note citing Machiavelli]). See below, pp. 386–91.
[125] *Ibid.*, II, ii, n. (369); IV, i (438–39).
[126] "Thus the law can well establish that there will be privileges, but it cannot give them by name to anyone; . . . it can establish a royal government and hereditary succession, but it cannot elect a king nor name a royal family" (*ibid.*, II, vi [379]). Cf. *ibid.*, n. (380); III, vi (408–13); III, iii (403–04); *Lettres Écrites de la Montagne*, v (P, III, 770–71).
[127] *Gouvernement de Pologne*, vi (P, III, 973–74). See below, chap. VIII, § 3A.

D · THE SOVEREIGN AND THE GOVERNMENT

Before turning to Rousseau's analysis of the founding of the institutions of civil society and the role of the legislator, it is necessary to elaborate what is perhaps the most original aspect of his political teaching, namely the distinction between the sovereign and the government.[128] Although the principle of the general will does not determine the appropriate form of government, this principle has as a corollary the necessity that *some* form of government be established:

> Just as a private will can not represent the general will, the general will in turn changes nature when it has a particular object, and cannot, being general, pronounce either on a man or a fact.[129]

It is inevitably necessary to apply general rules to particular cases, but in any particular case there is, properly speaking, no general will; the equity present in the enactment of a law is impossible when judging a violation of the law, because there is no "common interest which unites the rule of the judge with that of the party."[130] If the logic of the general will forces all citizens (including a potential murderer) to vote for a law establishing capital punishment for murder, a man guilty of murder cannot be expected to ignore his desire for self-preservation and vote his own execution.[131]

According to Rousseau, the logical impossibility that the sovereign, as sovereign, can execute the laws is apparent even in regimes where the populace judged particular cases:

> When the Athenian people, for example, named or removed its rulers, gave honors to some, imposed punishment on others, and by multitudes of particular decrees indistinctly exercised all the functions of government, then the people no longer had a general

---

[128] Surprisingly enough, this distinction has been largely ignored by most of the commentaries on the *Contrat social*. E.g., see the introductory essays in the editions of Jouvenel, Watkins, Guillemin, Vaughan, Lecercle, and Halbwachs previously cited. Yet in the summary of his political teaching in the *Émile*, Rousseau quotes more extensively from Book III, chaps. I–III of the *Contrat social* (i.e., from the analysis of the nature of government as distinct from the sovereign) than from any other part of the work. See *Émile*, v (G, 591–95).

[129] *Contrat social*, II, iv (P, III, 374).

[130] *Ibid.*

[131] Cf. *Geneva MS*, II, iv (P, III, 329). In this case, the distinction between "executing what one has promised" (i.e., the individual's obedience to the law on which he voted) and "willing it again, even when one has not promised to do so before" (i.e., the sovereign's right to change the law at any legitimately convoked popular assembly) becomes decisive. See the passage cited in n. 121 of this chapter.

will properly so-called; it no longer acted as sovereign, but as magistrate.[132]

The definition of the general will limits the acts of sovereignty to general laws, and thereby establishes a distinction between the functions of the sovereign and those of the government; these different functions must be performed in every legitimate regime, even if the body performing them is one and the same. Because "the executive power cannot belong to the generality in its legislative or sovereign capacity," every civil society must have a government which should not be "confused inappropriately with the sovereign."[133]

The establishment of a government is a "complex act" really "composed of two others, namely the establishment of the law, and the execution of the law."

> By the first, the sovereign ordains that there will be a governmental body established in such and such a form, and it is clear that this act is a law. By the second, the people names the rulers who will be charged with the established government. Now this nomination, being a particular act, is not a second law, but only a consequence of the first and a governmental function.[134]

At the outset, therefore, every people must necessarily act not only as the sovereign, enacting the laws, but as the first magistrate, appointing the rulers. To be sure, the fundamental laws can delegate the latter function—since it is one of government and not of sovereignty—so that subsequent to an original popular choice the rulers may be legitimately appointed without direct popular election.[135] But even in this situation, the sovereign retains the power to change the law establishing the form of government, and by this very fact, the populace also has the residual power to act as supreme magistrate by replacing the rulers in power without changing the form of government.[136]

This double capacity of the people to act as sovereign and as government is, for Rousseau, based both on logic and on experience;

---

[132] *Contrat social*, II, iv (P, III, 374). Note that Rousseau emphasizes the novelty of his position by adding that "this will appear contrary to common ideas."

[133] *Ibid.*, III, i (395–96).

[134] *Ibid.*, III, xvii (433).

[135] This is clearest when the magistracies in an aristocracy or monarchy are hereditary (*ibid.*, II, vi [379]; III, v [406]; III, vi [411]). Cf. *Second Discourse*, Part 2 (P, III, 186–87).

[136] *Contrat social*, III, xviii (P, III, 435–36).

such a "change of relationship" in a body which exercises juridically different functions:

> takes place every day in the English Parliament, where the House of Commons on certain occasions becomes a great committee in order to better discuss affairs, and thus becomes a simple commission instead of the sovereign court that it was the preceding instant.[137]

The difficulty with this conception is revealed by the fact that the English Parliament is not a true sovereign in Rousseau's terms; since a representative body is in principle merely a "trustee" of the sovereign people,[138] Rousseau's example casts a doubt on the practicality of having the populace act as the government as well as the sovereign.

Because the application of the laws to particular cases—the "acts of government" which characterize the "executive power"—are "naturally separated" from the enactment of the laws by the sovereign or "legislative power," the general will cannot be the agent which directly rules civil society:

> If it were possible that the sovereign, considered as such, had the executive power, right and fact would be so confused that one would no longer know what is a law and what is not, and the body politic thus denatured would soon be victim of the violence against which it was created.[139]

The popular claim to exercise governmental functions such as naming the magistrates is a residual claim based on "right," not on "fact"; although the principle of right is necessary to ensure that magistrates respect the law and the general will, attempts to realize the principle in the form of a direct democracy are imprudent:

> It is not good that the one who makes the laws should execute them, nor that the body of the people turn its attention from general considerations in order to give it to particular objects.[140]

Although direct popular government is not illegitimate, confusion between the sovereign and the government "denatures" the body politic because it undermines the limit of generality which defines the sovereign's legislative function and assures its equity.

[137] *Ibid.*, III, xvii (434).
[138] *Ibid.*, III, xv (429–30), where Rousseau explicitly cites the English Parliament and criticizes its claim to sovereignty.
[139] *Ibid.*, III, xvi (432).
[140] *Ibid.*, III, iv (404). Cf. *Économie Politique* (P, III, 264); *Second Discourse*, Ded. (P, III, 114).

The conception of the general will thus requires a distinction between the sovereign and the government, thereby raising the question of the particular form of political institutions appropriate to any given society. Having developed principles of political right that explain how obedience could be rational and legitimate, Rousseau therefore devotes the last two Books of the *Social Contract* to the subject of "Political Laws, which is to say the Form of Government."[141] Rousseau begins his analysis, in chapter I of Book III, by warning the "attentive" reader to study it "with reflection," thereby emphasizing the importance of the discussion which follows.[142]

Starting from the distinction, already noted, between "force" and "will" as the causes of all "free action,"[143] Rousseau asserts that:

> The body politic has the same sources of motion; one can distinguish in it, in the same way, force and will: the latter under the name of legislative power, the former under the name of executive power.[144]

The inevitability of the combination of will and force is, however, curiously qualified in this context: "Nothing is done, *or nothing ought to be done*, without their concord."[145] Evidently not all the acts of the body politic are "free"; it is always possible (if not likely) that political life be dominated by physical force, acting without reference to the source of legitimacy, the general will.

The healthy political order would therefore seem to be one of balance between will and force, based on the distinction between "executive" and "legislative power." Since the general will is inoperative without an "appropriate agent who will unite [the public force] and put it to work,"[146] the government or "supreme administration" should have the subordinate function of executing the com-

---

[141] See V, II, 22, cited in n. 19 of this chapter. I do not believe that J. H. Broome's characterization of the subject matter in the Four Books of the *Contrat social* is exact; cf. *Rousseau: A Study of His Thought* (London: Arnold, 1963), p. 54.

[142] "I warn the reader that this chapter should be read with reflection, and that I do not know the art of being clear for anyone who does not want to be attentive" (*Contrat social*, III, i [P, III, 395]).

[143] *Ibid.*, cited above, p. 69.

[144] *Ibid.* Note the importance Rousseau attaches to the terms *puissance législative* and *exécutive*—rather than *puissance législatrice* and *exécutrice* (which had been used by Montesquieu) (*Geneva MS*, III, i, n. [P, III, 334–35]; *Lettres Écrites de la Montagne*, vii [P, III, 833]). Rousseau insists on the form derived from an adjective, rather than from the noun *exécuteur*, in order to emphasize the "analogy" between these two forms of power (and, implicitly, to undermine the personalization of the sovereign's power).

[145] *Contrat social*, III, i (P, III, 395), italics added.

[146] *Ibid.* (396).

mands of the sovereign; the legitimate political order requires that the men who rule be subordinate to popularly enacted laws.

One of the obstacles to a proper understanding of the *Social Contract* today lies in the changed meaning of the terms that Rousseau so clearly tries to distinguish. The contemporary usage of the word legislation (i.e., all specific governmental actions enacted by a popularly elected representative assembly) is almost the opposite of Rousseau's meaning: he restricts the term "legislation" to the general or fundamental laws which are the "conditions of the civil association"; all particular actions of a government are called "decrees" or, more generally, "administration." Whereas Rousseau explicitly points to the imprudence of direct democratic government, when the contemporary usage of the word legislation is imposed on his thought, he appears to argue that the popular will should decide specific questions of public policy, ideally by a direct majority vote.[147]

Rousseau's condemnation of the "representation" of the sovereign is doubtless the chief source of the view that his principles require direct democracy.[148] But since he proposes representative institutions in his work on the *Government of Poland*,[149] his chapter on "Representatives or Deputies" must be considered in the context of his fundamental distinction between the sovereign and the government.

> The deputies of the people are therefore not, nor can they be, its representatives; they are only its commissioners; they cannot conclude anything definitively.[150]

The essential point is not that governmental functions cannot be delegated to individuals, but rather that these individuals cannot enact laws "definitively" on their own authority.

[147] E.g., Austin Ranney and Willmoore Kendall, *Democracy and the American Party System* (New York: Harcourt Brace and Co., 1956), pp. 9, 24, 48–51, 54–55, 62–64, 68, 74. Cf. Rousseau's insistence that foreign affairs are not in the competence of the sovereign (*Lettres Écrites de la Montagne*, vi [P, III, 826–27]), and his discussion of the establishment of tax rates as acts of "administration," to be determined by the government and merely assented to by the popular will (*Économie Politique* [P, III, 262–63, 269–78]).

[148] *Contrat social*, III, xv (P, III, 428–31). Rousseau's discussion of Roman politics and his assertions that a large electorate can assemble to act on political issues have also contributed to this interpretation (*ibid.*, III, xii [425–26]; IV, iii–iv [443–53]). Cf. also *Lettres Écrites de la Montagne*, v (P, III, 771), where "democracy" is the clearest example of "Republican" or legitimate government.

[149] *Gouvernement de Pologne*, vii (P, III, 978–89). See also *Économie Politique* (P, III, 270): "taxes can only be legitimately imposed with the consent of the people *or of its representatives*." Italics added.

[150] *Contrat social*, III, xv (P, III, 429–30).

When Rousseau asserts that "sovereignty cannot be represented for the same reason that it cannot be alienated,"[151] he invites the careful reader to refer back to the discussion of the inalienability of sovereignty:

> I say, therefore, that sovereignty, being only the exercise of the general will, can never be alienated, and that the sovereign, who is only a collective being, can only be represented by itself. Power can well be transmitted, but not will.[152]

Government may be viewed as the organization of power or physical force which is necessary to implement the common good as it is determined by the enlightened will of the body politic.

E · THE GEOMETRIC FORMULA FOR LEGITIMATE GOVERNMENT

According to Rousseau, the proper relationship between the sovereign and the government is an equilibrium that can be formulated in mathematical terms:

> It is in government that are found the intermediary forces whose relationships comprise that of the whole to the whole, or of the sovereign to the State. One could represent this latter relationship by that of the extremes of a continuous proportion, of which the proportional mean is the government. The government receives from the sovereign the orders that it gives to the people; and in order for the State to be in good equilibrium, it is necessary, everything considered, that there be equality between the product or the power of the government taken by itself, and the product or power of the citizens, who are sovereigns on one side and subjects on the other.[153]

A "continuous proportion" is a geometric relationship of the order:

$$A/B = B/C = C/D \ldots$$

Applying the mathematical proportion to the subject matter:

$$S/G = G/E \qquad \text{(Equation 1)}$$

[151] Ibid. (429).
[152] Ibid., II, i (368). Cf. III, xv (429): "The will is not represented: it is the same, or it is other; there is no middle term."
[153] Ibid., III, i (396). For clarification of the mathematical terms used by Rousseau, see Derathé's notes (P, III, 1472–76) and the works there cited. Cf. also Georges Beaulavon, ed., Du Contrat social (2d ed.; Paris: F. Rieder, 1914), pp. 212ff.

where S = sovereign; G = government; and E = State (the people as subject)

This continuous proportion exists if the terms of the equation are still equal when cross multiplied, so that:

$$S \times E = G \times G \text{ or } S \times E = G^2 \text{ or } \sqrt{S \times E} = G$$

Rousseau simply describes these equations in prose which seems awkward today due to changes in mathematical terminology.

Rousseau's choice of a mathematical relationship to represent the nature of the body politic has more significance than it has usually been given.[154] For example, Descartes—whose works Rousseau apparently knew well—claims that a careful consideration of the continuous proportion illuminates "all the questions that can be posed concerning the proportions or the relations of things and in what order they ought to be sought."[155] It could therefore be argued that Rousseau's use of this particular proportion is evidence of a desire to construct a theory of politics consistent with modern mathematical and physical science. One must immediately add, however, that the continuous proportion is also explicitly used by Aristotle in his formulation of the various kinds of justice, and that Plato's famous "divided line" is a geometric formulation of this very relationship.[156] Here again, Rousseau's philosophy can best be understood as a radical fusion of ancient and modern elements.

To this point, Rousseau merely provides an algebraic formulation of the principles of political right, requiring the subordination of the government to popularly enacted laws obeyed by the citizens.

Moreover, one could not alter any of the three terms without instantaneously breaking the proportion. If the sovereign wants to

---

[154] See *ibid.*, cited by Derathé (P, III, 1472–73); Halbwachs, ed., *Du Contrat social*, pp. 237, n. 1; 247–53; Lecercle, ed., *Du Contrat social*, pp. 116–17, n. 4; 119, n. 3; 120, n. 1.

[155] René Descartes, *Règles pour la Direction de l'Esprit*, vi, in *Oeuvres et Lettres*, ed. André Bridoux (Paris: Bibliothèque de la Pléiade, 1952), p. 55. Immediately before introducing the continuous proportion, Rousseau compares the function of government in civil society to "the union of the soul and body in man"—i.e., a central problem formulated by Descartes (*Contrat social*, III, i [P, III, 396]). For Rousseau's attitude toward Descartes as a representative of modern science, see *ibid.*, II, ix (388); *First Discourse*, Part 2 (P, III, 18n., 29); C. G., III, 356; *Institutions Chymiques*, I, iii (*Annales*, XII, 33); "Le Verger de Madame de Warens" (P, II, 1128), and Gouhier, "Ce que le Vicaire doit à Descartes" (*Annales*, XXXV, 139–60).

[156] Aristotle, *Nicomachean Ethics* V.1131a–b, 1133b; Plato, *Republic* VI.509d–510a.

govern, if the magistrate wants to give the laws, or if the subjects refuse to obey, disorder follows upon rule, force and will no longer act in harmony, and the dissolved state thus falls into despotism or anarchy.[157]

But Rousseau at once adds:

Finally, since there is only one proportional mean within each proportion, there is no more than one good government possible in a State. But as a thousand events can change the ratios of a people, not only can different governments be good for different peoples, but for the same people at different times.[158]

A necessary corollary of Rousseau's principles of political right is the decisive importance of finding the form of government that best suits each specific political society at a given time. The classical concern for the best regime is misleading to the extent that it directs the attention of political men away from the necessary circumstances which must be taken into account if political action is to succeed.[159]

Rousseau immediately uses the number of citizens as an example of the way his continuous proportion explains political life.

Let us suppose that the State is composed of ten thousand citizens. The sovereign can only be considered collectively and in a body, but each particular person, in his quality as a subject, is considered as an individual. Thus the sovereign is to the subject as ten thousand is to one, i.e., each member of the State only has one ten-thousandth part of the sovereign authority, even though he is subjected to it entirely. Let the people be composed of one hundred thousand men, the condition of the subjects does not change; and each carries equally all the empire of the laws, while his suffrage, reduced to one one-hundred-thousandth, has ten times less influence in drawing them up. Thus, the subject always remaining one, the ratio of the sovereign increases in proportion to the number of citizens. From which it follows that the more the State is enlarged, the more freedom is diminished.[160]

Since the ratio of the sovereign to the subjects increases as the number of citizens increases, the contribution of each individual to the making of the laws is reduced as the size of the community increases.

[157] *Contrat social*, III, i (P, III, 397).
[158] *Ibid.*
[159] *Ibid.* (398, 400); III, iii (403); III, vii (413); III, viii (414-19); III, ix (419).
[160] *Ibid.*, III, i (397).

Rousseau thereby deduces his preference for the small city as the most suited to justice—a prudential application of the principles of political right[161]—from a mathematical formula apparently expressing these principles in a universally valid way.

In order to prove that the continuous proportion accurately represents political life, Rousseau presents two relationships comparing different societies. His first proportion is:

> Now the less private wills are related to the general will, i.e., morals to the laws, the more the repressive force ought to be increased. Therefore, the government, to be good, should be relatively stronger in proportion to the greater number of people.[162]

In algebraic terms:

$$G_a/C_a = G_b/C_b \qquad \text{(Equation 2)}$$

where C = number of citizens.

Rousseau immediately adds a second general proposition:

> Since the enlargement of the State gives the depositories of public authority more temptations and means to abuse their power, the more force the government should have to restrain the people, the more the sovereign should have, in turn, to restrain the government.[163]

Or, in algebraic terms:

$$S_a/G_a = S_b/G_b \qquad \text{(Equation 3)}$$

Hence the proper ratio of the force of the sovereign to that of the government is determined by the same factor—the size of the political community—which determines the ratio of the force of the government to that of the subjects.

It appears, therefore, that Rousseau's conclusion is warranted:

> It follows from this double relationship that the continuous proportion between the sovereign, the prince, and the people is not an arbitrary idea, but a necessary consequence of the nature of the body politic. It also follows that one of the extremes, namely the people as subject, being fixed and represented by unity, every time

---

[161] *Ibid.*, III, xiii (427); III, xv (431).

[162] *Ibid.*, III, i (397).

[163] *Ibid.* (398). Rousseau adds that he is not speaking "of absolute force, but of the relative force of the different parts of the State" (*ibid.*), a qualification necessary if he is not to be guilty of a simple contradiction.

the doubled ratio [i.e., the cross multiplication of the four terms of the continuous proportion] increases or decreases, the simple ratio increases or decreases similarly, and that consequently the middle term is changed. Which shows that there is not a unique and absolute constitution of government, but that there can be as many governments different in nature as States different in size.[164]

Once again, Rousseau insists that the rigorous formulation of the relationships between sovereign, government, and subjects, as defined by the principles of political right, necessarily and logically entails the variability of political institutions in each society.

Since the continuous proportion seems to be the point at which Rousseau's purely formal logic defining the nature of law meets the prudential science of the legislator, it is of great importance to recognize that the apparent consistency of his argument cannot withstand mathematical or empirical analysis. To take the purely mathematical aspect first, even granting that there is a proportional relationship between the government and the population in two different regimes (Equation 2) and another proportional relationship between the sovereign and the government in these regimes (Equation 3), it need not follow that for each of the regimes, taken separately, Rousseau's continuous proportion exists. To be sure, it can readily be shown that both Equations 2 and 3 are determined by the number of citizens, and hence that these proportions are interdependent; for example, using the numerical example that Rousseau himself suggests:

$$G_a/10{,}000 = G_b/100{,}000$$

(Substituting the populations for C_a and C_b in Equation 2).

Solving this equation and Equation 3 for a common term (e.g., G_b):

$$G_b = G_a \times 100{,}000/10{,}000 \text{ and } G_b = G_a \times S_b/S_a$$

Since things equal to the same thing are equal to each other:

$$G_a \times 100{,}000/10{,}000 = G_a \times S_b/S_a \text{ or } 100{,}000/10{,}000 = S_b/S_a$$

This proof that Equations 2 and 3 are interdependent does not, however, permit one to derive the continuous proportion from them automatically, because the left hand members of Equations 2 and 3 need not be equal.[165]

---

[164] *Ibid.* Rousseau immediately warns, however, against taking the population as the sole measure of the "moral quantities" involved in the continuous proportion (*ibid.*).

[165] This can easily be discovered by substituting real numbers in these equa-

In the proportion between the government and the size of the population (Equation 2), Rousseau speaks explicitly of the *relative* force of two different citizen bodies, whereas in discussing the continuous proportion within a given society, he refers to the absolute force of the citizen as subject (which—given the rigorous equality of the law—is necessarily always the same and can be represented by unity).[166] But this means that Equation 2 can never be used as the basis of proving Equation 1: the ratio of the force of the government to the size of the population could conceivably be equal in two different societies, whereas the ratio of the force of the government to unity, being a different integer or whole number (since the denominator of the ratio is always 1), will be different for every society.[167]

It will be objected that Rousseau admits that the continuous proportion, especially if the force of the sovereign is represented solely by the population, cannot be taken as mathematically exact.

If, making fun of this system, one said that to find this proportional mean and form the body of the government, it is only necessary according to me to take the square root of the number of people, I would reply that I only take this number as an example; that the relations of which I speak are not measured only by the number of men, but in general by the quantity of action, which is composed by multitudes of causes; that at any rate if, in order to express myself in fewer words, I borrow the terms of geometry for a moment, I am not unaware nevertheless that geometric precision does not exist in moral quantities.[168]

This disclaimer only extends, however, to the *precision* with which the continuous proportion could be calculated, whether by the use of the population or any other measure of the "quantity of action," not to the very *logic* of the proportion itself. And yet, mathematically, that logic seems contestible to say the least.

The impossibility of deriving the continuous proportion from the "nature of things" is even more striking if one takes the trouble to consider Rousseau's analysis in the rest of the *Social Contract*. According to a "maxim of government" which Rousseau says is demon-

---

tions. And, of course, the term C in Equation 2 (the population) does not have the same meaning as the term E (the citizens as subjects of the state) in the continuous proportion.

[166] *Ibid.* (397, 398).

[167] I.e., the substitution of unity for C_a and C_b in Equation 2 gives only: $G_a/1 \neq G_b/1$ (unless the two governments are identical).

[168] *Ibid.* (398).

strated by "a thousand reasons," "the more the social bond is extended, the more it relaxes, and in general a small State is proportionately stronger than a large one."[169] In terms of the continuous proportion, this can only mean that the "quantity of action" of the sovereign is inversely proportional to the number of citizens; using Rousseau's numerical example in Book III, chapter i, the sovereign in a political community of 10,000 (S_a) is more active than the sovereign in a community of 100,000 (S_b). But according to the proposition summarized by Equation 2, the government of the *larger* community (G_b) must be more powerful or active than that of the smaller (G_a). It is therefore impossible to satisfy the condition of a "good equilibrium" specified in Equation 3, because insofar as the government acquires increased force merely to restrain a larger population, by definition the larger population is incapable of increasing its activity to restrain the government. The larger the political community, the more likely that the force of the government will be greater than the force of the sovereign.[170]

In fact, Rousseau makes it clear that the tendency of the force or quantity of action of the government to exceed the force of the sovereign is inherent in the nature of things. He asserts that there are "three essentially different wills in the person of the magistrate":

First, the will of the individual himself, which only tends to his private advantage; secondly, the will common to the magistrates, which is solely related to the advantage of the prince and can be called the corporate will, which is general in relation to the government and particular with relation to the State, of which the government is a part; in the third place, the will of the people or the sovereign will, which is general as much in relation to the State, considered as the whole, as in relation to the government, considered as part of the whole.[171]

Rousseau then goes on to describe the proper articulation of these three levels of will:

In a perfect legislation, the particular or individual will should be nothing, the corporate will of the government very subordinate, and, as a result, the general or sovereign will always dominant and the unique rule of all the others.[172]

[169] *Ibid.*, II, ix (386–87).
[170] Cf. *Dernière Reponse* (P, III, 87).
[171] *Contrat social*, III, ii (P, III, 400–01).
[172] *Ibid.* (401).

But this "perfect legislation," although in harmony with the "nature of law," is opposed to the "natural order" more broadly defined:

> According to the natural order, on the contrary, these different wills become more active as they are concentrated. Thus the general will is always the weakest, the corporate will has second place, and the private will is the first of all; so that, in the government, each member is first of all himself, and then magistrate, and then citizen: a gradation directly opposed to that which the social order requires.[173]

Nature tends "always" to be "directly opposed" to the requirements of a good polity; the natural love of oneself, corrupted into pride or vanity by society, can never be completely transformed into the exclusive love of one's fatherland which is necessary in the just city.

The natural tendency for the government (whose essence is *force*) to be more active than the sovereign (whose essence is *will*) explains a curious passage in Book III, chapter i. Rousseau suggests that the government can be analyzed in terms of the same proportion that he uses to describe the State as a whole:

> The government is, in a small way, what the body politic which contains it is in a large way. It is a moral person, having certain faculties, active like the sovereign, passive like the State, and which can be decomposed into other similar relationships, from which arises as a consequence a new proportion, another within the latter according to the order of tribunals, until one arrives at an indivisible middle term—that is, at a single ruler or supreme magistrate, who can be considered as the unity in the middle of this progression between the series of fractions and that of numbers.[174]

The last phrase of this paragraph indicates that, insofar as the proportion within the government is "like" the continuous proportion whose extreme terms are the sovereign and the subjects, the ratio of the sovereign to the government is a "fraction" and the ratio of the government to the subjects is a "number." Indeed, we have already seen this to be the case, since the subjects can be represented as an integer and the government is always more active than the sovereign.

Although it should go without saying that a fraction cannot be equal to an integer, a simple example of this fact is provided by estab-

[173] *Ibid.* (401). Cf. *Jugement sur la Polysynodie* (P, III, 644-45).
[174] *Contrat social*, III, i (P, III, 398).

lishing a progression composed of the number of chapters in each of the four Books of the *Social Contract*:

$$\frac{\text{Book I}}{\text{Book II}} \neq \frac{\text{Book III}}{\text{Book IV}} \text{ or } \frac{9}{12} \neq \frac{18}{9} \text{ or } \frac{3}{4} \neq \frac{2}{1}$$

Since Rousseau revised the chapter divisions of the *Geneva MS* (in which Book I had 7 chapters and Book II had 6), and on two occasions seemingly arbitrarily divided a single subject into three separate chapters, perhaps this example is not merely fanciful.[175] But be that as it may, a careful reading of the *Social Contract* proves that the realization of a continuous proportion in actual political life is simply impossible.

Rousseau's conception of a continuous proportion between the sovereign, the government, and the subjects is thus a mathematical formulation of his principles of political right which, like a frictionless surface, is of explanatory value only. Since this proportion simultaneously summarizes the conception of the general will and points to the necessary uniqueness of the form of government suited to each society, it is the link between his logical analysis of "the idea of the civil state" and his attempt to formulate a "science of the legislator."

3 · *Freedom and Order: the Tension between Politics and Morals*

A · THE ESSENCE OF ROUSSEAU'S CONCEPTION OF POLITICAL RIGHT

The foregoing analysis of Rousseau's principles of political right could be summarized as follows. The political community must have a voluntary convention as its basis, for only such a convention could produce a respectable reason for the obedience of men in society. The social contract, which defines this convention, consists of a total surrender of all rights by all citizens to the body politic as a whole; this surrender produces a sovereign, composed of all members of the society and alone capable of enacting the rules by which men will live together. These rules or acts of sovereignty are, by definition, only

---

[175] See *ibid.*, II, viii–x and III, xii–xiv. The chapters in each of these triads are so short that it hardly seems necessary for them to be separate; the former trio formed a single chapter (II, iii) in the *Geneva MS*. Given the inequality of length and subject matter in the various chapters of the final version, it is hard to believe that the specific divisions chosen by Rousseau are purely accidental. Of course there may be another explanation for division of Book II, chap. iii of the *Geneva MS* into three separate chapters, but commentaries have never explained it and it is at least conceivable that Rousseau decided (perhaps when adding the chapter on Civil Religion) to create a proportion out of the number of chapters in each of the four Books of the *Contrat social*.

legitimate when they proceed from the "general will," which is the enlightened self-interest of each member of the entire community when directed to the problems of the community. The generality of law, both in its objects and its source, provides a purely formal criterion of legitimacy, on the assumption that man freely wills his actions and cannot, by his very nature, will to do himself harm or injustice. Given this assumption, the natural impulse to self-preservation forces reasoning men to seek their own security in the security of a legitimate political society.

The nature of law requires a total surrender of natural right because only such a surrender makes possible freely willed obedience to enforced civil law. The strictly equal provisions of any just law, sanctioned by the force of the body politic, permit all citizens to secure their lives and property, the only condition which induces men to form the social contract and obey the laws. The principles of political right are, moreover, self-enforcing. Whenever the political community exceeds the bounds of legitimate law, as defined by the true general will, the social compact is by right destroyed and all men can again claim their natural rights. To regain his natural freedom, any individual need only leave the political association of which he is a member.[176] The surrender of man's claim to natural right does not destroy that prepolitical right because purely conventional duties cannot annihilate man's physical nature as an individual being. This does not mean, of course, that men actually do dissolve societies and reclaim their natural rights when the law is violated. On the contrary, this is rarely the case; "man is born free and *everywhere* he is in chains."[177]

Rousseau's principles can "render" civil society "legitimate" because he has discovered a formula which permits man in civil society to be "as free as he was before." This logical "idea of the civil state" cannot, however, exhaust the concerns of political thought. Because Rousseau places primary emphasis on the notion of freedom, his definition of the nature of the law does not resolve anything touching the way men actually behave or the proper order within civil society; presumably cannibalism, if authorized or prescribed by freely enacted law, is as legitimate as vegetarianism. But only if one studies the effect of law on men can political life be understood; to make the principles of political right meaningful, one must consider the manner in which

[176] *Contrat social*, III, xviii (P, III, 436 and n.); IV, ii (440 and n.).
[177] *Ibid.*, I, i (351), italics added. Note that this famous phrase might also be translated "man was born free" (*l'homme est né libre*), in which case it summarizes the teaching of the *Second Discourse* even more emphatically.

they are implemented. Since most men lack the "genius" to formulate appropriate legislation, Rousseau's conception of man's need for laws necessarily implies society's need for a legislator.[178] Hence the analysis of Rousseau's principles of right leads ineluctably to his understanding of the founding of civil society and the prudential rules for successful legislation.

B · THE MORAL RELEVANCE OF POLITICAL LEGITIMACY

This approach to Rousseau's political thought diverges in a decisive respect from one of the dominant interpretations of the *Social Contract*. Many commentators have insisted that the concept of the general will can only be understood in "moral" terms; unlike the contractual theories of Hobbes and Locke, Rousseau seems to infuse the conventional bonds uniting the political community with patriotic *sentiment*, without which his rational formula for legitimate obedience is impossible to understand.[179] Although the tone of Rousseau's works clearly justifies such an interpretation, a careful reading of the *Social Contract* and *Geneva MS* shows that the general will is presented as a rational construct explaining political right in a strict sense, as distinct from moral duty.[180] According to Rousseau's explicit statement, "moral freedom" is a consequence of political right and civil freedom, and it is the latter which is the topic of the *Social Contract*;[181] as was made even more evident in the *Geneva MS*, moral duty and virtue are derived from the principle of the general will and not vice versa.[182]

This problem can be restated somewhat more concretely by considering the fundamental paradox of Rousseau's political teaching. He incessantly appeals to the experience of Sparta and Rome as the models of civil life; in contrast even to modern Geneva, the classical

---

[178] The link between the need for laws and the need for a legislator was more clearly apparent in the *Geneva MS*, since Book I, chap. vii concludes with two parallel paragraphs, the first of which ends: "This is why the necessity of legislation arises," and the second of which ends: "This is why the necessity of a legislator arises" (P, III, 310-11).

[179] E.g., Jouvenel, "Essai sur la Politique de Rousseau," pp. 98–127, and esp. p. 106: Rousseau "moulded his *moral* notion of the General Will in a framework boldly constructed by Hobbes in order to receive a *juridical* notion of the general will." See also Watkins, "Introduction," p. xxiv: "The real novelty of Rousseau's theory is his attempt to apply the principles of natural morality to the determination of political legitimacy."

[180] See especially the distinction between "simple duty" and "strict right," *Geneva MS*, I, vi (P, III, 306), cited in n. 79 of this chapter. Cf. *Contrat social*, III, xviii (P, III, 435).

[181] *Ibid.*, I, viii (364–65), cited above, p. 53, n. 245.

[182] *Geneva MS*, I, ii (P, III, 286–89); II, iv (328–30).

city was motivated by virtue instead of bourgeois self-interest.[183] Yet Rousseau's attempt to return to the political practice of the Greeks and Romans, like that of Machiavelli, is based on the construction of a radically new or modern theory of political life. This rejection of the orientation of classic politicial philosophy is nowhere clearer than in the *Second Discourse*, which accepts the Hobbesian critique of traditional natural right and attempts to reestablish it on a basis consistent with the discoveries and presuppositions of modern science. Rousseau's principles of political right can therefore be best described as a reformulation of Hobbes' conception of the social contract.[184]

This attempt to return to the political model of the Greek *polis* without necessarily rejecting modern, materialistic physics has, as one consequence, Rousseau's emphasis on *freedom*. Classical thought was oriented to the question of the best political *order*; Plato and Aristotle sought to determine what would be the best regime. In contrast, Rousseau denies that there is any one ordering of a political community which is the best simply; instead, he develops a purely formal criterion of legitimacy which could be used to "establish" or render respectable all regimes.[185] As we have seen, Rousseau's attempt to describe the good life, in answer to the Platonic teaching, seems to be set forth in the *Émile*, a work which considers morality as the consequence of *private* education and denies that true freedom (i.e., moral freedom) is to be sought in civil society.[186] Rousseau's emphasis on man's natural independence and freedom thus seems to produce a political teaching which is not entirely appropriate as the basis of an appeal to the political model of the classical city.

Rousseau himself was, however, quite explicit concerning the articulation between "morality" and "politics":

> It is necessary to study society by men and men by society; those who would like to treat politics and morals separately will never understand anything about either of the two.[187]

"Morality" can be said to deal with "men," and "politics" with so-

---

[183] *First Discourse*, Part 1 (P, III, 12, 14–15); Part 2 (19–20, 23, 24n.); *Second Discourse*, Ded. (P, III, 113); *Lettre à d'Alembert* (G, 147, 176, 231); *Émile*, I (G, 9–10); *Contrat social*, I, vi, n. (P, III, 361–62); III, xi (424); III, xv (428–31); *Lettres Écrites de la Montagne*, vi (P, III, 809); ix (880–81); *Gouvernement de Pologne*, ii (P, III, 956–59).

[184] *Second Discourse*, Part 1 (P, III, 153–54); Part 2 (176–78); *Geneva MS*, I, ii (P, III, 284–89); *Contrat social*, I, vi (P, III, 360); IV, viii (463).

[185] E.g., *ibid.*, I, i (351); *Lettres Écrites de la Montagne*, VI (P, III, 811).

[186] *Émile*, I (G, 8–11); v (605), and above, chap. II, § 5.

[187] *Émile*, IV (G, 279).

ciety as a whole. The logic underlying political life provides a criterion of legitimacy that does not specify the kind of men required in order to perfect the political order; the moral teaching most appropriate for the natural man, as an individual living in society, is derived primarily from a natural religion and only incidentally concerns the principles of political right. Yet the apparent dualism is deceiving: since all men must now live in civil society, the individual has a moral duty to obey the laws, and the laws of any civil society inevitably form the moral character of the citizens.[188]

Rousseau's thought can ultimately be said to rest on a trichotomy between nature, morals, and politics. For example, in summarizing Émile's education, he remarks:

> Now, having considered himself by the physical relations with other beings, by his moral relations with other men, it remains for him to consider himself by his civil relations with his fellow citizens.[189]

It is this triple distinction between physical nature, morality, and politics which, in the form of the distinction between natural freedom, moral freedom, and civil freedom or the correlative excellences of natural goodness, humanitarian virtue, and civic virtue, gives Rousseau's philosophy its distinct character.[190] Whereas at first it appears that Rousseau, developing the ancient distinction between nature and convention, emphasizes the tension between the individual and society, in fact his conception of the human problem is far subtler; man's nature has a "moral side" (which can be described as his natural goodness), and conventional society necessarily engenders moral duties as well as political rights.

Rousseau's political principles are therefore closely related to his conception of human morality, and therewith to his conception of the corruption produced by society (and especially by enlightenment and reasoning). For this very reason, paradoxically enough, it is misleading to speak of Rousseau's principles of political right as having a "moral" character: by themselves, the rules of strict right do not and cannot insure the morality of the citizen, for civic virtue is the

---

[188] *Ibid.,* v (G, 571, 605–07); *Contrat social,* II, xii (P, III, 394); IV, ii (440); *Second Discourse,* n. XIX (P, III, 222–23).

[189] *Émile,* v (581). Cf. also Rousseau's description of the proper or philosophic method of studying hitherto unknown peoples as "natural, moral, and political history" (*Second Discourse,* n. X [P, III, 213–14]).

[190] See the concluding section of each of the chapters in Part I above, esp. 102–04 and 252–54.

result of the implementation of laws (and not of the philosopher's definition of their nature). This explains why, for Rousseau, the character of the citizens is determined by the "secret" intentions of the legislator; direct attempts to legislate personal morality—or indeed anything whatever concerning the morals of citizens that is contrary to existing public opinion—are bound to fail.[191]

It is worth emphasizing that on several occasions Rousseau asserts that it is the action of the *government*—and not of the sovereign—which determines the character of the citizenry.[192] In the *Political Economy* (which is concerned with the proper administration of civil society and is therefore directed more openly to the magistrate), Rousseau formulates an "essential rule of public economy" as follows:

If you want the general will to be fulfilled, make all the private wills approach it; and since virtue is only this conformity of the private will to the general, to say the same thing in a word, make virtue reign.[193]

The general will is in principle "indestructible" and in practice in conflict with the private will of each individual; morality therefore requires not the discovery of the principles of political right, but their effective realization in civil society.

Insofar as Rousseau's attempt to restore human morality is possible on the political level, the "moral" character of his thought is directly connected with the conditions under which legitimate institutions can be established in any given society. But, as we have seen, the realization of political right is a matter of "circumspection" or prudence, which can be illuminated by "maxims of government." Unlike the classics, who merely assumed that the statesman should be prudent if he wants to succeed, the modern foundations of Rousseau's theory of the general will forced him to elaborate a prudential "science of legislation."

[191] *Contrat social*, II, xii (P, III, 394); IV, vii (458–59); *Lettre à d'Alembert* (G, 174–82); *Second Discourse*, n. XIX (P, III, 222–23); *Nouvelle Héloïse*, Second Pref. (P, II, 24).
[192] *Économie Politique* (P, III, 251–52), in part cited above, p. 296; *Confessions*, IX (P, I, 404), cited above, p. vi. Cf. *Lettre à d'Alembert* (G, 182).
[193] *Économie Politique* (P, III, 253).

—VIII—

THE SCIENCE OF THE LEGISLATOR
(SOCIAL CONTRACT, CONCLUDED)

1 · *The Founding*

A · THE FUNCTION OF THE LEGISLATOR

It is no accident that the legislator or founder of the laws, whose function had been emphasized by Plato and other classical philosophers but is conspicuously absent in the works of Hobbes and Locke, has a central role in Rousseau's teaching. Since laws are impotent and civic virtue impossible without sound customs and public opinions, Rousseau's principles of political right must be put into practice by statesmen who take into account the unique traditions and situation of each society.

The lawgiver represents the implementation of political right in its purest form because the laws that constitute civil society must be founded by the work and art of man.

> Someone who dares to undertake the institution of a people should feel capable of changing human nature, so to speak; of transforming each individual, who by himself is a perfect and solitary whole, into a part of a larger whole from which this individual receives in some way his life and being; of altering man's constitution in order to reinforce it; of substituting a partial and moral existence for the physical and independent existence we all received from nature.[1]

Having denied that civil society is natural, Rousseau can consider legislation as the work of a single man who "transforms" the human condition.

The peculiar role of the legislator is underlined by Rousseau's insistence that this function has no status, strictly speaking, in political right.

> The legislator is in every respect an extraordinary man in the State.

[1] *Contrat social*, II, vii (P, III, 381).

— 354 —

If he should be such by his genius, he is no less so in his activity. It is not magistracy, nor sovereignty. This activity, which constitutes the republic, does not enter into its constitution: it is a specific and superior function which has nothing in common with human empire.[2]

Sovereignty cannot be attributed to the lawgiver, for Rousseau's principles of political right show that only the general will of the citizen body as a whole can be sovereign.

The one who draws up the laws, therefore, has or should have no legislative right, and the people itself cannot divest itself of this incommunicable right even if it wants to, because according to the fundamental compact only the general will can obligate the private individuals, and one can never be assured that a private will conforms to the general will until after it has been submitted to the free vote of the people.[3]

This inability of a private will—even that of the legislator—to have sovereign authority derives especially from the necessary immediacy or impermanence of the general will: "if it is not impossible that a private will agree on some point with the general will, it is at least impossible that this agreement be durable and constant."[4] Since "the law of today should not be an act of the general will of yesterday, but that of today," the sovereign "is always free to change" the laws, and the legislator cannot pretend to speak for the "actual consent" of the people in future times (even if he claims to enunciate the popular will at the moment of instituting new laws).[5]

Whereas the incompatibility between the individual legislator and the sovereign is a matter of right on which no compromise is possible, the distinction between the legislator and a magistrate is more a question of prudence or even common sense. To be sure, at first it appears that the lawgiver is not like a magistrate in an established regime, for even the best ruler "has only to follow the model that the other must propose"; if the magistrate must be subordinate to the laws, he cannot be their creator without risking great abuses of power.[6] Rousseau's examples, however, reveal the prudential character

---

[2] *Ibid.* (382). [3] *Ibid.* (383).

[4] *Ibid.*, II, i (368).

[5] *Geneva MS*, II, ii (P, III, 315–16). Cf. *Contrat social*, III, iv (P, III, 404), where the sovereign people is called the "legislator."

[6] *Ibid.*, II, vii (381). "If the one who commands men should not command the laws, the one who commands the laws 'should not command men; other-

of this distinction: Lycurgus, the model of the legislator, "abdicated the kingship" before "giving laws to his fatherland" and many ancient and modern republics adopted the "usage" of having a foreigner draft their laws; in contrast, the Roman Republic "nearly perished for uniting in the same heads legislative authority and sovereign power." As the Roman case makes clear, "legislative authority," far from being distinct from the magistracy, is akin to it; the Decemvirs of Rome (rather than the legendary lawgiver Numa) are the model of the inability of the legislator to attribute to himself "the right of making any law pass" on the basis of personal "authority."[7] According to the Dedication to the *Second Discourse*, in the best city only the magistrates have "the right" to propose new laws, but this right must be used with "circumspection."[8]

The parallel between the functions of the legislator and the magistrate requires emphasis if one is to understand Rousseau's conception of the founding of civil institutions. According to the principles of right, "the government is not the master of the law" (since only the sovereign populace can enact it), but in a sense the same limitation necessarily applies to the legislator; the prime difference between the legislator and ordinary magistrates is that the latter are obliged to respect existing laws whereas the former must destroy and replace all laws and customs that are incompatible with the general will and the true public interest.[9] But as Rousseau makes clear in analyzing Rome, the need to change old laws is not confined to the act of the founding; although Cicero "criticized" a fundamental change in the manner of voting "and attributed to it in part the ruin of the Republic":

I think, on the contrary, that the loss of the State was accelerated

---

wise the laws, ministers of his passions, would often merely perpetuate his injustices" (*ibid.* [382]).

[7] *Ibid.* (382–83). Rousseau's citation from Montesquieu (*ibid.*, 381) underlines this point by equating the legislator with the "rulers (*chefs*) of the republic": according to Montesquieu, "At the birth of societies, it is the rulers of the republic who create the institution, and afterwards it is the institution which forms the rulers of the republic" (*Considérations sur le Grandeur et la Décadence des Romains*, chap. I). Cf. Machiavelli, *Discourses*, I, xxxv.

[8] *Second Discourse*, Ded. (P, III, 114).

[9] *Économie Politique* (P, III, 247–50). In this text, Rousseau indicates the parallel between the tasks of the lawgiver and the magistrate by remarking that the latter should "follow in everything the general will," while the former should "conform the laws to the general will." The ultimate end of both the founding of political institutions and their "administration" is the maintenance of the moral character of the people insofar as is possible.

by not having made enough of such changes. Just as the regime for healthy people is not fit for sick ones, one must not want to govern corrupt peoples by the same laws that suit a good people.[10]

Since the need for innovation in the laws is ever present,[11] the problem of the founding is thus merely the problem of all government in its most radical form.

There are prudential reasons, however, for considering the act of legislation as if it were the work of a single man. Changes in the laws are dangerous because they undermine respect for law, not only on the part of the citizenry, but also by the magistrates themselves; new legislation in an established society is evidence of moral corruption, for it indicates that existing laws and customs are not sufficient to contain the private interests of men and direct them to the common good.[12] Since the government has a natural tendency to usurp the authority of the sovereign people, the more strongly legislation is connected with the action of a single lawgiver at the founding, the more sacred the laws will be and the less likely usurpation of power by the rulers. Precisely because the magistrates can at any time propose new laws, which they may be able to persuade the populace to enact, prudence suggests the importance of presenting the functions of the legislator and magistrate as fundamentally different.

The action of the legislator who proposes comprehensive institutions for a community has another advantage as well. The continued attempt to enact new laws as a response to existing deficiencies resembles the defects of "emergent government" at an earlier stage in human history.

Despite all the labors of the wisest legislators, the political state remained ever imperfect because it was almost the work of chance, and because, as it began badly, time in discovering faults and suggesting remedies could never repair the vices of the constitution. People incessantly mended, whereas it would have been necessary to begin by clearing the area and setting aside all the old materials, as Lycurgus did in Sparta, in order to raise a good edifice afterward.[13]

[10] *Contrat social*, IV, iv (P, III, 452–53).
[11] See *Lettres Écrites de la Montagne*, vii (P, III, 820, 825) and cf. Machiavelli, *Discourses*, III, i.
[12] *Second Discourse*, Ded. (P, III, 114); *Préface à Narcisse* (P, II, 971); *Contrat social*, III, xviii (P, III, 435); *Fragments Politiques*, IV, 7 (P, III, 493).
[13] *Second Discourse*, Part 2 (P, III, 180). Cf. *Contrat social*, II, viii (P, III, 384–85); *Gouvernement de Pologne*, vii (P, III, 975); and Machiavelli, *Discourses*, I, ix.

Since the establishment of laws is useless unless they are supported by common opinion and custom, it is futile to attempt to regulate defective behavior by legislation that does not go to the cause of existing vices. Most often, total reform is impossible: "Once customs are established and prejudices rooted, it is a dangerous and vain enterprise to want to reform them."[14] If the statesman's objective is civic virtue, the only chance for political improvement lies in extreme measures which uproot established traditions:

> To be sure, like some illnesses which overturn the heads of men and destroy their memory of the past, sometimes there are found, in the life of States, violent epochs in which revolutions do to peoples what certain crises do to individuals, in which the horror of the past takes the place of forgetting, and in which the State, having been set aflame by civil wars, is so to speak reborn from its ashes.[15]

Because it is impossible to overcome corrupted morals and make men truly free and virtuous without a "great revolution which is to be feared almost as much as the evil it could cure," the treatment of the laws as if they are the work of a single legislator has a double advantage: it discourages the enactment of new laws which will fail to have the intended effects, while pointing to the "rare events" or "exceptions" during which a truly legitimate republic, like those of Sparta and Rome, can be constituted.[16]

The possibility of establishing, at a single point in time, lasting political institutions which make men just and free is therefore an "exception" or "extraordinary" circumstance which nevertheless illuminates and indeed symbolizes the "ordinary" problems of political life; once the statesman knows the rules which should govern such a founding, he can easily deduce those which apply to the changes or modification appropriate to an existing regime. That such an act of founding is even possible can, of course, be denied—as it was by Burke and those nineteenth-century authors who insisted that political institutions can only be the result of historical growth. Rousseau's analysis of human evolution provides a response to this objection by pointing to the difference between the "social contract" and

---

[14] *Contrat social*, II, viii (P, III, 385).
[15] *Ibid.*
[16] *Ibid.; Observations* (P, III, 56). Cf. *Jugement sur le Projet de Paix Perpétuelle* (P, III, 600). On the relative importance of a single lawgiver in Sparta and in Rome, cf. Polybius, *Histories* VI.iii.

the enactment of laws; a "people suited for legislation" must be "already bound by some union of origin, interest, or convention."[17]

This difference between the social contract and legislation properly speaking is more extensively developed in the *Second Discourse*, where the original contract is presented as a specific act produced by the reasoning of one man; legislation, on the contrary, is described as an evolutionary process which takes place over a considerable period of time.[18] But given the conception of time which governs the *Second Discourse*—"the more slowly events followed each other, the more rapidly they can be described"—it is legislation which could conceivably take place in a short time, whereas the formation of the social bond appears to be the result of an "almost insensible progress from the beginnings."[19] The making of laws is the true opportunity for a political hero seeking lasting fame; men can rarely claim responsibility for the very existence of a society—and such claims are often mythical—but a great legislator can rightly be honored for having established all the laws, as did Mohammed, Moses, Lycurgus, Numa, and Calvin.[20]

B · ROUSSEAU'S MODIFICATION OF THE CLASSICAL CONCEPTION OF THE LEGISLATOR

Rousseau's emphasis on the making of the laws as the work of a legislator cannot be separated from his criticism of modern political life as radically inferior to that of the ancients.

> I look at modern nations and I see plenty of makers of laws and not one legislator. Among the ancients, I see three that merit particular attention: Moses, Lycurgus, and Numa.[21]

This return to a pre-modern conception is indicated at the outset of the chapter on the legislator by Rousseau's reference to Plato; having previously described the Emperor Caligula's analogy between "a

---

[17] *Contrat social*, II, x (P, III, 390).

[18] On the social contract, see *Second Discourse*, Part 2 (P, III, 176–78); on legislation, *ibid*. (180, 186–87).

[19] *Ibid*. (167), cited and analyzed above, pp. 166–67.

[20] *Second Discourse*, Part 2 (P, III, 180, 187); *Contrat social*, II, vii (P, III, 381–84); II, viii (385). Consider Rousseau's assertion that Numa, the lawgiver, and not the "fierce" Romulus, "was the true founder of Rome" (*Gouvernement de Pologne*, ii [P, III, 957–58]). Cf. Machiavelli, *Prince*, chap. VI and *Discourses*, I, xix.

[21] *Gouvernement de Pologne*, ii (P, III, 956). Cf. Aristotle's distinction between those who merely make laws and those who "frame constitutions" or regimes (*Politics* II.1273b–1274b).

shepherd," who is "of a nature superior to his herd," and the "shepherds of men, who are their rulers,"[22] Rousseau comments:

> The same reasoning that Caligula used with reference to facts,
> Plato used with reference to right in order to define the civil or
> royal man he seeks in his book on ruling; but if it is true that a
> great prince is rare, what will be the case for a great legislator?[23]

Referring to Plato's *Statesman*—obviously the dialogue in question[24]
—one finds not only the comparison between the true ruler and the
shepherd (based on an analogy between the "arts" of directing other
living beings), but a clear statement of the classical conception of the
legislator and the science or art of statesmanship.[25]

[22] "Just as a shepherd is of a nature superior to his herd, the shepherds of
men, who are their rulers, are also of a nature superior to that of their peoples.
According to the report of Philo, this is how the Emperor Caligula reasoned,
concluding well enough from this analogy that kings were gods or that peoples
were beasts" (*Contrat social*, i, ii [P, iii, 353]).

[23] *Ibid.*, ii, vii (381). In the first draft of the chapter on the legislator, the
references to Caligula and Plato were not divided (whereas in the final version they are in different chapters); originally Rousseau said: "In a word,
a God is needed to give good laws to the human species, and just as shepherds
are of a species superior to the beasts they lead, the shepherds of men, who
are their rulers, should be of a more excellent species than the peoples.
This reasoning that Plato used with reference to right in order to define the
civil or royal man he seeks in his book on ruling [*son livre du regne*], Caligula
used in fact, according to the report of Philo, to prove that the masters of
the world were of a nature superior to the remainder of men. But if it is
true, . . ." (*Geneva MS*, ii, ii [P, iii, 312–13]).

[24] This is made particularly clear by the reference to this dialogue under its
Latin title *Civili* in *Contrat social*, iii, vi (P, iii, 412 and n.).

[25] On the comparison of the ruler and a shepherd, see *Statesman* 261a ff.,
esp. 266e–268d. Note that the argument ends with the conclusion that there
is "one respect" in which "a king differs from all other herdsmen" (267e);
the analogy is explicitly treated as insufficient by Plato (cf. also 275d–276c
and the substitution of the art of weaving as the "example" of the art of the
statesman, 279b–283b and 287b). The remainder of Plato's dialogue, in many
ways the most important part, can be divided into the presentation of the
"legend" of the reign of Chronos (268d–274e) and the precise formulation of
the art of the statesman (275a–311c). According to the legendary "cosmic
history," time is divided into the age of Chronos—an era in which "God
himself assists the universe" directly, the motions of the heavenly bodies are
"reversed," and "all good things come without man's labor"—and the age of
Zeus, in which the universe is "released" by God, revolves in the direction
perceived at present as the result of the "innate force" built up in the prior
epoch, and in which men, being no longer born directly from the earth and
lacking divine guidance, must survive "by their own power" amid "disorder."
This account (effectively replaced in Rousseau's thought by the Newtonian
explanation of the movements of heavenly bodies and the analysis of human
evolution in the *Second Discourse*) leads Plato to the conclusion that the
statesman who is like a shepherd is "a god, not a mortal" and that he ruled

To understand Rousseau's position fully, it will be useful to restate the premodern view of the functions of the lawgiver as they are presented in the *Statesman*. For Plato, the political art is a "directive productive art," as distinct from the "instrumental" or "contributory" arts (like warfare) which produce the necessary means for civil life without establishing the use or end to which they are put.[26] Because this art directs other human activity, it requires knowledge which "will be found in the possession of one or two, or at most of a select few"; since most rulers lack this science, the identification of the true statesman requires a distinction between those who appear or falsely claim to "possess the art of ruling" and the few who actually have it.[27] For "men really possessed of scientific understanding of government," it is not essential that rule be in accordance with the laws or be willingly accepted by the people; all regimes under law are "mere imitations" or reflections of the regime which is simply best and which is ruled in accordance with wisdom.[28] Although the rule of law is inferior to the rule of wisdom, because laws are inflexible and cannot be varied to meet the exigencies of individual situations,[29] legislation is a practical necessity given the likelihood that those who exercise political power lack true knowledge.[30] The "second best" regimes—which is to say for practical purposes, every existing regime—must "forbid any individual or any group to perform any act in contravention of the laws," and in principle, laws should be understood as "written copies of the scientific truth in the various departments of life they cover." Because new legislation in an existing regime is only legitimate when in accordance with the science or truth about politics, the laws must be maintained without any change whatever, even if changes be desired by the many, except in the rare case in which a man with true wisdom—the statesman in the precise sense—acts as legislator.[31]

The Platonic conception of the primacy of scientific knowledge as

---

in the age of Chronos, not in the present cosmic era (275a); "those who rule these states of ours in this present era are like their subjects, far closer to them in training and in nurture than ever shepherd could be to flock" (275c). Despite Rousseau's modern cosmology, he shares Plato's account of the status of the human ruler.

[26] *Statesman* 287b–289d, 303e–305e. Cf. Aristotle, *Nicomachean Ethics* I.1094a–b; *Politics* III.1282b.

[27] *Statesman* 292e–293b, 300e. Cf. *Republic* I.339b–342b.

[28] *Statesman* 293c–297e; 302c; Aristotle, *Politics* III.1284a–b.

[29] *Statesman* 301b–c; Aristotle, *Politics* III.1286a.

[30] *Statesman* 300b–303b; Aristotle, *Politics* II.1272a; III.1282b, 1286a–1288a.

[31] *Statesman* 300c–301a. Cf. Aristotle, *Politics* II.1269a.

the sole criterion of true statesmanship thus has two important corollaries: first, in practice political life can only be salutary if it is subordinate to wise laws sanctioned by custom; second, only the statesman armed with political wisdom is capable of enacting new laws. Since a healthy civil society depends on "a right opinion concerning what is good, just, and profitable, . . . an opinion based on absolute truth and settled as an unshakeable conviction," the education of the young is decisive as a means of producing political unity and good customs.[32]

> It is the true statesman, in that he is the good and true lawgiver, who is alone able—for who else should possess the power—to forge by the wonderous inspiration of the kingly art this bond of true conviction uniting the hearts of the young folk.[33]

Above all, the lawgiver is to be understood as the human agent who, through wisdom, produces the common "conviction about values and standards" on which not merely obedience to the laws, but the virtue and unity of a political community rest.

It is not hard to see the parallels between Plato's conception of the statesman or legislator and Rousseau's political teaching.[34] The decisive difference between them arises from the conception of science and truth which Rousseau felt compelled to adopt; replacing "legends" dealing with "cosmic history" by modern natural science, and thereby recognizing the created character of human reason and intellectual ideas, Rousseau based his science of politics on the discovery that obedience can only be explained in terms of freedom and will. Rousseau's principles of political right thus give absolute priority to the voluntary acceptance of the laws, rather than their wisdom, for his science cannot claim to have a higher political status than the phenomenon of the general will it discovered; for Rousseau—unlike Plato—laws that do not have popular assent are not true laws.[35] Because Rousseau cannot admit that knowledge is, in political life, the sole criterion of the "true constitution" or the best laws, he abandons the attempt to define the best regime, and must consider the science of the legislator as a prudential science which guides the legislator in his understanding of the "invincible nature of things"; if the sov-

[32] *Statesman* 308d–309c, 310e–311a.
[33] *Ibid.*, 309d.
[34] See especially the emphasis placed on "public education" in *Économie Politique* (P, III, 259–62) and *Gouvernement de Pologne*, i (P, III, 954–55).
[35] Cf. *Statesman* 296b–297b, with *Contrat social*, II, vii (P, III, 382–83) and above, chap. VII, § 2C.

ereign will elects to ignore the truth, it does so in accordance with its right (although thereby acting imprudently).[36]

Rousseau's inversion of the classical priority of knowledge over freedom therefore creates a tremendous problem, for it entails a radical dependence of the legislator upon popular opinions.

> The wise men who want to speak their language to the vulgar instead of its own cannot possibly be understood. Now there are a thousand kinds of ideas that it is impossible to translate into the language of the people. . . . Each individual, since he only appreciates a plan for government that is related to his private interest, sees with difficulty the advantages he should derive from the continual privations that good laws impose.[37]

Since the private interests of the many are virtually certain to be opposed to new laws whose wisdom they cannot understand, the creation of political institutions seems to be a contradiction in terms.

> In order for an emergent people to appreciate the healthy maxims of politics and follow the fundamental rules of reason of State, it would be necessary for the effect to become the cause, for the social spirit that should be the work of the institution to preside at the institution itself, and for men to be, before the laws exist, what they should become by means of them.[38]

Knowledge of the principles of political right shows the necessity for free acceptance of the laws by the general will, but the science of the legislator reveals that the populace cannot be expected to adopt laws merely because they are in accordance with the "healthy maxims of politics" which compose that science.

As a consequence of his inability to employ coercion, Rousseau's legislator is "disarmed" by comparison to the classical lawgiver described by Plato.

> Thus the legislator, being unable to use either force or reasoning, necessarily has recourse to an authority of another order, which can win over without violence and persuade without convincing.[39]

[36] *Contrat social*, II, xii (P, III, 393–94); III, xviii (435).

[37] *Ibid.*, II, vii (383).

[38] *Ibid.* Note that it is the "maxims of politics" or "reason of State"—and not the principle of political right—that the people cannot be expected to understand; this sentence should probably be read in light of the distinction emphasized above, chap. VI, § 2E.

[39] *Contrat social*, II, vii (P, III, 383). Cf. *Jugement sur le Projet de Paix Perpétuelle* (P, III, 599), cited in n. 55 of this chapter.

Religion or popular superstition which unites a people prior to or independently of the laws is the only "sublime reason which is above the capacity of vulgar men" to which one can appeal in order to lead them to "obey with freedom." This appeal to "divine authority" is merely a means to a human end, dictated by the discoveries of political science.

Vain magical tricks form a passing bond; only wisdom makes it lasting.[40]

Religion serves as an "instrument" of politics at the "origin of nations," and without wisdom as its guide, is impotent to produce the lasting political glory which is the only true recompense of the legislator.

C · ROUSSEAU'S MODIFICATION OF MACHIAVELLI'S CONCEPTION OF THE LEGISLATOR

At this point, Rousseau adds a footnote quoting Machiavelli's *Discourses* in order to affirm the necessity of an appeal to God by every legislator:

In truth, there never was any remarkable lawgiver amongst any people who did not resort to divine authority, as otherwise his laws would not have been accepted by the people; for there are many good laws, the importance of which is known to the sagacious lawgiver, but the reasons for which are not sufficiently evident to enable him to persuade others to submit to them.[41]

Rousseau's quotation requires some comment because, as has been noted, Machiavelli is one of the authors most frequently cited with approval in the *Social Contract*. In addition to four footnotes in which Rousseau uses Machiavelli as an authority, in the chapter "On Monarchy" Rousseau criticizes the traditional opinion of Machiavelli:

It is natural that princes always give preference to the maxim that is most immediately useful to them. . . . This is what Machiavelli shows with clarity. In pretending to give lessons to kings, he gave great ones to the populace. *The Prince* of Machiavelli is the book of Republicans.[42]

[40] *Contrat social*, II, vii (P, III, 384).
[41] *Discourses on Titus Livy*, I, xi. Rousseau cites the Italian in a note; the translation used here is by Christian E. Ditmold in the Modern Library edition (ed. Lerner, p. 147).
[42] *Contrat social*, III, vi (P, III, 409). Cf. *Économie Politique* (P, III, 247), and above, pp. 308–10.

Rousseau's assertion, in a note added to the passage, that Machiavelli was "an honest man and a good citizen" should not be passed by too lightly;[43] when a book reputed to teach kings the most immoral methods of success is described by a philosopher as a "book of Republicans," an explanation is required.

Although it is neither possible nor relevant to prove whether Machiavelli really *was* "an honest man and a good citizen,"[44] it is useful to refer to the broad context of the passage that Rousseau cites in his chapter "On the Legislator."[45] Book I, chapter xi, of the *Discourses*, entitled "Of the Religion of the Romans," follows two other chapters which discuss the founding of Rome. In chapter ix, Machiavelli sets out to prove that "a sagacious legislator of a republic . . . should concentrate all authority in himself," and concludes from this that Romulus should be "excused" from blame for the murder of Remus and Titus Tatius:

> a wise mind will never censure anyone for having employed any extraordinary means for the purpose of establishing a kingdom or constituting a republic.[46]

If Machiavelli was a republican in Rousseau's eyes, then for Rousseau (as for Machiavelli) a just republic can be founded by means of wicked actions. Rousseau's treatment of the same example proves, surprising though it may seem, that this was his view: "the founda-

[43] The note, added after original publication, reads: "Machiavelli was an honest man and a good citizen; but attached to the house of the Medici, he was forced, in the oppression of his fatherland, to disguise his love of freedom. The choice of his execrable hero alone manifests enough his secret intention; and the opposition of the maxims of his book *The Prince* with those of his *Discourses on Titus Livy* and of his *History of Florence* shows that this profound political writer has until now had only superficial or corrupt readers. The Roman court [i.e., the Papacy] has strictly forbidden his book; I can well believe it, it is what he describes the most clearly" (P, III, 1480).

[44] For examples of recent interpretations of Machiavelli's essential intention, cf. Donald Atwell Zoll, *Reason and Rebellion* (Englewood Cliffs, N.J.: Prentice-Hall, 1963), chap. VI; Leo Strauss, *Thoughts on Machiavelli* (Glencoe, Ill.: Free Press, 1958), esp. pp. 278–99; and Max Lerner's introduction to the Modern Library edition.

[45] This is particularly appropriate because several commentators have spoken of the parallel between Rousseau's chapter on the legislator and the chapter of Machiavelli's *Discourses* which Rousseau quotes in it. Cf. Riechenburg, *Essai sur les lectures de Rousseau* (Philadelphia: [n. p.], 1932), p. 66n., and Derathé's n. (P, III, 1461–62).

[46] *Discourses*, I, ix (ed. Lerner, pp. 138–39). Note that this Machiavellian proposition does not occur in *The Prince*, and cf. Rousseau's comment quoted in n. 43 of this chapter.

tion of Rome was made by a troop of bandits."[47] Since Rousseau insists that justice is a human creation, he must admit, along with Machiavelli, that there are no natural or pre-political standards of morality by which the founder of a civil society can be judged.

Machiavelli continues his discussion of the founding by asserting that glory and praise are due to the founder of a good political order, whereas the founders of a tyranny are not only hated but insecure. The self-interest of a prince should lead him to be "fired with an intense desire to follow the example of the good," for only in this way can a prince "live securely" and gain "glory after death."[48] The end of the founding, according to Machiavelli, is the true self-interest of the lawgiver; the establishment of a just polity is merely a means to that end, since only just regimes survive long enough for their founders to gain immortal fame. Again, Rousseau asserts similar views, identifying virtuous political action as the "true self-interest" of the political man who seeks "distant glory" in "another" century.[49]

The chapter of the *Discourses* from which Rousseau quotes in his chapter "On the Legislator" refers to the legislation of Numa, who:

> finding a very savage people and wishing to reduce them to civil obedience by the arts of peace, had recourse to religion as the most necessary and assured support of any civil society.[50]

It was Numa who provided Rome with the laws which were most important for the greatness of that republic. Mere force, such as that employed by Romulus, does not produce a stable or disciplined political order; only when religion has taken root can a founder "introduce new and unaccustomed ordinances" without having to fear that his "authority" will prove "insufficient."[51] Rousseau's analysis follows Machiavelli in this detail as well, for Rousseau flatly asserts that "Numa was the true founder of Rome" precisely because his religious institutions "united the brigands [assembled by Romulus] into an indissoluble body by transforming them into citizens."[52]

For Rousseau, as for Machiavelli, the "first heroes were brigands,"

[47] *Préface à Narcisse* (P, II, 971n.). Cf. *Contrat social*, IV, iv, n. (P, III, 444); *Gouvernement de Pologne*, ii (P, III, 957), and above, chap. VI, § 2B; chap. VII, § 1A.

[48] Machiavelli, *Discourses*, I, x (ed. Lerner, p. 145).

[49] *Économie Politique* (P, III, 258); *Contrat social*, II, vii (P, III, 381).

[50] Machiavelli, *Discourses*, I, xi (ed. Lerner, p. 146).

[51] *Ibid.* (146–47).

[52] *Gouvernement de Pologne*, ii (P, III, 957–58); *Préface à Narcisse* (P, II, 971n.). Machiavelli goes on, however, to suggest that Numa's success was only made possible by the *virtu* of Romulus; since Numa was therefore dependent on "circumstances" or *fortuna*, it is Romulus—not Numa—whom

the emergence of justice is a human creation, and the men who first make the laws are themselves outside of the law. The legislator is thus not merely a wise man, but a political hero who must be prepared and able to perform lawless or even vicious actions in order to establish a good polity. The "virtue" of the philosopher is distinct from the "greatness" of the political leader precisely because the latter "only lives" for his fatherland and hence has no standard of virtue superior to the common good of his society.[53] In an early essay entitled "The Virtue Most Necessary for Heroes," Rousseau develops this contrast at greater length; although this work cannot be considered as a definitive statement of Rousseau's views, it is worth citing at least one passage which reveals the necessity and role of force in creating a solid political order.[54]

> Men do not govern themselves by such abstract views [as do philosophers]; one only makes them happy by forcing them to be so, and they must be made to feel happiness in order to make them love it. This is the occupation and the talent of the hero; it is often force in hand that he enables himself to receive the blessings of men, whom he at first forces to carry the yoke of the laws in order to subject them ultimately to the authority of reason.[55]

The hero should not be considered as "morally perfect," for he works for the "public felicity" as "a means of arriving at his personal glory"; "it is on injustice that most great men have founded the monument of their glory."[56]

The parallel between Rousseau's conception of the founding and

---

Machiavelli proposes as the model for "all princes" (*Discourses*, I, xix [ed. Lerner, pp. 173–74]). Rousseau does not go as far as this for reasons that should be apparent.

[53] *Économie Politique* (P, III, 255).

[54] *Discours sur cette question: Quelle est la Vertu la plus Nécessaire aux Héros, et Quels sont les Héros à qui cette Vertu a manqué? Proposée en 1751 par l'Académie de Corse* (P, II, 1262–74). According to Rousseau: "This piece is very bad, and I felt it so well after writing it that I didn't bother to send it. It is easy to do less badly on the same subject, but not to do well, for there is never a good answer to make to frivolous questions" ("Notice," *ibid.* [1262]). The question of the virtue of the hero may be "frivolous" because, as Rousseau concludes, "force is the true foundation of heroism" (1272). Rousseau's reluctance to see this piece published need not reflect disbelief in the ideas it contains, but rather the undesirability of writing on the subject. Cf. C. G., XIX, 45, 69, 70–71, 73, 92, 93, 99, 296–97.

[55] *La Vertu du Héros* (P, II, 1263–64). Cf. *Jugement sur le Projet de Paix Perpétuelle* (P, III, 599): "what is useful to the public is hardly introduced except by force, given that private interests are almost always opposed to it."

[56] *La Vertu du Héros* (P, II, 1265, 1272). Note also the use of legislators (and particularly Lycurgus) as examples of heroes (1267–68).

Machiavelli's is in a sense perplexing, for we have just seen that Rousseau considers the legislator in terms similar to those of Plato—and Machiavelli appears to be at the opposite pole from classical political philosophy, which he vigorously criticized.[57] Although Rousseau, like Machiavelli, attempts to return to the pagan political virtue of the Greeks and Romans, the same understanding of man which led Rousseau to modify the Platonic conception of the legislator leads him to diverge from Machiavelli as well. Whereas Machiavelli suggests that political action is the highest human possibility and that there is no insuperable tension between popular enlightenment and civic reform,[58] Rousseau's evolutionary understanding of man leads to a denial of the possibility of salutary political action under certain historical circumstances, and establishes the natural independence of man as a claim opposed to that of any political community, however just.

Rousseau thus places Machiavelli's conception of political action in a larger perspective, within which the philosophic life has a greater dignity than accorded it by Machiavelli, albeit a lesser status than in the thought of Plato. The science or knowledge of politics is something more than an instrument which can only be judged in terms of the good of civil society (as Plato would have admitted and Machiavelli denied), but the science of the legislator does not point to the philosophic quest as the end or perfection of human life (as Machiavelli would have admitted and Plato denied). The curious fusion of classical and modern themes, which characterizes Rousseau's principles of political right, is equally present in his science of legislation as well.[59]

[57] E.g., *The Prince*, chap. xv (ed. Lerner, p. 56); *Discourses*, I, Intro. (103).

[58] Hence *Discourses*, I, xi (the chapter quoted by Rousseau in his chapter "On the Legislator") concludes: "And although untutored and ignorant men are more easily persuaded to adopt new laws or new opinions, yet that does not make it impossible to persuade civilized men who claim to be enlightened. . . . Let no one, then, fear not to be able to accomplish what others have done, for all men (as we have said in our Preface) are born and live and die in the same way and therefore resemble each other" (148–49). On the resemblance between all men, cf. *Préface à Narcisse* (P, II, 969–70n.); *Second Discourse*, n. x (P, III, 208–14). If salutary political action is at least in principle open at all times and human wisdom incomplete when it is "disarmed" (i.e., politically impotent), theoretical speculation is in itself imperfect; Machiavelli thereby implies that the most excellent human life is that of the legislator who *uses* philosophical knowledge for the public good. Cf. the opening lines of *Discourses*, I, x (ed. Lerner, p. 141).

[59] Unfortunately, it is not possible here to go into the question of Rousseau's debt to Montesquieu in this respect. It is obvious that Rousseau considered the *Esprit des Lois* as a key source of the relationships which comprise the

2 · The Science of the Legislator: Maxims of Politics

A · HISTORICAL CONDITIONS OF THE FOUNDING

Lest it be thought that too much stress has been laid on the "science of the legislator," it is necessary to trace out the many propositions which Rousseau suggested as guides to the legislator or political man. In the *Social Contract*, the first generalization that is explicitly called a "maxim" of politics occurs (fittingly enough) in the chapter immediately following the discussion of the legislator:

> Free peoples, remember this maxim: one can acquire freedom, but never recover it.[60]

Rousseau thus restates his conception of history in practical terms, indicating the appropriate moment for enacting new legislation. Although the relevant theoretical principles have already been examined in Part I of this commentary, it is instructive to see how Rousseau formulates the historical limits on salutary political action in a specifically political perspective.

A nation, like a man, has "a time of maturity that must be awaited before submitting them to laws." Once "customs are established and prejudices rooted," reform is usually "vain and dangerous"; the sole exceptions are possible when a people "is only barbarous" and still "young" because a society in which "civic energy is used up" has become "incorrigible in growing old." But just as there is little chance that a morally corrupt people can be made free and virtuous, if one tries to civilize a nation too rapidly, "the work is ruined."[61]

> The Russians will never be civilized because they were civilized too early. . . . The Russian Empire would like to subjugate Europe and will be itself subjugated. Its subjects the Tartars or its neighbors will become its masters and ours.[62]

---

science of the legislator; see *Contrat social*, II, xi (P, III, 393)—utilizing *Geneva MS*, II, vi (P, III, 333). It would also be possible to show that Montesquieu, like Rousseau, was aware of the tension between classical and modern thought and attempted in a way to resolve it. But the manner of resolution is not the same, and despite Rousseau's great respect for Montesquieu, the latter is criticized for his failure to connect the study of "positive right" with a true understanding of universally valid principles of political right; see *Contrat social*, III, iv (P, III, 405); *Émile*, v (G, 584–85), and cf. Robert Derathé, *Rousseau et la Science Politique de Son Temps* (Paris: Presses Universitaires de France, 1950), pp. 281, 295, 300–01.

[60] *Contrat social*, II, viii (P, III, 385).

[61] *Ibid.* (385–86). Cf. *Émile*, IV (G, 402–03), and above, chap. v, § 2B.

[62] *Contrat social*, II, viii (P, III, 386). Cf. Voltaire's criticism of the predic-

Apart from the accuracy of this prediction—which has been at least partially confirmed to the extent that the Czarist regime was "subjugated" by some of its own "subjects"—Rousseau's example suggests clearly his understanding of the history of each civil society as an evolution from youth to maturity and old age.

Rousseau assumes that political change within society (as distinct from the origins of society as such) begins with savage or barbarian peoples, who can become civilized and free if they receive proper legislation, and then ultimately decline when inequality, enlightenment, and luxury develop as a consequence of the "inevitable tendencies" of civil society. Although often described as a linear decline from the goodness of the pure state of nature to the corruption of enlightened and despotic societies,[63] in many ways it would be more accurate to speak of a cyclical historical pattern. Since (at least in Rousseau's time) the immense majority of men still lived in uncivilized or savage society, and since civilized peoples can fall back into barbarism, the rise of new civil societies, especially outside Europe, seems continually possible. Because the institution of new laws would have the same consequences among such peoples as it did in previously civilized nations, Rousseau's notion of political and moral decline is best understood as part of a historical cycle which can repeat itself in the future.[64]

Rousseau's science of the legislator apparently presupposes this continuing possibility of instituting laws in previously uncivilized societies (which, with the possible exceptions of Corsica and Poland, are not in Europe). The appropriate moment for legislation is a delicate question, but the rare combination of historical circumstances can be defined:

---

tion, cited in Derathé's notes (P, III, 1467–69). Granted that Rousseau failed to predict the forces which actually did overthrow the Czarist empire, his assessment of the reforms of Peter the Great seems in retrospect more accurate than the praise of the *philosophes*.

[63] E.g., Bertrand de Jouvenel, "Rousseau the Pessimistic Evolutionist," *Yale French Studies*, XXVIII (Fall–Winter 1961) 83–96.

[64] See *First Discourse*, Part 1 (P, III, 9–11 and 11–12n.); Part 2 (20); *Second Discourse*, Part 2 (P, III, 187, 191); n. x (212–14); *Contrat social*, II, x (P, III, 391); III, xii (425–26); *Gouvernement de Pologne*, i (P, III, 954); *Constitution pour la Corse* (P, III, 902). Rousseau's continuing insistence on the feasibility of the small, agricultural society, defending itself without recourse to the sciences and arts which presuppose a large political community, suggests that he underestimated the irreversible character of modern technology. Cf. *ibid*. (902–08, 920–29, *et passim*); *Fragments Politiques*, VIII, i (P, III, 525); *Dernière Réponse* (P, III, 90–91).

What people, therefore, is suited to legislation? The one which, being already bound by some union of origin, interest, or convention, has not yet carried the true yoke of laws; one which has neither customs nor superstitions well rooted; . . . what makes success so rare is the impossibility of finding the simplicity of nature joined to the needs of society.[65]

The crucial point is that the existing bonds of a relatively simple people must not yet have been corrupted by an attempt to imitate the customs of European civilization. Since the latter tends to destroy the distinct national character on which healthy morals and patriotism depend, a society which is to receive good legislation must still maintain its native and unique traditions while its needs have progressed beyond those of a savage or uncivilized society.[66]

In addition to the general level of social development most conducive for the founding of a regime, Rousseau indicates more specific historical or political circumstances which the legislator must bear in mind:

> To these conditions for instituting a people must be added one which can replace no other, but without which they are all useless; it is that abundance and peace be enjoyed. . . . Should a war, famine, or sedition occur in this time of crisis, the State will be reversed without fail.[67]

Peace and prosperity are apparently absolutely necessary (albeit in themselves insufficient) preconditions for sound legislation because "tyrants" or "usurpers always bring about or choose these times of troubles to get passed . . . destructive laws that the people would never adopt in cold blood." This is a somewhat surprising remark, because two chapters earlier, Rousseau has described the legislation which founded the two greatest republics in history—Sparta and Rome—as the result of "violent epochs" of "civil war."[68] Rousseau's meaning, however, is clarified immediately; it is primarily foreign war or dependence on outside states (as, for example, would be rendered necessary by famine or natural catastrophe) which is inconsistent with the establishment of new political institutions; the people "suited for legislation" is:

[65] *Contrat social*, ii, x (P, iii, 390–91).
[66] *Gouvernement de Pologne*, iii (P, iii, 959–61); *Constitution pour la Corse* (P, iii, 902–04, 917); *First Discourse*, Part 1 (P, iii, 7n., 11–12n.).
[67] *Contrat social*, ii, x (P, iii, 390).
[68] Cf. *ibid.*, with ii, viii (385).

the one which does not fear being overcome by a sudden invasion, which can—without entering into the quarrels of its neighbors—resist each of them singly or gain the aid of one to repel the other . . . the one which can do without other peoples and which all other people can do without.[69]

Not merely peace, but self-sufficiency is necessary if a legislator is to succeed in the difficult task of establishing new laws.

Rousseau's remarks concerning the autonomy and peace necessary at the founding are presented briefly in connection with his discussion of the proper size of the political community:

> For all peoples have a sort of centrifugal force, by which they continually act against one another and tend to enlarge themselves at the expense of their neighbors, like the vortices of Descartes. Thus the weak risk being seen swallowed up, and none can preserve itself except by placing itself in a sort of equilibrium with all which makes the pressure everywhere just about equal.[70]

This mechanistic formulation of the so-called balance-of-power theory of international politics is not greatly developed by Rousseau in the *Social Contract*,[71] except for the indication that a state must be able to gain the aid of others against its possible enemies (unless it has the good fortune to be virtually isolated). In the context, Rousseau adds that the considerations of defense, being "external and relative, should be subordinated" to the "internal and absolute" criteria of a "healthy and strong constitution"; unlike Hobbes, for whom the size of a society should be determined by its needs of self-defense, Rousseau counts on alliances and a balance between the forces of

[69] *Ibid.*, II, x (390). Cf. *Constitution pour la Corse* (P, III, 902–03, 905, 921); *Gouvernement de Pologne*, iii (P, III, 959–60). Although Rousseau failed to follow this rule of prudence when agreeing to propose legislation for Corsica and Poland, the immediate historical consequences—the annexation of the former by France in 1769, and the partitions of the latter between Russia, Prussia, and Austria—bore out his maxim. So did the most successful example of new legislation in the eighteenth century—the United States.

[70] *Contrat social*, II, ix (P, III, 388).

[71] For Rousseau's most extensive analysis of international politics, see the *Extrait du Projet de Paix Perpétuelle de M. l'Abbé Saint Pierre* (P, III, 563–89) and esp. the *Jugement sur le Projet de Paix Perpétuelle* (P, III, 591–600). Rousseau's views on this subject have been clearly formulated by Stanley Hoffmann in "Rousseau on War and Peace," *American Political Science Review*, LVII (June 1963), 317–33; and "Rousseau, la guerre et la paix," *Rousseau et la Philosophie Politique* (Paris: Presses Universitaires de France, 1965), pp. 195–240.

rivals to secure the existence of every society, particularly at the founding.[72]

A legislator can only hope to institute a civil society if these internal and external historical conditions are met. In restricting the possibility of a new founding to these "rare" or "exceptional" cases, however, Rousseau does not limit the science of the legislator to the act which first establishes a regime. As we have seen, the need for legislation is a continuing one, and is particularly important once morals begin to decline; "one must not want to govern a corrupted people by the same laws which are suited to a good people." But whereas "upright and simple men" need only "good sense" to perceive the common good, so that "to the degree that it becomes necessary to promulgate new [laws], this necessity is recognized universally," as soon as "the social bond begins to relax" the guidance of political wisdom becomes essential for the statesman.[73]

Rousseau's maxims of politics are thus as relevant as a means of reforming existent regimes as they are for the original institution of laws, and in a sense are even more necessary among enlightened peoples (if only as a means of revealing the natural obstacles to reforms or palliatives for existing vices). Before turning to the maxims which refer explicitly to all political situations, however, it is necessary to consider Rousseau's propositions concerning the climactic and geographical conditions which must be particularly considered at the founding.

B · PHYSICAL CONDITIONS OF THE FOUNDING

Rousseau insists that laws will inevitably fail if they are based "on a principle different from the one which emerges from the nature of things":

> There are exceptions, I know, but even these exceptions confirm the rule in that they sooner or later produce revolutions which bring things back into the natural order.[74]

The natural order Rousseau has in mind includes factors of a physical nature, such as climate and geographical position, which commentators have often dismissed as being out of place in a work like

---

[72] *Contrat social*, II, ix (P, III, 388); III, xv (431 and n.); IV, ix (470). Cf. Hobbes, *Leviathan*, Part 2, chap. XVII (ed. Oakeshott, pp. 109–10); Aristotle, *Politics* II.1267a, 1721b; VII.1333b–34a; Plato, *Republic* IV.422a–423b.

[73] *Contrat social*, IV, i (P, III, 437–38); IV, iv (452–53).

[74] *Ibid.*, III, viii (416). Cf. *Lettre à d'Alembert* (G, 186), and *Contrat social*, II, xi (393), cited above, pp. 294–95, n. 135.

the *Social Contract*. Given the importance Rousseau was forced to attach to the science or art of legislation, the presence of such considerations no longer need be treated as a mere imitation of Montesquieu (however much Rousseau was indebted to him), and must be studied in the form Rousseau presents them.[75]

The question of the proper extent and population of the political community—which is to say, of the different kinds of laws suited to nations of different sizes—has already been mentioned with reference to defense from foreign attack. Although Rousseau considers the number of citizens as in itself determining many characteristics of political society—indeed we will return to this problem at length—he does not consider size solely in terms of population or territory in the abstract.

> A body politic can be measured in two ways, namely by the extent of its territory and by the number of its people; and between these two measures there is a suitable relationship in order to give the state its true greatness. Men make the State, and the land nourishes men; this relationship is therefore that the land be sufficient for the maintenance of its inhabitants, and that there be as many inhabitants as the land can nourish.[76]

It is the proportion between a state's population and the size and character of its territory which determines the "force" of a civil society, not either of these factors in isolation.[77]

This emphasis on proportions or relationships between different factors characterizes Rousseau's conception of the art or science of

[75] Cf. *Économie Politique* (P, III, 250). On the importance attached to climate and geography, see also *Constitution pour la Corse* (P, III, 906–07, 913–17). With reference to the chapter of the *Contrat social* most directly concerned with climate (III, viii), Derathé's note merely echoes the sentiment of most commentators: "This long chapter in which Rousseau examines the influence of climate on government is hardly appropriate in a work that treats 'principles of political right.' Besides the desire not to show himself inferior to Montesquieu, Rousseau ostensibly had not only the intention of filling out his book, but also to make less austere—by means of these concrete considerations—'the ungrateful material of the *Social Contract*, suited to few readers'" (P, III, 1484, citing letter to Rey, 4 April 1762, C. G., VII, 173). Derathé's interpretation is not supported by the letter in question, which speaks of the *Contrat social* as a whole; once it is admitted that the work treats of matters besides the principles of political right, the difficulty of guessing Rousseau's intention disappears.

[76] *Contrat social*, II, x (P, III, 388–89).

[77] Cf. Aristotle, *Politics* II.1265a–b; 1267b, 1270a; III.1276a; VII.1326a–b.

politics.[78] The balance between population and extent of land is crucial:

> for if there is too much land, its defense is burdensome, its cultivation insufficient, its product superfluous; it is a future cause of defensive wars; if there is not enough, the State is at the discretion of its neighbors for the supplement; it is the future cause of offensive wars. Any people which by its position has only the alternative between commerce or war is in itself weak; it depends on its neighbors, it depends on events; it never has anything but an uncertain and short existence.[79]

If the laws are to endure, the population must be suited to the specific territory which is the basic source of its means of preservation, for otherwise it will be dependent on chance and hence unstable.

The proportion required to insure the independence of a civil society cannot, however, be formulated in abstract terms:

> One cannot calculate a fixed ratio between the extent of territory and the number of men which are sufficient for each other—as much because of the differences in the qualities of land, in the degrees of fertility, in the nature of its productions, in the influence of climate, as by the differences to be noted in the temperaments of the men who inhabit them. . . . It is also necessary to pay attention to the greater or less fertility of women.[80]

Climate and geography have a dual effect, for they determine not only the characteristics of the soil and thereby the natural potentialities for feeding and supporting the citizens, but also the character of the population itself. This double importance is decisive for Rousseau, especially because (as we shall see) he does not seem to believe that technology can fundamentally reverse the political effects of the physical factors conditioning social life.

Rousseau admits explicitly that in considering natural phenomena as limits on political life, he follows Montesquieu:

> Freedom, not being the fruit of all climates, is not within reach of

[78] Cf. *Contrat social*, III, i (P, III, 400); III, ii (402); and C. G., II, 317: "things should be considered relatively in the physical order and absolutely in the moral order."

[79] *Ibid.*, II, x (389).

[80] *Ibid.* Note the contrast between the indeterminacy of this empirical relationship and the apparently fixed and certain ratios contained in the continuous proportion (*ibid.*, III, i, analyzed above, chap. VII, § 2E).

all peoples. The more one thinks about this principle established by Montesquieu, the more its truth is felt.[81]

Since—to quote the title of the chapter devoted to this subject— "every form of government is not suited to every country," the legislator must provide resources that will maintain the government (as distinct from the citizens themselves).

> In every government in the world the public person consumes and produces nothing. Where does the consumed substance come from? The labor of its members. It is the surplus of the private individuals that produces what is necessary for the public. From which it follows that the civil state can only subsist insofar as the labor of men produces more than their needs.[82]

Rousseau's premise follows necessarily from his formulation of the State as a "moral" or "conventional" person; his conclusion indicates the impossibility of civil society in a savage condition, where each man or family is self-sufficient.

Natural factors continue to influence civil society despite man's evolution away from the state of nature to the point at which individuals produce more than they need.

> Now this excess [of production over private consumption] is not the same in every country in the world. . . . This ratio depends on the fertility of the climate, on the kind of labor that the land requires, on the nature of its productions, on the strength of its inhabitants, on the greater or less consumption they need, and on several other similar relations of which it is composed.[83]

Rousseau then proceeds to analyze some of these relationships in more detail in order to determine "the form of government to which the force of climate tends."[84]

The production of surplus food must be considered with reference to the character of the inhabitants as well as the natural fertility in different climates.

---

[81] *Ibid.*, III, viii (414). The reference is to *Esprit des Lois*, esp. XVII, i-vi; XVIII, i-xiv; and *Lettres Persanes*, cxxxi. It is unfortunate that Derathé does not examine the relationship between this aspect of the *Contrat social* and Montesquieu; see *Rousseau et la Science Politique*, pp. 27, 53–54. Cf. Vaughan, "Introduction" (V, I, 71–86).

[82] *Contrat social*, III, viii (P, III, 414). Note that luxury, or in general any increases in the private needs of men, can therefore be condemned as reducing the surplus which is the means of supporting the government.

[83] *Ibid.* (414–15).   [84] *Ibid.* (415).

Let us suppose that of two equal pieces of land, one yields 5 and the other 10. If the inhabitants of the first consume 4 and those of the latter 9, the excess of the first product will be 1/5 and that of the second 1/10. The ratio of the two excesses being therefore inverse to that of the products, the land which only produces 5 will give a surplus twice that of the land that will produce 10.[85]

Land is generally more fertile in warm climates; even assuming soil of equal fertility, the colder the climate the more labor is required to produce an equal product—and hence "the surplus must necessarily be less" from a given area. In addition, "the same number of men consumes much less in warm countries"; "the closer one approaches the equator, the more peoples live on little." Similarly, in warm climates where few needs are imposed by "seasonal changes [that] are violent and quick," luxuries are less closely connected with utility (indicating the extent of natural surplus produced by the climate). Finally, "foods are much more substantial and succulent in warm countries," so that cold climates face "the visible disadvantage of having a smaller quantity of food in an equal product."[86]

These various relationships show that natural agricultural surplus tends to decrease as one moves "from the equator to the poles"; since this surplus is the source of support for government, climate tends to determine the suitable form of government.

Unproductive and sterile places where the product is not worth the labor should remain uncultivated and deserted, or only populated with savages; places where the labor of men only produces exactly what is necessary should be inhabited by barbarian peoples—any polity would be impossible there; the places where the excedent of

[85] *Ibid.* (416).

[86] *Ibid.* (416–18). Note that Rousseau ignores the possibility that at least some of these relationships—e.g., the amount of labor required to produce a given agricultural product—could be radically modified by technological innovation. Cf. *Esprit des Lois*, XVIII, vi and vii, in which Montesquieu discusses "Countries Formed by Human Industry" and the "Works of Man." In general, Montesquieu places more emphasis on the effects of climate and geography in conjunction with customs than does Rousseau. In contrast, Rousseau treats physical and natural characteristics in themselves in a somewhat more rigorous way than does Montesquieu; hence Rousseau tries to formulate propositions in terms of "ratios" or relationships, often in the form "the more *x*, the more (or the less) *y*." This produces an exposition that is much less anecdotal than that of Montesquieu, though the latter also formulates similar propositions. Although the general propositions in question appear to be forerunners of the hypotheses toward which modern political and social science is frequently directed, differences remain; see n. 92 of this chapter.

the product over the labor is mediocre are suited to free peoples—those where the abundant and fertile soil gives a great deal of product for little labor want to be governed monarchically.[87]

The connection between a warm, fertile climate and despotism, emphasized by Montesquieu, is particularly strong because:

> warm countries have less need of inhabitants than cold countries, and could nourish more of them; which produces a double surplus always to the advantage of despotism.[88]

Since a relatively dispersed population will be weak in the face of a government which can easily support itself by utilizing a large natural surplus, despotic rule is most suited to peoples living in hot climates.

The interest of these propositions lies not so much in their substance as in the way Rousseau presents them; Aristotle had long before connected free civil societies with intermediate climates.[89] Although Rousseau bases his analysis on natural regularities which are independent of human will and presumably cannot be ignored without political failure,[90] he does not announce the correlation between climate and types of regime as a natural inevitability; it is entirely possible that men can ignore the "nature of things" in establishing governmental institutions.

> Even if all the south should be covered with republics and all the north with despotic states, it would not be the less true that by the effect of climate, despotism is suited to warm countries, barbar-

[87] *Contrat social*, III, viii (P, III, 415–16). On the distinction between "savages" and "barbarians," cf. *Esprit des Lois*, XVIII, xi. Note that Rousseau emphasizes only agricultural modes of gaining subsistence, in sharp contrast to Montesquieu; cf. the importance attached to agriculture as the prerequisite for civilization, *Second Discourse*, Part 2 (P, III, 171–74).

[88] *Contrat social*, III, viii (P, III, 418). Cf. *Esprit des Lois*, XVII, iii–vii.

[89] "Those who live in a cold climate and in Europe are full of spirit but wanting in intelligence and skill; and therefore they retain comparative freedom, but have no political organization, and are incapable of ruling over others. Whereas the natives of Asia are intelligent and inventive, but wanting in spirit, and therefore they are always in a state of subjection and slavery. But the Hellenic race, which is between them, is likewise intermediate in character, being high spirited and also intelligent. Hence it continues free, and is the best governed of any nation. . ." (*Politics* VII.1327b). While Rousseau admits that differences in man's character can be deduced from climate, his emphasis on measurable phenomena contrasts sharply with Aristotle's concern with spiritedness (courage) and intelligence—both of which are, for Rousseau, largely due to human evolution rather than the direct consequence of nature. Cf. also *Esprit des Lois*, XVII, ii.

[90] Cf. *Contrat social*, III, xv, n. (P, III, 431).

— 378 —

ianism to cold countries, and the good polity to the intermediate regions.[91]

Rousseau's maxims are not scientific predictions—in part because no single factor such as climate operates in isolation, and in part because men can violate physical laws of nature, however imprudent it may be to do so. For this reason it is often incorrect to consider these general propositions as "scientific" in the sense of modern social or natural science; Rousseau is concerned with the regime which "suits" a given kind of people, and hence when he says that inhabitants of certain climates "should be" governed in a particular way, he does not imply natural necessity.[92]

Rousseau's analysis thus has the character of advice to the statesman; instead of presenting an objective analysis of the inevitable tendency of political phenomena, Rousseau tries to utilize a knowledge of such tendencies to prevent erroneous or imprudent legislation. The amount of territory in a new political community should be "extended a great deal in a mountainous country," whereas "one can narrow it at the edge of the sea, even among rocks and almost sterile sand."[93] Such choices are not merely tactical, since they determine the character and objective of the regime.

> For example, is the soil unproductive and sterile or the country too small for its inhabitants? Turn toward industry and the arts, whose products you will exchange for the foodstuffs you lack. On the contrary, do you occupy rich plains and fertile hillsides? On good land, do you lack inhabitants? Give all your cares to agriculture, which multiplies men, and chase away the arts. . . . Do you occupy extensive and commodious shores? Cover the sea with ships, cultivate commerce and navigation; you will have a brilliant and short existence. Does the sea only wash your coasts at almost inaccessible rocks? Remain barbarians and fish-eaters; you will live more tranquilly, perhaps better, and certainly happier.[94]

[91] *Ibid.*, III, viii (416).

[92] Cf. the distinction between "an ethical 'should'" and "a scientific 'should'" suggested by Bertrand de Jouvenel in his comparison of Rousseau's maxims of politics to "what we would call at present a 'positive law of political science'" ("Théorie des Formes de Gouvernement chez Rousseau," *Contrat Social*, VI [Nov.–Dec. 1962], 347). If many of the relationships discovered by Rousseau refer to "natural tendencies" (and imply a "scientific 'should'"), they result in prudential advice which is neither purely scientific nor purely ethical, being different in character from modern political science.

[93] *Contrat social*, II, x (P, III, 389–90).

[94] *Ibid.*, II, xi (392–93). Cf. the application of this advice, *Constitution pour la Corse* (esp. P, III, 907).

This direct address to those responsible for legislation shows how far Rousseau is from treating his maxims of politics either as "value-free" propositions or absolute ethical judgments; the four examples contain two choices which Rousseau considers inferior (communities based on the development of industry and dependent on external trade) and two modes of establishing or maintaining a salutary society (the agricultural civil society and the uncivilized or barbarian people, both capable of independence and freedom).

Since the act of legislation is concerned with "the particular system of institution which is the best, perhaps not in itself, but for the State to which it is destined," climate and geography may dictate legislation which is radically inferior to the best regime—or even to a legitimate one.[95] Consideration of the physical necessities which condition politics is thus a means of achieving the most decent solution of the unique problem posed by each human society.

> In a word, beside the maxims common to all, each people contains in itself some cause which orders it in a particular manner and makes its legislation suited to it alone.[96]

Since we have considered Rousseau's analysis of the varying effects of geography, climate, and history, there remain to be analyzed these "maxims common to all peoples." In so doing, we will see more clearly how Rousseau's political preferences rested on an analysis of political phenomena that is largely independent of—albeit complementary to—his principles of political right.

C · THE CHARACTERISTICS OF CIVIL SOCIETY

Rousseau's understanding of social life has had a great impact on what is now called the science of sociology—i.e., the objective study of societies without reference to questions of political right (and often without reference to politics in a broader sense).[97] This is not accidental, for Rousseau considered customs and moral standards—the *moeurs* of a people, to use the untranslatable French word—to be a decisive factor in political life.

> It is useless to distinguish the morals (*moeurs*) of a nation from the objects of its esteem; for all these things depend on the same principle and are necessarily mingled. Among every people in the

[95] *Contrat social*, II, xi (P, III, 392); III, ix (419); III, xv (430–31).
[96] *Ibid.*, II, xi (393).
[97] See esp. Émile Durkheim, *Montesquieu et Rousseau* (Paris: Rivière, 1953), *passim*.

world, it is not nature but opinion which decides the choice of
their pleasures. . . . One always loves what is beautiful or what is
found so, but it is on this judgment that one is mistaken; it is therefore this judgment that has to be controlled.[98]

Men living in society are necessarily governed by passions, but these
passions can be given "new directions" that differ from the self-interested desires that dominate modern, corrupt European societies.

> A man who would not have any passions would certainly be a very
> bad citizen: but if one cannot teach men to love nothing, it is not im-
> possible to teach them to love one object rather than another, and
> what is truly beautiful, rather than what is deformed.[99]

The fundamental question implicit in political action is therefore the
orientation to be given to *moeurs* and the determination of the "objects of esteem" among a people.

The legislator must begin from the knowledge that the character
and prejudices of men are ultimately the consequence of political
institutions:

> The opinions of a people arise from its constitution; although the
> law does not regulate morals (*moeurs*), it is legislation that creates
> them.[100]

"The true constitution of the State" and "the most important of all"
the laws are "engraved not in marble nor in bronze, but in the hearts
of the citizens." But because "public opinion cannot be submitted to
constraint," it is impossible to order people to believe and behave in
a specific way. Hence Rousseau describes "morals, customs, and above
all public opinions" as:

> a part [of the laws] unknown to our politicians, but on which de-
> pends the success of all others: a part with which the great legisla-
> tor is concerned in secret, while he appears to limit himself to par-
> ticular rules which are only the supports of the arch, of which

[98] *Contrat social*, IV, vii (P, III, 458). As Rousseau notes in this chapter,
the *Lettre à d'Alembert* is particularly crucial as a presentation of his conception of the political relevance and character of *moeurs*.

[99] *Économie Politique* (P, III, 259).

[100] *Contrat social*, IV, vii (P, III, 459). Cf. *Économie Politique* (P, III, 251)
and esp. *Fragments Politiques*, VI, 8 (P, III, 513): "In any government that
might be, a wise administration can form public morals by education and by
custom, and so direct the inclination of private individuals that they generally find themselves more content with the government under which they
live than they would be under any other, be it better or worse indifferently."

morals (*moeurs*)—formed more slowly—at last form the immoveable keystone.[101]

Since a government influences the morals and manners of citizens "only by its primitive institution" and not by legal punishments, the legislator must direct himself to establishing a conformity between the unwritten "laws" of custom and the written legislation he institutes.[102]

Because every individual is naturally concerned with his own preservation and comfort, this conformity between law and custom requires the greatest possible development of the artificial bonds representing civil society, which replace "the forces belonging to man" by nature.

> The more these natural forces are dead and annihilated, the more the acquired ones are great and durable, and the more also the institution is solid and perfect.[103]

If the opinions and passions of men were perfectly oriented toward the good of society, it would be virtually unnecessary to "add laws."

> The better the State is constituted, the more public affairs outweigh private ones in the mind of the citizens.[104]

Civic virtue, which consists in the implantation of a way of life in which the individual prefers the common good above all else, presupposes that the "will" of the individual is trained to orient itself to the community as a whole, rather than to his "private affairs"; such a way of life depends more on customs and opinions than on the laws in a narrow sense.

This primacy of habitually accepted standards or prejudices explains not only why laws are in themselves incapable of reforming corrupt men—for there are "a thousand ways of eluding the law" if one's passions are opposed to it—but why a well-governed state "needs few laws."[105]

---

[101] *Contrat social*, II, xii (P, III, 394). Cf. *Émile*, v (G, 600): "the apparent form of government" is less important than "the effects it produces on the people and in all levels of administration." On the impossibility of coercing public opinion, see esp. *Lettre à d'Alembert* (G, 176–82).

[102] *Ibid.* (182). See also *Fragments Politiques*, IV, 9–11 (P, III, 494–95); 14 (496); 23 (498); XVI, 6–7 (555–56).

[103] *Contrat social*, II, vii (P, III, 382).

[104] *Contrat social*, III, xv (P, III, 429). Cf. *Second Discourse*, Part 2 (P, III, 187–88).

[105] *Ibid.*, IV, i (437); IV, iv (453); *Gouvernement de Pologne*, x (P, III,

If I was asked what is the most vicious of all peoples, I would reply without hesitation that it is the one with the most laws.[106]

Because laws can never succeed unless they are supported by the moral habits of the citizens, all changes in laws—and indeed, in customs of any kind—are intrinsically dangerous.[107] In the good regime, harmony between public opinion and the laws insures that existing legislation will continue to receive the assent of "the general will of today" because "it must be thought that it is only the excellence of ancient wills which could have conserved them for so long."

This is why, far from weakening, the laws acquire new force incessantly in any well constituted State; the prejudice of antiquity makes them daily more venerable; in contrast, wherever the laws grow weaker in aging, that proves that there is no more legislative power, and that the State is no longer alive.[108]

Although the logic of political right emphasizes the legitimacy of changing the laws at any time, the art of politics is directed to the development of habits and opinions which render the exercise of this right unnecessary.

To achieve morals and customs which support the laws, the latter must always be respected:

No law must ever be allowed to fall into disuse. Should it be indifferent, should it be bad, it is necessary to abrogate it formally or to maintain it in vigor. This maxim . . . is fundamental.[109]

"Despotism always requires" that one adopt, as in France, the "maxim of State of closing one's eyes to many things"; in contrast a healthy regime must have "few laws, but well-digested and, above all, well-observed ones." While law enforcement is necessary, it should not be difficult if the legislation is well-adapted to the opinions of the populace.

In particular, recourse to capital punishment indicates political cor-

---

1000–01); *Second Discourse*, Part 2 (P, III, 187–88); *Fragments Politiques*, IV, 6 (P, III, 492).

[106] *Ibid.*, IV, 7 (493). Cf. *Économie Politique* (P, III, 253): "The more you multiply laws, the more you make them scorned."

[107] *Contrat social*, III, xviii (P, III, 435); *Préface à Narcisse* (P, II, 971); *Gouvernement de Pologne*, i (P, III, 954–55). This is, of course, the central theme of the *Lettre à d'Alembert*.

[108] *Contrat social*, III, xi (P, III, 424–25). Cf. *ibid.*, II, vii (394).

[109] *Gouvernement de Pologne*, x (P, III, 1002).

ruption, especially since the end of civil society is the preservation of its members:

> The frequency of capital punishment is always a sign of weakness or laziness in the government.[110]

Although the death penalty is necessary for those "who cannot be preserved without danger," "good morals" are the means by which a "wise administration . . . maintains respect for the laws, love of the fatherland, and the vigor of the general will"; it is not so much coercion as education which is the means of insuring obedience to the laws.[111]

Since "it is no longer time to change our natural inclinations when they have established their course and habit has been combined with *amour-propre*," the formation of morals depends decisively on the upbringing of the youth.

> Public education under rules prescribed by the government and under magistrates established by the sovereign is therefore one of the fundamental maxims of popular or legitimate government.[112]

Such education cannot succeed, however, unless it has the support of "authority" and "example"; the most fitting teachers of the young are "famous warriors" and "upright judges" who have "worthily fulfilled" official functions, for otherwise it will be clear that "public confidence" does not consider education to be "the most important business of the State."[113] Private education, like that of the Romans, is only compatible with a virtuous citizenry if fathers have "unlimited power over their children" and are "more feared than the magistrates"; in Rome, each father was "the censor of morals and the avenger of the laws."[114]

Since legal constraint is ineffective as a means of changing public education, it is not possible to establish public censorship as "the arbiter of public opinion," but only as its "declarator":

> Censorship can be useful for conserving morals (*moeurs*), never for reestablishing them. . . . Censorship maintains morals by preventing opinions from being corrupted, by conserving their upright-

[110] *Contrat social*, II, v (P, III, 377). Cf. *Économie Politique* (P, III, 256–57).
[111] *Contrat social*, II, v (P, III, 377); *Économie Politique* (P, III, 259). Cf. *Gouvernement de Pologne*, iv (P, III, 669–70).
[112] *Économie Politique* (P, III, 260–61).
[113] *Ibid.; Gouvernement de Pologne*, iv (P, III, 966–69).
[114] *Économie Politique* (P, III, 262).

ness by means of wise applications, sometimes by fixing them when they are still uncertain.[115]

Public opinions are by their very nature volatile, consisting of popular reactions to day-to-day affairs; morals and customs, although more general than the particular objects which popular prejudices identify as the "noble," "beautiful," or "good," must be protected by preventing erroneous public judgments. Even in corrupt society, political reform must begin with a redirection of popular praise and blame, although in the latter situation at first it is essentially private morals which must be altered.[116]

Rousseau's emphasis on the overwhelming importance of popularly accepted moral standards is obviously connected to his conception of the general will. His treatment of political phenomena goes beyond this principle, however, for he is concerned with the conditions that are conducive to civic virtue, healthy public opinion, and political freedom. The first of these is that the political community be distinct from humanity as a whole:

> It seems that the sentiment of humanity evaporates and is weakened in being extended over the entire earth. . . . Interest and commiseration must be in some way limited and compressed in order to give it activity. Now as this inclination in us can only be useful to those with whom we have to live, it is good that [the sentiment of] humanity, being concentrated between the citizens, gains new force in them by the habit of seeing each other and by the common interest that unites them.[117]

Because the sentiments and affections underlying civil society are incapable of infinite extension, Rousseau denies the possibility of a universal society of all men, and insists on the necessity of basing morality and justice on an exclusive community.[118] Indeed, Rousseau's criticism of Christianity is precisely that, being akin to the natural

---

[115] *Contrat social*, IV, vii (P, III, 459).

[116] Cf. *Lettre à d'Alembert* (esp. G, 182); *Nouvelle Héloïse*, Second Pref. (P, II, 17–26); *Émile*, I (G, 18); *Second Discourse*, n. XIX (P, III, 222–23); *Constitution pour la Corse* (P, III, 937).

[117] *Économie Politique* (P, III, 254–55). Note that Rousseau here treats "the sentiment of humanity" as a single "inclination" even though it is composed of "interest and commiseration"; cf. *Second Discourse*, Pref. (P, III, 126) and above, chap. I §§ 4E–5 and chap. III, § 2E.

[118] *Geneva MS*, I, ii (P, III, 282–88); *Second Discourse*, Part 2 (P, III, 178–79); *Émile*, I, (G, 9–10). See esp. above, chap. I, § 5.

religion, it encourages bonds between all men as men which cannot possibly have a political expression.[119]

The inevitable particularities of human passions and interests produce a limit on political society to which Rousseau attaches great importance:

> The more the social bond is extended, the more it relaxes, and in general a small State is proportionally stronger than a large one. A thousand reasons demonstrate this maxim.[120]

Although it will be necessary to consider some of Rousseau's reasons for this maxim when discussing the relationship between the government and society as a whole, size also influences the cohesion of the citizen body more directly. Since legitimate rule requires that each citizen have the sentiment that he contributes equally to the laws, the larger the community, the smaller the influence of the individual in the enactment of the laws.

> From which it follows the that the more the State is enlarged, the more liberty diminishes.[121]

Expansion of a civil society is therefore dangerous, because it tends to destroy the uniformity of morals and customs as well as the sense of identity on which a healthy community rests.[122]

Mere size, however, is but one of the factors which must be considered in order to insure the coincidence of laws and habits needed in a healthy political community. In this perspective, Rousseau's conception of the general will can be understood—as indeed many commentators have pointed out—as a "sociological" description of the conditions in which private interests are directed to the common good. After describing the general will as "the sum of the differences" of each private will, as distinct from the "will of all" (which is simply "a sum of the private wills"), Rousseau adds:

> If, when a sufficiently informed people deliberates, the Citizens have no communication among themselves, from the great number

[119] *Contrat social*, IV, viii (P, III, 465–67).
[120] *Ibid.*, II, ix (386–87).
[121] *Ibid.*, III, i (397). In his perceptive discussion of this maxim, Jouvenel points out the difference between Montesquieu and Rousseau in their analyses of the size of a political community ("Théorie des Formes de Gouvernement chez Rousseau," pp. 345–46). See also above, pp. 342–46.
[122] *Dernière Réponse* (P, III, 79); *Gouvernement de Pologne*, v (P, III, 970–71). One reason for this, apparently, is that geography and climate have such a necessary influence on *moeurs*; see this chapter, § 2B, and the passage cited at n. 146.

of small differences would always result the general will, and the deliberation would always be good. But when cliques or partial associations are formed at the expense of the large association, the will of each of these associations becomes general in relation to its members and particular in relation to the State; one can say that there are no longer as many voters as there are men, but only as many as there are associations. The differences become less numerous and give a less general result.[123]

Since this passage seems anachronistic in the modern industrial democracies of the West, where political life is dominated by the competition of political parties and private interest groups, it is particularly important to analyze Rousseau's meaning with care.

Rousseau did not assume that political life concerns the relationship between citizens solely as isolated individuals:

Every political society is composed of other, smaller societies of different kinds, each of which has its own interests and maxims; but these societies that everyone sees, because they have an external and authorized form, are not the only ones that really exist in the State. All the private individuals that a common interest unites compose so many others, permanent or passing, whose force is no less real for being less apparent, and whose various interrelations, when well-observed, are the true knowledge of morals (*moeurs*).[124]

---

[123] *Contrat social*, ii, iii (P, iii, 371–72). Although this passage has often been interpreted as an attack on every form of political party or interest group (e.g., Lester G. Crocker, "Rousseau et la Voie du Totalitarisme," *Rousseau et la Philosophie Politique* [Paris: Presses Universitaires de France, 1965], pp. 109–10), it is in part merely a demand for the universal secret ballot and in part an attack on the division of the French *parlements* into three estates (which, with the exception of Languedoc, tended to vote separately). On political practices in France at the time of Rousseau, see Alexis de Tocqueville, *L'Ancien Régime et la Révolution*, in *Oeuvres Complètes*, ed. J.–P. Mayer (Paris: Gallimard, 1952), Vol. ii, Part 1, esp. Appendice, p. 260. Similarly, voting in local government was often by corporation; hence Tocqueville remarks, in his long note on the government of Angers, that "the deputies from the sixteen parishes . . . who participate in the general assembly are chosen by companies, bodies, or communities, and they are strictly the commissioners (*mandataires*) of the small body from which they are deputed. They have, on every matter, instructions that bind them" (*ibid.*, p. 281). Cf. *Gouvernement de Pologne*, vii (P, iii, 978–79).

[124] *Économie Politique* (P, iii, 245–46). Cf. the so-called "group theory of politics" developed by American political scientists; see esp. David Truman, *The Governmental Process* (New York: Alfred Knopf, 1951). Chief among the "external and authorized" associations in eighteenth-century France was, of course, the Catholic Church. Cf. Hobbes, *Leviathan*, Part ii, chap. xxii (ed. Oakeshott, pp. 153–56).

The distinction between the private will of the individual and the general will of the group applies to all politically relevant collectivities, including these subordinate or partial associations.

> The will of these particular societies always has two relations; for the members of the association, it is a general will; for the large society it is a private will, which is very often right in the first respect, and vicious in the second.[125]

The problem of partial associations in civil society thus depends on the relationship between the common interest of these groups and the general interest of the society at large.

Rousseau assumes that the natural effect of groups is to create a tension between the duties of men and their interests:

> It is true that the particular societies being always subordinate to those that contain them, one should obey the latter preferably to the former, that the duties of the citizen precede those of the senator, and those of man precede those of the citizen. But unfortunately personal interest is always found in an inverse ratio to duty, and increases to the degree that the association becomes narrower and the engagement less sacred.[126]

Since the society of all mankind is a "chimera," the broadest feasible political collectivity is a civil society, and the problem raised by lesser associations, whether formal or informal, is that they create a common interest among their members which has the status of a private interest in the eyes of other citizens.

According to the "natural" ordering of wills, the individual follows his purely private self-interest rather than the common interest; by extension, he tends to follow the group interests closest to this particular will rather than the general will of the entire society. Rousseau's analysis of the interaction between the private will of the magistrate, the common will of the body of rulers, and the general will of the people, as described in the *Social Contract*, is thus but one example of a general phenomenon of social life; it is inevitable that "these different wills become more active in proportion as they are concentrated."[127] Particular associations, by increasing the activity and force of interests which have only a "private" character with

[125] *Économie Politique* (P, III, 246).
[126] *Ibid.*
[127] *Contrat social*, III, ii (P, III, 401). See above, pp. 346–47, where this chapter is analyzed.

respect to the society at large, reduce the likelihood that a public deliberation will enunciate the general will.

The extreme danger is that a single group—be it the "body of rulers" or any other association—will dominate the entire society.

> When one of these associations is so large that it wins out over all the others, you no longer have as a result a sum of differences, but a single difference; then there is no longer a general will, and the view which wins out is only a private view.[128]

Whereas everyone can respect a judgment of the true general will because it is the sum of the "great number of little differences" between each citizen, the minority cannot accept the opinion of the majority if the latter has the status of "private advice" motivated by an interest less general than that of the society as a whole. Rousseau thus indicates both the danger a "tyranny of the majority" and the illegitimacy of claims by a single political party or group to represent the general will.

Should those in power succeed in substituting the general will of their particular association for the freely expressed will of the entire citizen body, "the State shrinks":

> When the prince . . . usurps the sovereign power . . . the large State is dissolved and another is formed within it, composed only of the members of the government, and which is no longer anything to the rest of the people but its master and its tyrant.[129]

Whatever the effects of Rousseau's doctrines historically speaking, he was well aware of the disastrous political effects that could be produced by a modern totalitarian regime, in which a single party pretends it is the sole valid "representative" of the common good.

To prevent this danger of tyranny, it is essential that private associations, which can easily gain control of the government if their force is unchecked, be limited. Although the surest means of so doing would be "that there are no partial associations in the State," as in "the unique and sublime institution of the great Lycurgus," such a solution is scarcely practical; wherever private interests are not as entirely directed to the common good and supported by such patriotic morals and customs as existed in Sparta, partial associations are the necessary consequence of political life.

If there are partial societies, it is necessary to multiply their num-

[128] *Ibid.*, II, iii (372).
[129] *Ibid.*, III, x (422).

ber and prevent their inequality, as Solon, Numa, and Servius did.[130]

As soon as there are very many interest groups of relative equality, they pose little danger because the differences of interest between them become smaller and more frequent, and the chances of a single one gaining a majority correspondingly reduced.[131]

Rousseau's emphasis on the necessity of equality in the healthy society can be viewed, in a sense, as a direct outgrowth of his analysis of the play of private and group interests. To insure that every citizen has an interest in the maintenance of the laws, there must be relative equality of wealth[132]—and of power.

> With respect to equality, one should not understand by this word that the degrees of power and of wealth be absolutely the same, but that, with respect to power, it be beneath all violence and never be used except in virtue of rank and the laws, and with respect to wealth, that no citizen be so rich that he can buy another, and none so poor that he is forced to sell himself.[133]

Factual inequalities of status and wealth are perfectly consistent with a solid regime provided they cannot be used on a personal basis to make some citizens dependent on others; as long as the privileges accorded to different economic classes are authorized by law, the poor may even be effectively disfranchised in a legitimate regime. In this respect, Rousseau's praise of the political institutions established in Rome by Servius is sufficient evidence that Rousseau was not a simple egalitarian in the extreme sense often attributed to him.[134]

---

[130] *Ibid.*, II, iii (372). Note that it is the Roman constitution, founded by Numa and reformed by Servius—and not Sparta—that Rousseau analyzes as a model of the legitimate republic in Book IV. Cf. the passage from Machiavelli's *History of Florence*, which Rousseau cites at this point, with *Discourses*, I, iv-vi (ed. Lerner, pp. 119–30). See also Derathé's notes (P, III, 1456–57).

[131] Cf. Hamilton, Madison, and Jay, *The Federalist Papers*, esp. the famous numbers 9 and 10 (New York: Modern Library, n. d.), pp. 49–62.

[132] See *Contrat social*, I, ix, n. (P, III, 367), cited above, p. 183.

[133] *Ibid.*, II, xi (391–92).

[134] Cf. the reference to Servius in *ibid.*, II, iii (372), cited in n. 130 of this chapter, with IV, iv (447–49, 450–51), where Rousseau analyzes the Servian institution of the Centuries. In the resulting assembly, the first or wealthiest of the six classes of citizens had an effective majority by itself. Yet Rousseau concludes that "all the majesty of the Roman people was only found in the Centuriate assemblies" (*ibid.* [452]). Rousseau was perfectly aware of the problem: "in the Centuriate assemblies, affairs were decided by the plurality of money much more than the plurality of votes" (451); "in order that the

The difficulty created by inequalities of wealth and power is that they can only be restrained, as was the case in Rome, by very strict moral standards.[135] Without customs which produce "moderation of goods and credit among the great, and moderation of avarice and envy among the small," social inequality is dangerous because it produces irreconcilable private interests and the resulting refusal of either the poor or the rich to respect the laws. Especially under modern conditions in which men lack moderation in their desires for personal gain, the only tolerable solution is relative equality of wealth and power.

It is therefore one of the most important matters for the government to prevent extreme inequality of fortunes, not in removing riches from their possessors, but in removing from all the means of accumulating them, not in building poorhouses, but in keeping citizens from becoming poor.[136]

Since the expropriation of private property from specific persons is impossible according to the law—the rich could not conceivably will, as their own private interest, an act which would undermine the property right in itself—it is necessary to prevent inequality by regulating the methods of accumulating wealth. Hence progressive taxation (i.e., taxes which increase according to the wealth of citizens) and inheritance taxes—if not the prohibition of inheritance—are to be preferred to confiscation, which can only result in irreconcilable opposition between the rich and poor.[137]

The equality necessary for political stability is not restricted to

---

people would not so fully see the consequences of this last form [of voting], Servius pretended to give it a military air" (447). On the operation of the Centuriate assembly, see Lucy Ross Taylor, *Party Politics in the Age of Caesar* (Berkeley and Los Angeles: University of California Press, 1961), esp. chap. III. Taylor's remarks on the anti-popular role of Cato, as leader of the "optimates," are also a helpful corrective to Rousseau's praise of Cato as an exemplar of civic virtue; see chaps. VI, VIII, *et passim*.

[135] Hence Rousseau comments, with respect to the division into Centuries: "only the simple morals of the first Romans, their taste for agriculture, their scorn toward commerce and toward lust for gain, could make it practicable" (*Contrat social*, IV, iv [P, III, 448]).

[136] *Économie Politique* (P, III, 258).

[137] *Économie Politique* (P, III, 262–64, 269–78); *Constitution pour la Corse* (P, III, 930–37); *Gouvernement de Pologne*, xi (P, III, 1006–12). Note Rousseau's criticism of Montesquieu's views concerning the tax system suited to a free people; cf. *Économie Politique* (270) and *Gouvernement de Pologne* (1010–11), with *Esprit des Lois*, XIII, xiv.

questions of wealth and personal power. Rousseau was also concerned with the effects of unequal distribution of population throughout the territory of a society. He connected social inequality with the development of cities, in which a large population is inevitably dependent on the cultivation of commerce, the arts, and industry; given the limited nature of man's physical needs, such activities are necessarily oriented to luxury and thereby accentuate the distinction between the rich (who use and profit most from them) and the poor— especially the farmers.

> Populate the territory equally, extend everywhere the same rights, carry everywhere abundance and life; it is thus that the State will become at the same time the strongest and the best-governed possible. Remember that the walls of cities are only formed from the debris of houses in the fields. For every palace I see built in the capital, I imagine a whole countryside reduced to ruin.[138]

Or, as Rousseau puts it in the *Émile*:

> Two states equal in size and number of men can be very unequal in force; and the more powerful of the two is always the one whose inhabitants are the most equally spread over the territory.[139]

Rousseau's persistent preference for the small agricultural community is thus based on the general proposition that the development of large-scale urban life necessarily produces inequality and moral corruption.[140]

The same reasons explain Rousseau's assertion that, where a large society is unavoidable, a single capital city is dangerous because it will attract a disproportionate share of population and wealth.

> If one cannot reduce the State to its proper limits, there still remains one resource; it is not to allow a capital, to have the government reside alternatively in each city, and thus to assemble in turn the estates of the country.[141]

As is evident, Rousseau's conception of the effects of urbanization and industrialization, as well as his preference for a rustic way of life, are sharply divergent from current attitudes and seem largely irrele-

---

[138] *Contrat social*, III, xiii (P, III, 427).

[139] *Émile*, v (G, 599).

[140] *Économie Politique* (P, III, 258); *Lettre à d'Alembert* (G, 168–73); *Émile*, IV (G, 252–53); v (599–600); *Dernière Réponse* (P, III, 79n.); *Constitution pour la Corse* (P, III, 907, 911).

[141] *Contrat social*, III, xiii (P, III, 427). Cf. *Constitution pour la Corse* (P, III, 911–12).

vant to modern experience. However that may be, his conception of the science of the legislator is not restricted to these concerns; Rousseau analyzes the necessary consequences of different forms of government in a manner which is not, strictly speaking, dependent on his own preference for the small, agricultural city-state.

D · THE EFFECTS OF DIFFERENT FORMS OF GOVERNMENT

Rousseau's use of a continuous proportion between the sovereign, government, and people has already been discussed in the context of his principles of political right, which this relationship summarizes in geometrical terms.[142] The equilibrium defined by the continuous proportion can also be viewed, however, as the basis of numerous maxims of politics. The most obvious is that:

> Since there is only one proportional mean within each proportion, there is no more than one good government possible in a State.[143]

Rousseau therefore discusses the various forms of government in detail, dismissing as irrelevant the abstract question of "which is absolutely the best government."[144]

The first term of the continuous proportion—the ratio of the sovereign to the government—is of considerable interest to Rousseau, especially because it is connected to the inverse relationship between size and political cohesion, strength, or morals—not to mention the freedom of the citizen. In a large society:

> the people has less affection for the rulers it never sees, for the fatherland which is to its eyes like the world, and for its fellow citizens, most of whom are foreigners to it.[145]

Even more important, in a sense:

> the same laws cannot be suited to so many different provinces which have different morals (*moeurs*), which live under opposed climates, and which cannot suffer the same form of government.[146]

It follows that the larger the State, the less likely that the political institutions will truly reflect the sovereign general will.

We have already noted Rousseau's dual propositions that, in order to maintain the equilibrium defined by the continuous proportion,

---

[142] See above, chap. VII § 2E.
[143] *Contrat social*, III, i (P, III, 397).
[144] *Ibid.*, II, ix (392–93); III, i (398, 400); III, ix (419).
[145] *Ibid.*, II, ix (387).
[146] *Ibid.*

"the government . . . should be relatively stronger in proportion as the people is more numerous" and "the more force the government should have to restrain the people, the more the sovereign should have, in turn, to restrain the government."[147] The second requirement naturally contradicts the first, however, because the increased size of a population renders it less capable of opposing the government. In order to strengthen the sovereign against the government, Rousseau's main practical suggestion is repeated "assemblies of the people":

> The more force the government has, the more frequently the sovereign should show itself.[148]

But the larger the society, the more difficult frequent assemblies, and hence the more likely that the continuous proportion will be violated in fact.[149]

The same considerations are apparent with reference to the relationship of the government to the people as subjects, which forms the second term of the continuous proportion:

> Administration becomes more difficult over large distances, just as a weight becomes heavier at the end of a long lever.[150]

This analogy between the force of the government and a lever represents Rousseau's manner of analyzing the relationships within civil society, for he returns to it in discussing the density of population:

> The advantage of a tyrannical government is therefore in this respect to act over long distances. With the aid of the points of support it gives itself, its force increases at a distance like that of levers. The force of the people, on the contrary, only acts when concentrated.[151]

At this point, Rousseau adds a note with reference to his two uses of this analogy:

> This does not contradict what I said before in Book II, chapter ix, concerning the inconvenience of large States; for it was a question there of the authority of the government over its members, and it is a question here of its force against the subjects. Its spread out members serve it as points of support [fulcra] in order to act at a distance on the people, but it has no fulcrum for acting directly

[147] *Ibid.*, III, i (397–98), cited above, p. 343.
[148] *Ibid.*, III, xiii (426).
[149] Cf. *ibid.* (427); III, viii (418); III, xv (429–31).
[150] *Ibid.*, II, ix (387).   [151] *Ibid.*, III, viii (418–19).

on its own members. Thus in one case the length of the lever makes its weakness, and its strength in the other case.[152]

The weakness of the government of a large state vis-à-vis its own officials must therefore be distinguished from its relative power vis-à-vis the citizen body.

This *internal* weakness of large scale government is a general phenomenon.

> The total force of the government being always that of the State, does not vary; from which it follows that the more it uses this force on its own members, the less remains for it to act on all the people.[153]

Rousseau then immediately deduces what he calls a "fundamental maxim":

> The more numerous the magistrates, the weaker the government.[154]

This proposition has as its corollary:

> When the functions of the government are divided among several tribunals, the least numerous acquire sooner or later the greatest authority—if only because of the ease of expediting affairs, which brings them to it naturally.[155]

These maxims—which should be empirically verifiable[156]—thus lead

---

[152] *Ibid.*, n. Note Rousseau's tacit appeal to the self-interest of the ruler, whose control over his subordinates is greater in a smaller community; large-scale tyranny is self-defeating for the tyrant.

[153] *Ibid.*, III, ii (400).

[154] *Ibid.* Rousseau demonstrates this maxim by elaborating the distinction between the private wills of individuals, the common will of magistrates, and the general will (see above, pp. 346–47, 388); he argues that the "private will has much more influence in the acts of government than in those of the sovereign" and, after comparing the relative force of the government to the absolute force of the State, he makes the pragmatic observation that "the expedition of business becomes proportionately slower as more men are interested with it" (*ibid.* [400–02]).

[155] *Ibid.*, III, iv (404–05).

[156] For example, it could be argued that the inverse proportion between the force employed by rulers on their own agents and on the citizen body was reflected in the history of the Soviet Union, where (at least under Stalin) there seemed to be an oscillation between periods of purges and repression within the party and governmental hierarchies, and periods of pressure on the public at large. Similarly, the tendency of power to gravitate to ruling bodies composed of few men, particularly in modern times, is a frequently noted phenomenon. On the latter, see Bertrand de Jouvenel, *Du Pouvoir*

Rousseau to interpret the traditional distinction between monarchy, aristocracy, and democracy in terms of the relative force of the government over its own members and the citizen body.

Rousseau combines the maxims concerning the internal characteristics of governments of different sizes with the propositions dealing with the population as a whole:

> I have just proved that the government relaxes in proportion to the multiplication of magistrates, and I have previously proved that the more numerous the people, the more the repressive force should augment. From which it follows that the ratio of the magistrates to the government should be inverse to the ratio of the subjects to the sovereign. That is, the more the State is enlarged, the more the government should shrink, so that the number of rulers diminishes in proportion to the increase in the populace.[157]

The latter relationship is not an empirical proposition or a "positive law of political science" (to use Jouvenel's term), because it indicates the form of government which "should" be adopted if it is to "suit" the society to be ruled:[158]

> If in different States the number of magistrates should be in inverse proportion to that of the citizens, it follows that, in general, democratic government suits little States, aristocracy mediocre ones, and monarchy large ones.[159]

Rousseau was well aware of the "multitude of circumstances which can provide exceptions," and his description of the evolution of Roman institutions is ample evidence that he knew of cases which did not follow his prudential rule.[160]

The multiplication of levels of administration, each of which must be supported by taxes, increases the cost of government without bringing with it any real advantages:

(Geneva: Bourquin, 1947); and "The Principate" (paper presented to the Sixth Congress of the International Association of Political Science, Geneva, September 1965).

[157] *Contrat social*, III, ii (P, III, 402). Note that the continuous proportion, insofar as the number of citizens is taken as a representative measure of the extreme terms, would lead to exactly the opposite conclusion. Cf. *ibid.*, III, i (398) and above, pp. 340–48.

[158] Cf. Jouvenel, "Théorie des Formes de Gouvernement," p. 347.

[159] *Contrat social*, III, iii (P, III, 403–04).

[160] Cf. *ibid.* (404) with III, x, n. (421–22) and IV, v (455): Rome had more ruling magistrates toward the end of the Republic than under the Tarquins.

The farther contributions go from their source, the more they are burdensome. It is not on the quantity of taxation that their weight must be measured, but on the distance that they have to travel to return to the hands from which they left.[161]

"Rapid and well-established circulation" of finances does not weigh heavily on the citizens, even if their taxes are large, whereas:

however little the people gives, if this little doesn't come back to it, in always giving it is soon worn out. . . . From which it follows that the greater the distance between the people and the government, the more the tributes become burdensome: thus in democracy the people is the least taxed, in aristocracy it is more, and in monarchy it carries the heaviest weight.[162]

This proposition permits Rousseau to assert that the various forms of government are suited to different states as a function of their wealth as well as their size:

Monarchy therefore is only suited to rich nations, aristocracy to States mediocre in wealth as well as size, and democracy to small and poor States.[163]

Since, as we have seen, wealth—at least insofar as a natural surplus is concerned—is connected with climate, Rousseau's correlation of the form of government with the wealth and size of the society is also a correlation with climate: the political option is fundamentally between large, wealthy, and morally corrupted despotic regimes in warm climates; mediocre, relatively poor, and possibly healthy republics in intermediate climates; and the very small, free, barbarian populations in extreme and relatively unfertile or cold regions. But instead of presenting this option in its simple form, Rousseau decomposes it into the subordinate relationships which account for these tendencies, thus providing the greatest possible scope for a prudential consideration of the conditions influencing a given society.

Although the forms of government are virtually infinite in number, for practical purposes the traditional distinction between monarchy, aristocracy, and democracy can be used to clarify the choices made by the legislator.[164] Departing from common usage, Rousseau does not consider a republic to be a form of government:

161 *Ibid.*, III, viii (415).
162 *Ibid.*   163 *Ibid.*
164 *Ibid.*, III, iii (403); III, vii (413).

I therefore call a republic any State ruled by laws, under whatever form of administration there might be. . . . All legitimate government is republican.[165]

As he adds in a note to clarify this use of the word "republic":

I do not mean by this word only an aristocracy or a democracy, but in general any government guided by the general will, which is the law. To be legitimate it is not necessary that the government be confused with the sovereign, but that it be its minister: then even monarchy is a republic.[166]

Despite the possibility of what would today be called "constitutional monarchy," however, kings usually claim to be sovereign; for practical purposes, choice is between what is popularly called monarchy and a republic or democracy.[167]

Assuming the existence of legitimate laws, a democracy can be defined in precise terms as government by "all the people or the greater part of the people," aristocracy as government in the hands of "a small number" (such that "there are more simple citizens than magistrates"), and monarchy as "government in the hands of a single magistrate from whom all the others hold their power."[168] In its pure form, each kind of government has specific requisites in order to succeed.

A pure democracy is the most difficult to achieve:

Besides, how many things that are difficult to unite are presupposed by this government? First a very small state . . . second, a great simplicity of morals (*moeurs*). . . . Then, a great deal of equality in rank and wealth. . . . Finally, little or no luxury.[169]

Although "in the strict sense of the term, a pure democracy has never existed," more or less democratic regimes are possible; they tend, however, to be unstable:

There is no government so subject to civil wars and internal agitation as the democratic or popular one, because there is no other which tends so strongly and so continually to change its form, nor which requires more vigilance and courage to be maintained in its own [form].[170]

[165] *Ibid.*, II, vi (379–80). [166] *Ibid.*, n. (380).
[167] See n. 189 of this chapter.
[168] *Contrat social*, III, iii (P, III, 403).
[169] *Ibid.*, III, iv (405).
[170] *Ibid.*

In itself, this weakness has its advantages, as Rousseau later points out (referring to Tacitus and Machiavelli as authorities), because "a little agitation" resulting from "freedom" is more conducive to "making the species prosper" than is peace.[171]

The true danger of direct democracy is that it leads to a confusion of the sovereign and the government, thereby contradicting a fundamental requirement of the principles of political right.[172] Moreover, the mode of election appropriate to a democracy is the choice of magistrates by lot:

> In any true democracy, the magistracy is not an advantage, but a burdensome obligation, that cannot be justly imposed on one private person rather than on another. The law alone can impose this obligation on the one on whom chance falls. For then the condition being equal for all and the choice not depending on any human will, there is no particular application which changes the universality of the law.[173]

But the election of magistrates by lot is without "inconvenience" only where men are so nearly equal, "in morals (*moeurs*) as well as in talent," that the selection of one citizen rather than another is "virtually indifferent"; since this condition is impossible, particularly with reference to the highest offices, democracy will often result in the election of inferior men.[174]

In its "elective" form, aristocratic government—as distinct from aristocratic sovereignty—is "the best" of all political institutions precisely because "it is against the natural order that the large number govern and the small number be governed."[175]

It is the best and most natural order that the wisest govern the mul-

---

[171] *Ibid.*, III, ix, n. (420): "Tumults, civil wars greatly anger rulers, but they do not create the true misfortunes of peoples, who can even have repose while there is dispute over who will tyrannize over them. . . . A little agitation gives energy to souls, and what makes the species truly prosper is less peace than freedom." Cf. also the passage from Machiavelli quoted in *ibid.*, II, iii (372).

[172] *Ibid.*, III, xvi (432). See above, chap. VII, § 2D.

[173] *Ibid.*, IV, iii (442). Rousseau criticizes Montesquieu's reasoning in this context—a criticism which arises because Rousseau considers the problem from the point of view of "right," not from the perspective of the likely characteristics of democracies.

[174] *Ibid.* (443); III, iv (404–06).

[175] *Ibid.*, III, iv (404); III, v (406). Cf. *Lettres Écrites de la Montagne*, vi (P, III, 809): "The best of governments is aristocratic; the worst of sovereignties is aristocratic"; and *Jugement sur la Polysynodie* (P, III, 645): "aristocracy [is] the worst of sovereignties."

titude when one is sure that they will govern it for its profit and not their own.[176]

The requisites for an aristocratic regime in which the government does not usurp the sovereignty are intermediate or moderate in character:

> There should not be a State as small nor a people as simple and as upright . . . as in a good democracy. Nor should there be such a large nation that the rulers, dispersed to govern it, can decide for the sovereign each in his own department. . . . Aristocracy requires . . . also . . . moderation among the rich and contentment among the poor, for it seems that a rigorous equality would be misplaced there.[177]

Sparta and Rome, the models of free government, were elective aristocracies (as distinct from the natural aristocracy of age suited only to "simple" or primitive peoples, and hereditary aristocracy which is "the worst of all governments" because the rulers perpetuate themselves in office and hence easily usurp sovereignty).[178]

As the distinction between elective and hereditary aristocracy indicates, the mode of selecting magistrates in an aristocratic regime is decisive. Election is superior because, while tending to result in the appointment of men of wealth who "can better give all their time" to their functions, it leaves room for "sometimes teaching the people that there are more important reasons for preference in the merit of men than in their wealth."[179]

[176] *Contrat social*, III, v (P, III, 407).

[177] *Ibid.*

[178] *Ibid.* (406–07). On the "undemocratic" character of Sparta—and particularly the inequalities of wealth there—see Aristotle, *Politics* II.1269b–1271b.

[179] *Contrat social*, III, v (P, III, 408). At this point Rousseau indicates his divergence from the classics by applying Aristotle's description of oligarchy (government of the wealthy) to aristocracy (according to Aristotle, government by the best). Cf. *Politics* III.1279b. Whereas Aristotle speaks of a sixfold distinction of governments into the three legitimate forms of monarchy, aristocracy, and democracy and their corresponding corruptions—as does Plato in the *Statesman* (291d–292a, 300e–301d, 302c–303b)—for Rousseau there are only three true forms of government, solely determined by the number of rulers and all subject to the same principles of political right; the "abuse of government" when these principles are not respected produces three forms of anarchy—"ochlochracy," "oligarchy," and "tyranny" or "despotism"—none of which are forms of government properly so-called (*Contrat social*, III, x [P, III, 423]; III, i [396]). Cf. Hobbes, *Leviathan*, Part II, chap. xix (ed. Oakeshott, p. 121), and the explicit criticism of Aristotle in *Contrat social*, III, x, n. (423). The consequence of Rousseau's shift from the classification of Aristotle is that the forms of government no longer refer to

It matters a great deal to regulate the form of the election of magistrates by law; for in abandoning it to the will of the prince one cannot avoid falling into hereditary aristocracy.[180]

Lot, choice, or mixed rules of designating magistrates can be utilized in an aristocracy, but election by "choice" (i.e., the selection of magistrates among the competing candidates) "should fill the positions which need specific talents, such as military posts." In contrast, election by lot is appropriate not only in pure democracy, but for positions in an aristocracy where "good sense, justice, and integrity are sufficient, such as in the justiciary, since these qualities are common to all citizens in a well-constituted state."[181]

In any event, public employment should not be a "trade" or lifelong "condition" of any individual. As Rousseau put it in applying his political teaching:

Every public man in Poland should have no other permanent condition than that of a citizen. All the posts that he fulfills, and above all those that are important . . . should only be considered as trial positions and degrees to climb higher after having merited it. I exhort the Poles to pay attention to this maxim, on which I will often insist: I think it is the key to great energy in the State.[182]

While one consequence of this maxim is that—as Rousseau never tired of insisting—only a citizen army is consistent with freedom and mercenary troops are to be avoided at all costs,[183] the primary consequence is a "gradual progress" through the various offices and magistracies, open in principle to all and rewarding only those of merit.[184]

---

the *regime* or *politeia* in the sense of a political order determining the way of life of the people. Rousseau distinguishes more sharply between political institutions and *moeurs* than did the classics because his science of the legislator is based on a theory of human evolution according to which the rise of moral corruption is a historical inevitability, to some extent independent of the form of administration of a political society.

[180] *Contrat social*, III, v, n. (P, III, 407).

[181] *Ibid.*, IV, iii (442–43). By implication, of course, the highest civil magistracies are akin to military commands (*ibid.*, III, xviii [435]) and should be elected by choice. But note the combination of lot and election in selecting the king according to the *Gouvernement de Pologne*, xiv (P, III, 1030–33).

[182] *Ibid.*, iv (P, III, 967). Cf. *Constitution pour la Corse* (P, III, 946).

[183] *Dernière Réponse* (P, III, 82); *Économie Politique* (P, III, 268–69); *Constitution pour la Corse* (P, III, 948–49); *Gouvernement de Pologne*, xii (P, III, 1013–18); *Contrat social*, III, xv (P, III, 428).

[184] See esp. *Gouvernement de Pologne*, xiii (P, III, 1020–29) as well as iv (969); vii (991–93); x (1000–02); xi (1010); *Économie Politique* (P, III, 261); *Constitution pour la Corse* (P, III, 919, 934, 947, 948).

Rousseau's explicit preference for elective aristocracy has not been sufficiently considered in the interpretation of his well-known chapter "On Deputies or Representatives" in the *Social Contract*. His condemnation of the surrender of sovereignty to a representative assembly does not mean that Rousseau ignored the need for a parliament; on the contrary, he expected that the laws would be prepared for popular enactment by representatives: "the deputies of the people . . . are only its commissioners; they can conclude nothing definitively."[185] Since the ministerial character of magistrates or deputies is a direct consequence of Rousseau's principles of political right, the status of representative government depends on the extent to which the strict principles of right can legitimately be modified when put into practice. For the moment, it is sufficient to note that this problem necessarily arises in his thought because of his preference for elective aristocracy (which, in current terms, is merely another name for parliamentary or representative government).[186]

Monarchy is the form of government with the "most vigor," but also the most likely to be dominated by the "private will" of the ruler, so that "the very force of the administration is incessantly turned to the prejudice of the State." Monarchy presupposes a large community because it cannot operate without "intermediate orders: it is necessary to have princes, the great, nobility . . . none of which is suited to a small State."[187] It is the most risky form of government because the dependence on a single man implies that its "greatness or extent was measured according to the faculties of the one who governs it." Elections are dangerous because the great power of the king invites corruption in the process of choice, but the recourse to hereditary rule is even worse because it produces rule by "infants, monsters, imbeciles," and the "regents" who must exercise their power; since each successive ruler has the sole power to appoint all other magistrates, consistent public policies are impossible under monarchy.[188] For all practical purposes, therefore, it is possible to distinguish between "republics" and "monarchies" because the latter are rarely

---

[185] *Contrat social*, III, xv (P, III, 429–30), cited above, p. 339.

[186] See § 3 of this chapter as well as above, p. 334, n. 127. In current terms, the practical problem of Rousseau's principles of right could be stated as follows: to what extent is it absolutely necessary, for government to be legitimate, that the laws elaborated by representative institutions be submitted to popular referenda?

[187] *Contrat social*, III, vi (P, III, 408–11).

[188] *Ibid.* (411–12); IV, iii (443). Cf. *Second Discourse*, Part 2 (P, III, 187, 194).

if ever legitimate in their pure form, and degenerate easily into despotism or tyranny.[189]

E · THE DECLINE OF POLITICAL INSTITUTIONS

Like Rousseau's maxims concerning the proper historical moment of instituting legislation, the "inevitable tendency" of the executive power or government to usurp the legislative or sovereign authority of the people must be understood in the context of his general conception of historical evolution. Because this pattern is treated extensively in the *First* and *Second Discourses*, a summary will suffice at this point:

> Just as the private will incessantly acts against the general will, so the government makes a continual effort against sovereignty. The more this effort increases, the more the constitution is altered, and . . . it must happen sooner or later that the prince finally oppresses the sovereign and breaks the social treaty.[190]

This tendency has two sets of causes: some are intrinsic to the work-

---

[189] *Contrat social*, III, vi (P, III, 410, 412–13); III, viii (416); III, x (422–23n., 423 and n.); III, xii (426); *Lettres Écrites de la Montagne*, v (P, III, 770–71); vi (811). Rousseau introduces a distinction between the tyrant (the "usurper of royal authority") and the despot ("the usurper of sovereign power"): "The tyrant is one who comes up against the laws to govern according to the laws, the despot is one who puts himself above the laws themselves" (*Contrat social*, III, x [423]). Cf. the distinction in d'Argenson's *Considérations sur le Gouvernement Ancien et Présent de la France* (ed. 1764, p. 14): "Despotism is called an authority which claims to be independent of any fundamental or particular law. Tyranny is the factual abuse, from the power that Despotism (if it exists somewhere) claims to have by right." Since Rousseau himself nowhere seems to rely on the distinction between tyrant and despot, following instead "the common meaning" according to which "the tyrant is a king who governs with violence and without reference to justice and laws" (cf. *Contrat social*, III, x [423] with III, viii [418-19]), his introduction of a "precise meaning" of the term requires explanation. Rousseau says he is returning to the usage of Greek political practice—he cites Cornelius Nepos and Xenophon's *Hiero* as authorities—as a means of criticizing Aristotle's definition of the king as one who rules for the "utility of his subjects." Hence Rousseau concludes that "it would follow from Aristotle's distinction that since the beginning of the world there would not yet have existed a single king" (*ibid.*, III, x, n. [423]); cf. n. 179 of this chapter. On the validity of Rousseau's interpretation of Xenophon's *Hiero*, it is absolutely necessary to consider Leo Strauss, *On Tyranny* (rev. ed.; Glencoe: Free Press, 1963) chap. IV, esp. p. 126, n. 7. On the reduction of all forms of government to the alternative between republics and monarchies, see Machiavelli, *The Prince*, chap. I.

[190] *Contrat social*, III, x (P, III, 421). Cf. III, ii (400–01); III, xi (424–25); III, xiv (428); III, xviii (435).

ings of governments, others result from the evolution of civil society as a whole.

Taking the latter first, we have already analyzed Rousseau's fundamental proposition that enlightenment produces social corruption, releasing personal interests and destroying morality and civic virtue; in the *Social Contract*, Rousseau contents himself with a brief reference to the central thesis of his *First Discourse*.[191] The substitution of money for civic duty is more explicitly attacked,[192] as is the tendency of luxury to produce despotism.[193] More broadly, Rousseau, restates the thesis of his *Second Discourse* by asserting the natural tendency toward an increase in social inequality:

> It is precisely because the force of things always tends to destroy equality that the force of legislation should always tend to maintain it.[194]

The unnatural character of civil society makes it impossible to hope for the perpetual existence of political institutions, and the art of politics is merely to retard the inevitable decline as much as possible.

The necessary corruption of civil society is subtly revealed by Rousseau's criterion for a "good government":

> All things otherwise equal, the government under which, without foreign means, without naturalization, without colonies, the citizens populate and multiply the most, is infallibly the best.[195]

But since increased population results in a weakening of the social bond as well as the need to increase the repressive power of the gov-

---

[191] "Those [centuries] in which letters and arts have flourished have been too much admired, without penetrating the secret object of their culture, and without considering their deadly effect" (*ibid.*, III, ix, n. [420]). See above, chap. v.

[192] "It is the bother with commerce and arts, the avid interest for gain, the softness and love of commodities, which change personal services into money. . . . Give money, and soon you will have chains" (*ibid.*, III, xv [429]). Cf. II, xi (329); *Constitution pour la Corse* (P, III, 904–08, 911–12, 916–17, 920–39); *Gouvernement de Pologne*, xi (P, III, 1003–10).

[193] *Contrat social*, III, viii (P, III, 415–18).

[194] *Ibid.*, II, xi (392).

[195] *Ibid.*, III, ix (420). Cf. *Émile*, v (G, 598–99). Rousseau meant this suggestion seriously, to the extent that he considered increases in population to be the natural consequence of a healthy agrarian society, and population decline to be inevitable in enlightened societies; see esp. *Second Discourse*, n. IX (P, III, 202–05); *Constitution pour la Corse* (P, III, 904–05). There is perhaps no other proposition of Rousseau's science of the legislator, however, which shows more strikingly the alteration of political phenomena produced by modern science and technology; at present, some would be tempted to reverse Rousseau's maxim.

ernment, the very success of a good regime tends to lead to its own downfall.[196] Fame in itself is a sign of "decline."[197]

The natural tendency of even healthy civil societies to expand, to develop enlightenment, and to become corrupted is paralleled by the internal dynamics of political institutions:

> Government shrinks when it passes from the large number to few, that is from democracy to aristocracy and from aristocracy to royalty. That is its natural inclination.[198]

In part, this tendency is the result of a decline in the force of any government over time.

> In fact, government never changes its form except when its exhausted energy (*ressort usé*) leaves it too weak to be able to preserve its own form. . . . It is therefore necessary to rewind and tighten the spring (*ressort*) to the extent that it gives way, for otherwise the State that it supports would fall into ruins.[199]

As this return to the analogy between a government and a watch or machine run by springs suggests, political institutions tend to wear out because the cooperation of large numbers of magistrates presupposes a strong "common will" within the government; as the private interests of rulers are released from subordination to the general will by the decay of civic virtue, the tendency toward an aristocracy or monarchy which usurps sovereign authority becomes inevitable.

The sole means of preventing or at least delaying this decline is frequent popular assemblies, which restrain the government by making it dependent on the sovereign people:

> There must be fixed and periodic [assemblies] that nothing can abolish or adjourn, such that on the indicated day the people is legitimately convoked by the law, without the necessity of any

---

[196] *Constitution pour la Corse* (P, III, 907). Cf. Aristotle's remarks on the necessity of limiting the population of the city if it is to be stable (*Politics* II.1265a–b; VII.1326a–b).

[197] "A people only becomes famous when its legislation begins to decline" (*Contrat social*, II, vii [P, III, 381]). Cf. *Émile*, III (G, 224, n.): "I hold it impossible that the great monarchies of Europe still have a long time to last: all have shined, and any state that shines is on its decline. I have my own opinion of the more particular reasons for this maxim; but it is not appropriate to say them, and everyone only sees them too well."

[198] *Contrat social*, III, x (P, III, 421).

[199] *Ibid.* (422). The play on the double meaning of the word *ressort*—meaning either energy or a spring—is particularly clear in this passage.

other formal convocation . . . the more force the government has, the more frequently the sovereign should meet.[200]

Rousseau attached great importance to this device of frequent popular assemblies which the government cannot prevent without openly violating the law, and in which the sovereign people could change the form of the government or replace the magistrates if it so desired.[201] But for this very reason these assemblies are dangerous once a people becomes morally corrupt, for the people are easily "fooled" by demagogues.[202]

Another method of restraining this tendency to decline consists, according to Rousseau, in the imitation of certain institutions employed in Rome; what is usually considered as his "digression" concerning the Roman constitution must be seen in this perspective. Rousseau indicates early in Book IV that he will suggest further "practical means for preventing the abuse" of the substitution of private wills for the general will (in addition to the device of frequent popular assemblies presented in Book III).[203] Apart from the particular method of "collecting votes in the assembly of the people," which in the most important case consisted in dividing the Roman population into classes that effectively disenfranchised the poor,[204] the devices of particular importance are the tribunate, the dictatorship, and censorship.

Of the first of these Roman institutions, Rousseau says:

The tribunate is not a constituent part of the city, and should not have any part of the legislative or executive power. But it is in this very fact that its power is greater: for being unable to do anything, it can prevent everything. It is more sacred as the defender of the laws than the prince who executes them or the sovereign who gives them.[205]

[200] *Ibid.*, III, xiii (426).

[201] *Ibid.*, III, xiv (427–28); III, xviii (435–36). Cf. *Gouvernement de Pologne*, vii (P, III, 978), where Rousseau claims that "before the *Social Contract*, where I give" this method of preventing usurpation, "no one thought of it."

[202] *Ibid.*; *Contrat social*, II, vi (P, III, 380); III, iv (404); III, xiv (428); IV, i (438); IV, iv (452–53); IV, vi (456–57). This caution would apply equally well, of course, to popular elections and referenda in large modern societies.

[203] *Ibid.*, IV, ii (441). For the conventional interpretation of the chapters that analyze Rome, see above, n. 21 of chap. VII.

[204] *Ibid.*, IV, iii (443); IV, iv (444–53, esp. 450–52). See n. 134 of this chapter.

[205] *Ibid.*, IV, v (454). The parallel between the role of the legislator (who has neither sovereign nor executive power) and the tribunate suggests that the latter acts as the institutionalized representative of the former. Perhaps it would

This negative power is not to be feared as being too weak—since weakness "is not in its nature"—but:

> whatever force it has in excess, it reverses everything. . . . It degenerates into tyranny when it usurps the executive power, of which it is only the moderator, and when it wants to dispense laws, which it should only protect.[206]

The difficulty with this device, as Rousseau indicates by giving the example of the Spartan Ephors, is that although such a power can be "without danger" as long as good morals exist, it may "accelerate corruption once begun"; the best method of limiting this tendency is to "not make this body permanent, but to regulate the intervals during which it would remain out of existence." Even so, the tribunate is subject to the same logic of decline as other political institutions, and cannot in itself prevent the ultimate usurpation of sovereign power.[207]

The other devices employed in Rome and proposed by Rousseau as a check on political decline are the institution of dictators in times of crisis and of censors to maintain morals. Both functions, however, are more suited to preserving a society that is still healthy than to reforming one that is beginning to become corrupt. During crises, when the "inflexibility of the laws" creates a danger of the "loss of the State," it may be necessary "to name a supreme ruler who silences the laws and suspends sovereign authority for a moment." Since such a magistrate "can do anything except make laws," as long as the powers of a dictator are limited to very short periods of time they are not dangerous. But in corrupt periods politicians will be tempted to prolong the dictator's mandate or to violate the laws governing it; moreover, as the example of the Romans shows, the "fear" of such a power may lead to a refusal to name a dictator when necessary, even

---

not be too misleading to consider the United States Supreme Court as something akin to the institution Rousseau has in mind. But it should be added that the Roman tribunes were considered as spokesmen for the *populares* or people; see, e.g., Taylor, *Party Politics in the Age of Caesar*, pp. 5–6, 14, *et passim*. Rousseau was, of course, well aware of this and describes a tribune as "a simple officer of the people" who made "proud patricians" give way, *Contrat social*, IV, v (454).

[206] *Contrat social*, IV, iv (P, III, 454).

[207] *Ibid.* (454–55). Cf. the phrase "seditious tribunes" (*ibid.*, IV, iv [449]) and the criticism of the Tribal Assemblies, "in which the tribunes were elected and passed their plebiscites" (*ibid.* [451]). Note that according to Rousseau, the power of proposing new laws should be restricted to the magistrates proper (i.e., the "executive power"), and hence should not belong to the tribunate, as it did in Rome.

though this may be simply "circumspection" with "little reason."[208] In the same manner, as has already been noted, censorship "can be useful for maintaining morals, never for reestablishing them"; in corrupt, modern times, "such tribunals would soon have overturned everything among us."[209]

Ultimately, Rousseau relies far more heavily on the institution of civil religion to restrain the inevitable tendency to moral corruption and despotism than on particular institutions imitating the Roman constitution. It may well be that a sense of the weakness of formal political institutions in the face of declining morals led Rousseau to add the celebrated chapter viii of Book IV after having completed his draft of the *Social Contract*.[210] In any event, this chapter makes it clear that without "a religion which makes [each citizen] love his duties," civil society is extremely vulnerable. Since the relation between a civil religion, establishing "sentiments of sociability without which it is impossible to be either a good citizen or a faithful subject," and Rousseau's natural theology has already been discussed,[211] two points suffice here. The first is Rousseau's direct attack on the disastrous political effects of Christianity, on the grounds that it creates a "double power in perpetual jurisdictional conflict that has made any good polity impossible in Christian States." Although particularly critical of Catholicism, "a religion of the priest," even "the pure and simple religion of the Evangile, the true Theism" (i.e., a religion like that of the Savoyard Vicar) destroys the citizen's pride "in the glory of his country" and is totally contrary to the "social spirit"; a "Christian Republic" is a contradiction in terms because "each of these two words excludes the other."[212]

The second is Rousseau's practical conclusion that, within the limits of a civil religion defined by the sovereign (i.e., by the laws), tolerance of private belief is necessary:

Now that there is no longer nor can there be an exclusive national religion, one should tolerate all those that tolerate others, insofar

[208] *Ibid.*, IV, vi (454–58).

[209] *Ibid.*, IV, vii (458–59); *Second Discourse*, n. XIX (P, III, 222).

[210] On the circumstances in which the chapter on "Civil Religion" was composed and added to Rousseau's manuscript, see the Letter to Rey, 23 December 1761 (C. G., VII, 2) and Derathé's n. (P, III, 1498).

[211] *Contrat social*, IV, viii (P, III, 468). See above, chap. II, § 3.

[212] *Contrat social*, IV, viii (P, III, 462–67). While Rousseau explicitly refers to Hobbes in his critique of Catholicism (463), his attack on the adverse political effects of the natural religion of the Evangile is obviously also inspired by Machiavelli. Cf. Robert Derathé, "La Religion Civile selon Rousseau," *Annales*, XXXV, 164–65.

as their dogmas have nothing contrary to the duties of the citizen.[213]

The discovery of the "true theism" represents a practical limit on the perfection of civil society which is somehow irreversible (at least for European civilization); the moral corruption which permits Rousseau to teach publicly his purely personal religion means that it will never again be possible to return to the politically healthy paganism of the ancients, based "on errors and lies" that are revealed by the discovery of "natural divine right" by Jesus or by Rousseau (speaking through the Savoyard Vicar).[214]

Ultimately, neither political institutions nor a civic religion can effectively preserve civil society from the decline which is part of the "nature of things." The most one can hope for is that prudent use of these means, illuminated by a knowledge of the historical tendency of all social life and the maxims of politics, will moderate or delay the effect of moral corruption and, once it has occurred, render possible the tranquil life of the few decent men who remain at the margins of a decadent or despotic civil society. The limits of the science of the legislator point to the legitimacy of a withdrawal from civil society by the philosopher (whose works are motivated by a concern for the happiness of the human race) or by the *promeneur solitaire* (who is concerned solely with his personal goodness and happiness). It is fitting that the *Social Contract*, by concluding on the note of religious toleration and the impossibility that any regime—even the most excellent—could "oblige anyone to believe" in the dogmas of civil religion, reveals Rousseau's continuing claim against all civil society in the name of nature.[215]

---

[213] *Contrat social*, IV, viii (P, III, 469).

[214] *Ibid*. (464–65).

[215] *Ibid*. (468–69). In his comments on the civil religion, Derathé is disturbed by the realization that Rousseau's defense of tolerance is not truly "liberal": "according to Rousseau, the State has the right and the duty of penetrating into consciences to proceed to an *inspection* which, in my eyes, is terribly similar to an inquisition" ("La Religion Civile selon Rousseau," p. 167). A careful study of the relevant texts would show that Derathé fails to consider Rousseau's distinction between actions and beliefs (cf. the remarks of Jean Fabre, R. A. Leigh, Pierre Burgelin, and Sven Stelling–Michaud, *ibid*., pp. 171–72, 174–76). Moreover, Derathé's use of the standards of "liberal" society to judge Rousseau is rather misplaced, for Rousseau never failed to criticize this conception of political life. The dogmas of civil religion are presented as a matter of "right," distinct from the "political considerations" necessarily governing the application of the "principles" of political right. Moreover, Rousseau's principles define a closed or self-sufficient political community, governed by *laws* based on universally shared *prejudices* and morals. Cf. *Con-*

A · THE FLEXIBILITY OF PRINCIPLES OF POLITICAL RIGHT

Examination of Rousseau's science of the legislator shows conclusively that he did not content himself with the formulation of abstract principles of political right. Like a frictionless surface in mechanics, Rousseau's principles of legitimacy (symbolized by the concept of the general will) can never be fully realized in practice; they can only be applied to political reality if the particular circumstances of each society are fully taken into account. Rather than leave such questions of practical application entirely to the prudence of the individual statesman, Rousseau considered it necessary to develop a science of the conditions that will determine how close one can come, in any given society, to satisfying all the requirements of "strict right."

The general rules guiding political prudence do not have any simple relationship to the logic of the general will, for in some cases they merely complement it (by indicating the circumstances in which a healthy regime is possible), whereas in others they modify what appear at first glance to be invariable principles (by revealing the inherent contradictions between "the nature of things" and the requirements of political right). But even the latter maxims—such as those which reveal that the continuous proportion between sovereign, government, and people is impossible to achieve—are *logically* consistent with the principles of political right; they merely indicate why the human condition does not allow political perfection. It is therefore hard to see why many commentators have accused Rousseau of the "contradictions" which, according to Jean Jacques, were essentially in the "things" and not in his doctrines.[216]

---

trat social, IV, viii (P, III, 467). Ultimately, few liberals have recognized that *every* society is, to some extent, closed.

[216] For example, Lecercle analyzes Vaughan's distinction between the "abstract" and "concrete" parts of the *Contrat social* as follows: "These two parts are not in agreement. For, having asserted that there is only one possible formula for the contract and that the slightest variation makes it illegitimate, he starts to study the concrete geographical and historical conditions in which the legislator must operate, and he sees, following Montesquieu, that all peoples are not ready for freedom. . . . Is there a contradiction? Yes, because the point of departure is idealist. Rousseau at first defines an ideal without contact with the real, and he has plenty of difficulty in getting back to reality. . . . Thus Rousseau defines the democratic ideal in the absolute. Legislators will convert what they can of [the ideal] into facts, taking into consideration natural necessities" ("Introduction," *Du Contrat social* [ed. Lecercle, pp. 30–31]). The point, of course, is that Rousseau saw the difficulty so well that he tried to show the legislator precisely what the "natural necessities" were and how the

To trace out fully the manner in which Rousseau conceived of his political thought as a guide to sound political action, it would be necessary to study in detail the relationship between the *Social Contract* and the works in which Rousseau applied his teaching to concrete circumstances. Although the most obvious of these works are Rousseau's constitutional proposals for Corsica and Poland (in which he acts as legislator or advisor to the legislator), it would be equally necessary to consider his two major studies of Geneva: the *Letter to d'Alembert* and the *Letters Written from the Mountain*. Because such a task is far beyond the limits of this work, a single, albeit crucial example will have to suffice.

Since the inalienable sovereignty of the people and the ministerial character of magistrates or deputies are two of the central principles of political right, it is appropriate to indicate how Rousseau interpreted them in proposing a constitution for Poland. Although it would be preferable to reduce the size of Poland or to make it a "federated government" in which each Palatinate would have its own "particular administration,"[217] Rousseau consents to propose institutions for a central government (despite his preference for the small city).

One of the greatest inconveniences of large States . . . is that the legislative power cannot itself appear in them, and can only act by deputation. That has its bad and its good, but the bad predominates. The legislator in a body is impossible to corrupt, but easy to fool. Its representatives are fooled with difficulty, but easily corrupted.[218]

To check this evil, Rousseau proposes to make it difficult for an individual to participate in "two consecutive" Diets or parliaments and, more particularly, to "subject the representatives to follow exactly their instructions and render strict account to their constituents."[219]

Rousseau underlines the flexibility of his principles by the way in which he describes the Polish Diet, whose members (nonces) were to be elected by Dietines containing all citizens (in effect, the nobles only).[220] Rousseau insists on the ultimate necessity of enfranchising

---

principles of right would have to be modified in order to be put into practice. If this is "contradictory," then any applied science must be said to contradict the theoretical science upon which it rests.

[217] *Gouvernement de Pologne*, v (P, III, 970–71).

[218] *Ibid.*, vii (978–79). Note how Rousseau's judgment rests on his preference for virtue over enlightenment.

[219] *Ibid.* (979–81). Cf. n. 123 of this chapter.

[220] *Ibid.*, vi (972–74); vii (979–80).

the serfs and bourgeoisie so that they may participate in the Dietines, explicitly equating this requirement of his principles of political right with the "law of nature":

> The law of nature, that holy, imprescriptable law which speaks to the heart and reason of man, does not permit that the legislative authority be thus restricted [i.e., to the nobility], and that the laws oblige anyone who has not voted personally, like the nonces, or at least by his representatives, like the body of the nobility.[221]

In terms of strict right, universal suffrage seems to be prior to direct legislative action by the sovereign peoples (despite the fact that both seem to be equally necessary according to the *Social Contract*).[222] The Diet, composed of popularly elected deputies, is effectively "the sovereign authority," and is "by its nature above the law"; although the constituents can punish the nonces for violating their instructions (with death if they so desire), they must "fully obey, always, without exception, without protest" any laws passed by the Diet (though, to be sure, with the right to make "representations" at its next session).[223]

Rousseau flatly states that these representative institutions are legitimate and consistent with his principles of political right:

> The principles from which these rules are deduced are established in the *Social Contract*.[224]

Indeed, even in the *Social Contract* itself it appears that the election of a parliament is not contrary to right, provided that the deputies are strictly held to account and are responsive to their constituents.

> The English people thinks it is free; it is greatly mistaken, it is only free during the election of members of Parliament; as soon as they

---

[221] *Ibid.*, vi (973). Rousseau adds: "One doesn't violate this sacred law impudently": the weakness of Poland is its punishment for violating the principles of right, which are perhaps called a law of nature because they cannot be ignored without harmful consequences. This passage is one of the most explicit equations of Rousseau's principles of political right with the law of nature that I have found in his works.

[222] Cf. *Contrat social*, II, i (P, III, 368–69); II, iv (373); III, xv (429–31); IV, i (438–39).

[223] *Gouvernement de Pologne*, vii (P, III, 980–81).

[224] *Ibid.* (981). The rules in question concern the provisions regarding the Polish Diet which have just been discussed. In the chapter dealing with the Diet, Rousseau refers to the *Contrat social* by name on three other occasions (*ibid.*, 977, 978, 988), thereby emphasizing the consistency between his practical proposals and his principles of right.

are elected, it is enslaved, it is nothing. In the short moments of its freedom, the use it makes of it certainly shows it deserves to lose it.[225]

While it is obvious that Rousseau's conception of the legitimate form of representation is different from that of Burke (according to which the representative need not follow the express wishes of his constituents),[226] it should be apparent that the principles of right do not preclude a well-regulated parliamentary government in societies which are too large to permit any other solution. "The same principle should occur in every well-constituted State" (i.e., the laws should be enactments of the general will), but this principle must be implemented "more or less . . . according to the form of government"; because a perfect political institution is impossible, the closer the approximation to the principles of political right, the better the regime.[227] These principles are "rules for observations" concerning political life or "a scale to compare to the measures one makes," not practical proposals in themselves.[228]

B · THE STATUS OF POLITICAL PHILOSOPHY

The flexibility with which Rousseau assumed his theoretical ideas would be applied to political life reflects his general conception of the relationship of philosophy to human practice. Rousseau continuously insisted that actions are more important than words. Immorality is, essentially, saying one thing and doing another—or violating a general rule which everyone else obeys and from which the corrupt individual exempts himself while pretending to obey. Rousseau criticized the popularization of scientific knowledge because he thought it contributed to such immorality; he did not condemn philosophy or science in every form, but only when studied or "cultivated" by the people (as opposed to "the few").

In this sense, actions—and hence practical utility—provide a criterion for judging thought. But pure thought or philosophy is the search for truth as an end in itself; this quest is, indeed, only "nat-

[225] *Contrat social*, III, xv (P, III, 430). Note that the English *are* free when electing their representatives, and that Rousseau's criticism is directed to the way the English *use* their freedom to vote. The corruption of the English electoral system in Rousseau's time must, of course, be kept in mind when reading this passage. Cf. also the equation of "the consent *of the people* or of *its representatives*" (*Économie Politique* [P, III, 270]).

[226] Edmund Burke, "Speech to the Electors of Bristol," in *Works*, 9 vols. (Boston: Little, Brown & Co., 1839), II, 10–14.

[227] *Contrat social*, III, ii (P, III, 401); III, iv (405). See above, chap. VI.

[228] *Émile*, v (G, 585, 597).

urally good" because it is the *action* of an isolated, self-sufficient human mind, seeking wisdom for its own worth, independent of any social considerations of utility. As a result there is a disproportion between science and society, or between the ultimate activity of the individual philosopher (the search for truth in solitude) and the criterion of utility in social actions (the virtue of the citizen).[229]

The definition of immorality as exempting oneself secretly from generally binding rules applies to the action of the solitary philosopher as well as to any other man. Although doubting socially accepted dogmas, he appears to obey their external commands; if he also isolates himself as a useless member of society, Rousseau does not hesitate to call the learned man—or any man—a "rascal" or "the most wicked of men." Rousseau's condemnation of the "idle" philosopher in the name of civic virtue does not, however, detract from the intrinsic superiority of the solitary dreamer or thinker. The true philosopher simply rejects the claims of social morality in the name of personal independence and natural goodness. The moral consequences of the *re*-search for truth (which every wise man must make for himself) are irrelevant to the "god-like" freedom it gives to the researcher.

One must, however, distinguish the immorality of teaching or employing the search for knowledge (which, being social, can be judged in terms of morality) and the personal quest for wisdom (which is trans-social or naturally good). Rousseau did not mean that the findings of philosophic inquiry are always unrelated to social action. The notion that the philosopher and his society are intrinsically opposed to one another is, in itself, a truth of philosophy; the true philosopher knows that the search for wisdom, beneficial to himself, may harm others if openly taught—and thereby recognizes that certain kinds of knowledge should guide public activities if they are to be healthy or successful.

It follows that, even in isolation, the wise man must decide whether to maintain silence or to use his wisdom in society for the good of others. Rousseau personally chose the second course (at the cost, according to his own account, of personal misery). He related his thought to action by publishing his major works for public consumption, and by applying his abstract ideas to particular cases (be it his own life or the projected constitution for Poland). Even if this was merely because he lived in a corrupt era, it implies that sometimes the public demonstration or diffusion of theoretical knowledge is pru-

[229] Cf. above, chap. v.

dent. Furthermore, Rousseau claimed that the truth is universal and said that he wrote for all time, not merely for his corrupt fellows; to some extent, knowledge is necessary as a means of assuring human happiness.

It is important, however, to distinguish two kinds of knowledge: philosophy proper (metaphysics or the truth about the whole), which is *always* open to "insuperable doubts" and is never really known by men; and the contingent understanding of experience, which can be known (though the truths so discovered can never transcend the realm of the experience concerned). Metaphysics is almost always socially dangerous because it can destroy healthy belief without ever truly establishing moral or political duties; given the limitations of human reason, the stage of doubt engendered by an attempt to understand the inner nature of the universe can never be replaced by knowledge that is demonstratively certain to others.

In contrast, philosophy or science based on and confirmable by experience, when properly used by the few who are truly wise, can be socially useful. In corrupt circumstances, the open teaching of the truth undermines unjust prejudices, making possible salutary change; moreover, such reforms must be directed by prudence, whose most important lesson is that all change need not be for the better. Where all popular faith has been effectively destroyed and replaced by hypocrisy and vice, it may even be suitable to discuss metaphysical questions in public, provided that in so doing one leads the common men toward healthier or more natural prejudices consistent with virtue— or at least with goodness.

Inside the perfectly just society, the open exchange of truth, which necessarily implies philosophical doubt of social customs and dogmas, is replaced by public opinion, healthy prejudice, and educational institutions based on a common faith. But all of these social institutions have been created by man, and the legislator or statesman, to establish or maintain popular morals, needs knowledge of men and their behavior. Even the restraints on the public dissemination of science in the virtuous civil society are based on the truth that such an action destroys morality. Hence Rousseau's thought implies that, in every possible case, the discoveries of science or philosophy must influence human life.

It might be objected that Rousseau did not believe in the possibility of salutary action except in rare cases because he saw history as a necessary degeneration from a primitive golden age. Even granting that he was a "pessimistic evolutionist" (to use Jouvenel's phrase),[230] it would not follow that Rousseau was indifferent to action in this world. On the contrary, since the good act is normally a matter of choosing the lesser evil, knowledge of the necessary rules governing social change is only useful as a guide to action. Rousseau did not analyze the state of nature to induce men to universal quietism, but rather to provide a criterion of judgment that would not, at the same time, impel men to actions doomed to failure. Of course, Rousseau was well aware that knowledge is not the *only* thing necessary for success—in politics one also needs luck and a certain boldness. He knew that the characteristics of the philosophers are not those of the political hero, but he insisted that the latter can, without prudence, do far more harm than good. And for Rousseau, prudence can only be firmly established on knowledge of man and physical nature.

At the end of his career, as at the beginning, Rousseau believed that his defense of human freedom in its various forms was a defense of the "truth." Rousseau's motto thus points to the sovereign status of philosophy—and especially political philosophy—as the science which determines that most important of all questions, how man should live: *Vitam impendere vero.*

C · A FINAL COMMENT: ROUSSEAU AS A WRITER

For some, the foregoing analysis will have been gravely deficient in one respect: in treating Rousseau as a philosopher, his status as a writer or artist has generally been ignored. Although the most obvious indication of this bias lies in the failure to analyze his great novel, the *Nouvelle Héloïse*, Rousseau's influence on the style and substance of modern literature could be shown equally well from his more philosophical writings. In any event, many commentators would argue that the origins of the romantic period, if not of modern existentialism, can be traced to Rousseau's appeal to sensibility and nature, to his quest for a unified and truly happy existence, or to his attempt to depict the inner life of an artistic or sensitive soul (as, for example, in the *Confessions, Dialogues,* and *Reveries*).[231]

---

[230] Cf. Bertrand de Jouvenel, "Rousseau the Pessimistic Evolutionist," pp. 83–96; and *idem.,* "Rousseau, Évolutionniste Pessimiste," *Rousseau et la Philosophie Politique* (Paris: Presses Universitaires de France, 1965), pp. 1–19.

[231] E.g., Georges May, *Rousseau par lui-même* (Paris: Seuil, 1961), p. 177, *et passim;* Daniel Mornet, *Rousseau: l'homme et l'oeuvre* (Paris: Hatier-Bovin, 1950), pp. 99–100, 166, *et passim*; Jean Starobinski, *Rousseau: le transparance et l'obstacle* (Paris: Plon, 1957); Pierre Burgelin, *La Philosophie de l'Existence de J. J. Rousseau* (Paris: Presses Universitaires de France, 1952). But cf. J. H. Broome, *Rousseau: A Study of His Thought* (London: Arnold, 1963), pp. 209–10.

Before presenting a critical appreciation of Rousseau's political philosophy, these remarks are in order if only to suggest the necessarily incomplete character of any book on Rousseau, however extensive. The foregoing analysis has attempted to present a coherent commentary on the major works of Rousseau's philosophic "system." In so doing, the intention has been to explain, insofar as possible, everything in these texts (rather than to select particular passages in order to highlight one or another of the many themes which the reader of Rousseau is led to consider). In the last analysis, however, his books are still living precisely because they concern our own lives and problems, and not merely because they present Rousseau's overall system. Having attempted to look at the texts from the inside, as it were, to see Rousseau's meaning, it is now necessary to view them in terms of the problems of our own day. That this is even possible is sufficient evidence of Rousseau's greatness as a writer and thinker.

CONCLUSION:
SOME CRITICAL REFLECTIONS

1 · *The Continuing Relevance of Rousseau's Political Philosophy*

One of the greatest problems in studying a political philosopher is caused by a confusion of two different levels of analysis. The study of Rousseau's philosophic works is merely a sterile exercise if their relevance to persisting human and social problems is not seen, but all too often it is hard to know where Rousseau is being analyzed and where the commentator is introducing his own attitudes and ideas. Although a desire to avoid this confusion has led me to discuss Rousseau's "system" on its own terms, such a textual analysis would be incomplete without a few comments concerning the relevance and validity of Rousseau's philosophy.

Rousseau himself pointed out that his thought was in many respects paradoxical; as he remarked in the *Émile*: "I would rather be a man of paradoxes than a man of prejudices."[1] Whatever the aspects of Rousseau's personal character which reinforced this tendency, he claimed that paradox was an inevitable consequence of philosophic "reflexion," and it is not hard to see that what so often appear to be Rousseau's contradictions arise from the intellectual problems as he saw them. For Rousseau, the nature of man and society could not be understood without reference to the tension between classic thought, especially as represented by Plato, and the scientific tradition originated by such thinkers as Machiavelli, Hobbes, and Bacon; precisely because he accepted many of the innovations of the moderns, Rousseau felt the necessity to reassert themes that had been emphasized by the ancients.[2]

Today, under the overwhelming impact of the successes of modern natural science, there are few who turn to classical philosophy on the assumption that it contains valid truths; the study of works which Rousseau took most seriously has largely been relegated to

[1] *Émile*, II (G, 82).
[2] See above, esp. chap. II, § 5; chap. IV, § 3; chap. VIII, § 1.

specialists in the history of ideas. At the same time, however, there is a growing awareness that the pursuit of technological progress and the increased satisfaction of material wants are insufficient as ends in themselves. If, as seems entirely likely, the next century will witness the discovery and control of the genetics of human reproduction, to what use will such power over nature be put? The development of nuclear weapons (not to mention the emergence and spread of totalitarian regimes, based on modern technology and established in the name of material well-being) should be sufficient evidence that the proper ends of human life are not sufficiently defined by a projection of the progress of natural science into the political sphere.

Because criticism of the effects of unrestrained scientific development served as Rousseau's philosophic point of departure, his thought remains highly relevant to contemporary problems. The dilemma now facing political philosophy—which was also Rousseau's dilemma—has been nowhere stated with more clarity than in the following passage by Leo Strauss:

> We are all in the grip of the same difficulty. Natural right in its classic form is connected with a teleological view of the universe. All natural beings have a natural end, a natural destiny, which determines what kind of operation is good for them. In the case of man, reason is required for discerning these operations: reason determines what is by nature right with ultimate regard to man's natural end. The teleological view of the universe, of which the teleological view of man forms a part, would seem to have been destroyed by modern natural science. . . . Two opposite conclusions could be drawn from this momentous decision. According to one, the nonteleological conception of the universe must be followed up by a nonteleological conception of human life. But this "naturalistic" solution is exposed to grave difficulties: it seems to be impossible to give an adequate account of human ends by conceiving of them merely as posited by desires or impulses. Therefore, the alternative solution has prevailed. This means that people were forced to accept a fundamental, typically modern dualism of a nonteleological natural science and a teleological science of man. . . . The fundamental dilemma, in whose grip we are, is caused by the victory of modern natural science. An adequate solution to the problem of natural right cannot be found before this basic problem has been solved.[3]

[3] *Natural Right and History* (Chicago: University of Chicago Press, 1953), pp. 7–8.

Rousseau's thought provides a clear example of the "typically modern" predicament defined by Strauss, for it is based on an acceptance of modern natural science and a rejection of hedonist political orientations.

Rousseau tried to discover a means of returning to the classical practice of political and social life, on the presumption that the good for man can be defined with reference to his nature. Yet to do so, he relied on a scientific study of the evolution of the human species (the *Second Discourse*) and an analysis of individual human development in terms of sensations and experience (the *Émile*). Hence the weaknesses and strengths of Rousseau's philosophical system illuminate the continuing questions of political philosophy.

This is not to say that Rousseau's own system is, in contemporary times, a satisfactory one. As Bertrand de Jouvenel has pointed out:

> All social evolution of the last two centuries has been contrary to the preferences of Jean-Jacques, as—incidentally—he had foreseen. His preference was for a rural society, in which men were in contact with nature, in which their principal activity was subsistence agriculture mixed with artisanal tasks, in which production for the market had little place, in which the division of labor was not extensive, in which taxes were paid in nature rather than in money, in which the development of needs and foreign commerce was discouraged, in which morals were stable, in which the State was small, in which institutions tended to maintain and accentuate distinctive national characters.[4]

The fundamental opposition between Rousseau's preferences and those of the present day (the latter being akin to enlightenment views that Rousseau bitterly attacked) has often been masked by the superficial similarity between his democratic principles and modern political ideas. Again, to cite Jouvenel:

> Aside from the influence of Rousseau on our sensibility, which is immense, his influence on our ideas presents a paradox. For the political ideas of the *Contract* have profoundly affected us, but the social ideas, which have a much larger place in the work of Rousseau, have not done so at all.[5]

It would seem that Rousseau's conceptions of the general will and

---

[4] "Rousseau, évolutioniste pessimiste," *Rousseau et la Philosophie Politique* (Paris: Presses Universitaires de France, 1965), p. 18.
[5] *Ibid.*

popular sovereignty have been of continuing influence despite—or is it because of?—the current irrelevance of Rousseau's own practical conclusions.

This paradox suggests that it is necessary to set to one side Rousseau's ideal of the small, agricultural, unenlightened society; only if we see more deeply into the relevance of his philosophic principles can we judge whether his rejection of the evolution of modern political society is an anachronism or a highly pertinent warning. In so doing, it will be convenient to begin with Rousseau's political teaching before turning to the *Émile* and the two *Discourses*.

2 · The Failure of Rousseau's System

A · THE *Social Contract*: THE UNTENABILITY OF ROUSSEAU'S
PRINCIPLES OF POLITICAL RIGHT

The very possibility of distinguishing between Rousseau's own preference for the classical city and his principles of legitimate government is far from accidental; it results from his distinction between "political right" and the "science of legislation." Since the conception of the general will in no way determines what is willed by the sovereign people, a regime oriented toward commerce, industry, and enlightenment can be, according to Rousseau's own principles, as legitimate as the kind of city he personally preferred; the only condition is that the ends of political society be consistent with general laws enacted by the citizen body as a whole.

The resulting approach to politics is obviously an attempt to resolve the modern "dilemma" defined by Strauss. Rousseau's principles of political right could appear to be consistent with a nonteleological science of man, for his formal logic of civil obedience is derived from the properties of the will acting in a Hobbesian state of nature. At the same time, Rousseau could claim to give due weight to man's natural ends by developing a science of legislation that reveals the impossibility of promoting or sustaining civic virtue in large-scale, enlightened, commercial societies (which seemed to be the inevitable consequence of Hobbesian or Lockean political philosophy).

Although Rousseau may have seen the political problem raised by the triumph of modern natural science more clearly than did the *philosophes*, the repeated misunderstanding of his protest against an industrialized urban civilization suggests that his solution suffers from a grave weakness. Rousseau's definition of political legitimacy is constructed on the assumption that the principles of right are similar to the principle of a frictionless surface in mechanics. As a result, Rousseau was forced to invert the priority of means and ends in his political teaching: the principles of right, being incapable of distinguishing the proper objectives of civil society, have the character of means to the end of securing obedience; in contrast, the science concerned with the ends of civil society becomes a prudential concern of secondary importance.

Reflection upon Rousseau's analogy between political right and a frictionless surface indicates more fully the danger of this derivation of formal conceptions of legitimacy from a nonteleological science of man. Modern physics has discovered that the laws of mechanics predict motion only within certain external conditions or parameters; at given levels of temperature, velocity, or mass, relationships that hold on the earth's surface no longer obtain. It has also been found that all the properties of moving bodies cannot be simultaneously measured with infinite accuracy; at some point, increased precision with reference to mass entails uncertainty with reference to velocity (and vice versa). As a consequence, it can be said that mechanical phenomena cannot be understood or measured without prior definition of the conditions being considered.

In natural science, such definitions or hypotheses do not create serious theoretical problems for two reasons. First, it is now generally accepted (as indeed Rousseau foresaw) that the propositions developed by natural scientists have only a hypothetical or conditional character, subject to further revision or rejection on the basis of new experiment and evidence. Second, the adoption of hypothetical conditions as the limit for one set of experiments or theories does not preclude the adoption of different parameters in other areas of inquiry; physicists and chemists can and do treat the same phenomena on the basis of different assumptions, with the ultimate hope that even if their immediate results are not convergent, a consistent explanation can or will be found.

Although the same remarks could be made concerning theories of man and society, the extension of scientific methodology to human affairs is open to an important objection. Whereas the atoms manipulated in an atomic accelerator are (as far as we can tell) indifferent to the physicist's objectives, the ends defined by statesmen are of vital concern to the men affected thereby. The environmental conditions that affect a political community are not always variables about which the citizen is indifferent; even if the influence of climate, history, or geography is hypothetical in the sense that it can be studied on a comparative basis and perhaps changed by human action, in the immediate present there are limits on economic development or political organization which cannot be modified at will. Since the pursuit of specific objectives by those exercising political power precludes contrary "experiments" within a single society, theories or ideas about politics, once widely disseminated, have a radically different character than scientific hypotheses concerning physical nature. Although the latter are not, by their nature, mutually exclusive, the adoption of political goals (even if supposedly based on a science of man) inevitably precludes the acceptance of contrary principles.

Rousseau was fully aware—as few thinkers of his time or ours—of the gap between scientific propositions and the assumptions or prejudices governing civil society. But his principles of right, seemingly consistent with a nonteleological natural science, appear impotent as a means of inhibiting the most enormous social experiments conducted in the name of scientific or pseudo-scientific theories of human nature; the most obvious of these theories—that of Karl Marx —has produced totalitarian political systems that sharply contradict Rousseau's own preferences, but could conceivably be justified in terms of the enlightened or true self-interest of a citizen body which has absolute sovereignty.

If Rousseau can hardly be taxed with responsibility for twentieth-century totalitarianism (and much less a preference for it), his principles are open to a subversion of this kind because he divorced the proper ends of man and society from his principles of political right. Having defined a logic of civil obedience that is purely formal, Rousseau tacitly admitted that the prudential science defining the good civil society was not an intrinsic or necessary part of his principles of political right, but merely a guide to their successful implementation. Rousseau was therefore forced—along with Machiavelli and Hobbes—to treat the difference between various forms of government primarily as a technical problem whose solution depends on knowledge of the "natural tendencies" of politically relevant phenomena. But as soon as the triumph of modern technology permitted man to conquer the natural relationships which Rousseau thought were "invincible," his definition of the *necessary* superiority of the simple, agrarian city became an anachronistic and purely personal preference—one is tempted to say, a pious wish—which can be rejected without abandoning his principle of popular sovereignty.

Rousseau was probably aware that his teaching concerning the general will could be subverted, and used to erect corrupt or tyrannical political systems; indeed, this may explain the blurring between principles of right and prudential maxims of government which characterized his revision of the *Geneva MS*. But because Rousseau defined political right in terms of the *will* as an abstract phenomenon, distinct from that which is willed, his thought could not be freed from this danger by such a superficial change.

Rousseau's legislative or political science is superior to those current scientific analyses of political life which imitate the natural sciences on the assumption that the ends or values of a society are beyond rational discussion, and hence must be taken as given. In contrast, Rousseau insists that this question is and must be part of any sane analysis of politics: "it is necessary to know what should be to judge well concerning what is."[6] But the attempt to divide the question of "what should be" into a definition of rightful obedience (as universally valid as the principles of mechanics) and a specification of the natural rules governing political success merely permits the characteristic problem of modern political philosophy to recur under a different guise.

This problem is often posed in terms of the concept of freedom. Rousseau's principles establish civic freedom and equality as the ends of political society. But as we have seen, equality is subject to prudential variations, for it is ultimately a means to freedom; the political models chosen by Rousseau—Sparta (which was based on the radical enslavement of the Helots) and Rome (whose laws effectively disenfranchised the poor in the most praiseworthy epoch of the republic) —show clearly enough the extent to which equality is of secondary priority. It is as an apostle of man's natural freedom that Rousseau condemns the development of property and the moral inequalities which necessarily arise in civil society.

By placing man's natural freedom at the core of his political philosophy, Rousseau increased the importance of determining the ends for which freedom can properly be used. At the same time, he was unable to define such ends in terms of political right by anything except an analogy with man's natural state, where the end of freedom was self-preservation in accordance with natural impulses. But as he so strongly insisted, the impulses arising in civil society are largely artificial and can be manipulated by governments: "it is certain that peoples are in the long run what the government makes them."[7] Since the return to the life of the savage is precluded by human evolution,

[6] *Émile*, v (G, 585).
[7] *Économie politique* (P, III, 251).

the healthy prejudices or opinions which should govern and restrain the artificial wants created in society cannot follow from the concept of freedom in itself. Rousseau was thus forced to relegate his own conception of the proper civic society to the status of a personal belief, subordinate to—and detachable from—the primary assertion that political life must be understood in terms of freedom.

B · THE *Émile*: THE UNTENABILITY OF ROUSSEAU'S CONCEPTION
OF THE CONSCIENCE AND FREEDOM

The decisive status of freedom and the questionable character of this concept as the basis of a political philosophy is nowhere more apparent than in the *Émile*. Analyzing the supposedly natural pattern of human development within society, Rousseau attempted to determine the natural limits on human freedom in order that the end or good life for man, as an individual, could be defined without ambiguity. To do so, it was necessary to study human education in terms of physical sensation, for otherwise Rousseau's philosophy would have been open to the objection that it ignored the findings of materialistic or nonteleological natural science. But Rousseau was passionately concerned to show that, on the basis of an analysis of physical sensations and experience, it was possible to describe a *natural man*, free from the variable social prejudices of time and place; only in this way would it be possible to suggest the end for the individual as a thinking being.

Rousseau could not leave this end as freedom in the abstract, for he admitted that the free pursuit of the means to satisfy desires and impulses, however circumscribed and good it may have been in the state of nature, was easily corrupted within civil society. Since Rousseau believed that civil society was unnatural and that it tended to moral decline and political tyranny, he could not define standards of social morality on the assumption that the just is identical to the legal. Doubting the practicability of his own political teaching in most modern States, and being opposed to that of Hobbes, Rousseau therefore tried to elaborate a natural morality for the individual living in corrupt times.

He was therefore forced to ascertain certain natural characteristics or impulses which are not subject to modification or destruction within society. From the moral perspective, the crucial aspect of this ineradicable nature of man is not freedom, but the conscience; this natural sentiment, derived from a careful training of pity, is an ingenious attempt to show that natural impulse is not simply governed by the desire for self-preservation. If pity is natural, there exists a physically determined impulse directed to the well-being of others rather than the immediate satisfaction of personal wants. The conscience, as a manifestation of social or "moral" sentiment in a rational being, can thus be considered natural, since it does not depend on the prejudices or customs of given civil societies. Insofar as Rousseau's premises are granted, it would appear that he has found a means of conciliating a materialistic explanation of the rise of the conscience and morality with a teleological conception of that which is naturally good for man.

The conception that freedom and the conscience are the essential natural characteristics of man is, however, open to question. Rousseau was well aware that the choice of certain objects as "good" and others as "bad" was the consequence of education in society and hence conventional. But he insisted that love of the good and aversion for the bad, in the abstract, were a natural consequence of the release of the conscience once men have learned to reason. This defense of the natural status of the conscience presumes that a human faculty, held in potentiality in the state of nature, could be released by conventional education within society.

Such an understanding of human nature is entirely tenable, and could be consistent with the most thoroughgoing materialist or non-teleological physics; it is perfectly comprehensible that, as the result of accidental causation, new forms or modes of being come into existence which were not actually present from the outset and yet are natural. In this respect, however, the traditional conception of reason as the basis of morality and natural right is as defensible as Rousseau's substitution of the conscience. Indeed, it is curious to note that Rousseau's attempted compromise with a materialistic science is far weaker than the classical understanding elaborated, for example, by Plato; whereas reason and the principles of logic appear to be characteristic of any calculating beings produced by accidental causation (including, one might argue, computers), the sentiments Rousseau attributed to natural man can be traced to the particular conventions arising under certain historical conditions.

The possibility that the conscience, unlike reason, is *totally* a product of man's training in society deserves serious consideration, for it perhaps explains why the *Émile*, unlike the *Social Contract*, is little read today as a serious philosophic work. Studies of the social primates (the animals most nearly resembling our evolutionary ancestors) and of primitive human societies reveal the close relationship between aggression within the species, the establishment of hierarchies within the group, and social bonds. More to the point, one scientist has written: "The use of intelligence for the fabrication of tools may have been a major contributing factor in the resolution of man's social conflicts."[8] As the experience of Nazi Germany graphically illustrates, Rousseau's premise that the conscience or pity is a more fundamental human attribute than reason can—to say the least —be opened to scientific doubt.

The same conclusion can be reached with respect to the sentiment of freedom itself, for modern psychology suggests that the sense of being free is determined by the relationship between what an individual believes *should* be the permissive range of action and what actually *is* permitted in a given environment. Since personal beliefs concerning appropriate behavior are subject to conditioning or social custom, what is free for one individual in one setting is repression for another. Rousseau was aware of this possibility, as is evident from his comments on slavery: "Slaves lose everything in their chains, including the desire to leave them; they love their slavery. . . ."[9] But if the slave can *feel* free, this feeling cannot define the ends for man—at most, it defines a stable condition in which men are satisfied by the potentialities opened to them. A rational definition of the situations which are *truly* free, whether for the individual or the citizen, is the necessary prerequisite for using freedom to define man's end, because this concept, insofar as it is used to characterize human nature, is empty and does not preclude the training of men to accept voluntarily the most abject and indecent standards of behavior.[10]

---

[8] M.R.A. Chance, "Resolution of Social Conflict in Animals and Man," in *Conflict in Society*, A.V.S. de Reuck and Julie Knight, eds. (London: J. & A. Churchill, 1966), p. 34. On the evidence concerning man's evolutionary origins and the relationship between human behavior and animal instinct—problems to which I will return in assessing Rousseau's *Second Discourse*—see Robert Ardrey, *African Genesis* (New York: Atheneum, 1961) and *The Territorial Imperative* (New York: Atheneum, 1966); Konrad Lorenz, *On Aggression* (New York: Harcourt, Brace, 1966); J. N. Spuhler, ed., *The Evolution of Man's Capacity for Culture* (Detroit: Wayne State University Press, 1959). These works, and the many others cited in them, reflect the emergence of a new science ("ethology" or the study of animal behavior), which permits us to reconsider the question of human nature from a new perspective. While it now seems possible to speake of natural roots for morality (see, for example, chapter VII of Lorenz's work, entitled "Behavioral Analogies to Morality"), the conscience does not seem to be an adequate ground for analyzing the phenomena in question.

[9] *Contrat social*, I, ii (P, III, 353).

[10] Cf. Robert Waelder, "Protest and Revolution against Western Societies," in *The Revolution in World Politics*, Morton A. Kaplan, ed. (New York: John

C · THE "PROFESSION OF FAITH": THE UNTENABILITY
OF ROUSSEAU'S METAPHYSICS

The necessity of defining human freedom in substantive terms, rather than as an absence of external constraint on the will, obviously concerned Rousseau himself. If his political teaching attempted to solve this problem by a definition of the healthy society which is, in the last analysis, separable from the principles of right, Rousseau's moral teaching for the individual rested on a conception of metaphysics and natural religion which is separable from his analysis of man's physical and mental development. But whereas this characteristic dualism resulted in the adoption of only part of Rousseau's political teaching, it has led to the total abandonment of his moral teaching (with, revealingly enough, a residual acceptance of many of his educational proposals).

It is no exaggeration to say that Rousseau's attempt to reconcile materialist physics and traditional morality by elaborating a natural religion is totally obsolete; like his preference for agrarian cities, it seems largely of antiquarian or biographical interest. The reason lies most particularly in the arguments in favor of metaphysical dualism presented by the Savoyard Vicar (and apparently held personally by Rousseau). The discoveries of modern physics have simply obliterated the distinction between "communicated motion" and "spontaneous motion," in turn derived from the conception that matter is naturally at rest; once it appears that the motion of matter (energy) and matter itself (mass) are different forms of the same phenomena —and that mass can be converted to energy, or vice versa, by purely material causation—Rousseau's reasoning falls to the ground.

From this perspective, it becomes obvious to the critic that Rousseau shifted (one wonders whether consciously or not) from the consideration of physical motion to the felt *sensation* of motion when presenting the Savoyard Vicar's metaphysics; to the argument that spontaneous and communicated motion are distinct, Rousseau adds a footnote in his own name that tacitly equates spontaneous motion and feeling.[11] This equation is a particularly clear example of the

---

Wiley, 1962), p. 7, and *idem.*, "The Concept of Justice and the Quest for an Absolutely Just Society," *Journal of Criminal Law, Criminology, and Police Science*, Vol. 57 (1966), esp. 3.

[11] When the Vicar describes the "visible universe" as "disparate and dead matter," Rousseau notes: "I have tried my best to conceive of a *living* molecule, without being able to succeed. The idea of matter *feeling without having senses* seems to me unintelligible and contradictory" (*Émile*, IV, "Prof. of Faith" [G, 329 and n.], italics added).

— 428 —

extent to which Rousseau emphasized sensation as the crucial element of life; whereas modern biologists and biochemists situate the distinction between organic and inorganic matter at the level of molecules of a certain size and complexity—and, in any event, modern physics assumes that internal motion is common to all atoms—Rousseau assumes that spontaneous physical motion must necessarily imply conscious sensation (which, according to the modern view, is only an attribute of particularly complex living organisms).

Rousseau was, of course, aware of the impossibility of proving the dualist metaphysics he derived from his analysis of matter. But having tried to establish a moral teaching compatible with modern science, it is indeed a cruel twist of fate that his metaphysical arguments have been rendered not merely dubious, but simply ridiculous by subsequent developments in the natural sciences. What Rousseau admitted to be a purely personal belief in the spirituality of the soul and the existence of God is thereby deprived of the little rational support which he was able to create for it. As a consequence, the image of Émile as the natural man can no longer claim philosophic value as a definition of the good life; it is, in the last analysis, a prescription for the private life of a given class of men at a given time, and not for man as man.[12]

[12] Although Strauss describes this aspect of Rousseau's thought as a return to "the noblest concern of the bourgeois" (*Natural Right and History*, p. 291), one could also describe Rousseau's image of the natural man as a family-oriented aristocrat. The *Émile* was directed to that class (not to the bourgeoisie), and aside from Saint Preux, all the central protagonists of the *Nouvelle Héloïse* are members of the nobility; in this perspective, Rousseau's friendship with so many French nobles takes on fuller meaning. But while the good life as described in the *Nouvelle Héloïse* and *Émile* seems particularly oriented to a certain kind of aristocrat, Rousseau himself came from what has been called the *petite bourgeoisie*: "it should not be forgotten that Rousseau was, from his childhood to his death, an artisan, bureaucrat, or minor employee just as much as a writer" (Michel Launay, "La Société Française d'après la Correspondance de J.-J. Rousseau," Société des Études Robespierristes, *Jean-Jacques Rousseau* [Gap: Imprimerie Louis-Jean, 1963], p. 22). Launay's article, esp. pp. 21–39, presents interesting evidence of Rousseau's role as a representative of those petty bourgeois who rejected the rise of industrialism and capitalism. In the last analysis, Rousseau's view of the good life is perhaps best understood as an appeal to all those, both aristocrats and common men, who opposed the modern industrial system; insofar as he transcends the interests of a given class, it is in the name of an attack on the economic and political principles of a specific era. This underlying theme explains the connection between the familial life of Émile or Julie and Rousseau's own existence as the *promeneur solitaire*; both are ultimately solutions for individuals who can be described as "classless" (*déclassée*) during the period of industrialization. Insofar as Rousseau speaks to "man as man," therefore, he does so from the perspective of a specific historical epoch (and hence primarily with reference to those who are cut off from the classes which characterize political society as we know it today).

Rousseau's attempt to develop a conception of human nature that was free from metaphysical implications was thus a double failure: at bottom, Émile's morality is based on a belief in natural religion which is dependent upon acceptance of an admittedly dubious metaphysics; and this metaphysics in turn has appeared, at least in the form presented by Rousseau, to be simply inconsistent with modern natural science. It follows that insofar as Rousseau's analysis of the natural development of man was intended to establish philosophic conceptions of moral freedom and human virtue, his system is a failure. What remains—namely his keen insight into human character, and especially into the artificiality of most wants and desires within advanced civil society—is a necessary corrective to many oversimplified current opinions, but is in need of a more satisfactory philosophical foundation.

D · THE *Second Discourse*, PART 1: MAN AS A SOCIAL ANIMAL

In this context, the *Second Discourse* appears as the single work on which Rousseau's philosophic system turns, for in it he established the primacy of natural freedom as the criterion for political philosophy. To be sure, Rousseau attempted in this work to protect his position by substituting the concept of human perfectibility for freedom, in order to insure that his dubious metaphysics would not infect his philosophical understanding of human nature. But here again the development of modern science has been cruel to Jean Jacques: once the evolutionary analysis he himself applied to man was generalized to all animal species, it became clear that, within certain limits at least, evolution and a process of self-perfection in response to the needs of survival were characteristic of all animals. Darwin's biological theories, subsequently confirmed by experimental evidence of the natural selection and modification of different species, render impossible a distinction between man and other animals on the basis of perfectibility, revealing the extent to which this notion was essentially a scientific or formalistic equivalent of Rousseau's concept of freedom.

To be sure, Rousseau's analysis is not thereby rendered totally irrelevant; he can still speak of the natural freedom of an isolated animal as an objective phenomenon in the sense that such an animal may not be dependent on any other member of its species. But the obliteration of the line between man and other animals makes it clear that the savage of the pure state of nature—or the higher primates from which homo sapiens developed—were merely animals, although

— 430 —

certainly animals of exceptional adaptability and learning capacity. At this point, it becomes difficult to see why the pure state of nature should be established as the criterion for civilized human life, since the acquisitions of the human species as it has evolved seem more relevant to political and social problems than any presumed characteristics shared with man's biological ancestors.

Even should this conclusion be contested in general, the description of man's primitive state in Part 1 of the *Second Discourse* is subject to grave reservations. It has been emphasized that Rousseau was well aware of these reservations concerning one capital point, namely the total isolation of man in the pure state of nature; Rousseau apparently presented this image in order to strengthen his contention that man was naturally free, since he knew of and even admitted the possibility that a continuing family relationship existed from the earliest times.

On this point, modern anthropology has provided evidence indicating that Rousseau's conception of human self-sufficiency cannot be presented as the original or animal condition from which man has evolved. Both higher primates, such as baboons and orangoutangs, and the simplest men studied by anthropologists in the last century have tended to live in small bands, usually larger than a single nuclear family. In itself, this would not be devastating for Rousseau's position were it not for the decisive role of leadership in these small groups: among both the higher primates and the simplest primitive tribes, the band is often led by an elder or dominant male, and individual behavior seems to be strongly conditioned by the activities of the group as a whole and the leader in particular.

Even if one were to base political philosophy on the animal beginnings, therefore, it would be necessary to conclude that man is naturally social and that, far from being totally independent, his survival depends to a certain extent on cooperative behavior. It is significant, for example, that violence within bands of higher primates tends to occur when the previously accepted ordering of individuals is challenged, particularly by a contest for leadership.[13] If, in this respect, the behavior of men in highly developed societies seems hardly unique, it also follows that violence in the state of nature is not solely due to the conflicting pursuit of self-preservation by isolated individuals. The discovery that even animal groups are organized in

[13] E.g., S. L. Washburn and I. De Vore, "The Social Life of Baboons," *Scientific American*, Vol. CCIV (June 1961), 70. See also the references in n. 8 of this chapter.

predictable ways suggests that it is not primarily or solely individual freedom which characterizes the phenomenon of human life; the order of social groups would appear to be as natural as the freedom which, for Rousseau, alone characterized man's primitive condition.

This does not mean, however, that Rousseau's evolutionary analysis of human nature is totally indefensible. In particular, his own awareness of the possibly social character of primitive life must be recalled; the decisive aspects of man's animal condition are stupidity, inability to reason, and the absence of language. On this point, it would be hard to deny that Rousseau's analysis deserves consideration; from this perspective, the *Second Discourse* remains a significant philosophical book. Since Rousseau admitted the possibility of animal cries and a simplistic "mechanical prudence," his view of the ignorance of primitive man by comparison with civilized man has not been overthrown by modern anthropology; given the discovery of refined implements and cave paintings (the latter being more significant as evidence of evolved religious beliefs than of artistic ability) which date back 40,000 years and more, Rousseau's reference to the "thousands of centuries" required "to develop successively in the human mind the operations of which it was capable" seems highly respectable.[14]

Rousseau's denial of the natural status of reason appears tenable largely because on this point he was attacking the traditional definition of man in the name of modern natural science (which, in this respect at least, has partially confirmed his "boldness"). But we may still question Rousseau's assertion that "on the principles I have established, one could not conceive of any other system that would not provide me with the same results";[15] despite the soundness of his view that man is the product of evolution, the existence of social groupings and human interdependence from a very early—if not the earliest—times has more of an impact on Rousseau's principles than he himself foresaw.

This is particularly apparent with reference to his attempt to replace sociability by pity as the basic natural impulse complementing the drive to self-preservation. As we have seen, pity is the root of all social affections and virtues according to Rousseau, but its natural status is questionable; in the pure state of nature, Rousseau was unable to provide conclusive evidence that pity operated effectively (and even implied that it did not do so). This means that for Rous-

[14] *Second Discourse*, Part 1 (P, III, 146).
[15] *Ibid.* (162).

seau pity has the same character as the conscience or reason: it is a potential human faculty released by the perfection of the species. Even granting that this evolution was the consequence of external or accidental causes, modern science has failed to establish any particularly natural priority of pity over reason.

On the contrary, the analogy of the higher primates living in simple bands would indicate that Rousseau's sharp distinction between love of oneself and *amour-propre* is questionable. Apparently even chickens and birds, not to mention baboons, have sufficient ability to calculate (or "reason" in the narrowest sense) to compare themselves with others, to recognize one member of the band as leader, and on occasion to engage in combat to dispute this primacy. If pride or *amour-propre* is the consequence of social life, and social life is natural to man, it would follow that *amour-propre* is at least as primeval as pity. Indeed, given Rousseau's admission of the weakness of pity in primitive beings and the absence of proof that mutual assistance among higher primates or primitive men is based on pity (as distinct from social habit and affection), it would appear that Rousseau's description of the order in which human sentiments arise should be reversed; pity, like the humanitarian virtues Rousseau derived from it, can probably be taken as a feeling characteristic of civilized life.[16]

Rousseau's insistence that pity is natural even for primitive man must therefore be seen as part of his general attempt to base a philosophic understanding of human nature on sentiments, an attempt which can be called "romantic" in the sense that it exalts natural impulses in place of reason. But Rousseau's philosophy as a whole, whatever its romantic elements, had a "tough" or "hard" side which cannot be dissociated from his attempt to build upon natural science. Since this effort has been rendered suspect, if not obsolete, by subsequent scientific hypotheses, it is tempting to overstate the sentimental aspects of Rousseau as a thinker. Indeed, this may well account for the widespread tendency to consider Jean Jacques as a literary figure rather than as a philosopher.

E · THE *Second Discourse*, PART 2: THE ORIGINS

OF CIVIL SOCIETY

It might be thought that the foregoing remarks concerning the natural sociability of man dispose of Rousseau's position in the *Second*

---

[16] In addition, there is now good ground for believing that one of the roots of social bonds, in addition to a general gregariousness, is aggression between members of the same species. Cf. Lorenz, *On Aggression*, esp. chap. VI ("The Bond").

Discourse, most particularly because they show the impossibility of adopting a contractual view of the origins of civil society. Surprisingly—and this will not be the last of the paradoxes of the continuing relevance of Rousseau—this is not the case. Quite the contrary, Rousseau's awareness that the family might be natural in the pure state of nature, while it does not suffice to justify his conception of the "simplest operations of the human soul," does indeed save much of his evolutionary analysis from being merely of historical interest. It should not be forgotten that Rousseau himself does not derive *all* society from contract, but only civil societies based on consciously man-made laws (as distinct from the slowly evolved customs and *moeurs* which characterize savage society).

From the perspective of modern anthropology, the astonishing point is not that a contractual explanation is untenable, but rather that some scholars (notably Lévi-Strauss) insist on the conventional character of primitive and pre-civilized societies; it may be, on this point, that Rousseau's error was to place the social contract too late in history! To be sure, it is not a question of a specific historical event —this would hardly be possible if man is naturally social, and in any event was never seriously claimed by Rousseau. The allegory of a contractual settlement between previously isolated individuals is mainly significant as an indication that the members of any human group consider social obligations as reciprocal *conventions*. This conception has two aspects: first, the members of any human group are ultimately aware that the pattern of their social interaction is a custom or "way" of doing things, subject to violation by individuals and —at least in some cases—to change; second, obligations are seen as reciprocal duties between individuals, rather than as a result of an unquestioned surrender of authority to men who then unilaterally impose duties on other members of the group.

Insofar as anthropological studies have concerned the simplest human societies (and insofar as these societies represent earlier stages of human evolution), it appears that groups of *men*—as distinct from animals—are conscious of the mutual character of their obligations as well as the customary or traditional origin of their modes of behavior. In this sense, something like a conventional bond seems to have existed in primitive societies prior to political organization on the basis of consciously man-made laws, manipulated more or less at will by those in authority.

If so, Rousseau's conception of the social contract must be preferred to that of Hobbes, for the dominance of an individual leader

(even among higher primates) cannot be taken as evidence of a re-
nunciation of natural rights by all other members of the group; on the
contrary, primitive bands seem to repose on tacit considerations of
mutual advantage which, when violated, can produce contests for
power or disruption of the group. But, curiously enough, the preemi-
nence of a single leader under these circumstances apparently depends on the nonmaterial gratifications enjoyed by those with authority. Hence the Hobbesian insistence on the natural status of pride
—denied by Rousseau—appears to be connected with a type of conventional bond not totally unlike that specified by Rousseau in his
critique of Hobbes![17]

Having said this much, it does not follow that Rousseau's outline
of human evolution as a whole—admittedly more hypothetical than
his denial of rationality and language in the pure state of nature—
withstands the test of recent scientific discoveries. In particular, his
attribution of the origin of property to the epoch in which agriculture and metallurgy were developed does not seem to be tenable.
Bands of higher primates (and other animals as well) often treat
their habitat as a possession to be defended, by violence if necessary,
against outsiders—much in the way Rousseau pictured the primitive
family's defense of its homesite early in the evolutionary process.
More significant, primitive tribes (according to Rousseau's analysis,
savage societies prior to the origin of property and civil law) have
virtually always clearly evolved concepts of private or communal
property as distinct from tenuous possession. Indeed, much of the
customary behavior among primitives is concerned precisely with the
allocation and ownership of goods, be they wives, animals, tools and
weapons, houses, or land; even among hunters and gatherers, whose
mode of subsistence is the simplest known and directly parallel to
that of higher primates, such notions of property exist.[18]

As with the social contract, therefore, it is necessary to place the
emergence of property at an earlier epoch than was admitted by
Rousseau, doubtless because man the tool-maker developed foresight
and reason (albeit to a limited extent) at a far earlier epoch than

[17] For characteristic descriptions of the simpler forms of primitive society
as studied by modern anthropology, see I. Schapera, *Government and Politics
in Tribal Societies* (London: Watts, 1956); Lucy Mair, *Primitive Government*
(Baltimore, Md.: Penguin, 1962), esp. pp. 35–36; Robert Lowie, *Primitive Society* (New York: Harper Torchbook, 1961), chap. XIII. The best introduction
to the work of Claude Lévi-Strauss is probably *Tristes Tropiques* (Paris: Union
Générale d'Éditions [Le Monde en 10/18], 1962).

[18] Cf. Schapera, *Government and Politics in Tribal Societies*, chap. I, with
Ardrey, *The Territorial Imperative*.

Rousseau thought possible. The result of these findings of anthropology, insofar as they are relevant to political philosophy, is that it is no longer possible to speak of the establishment of laws and civilized society as such a sharp break from the preceding stage of savage or primitive life. Exactly what characteristics *are* implied in the origins of what can be called civilization have not been fully defined, but certain of them can be suggested: first, a surplus of the means of subsistence; second, larger scale and more complex social organization, in which certain sub-groups are capable of manipulating such a surplus and devoting it to activities not immediately required for the self-preservation of all members of the society; and finally, advanced techniques, the most important of which—though perhaps it is not a necessary pre-condition for all civilizations—being the art of writing. A division of labor based on the establishment of property does not seem to be among these conditions, for uncivilized tribes often develop cooperative modes of behavior and frequently specialize certain tasks (most notably magic or religion).

The prerequisites for civil society are clearly not the consequence of a particular human agreement or social contract, but rather seem to have evolved under peculiar conditions at widely separated points on the globe and at different times. Moreover, the origin of higher civilizations does not seem to be connected with a voluntary surrender of rights to a community as a whole, as is the case in Rousseau's conception of the "right" or legitimate origin of civil societies; on the contrary, whereas the simplest primitive communities are characterized by a quasi-contractual relationship of mutual benefits for individuals or kinship groups, the earliest civilizations seem to rest on superior force or violence, which permitted one group to dominate another in order to form a larger and more complex society than was hitherto possible. This pattern is found among primitive societies with more complex political institutions as well, since the emergence of larger social systems capable of producing a surplus of goods at the disposal of a select sub-group has often been the consequence of violence rather than voluntary submission or contract.

Rousseau was, of course, totally aware of this possibility, and indeed—as has been shown—admitted that civil society probably originated as a result of force rather than from a free social contract. But if so, it seems hardly necessary to base political right on a presumably logical explanation of the kind of agreement which *could* have explained the origin of civil society had it been willingly adopted by free individuals. On the contrary, Rousseau's pessimism concerning the corrupting effects of civil society would have been more fully confirmed had he emphasized to the full the autocratic political tendencies found in virtually every community which first developed a higher civilization. Whether one thinks of the great Middle Eastern civilizations (Egypt, Babylonia, Assyria), those of the Far East (China and India), or those of the Western Hemisphere (the Incas and the Aztecs), the contrast between the relative freedom of the most primitively organized savage societies and the despotic tendencies of early civilizations is quite remarkable.[19]

We are thus led to the astonishing paradox that precisely because Rousseau's conception of human evolution has been largely contradicted by more recent scientific enquiry, his criticism of the development of large-scale, civilized, political societies has a certain—if only nostalgic—validity. Be that as it may, the admission that man is by nature a social being from his very beginnings casts doubt on the possibility of constructing a theory of political right in the particular terms chosen by Rousseau: if a contractual formulation for the basis of society is tenable, it seems to refer to a primitive or savage stage of social development and not to civil society, and in any event cannot be defined in terms of a free surrender of natural rights to a political community conceived of as an egalitarian body of previously free and independent individuals.

When considered in the light of the deficiencies of Rousseau's political teaching proper, as well as his conception of Émile as the natural man, these criticisms of the *Second Discourse* mean that freedom cannot be taken, at least as Rousseau took it, as the unifying concept in political philosophy. Whether one considers the simplest bands of higher primates or men, or the earliest civilizations—not to mention the highly developed political societies of our own day—it appears that the decisive problem for political right is the order or character of the social community.

Men cannot be considered as having been naturally free in the state of nature, if by this it is meant that he was isolated and hence the sole judge of his rights and duties (without reference to common customs or obligations shared with others). Man cannot be considered as morally free only when he has accepted, voluntarily, obligations derived

[19] Cf. Aristotle, *Politics* VII.1327b, cited above in n. 89 of chap. VII. On the origin of civilization and its connection with social coercion, see V. Gordon Childe, *Man Makes Himself* (New York: Mentor, 1951), esp. pp. 90, 106–12; Lewis Mumford, *The Transformations of Man* (New York: Harper, 1956), esp. pp. 44–70; S. N. Eisenstadt, *The Political Systems of Empires* (London: Free Press of Glencoe, 1963), pp. 13–16.

from a natural religion based solely on the arguments presented by the Savoyard Vicar, for these arguments have been made irrelevant by modern natural science. And societies cannot be considered as politically free when their rulers claim to be subject to the general will and permit the citizens to ratify their decisions in popular plebiscites, for modern technology has permitted men to establish the most thoroughgoing tyrannies while claiming to satisfy such formal criteria.

Insofar as political philosophy is defined as the quest for the just and the good for man in society, this quest cannot be separated from the question of the organization and ends of human society. In this sense, Rousseau's philosophy must be accounted as a failure precisely because his emphasis on freedom was an attempt to avoid this question in terms of right, displacing it instead to the realm of his prudential "science of the legislator." The assumptions that nature is "invincible" and that large-scale, commercial, and enlightened societies are ultimately doomed to destruction seem hardly self-evident at a time when science is conquering nature and the kind of community Rousseau thought most natural is being irreversibly destroyed by modern technology.

3 · *Rousseau's Most Defensible Work*: the First Discourse

It remains only to discuss the first of Rousseau's "major writings" and the one he himself felt the least perfect—a judgment shared by many critics. For Georges May, the *First Discourse* presents Rousseau's fundamental criticism of progress and moral corruption

in the weakest and perhaps most false form. Attributing the moral corruption of civilized man to the external forms of civilization in this work, he enclosed himself in a vicious circle from which he proceeded to spend the rest of his life trying to escape.[20]

For Bouchardy:

detached from its biographical context, it [the *First Discourse*] would doubtless lose the largest part of its interest for today's reader.[21]

If the fundamental structure of Rousseau's philosophic system is open to grave question, it would seem to follow that this work—the weakest link—need not deserve serious consideration. Yet the ultimate paradox of Rousseau is that the contrary is true: the *First Discourse*,

[20] *Rousseau par lui-même* (Paris: Seuil, 1961), pp. 50–53.
[21] "Introduction, *Discours sur les Sciences et les Arts*" (P, III, xl).

despite its rhetorical overstatement and "absolute lack of logic and order,"[22] remains Rousseau's most relevant philosophic work.

Lest this appreciation seem too shocking, it must first be noted that —as has been argued in chapter v—the *First Discourse* contains the germ of Rousseau's entire system. Yet in it Rousseau presents his ideas in a partial way, because he does not as yet commit himself to his ultimate definitions of moral freedom based on natural religion, natural freedom based on man's isolation in the state of nature, and civil freedom based on the formal logic of the general will. The arguments above have questioned the validity of the philosophic system which Rousseau elaborated to sustain his protest against the enlightenment, and not that protest itself; hence the critical rejection of his later works need not necessarily lead to a dismissal of the work which, to use May's terms, "sealed his destiny."

One can go further. The fundamental elements of Rousseau's *First Discourse* have a subtle connection with the remainder of Rousseau's thought which Jouvenel has aptly described as follows:

> The attack on the sciences and arts ultimately appears only as an attack appended to the cause that Rousseau was to sustain all his life, but it is an attack profoundly connected to it. And if he at first exaggerated their responsibility, most of the blows against them in the first *Discourse* remain valid in his corrected system.[23]

In this sense, one can say that the critique of the effects of the enlightenment, based on the inevitability of a tension between science and society, is both characteristic of Rousseau's philosophy and separable from his mature system.

This is not to say that the historical arguments proposed by Rousseau are always tenable as they stand, nor that his criticisms of eighteenth-century enlightenment exactly fit twentieth-century society. But beneath the arguments Rousseau directed to his contemporaries is a logic that he thought true in all times and places; the *First Discourse* was intended to "live beyond its century."[24] A glance at our own times reveals the surprisingly great extent to which Rousseau succeeded in this respect.

To begin with the most obvious fact of political life today, Western industrial societies have continued to develop and cultivate science

---

[22] *Confessions*, VIII (P, I, 352).
[23] "Essai sur la Politique de Rousseau," in J. J. Rousseau, *Du Contrat Social* (Geneva: Éditions du Cheval Ailé, 1947), p. 28.
[24] *First Discourse*, Pref. (P, III, 3).

and technology, as indeed Rousseau expected would be the case. This "progress" has coincided, as Rousseau predicted, with an expansion of the size of political communities, with an increasing economic and political interdependence of States, and above all, with a creation of new needs and demands whose satisfaction has become the primary end of the endeavors of most men and politicians. If the consequence has not always been "slavery" in the advanced industrial societies, it is nonetheless true that in some countries this epoch has produced a despotism based on advanced technology, permitting total control and mobilization of huge populations to a degree apparently never before attained (even in the despotisms of the earliest high civilizations).

Rousseau's principal point in the *First Discourse* was not, however, the specifically *political* risks of enlightenment; he was mainly concerned with morality. On this level, it is hard to deny that, to say the least, a moral uneasiness (if not nihilism) has coincided with unprecedented advances in scientific culture. Rousseau condemned the "base and deceptive uniformity" coinciding with material progress among "the men who form this herd called society"; leaving to one side impressionistic criticisms of current "conformity," it suffices to mention the sociological analyses of "mass society," vulnerable to manipulation by new means of communication and deprived of the social roots and beliefs which supported the moral standards of earlier generations.[25]

Rousseau attached particular importance to the effects of "luxury" (i.e., to the creation of new desires and wants which are not physically necessary—and, for that very reason, are all the more compelling as motives for behavior). Of all the statements in Rousseau's works, perhaps none rings truer today than his characterization of the results of this development: "Ancient politicians incessantly talked about morals and virtue, those of our time talk only of business and money." Given the unquestioned acceptance of the pursuit of wealth and material well-being in modern industrial society, Rousseau's insistent challenge commands attention: "what will become of virtue when one must get rich at any price?"[26]

To convince oneself that this question is not simply a matter of

---

[25] *Ibid.*, Part 1 (P, III, 8). Cf. José Ortega y Gasset, *The Revolt of the Masses* (New York: Norton, 1932); William Kornhauser, *The Politics of Mass Society* (Glencoe: Free Press, 1959); Herbert Marcuse, *One Dimensional Man* (Boston: Beacon Press, 1964).

[26] *First Discourse*, Part 2 (P, III, 19). For a typical example, see Barbara Ward, *The Rich Nations and the Poor Nations* (New York: Norton, 1962). The few modern exceptions to Rousseau's generalization prove its relevance,

rhetoric, one need but glance at some of the simplest news items as reflections of the morals of our time. On the political level, consider the striking contrast between Nathan Hale's dying words and the behavior of his modern American counterpart, Francis Gary Powers. On the private level, the quest for profit leads to the creation of artificial needs, the exploitation of the poor (who often pay more for inferior goods), and the pollution of public waterways and air spaces. To be sure, one can reply by pointing to innumerable examples of civic or moral virtue in recent times, but it would be folly indeed to deny that our age is above all marked by a hedonist quest for objects and pleasures, a quest which raises profound questions concerning the status of morality.

It has not been sufficiently recognized, in this respect, that Rousseau's critique of the "degrading" moral effects of "a multitude of futile concerns" released by the cultivation of artificial needs is not attributed to the sciences and arts as the direct or primary cause: "luxury rarely develops without the sciences and arts, and they never develop without it."[27] Enlightenment is a concomitant of the legitimized search for personal gratifications, but the latter can exist without the former and hence is not caused by it in any simple sense. This is particularly important because it exonerates Rousseau from at least one criticism of his *First Discourse* which would otherwise deserve serious consideration.[28]

Whatever the causal process involved, an objective consideration of our own era confirms Rousseau's claim that the pursuit of luxury and wealth based on scientific and technical progress coincides with grave social and moral problems. That many of the modern arts are, to use Jouvenel's phrase, "an educator of voluptuousness"[29] is amply revealed by the verses of the popular music dispensed on radios and

---

for those who speak of "morals and virtue" in political life today are most often men whose lives or political preferences are oriented to the pursuit of "business and money."

[27] *First Discourse*, Part 2 (P, III, 19, 20).

[28] Cf. Jouvenel's comment: "Can it be said that the social transformation which dissolves morals has the sciences and arts as its cause? . . . Rousseau wanted the sciences and arts to play a causal role. . . . This bold affirmation greatly contributed to the fracas concerning the *Discourse*. But far from being necessary to Rousseau's system, it establishes it falsely and weakens it" ("Essai sur la Politique de Rousseau," p. 27). Note that the subject of the *First Discourse* is: "Has the restoration of the sciences and arts *tended* to purify morals?" Although Rousseau speaks of "the evils caused by our vain curiosity," he is so far from attaching sole causal responsibility to the sciences and arts that he explicitly indicates that they arise from vices—i.e., from pre-existing moral deficiencies (*First Discourse*, Part 2 [P, III, 18]).

[29] Jouvenel, "Essai sur la Politique de Rousseau," p. 28.

records, not to mention certain aspects of modern literature. With respect to the effects of the theatre, especially as Rousseau later specified them in the *Letter to d'Alembert*, Jouvenel's statement is so apt that one cannot but cite it:

> How can its prophetic character not be recognized today? When it was written, spectacles were only the food of a slim stratum of the population. The frequentation of spectacles has only been able to become a habit for an entire people in our days. One must be indeed blind not to admit the disastrous effect. . . . Who would dare deny that movies have made souls more impressionable and more mobile, have disposed hearts to follow their most superficial impulsions and to create new ones, have provided minds with false images and taught them to be fooled by pretenses? Who would not assert that today's men seek everywhere—and particularly in public life—romanesque lies and dramatic emotion for which the screen has given them the taste.[30]

As for Rousseau's attack on orators, as Jouvenel has pointed out, the modern equivalent is that

> art of persuasion which, provided with stentorian instruments, is called propaganda. . . . Can we believe that it makes citizens, when we see that it makes barbarians?[31]

That one of the most perceptive political scientists of our day should find such striking confirmation of Rousseau's central thesis is, in itself, disturbing evidence that the *First Discourse* cannot be complacently dismissed from philosophic consideration.

Perhaps more revealing than the analysis of contemporary life in the West (on which, after all, perspective is difficult to gain) is the general pattern of historical development in the mid-twentieth century. Rousseau reminded his readers of the conquest of wealthy empires by poorer rivals, and it requires particular obtuseness to fail to see, in the process of decolonization, the successful challenge to Western democracies by underdeveloped or backward peoples with but a fraction of the economic and military power of their former colonial conquerors. Increasingly, present world affairs are being seen as a contest between the developed societies of the Northern hemisphere and the poorer peoples of the Southern hemisphere, a contest in which the industrialized West is increasingly unable to impose its will on peoples it formerly dominated with ease. Whatever the immediate

[30] *Ibid.*, p. 29.   [31] *Ibid.*, p. 30.

successes due to accumulated military and technological superiority, the long-range implications of this challenge to the great industrial powers cannot be ignored without totally misunderstanding the predicament of modern man.

If the *First Discourse* is, of all Rousseau's philosophic works, the one which speaks most directly to the crises of our time, how are we to account for this paradoxical fact? Jouvenel, who has seen this relevance more clearly than any other recent commentator, implicitly points to the answer by emphasizing the source of Rousseau's inspiration:

> Why seek obscure precursors for Rousseau? He has all of classical antiquity. His protests against a society carried away by the taste for wealth, the seductions of curiosity, and the attraction of new things, his idea of a community formed for virtue and constant in the simplicity of its morals, all of that is in Plato, Plutarch, Seneca, Tacitus.[32]

Since Rousseau's return to positions held by classic philosophy seems to be the most illuminating teaching he has left us, his failure to reconcile these traditions with modern science suggests—and this is the ultimate paradox—the necessity of returning to these classics themselves. The basic problem "caused by the victory of modern science" remains to be solved; our predicament requires, as for Rousseau, a confrontation of the scientific optimism of modern opinion with the political pessimism of ancient philosophy.

[32] *Ibid.*, p. 35. See also pp. 21, 25–26, 29, 32, 36–38, 41–42, 44, 56, 64–65, 89–91, 138–43, 149, 153–54.

SELECTED BIBLIOGRAPHY

This bibliography does not claim to be exhaustive, since very complete listings of the commentaries and editions of Rousseau's writings are already available in the *Annales de la Société Jean-Jacques Rousseau*. Instead, it has seemed more useful to present a representative sample of relatively recent primary and secondary sources, with annotations that may be of assistance to the student. References to works written before 1930 will be found in abundance in more recent scholarship; see especially the books listed below as #33 and #35. It must be added at once, of course, that the critical remarks below represent personal assessments which would often *not* be shared by other scholars.

I. EDITIONS OF ROUSSEAU'S WORKS

A. In French

1. *Oeuvres Complètes*. Edition published under the direction of Bernard Gagnebin and Marcel Raymond.
   Paris: Bibliothèque de la Pléiade [Gallimard], 1959-present.
   Definitive scholarly edition, following original spelling, punctuation, and capitalization. Extensive introductions, notes, and variants to each work as well as bibliographical notices.
   Vol. I: *Confessions, Rousseau Juge de Jean Jacques, Rêveries d'un Promeneur Solitaire*, autobiographical fragments and biographical documents (1959). Ed. Bernard Gagnebin, Marcel Raymond, Robert Osmont.
   Contains a useful chronology as well as the essential materials for understanding Rousseau's biography.
   Vol. II: *La Nouvelle Héloïse*, theatre (including *Préface à Narcisse*), poetry, literary essays (1961). Ed. Henri Coulet, Bernard Guyon, Jacques Scherer, Charly Guyot, Bernard Gagnebin.
   Guyon's introduction to the *Nouvelle Héloïse* is particularly useful.
   Vol. III: *Discours sur les Sciences et les Arts*, writings in defense of *First Discourse, Discours sur l'Origine et les Fondements de l'Inégalité, Économie Politique*, first version of *Contrat social* (*Geneva MS*), *Contrat social, Fragments Politiques*, writings on the

Abbé St. Pierre, *État de Guerre, Lettres Écrites de la Montagne, Projet de Constitution pour la Corse, Considérations sur le Gouvernement de Pologne, Depêches de Venise* (1964). Ed. François Bouchardy, Jean Starobinski, Robert Derathé, Sven Stelling-Michaud, Jean-Daniel Candaux, Jean Fabre, Bernard Gagnebin.

Indispensable working instrument for all future work on Rousseau's political philosophy. Among the various introductions, frequently of use, the essay by Fabre on the *Considérations sur le Gouvernement de Pologne* deserves special note. Volume is occasionally marred by typographical errors and misinterpretations in the editorial notes.

2. *The Political Writings of Jean Jacques Rousseau.* Ed. C. E. Vaughan.

2 vols.; Cambridge: Cambridge University Press, 1915. Reprinted, Oxford: Basil Blackwell, 1962.

Prior to the Pléiade, the best scholarly edition. Modernized punctuation, capitalization, and spelling. Vaughan's remarks in the general introduction (Vol. I) are often highly debatable.

Vol. I: *Second Discourse, Lettre à Philopolis, Économie Politique, État de Guerre*, fragments, writings on the Abbé St. Pierre, Diderot's *Droit Naturel*, and the *Geneva MS* (first version of *Contrat social*).

Vol. II: *Contrat social*, last four *Lettres Écrites de la Montagne*, passages illustrating the *Contrat social* (including selections from the *Émile*), *Projet de Constitution pour la Corse, Considérations sur le Gouvernement de Pologne*.

3. *Du Contrat Social, Discours sur les Sciences et les Arts, Discours sur l'Origine de l'Inégalité, Lettre à d'Alembert, Considérations sur le Gouvernement de Pologne, Lettre à M. de Beaumont.*

Paris: Garnier, n.d., ("Classiques Garnier").

Currently published vulgate of these works. Numerous textual errors; few editorial notes. (For the *Contrat social*, a ready indication of whether any given edition has been properly established is found in the first sentence of Book III, chapter ii, which should read: " . . . *il faut distinguer ici le prince et le gouvernement.*" Garnier, following Hachette and other 19th-century vulgate editions, reads "*principe*" instead of "*prince.*")

4. *Correspondance Général de J. J. Rousseau.* Ed. Théophile Dufour and P. P. Plan.

24 vols.; Paris: Armand Colin, 1924-1934.

An invaluable source, despite scholarly faults (which have led to the preparation of a new edition of the correspondence—see #5).

5. *Correspondance complète de Jean-Jacques Rousseau.* Ed. R. A. Leigh.

    Geneva: Institut et Musée Voltaire, 1965-present.

    A truly scholarly edition. Only Vols. I-IV have appeared to date.

6. *Discours sur les Sciences et les Arts.* Ed. George R. Havens.

    New York: Modern Language Association of America, 1946.

    Excellent critical edition. Introduction includes a valuable analysis of the history of the *First Discourse.*

7. *Discours sur l'Origine et les Fondements de l'Inégalité parmi les Hommes.* Ed. Jean-Louis Lecercle.

    Paris: Éditions sociales, 1954.

    Introduction resumes Rousseau's life and emphasizes the dialectical, but pre-Marxian character of his thought. Text follows Vaughan.

8. *Du Contrat Social.* Ed. C. E. Vaughan.

    Manchester: University Press, 1918.

    Excellent critical edition of the text, with lengthy introduction subject to many of the same reservations as indicated for #2.

9. *Du Contrat Social.* Ed. Maurice Halbwachs.

    Paris: Aubier [Éditions Montaigne], 1943.

    Extensively commentated critical edition. Introduction emphasizes the philosophic antecedents of Rousseau, with particular emphasis on Hobbes.

10. *Du Contrat Social.* Ed. Bertrand de Jouvenel.

    Geneva: Éditions du Cheval Ailé, 1947.

    One of the most beautiful editions. Supplemented with notes containing the marginalia of Voltaire and other contemporaries. On the excellent introduction, see #47.

11. *Du Contrat Social, Discours sur les Sciences et les Arts, Discours sur l'Origine de l'Inégalité parmi les Hommes.* Introduction by Henri Guillemin.

    Paris: Union Générale d'Éditions ["Le monde en 10/18"], 1963.

    Introduction is a marvelous example of criticism based on secondary sources and quotations out of context. Text follows vulgate (cf. #3).

12. *Du Contrat Social.* Ed. J.-L. Lecercle.

    Paris: Éditions Sociales, 1963.

    Introduction is a curious blend of traditional French analysis and Marxist criticism. Text follows Vaughan.

12a. *Du Contrat Social.*
  Paris: "Garnier-Flammarion," 1966.
  New paperback edition.
13. *Émile ou de l'Éducation.* Ed. François and Pierre Richard.
  Paris: Garnier, 1961 ("Classiques Garnier").
  Most readily available edition (in the absence of the relevant
  volume of the Pléiade). Introduction merely outlines Rousseau's
  argument, emphasizing its place in French literary and pedagogic
  history. Typographical errors are not lacking in the text; notes
  are not without errors of interpretation.
13a. *Émile.*
  Paris: "Garnier-Flammarion," 1966.
  New paperback edition. Should not be confused with the
  "Classiques Garnier" edition (preceding entry), which has been
  cited throughout this volume.
14. *Émile.* Introduction by Henri Wallon, with notes by J.-L. Lecercle.
  Paris: Éditions Sociales, 1958.
  Selections only. Introduction summarizes the entire work, and is
  complemented by an essay on "*Émile* dans l'histoire" by J.-L.
  Lecercle.
14a. *Essai sur l'Origine des Langues.*
  In *Les Cahiers pour l'Analyse*, No. 4 (Sept.-Oct. 1966).
  Facsimile reproduction of 1817 edition serves as appendix. The
  issue itself suggests the persisting relevance of Rousseau's thought.
15. *Les Rêveries du Promeneur Solitaire.* Ed. critique by Marcel
Raymond.
  Genève: Droz, 1948.
  Introduction emphasizes the almost mystical character of Rousseau's return to the sentiment of existence in his late years. Critical edition of the text is supplemented by variants, notes, the
  text of the "cartes à jouer," and three contemporary descriptions
  of Rousseau's last years (by Dusaulx, Corancez, and Bernardin
  de Saint Pierre).
15a. *Lettre à d'Alembert.*
  Paris: "Garnier-Flammarion," 1967.
  New paperback edition.

B. English Translations

16. *Rousseau: Political Writings.* Trans. and ed. Frederick Watkins.
London: Thomas Nelson, 1953.

Solid translation of *Social Contract, Considerations on the Government of Poland*, and Part I of *Constitutional Project for Corsica*. Introduction emphasizes the relevance of Rousseau to modern liberal democratic and totalitarianism.

17. *The First and Second Discourses*. Ed. Roger D. Masters; trans. Roger D. and Judith R. Masters.
    New York: St. Martin's Press, 1964.
    Translation accompanied by notes and an introduction.

18. *Confessions*.
    2 vols.; London: J. M. Dent [Everyman's Library], 1951.

19. *Considerations on the Government of Poland*. Trans. Willmoore Kendall.
    Minneapolis: Minnesota Book Store, 1947.

20. *Creed of a Priest of Savoy*. Trans. Arthur H. Beattie.
    New York: Ungar, 1956.
    Translation of the "Profession of Faith of the Savoyard Vicar."

21. *Émile*. Trans. Barbara Foxley.
    London: J. M. Dent [Everyman's Library], n.d.
    Only currently available translation of the *Émile* in its entirety. Rendering is unfortunately loose (e.g., *"l'auteur des choses"* in the opening sentence is translated by the word "God").

22. *Émile, Julie, and Other Writings*. Ed. R. L. Archer.
    Great Neck, N.Y.: Barron's Educational Series, n.d.
    Selections only.

23. *Politics and the Arts: Rousseau's Letter to d'Alembert*. Trans. and ed. Allan Bloom.
    Glencoe, Illinois: The Free Press [Agora Editions], 1960.
    Careful translation of the *Lettre à d'Alembert*, with helpful introduction and notes.

24. *Social Contract, Discourse in Arts and Sciences, Discourse on Inequality, Political Economy, Considerations on the Government of Poland*. Ed. G.D.H. Cole.
    New York: E. P. Dutton [Everyman's Library], 1950.
    Translation, which appears to be merely a revision of an anonymous 18th-century edition (cited in the bibliography without an indication of this fact), is often inaccurate, and the edition itself sadly incomplete (only a few of Rousseau's notes to the *Second Discourse* being included).

25. *Social Contract*. Ed. Charles Frankel.
    New York: Hafner, 1947.
    A competent edition, based on a 1791 translation.

26. *Social Contract*. Trans. and ed. Willmoore Kendall.
   Chicago: Henry Regnery [Gateway Editions], 1954.
      Questionable translation for critical study, most particularly
      because Kendall inserts (in italics, to be sure) qualifying phrases
      which presumably illuminate Rousseau's meaning and are often
      debatable. Also has the disadvantage of carrying Rousseau's
      footnotes into the text.
26a. *Social Contract and Discourse on the Origin of Inequality*. Ed.
   Lester G. Crocker.
   New York: Washington Square Press, 1967.
      Suffers, like the Cole edition, from the failure to translate almost
      all of Rousseau's notes to the *Second Discourse*.
27. *Index Général des Oeuvres de J. J. Rousseau*
      In preparation by a group of French scholars; available only
      by subscription. When completed will give the reference to all
      nouns, qualifying adjectives, verbs and substantive adverbs in
      the major works of Rousseau. Will be a valuable tool in future
      research.

II. COMMENTARIES

A. Books and Articles

28. Benda, Harry. "Rousseau's Early Discourses (I) and (II),"
Political Science (Wellington, New Zealand), v (Sept. 1953) 13-20;
and (March 1954) 17-28.
      Attempt to trace the evolution of Rousseau's thought from the
      First Discourse and the essays defending it to the *Second Dis-
      course*. Exaggerates the discontinuity of Rousseau's thought and
      fails to make certain crucial distinctions (e.g., the difference
      between "goodness" and "virtue").
29. Broome, J. H. *Rousseau: A Study of His Thought*.
   London: Edward Arnold, 1963.
      Introduction to Rousseau's writings which attempts to give a
      balanced view of his many facets. As is inevitable in such a
      work, many detailed points of analysis are open to debate.
30. Burgelin, Pierre. *La Philosophie de l'Existence de J. J. Rousseau*.
   Paris: Presses Universitaires de France, 1952.
      One of the rare commentaries which treats Rousseau as a phi-
      losopher while emphasizing the intimate connection between his
      life and writings. Organized thematically and drawing from the
      entire range of Rousseau's writings, it provides many suggestive
      insights.

31. Cassirer, Ernst. *The Question of Jean Jacques Rousseau.* Trans. and ed. Peter Gay.

New York: Columbia University Press, 1954.

In a notable attempt to state the unity of Rousseau's thought, Cassirer presents what is generally described as a "neo-Kantian" interpretation, emphasizing the extent to which Rousseau's position rests on a radical reanalysis of human rationality deriving morality from the law discovered by reason. Compare the critical remarks in the Appendix to #34.

32. Cassirer, Ernst. *Rousseau, Kant, and Goethe.*

Princeton: Princeton University Press, 1945. Reprinted as a Harper Torch Book, New York: Harper & Row, 1963.

The essay "Kant and Rousseau" attempts to show the link between the two philosophers as a key expression of the Enlightenment (see #31).

33. Cobban, Alfred. *Rousseau and the Modern State.*

London: George Allen & Unwin, 1934. Reprinted, Hamden, Conn.: Shoe String Press, 1961.

A defense of Rousseau against the charge of being a supporter of despotism, placing emphasis on the application of Rousseau's principles and the extent to which his thought illuminates the problems of modern democracy in the West. Chapter II gives a useful survey of many characteristic interpretations of Rousseau.

34. Derathé, Robert. *Le rationalisme de Jean-Jacques Rousseau.*

Paris: Presses Universitaires de France, 1948.

An attempt to save Rousseau from the criticism of being an anti-rationalist. Underestimates Rousseau's analysis of the importance of passion and sentiment as the basis of civic virtue and healthy *moeurs*, not to mention the philosophical significance of his denial that man is naturally rational.

35. Derathé, Robert. *Jean-Jacques Rousseau et la Science Politique de Son Temps.*

Paris: Presses Universitaires de France, 1950.

An exhaustive attempt to situate Rousseau's works in the context of the philosophical and juristic schools of "natural right" in the 17th and 18th centuries. The title is misleading insofar as the influence of Montesquieu is omitted (as well as lesser figures like d'Argenson); but the comparative analysis of the concepts of political right as developed by Rousseau and by Hobbes, Pufendorf, Grotius, Barbeyrac, Locke, and other jurists is often useful. Extensive bibliography.

36. Durkheim, Émile. *Montesquieu et Rousseau, Precurseurs de la Sociologie.*

Paris: Marcel Rivière, 1953. English translation, Ann Arbor: University of Michigan Press, 1960.

Contains an illuminating analysis of the *Contrat social,* most particularly of the theory of the general will.

37. Green, F. C. *Jean Jacques Rousseau: A Critical Study of His Life and Writings.*

Cambridge: University Press, 1955.

An attempt to provide a comprehensive biographical study of Rousseau and his thought. As with many such studies, treats Rousseau's major writings in terms of his personality, often underestimating their philosophical character.

38. Grimsley, Ronald. *Jean Jacques Rousseau: A Study in Self-Awareness.*

Cardiff: University of Wales Press, 1961.

An analysis of Rousseau primarily from the psychological perspective. Sometimes marked by a certain animosity toward Rousseau.

39. Grimsley, Ronald. *Jean d'Alembert (1717-1783).*

Oxford: Clarendon Press, 1963.

Chapter vi contains a good discussion of the relations between d'Alembert and Rousseau.

40. Groethuysen, Bernard. *J. J. Rousseau.*

Paris: Gallimard, 1949.

Posthumously published from notes; a frequently illuminating commentary—indeed, often a dialogue with Rousseau. Despite the tendency to reduce philosophic questions to those of personality, it contains many useful insights (especially concerning Rousseau's political and religious teaching).

41. Guéhenno, Jean. *Jean Jacques Rousseau.*

3 vols.; Paris: Grasset, 1948 [vol. i: *En marge des Confessions* (1712-1750)]; Paris: Grasset, 1950 [vol. ii: *Roman et verite* (1750-1758)]; Paris: Gallimard, 1952 [vol. iii: *Grandeur et misere d'un esprit* (1758-1778)] English translation, 2 vols.; New York: Columbia University Press, 1966.

An extensive attempt to reconstruct an accurate biography, confronting the *Confessions* with evidence from Rousseau's correspondence and his other writings.

42. Havens, George R. "Hardiesse de Rousseau dans le *Discours sur l'inégalité," Europe* (November-December 1961) pp. 149-58.

Valuable statement of the originality of Rousseau's philosophic perspective in the *Second Discourse*. This issue is devoted entirely to Rousseau, and contains a number of other useful articles (cf. #55).

43. Haymann, Franz. "La loi naturelle dans le philosophie politique de J. J. Rousseau," *Annales*, xxx (1943-1945), 65-109.

An attempt to refute Vaughan's thesis that Rousseau rejected natural law "root and branch." Although the interpretation differs sharply from that given here, Haymann's thesis has been influential among French critics and is followed by Derathé (see #35).

44. Hendel, Charles W. *Jean-Jacques Rousseau: Moralist.*

2 vols.; London: Oxford University Press, 1934. Reprinted, Library of Liberal Arts, Indianapolis and New York: Bobbs-Merrill, 1962.

One of the most extensive surveys of Rousseau's philosophy and writings. Although in many cases Hendel merely summarizes texts with the aid of extensive quotations, his interpretation is usually balanced and his comparisons with other philosophers extraordinarily useful.

45. Hoffmann, Stanley. "Rousseau on War and Peace," *American Political Science Review*, LVII (June 1963), 317-33.

A probing analysis of Rousseau's teaching as it applies to international relations. Marred by an overly schematic conception of the stages of human evolution as defined in the *Second Discourse*. (See also #63.)

46. Jimack, Peter D. *La Genèse et la Rédaction de l'Émile de J. J. Rousseau.*

Geneva: Institut et Musée Voltaire, 1960 [*Studies on Voltaire and the 18th century,* vol. XIII].

Although treating the *Émile* more as a work of pedagogy than of philosophy, Jimack's analysis is indispensable for all questions concerning the elaboration of the manuscript and the history of its publication. The discussion of sources in Part III is largely in terms of specific details, leaving to one side the fundamental philosophical problems posed by Rousseau.

47. Jouvenel, Bertrand de. "Essai sur la Politique de Rousseau," in J. J. Rousseau, *Du Contrat Social.*

Geneva: Éditions du Cheval Ailé, 1947.

One of the most perceptive interpretations of Rousseau's political thought. Despite an occasional slip in the details of textual analysis, it gives an accurate assessment of the importance of classical philosophy for Rousseau, as well as of the different aspects of his system. (See also #48, #61, #63.)

48. Jouvenel, Bertrand de. "Théorie des Formes de Gouvernement chez Rousseau," *Le Contrat social*, VI (Nov.-Dec. 1962) 343-51.

The first systematic attempt to discuss Rousseau's "maxims of government" as distinct from his principles of right. A particularly important article, despite a tendency to overstate the similarity between Rousseau's descriptive propositions and modern political science.

49. Krafft, Olivier. *La Politique de Jean-Jacques Rousseau: Aspects Méconnus.*

Paris: Librairie Générale de Droit et de Jurisprudence, 1958.

An interesting example of the possibilities of applying Rousseau's ideas to contemporary political and legal problems. Although Part I ("Égalité") is not particularly illuminating as a study of Rousseau's system, Part II ("Modes de Gouvernement") contains some astute critical analysis, emphasizing his hostility to representation and directly democratic government.

50. May, Georges. *Rousseau par lui-même.*

Paris: Seuil ["Ecrivains de Toujours"], 1961.

An introduction to Rousseau's life and works emphasizing his literary and biographical interest, rather than his status as a serious philosopher.

51. Morel, Jean. "Recherches sur les sources du *Discours de J. J. Rousseau sur l'origine et les fondements de l'inégalité parmi les hommes,*" *Annales*, V (1909) 119-98.

Extensive analysis of the modern sources of Rousseau's *Second Discourse.*

52. Mornet, Daniel. *Rousseau, l'homme et l'oeuvre.*

Paris: Hatier-Bovin ["Connaissance de Lettres"], 1950.

A compact introduction to Rousseau, placing him in the perspective of his times. Most valuable from the literary perspective.

53. Proust, Jacques. *Diderot et l'Encyclopédie.*

Paris: Armand Colin, 1962.

Contains, especially in chapter X, a valuable discussion of the relationship between Diderot and Rousseau, citing the relevant scholarly literature.

54. Shklar, Judith N. "Rousseau's Images of Authority," *American Political Science Review*, LVIII (Dec. 1964), 919-32.

Although specific formulations could be questioned, contains some suggestive ideas about Rousseau's attitudes to personal authority and leadership, especially with reference to the *Nouvelle Héloïse*.

55. Starobinski, Jean. "Tout le mal vient de l'inégalité," *Europe* (Nov.-Dec. 1961), pp. 135-49.

Connects Rousseau's personal experience with his philosophic insight.

56. Starobinski, Jean. *Jean Jacques Rousseau: le transparence et l'obstacle.*

Paris: Plon, 1957.

A suggestive analysis attempting to show that Rousseau's character and personality provide the essential themes (man's alienation from other men and his quest to overcome it) of Rousseau's writings. Treats Rousseau primarily as a literary figure.

57. Strauss, Leo. "On the Intention of Rousseau," *Social Research*, XIV (Dec. 1947), 455-87.

Careful and suggestive analysis, placing Rousseau's work in the context of the problems posed by classical philosophy.

58. Strauss, Leo. *Natural Right and History.*

Chicago: University of Chicago Press, 1953.

Chapter VI contains a subtle, highly compressed analysis of Rousseau's political philosophy in the context of the major issues presented by the doctrine of natural right. Underemphasizes the *Émile*.

59. Thomas, Jacques-François. *Le Pélagianisme de J. J. Rousseau.*
Paris: Nizet, 1956.

An attempt to show that Rousseau, while not strictly speaking guilty of the theological heresy of Pelagianism, represents the spirit of this belief that man can secure grace by his own efforts. An example of criticism based almost entirely on secondary sources.

60. Weil, Eric. "J. J. Rousseau et sa Politique," *Critique*, LVI (January 1952), 3-28.

Review of a number of commentaries (including #30, #34, #35). Suggests the basis on which both the neo-Kantian and existentialist interpretations of Rousseau can be accepted.

60a. Winwar, Frances. *Jean-Jacques Rousseau: Conscience of an Era.*

New York: Random House, 1961.

Popular biography.

— 455 —

B. Collections of Articles

(Only articles that are particularly important from the perspective of political philosophy are indicated.

61. "Jean Jacques Rousseau," *Yale French Studies*, XXVIII (Fall-Winter 1961-1962).

L. G. Crocker, "The Priority of Justice or Law"

M. Dickstein, "The Faith of a Vicar: Reason and Morality in Rousseau's Religion"

J. Starobinski, "The Illness of Rousseau"

B. de Jouvenel, "Rousseau the Pessimistic Evolutionist"

P. Burgelin, "The Second Education of Emile"

Annotated bibliography of recent works. Jouvenel's piece is of particular importance. On the biographical level, Starobinski's analysis is especially acute (cf. also #55, #56).

62. *Présence de Jean-Jacques Rousseau*. Comprises vol. XXXV of the *Annales*, containing papers presented at the "Entretiens sur Jean Jacques Rousseau" held in Geneva 16 and 17 July 1962.

Paris: Armand Colin, 1963.

P. Burgelin, "L'éducation de Sophie"

H. Goutier, "Ce que le Vicaire doit à Descartes"

R. Derathé, "La religion civile selon Rousseau"

J. Fabre, "Réalité et utopie dans le pensée politique de Rousseau"

B. Baczko, "Rousseau et l'aliénation social"

R. A. Leigh, "Vers une nouvelle édition de la correspondance de Rousseau"

The bibliography and listing of various colloquia during the "Année Rousseau" in 1962 are useful.

63. *Rousseau et la Philosophie Politique*. Annales de la Philosophie Politique, vol. 5.

Paris: Presses Universitaires de France, 1965.

B. de Jouvenel, "Rousseau, évolutionniste pessimiste"

P. Burgelin, "Hors des ténèbres de la nature"

I. Fetscher, "Rousseau, auteur d'intention conservatrice et d'action révolutionnaire"

C. J. Friedrich, "Law and Dictatorship in the *Contrat social*"

L. G. Crocker, "Rousseau et la voie de totalitarisme"

J. Plamenatz, " 'Ce qui ne signifie pas autre chose, sinon qu'on le forcer d'être libre' "

R. Derathé, "Les Rapports de l'exécutif et du législatif chez Rousseau"

BIBLIOGRAPHY

S. Cotta, "Théorie religeuse et théorie politique chez Rousseau"
S. Hoffmann, "Rousseau, le guerre et la paix"
   As a whole, a representative sample of recent Rousseau scholarship. The essays by Jouvenel (see also #61), Fetscher (see also
   #64), Derathé (see also #35), and Hoffmann (see also #45)
   are particularly useful. In contrast, the debate between Friedrich
   and Crocker deforms the fundamental issue.

C. German Commentaries

64. Fetscher, Iring. *Rousseaus Politische Philosophie.*
   Neuwied: Hermann Lachterhead Verlag, 1960.
65. Rang, Martin. *Rousseau Lehre von Menschen.*
   Gottingen: Vandenhoeck & Ruprecht, 1959.
66. Vossler, Otto. *Rousseaus Freiheitslehre.*
   Gottingen: Vandenhoeck & Ruprecht, 1963.

INDEX

academies, 231-33
Academy of Dijon, xii, 106-07, 108*n*, 111-12, 119*n*, 159*n*, 205, 206*n*, 209-13, 215*n*, 218, 228*n*, 232-33, 309*n*
adolescence, 37-48
Aeneas, 302
Africa, 252
Alexander the Great, 220, 221
amour-propre, 38-41, 44-47, 298; and conscience, 82
Angers, 387*n*
Anytus, 241*n*
Apollo of Delphi, 104*n*
Aquinas, St. Thomas, 79*n*, 201-02, 329*n*
Ardrey, Robert, 427*n*, 435*n*
aristocracy, 399-402
Aristotle, 7, 23*n*, 45*n*, 46*n*, 64*n*, 92-93, 107, 112-13, 134*n*, 159*n*, 192*n*, 201, 249*n*, 250, 279, 295, 309*n*, 341, 351, 359*n*, 361*n*, 373*n*, 374*n*, 378, 400*n*, 403*n*, 405*n*, 437*n*
Arouet, *see* Voltaire
arts, and corruption, 235-43
assemblies, popular, 394, 405-06, 411-13. *See also* Centuriate assembly, Tribal assembly
Athens, 219, 221-23, 229*n*, 240-41, 242, 247
Austria, 220, 372*n*

Babbitt, Irving, 90*n*
Bacon, Francis, 52*n*, 228*n*, 418
Baczko, Bronislaw, 180*n*
Barbeyrac, Jean, 78*n*, 187*n*, 188*n*, 199*n*, 309*n*
Barrillot et fils, 207*n*
Bayle, Pierre, 309*n*
Beaulavon, Georges, 340*n*
Benda, Harry J., 234*n*, 248*n*, 249*n*
Berkeley, Bishop George, 229*n*
Bloom, Allan, xv, 205*n*
Bodin, Jean, 309*n*
Bonnet, Charles, 174
Bouchardy, François, 206*n*, 208*n*, 232*n*, 233*n*, 249*n*, 438
Broome, J. H., vi*n*, 338*n*, 416*n*
Buffon, Comte de, 114*n*, 115, 116*n*, 121*n*, 122*n*, 176*n*
Burgelin, Pierre, vi*n*, 8*n*, 21*n*, 112*n*, 409*n*, 416*n*
Burgundy, Duke of, 220*n*

Burke, Edmund, 358, 413
Burlemaqui, Jean-Jacques, 78*n*, 302*n*

Caesar, Julius, 237*n*
Caligula, 309*n*, 359-60
Calvin, John, 359
Canada, 281*n*
Candaux, Jean-Daniel, 199*n*
Cannae, 237*n*
Caribs, 173*n*, 180*n*
Carthage, 220, 221, 237*n*, 246*n*, 310*n*
Cassirer, Ernst, 99*n*, 306*n*
Cato, 247, 304*n*, 391*n*
Centuriate assembly, 390-91*n*
Chance, M.R.A., 427*n*
Chardin, Jean, 309*n*
Charles VIII (King of France), 237*n*
Childe, V. Gordon, 437*n*
childhood, early, 30-34; later, 34-37
China, 219-20
Choiseul, Duke of, 308*n*
Chronos, Age of, 360-61*n*
Cicero, 45*n*, 93, 309*n*, 356
Cineas, 246
citizen, 10-14, 23-24, 92-95, 297-98. *See also* virtue, civic
Citizen of Geneva, Rosseau as, 205, 207-08, 215*n*, 226
civic virtue, *see* virtue
civil freedom, 252-54, 314-18, 322-23
civil society, idea of, 285-91. *See also* nature of law
civil society, origins of, 181-87; and natural right, 158-64
Clarke, Samuel, 58, 82
climate, 373-80
Cobban, Alfred, 77*n*, 301*n*, 306*n*, 317*n*
Comte, Auguste, 5
Condillac, Etienne Bonnot de, 29, 52, 131, 133, 148*n*
conscience, 74-89, 212, 296, 425-27
continuous proportion, 340-48, 393-94, 396*n*
Conzié of Charmettes, Count, 69*n*
Cornelius Nepos, 309*n*, 403*n*
Corsica, 233*n*, 258, 370, 372*n*, 411
Cramer, Philibert, 3*n*
Crocker, Lester G., 52*n*, 294*n*, 387*n*
Cumberland, Richard, 263
customs and morals (*moeurs*), 380-93

— 459 —

d'Alembert, Jean Le Rond, 309n
d'Argenson, Count Marc-Pierre de Voyer, 307n
d'Argenson, Marquis Réné-Louis de Voyer de Paulmy, 307-08, 309n, 327, 403n
Darwin, Charles, 430
Decemvirs, 309n, 356
Delphic oracle, 239-41
democracy, 398-99
Derathé, Robert, vin, ixn, 77n, 136n, 137n, 152n, 199n, 257n, 259n, 261n, 264n, 282n, 302n, 305n, 308n, 311n, 316, 317n, 318n, 319n, 340n, 341n, 365n, 369n, 370n, 374n, 376n, 390n, 408n, 409-10n
Descartes, René, 59, 61n, 64n, 113n, 228n, 341, 372
despotism, 403n. See also tyranny
DeVore, Irven, 431n
dictator, 407-08
Diderot, Denis, ix, xii, 97, 107n, 187n, 189n, 201n, 203n, 206, 259n, 261-68, 273, 323n, 324n
Dionysius the Younger, 309n
Duchesne, Nicolas-Bonaventure, xiii, 206n
DuPan, Jean, 195n
DuPeyrou, Pierre-Alexandre, xviin
Durkheim, Émile, 325n, 380n
Dutch, 220, 221, 237n, 246

education, defined, 5; methods, 18-20; public, 384
Egypt, 219
Eisenstadt, S. N., 437n
England, 220, 221, 281n, 412-13; Parliament, 337
Enlightenment, and corruption, 218-25
Ephors, Spartan, 407
epigraphs: *Émile*, 15 & n; *Second Discourse*, 112; *First Discourse*, 208, 211n; *Contrat social*, 302
equality, 328, 390-92; and freedom, 424
eternal law, 201
exegesis, organization of, v-vii; method of, x-xvi

Fabre, Jean, 306n, 409n
Fabricius, 246
family, 165-75; in state of nature, 125-32; and political right, 276-79
females, 21-27

Fénelon, François de Salignac de La Mothe, 307n
Fetscher, Iring, 251n, 300n
France, 225, 237n, 246n, 281n, 372n, 387n
Franks, 220, 221, 237n
Frederick the Great, 306-07, 308
free will, *see* freedom; will
freedom, 41-42, 52-53, 62, 69-73, 93-95, 124-25, 424-25, 427-28, 430-38; distinction of natural, moral, and civil, 53, 73, 102-04, 252-54, 352; in state of nature, 147-51, 156-57; and political right, 283-84; and political order, 351-53; "force him to be free," 329-31. *See also* civil freedom, moral freedom, natural freedom
frictionless surface, model of general will, 285-86, 290, 327, 422, 424
friendship, 43-46
Fustel de Coulanges, Numa Denis, 245n

Gauls, 220, 221, 237n
general will, 42, 51, 190, 323-34; of human species (Diderot's conception), 264-65, 268, 273. *See also* frictionless surface, nature of law, social contract
Geneva, 54, 192-95, 249n, 258, 304n, 350, 411
Genoa, 233n
geography, 373-80
Germans, 219, 246
Glaucus, 114
glory, 366-67
God, 65-68. *See also* religion
golden rule, 274-75
goodness, 41, 43, 68n, 95-98; distinct from virtue, 12; based on freedom, 52. *See also* natural goodness, virtue
Gorgias, 241n
Goths, 237n
government, legitimate, 189-95; distinct from sovereign, 335-40; forms of, 393-403; geometric formula for, 340-48
Greece, 219, 220, 221-23, 236n, 237n, 243n, 245, 246
Green, F. C., viin, 97n
Grimsley, Ronald, viin
Groethuysen, Bernard, viii, 55

solitary dreamer, 96-99, 103, 104, 111*n*, 146, 254, 409, 414, 429*n*
Solon, 390
sovereign, distinct from government, 335-40; limits on, 316-23
Spain, 220, 221
Sparta, 23-24, 186, 221-23, 246, 251, 297, 299*n*, 334*n*, 350, 357, 358, 371, 389, 390*n*, 400, 407, 424
Spencer, Herbert, 5
Spink, John S., 54*n*
Spinoza, Benedict de, 78*n*, 164*n*, 198, 202, 229*n*, 230, 269*n*
Spuhler, J. N., 427*n*
Stalin, Josef, 395*n*
Starobinski, Jean, vii*n*, 90*n*, 109*n*, 117*n*, 118*n*, 134*n*, 139*n*, 150*n*, 152*n*, 161, 180*n*, 182*n*, 195*n*, 200*n*, 416*n*
state of nature, 11, 116-57
Stelling-Michaud, Sven, 409*n*
Stevens, Wallace, xxv
Strauss, Leo, 52*n*, 54*n*, 58*n*, 62*n*, 71, 73*n*, 97*n*, 107*n*, 109*n*, 118*n*, 142*n*, 152*n*, 157*n*, 189*n*, 199*n*, 203*n*, 211*n*, 212*n*, 228*n*, 231*n*, 241*n*, 269*n*, 285*n*, 287*n*, 290*n*, 296*n*, 365*n*, 403*n*, 419-21, 429*n*
Swiss, 219, 220, 221, 233*n*, 237*n*, 246, 333

Tacitus, 188*n*, 219*n*, 309*n*, 399, 443
Talmon, J. L., 89*n*, 294*n*, 325*n*
Tarquins, 396*n*
Taylor, Lucy Ross, 391*n*, 407*n*
theory and practice, 410-16
Theseus, 270
Thielemann, Leland, 262*n*
Thomas, Jean-François, vi*n*, 54*n*
Thoth (Egyptian God), 225
Thucydides, 229*n*, 331*n*
Titus Tatius, 365
Tocqueville, Alexis de, 5, 387*n*
Trasimene, 237*n*
Treaty of Paris, 281*n*
Tribal assemblies, Roman, 407*n*

Tribunate, Roman, 406-07
Truman, David, 387*n*
Turnus, 302
tyranny, 195-97, 389, 403*n*

United States of America, 372*n*, 407*n*
unnamed naturalist, *see* Leroi, M.

Vandals, 220, 221, 237*n*
Varro, 309*n*
Vaughan, C. E., 77*n*, 99*n*, 112*n*, 142-43*n*, 248*n*, 261, 264*n*, 265*n*, 269, 305*n*, 307*n*, 318*n*, 335*n*, 376*n*, 410*n*
Venice, vi*n*, xii, 310
vice, 179-80; in eighteenth century, 213-18
Virgil, 302
virtue, 42-43, 95-98; distinct from goodness, 154-55, 159; humanitarian (*humanité*), 49-50, 80, 247, 273; civic, 51, 246-47, 252-53, 272-73; and science, 209-13
Voltaire, 8*n*, 68*n*, 88*n*, 171*n*, 216*n*, 229*n*, 289, 369*n*
Vossius, Isaac, 133*n*

Waelder, Robert, 427*n*
War of Devolution (1667-68), 187*n*
Warburton, William, 309*n*
Ward, Barbara, 440*n*
Washburn, S. L., 431*n*
Watkins, Frederick, 294*n*, 325*n*, 333*n*, 335*n*, 350*n*
Weil, Eric, 203*n*, 304*n*
will, 64-72, 285, 289-90, 324-25, 333; in state of nature, 147-51, 156-57; private and general, 326-28, 346-47; of all, 326. *See also* freedom
Wilson, Arthur M., 206*n*, 262*n*
Wurtenburg, Duke of, 18*n*, 306*n*

Xenocrates, 107
Xenophon, 403*n*

Zoll, Donald Atwell, 365*n*